Bill's Way

Bill Ritchie

 A catalogue record for this book is available from the National Library of Australia

Copyright © 2024 Bill Ritchie (Estate)
All rights reserved.
ISBN-13: 978-1-923174-43-6

Linellen Press
265 Boomerang Road
Oldbury, Western Australia
www.linellenpress.com.au

Contents

Preface 1

Chapter 1 - My Story Begins...3

Chapter 2 - My Family and Me 12

Chapter 3 - Naval Entry..41

Chapter 4 - RAN Station 284..57

Chapter 5 - HMAS *Moreton* 63

Chapter 6 - HMAS *Gerard*..65

Chapter 7 - HMAS *Madang* 72

Chapter 8 - HMAS *Broome*...75

Chapter 9 - HMAS *Platypus* 78

Chapter 10 - HMAS *Bathurst* 82

Chapter 11 – HMAS Platypus 2nd Time 91

Chapters 12, 12A & 12B 92

Chapter 12A 97

Chapter 12B 98

Chapter 13 - HMAS *Watson* (1st Stint)..100

Chapter 14 - HMAS *Bataan*..108

Chapter 15 - HMAS *Watson* (2nd Stint) 137

Chapter 16 - HMAS *Albatross*..141

Chapter 17 - HMAS *Sydney* 149

Chapter 18 - HMAS *Watson* (3rd Stint)..200

Chapter 19 - HMAS *Vengeance*..207

Chapter 20 - HMS *Dryad*..224

Chapter 21 - HMS *Tumult* 240

Chapter 22 - HMS *Sheffield*..249

Chapter 23 - Homeward Bound and A New Home 268

Chapter 24 - HMAS A *Watson*..273

Chapter 25 - HMS *Dryad*..281

Chapter 26 - HMS *Ark Royal* 286

Chapter 27 - 890 Squadron 300

Chapter 28 - Returning Home 306

Chapter 29 - HMAS *Melbourne* 309

Chapter 30 - HMAS *Stuart* 323

Chapter 31 - HMAS *Watson* 338

Chapter 32 - HMAS *Perth* 342

Chapter 33 - HMAS *Watson* 366

Chapter 34 - HMAS *Melbourne* 368

Chapter 35 - Navy Office (Russell) Canberra 389

Chapter 36 - HMAS *Melbourne* 401

Chapter 37 - HMAS *Watson* 422

Chapter 38 - Navy Office 426

Chapter 39 - Western Australian Naval Support Facility 430

Chapter 40 - Harold E Holt 460

Chapter 41 - Return to HMAS *Stirling* 472

Chapter 42 - Retirement 474

Our Poppy - Poem 491

Associations and Memberships 492

Legacies 492

Appendix 494

Ships W G Ritchie Served in 495

Ashore and at Sea 495

Cyclone Tracy 503

OBN Details - Bill Ritchie 508

Preface

This book is dedicated to the life of my dad, William (Bill) Gray Ritchie, the firstborn child of Walter and Laura (Ruby) in Kalgoorlie on March 1st 1926. A younger brother, Harry, and sister, Janet, followed two years apart. The family were the average battlers of the era living in a small but accommodating house in Lewis Street. With the arrival of Janet, Bill from a young age slept outside on the verandah, except when rain intruded when he was allowed to sleep inside.

After these humble beginnings, with little or no excesses and early life illness, he worked in mining as a trainee surveyor. Bill then joined the Navy at the age of eighteen. This took him to the other side of Australia for training as a Radar Operator, a new technology recently developed, before being sent off to join boats serving in the Second World War. He served in the RAN for over thirty-nine years, actively involved in five wars and conflicts. He served on over twenty naval vessels and numerous naval bases, retiring with the rank of Commander after a stint as commanding officer (Aus) of the Harold E Holt base in Exmouth and a final stint as Executive Officer of HMAS Stirling.

He met Mum (Joan) whilst based in Sydney and went on to marry her in London in December 1955 whilst there on one of his two stints with the RN for officer training in England. They would have four children – Anthony, Anne, Peter and Walter.

In his later working life and in retirement from the RAN, he would go on to either volunteer his services and or become a member of many organisations, mainly those based around the Rockingham area, many of which he would be awarded Life Membership of. He was also awarded Member of the Order of Australia as well as the recipient of seventeen service medals.

The contents of this book were written in his own words in the later years of his life, most from memory, some from research, and I have done my best to complete some insight into his retirement years as he passed away prior to finishing that period of his life. Dad had a heart attack at age 57, the year of his retirement. He would go on to live to the ripe old age of 97, living at home in the family house in Shoalwater, prior to passing away peacefully in his sleep in Hollywood Hospital on November 28th, 2023.

Firstly, I would like to acknowledge the support Mum Joan put into Dad's career and general life over the 56-plus years of their marriage until her passing in 2012; a lot of time was spent raising the four children whilst Dad was away at sea.

I would also like to acknowledge the time and effort my sister Anne made in Dad's later years, assisting him with the various errands and housework that needed to be done.

Son Peter.

Chapter 1

My Story Begins

My Ancestors

During my research, I discovered that the name Ritchie is a derivative of Richard and came about when Europeans came to Scotland around 1450. I also discovered that it is a Sept of the Macintosh Clan. So, what do I know about my ancestors?

It appears that my original ancestors lived in the village of Pitsligo, near Rosehearty, on the northeast coast of Scotland. Between 1750 and 1860, the Scottish Highland Clearances saw the people removed from these areas to the south, and my ancestors relocated to Linlithgow, which is on the road between Edinburgh and Glasgow.

So now let me introduce my **Great-Great-** and **Great-Grandparents**

My Great-Great-Grandparents were **William Ritchie** (b 12/3/1792 in Linlithgow). He married **Elizabeth Miller** (b 30/5/1797) and died on 24/12/1819. They had ten children. Elizabeth died on 11/6/1839, aged 42. Subsequently, William married **Catherine Munro** on 21/5/1841.

My Great-Grandparents were **Walter Ritchie** (b 17/6/1836 in Linlithgow). **Walter** died on 17/7/1916, aged 80. He married **Janet McLeish** on 12/6/1860. **Janet** (b 7/5/1842) died on the 30/3/1930, aged 87. They had ten children.

- **Margaret** married Robert Childs.
- **Elizabeth** married George Mounsey.
- **William** married Isobella Baker.
- **Christina** married Lancelot Mounsey.
- **Catherine** married George Proud.
- **Walter died young.**
- **John** married Annie Thomas.
- **Janet** married Thomas Evans.
- **Mary Carmichael** married Stanley Douglas.
- **Isobella Watt** married Albert Hocking.
- **Walter Robert Alexander,** the youngest was my dad.

On the next page is a photo of the family (with my dad as a baby on his Mum's lap) (left), and Walter and Janet McLeish (right).

The Ritchie Family

Walter and Janet Ritchie (nee McLeish)

My Father

My father, **Walter Robert Alexander Ritchie**, was born in Broomfield, near Ballarat, Victoria, on the 15/10/1883 and died on 23/9/1976, aged 92, in Perth. He was buried in September 1976 in Karrakatta Cemetery, Western Australia. We have no information on his early childhood and schooling. A Victorian cousin sent me a picture of a school in Ballarat that she believed my father went to.

It appears my father came to Western Australia with his father and brothers, William and John (Jack). They prospected for gold somewhere in the Eastern Goldfields. The exact area is not known. The sisters, Mary Carmichael, Isobella (Belle) and Elizabeth (Bessie) and Catherine (Kit) followed. Some of the girls were to look after the camp whilst the men searched for gold.

Kit, Mary, & Belle Ritchie

An Aside. Mary went on to marry a Stan Douglas. I remember two of their sons, who, with their father, operated a mine near Menzies. The Douglas family often visited Kalgoorlie and would call into 88 Lewis Street for a chat or a meal. I remember the dad, Stan, was a bit of a character. As a small child I remember being taken to Menzies, where Mary was operating a small shop. On one occasion, she allowed me to go and select a chocolate from the shop. I also remember being taken out to their small mine in the bush to spend the night or two with Stan and one of the sons. They took me rabbit shooting and allowed me to shoot at one of the rabbits, however I missed.

Kit married George Proud who had a mine near Kalgoorlie. Their daughter Dora used to send my father a diary each year while he was away at World War I. Later, Kit and Dora moved to Sydney, where Dora married Edward (Ted) Edmunds. They were to become great friends to me while serving in Sydney and the Navy. Kit died in 1960 whilst I was serving at HMAS *Albatross*, which is near Nowra in southern New South Wales. Their son George died a few years ago and I see the other son Don, and wife, Sandra, during my annual visits to Sydney to see my eldest son Tony, wife Tara and the Triplets. Uncle George often came to 88 Lewis Street for Sunday lunch and would cut my hair with hand clippers which could be quite blunt and a hair or three were pulled out of a protesting child.

My Story Continues

For some reason, my father split up with his brother William and seems to have spent some time in the Eastern Goldfields and Kalgoorlie, and as far north as Broome, until he enlisted in 1915 in Kalgoorlie. The story of the split is not really known but is thought to be over my dad finding some gold and the need to register a claim for that area. Being underage, Dad could not register the claim, and his brother went in and found the Registry Office closed for the day. When he went the next morning to register the claim, he found it had already been registered. That is, it had been jumped.

It is probably not too hard to conclude that the brother unwittingly revealed the location of the find whilst having a drink the night before. *(LOOSE LIPS SINK SHIPS)*. The fact my dad never drank, as far as I know, may confirm this assumption.

My father probably continued in the mining sector. He recounted how, when in the Assay work area, he realised there were no old men in that sector and formed the conclusion that the mercury used in the process killed them off. It is not known when he went into the shop/wholesale/retail business as a travelling salesman. I assume that he decided to work in that area rather than search for gold. It appears he may have settled in Kalgoorlie for he enlisted for WWI from there. A photograph I have of him is when he was part of the Railways Football team in Kalgoorlie.

Enlistment

My father enlisted on the 27/2/1915. He was sent to Black Boy Hill Camp on the Darling Range Scarp east of Perth. This area has now become known as Greenmount.

He was selected to become a Medical Orderly and sent to Rockingham, south of Perth, to join the 2nd Australian Field Hospital for training et cetera. This area was also being used by the WA 10th Light Horse for training. My father's diaries have made it clear he would have preferred to have been in the Lighthorse Group. However, and no doubt because of his age, he was selected as a Medical Orderly. Also, he was pretty good shot with a rifle.

He was sent to Egypt with the Hospital and joined a Hospital Ship sailing for Lemnos, where the Hospital was to be or was located, in support of the Gallipoli landings. However, the ship was diverted as it was about to enter Lemnos and was sent to support the Beach Landings.

No. 2427. L/Sgt. W. R. Ritchie From Kalgoorlie. 33rd. Rfts. Enl. 27/2/15. Rt. 17/8/19. Transferred to 4th. L/Horse Field Ambulance.

In a letter I came across later in my research, he wrote to the authorities claiming the "A" (Anzac letter) those who landed at Gallipoli were awarded to wear on their colour patch. It appears that he spent five or more days on the beach tending to the wounded.

He also made a remark that, on one occasion, he went up to see his Light Horse mates at the front. As he made his way across some open ground, he attracted machine-gun and rifle fire. Fortunately, he was not hit.

After the evacuation from Gallipoli, he returned to Egypt and, at some point, was able to transfer to a Light Horse Regiment as a medic.

Later, he served in Palestine and Syria. He was at Beersheba during the famous Australian Light Horse charge to attend the wounded. He would have been back behind the starting line of the charge. He returned to Australia in 1919 and went back to the Eastern goldfields, resuming employment as a storeman. Exactly where, I have not been able to find out, and I'm guessing it may have been Beria, a mining area north of Kalgoorlie.

At some point, he must have returned to Kalgoorlie, and I have assumed he was living in Mrs Geddy's Boarding House in Victoria Street, Kalgoorlie, and working for J & W Batemans, a wholesale business covering a wide range of goods. They supplied Kalgoorlie and the area nearby as well as sheep stations much further afield.

My Mother Ancestors

Great-Grandparents

My Great-Grandparents, on my mother's side, were James Cope (b????/18??), who came to Australia as a Prison Warder in 1867 on the *Norwood*.

The following remarks I found in a book whilst I was researching for information. The author's name is not noted.

- It appears that he had been serving in the army in Cork, Ireland before returning to Barbados and then Gibraltar from this deployment. These deployments by the regiment were usually for two years. The author of the article quoted records that show that on two occasions, he had been promoted to Corporal but, on each occasion, lost rank due to being disciplined.

- He joined the London Metropolitan Police on 29 August 1850 and resigned on 11 August 1856. In the latter year, her Majesty's Secretary of State applied to a commissioner of police for London for volunteers to join the Convict at Bermuda. The author of this article had no information on his service during that time.

- He was serving at Gibraltar in 1866 when he volunteered to join the establishment the Convict Establishment in the Swan River Colony. On 18/6/1866, James returned to England, escorting prisoners from Gibraltar. He had applied for transfer to the Swan River Colony to join his brother Thomas who was a pensioner guard.

- Certificates from acting Medical Officers in Chatham and Milbank prisons show that the men who had been selected for service in Western Australia were in health and capable of performing the duties of the water in Western Australia. They show that Assistant Warder Cope had great experience in dealing with convict and had the selected to transfer to Western Australia with the consent of the authorities at Gibraltar on excellent character which he bears.

- On 25 March the *Norwood* picked up the Pensioner Guard in Gravesend. The writer of this article I am quoting could not find any record of James' marriage that had produced James Alma. Family scuttlebutt is that his wife may have been Spanish. There is a suggestion in some family records that her name was Isobella. James Alma's birth in 1854 would have been whilst his father was serving in the Metropolitan Police in London. The author of the article had, at the time, not accessed Police Records.

- After arrival in Fremantle, James worked in the Fremantle Prison and that pervaded from acting Warder to Warder. Being a widower, he was given permission to live in the Gatekeeper's cottage with his son. The areas where he supervised convicts were as follows: Albany Road between Canning Bridge and area Narrogin between 1867 and 1869. The guards lived in tents or barracks.

- On 18 May 1870, James Alma Cope apprenticed to John Pedler of Perth, as a saddler and a harness maker, and I have a copy of the indenture. It shows a premium divided into payments of £10, one at the time of signing and the other after six months. James Elma was to be paid nothing for the first three years and in the fourth year, four shillings per week. In the fifth year, six shillings per week. Clothes and washing to be found by the parents of James Alma Cope. From what we can gather, James Alma pricked his finger with the Sadler's needle and died on 25/7/1880.

Here ends the summary by an unknown researcher. A bit long but interesting.

Continuing My Great-Grandparents (Mum's side)

James went on to marry Ellen Twohig (b. 1846 and died 29/7/1917). She came from Cork and had landed in Fremantle due to severe sea sickness on the voyage out from England. She had been going to an uncle in New South Wales.

On retirement, James and Ellen moved to Jarrahdale where Ellen set up a Boarding House. James found employment in the Timber Mill. They had five children: William James (Bill), Elizabeth Catherine (Kit), **Thomas James** (Tom) (my grandfather), Rosanna (Rose) and Ellen Mary (Nell).

No 2 Boarding house Jarrahdale

Thomas James Cope and Laura

An Aside. The story goes that the original Ellen's Boarding House had a large Jarrah tree alongside it and Ellen was frightened branches could fall and damage the house. She employed the best tree cutter in the district, who assured her that he could cut the tree down without damaging the house.

Unfortunately, the tree fell right across the house and destroyed it. Subsequently, the Timber Company provided what was their Recreation Hall, and this was modified into a Boarding House with some small cabins adjacent. The whole area was fenced, and Ellen was not allowed to graze her cows outside the fenced area.

My Mother

My Mother was born at Jarrahdale on the 13/8/1898 and was christened **Laura Ruby Cope (Ruby)**. Her father was **Thomas James Cope**, (b ??/??/18?? d 19/4/1920) who had married **Laura Woolston** (b.5/6.1874 d 19/8/1898 at Jarrahdale).

Laura Woolston worked as a maid in Ellen Cope's Boarding House, having come to Western Australia with two brothers who worked in the timber industry. Unfortunately, Laura died some days after the birth. My mother would have been taken to her grandmother's Boarding House when she left the hospital.

Grandmother Ellen Cope initially looked after her granddaughter Ruby after Laura's death. Later, one of her daughters, Ellen, who came to be known by me as Auntie Nell, and her husband, Harry (A.A Henry Martin (Uncle Harry)), took over the raising of Ruby. The Martins had previously lost James and Andrew as babies.

Harry Martin came to Western Australia at the age of 12 or so. I do not have any information on his early days in WA except that he came to the timber industry from the Goldfields.

From a book titled "The Timber People, A History of Bunnings Ltd", there is a statement that he was a respected builder and millwright, and he had a company named **Harry Martin and Co.** and became involved with Bunnings Ltd, who provided construction materials, such as timber, to those requiring it.

Harry was joined by a young Charles Bunnings who looked after surveying and materials for Uncle Harry's Company. This company was contracted to build a concrete bridge over the Morowa River at Malinu Springs and another over the Gascoyne River.

I understand the bridge over the Gascoyne River at Carnarvon was the first concrete piered bridge built in Western Australia, and possibly Australia. The company also built some north-west roads.

Harry Martin is reported as being an exceptional manager of various sawmills, a tough, outspoken but fair man. It is reported that no man dared cross Martin. He was also a maker of fine furniture and other such items as jewel boxes. I used to watch him in this activity when down from Kalgoorlie, very interested in the way he would prepare everything so that when they were put together there was no gap to be seen between two adjacent pieces. He could use either hand efficiently.

I'm led to believe that Harry Martin insisted on no grog being available in camp during construction. There is a story that, when building the bridge over the Gascoyne River, he picked up that somehow grog was coming into the camp, although they were a considerable distance from any town or pub. After the men had left the camp to work on the bridge, he searched all their belongings and the bush around the camp and did not find any grog.

One night, while inspecting the work that had been done and preparing for the next day's work, he noticed a cord hanging out of one of the piers that the scaffolding had been built around, ready for concrete to be poured in a day or two's time. His curiosity aroused, he pulled on the cord and found a full bottle of whiskey at the end. He lowered the bottle back into the scaffolding. Next morning, when they began to pour the concrete, he insisted that the first prepared scaffolded pier that the concrete was to be poured into was the one where the whiskey was hidden. There were protests, of course, but he just smiled and observed that the job was done correctly. He subsequently found out that one of his sister-in-law's sons, David H, who drove the truck into town for supplies, had brought it on site for one of the workmen.

Some pictures of my mother as a young lass

Ruby is in back row on the right-hand side
From the picture above, she appears to be involved in dress up or theatre/plays.

Ruby as a teenager.

As my mother grew up, she spent a lot of the time travelling and living in various places in Western Australia as Uncle Harry took on work. Somehow my mother obtained an education.

I have seen a picture of three Sisters of Mercy, and their names, so I assume she spent time somewhere with these sisters or she did it by correspondence. We will never know.

Auntie Nell and my mother outside one of their homes.

Uncle Harry later built the house in Seventh Avenue, Maylands, where we children and our mother would spend Christmas each year. My dad worked over Christmas and could not come to Perth. In fact, he only went with us once, and that was when we went to Mandurah for Christmas, and Uncle Harry erected a large Bell Marquee.

Uncle Harry also worked south of Perth, and it appears that my mother had a job working in a Post Office at Bridgetown, possibly whilst Uncle Harry was building the Bridgetown bridge over the Blackwood River.

Note. A friend showed me a paragraph from a book she was reading. The author stated that a very pleasant lady at the Bridgetown Post Office was very helpful when attending to his requirements. He went on to quote her name as Ruby Cope.

My Grandfather

Thomas James Cope worked on the railway that carted timber from the timber mills in Jarrahdale to the jetty in Rockingham. One night, working as a brakeman who would jump from carriage to carriage applying the brakes to each carriage on the descent down the scarp, on arrival into Rockingham, he was nowhere to be found. Retracing the journey, he was found deceased on the Mundijong plains, where it is thought he had fallen whilst jumping from one carriage to another. On a previous trip, the train had a derailment thought to be around the Duckpond Road/Telephone Lane area, and he was found trapped under a carriage. He survived this incident.

Chapter 2

My Family and Me

1 March 1926 to 24 July 1944

Introduction

Let me now turn to what I know of my parents' meeting and subsequent marriage. I will then cover the birth of myself, my brother and my sister, and some information on my growing up until I was accepted by the Navy.

Parents Courtship

We were never told how my mother and father came to meet. But Surprise! Surprise! Thanks to an old Post magazine I picked up when having a haircut, I found an article written by my father. He was managing a mobile store at the end of a rail line where men were cutting wood for a mine in Beria. Among his comments was:

"there were no women at the woodcutter's camp except for a Mrs Starsavech, the wife of a woodcutter."

Towards the end of the article, he went on to say:

"the only other woman they saw was the Lady who brought out the pay from time to time to pay the wood cutters."

In closing, his final comment was:

"and I went on to marry her."

I have no other details of my mother's courtship with my father and how they fell in love. They must have been able to get together when Uncle Harry was camped near Beria. Also, Uncle Harry may have been building roads somewhere near Kalgoorlie at some time and my father was probably working in Kalgoorlie at that time. We do know that he proposed to my mother at the wishing well in Kings Park in Perth. I remember going with him, and brother Harry and his wife, to this wishing well in Kings Park, where he indicated that was where he had proposed to my mother.

My mum had been raised a Catholic; Dad was, if anything, a Presbyterian; although when asked by me it was always *"Bush Turkey."* Auntie Nell forbid the marriage, probably because my father was not a Catholic, and was much older than my mother. That did not stop my mother leaving for Kalgoorlie to marry my father. *See Aside for another Surprise.*

An Aside. Before becoming employed as the Executive Officer of HMAS Stirling, I had been responsible in Canberra as the Liaison Officer during the design stage of this facility. One person I came to know well, both in Canberra and in setting up the Base, was a WA Department of Housing Construction Official who became the Project Director. His name was Jim B. We became the best of friends.

During one of our monthly luncheons at HMAS Stirling, his wife slipped me a small photograph of a young child looking out the side of the car. I recognised the photograph, as it was one of me in my Uncle Harry Martin's Buick when I was two. I was staying with them at the time of my brother's birth in Perth. When I quizzed the wife about how she had a photograph of me, she said that Jim's mother had given it to her to give to me.

I visited Jim's mum before she died. Her father was a piano tuner and salesman. While visiting the town of Bridgetown, he was approached by Uncle Harry concerning the purchase of a piano for my mother to learn to play. Uncle Harry found out that this father had a daughter about my mother's age and invited him to bring his wife and daughter down the next time he came.

Apparently, a great friendship developed between the daughter and my mother, and she often stayed with that family in Perth. Mrs B also gave me a few instances of how the two girls sometimes were in trouble with the father. She also recounted that she was the only person to see my mother off at Perth railway station when my mother was leaving to go to Kalgoorlie to marry my father. She said my mother showed her the wedding shoes and they turned out to be exactly the same as Mrs Buchanan had bought for her wedding.

My Parents' Marriage.

On arrival in Kalgoorlie, my mother went to stay with a Mrs Love, (a widow) and her two daughters, Eileen and Rita, in Lewis Street, Lamington. Mrs Love was to be the chaperone to my mother until my mum and dad married. Mrs Love gave Mum a Blue Bird tea set as a wedding present when she married.

The following is an extract of a paper record of my parents' marriage in 1923.

> *"A quiet and pretty little wedding in St Mary's Church, Kalgoorlie, on November 17, when Walter, youngest son of Mr & Mrs Ritchie of Ballarat, was married to Ruby, only daughter of Mr & Mrs Cope of Jarrahdale. The Rev Father Langmead officiated.*

Their initial residence was in Boundary Road, Kalgoorlie. They then purchased a house at 88 Lewis Street, a short distance from, and on the opposite side of the street to where Mrs Love and her girls lived.

I have no idea how the Loves came into my mother's life. It may have been that they met my mother at the Catholic Church when Uncle Harry was constructing the bridges for a railway line between Kalgoorlie and Leonora. Auntie Nell and my mother could have been with Uncle Harry at this time, and my father could have been working in Kalgoorlie.

However, several times, I do remember my mother visiting and taking me to the Love's. I would sit on the back steps and be given a cool drink.

Soon after moving into their new home, Mum asked Mrs Love over for morning tea on a Sunday after Mass. Dad was told to put a shirt on and join the ladies.

Wedding Photo of Walter and Ruby

88 Lewis Street (Corner of Campbell Street)
The layout of the house is set out below.

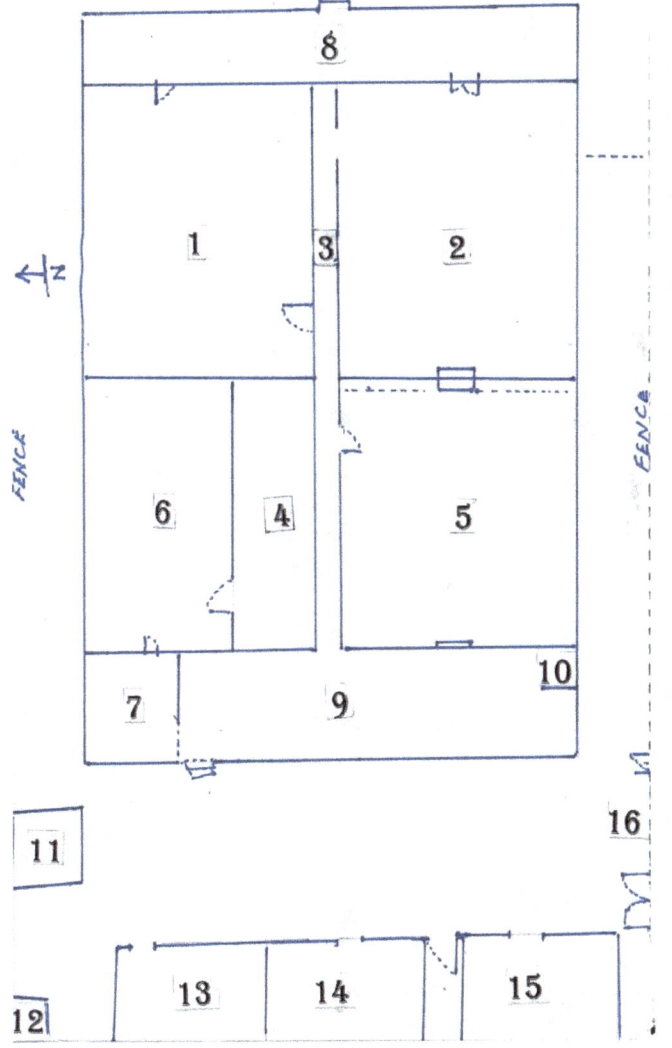

THE HOUSE consisted of one main **Bedroom (1)** on the north side of the house with a similar sized **Lounge room (2)** on the opposite side of a **Passageway (3)** that led from the front door to what was known as the **Lobby (4)**. Behind the Lounge was the Kitchen **(5)** of similar size to the bedroom/lounge. A common brick chimney was shared between the kitchen stove and the grate in the Lounge Room. I cannot recall if the Lounge fireplace was ever used during my time living there.

Behind the main bedroom was a small area known as the **Back Room (6).** This contained a single bed some cupboards and an old fireplace. This was the children's bedroom, until they were old enough to sleep on the front veranda. In other words, used, particularly in winter, for breakfast or a snack. There was a chair or two placed around the kitchen table. Across the front of the house was a **Veranda (8)** with a step. There was a trellis with vines across the front veranda that provided some protection from the elements.

There was also a **Veranda (9)** across the back of the house. The northern end had been enclosed to form a **Bathroom (7)** that had a door to the veranda and one from the Back room. At the other end of the veranda was a large **Coolgardie Safe (10)** standing in a tray of water. The top was pyramid-shaped with a dripping tap over the apex that kept the hessian sides damp and allowed butter and the like to be kept cool during the heat of the day. This Safe stood in a tray of water to stop ants and other insects from getting into the safe.

There was a small step by the bathroom leading to the backyard. A large wooden box was situated on the back veranda and contained the chopped-up wood for the kitchen fire. I also remember a small water bag located on this veranda close to the door to the Lobby. Later, a large fresh water bag with a hose from the bottom replaced the smaller bag. There was no Coke or similar in those days.

There were no overhead fans in any of the rooms; no radio, telephone, and television weren't heard of in those days.

Separate from the house was a **Wash House (11)** containing two wash tubs, with a scrubbing board and a hand ringer in between the two tubs. Cold water taps were located above each tub from memory. The copper adjacent to the tubs was wood-fired and just outside the entry to the Wash House. The water for the copper was taken from a rain tank alongside the back veranda or filled with water from the taps over the wash tubs.

The **Dunny (12)** was located in the corner of the back, and next door's fence. It consisted of a small hut with a door. There was a wooden seat with a hole in the middle that sat over the dunny pan that collected discharge from one's bowels. Each week the dunny man would come and collect the pan from under the seat using a door in the back fence that opened into the back lane. The toilet paper was pages from the newspaper torn to make toilet paper. This was hung on the hook on one side of the Dunny.

Three **Horse Stables (13,14,15)** and the **Feed Room**, located between stables (14 and 15) abutted our back fence. There was a small and large gate (16) that opened onto the road alongside the southern fence. The stables were fenced to keep the horses in their stable areas. The stable nearest the dunny was used as a storage space for boxes, suitcases, and lots of odd pieces. I was forbidden to touch anything in this Stable. Ha, ha, ha.

Alongside the end wall, nearest the dunny, was where the manure was heaped and allowed to break down.

Furnishings

I think it appropriate to mention the furnishings for, by today's standard, they were basic. The Main Bedroom contained a large, iron double bed and a standalone large wardrobe at the foot of the bed, as well as a wash basin stand with a water jug and basin on one side of the bed. There was a dressing table near the wash basin stand, and on the other side of the bed, by the door to the front veranda, was another small table behind which was a gun. As shown in the sketch, there was also a door to the passageway.

The Lounge room contained a three-piece lounge and a fireplace with a mantle above. On one side of the fireplace was a picture of my Cope grandparents and, on the other, a wedding picture of my parents.

The Passageway had a small stand and I remember there were hooks for hanging coats and a place for a brolly.

The Lobby contained a dining table on one side and near the walls of the back room. There was a long wooden stool against this wall on which we children sat. My father always sat at the end nearest the back veranda and my mum would sit facing opposite us on the chair. If there were visitors staying, they would sit alongside my mother or at the other end of the table to my father. Initially, there was no ice box. Later, an ice box was placed against the back wall of the lobby and used in the summer months.

The Kitchen had a large table that stood under the window opening onto the back veranda. There were some chairs around the table and there was a sideboard on the southern wall for crockery and cutlery. There was a bench between this wall and the stove. There was a sink in this bench; I can't remember if there was a tap over the basin, and I certainly remember there being no drainage pipes from the sink. Washing up dishes was done in a large basin on the table, with hot water being boiled on the stove. I think there was also another bench from the stove to the wall with the lobby. It was a wood-fired stove. The washing-up water was thrown under a small tree in the backyard.

As a child, I was washed in a tub on the kitchen table until I could use the bathroom and bath by myself. To make toast, it was necessary to place the bread on a 3-pronged wire fork browning one side then the other from the opening to the wood fire.

Something that has stuck in my mind all these years was that at the end of the week, on my father's return from work, he would go to the sideboard and place his pay in a small container. I think he kept what he needed for his recreational activities – card playing.

Mum Ironing. I remember when Mum was ironing in the Lobby, one of my very early duties was to bring out a hot iron from the top of the kitchen stove and take the cool one back to the stove for reheating.

Later, when the house was rewired, power points were placed in each of the rooms. The one in the kitchen was used to boil water, the one in the lobby was used by my mother for ironing, and the one in the main bedroom was for a bedside light. There was also one in the Lounge room, and much later, I believe a radio of some kind was placed in that room.

The Back Room had an old unused fireplace in the centre of the outer wall. My father's old tin trunk containing his military uniform and other items of memorabilia was placed in the space and there were strict instructions we were not to touch the tin trunk. (ha, ha, ha). There was a single bed with a bedside table and a large linen cupboard against the rear wall, located between the door from the lobby and the bathroom door.

Bathroom. This contained a full-sized bath with a shower over one end. There were two shower curtains. A wood chip water heater was sited against the outer wall alongside a table and hand basin. My father's razor strop was hung on the door to the veranda. This door was never opened in my time.

Clothesline. Two cross pieces on poles, some distance apart, with wires between, provided a place to hang out the washing. To take the sag out of the lines and to prop up the centre of the clothesline and so keep the washing from touching the ground was a clothesline prop (a long pole with a fork at one end).

Stables (13,14,15). Usually there were two racing horses in the stables, sometimes three, that my father trained and raced.

Front Veranda. The front veranda was our bedroom; the back room and lobby were equal in size to the main bedroom and passage. The lobby was the main dining area, although the kitchen area also had a table.

My Birth

On the 3rd of March 1926, the Kalgoorlie Miner announced that a son had been born to Walter Robert and Ruby Laura Ritchie (nee Cope) on the 1st of March 1926 at a Nursing Home in South Kalgoorlie. On leaving the Nursing Home, I was taken home to 88 Lewis Street, Lamington. The couple would have been extremely happy because on a previous occasion, my mum had miscarried when she'd tried to reach something at the top of a tall wardrobe. (told to me by my mother) I was baptised Bill Gray Ritchie after one of my father's Light Horse mates from WWI. However, the Register of Births would not accept Bill as a proper name, and I was registered as William Gray Ritchie.

While some of my memories are sketchy, I would have first been put in a cot in my parents' bedroom and later moved to the back room and then the front veranda. Initially, the only protection from the elements on the veranda was a trellis with the vine on the front side of the veranda. The southern end was three feet (one metre) above ground level, and one had to be very aware on a dark night not to walk the wrong way to the front door.

My brother **Harry** arrived on April 3, 1928. Harry was born in Perth, and during the latter part of my mother's pregnancy, we lived with my Aunt Nell and Uncle Harry at 127 Seventh Avenue, Maylands, a suburb of Perth.

I had accompanied my mother to Perth and was looked after by my Auntie Nell. I can remember being told I had a baby brother and, although I seem to recall being taken to the hospital, my mother was in to see this brother of mine. I cannot remember being taken to the ward and seeing my brother. However, I do recall being taken to the chocolate factory on Guildford Road, run by my Uncle Athol C, my mother's half-brother from her father's second marriage. I had a feast.

When we returned to Kalgoorlie, I do not know. I believe it would have been as soon as my mother had recovered enough to undertake the journey back to Kalgoorlie by train. I remember another of my uncles and aunts lived not very far away from the Chocolate Factory. I can't recall if I went to the chocolate factory again.

On our return home with Harry, I was required to sleep on the front veranda. My bedding consisted of cotton sheets, one blanket and a counter-pain. In winter, it could be very cold in Kalgoorlie. To keep warm, I would grab sheets of newspaper and put them between the blanket and the counter-pain. A hot water bottle helped warm the bed.

As previously stated, the only protection from the elements was a trellis along the front of the veranda with a vine growing along it. When there was a dust storm or rain, I would move into the lounge room with my blankets and sheets and sleep on the lounge or in the two lounge chairs pulled together. As Harry and I grew older there was always a bit of an argument as to who should get to sleep on the chairs as opposed to on the lounge. You couldn't fall out of the chairs. You could roll off the lounge.

The Great Depression

When I was about 3½ years old, the Great Depression began on Black Tuesday, 29th of October 1929. So began a time of extreme hardship for the people of Australia and elsewhere. Even before the devastating stock market crash on Wall Street in New York, United States of America, unemployment in Australia was already 10%. This collapse of the stock market trading signalled the beginning of a severe depression for the whole industrialised world; Unemployment in Australia more than doubled to over 21% in mid-1930 and reached its peak in mid-1932 when almost 32% of Australians were out of work.

Fortunately, my father remained in employment throughout the Depression. However, people were forced into all sorts of tricks and experiences to survive. There were all sorts of shabby and humiliating compromises. In thousands and thousands of homes, fathers deserted the family and went on the track (became itinerant workers), or perhaps took to drink.

I still have memories of men coming through our side gate to our back door and seeking any bread or tea. We really did not have much to give, my mother always kept the morning teapot and whatever bread she could spare to give to these people. I remember something else which they greatly appreciated. The first comment is, except for one fellow, every person who came through that gate chopped up some of the wood by the gate before he left. The second was in the middle of winter, a chap arrived wearing only a shirt and slacks. When my mother asked him if that was all clothing he had, he replied yes. She told him she had a sweater that had a few holes in it and he was very happy to accept that. I seem to remember he gave a bit more time cutting up the wood.

Other social consequences of the Great Depression included working-class children leaving school at 13 or 14 years old and every woman carrying a greater domestic burden. Homemaking was still considered a woman's role, so even if the woman had worked all day scrubbing someone's floors to bring in some money, her unemployed husband still expected her to cook dinner and keep the house in order.

My Childhood Pre-School

My earliest recollections are of being able to roam around the street and to play on the jingers used for carting large loads, such as houses or part of a house, and harness equipment for camels. It was located on the large open block opposite our house. My mother always insisted I wear sandals when playing in this area. Nails and other metal lying on the ground meant it was possible to be infected by tetanus when something pierced your skin, especially the soles of the feet. She obviously knew of young James Cope's death due to Tetanus.

Janet's Arrival

My sister Janet arrived on the 10th of May 1930. She was born in a Maternity Hospice alongside the Kalgoorlie Fire Station. My cousin Nell Hughan had come to Kalgoorlie to look after me whilst my mother was in hospital. I can remember being taken to the hospice but cannot recall being taken up to the ward to see my mother and sister.

What I do remember is being allowed to climb all over the fire engine and have a fireman's helmet placed on my head.

Messages

When playing somewhere in the street I would smell biscuits or cakes being removed from the oven. I would knock on the back door of that neighbour's house asking if there were any messages they needed. Mostly a treat would be offered. From early on, there was one house that I knew I was not to go to. It was on the opposite side and down the street from ours occupied by the Taggart family.

Life is Strange. Later in life, while the Executive Officer of HMAS *Stirling*, I received a phone call from a lady who identified herself as someone from the local Historical Society. I was asked if it was possible to arrange a visit to the HMAS *Stirling* on Garden Island for an elderly lady to view a large Norfolk pine tree that had been planted by the person's parents many, many years ago – when people had holiday shacks on Garden Island. When I asked for the car number that would be bringing the two ladies to the island, I was told that I would need to provide the car. My answer was "Really?" The reply was, "Billy Ritchie, I threw you out of my kitchen often enough when you were small." When I asked the name again, she said, "Nora Taggart!" I then knew exactly who it was and provided a car and personally escorted the pair to the tree.

When Janet arrived home, it was not long before brother Harry joined me on the front veranda – that was our bedroom.

An Aside. As Stipendiary Steward, my father would walk from the mounting yard alongside the racing track to the tower where he could observe the race. Many people, ladies in particular, would ask him who he thought would win. Starting at the first horse number in his race book, he would give each a number and, if necessary, start again if there were more requests than horses in the race. So, there would be at least one person who had the winner. My mother, a keen punter, would not be impressed when some lady came up and told her that my dad had given her a winner She would retort, "He never gives me any winners." (I learnt what he did by watching him after I sold my race books.)

A Bluebird Tea Set was bought out for the occasion. When Dad took his first sip, his comment was, "Where did you get these cups?" After a few more sips, he said, "A man can't drink out of these fool cups and stop kicking me under the table."

Dad did not make a good impression on Mrs Love.

Note: This Tea Set and my mother's wedding ring are my brother Harry's most prized possessions.

There were few cars in those days. The greengrocer, baker and milkman all had horse and carts with their wares displayed. Sometimes I would be allowed to sit in front of the cart and accompany the driver up the street and eventually get off and run back home.

Billy Ritchie

As I became more adventurous, I began climbing trees alongside of the house. There was a girl named Verity who lived just down the street and, as we got older, she would join us and climb trees and other activities we were up to. One day she came along and said that her mother told her she was not to climb trees or play with us anymore. We never questioned why.

Mrs Geddes Boarding House.

The relationship of Mrs Geddes and my parents is not known. I have assumed that my father probably boarded there at times and probably prior to his marriage to my mother.

From time to time, I, and later Harry and Janet, would be taken to a Boarding House almost opposite the Catholic Church. This was run by Mrs Geddes herself and we would be entertained to what I thought was a wonderful lunch. We would sit at the long tables, with nice plush chairs, and be brought out meals. After the meal, I would be taken away by the staff to be shown the kitchen, pantry and the general preparation area while the adults talked. Sometimes I would be taken into the cool room where there were all sorts of meat carcasses hanging from rails. Sometimes, I would be given a piece of fruit or, on a special occasion, an extra sweet dish.

Mr Geddes was a pompous Englishman, always attired in the suit, with a waistcoat, and the necessary fob watch. He wore a bowler hat and carried a walking stick or cane. And, as far as I am aware, he never contributed to the running of the Boarding House. He was known to try and make advances to the chambermaids working for Mrs Geddes. He would try and get a girl alone when she was making up a bed and/or cleaning a room. He would threaten her with the sack if she told anyone.

It was his motive operandi to take off his shoes to reduce the noise as he crept up to the unsuspecting lass. A new girl was an obvious target. The senior chambermaid made sure the door was wide open and inviting for Mr Geddes to see the new girl alone in the room making up the bed. He fell for the bait and, on one occasion, as he was sneaking up on the girl who was bending over the bed, he let out a large cry of pain and started hopping around the room. The senior chambermaid had sprinkled brass drawing pins all over the floor from the entrance doorway to the bed. Mr Geddes made a hasty retreat and, after that, was never so keen to sneak up on the chambermaids.

Mrs Geddes also had a very nice home, not very far away from the Boarding House and there was a very nice park opposite. On occasion, she entertained us with afternoon tea at the house. I would be allowed to go and play in the well-grassed and tree-covered park. I had many happy times exploring the park and looking for insects or other interesting flora. At that time, the Kalgoorlie Swimming Pool was adjacent to the park. I was forbidden to go to the pool as I could not swim and often listened with regret to the happy noises and shouts coming from the pool.

Church

I can recall, that after my brother was born, walking beside my mother, who was pushing a pram with Harry in it. We were going to Church that was over a mile plus from home. Later, we would go to the local Sisters of Mercy Convent School where Mass would be celebrated in one of the school rooms. This was less than half the distance to the Church from home.

From time to time, there would be a Mission at the Church, presented by Priests of the Redemptus Order. I still remember their homilies, where they would pound the pulpit to emphasise the point they were making. Not too sure if I took too much notice of what they were saying, but I now realise this approach helped to embed some of my faith subconsciously.

Sometimes, when visiting the Boarding House, my mother would go to Confession in the Church, and I would be sat in a pew nearby until she was ready to leave. When I asked questions about what went on in the Confessional, I was put off with the statement that "you will learn soon enough."

One day, I ducked out of the Boarding House and waited until no one was making to enter the Confessional, and I went in. When asked to confess my sins I was initially silent. The priest then went through the Ten Commandments individually. When he came to "Thou Shall Not Kill" I confessed that I had killed a lot of flies, spiders, and a couple of lizards. He blessed me and I left. I later found out that he related this incident when he was dining out with other parishioners.

Another thing I remember about going to Mass in the Church (not the Convent) was how each of the three Societies would attend Mass. There were the Children of Mary, who would attend one week and sit as a group in the front pews on the left as you faced the Altar; the next week, the women's Sacred Heart group would sit in the same pews that the Children of Mary had occupied. The men's Holy Name Society would occupy the front pews on the right-hand side as you faced the Altar on the third week. I joined this group as soon as I was able.

Dance Night.

There was a regular weekly dance night in the Church Hall, however, I never got to learn to dance until much later in life. On occasions I stood at the door watching, but never went in.

Movie Pictures

There were two main cinema theatres and a smaller indoor theatre. One was at the top of Hannans Street, named the Cremorne, and at the other end of Hannans Street was the Regent. Both these theatres had outdoor garden areas for the showing of movies in the summer months. The Cremorne Gardens was separated from the main theatre by a pub whilst the Regent Gardens were adjacent to the main theatre. The indoor theatre, the Majestic, was about 1/3 of the way from the Cremorne to the Regent, in the main shopping area. There was also another theatre and gardens, the Palace, in nearby Boulder.

As a treat, when young, my mother would take me to the indoor movies at the Majestic. Sometimes, after the pictures, I would be taken into Tippett's Tearooms next door, and be treated to a drink and a large cream puff. When old enough to be trusted on my own, I was given the money to go to the pictures and to buy a drink.

The outdoor theatres had deck chairs in front of the screen and behind them were the stalls. At the Cremorne Gardens, a 3-foot, high fence separated the two. Girls would be given the price to sit in the deckchairs, and invariably the boys were only given money for the stalls. When the lights went out, there would be boys jumping over the fence going to sit with their girlfriends in the deck chair. When the film ended there would be a rush to get back over the fence again before the lights came on.

During the break in the movie, there would be a rush to the shop across the road to buy a drink and an ice cream or chocolate. When in the shop, the boys, with girlfriends, tended to hold back buying, so as not to reveal what they were buying for the girlfriend. When the bell went to signal the movie was about to restart, there was a rush to the counter and then to the theatre to jump the fence again. As I did not have a girlfriend, I was quite amused by these going-ons.

After the movie was over, the girls, who didn't have boyfriends, would walk two or three together going home. It was not unusual for the boys to block their path several times using their bikes, so the girls would arrive home late and would get into trouble.

One girl had a father who was a reasonably heavy drinker. He would fall asleep waiting for her, and she would get a dressing down if late, and maybe a smack or two to reinforce his anger. Just to make sure he was awake, boys would throw stones onto the galvanised tin roof as she was walking to the front door. An angry father would read the riot act to his daughter.

Aside. During one of my Naval leaves, and I must've been over 21, I went to say hello to the daughter of one of our family friends who was working as a barmaid in the Palace Hotel, on the corner of Hannan Street. I was in uniform. A man came and sat beside me. I recognised him as the father referred to in the above paragraph.

He said, "Sailor, would you like to join me in a drink."

I replied, "Only if I can buy you one in return."

He agreed, and we settled into a conversation about my time in the Navy, what I had been doing and that sort of thing.

When there was a pause, I said, "What is your daughter doing these days?"

He sat bolt upright and, in a slightly angry voice, asked, "How do you know my daughter?"

I laughed before answering, "How many bricks do you have on your roof."

His response was, "How do you know about them?"

I replied, "One or two of them would be mine."

He said, "Really," and I apologised for my foolish boyhood behaviour. He forgave me and told me his daughter was married and not living in Kalgoorlie. Sins of the past do catch up.

Let me return to my story.

Riot

I was rising eight years old when my father came home in the middle of the day and ordered us not to go outside our fenced area. When he left, he had his rifle with him and was made a Special Constable. The only comment was that there had been trouble in Boulder near where the mines were.

The reason for this situation was that the celebration of the 1934 Australia Day in Kalgoorlie and Boulder resulted in a riot. The events that led up to this riot were sparked by the accidental death of a local sporting identity and miner. The inebriated miner had been twice ejected from the Home and Home hotel by the Italian Barman. He subsequently died. The mob, mainly Southern European settlers, attacked, destroying commercial and private property. Three people were killed, including a young Croatian miner from Dalmatia, and over 90 people were arrested. The goldmines were closed for a week. The event left a deep scar that took decades to heal and was the main cause of insecurity that undermined the social fabric of this important mining area made up of diverse communities. Foreigners were marginalised and discriminated against in this settlement established several decades earlier. They did not have equal access to work as their Australian/British neighbours.

Schooling

Before I was of school age, my mother introduced me to the alphabet and small words that I would be taught to pronounce. Also, what each number represented. Emphasis was placed on the pronunciation of a letter or number. I was taught simple adding up and subtracting with the numbers 1 to12. I was also taught how to hold a pencil and how to write a word, quite clumsy of course. She also taught me how to use the knife and fork or spoon when there were several of each on the table in front of me.

This training helped when I began school as I had a basic knowledge of words and numbers and what they meant.

My First School was at St Mary's Catholic Primary. This was adjacent to the St John's of God Hospital, near the main shopping centre of Kalgoorlie. It was run by the Sisters of St John Of God, who were responsible for the hospital. The Sisters wore a very large, white head covering which fascinated me. When I was enrolled, I remember that most of the students were girls and there were only about five or six boys like me. I wasn't there long before I, and some of the other boys, were transferred. I then began school at the Sisters of Mercy Convent School, Butler Street, which was much nearer my home. This school had quite a fair proportion of boys to the girls.

When the bell rang at the start of the school day, we would form a queue behind our Class Teacher. I think the National flag was hoisted, and maybe we recited the National Anthem, and then we advanced into the classrooms.

One Sister I remember well. She had no hesitation in slapping the cane on your desk to gain attention if your mind was straying or if you were misbehaving or to give you a few cuts on the hand if you were behaving badly. Most of the other Sisters taught in a way that kept your attention and rarely used the cane. I enjoyed schooling. The younger classes would get the breaks earlier than the older ones. We would enjoy taking turns on the swing until the elder students came out. They would take over pushing the swing, so you went right up until you were almost parallel with the ground. This is very frightening and, of course, the younger students would abandon using the swing.

I can't remember the results of any exams. I think I would have been in the middle of the pack or just above. Certainly not the best learner.

Occasionally, one of the students would be sent to help the Sister in the Convent kitchen. Such things as peeling potatoes and helping with other vegetables and chores was the order of the day. Very occasionally, the supervising Sister would give you a reward. However, like most people of those days they could not afford any luxuries of any kind, so it was a special treat.

The Bike Incident. There was one incident I certainly remember clearly from my days at the Convent. It was about riding a bike. The only people who owned bikes tended to be those people who needed a bike to get to work. Very few children had them. The cost of a bike for a child was usually beyond the finances of most people.

One of the boys, named Wacker, who was in my class, brought a bike to school and challenged the gathering with, "I bet none of you can ride a bike." He challenged anyone who thought they could to come forward. One of the boys of my brother's age, whom I often joined in games, said, "Bill Ritchie can." He had obviously seen me and the chap next door helping me learn to ride. I wasn't particularly impressed by his statement.

Wacker then challenged me to show what I could do. Apprehensively, I got on the bike, which was small enough for me to reach the pedals, and slowly took off riding around the tennis courts of the school, gaining more confidence the further I went. Having proved the point, I found there were no handbrakes, and I had not yet learnt to put my foot on the back wheel to stop. I bought the bike alongside a tennis net that was up, and slowing down, I was able to grab the net and stop the bike. However, ever so slightly, the pedal caught in the netting and bent the pedal somewhat. Wacker yelled at me that he was going to kill me. Just then the bell rang for us to line up prior to going into the classroom again. I made a beeline to be first in the queue and stood behind the Nun at the head of the queue. I managed to avoid him throughout the rest of the day and made sure I went home by a different way than normal. Strangely, he never brought up the matter again. Apparently, his younger brother, also known as Wacker, was in my brother's class. Their sister, Mollie, went on to become a Nun.

The Four R's. Learning the 4R's – Reading, wRiting, and aRithmetic, as well as Religious Instruction, kept our minds active. With writing, we were taught how to hold a pencil and used paper that had lines across. This allowed us to be taught the correct slope and height of each letter and, all these years later, I still have a neat hand, when I apply myself.

The Nuns got to know you and your family very well. One of the Sisters I liked quite well was the Mother Superior who taught us. I can't remember what the subject was. Like all Sisters, she was stern in her approach. I always found her helpful, if I indicated I didn't quite understand the question or how to answer. Here I digress again.

Unlikely meeting. My Naval Annual Leave was usually six weeks and around Christmas time. I would spend time with my family in Kalgoorlie and catch up with any friends who were not away in the Defence Forces. After a week or two I would travel to Perth, staying at my Auntie Nell's. The last week or two would be back in Kalgoorlie with family. It was here I would catch the train back East.

Returning from Perth on one occasion, two Sisters of Mercy joined the train at Coolgardie, about twenty miles or so from Kalgoorlie. They came into the compartment I was in on my own and sat diagonally opposite me. I immediately recognised the senior Sister from my days at the Convent School. I was in uniform and much older than when she had last seen me, probably nine or ten years. When she did not say anything, I made the comment that "You have obviously forgotten me, Sister." A big smile appeared on her face and her reply was "Never, Billy Ritchie." We discussed what I had been up to since I joined the Navy.

Bonfire Night

This occurred in November each year, and a pile of old dried branches would be lit on the vacant block behind our house. Those attending would let off all sorts of firecrackers. Sparklers were favourites, as were jumping jacks and other sorts of crackers. Sometimes, there would be skyrockets as well. Next morning, we would be out looking for any crackers that had not gone off.

It was not unusual for someone to place a heavy cracker in someone's letterbox and destroy it. Fortunately, I avoided doing this.

A Fancy-Dress Ball

A Ball was held in the Kalgoorlie Council Hall each year and children would look forward to parading in their fancy clothing, most handmade by the mothers. My mother made several outfits over the years, and we enjoyed ourselves parading before those present.

Navy Interest

I am not sure how it came about, but around the age of nine or ten I must have seen a movie, or read a book, magazine, or something, that revealed the exploits of the group of sailors who had to haul an artillery piece up a mountain, covered in thick forest and with hardly any paths to get into the top. When the gun was finally in position, it dominated the bay below. Something in the trials and tribulations of the sailors, and the successful engaging of the ships in the harbour, inspired my imagination. From that day forward I seem to have formed the opinion that I would become a sailor in the King's Navy.

On one occasion, when at a school chum's house doing homework, his mother asked me what I wanted to be when I grew up. I had no hesitation in saying a sailor. She then gave me a serious lecture on the last thing I should do was to become a sailor, because she had a relative who had served in sailing ships and had fallen and been killed. She emphasised how dangerous it was to be at sea even in peacetime. I listened, absorbed, and thought about what she had said. However, it never took away the desire to join the Navy.

Christian Brothers College (CBC)

Eventually, the time came to move on from the Convent and start at the Christian Brothers College; this was a School for Boys only. It was also the other side of the main street of Kalgoorlie. Unless you were given a tram fare, it was a good walk to get to school, probably one and a half to two miles or so.

Alongside the School was Ryan's Tuckshop. Mr Ryan was the brother of one of the Christian Brothers in the school, who taught leaving and sub-leaving classes. Very occasionally, I would be given a three-pence or sixpence to buy a pie or a pastie for lunch. Normally, our lunch was sandwiches from home. Mr Ryan would take orders for pies and pasties before school started and then he would ride up to Trahare's Deli just before lunch and bring the orders back in a big basket.

In front of the school was a large park, known as Commonwealth Park, that, from memory, had a cricket pitch and tennis courts. Later, a full-sized Olympic swimming pool was built there. I know we also had some other sports activity in the park. Later I played tennis on the courts and, as a result, I was able to leave my bike at a nearby home of three of the girls I played tennis with or when visiting the pool.

Unlike today's classes, there were ten subjects, which included geography, math, geometry, history, mostly and not necessarily all about Australia. Of course, being a Catholic School, one of the subjects was religious instruction.

The Christian Brother in charge of my first class was patient and kind and helped me where necessary. I found, if I paid particular attention to what he was saying, it would stay in my mind. I was able to keep up with his teaching although some boys found it a bit harder.

All the bright boys sat in the front rows; students like me sat behind them; those who were slow to pick up sat at the back. One thing I was to recall later in life was once we were given a task, the teachers would move to the back of the class. I always thought they were watching for someone to be talking or cheating and not getting on with what he had set us to do. I realised later that they went to the back of the class and helped those who were slow.

One of the Brothers would take boys who had a bike into the bush and teach them bush craft. When I finally got a bike, I used to enjoy these outings. I especially remember one instance where we came to a sizeable rocky hill and stopped for a break. Brother took us up the side of the hill where there were some stones piled one upon the other. He carefully began removing some from the top and revealed a pool of water. He told us this was used by Aboriginals and, if we ever used this to have a drink of water, we must carefully put all the stones back as close to what they were. Perhaps my first lesson in Aboriginal culture.

In year 9 class, I found myself being taught math or arithmetic by a brother we named Basher W. It was not always the first class of the day. As you can imagine, when we went into class, and there was no teacher, there would be a lot of teasing or messing around. On his arrival, one of the ways that Basher got our attention for what he was to teach that day, was to pick out four or five boys in the class and bring them to the front. He would ask them to hold out their hand and he would give them six of the best with his strap.

When asked, "What was that for, sir?" he would just smile and say, "You know what it's for." However, it made sure we all paid attention for the rest of the class. We soon learned that if you were right-handed, you put out your left or vice versa. As I look back on my grounding in math, his method of gaining attention has stood me in good stead throughout my life. He tended to rotate those he punished each day.

Only one other teacher could be ruthless and handy with a strap if you weren't paying attention. Later, after I had left the school, he had left the Brothers and was running a jewellery and gift shop in Kalgoorlie which I visited one time when on leave. I called into the shop to say hello and it was obvious he didn't want to know me. I never knew the reason why he left. I have always assumed that he had found someone he went on to marry.

As I look back over the cane at the convent, or the strap at the college, neither did any damage to my thinking of corporal punishment as an abuse.

One Punch

Sometimes, when going home from CBC, there would be a group of boys from the local State School who would stop you, and you could get into a punching match. I used to keep a good eye out for these groups and usually avoided them wherever they were.

However, on one occasion, I looked up a particular back lane, a short distance from the school, that I often took to avoid these gangs. Seeing no evidence of such, I started up the lane.

Suddenly, a group of boys appeared and surrounded me. They had been hiding in a recess in the back fences that allowed cars to turn into the backyards. They were urging someone bigger than myself to take me on.

My father had instructed me that, if I ever found myself in such a situation, to make sure I made the first punch and hit the opponent's nose so it bled. As my opponent kept poking me in the chest, urging me to come on, I slowly pushed my hand back behind me and with a closed fist, swung my first and only punch, hitting my opponent's nose very hard. Blood went everywhere. I jumped back and adopted a very aggressive boxer stance, inviting anyone want to be next. The mob scattered, and I was able to continue my way home. On future occasions, I could pass them by, and they would say hello and how's it going. It was to be the only time in my life that I had to throw a punch.

Hand Ball Court

There was a Handball Court against the back fence of the College. There was some competition to be first at school with a tennis ball, so you would play the first game and continue until beaten. I often tried to be the first and became quite good at the game.

Sequence. Later in life, when undergoing my second time on a course as an Officer in England, I was invited to have a game of squash with one of my British classmates. I told him I had never played the game, so we commenced with a general hit-up on the court, and after a time, he asked me if I would like to have a game. During and after the game he accused me of lying about having not played. I told him I did not lie, and that I had never had a squash racket in my hand before that day. He wasn't convinced. When I asked what the problem was, he stated that somehow, I seemed to get in the right place to return the ball all the time. I had no idea what he was talking about.

A considerable time after the course ended, I was looking back over it, and the squash game came to mind. It then dawned on me that it was my handball experience that came to the fore. We had both gone our different ways and I was never able to enlighten him of this fact.

Boy Scouts

When I was about eleven, I must've been sick, as I remember being in the back-room bed, when my mother brought in an old magazine called Boy Scouts Own. After I had read the magazine, and recovered, my mother asked if I thought I would like to join the Boy Scouts. As there were not any boys of my age in our area, I agreed and joined the First Lamington, Second Western Australian Boy Scouts Group. Here I met boys of my own age and older and was able to fit in well with them even though I was a Catholic and they were all not Catholics.

Scouts Law

I had some trouble learning the Scouts Law to gain my Tenderfoot Badge. One of the older scouts came to help me and taught me the following ditty, that I have used to guide my life ever since. The Ditty goes like this:

Trustee-Loyal-Helpful

Brotherly-Courteous-Kind

Obedient-Smiling-Thrifty

Pure as the Rustling Wind.

Along with the requirement of the three R's – Responsibility Reliability and Respect – a person will become a very valuable member of Society if they practice what this ditty says. As I write these words, they are what is very missing in the current generations. This should be explained and taught to all children by the age of four or five.

Other Scouting Activities. From time to time, we would go into the bush camping, sometimes only three or four boys on our own or, on other occasions, quite a number. Usually, we would go to a place on the water pipeline to Kalgoorlie where there was a tap, and we could get water. We would be camped nearby. I remember, on one occasion, we were barbecuing some steaks and some Aborigines came along and talked to us. However, when they left, we found some of our steaks had been pinched. However. it certainly didn't make me detest Aboriginals.

There was also an **Annual Scout Jamborette** held at Point Walter Reserve on the Swan River in Perth during the Christmas School holidays. I was able to go to these each year if I saved up thirty shillings from working at my father's place of employment. Afterwards, I would spend time with my mother, brother and sister at my Uncle Harry and Auntie Nell's place.

One of the highlights at the Jamborette was to be taken to look at various places of Industry or similar. We all would get a biscuit or two at the Biscuit Factory, cake or whatever at a Bakery. I especially remember, at one stage, we were taken to an airfield, and were able to see the latest fighter aircraft; I have an idea it was a Spitfire. It would have been after the Japanese entered the war. Some of us wanted to visit a warship or submarine berthed in Fremantle harbour. Unfortunately, these were off-limits.

One highlight I remember well was when, at one of the Jamborettes after World War II started, there was a sailor who had been a Scout before joining the Navy. He attended the camp with his hammock and slung it between two trees. He would lash up the hammock each morning. We were all interested in this style of bed and quizzed him about how he used it in a ship. This would have been when I was about sixteen.

12 Minute Mile. One of the things we learnt was to cover a mile in twelve minutes. Each year in Kalgoorlie, we would go to the racecourse and compete against other Scout Groups in the District to see who could cover the one mile in exactly twelve minutes. The technique was to run fifty and walk fifty paces. Our group used to practice regularly at our Scout meetings and became very proficient in covering the distance in exactly or close to twelve minutes.

13 Minute Mile and a Half. Later, in my Navy career, at the age of 56, I had to prove I could cover a mile and a half in thirteen minutes. Before the time came to do the test, I would practice using my Boy Scout training by increasing the running to seventy-five paces and this basically met the requirement. However, in my last year of doing this test, the Physical Trainer Instructor (PTI), supervising my test told me I had failed, although, by my watch, I was under thirteen minutes. I wasn't impressed, and I did it again and passed basically with the same time on my watch. I appreciated he was taking the Mickey. Today the PTI is one of my friends.

Play Mates in Perth

One of the next-door neighbours to my Auntie Nell had a girl about my brother's age and a boy some year or two younger than my brother. The girl's name was Elsa. We were permitted to play with her and her brother, either in our aunt's yard or in their yard. Over the years we became good friends, and I took Elsa out to the beach or to the pictures when I was on leave in Perth before proceeding to the war area.

Aside. When I was coming home from World War II, as I will relate later, HMAS *Fremantle* visited Fremantle on her way east to Melbourne to pay off the ship. Unless on duty, we had overnight leave, and I caught up with Elsa, taking her on board the ship and showing her around. Whilst on the upper deck, she asked if she could have a picture with the mast in the background, and I took such a picture for her in the mast structure.

Many years later Elsa was having a meal with her friends and her boyfriend, and the group were showing one another their photographs. When Elsa produced the picture I had taken of her against the mast of HMAS *Fremantle*, her boyfriend, who had been in the Navy, and later married Elsa, was very irritated that she'd been out with another sailor.

He quizzed her on the name of the sailor, and her reply was that you would not know him, as when on holidays he used to stay next door to her place over many years. He insisted that she tell him the name. She eventually said his name was Bill and he came from Kalgoorlie; he became very interested and asked the surname. When told 'Ritchie', he broke into a big smile and announced that he had done his initial Navy training with a Bill Ritchie from Kalgoorlie. Yours Truly. They were happily married later, and I used to see them every time I came on leave and later when I was posted to set up HMAS *Stirling*. What a small world.

Pocket Money.

So that I could earn some pocket money, my father employed me at his place of work where he was the senior storeman. I would wash and clean wine and beer bottles (26oz) so they could be reused. The main need was to remove the labels and ensure the bottle was not damaged and thoroughly cleaned. It wasn't a particularly hard task. However, in wintertime, the water could be ice cold, so you would need to boil some water in an old kerosene tin to provide suitable warm water for the cleaning. Other jobs were in the store house, where my father worked. I would be required to locate items from the shelves that were needed to fill a particular order. If there were biscuits to be selected, you may find a torn package in the tin holding the biscuits and would help yourself to one or two, making sure Dad didn't know about it. There were occasions when I helped at Stock-take time.

Sometimes, I would accompany the delivery driver, Alf, on his rounds in a very ancient truck and help deliver the various goods. Riding around in a truck in those days was a bit special, and you saw a lot of the town I normally did not visit.

One other task my father put me to work on was the filling of bottles with Port wine and labelling the bottles. Sometimes, I would feel a bit woozy when I finished. I never realised at the time that the fumes were affecting me when I was bottling, and, surprisingly, I never thought to taste the Port. My brother Harry also washed bottles, and in the winter, Stanley, one of the clerks, would bring a few potatoes and onions up to the bottle washing area, and they would be cooked in the ashes of the fire used to heat the water.

Bicycle. My father bought me an old bike from a Police Auction of unclaimed goods and chattels. It had fixed gears, no mudguards no brakes. I had grown enough to be able to reach the pedals, and it was much easier to ride to school than to walk. I soon learnt to put my foot on the back wheel whenever I wanted to stop.

One day, my father advised me that if I wanted a new bike, I would need to get a part-time job to pay for it. I was galvanised into action. I took up selling chocolates and other goodies in a tray at the football matches and selling Race Books at the Racecourse. When there was a midweek race meeting, I would be allowed out of school to carry out this task. Eventually, I was able to buy a new racing bike with gears and brakes, mud guards, light and generator. I felt as if I had won the lottery. Finally, the bike was paid for. It was lovely, a racing bike; I sometimes joined other boys and would race around the mini velodrome-like track surrounding the football field at the Kalgoorlie Oval.

Horse Riding

One thing my father taught me was how to saddle and ride a horse. I became a proficient rider. He also taught me how to hitch up a buggy and to drive it.

Outside, Street side Fence at Side of Home. Bill in the saddle

Back to Schooling.

Each Christmas we went to Perth. My mother would buy stationary, such as notebooks and other items we would need for the coming school year. The reason was they were much cheaper in Perth than in Kalgoorlie.

When I entered what would be Year 10 today, we had a new Principal arrive from the East Coast. He required that we have loose-leaf folders, with suitable lined paper to be kept in the folders. Also, there were several other items that he required us to have. No doubt he was used to having students from well-off homes in the East who were able to buy these items for use in his past school in Melbourne. Like others, my parents just did not have the funds to cover this impost.

One of the first things he did was to set us a series of maths questions to find out what our standard was. It was our first class after the Christmas holidays. Two of us in the class had topped the State in Maths the previous year with scores of 100%. Because it wasn't a test, and we had been away for something like six to eight weeks on Christmas holidays, we didn't concentrate on trying too hard in our answers to the questions. The questions were similar to the annual test we had undertaken. He was furious at the results made his thoughts known, and made a few unsavoury comments about the standard we were at. He also became very hard, and his attitude to our learning would today be intolerable. However, most of us made sure we then paid attention to achieve the results he was looking for.

It didn't take long before many of my classmates left the school because of the stress of trying to learn under him. I convinced my mother and father that I could go to the School of Mines (SoM) and do the Year 10 (then known as Junior year) subjects to pass, and it would be in good stead for my first year of gaining employment in the mining industry. Several of the subjects were related to what I had been doing in secondary school, Maths, Drawing and English and were part of the Year 10 testing schedule. The main ones I had to pick up from scratch was Physics and Chemistry. This gave me five subjects to allow me to pass the Year 10 examinations. Just in case I failed one of the subjects I attended the Boulder Technical College and undertook Metalwork that was included in Year 10 tests.

School of Mines. (SOM)

I had no trouble fitting into the class routine and learning, especially with the three subjects I had been doing at CBC. However, because I joined the class part of the way through the first term I really had to try and catch up with what I had missed. In the case of Chemistry and Physics, I was paired with a young girl, Pat G, at the laboratory bench. She helped me try and catch up as best I could, working at her home. I attended the school for three days a week and the Tech one day. After the first term, thanks to Pat's help, I was able to eventually catch and keep up in all the subjects. Even today, 80 years later, Pat remains on my Christmas card list. When stationed in Canberra I managed to meet up with her and her husband.

At the end of first term at SOM, we were given three-hour tests in each subject. In the math test I found I had no idea about four of the eight questions. I had completed the four within 30 minutes of the test beginning. I tried to work out answers to the other questions but had absolutely no idea how to answer them. They had been taught before I joined the class. I finally gave up, handed in my answers to the teacher and proceeded to the door. He stopped me leaving whilst he looked at my answers. He said you have only answered four questions. I replied, equal marks for all questions so that's 50% in what I have handed in. When the results came back, I had 50%.

Aside. Dad and Teacher. I was to later learn that my dad and the teacher were in the same Club and played cards together. The teacher told my dad of my cheeky response and how he had been unable to take a mark off the answers or even for the neatness of my presentation. Many years later, when on leave, I was to meet the teacher again and he asked me why I had not tried to answer the other questions. I told him that I had no idea of any of those questions; I didn't know how to answer because of my late start in the class. He also made a statement that my father was as straight as a gun barrel and could not be bought. His comment was that he hoped I would be like my father. I certainly have tried to make sure that I was always straight.

Employment

Sometime during my first year at the School of Mines, my dad told me that his great friend Bill M, Underground Manager of one of the mines associated with the Lake View and Star Mines, advised him of a job vacancy in the Lake View and Star Mining Survey Office. Dad thought I should apply. I made an application and was accepted as a Junior Surveyor. I was required to continue my study at the School of Mines. I would ride my bike in the morning from home to the office, some four or so miles from home – usually with a headwind – work, then spend three or four nights, up to three hours, at School of Mines or the Technical College. Fortunately, I had a light on my bike, so night-time did not present much of a problem. In winter, I trained and played with one of the Boulder City teams in the local AFL competition. The reason was, by the time I would reach Kalgoorlie, it was usually dark and most of the training would be over.

An Aside. In my father's diaries I have found notations made about a Bill M being in a unit he was in. As I have done my family research, I have found that there are M's back in my ancestral line, so it is possible that they were related.

Underground

There were several aspects of this job I had to learn, the first of which was to be the offsider for one of the Mining Surveyors, who would go underground to where the miners were tunnelling following any indication of gold. The Surveyor would always carry his theodolite that worked out the direction, while the assistant would carry a bag containing the spikes, odds and ends and tape measure used to measure distance of the areas that had been mined since the last survey.

Quite often we would leave the surface around 8 AM and return any time up to 4 PM or so when we would shower and wash our overalls so they would be dry by the next morning. When in a stope or drive, it was not unusual to find in one section there was a good airflow cooling the area and another where cooling had yet to be put in and it was very hot.

The job was to calculate the quantity of ore blasted from the face of the stope so that the miners' pay could be determined. The Surveyor would use his theodolite to work out the direction the tunnel had gone from a marker on the floor of the tunnel. I would run the tape to the stope face, and the Surveyor would record this and then measure the width and height at the stope face.

Ore blasted from the face of the stope was usually dragged by a scraper to the ore pass at the bottom, where there was a chute with a control gate that discharged into a drive. Battery-powered locomotives pulling a string of side-tipping trucks carried the ore to the shaft, where it would be poured into a skip and hoisted to the surface for treatment. When the skip reached the surface, the contents would be tipped out into a bin and, from there, would be taken to the Crushers and then onward to other parts for processing. Samples would be sent to the Assayers to analyse what was in the rock and note the amount of gold or otherwise.

Back in the office, the Surveyor would use the bearing and distance to work out how much had been removed in the area mined from the last survey and mark it on a chart. The Surveyor would then calculate the actual amount removed and work out the total. (by hand)

The assistant was required to first add up by hand to verify the Surveyor's total and then produce the printed result on an old hand-operated calculator. Sometimes, a wrong figure would be pushed on the calculator, and the Surveyor's and assistant's by-hand verification figures did not match. This meant checking by looking at the paper copy from the calculator to find where an error had been made. A corrected paper copy was used as a record.

Subject To Jokes

On joining the office, like most workplaces, there would be efforts to embarrass the new boy. In my case, I was sent to the main store to get a tin of striped paint. I arrived at the store and was told it would take a little while to mix the paint. Being awake to the joke I took off riding my bike round the mine site to fix in my mind the various buildings and what they did.

I called into the foundry and talked to the foreman, Jim M, a great friend of the family, and who had tried me out to be a blacksmith's assistant before the Surveyor job became available. I think I even went outside the perimeter of the mine site and looked at some of the old workings. Eventually when I got back to the store, they told me they couldn't mix the paint because they were one colour short, and it was on order.

I returned to the office where I was quizzed on where the hell I had been. I replied I had been waiting for the paint to be mixed and taken the opportunity to familiarise myself with the various buildings and activities in that area. I said the store people told me they had to order one colour in. I have an idea it was realised I was awake to the joke and there were no more attempts to embarrass me.

Underground Ladders

When working underground, you would be lowered in a cage to the level where you were to work. Later, the cage would be replaced by a skip that took the ore to the surface. When the skips were working, it would be necessary to use the ladders in the shaft to move from one level to the next. We always started on the upper-level job first and then climbed down a ladder in the shaft. One had to be very aware that there might be a missing rung or two in the ladder and you soon learnt to have two hands and one foot, or two feet and one hand, on the ladder. Remember, you would have a weighty bag slung over your shoulder and it would be a long way to the bottom of the shaft in the event of a fall.

Navy Application

When I turned seventeen on 1 March 1943, I obtained my parents' permission to apply to enter the Navy for service in World War 2. I received a train ticket to Perth and was interviewed and medically examined. I passed A1 and returned home, thinking I would be called up in the not-too-distant future. Imagine my dismay and great disappointment when I received a letter advising that although I was A1, they could not accept me as I was man-powered working in the mining industry.

Volunteer Defence Corp. (VDC)

As young lads, some of us would pull the targets in the butts and mark the shot on the target for the Rifle Club members on the local rifle range. Some of the shooters were World War I veterans, and at the end of their competition, we lads would be given five rounds so we could learn to shoot a .303 rifle. With the instruction, we learnt how to hold the rifle, aim and squeeze, not pull the trigger. The rifle kick was a bit hard on young shoulders if you did not hold the rifle tightly enough.

Some of the Veterans joined the Volunteer Defence Corps and, on my rejection by the Navy, I thought I would do my bit for the War by becoming one of them. Besides not being the best Drummer boy, I was taught how to strip and clean the various rifles and submachine and machine guns the group had. I also learnt Squad Drill, the Army way, and on one occasion we had a bivouac and training, with live firing with imaginary targets in the sandhills around Esperance on the south coast. Next, let me discuss how my life was turned upside down in the latter part of 1943.

Scarlet Fever.

I can't remember whether it was in 1943 or earlier that my brother Harry had Scarlet Fever and was hospitalised in the Kalgoorlie District Hospital. One night, he decided he'd had enough of the hospital and decided to make his departure. He managed to escape through a hole in the fence around the hospital and made his way home in a roundabout way, so avoiding searchers who were out looking for him. Eventually, he arrived home.

I woke up when a policeman knocked on the door. I think my mother answered to be told Harry had escaped from the hospital and they were searching for him. My dad quickly dressed and joined the search party.

Not long after he left, I found Harry crawling into bed with me. He was very cold and snuggled up very close. My dad returned shortly after and was advised Harry was with me in bed. He immediately went to one of our neighbours, who had a telephone, and advised the hospital and borrowed the neighbour's car and used it to take my brother back to the hospital. Eventually, Harry was released and re-joined the family.

My Hospitalisation

Sometime in the latter months of 1943, I developed a severe temperature of around 106 or 107. I was hospitalised in the same hospital Harry had been in and underwent quite a few procedures to try and get my temperature down. Nothing worked, and I found myself transferred to a ward where there were a few very elderly patients. It was the Male Death Ward. On several nights in this ward, I would be woken up by noises from an adjacent or bed opposite. When I asked what was going on, I would be told to go back to sleep, which I did. However, in the morning I noticed the made-up bed where there had been the noise. When I asked the nurse where he was, she advised he had left. In my state at the time, it never dawned on me that he had died.

Out of Body Experience.

One day, I was expecting my mother and father to visit, but they did not arrive at the time expected. It appears they were at the end of the veranda, at the opposite end to where my ward opened onto that veranda. Suddenly, I experienced myself flying towards where my parents, the doctor and matron stood discussing what to do with me. I was able to listen in and remember the doctor saying, they had tried all known methods of medicine to get my temperature down, and he was at wits end to what to do.

My father, a WWI Medic, then said, "There must be something you can do."

I still remember the doctor saying the only thing he could think of was that the Defence Force was using a drug called Sulphurmulamide with some success, and he would like to try it. I think he stated that it had not been used to his knowledge to bring down temperatures. My parents approved and I began to take this medication.

Within a day or so my temperature had dropped to normal, however a big red rash appeared on my chest suggesting that I had Scarlet Fever. This was cleared up and I went home. However, see **Village Idiot** below.

When I told my mother sometime after I got home that I had overheard the conversation between her, Dad, the doctor and matron, she told me I couldn't have because of the distance they were from the ward. However, she was shocked when I repeated the exact words that had been spoken, and she realised I must have had an out-of-body experience. She insisted, with great emphasis that I was never to repeat this conversation again or speak of an Out of Body experience. I often wondered why she made this remark. I came to believe that she thought I may have inherited something from my great-grandmother, Ellen Cope, who was very Irish and was said to have the Third Eye.

The Village Idiot

One morning I woke up and got out of bed as usual. When I went to walk from the bed to the front door to enter the house, I stepped backwards towards a 3-foot drop off the veranda. I immediately stopped and tried to get back into bed by stepping to the left, but I went to the right. My movements were 180° out of kilter. I was thinking what to do, and I decided to put my leg to the right, and it went left, and when I decided to push the leg back, it went forward. I decided to try for the door by thinking 180 degrees out of phase. I was able to make it to the inside and I gave my mother a fright when I told her my problem.

I was still taking the medicine given to me in the hospital that had reduced my temperature. The doctor had no idea what was wrong. I was not allowed to stay at home if there was no one there and people became aware of this kid who had a problem. The Survey Office was advised that I was not fit to carry on at that time. No medicine seemed to help and I suggested my parents advise the Survey Office to find someone else to fill my position.

In December, a decision was made that I stay at home with my father for Christmas rather than try and go on the train to Perth. Mum departed with the other two children, and I stayed home forbidden to leave the house, and I followed these instructions.

I think it was Christmas Day 1943 when my father took me to lunch at a small Café in Kalgoorlie. When the meal was served, my father cut everything up so that I could use a spoon and a fork to feed myself as I had been doing successfully at home. However, one of the problems I had acquired was that my hands would sometimes sort of flip upwards unexpectedly. Somehow, I thought I had managed to control the urge.

However, shortly after I began eating, the spoon went over my shoulder one way and the fork over the other. My father was horrified and embarrassed. He grabbed me by the scruff of my neck, pulled me out of my chair and took me outside and told me not to move. I was quite scared and shaken by what had happened. Dad returned inside to apologise to those who had collected the spoon and fork, paid the bill, and took me home. When we got home my father told me to stay in the lobby and not move. He collected all my sulphur tablets and took them outside and buried them. I was crying about him taking the tablets. When he came back, he told me to stop crying and not be a sook.

At this stage, I was sleeping in the back room in the bed. Sometime after the tablets were buried, I woke up feeling quite different and when I got out of bed, I found that my movements had returned to normal. Shortly after this, I seem to remember going to Perth and staying with Bill M, the Mine Manager's sister, and her daughters in Cottesloe. Their daughter-in-law was a WRAN Communicator serving on Rottnest Island. She would come home when off duty. The other daughters worked in the city. The son and husband of the WRAN were in the Navy. It turned out that he was the Captain of the Corvette that accompanied HMAS *Fremantle* down the West Coast after World War 2. I was serving in HMAS *Fremantle* at that time.

After returning home, after my holiday at Cottesloe, my dad suggested I should look for a job and contribute to the running of the home. His great friend, Bill M, the Mine Manager, advised that one of the mines, Paringa, was looking for someone to be trained as a cadet in the Industrial Chemistry Section of the Mine. I can't be sure, but I must've been close to eighteen at that time. During the interview, the chemist had been made aware of my past problems and agreed to give me a three-month trial as a labourer before signing on as a cadet in Industrial Chemistry. I made it quite clear that I hoped the Navy would call me up. Like everyone else, he thought that would not happen due to my village idiot period. My job was to take ore samples off an elevator of ore and, using a dolly pot, crush the ore into a powder. It was hard work. The chemist would use this powder to assess how much gold might be in that sample.

As the work was hard, I soon realised I was basically fit again, so I made another request to join the Navy. I was sent for within a few weeks, went to Perth, and passed A1 again.

Call Up

On turning eighteen, I was required to report to a Registration Centre in Kalgoorlie to be registered for Citizen Military Service. As I said above, I had fully recovered from the Scarlet Fever and being the Village Idiot. Knowing I could not avoid registering, I turned up at the appointed time and was greeted at the entrance door by a man, who was the Surface Manager for Lakes View and Star. I knew him quite well because he quite often visited the Survey Office. He took my notification and said, "You don't have to come in, Bill, we know all about you." I asked him if he was sure I did not have to sign anything. He nodded, so that was my registration.

Aside. Many, many years later, when serving in HMAS *Melbourne*, the ship visited Fremantle, and the Surface Manager's son was a helicopter pilot on board. The son asked me to act as an escort to his father and mother whilst he was flying, and I happily agreed. I met the father and mother at the gangway and gave them a bit of a Cook's tour around the ship before we sailed and then to look at the flying and recovery operations. He wasn't particularly friendly or talkative. I just did what I had to do. After the flying operations finished, his son joined and took over caring for his parents. I wondered if the father's attitude had anything to do with my Registration for Military Service and seeing me as a Lieutenant Commander.

Navy Application

When I fronted up to the Medical Officer (MO) he said, "Haven't I seen you before?" My reply: "Yes, a year ago and you passed me A1." He said "We don't need to test you so get out of here." However, I insisted he checked all my vital bits and pieces which he did and said, "You're still A1."

I returned to Kalgoorlie and informed my Industrial Chemist boss that I had again been passed A1 for the Navy. He nodded, thinking there was no way the Navy would take me. However, within a month I was on my way to Perth to sign up.

So ended my civil employment. My Naval one was about to begin. When I told my parents, they had no objection to my going away in the Navy.

HERE ENDED MY CIVILIAN LIFE for 39 years.

Chapter 3

Naval Entry

26 July 1944 to 5 January 1945

Induction

Shortly after returning to Kalgoorlie after my final medical, I received my Call-up notice with a train ticket to Perth. I was instructed to report to the Recruiting Centre, Perth, on 26 July for Induction into the Royal Australian Naval Reserve. This I did with others, and the chap standing behind me was Jack L, who was to become a mate for life. We were then advised we would be travelling east by train and to be at the Perth Interstate Rail Centre at a given time and date. From memory, there were about twenty-four of us in the group.

Train Trip

We embarked on the train and proceeded to Kalgoorlie with eight to a compartment. We sat up all night on the trip. On arrival in Kalgoorlie, we detrained and transferred to the Trans Train that would take us as far as Port Pirie where we would transfer to a South Australian train that was to take us to Adelaide. I was able to dash home and see Mum before I had to board the train east.

Reason for Changing Trains. Each State had a different Rail Gauge (distance between the rail tracks) at that time. In WA, it was 3 feet 6 inches; in South Australia, it was 5 feet 4 inches and in New South Wales, it was 4 feet ? inches.

Departure Kalgoorlie.

Departing Kalgoorlie Station, the train stopped at Parkston, a few miles out of town, to embark other passengers and, I believe, to attach rail cattle trucks in which soldiers were entrained.

Compartment. On the Trans Train, it was again eight to the compartment. As we were going to spend several nights on the train, a round-table conference was held to decide how we were going to arrange our sleeping spot. It was agreed that two would lie head to toe on the two seats and floor, leaving the two lightest weights to sleep on the luggage racks on either side of the compartment above each seat. Muggins was one of the lightest.

A Prisoner of War Compound, with Italian POWs, was not far from the station and it was possible to see the inmates at the fence looking to see what was going on. We were not allowed to approach them.

Cattle Trucks (Exotic Accommodation)

There were paillasses for each soldier to sleep on. Certainly, a poor mattress because it was not that thick.

Stops. The locomotive was steam-driven, and as we made our way across the Nullabor, it would stop at small railway settlements for water. If it coincided with a mealtime, we would be lined up alongside the track to be fed food prepared in a carriage that had been stripped of compartments and converted into an Army Mobile Galley.

Help in Galley. On some later trips, when coming on leave, some of us would be detailed to help the cooks by peeling spuds and other tasks like serving the food or washing up. Generally, the food was good and could not be complained about.

It was a single rail track, and at other times it would be diverted to a side track to allow a freight train to pass.

South Australia

After entering South Australia, the first stop was Port Augusta and then on to Port Pirie. Here we had to change trains for Adelaide. There was a pub nearby, and of course, there was a beeline for the pub, and by devious means, bottles were smuggled onto the train.

Next stop Adelaide, where we would be de-trained with our small overnight bags. I think we were billeted in Kensington Barracks until the next day's train to Melbourne. We were able to have a shower and get some decent sleep. Having little money, we did not stray far.

Enroute Melbourne

I cannot remember if it was this trip or later that we were pulled up alongside a goods train and a few adventurous souls looked under the covers of the adjacent train and found it was carrying beer. No need to explain how beer bottles were being thrown out windows on the rest of the journey. At some stage, there was a search by the senior military, and I do not think they found anything. Such is the ingenuity of soldiers and sailors.

Melbourne

We arrived at Spencer Street Station early on a Sunday morning and, having de-trained, were met by a Naval Regulator who provided each of us with tickets to Crib Point, near our destination, the Naval Training Establishment of HMAS *Cerberus*. We were instructed to be at Flinders Street Station by a certain time to catch the Liberty Men's train leaving after dark. (I cannot remember the time). We were told we were free to have a look around Melbourne City, but make sure we did not miss the train. No meals were provided. Our small group of three or four did not have much cash. I had enough to buy a coffee, the last of my cash, and someone bought a pie, and each got a bite of it. The next time we had anything to eat is set out below.

With the many Libertymen, we entrained and proceeded to Crib Point where the Libertymen rushed off and we newcomers were formed up in threes and marched (walked) into HMAS *Cerberus*.

HMAS *Cerberus*

HMAS *Cerberus*

The picture on the previous page gives an overview of the size and layout of this establishment, which was officially opened in September 1920.

I will only describe in detail our arrival and those events, or incidents, that I feel appropriate. Others I will brush over to make you aware of the sort of training we underwent. Where there is something or incident to relate, it will be in italics.

Arrival and Settling In.

Following our arrival at Crib Point, we fell in and formed into three lines. As we marched past the Barrack Blocks, we were greeted by "You will Be Sorry" coming from those Blocks. At the Regulating Office, we were checked in, handed our Identity Card and informed what Block we were to occupy. At some time, we were taken to our Block, allocated lockers, then we were off to the Dining Hall for a meal. We were the only group in this block.

The meal consisted of cold pork chops, no doubt cooked about five or six hours earlier, and uneatable. A Bread-and-Butter Custard had to do.

Then it was off to the Store to draw our hammocks and bedding before arriving at our Accommodation Block, which was about three along from the Regulating Office. Here, we were instructed on how to assemble our hammocks by attaching the rope end arrangements to each end and then how to secure them to the overhead hammock rail. Our bedding was then placed in the hammock and made ready for us to swing up and bed down for the night.

The fun then began as we were shown how to get into our hammock. This meant grasping the rail above the head, and the head on the hammock was tied, too. We were shown how to swing our legs and body up and get our legs and body across the hammock lengthwise. Then, push the hammock sides apart and get your body onto the bedding. Most of us had to have several goes before we made it into the hammock. Then it was a visit to the bathroom for a cleanup, wash and go to the toilet and then into sleeping attire and swing up and crash. (sleep) No need to rock the hammock. The time would have been getting on for midnight or thereabouts. It was the end of an extremely long and tiring day.

The First Full Day

Wakey, Wakey. At 6 am, we were awoken by the Senior Sailor in Charge of our Block yelling Wakey, Wakey, Rise and Shine and whacking the bottom of the Hammocks with a stick, the Navy way of waking you up. We then got dressed, and we were shown how to ash up and stow our hammocks and put them in the hammock bin. Then shower and shave and off for breakfast.

I cannot remember what I had, except the cereals and porridge got a good work over as did the toast, marmalade, and tea/coffee.

Outfitting.

We were then marched to the Clothing Store and fitted out with our uniforms, shoes and boots, socks, stockings, underwear, lanyards, Seaman's knife and other items such as towels, toiletries, and a small sewing kit. Then back to the Accommodation to be instructed on donning the uniform, square neck shirt, top part of the uniform, square collar etc., Bell Bottoms (trousers that flared out at the bottom). Instead of the normal buttons on the front of the trousers, there was a small flap, with a couple of buttons, it was covered by another flap that went across the stomach, securing the top flap on either side of the front of the body. Finally, we had the appearance of a sailor.

Aside: When we asked why the flap and bell-bottom trouser legs, we were told that this allowed one to get out of the trousers quickly if one finished up in the water. Something that the Navy of today has forgotten.

With our caps we were given a Tally Band, with the letters HMAS that went around the cap. We were shown how to tie a bow to secure it to the cap.

It was during this period of settling in that two extra members were added to our class. They had been ill and not been able to complete their course, so they joined us. They settled in very well and they accepted that we had a slightly different outlook on life than those from the eastern states. After the war, one of these two became a dentist and I visited him several times during trips to Newcastle.

Daily Routine.

Each day there was a programme that laid down what instruction we would be doing. In the beginning, there was Squad Drill, Physical Training, Lectures and Other activities that would train us to be sailors.

Squad Drill

It was not long before we were introduced to Squad Drill.

Having been in the VDC, I had done most things except the Navy way of Army one as was the salute.

The need to form up in three lines, come to attention and stand easy, turn left or right, how to open ranks, where the front rank took one pace forward and the rear one pace back. Then learning how to march with the foot that was to make the first movement and the swinging of the arms in the correct way. All the Parade movements were learnt and practiced. We were taught how to make the Naval salute correctly.

One of our members, nicknamed Gandhi, had a problem with marching. He would swing his arm forward on the same side as his leg instead of it going backwards as the foot went forward. Eventually, he was able to do it properly. I will mention Gandhi much later in my story.

Rifle Drill.

After we had mastered Squad Drill, we were introduced to rifle drill and began the task of Sloping Arms, Ordering Arms, Presenting Arms, Reversed Arms, and so on. Soon, we were doing Squad Drill with rifles and various marching with rifles, etc. Eventually, we were brought to the required standards.

Physical Training.

Mixed up in the daily routine were trips to the Drill Hall, where the Physical Training Instructors (PTIs) began the task of bringing our fitness up to the required level. We ran around the gym, climbed the ropes, and hung off the wall racks. Our tortured muscles were given a thorough workout each time we visited the gym. We did at least one cross-country run and other runs around the Parade ground or the gym to get the fitness standard required.

There was, I think, a 55m swimming pool where we were required to prove that we could do a length fully clothed. Fortunately, I was able to drag myself all the way without stopping which was classified as a pass for the Swimming test.

Weekend leave.

Eventually, we were given our first weekend leave and caught the train to Melbourne. Unfortunately, my friend Jack, being under 18, was not allowed to stay at Navy House in the Melbourne CBD. He had to go to an Annex in one of the suburbs. He would catch a tram into the CBD, and we looked around, had a meal, and went to a picture or something like that. After that, he returned to the Annex to sleep.

I was able to go to Mass on Sunday as the church was not far from Navy House.

On Sunday, Jack brought his overnight bag with him and left it with mine at Navy House. We went for a meal, to a picture show and we just wandered about. At the appointed time we boarded the train back to Cerberus after collecting our overnight bags.

We would be allowed leave every fortnight until we qualified.

Edithvale Home. On the second of our weekend leaves, Jack rang me at Navy House and said there was an invitation to a 17th Birthday party on Saturday at Edithvale, a suburb on the rail line back to Cerberus. There was overnight accommodation if we wanted to stay after the party.

When we got to Edithvale, we were met and taken to the house. We were introduced to the Birthday Girl and her family. The girl had an older young lady as her guardian/companion who went everywhere with her. Eventually, three or four other girls arrived. They were the Birthday Girl's friends. There were two or three other sailors present.

It was an enjoyable party. When the party finished, the men went to an adjacent building to the home to bed down. We went to get into bed and found each bed had been short sheeted; we could hear the girls giggling outside so we knew who was responsible. We resisted retaliating as their bedding was in the house.

Next morning, us bronze Aussies dressed casually, with bathers on under our clothing, and proceeded out the back gate of the property onto the beach. Stripping off, we all raced into the water and had only gone a few strokes before we realised the water was freezing. All left the water, ran up and down the beach to get warm, and the girls were all laughing at us at our predicament.

We were taken for a tour up into the Dandenong Hills after breakfast and an invitation was made that anyone who wanted to come each leave weekend was welcome to come and spend the weekend. The parents advised us that they had been doing this for some years for recruits from Cerberus. Jack and I took up the offer. Interestingly I stayed in touch with the Birthday girl and met up with her on several occasions when in the Melbourne area or touring Victoria. I was able to see her shortly before her death some years ago from when I write.

As a result of this weekend, I was asked by one of the girls if I would like to come to her place and meet her parents. Sometime after that, we would meet up and go to the pictures or beach or something similar I would accompany her home on the tram and see her to her front gate and say goodnight. I'd then catch a tram back into Melbourne to the Navy Club.

Her parents and sister basically accepted me as one of the family. In later years, whenever there was a ship I was on, or I was visiting Melbourne, I would meet up with this young lady. This relationship continued until the girl died just a few years ago. I was lucky enough to be in Melbourne and able to see her after she had been hospitalised sometime before her death. I would have liked to have married her, however, she advised me.

Later in our relationship, she wanted someone who was home all the time.

These weekends at the Birthday girl's home continued until we left Cerberus. When on any occasion I was in Melbourne on a ship, I made sure to visit the family and thank them for days gone by.

Back to Cerberus and Training

On return to Cerberus after our first-weekend leave, we continued our training.

Gunnery Training.

Gunnery training is set out below.

Machine Guns. We were trained in the Vickers heavy machine gun, the Bren and Lewis light machine guns, and Tommy and Owen Guns.

Incident. Our introduction to the Lewis gun was under the shelter of the Covered Parade Ground. The gun was taken from its large wooden box, with rope handles at each end. The instructor placed the gun on a canvas spread and proceeded to pull it apart. He then asked if anyone would like to try and put it together again. He asked each member of the class individually. No one put his hand up. I was the 26th and last one he asked. Having had to do it in the VDC, I said, "If no one else wants to have a go, I'll have a try." I proceeded to put the gun together and, in about one minute, had completed the task, reporting "Ready to fire." The instructor was more than a bit stunned, I think, and said, "Smart Bugger," and then "See that box the gun came in, pick it up behind your back and go for a run around the Covered Parade area whilst I teach these others what to do."

No question about how I knew what to do. The box that I had to carry was rectangular; the ends and lid and bottom the sides were about 2.5cm x 2.5cm thick and were quite long. I was only just able to reach the rope handles at either end. It was quite heavy I can assure you. So off I trotted slowly around the Parade ground until the session ended. If I stopped to catch my breath, there would be a shout to "get moving."

(Navy Rule – never volunteer you know anything.)

Gun Mounts. 4" Gun. After all the previous gunnery training, the time arrived to introduce us to the heavy stuff. We were trained to aim, rotate the gun, and load the 4" shells working as a team. The job of loader required you to push the shell into the gun barrel and have your hand knocked away to the side when the round was in. One was worried that your hand would be jammed in the loading mechanism. Fortunately, the instructions on how to do this were good and no one hand was caught.

Tommy and Owen Guns. We were taught how to load, aim, and fire each of these guns; we were taught how to clean them and generally assemble them. We were able to fire a few rounds and one of the things I learnt was that the Tommy gun tends to pitch up and move slightly to the right when fired on automatic.

Rifle Range

The time came for us to fire the Lee Enfield .303 rifle. We were taken to the Rifle Range and given 12 rounds to test our skill. If you were a very good shot, you could be awarded your Rifleman's badge to wear on your arm and your pay would receive a slight increase *each week*.

Incident. When my time came to fire, I was confident that I would do well, knowing how I had become quite a decent shot after pulling butts for the local rifleman at home. How wrong you can you be.

The Range Instructor was an imposing Sergeant Major, Royal Marines. He made sure that you had the gun securely held and repeated the instructions of keeping the rifle steady and the fore sight in the correct position within the after sight.

I took aim, with sights correctly aligned, so I thought, and squeezed the trigger. I was surprised that there was no mark on my target. I noticed two markers on the target to the left of my target and realised my shot was one of them. I could not work out what was wrong and decided to try again. This time I aimed to the right on the edge of my target on the side opposite to where I had hit the other target. Again, I made sure my fore and after sights were in the right position as I aimed and fired. I expected my shot to hit the left on the bullseye. Instead, it was on the right-hand edge of my target.

I called out to the Sergeant Major that there was a problem with the sights and asked if I could have another rifle. He came, took the rifle, and checked the number on the rifle butt, fiddled with the fore sight, aimed, and fired. He scored a bullseye and said 'nothing wrong with this rifle'; he told me to keep using it. I woke up that the foresight was loose.

Before each shot, I tried to make sure the fore sight was centered and I think I got a couple of bulls and the rest inners, not enough to get crossed rifles. I wasn't a Happy Chappie.

Bren Gun Firing

Finishing instructions on this gun, we were given the opportunity to fire it. Instead of the rifle range, we were to fire it down Hans Inlet, which led to Westernport Bay. We were to fire down the middle of the inlet. While I was aiming, I noticed a white swan swim out from the reeds on one side of the inlet. I just lined up my sight behind the swan and, having been given the order of the fire when ready, I fired a single shot. It hit the water just behind the swan who leapt up and paddled quickly back into the reeds. The instructor shouted, **"Stop Firing"** and gave me a blast for firing. I told him I was sorry but had just pulled the trigger as he was issuing the order.

In between all the Gunnery Stuff, we were also instructed in other various seamanship activities.

Seamanship

Knots. Our Seamanship training began with instruction on how to tie all the knots we would use whilst in the Navy. It was explained that if you did as you were taught, you would be able to undo the knots should they be very tight. My Boy Scout days had shown me how to tie a reef knot, bowline, double bowline, and sheepshank. I think I learnt some others that I can't remember.

Splices. We were taught how to join two pieces of rope and form a loop with splicing. Rope splicing was not difficult to learn. However, wire splicing was a different kettle of fish and a bit harder to learn. I seem to recall that we had to do a rope splice to pass out, and I am not sure about the wire splice.

Boat Pulling (Rowing)

Our training introduced us to three types of rowing boats. The first was the 32ft cutter, then the 27ft Waler and finally the sailing Dingy.

However, the next day, we had to move all our goods and chattels into the block alongside the MAA's office so he and his staff could keep a close eye on us.

32 Foot Cutter. This was manned by twelve oarsmen and a coxswain who steered the boat. Two men sat on each thwart and each man had a number starting from the one seated at the front of the boat.

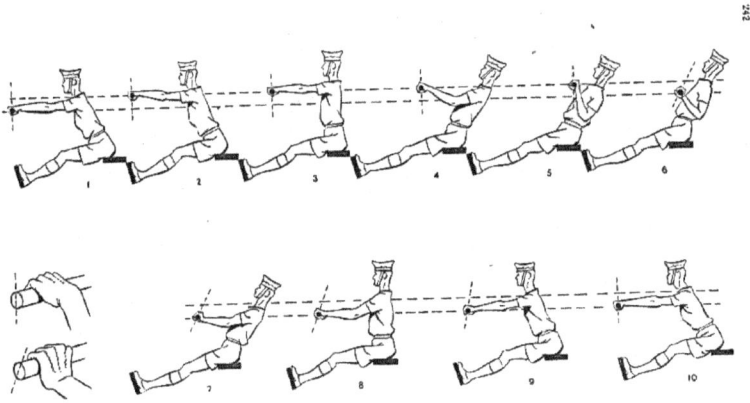
See the Pulling Cycle in Picture

The starboard side oarsman at the front of the boat acted as bowman, letting go of the line at the front of the boat. No 12 on the rear thwart was the stroke who was used to guide those pulling. (Pulling is a naval term for rowing.) All the other crew members would be behind him so they could keep an eye on his movements to coordinate theirs.

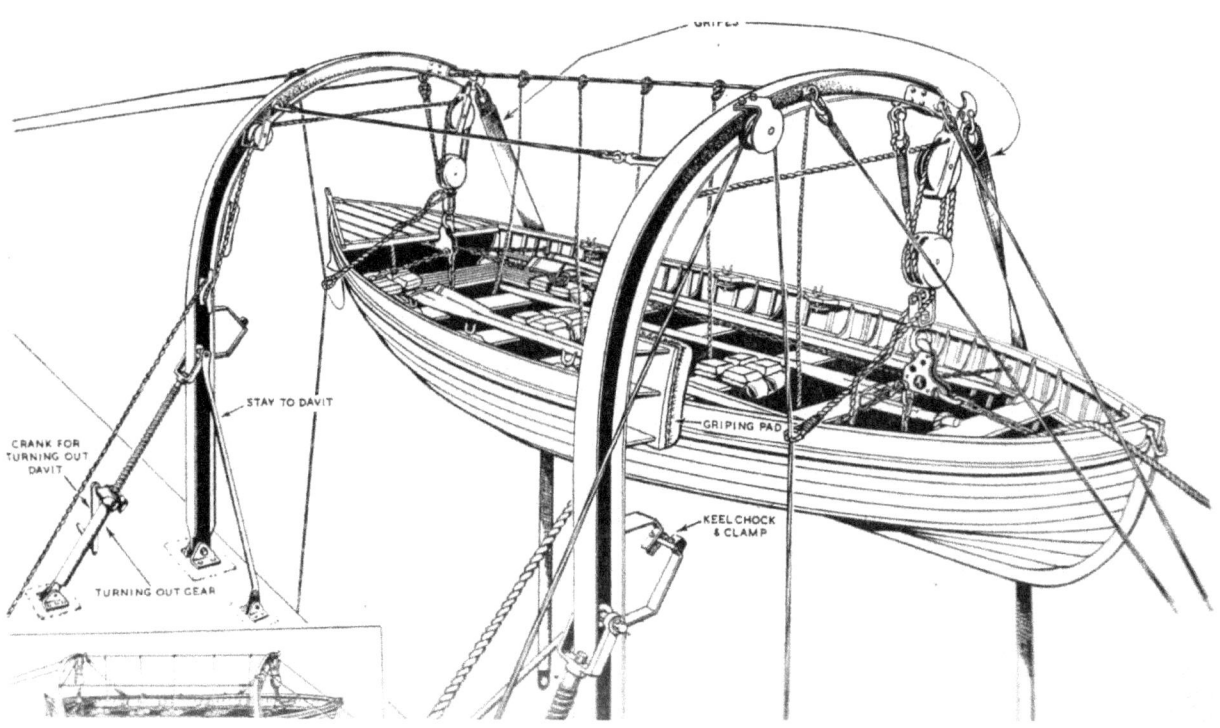

27 Foot Whaler. This boat had five crew and a helmsman on the Tiller. No1 (Bowman), 3 and 5 (Stroke) sat on port side with oars out to starboard. The other three sat on the starboard side with oars out to Port.

We were instructed on the lowering and hoisting of a boat from davits. An example is in the picture above. This is of a 27ft Whaler in the davits, swung outboard.

Lowering and Rehoisting a Whaler.

There is a disengaging arrangement under the lower blocks that is actioned by the Coxswain as the boat is lowered and reaches water level. The Coxswain releases the locking device, and both blocks are released simultaneously, and the boat is free and able to move away from the ship or wharf. There is also a line that passes from the ship to the bow of the Whaler, and once in the water, this is slipped so the Whaler can pull away from the ship side.

Returning to Ship

On return, the disengaging gear is locked, and the Bowman hooks on the front block and raises his hand to indicate the block and gear are locked. The Coxswain then hooks on the rear block. This must be done within seconds of one another, particularly if there is sea running.

The actual lowering is done by a winch in big ships and by several sailors lined up, side by side on either side of each fall. The order is given to take up the slack (ropes through the two blocks to lower and hoist). When ordered, the ropes are individually pulled tight and then at the order "marry", sailors' hands would take both ropes in their hands to ensure the boat is lowered horizontally, easing out as directed by the Supervisor.

When hoisting it is the same, the slack is taken up and then two hands placed over both ropes and at the order to hoist, the sailors move quickly away from the Davits until the order to stop is given when the boat is at the ship's deck/wharf level, so passengers and goods can be unloaded when this has been done but is secured.

Sea boat

We learnt what a sea boat was on the ship. It was the boat that could be launched quickly should there be a requirement, like a man overboard, or some other incident, requiring a boat to be in the water no matter where you were at sea. There are further comments in the Whaler in later chapters.

Swimming Test

Each member of the class was required to show they could swim the length of the swimming pool fully clothed. It was a bit harder than I thought, but I managed to pass and be accredited as a pass for the swimming test.

Divisions

Divisions were where each group was formed up and marched onto the Parade Ground where they were inspected by a Senior Officer. There would be a Guard and Band as part of the ceremony. At the conclusion of the Inspection, after any speech, or religious service, each group would be made past the Reviewing Officer who took the Salute as we marched by his position.

Sunday Church Service

On the Sunday, when the Inspection had been completed, it was time for Prayers. The senior Religious Person would take over.

In my time, Roman Catholics would fall out, and we would go to an area alongside the Drill Hall. Usually, the senior Catholic would invite everyone to pray a decade or two of the Rosary.

It was interesting to see the non-Catholics, who had fallen out to have a smoke0 and would be looking round, not being familiar with the Rosary. If there was an Officer present, he would make it quite clear to the non-Catholics that he wasn't impressed and, if he caught them doing it again, he would have no hesitation in running them in the skulking.

I'm not sure what happens these days.

Some Incidents Worth Mentioning

For some reason, those from the Eastern States tended to look on us Western Australians with some disdain, whether it was while playing football or in other activities.

There was one occasion when those in the Victorian accommodation block raided our accommodation when we weren't there, messing things up and we were held responsible for it during an inspection.

Two of our members managed to lead a firehose from the hydrant and put the nozzle through the window of the Victorian's accommodation block and jammed the window down on the nozzle. We all made sure our group were in their hammocks sleeping when the water was turned on. You can imagine the scene.

It didn't take long before the Master at Arms (MAA) and staff arrived. They burst through our door and found everyone, including the tap-turner-oners, in their hammocks and apparently asleep. We protested our innocence at being woken up. I think the MAA decided he couldn't prove it was us, and the matter was left there. However, the next day, we had to move all our goods and chattels into the block alongside the MAA's office so he and his staff could keep a close eye on us.

Another Incident.

On another night, the Duty Petty Officer came and turfed us all out of our hammocks and lined us up on the road outside with our hammocks on our shoulders. He commanded us, in a slurred voice, to Frog March to the end of the road and back. It was very dark and as we frog marched off, he sat on the side of the road, and we noted his head nodding. So, we made a lot of noise the first few yards then slowly reduced the noise until no further than about 30 or 40 yards from him. We waited a short while before reversing our noise, really stomping as we came back alongside him. He woke up as we pulled up and told us to get to bed. This we did.

We knew about this Petty Officer and that he had been on HMAS *Australia* when it was hit in World War II. He had PTSD (as it is now called) and had been sent home. He drank heavily to try and blot out his memories. We really felt sorry for him and took the matter no further.

Soundings (Finding Depth)

Heaving the Lead. To find the depth of water under a ship, a procedure called **Heaving the Lead** was used. The person doing this would stand at the ship's side, or on a platform attached to the ship's side, and swing a rope line, with the weight at the end, backwards and forwards until he had enough momentum for it to circle over his head and for him to let it go at a line parallel to the water. He would let it go forward as far as possible. The weight would sink, and as the ship moved ahead, the line would become vertical at the time it passed under the platform. The linesman would check it was on the bottom of the sea and work out, from markings on the line, the actual depth. There were coloured markers placed at intervals along the rope, and their colour would enable the depth to be calculated and reported to the bridge.

Anchoring and Towing

We were given instruction on Anchoring the small craft, and that of an actual warship. I won't expand on this here.

Duty Weekend.

On the weekend we could not go on shore leave, we would be known as the Duty Watch. One of the duties was to clean out the Bathroom and Heads (toilets) areas. On one occasion I was paired with this more senior able seaman to clean a set of heads and washbasins. After we had finished, he switched on some music and began to dance, using the mop as his partner. I laughed and he said he was practicing his steps for the next occasion he went to a dance.

I asked if he could teach me a few steps and he proceeded to teach me how to waltz; he took the lady part. And that was the beginning of my dancing career. At that time, I never had a chance to learn any more steps before it was time to leave Cerberus.

Kit Inspections

From time to time, we would be required to lay out our kit in a prescribed manner. Our spare hammock would be laid on the floor and each item would have to be neatly folded and placed in an allotted position that we had been taught. I suppose these inspections were to make sure that we were washing and ironing our clothing.

Finally, after several tests, we were told we had passed Recruit training and were ready for postings to a ship or further training in the Specialisations selected. There was a passing-out Parade and Inspection before we could pack our bags and hammocks.

A few last comments on how I became a Radar Operator.

Specialist Training.

I had given no thought to what Sub-specialisation I would apply for after Recruit Training. One day, towards the end of the Recruit Training, my friend Jack came and asked what Subspecialised training I was going to apply for. I said I had not thought about it but supposed it would be Gunnery.

He then suggested that I apply for Radar, a word I had never heard or read about. He explained that one of his girlfriend's fathers, who worked in the PNG (Postal Service), when Jack was working there, was an Electrical Engineer and had lent Jack a magazine describing radar and its operation and uses.

Jack then proceeded to explain the basics, informing me that it was a directional radio beam that, when the beam hit a solid object, it reflected, and because the speed of the radio wave was known, it was possible to work out the range of the solid object by knowing time taken from start to return divided by two. Knowing the bearing the beam was sent out on, and the range, it was possible to plot the range and bearing of a target or land.

Jack and I applied to specialise in Radar operation and were duly interviewed. At that time, I could never imagine where this decision to apply for Radar Training would lead me.

At the interview, I was asked why I wanted to be a Radar Operator. I replied that because it was new, I had the desire to learn as much as I could about Radar and its operation.

The first question put was to go to a map on the wall and tell them what was located at a certain latitude and longitude and report it to the Board (Interviewers). As I walked towards the map, I picked up some latitude and longitude figures on the side of the map and, by the time I had got there, I was able to place my finger on the small island and report the name of that island. I received a very well done from the Board. The next question was to describe what I knew about Radar. I stated I knew next to nothing about it. It was hard to find any information on it. However, what I had learned was that it consisted of a radio beam that could be focused to give the direction of the contact. I understood the speed of radio waves could be measured by dividing the time taken from transmission to reception, and dividing it by two, the actual range could be worked out. Once plotted, and if there was any movement between plots, it could be a target. If there was no movement, it was most likely a stationary object like land.

I was then told to go to the fireplace in the room and repeat the words they gave me. Using my normal voice, I repeated the sentence to be greeted by, "Speak like a woman, man." I then pitched my voice exceedingly high pitch, and this seemed to be accepted. I think they thanked me, and I left the room. Later, I learnt I had been selected for Radar Training.

Note. In difficult radio interference conditions, a high-pitched voice could often be heard whilst a lower pitch was distorted and could not be deciphered.

Reflection

As I write this, something like 77 years later, I am reflecting on my friend Jack's pressure to apply for radar and the effect it had on my life and Naval Career that was to follow. Today I am considered the father of the Radar Branch, which is not true as they were the original WWII operators, known as Radar Direction Finding (RDF), who preceded me. I was one of the early RPs (Radar Plotters) when plotting was added to the training of the radar operator.

I have a building at the training establishment, HMAS *Watson*, in Sydney named "The Ritchie Building" that I had the pleasure of opening after I had retired. I assume I was selected for my many years involved with the Training of Radar Plotters.

Home Leave

In my case, I was given a train ticket back to Western Australia and reversed the changing trains until we reached Kalgoorlie, where I was able to have some leave.

Christmas Leave.

I will finish this chapter with a brief description of my Christmas leave. On arrival in Kalgoorlie, I made my way home with my bag and hammock and was welcomed by my mother, brother and later my dad. I cannot remember if my sister was living at home or with my aunt in Perth.

I was able to catch up with a few old friends and completely relax from being under Naval Discipline.

My bed was on the front verandah, and I enjoyed being in that bed again.

I went swimming, played tennis, went to the pictures, or just loafed at home.

All too soon it was off to Perth to Uncle Harry's and Auntie Nell's for Christmas.

Perth

Here again I met up with old friends, especially Jack, my mate.

Christmas Dinner took place at Uncle Harry's home with his usual guests. During lunch I was quizzed about my experience so far of the Navy.

I caught up with an old Kalgoorlie girlfriend who was at university and of course my uncles and aunts who lived in the adjacent suburb of Maylands.

I returned to Kalgoorlie for another two weeks before embarking on to the Trans train to Port Pirie.

Kalgoorlie to Sydney

I opted for a Cattle Truck, and most of my Navy friends on the train still thought I was mad. However, with no sleeper I wasn't going to be in the luggage rack of the train when I could enjoy my hammock.

Naturally the soldiers in the cattle truck with me were amused and asked if they could have a go at getting into the hammock. You can imagine the laughter as some of the soldiers found the hammock could roll before they got into it, and a number finished on the floor.

Until I got a sleeper, and there were no cattle trucks, I always took my hammock crossing the Nullabor.

From Adelaide, it was on to Melbourne and there I boarded the train to Sydney. There were no cattle trucks on this train, and I had to sit in the compartment and place my bag and hammock in the luggage van.

I can't remember staying in Melbourne overnight, and I believe we boarded the train to Sydney a short time after arriving in Melbourne.

From Melbourne, we proceeded to Albury, and arriving there, we had to change trains again. We were able to get a hot drink and something to eat that was provided by staff or volunteers. I do know it was cold and I enjoyed the warm drink. Then it was on to Sydney.

I joined my fellow classmates, and we made the best of sitting up for the trip first to Adelaide, where we stayed overnight, then onto Melbourne and Albury, where we again changed trains due to the rail line gauge.

Thanks to a Red Cross group of ladies, we were able to get a cup of hot coffee and something to eat at Albury.

Then, I went to Sydney and joined HMAS *Watson*, which turned out to be RAN Radar Station 284, where I trained as a radar operator.

Chapter 4

RAN Station 284

6th January 1945 – 10th April 1945

Initial Radar Training.

On arrival at Central Railway Station, Sydney, a member of the Rail Transport Office led me to a truck, and I was taken to HMAS *Penguin*, located on Middle Head at the entrance to Sydney Harbour. RAN Radar Station 284 was on South Head of the entrance to the Harbour, and there was no accommodation there for Navy personnel.

The Army personnel manning guns on the cliff top had accommodation in a two-storey brick building located below the guardhouse to the radar station. I believe there were several houses for Army Officers located closer to the harbour and lower down from the cliffs.

Each morning of the course, the Trainee Radar Plot group would board a tug at the HMAS *Penguin* jetty in Balmoral Bay and be taken across to Watsons Bay Wharf. After rounding Middle Head and entering the main channel into the port of Sydney, we were required to go through an entrance to the antisubmarine boom nets that stretched from one side of the harbour to the other. At the Watsons Bay wharf, where we disembarked, the tugs coming alongside this wharf were something to behold, and invariably, it took some time to secure the tug. The trainees made their way through the Army area, up what was really a steep goat track, to the guardhouse and classrooms. Some trainees lived ashore.

RAN Station 284

Guardhouse. As we checked in through the guardhouse, we were given a small ticket to be used for our lunch. There were no dining facilities at that time. Before proceeding further, I will comment on the few buildings that made up RAN Station 284. I have already mentioned the guardhouse.

Administration and Training Blocks There was a sloping concrete path from the guardhouse up to the Administration block. This building has the Admin Office, classrooms, and a cinema

B Block. Further south, and closer to the cliffs, was another brick building, known as B Block, containing all the Radars.

Radio Operating Procedures Classroom Behind that, there was a small building containing the facilities for teaching Radio Operating procedures. These last two buildings overlooked Watsons Bay shops and the notorious Watson Bay Gap where, from time to time, people would jump off the cliff to end their lives.

Instruction

We were taught the theory and basic circuitry of the different Radars designed and built in England and one designed and built in Australia by AWA. The designation of this Australian radar was A276. We were informed of the history of radar and how it was used to detect ships, aircraft, and land, and that heavy clouds could also be picked up.

Radar Display. The class was taken to B Block, introduced to one of the radars, and shown the Radar Display. The display was about six to eight inches across. There was a pulsing green line running across the middle, called a Trace. This had a small amount of interference on it, and this was known as the Ground Wave. If a Radar Contact, known as an Echo, was made, it would appear as a pulsating blimp above the ground wave.

Range Calculation. The speed of the radio pulse was known, and it would be reflected once it hit an object, plane, land etc. By dividing the time taken electronically for the radar pulse to go out and back it was possible to develop a distance.

Range Scale. There was a range scale under the Trace, and this allowed the range to be calculated.

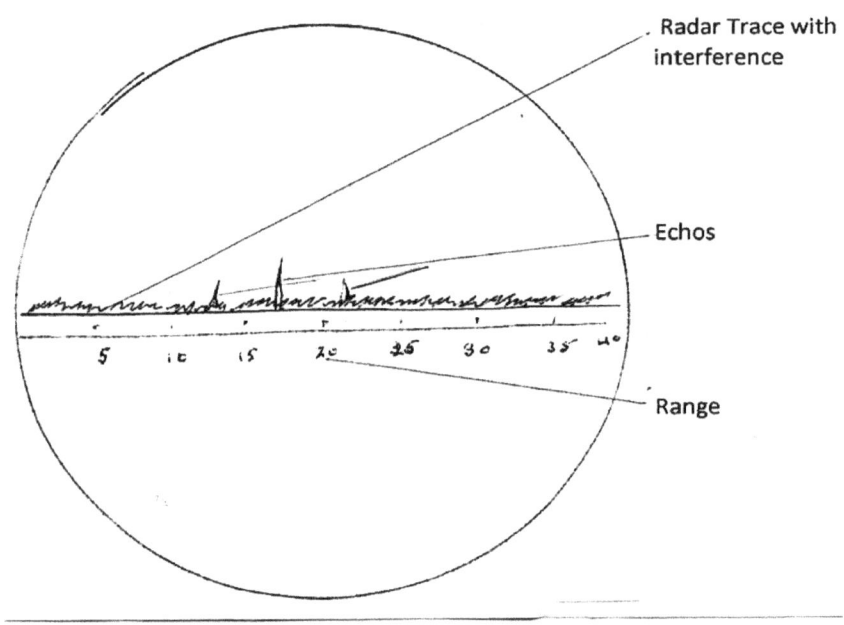

Aerial Control. The aerial could be turned about 190 degrees either way; there was no 360-degree rotation. Except for one radar that was controlled by hand from above the head, the others were hand-controlled electronically.

Radar Aerials allowed the radar transmission to be focused so, if a contact appeared, the aerial would be swept through the contact both ways to establish its central bearing from the ship. This bearing, with distance from the range scale, would be reported to Bridge with the range as "contact bearing 260 zero range 30 mile.". They would plot it on a chart. In those early days, there were no dedicated plotting tables.

Each operator usually spent twenty minutes looking at the screen before he was relieved. This rotation was necessary because of the intense concentration needed. The cabinet the operator sat in was usually dimly lit to be able to see the screen.

Other Training and Tests

We were introduced to Nautical charts, Plotting techniques, **Relative Velocity** and other items, that were a necessary part of the qualification that was required for all Radar Operators. We practised operating both Surface and Air radars. My qualifying test was to find a ferry running between Manly, on North Head, and Circular Quay in the city. As you can imagine the landmass of South Head, on one side of the harbour and Middle Head on the other, and a cloud mass created a lot of solid contacts, and there was considerable interference on the A scope. However, I was able to pick up the moving ferry despite all the interference, and that satisfied the Examiner. I don't seem to remember detecting any aircraft, and I cannot remember using any sort of automated plotting table at that time.

There were two types of radar training. The one I undertook – Surface and Air Search – and the other was instruction on radar used for the ranging of guns.

Radio Operating Techniques,

We were taught radio operating procedures. It was interesting to learn the correct procedure. Instructors were either a Petty Officer or a Leading Seaman. It was a Leading Seaman instructor who taught us how to receive and send messages by radio. He taught us how to pronounce the alphabet, such as A for Alpha, B for Bravo, etc. We were taught not to speak too fast, for if there was any interference, it could be difficult to interpret.

Aside. I believe Jack L and I were the only Ordinary Seaman in the class of seven or eight. On one occasion, during the Radio operating procedures lesson, one of the Able Seamen said he needed to go to the Heads (toilet) in a hurry and left the class. Shortly after, a second Able Seaman made the same request indicating that it must have been something that he and the other chap had eaten. Before long, all the Able Seamen had left the class indicating they had stomach pains.

Finally, the Leading Seaman realised there was something going on and stopped instructing Jack and me and went looking for the rest of the class. I took the opportunity to use the Heads (toilet) in B block, and I was heading towards the B Building doorway when I noticed one of the Able Seamen from the class, with one of the large Navy teapots, disappearing over the side of the cliff. Initially, I thought he had fallen, then realised that there must be some form of path on the outside of the cliff that he had taken. I didn't say anything when I returned to the classroom.

I later found out that the entire class, less Jack and me, had gone to a small cave in the cliff face and were having a smoke and a cuppa tea. They did not reappear until sometime later, just before the class was due to end. On reflection now, all these Able Seamen who absconded from the class were experienced veterans, and they had a fair idea of the correct procedures due to their earlier wartime experience. I think the Leading Seaman realised it was useless to report them, so they got away with this indiscretion. For Jack and me, it was part of learning the wiles of Seamen. On one occasion, I too went down the cliff face to a small cave.

Lunch time

There was no Mess on the Base, and it was necessary to proceed to the Church of England Hall in Watson's Bay, where the Ladies of the Parish prepared lunch. This meant going down the goat track, out past the shops and up a hill. Here we would hand our ticket in at the door and be shown to a table and served. There were doors at each end of the building. If we were very hungry and smart, we would watch for when the ladies were showing people to a place and slip into the group from this other door. Later we would present at the front door with our ticket.

The meals were certainly nice. Things in short supply were provided by the Authorities to make sure we received a good meal.

Return to HMAS *Penguin* and Short Leave

On completion of instruction for the day, the various classes billeted in HMAS *Penguin* would proceed down the goat track to the Watsons Bay wharf to board the tug waiting to take us back to HMAS *Penguin*. Here, I will mention that one morning, as we were coming over from HMAS *Penguin* to RAN Station 284, there were several heavy cruisers leaving the harbour. This was the first time I had seen such a large warship, as the only ships I was acquainted with were ones the size of Destroyers, Corvettes, or tugs. On another occasion, just before we had completed the course, we saw HMAS Australia entering the harbour after she had been damaged in fighting off the Philippines.

The final part of the course was to go to sea and practise under sea-going conditions.

Sea Training

From 11 to 17 April, on completion of practical tests, the class embarked for sea training in HMAS *Yandra*. Sea training gave the class practical experience at sea in using radar under actual sea conditions.

HMAS *Yandra*

It was perhaps the most interesting part of the course. There were not a lot of contacts as you can imagine. However, on occasions we did pick up an aeroplane and were able to see the type of pulse. the ship called into Eden for an overnight stay towards the end.

Besides Radar Sea Training, the ship also carried out sea training for Sonar Operators.

Shore Leave (From HMAS *Penguin*)

Unless in the Duty Watch, leave would be granted, and one was able to visit the local shops or catch a bus into the Sydney CBD and take in a movie or just wander around and have a meal. However low pay saw me only go ashore at the weekend.

Hyde Park

In Hyde Park, in the Sydney CBD, there was a large marquee where you could get a meal, listen to the music and later the ladies would be available for a dance. I seem to remember it was called **The Anzac Buffet**. As an Ordinary Seaman, I think we had to be back at Penguin by midnight or something like that. What I didn't know then was that a young lass, who often played the piano and whom I never got to meet at that time, would become my wife.

End of Course

Finally, the course came to an end, and each of us was given details of our next draft. All the class, except myself, were being sent to ships. My draft was to HMAS *Moreton*, in Queensland, for onward air passage to New Guinea as the spare Radar Operator for ships operating in the south-west Pacific. I had a Priority 2 air ticket.

Here, I am including my train trip to Brisbane and staying at HMAS *Moreton* for a short time, rather than include the details in a separate chapter.

I joined the train at Central Station for the trip to Brisbane. There were eight in the compartment, a mixture of soldier types and me the only Matelot. We all had to sit up for the trip. I can recall that, as night fell, it was bitterly cold. Fortunately, there was some heaters under the seats that took the chill off, but it was still very cold.

I cannot remember the stop; however, I do remember, with some affection, the Red Cross ladies who were manning a coffee/tea area where some sandwiches were also provided. While I was having a coffee, I was standing alongside some soldiers, all wearing their warm, long, service greatcoats. My protection from the cold was the Navy Burberry designed to keep off the rain, not the cold. At that moment, one of my father's last comments to me before I left home was to make sure I got the longest greatcoat possible and not to worry about its fitting. Oh, for a Navy Greatcoat. Many years later, I bought a long Navy Greatcoat whilst studying to be an Officer. When I returned from England, my dad saw it and confiscated it, saying I wouldn't need it in Australia.

Chapter 5

HMAS *Moreton*

11 April 1945 to 17 April 1945

Arrival

On arrival at Brisbane Railway Station, I was led to a small truck, where, after throwing my bag and hammock in the back, I was taken to HMAS *Moreton*. I completed the draft in routine and was allocated to a large accommodation block. Here, we slung our hammocks from the rafters, and I was given a locker for my gear. I was to wait until there was a seat on an aircraft to take me to New Guinea.

Moreton **Duties**. The basic routine for people like me, waiting for transportation further north, was rising each morning to lash up and stow the hammock, have a shower, go to breakfast, and each morning be employed cleaning duties in the accommodation, latrines, or sweeping the road and painting the roadside kerbs. On an afternoon, we usually had a make-and-mend (time off) to go on short leave. If a Brisbane native, they usually got overnight leave.

With little money to spend, I stayed on board almost every day. However, one of the local lads told me a good place to get a cheap wholesome meal was Mumma Maria's. I found my way there by tram and the meal that night was Spaghetti Bolognese. I couldn't remember ever having this dish before. This was served on large platters to tables where there were about 10 or 12 people. There were no chairs just long stools on either side. The table was covered in a white linen tablecloth with matching napkins.

On my first night, I was surprised to see several people in formal wear such as the ladies in long dresses and the men in tuxedos. Apparently, this was not unusual as people grabbed a meal before going onto some social function and dancing the night away. You could eat as much as you liked as they replaced the empty platters from time to time.

The second time I went there I was served a very nice steak and salad.

When I stayed on board of an afternoon, I spent it reading magazines or a book. There were no comfortable chairs in the Accommodation block, so I used to lie on top of the hammocks in the hammock bay, where all hammocks were kept during the day.

Departure

One afternoon, whilst I was laying on the top of the hammocks, a member of the Regulating Staff asked if my name was "Ritchie" and when I said yes, he said "Get your bag and hammock

– you are on your way," so dutifully I changed into my uniform, cleared the locker, and was led to a small truck and placed my bag and hammock in the back. I sat in the front seat. So here I was on my way out to the battle zone by air. Ha. Ha, ha.

As I didn't know Brisbane, I just sat back and enjoyed the ride. However, I was surprised when the truck drove onto the wharf on the Brisbane River. When I questioned the driver as to why I was not going to the airport, he informed me that I was going to HMAS *Gerard*. I protested that they had picked the wrong Ritchie, as I had found out there were two other Ritchie's in our block.

HMAS *Gerard*

The wharf turned out to be one connected with the Sugar trade. When I looked around for a ship, there was none to be seen. When I asked the driver, **"Where is the ship?"** he pointed to the side of the wharf, and I then noticed about 12 inches of mast above the edge of the wharf. Looking over the side of the wharf I looked down on a small ship and was told to get on board. I told the driver I was supposed to be going by air to New Guinea on a category two flight. He told me to get on board and do what I was told. The driver lowered my kitbag and hammock down to the ship. Still protesting, I climbed down the vertical ladder on the side of the wharf and boarded HMAS *Gerard*, for my category two air flight to New Guinea.

The new episode was about to begin in my life.

Chapter 6

HMAS *Gerard*

18 April 1945 to 17 June 1945

Dimensions	Displacement	Engine
112.2' x 24.8' x 8.5'	194 Tons Gross	187hp

Armament

1 x 12 pounder HA	1 x 20mm Oerlikon	2 x Vickers .303 inch MG

Introduction

HMAS *Gerard*, **my first active Naval ship,** had been operating in the wheat trade in Spencer's Gulf until she was requisitioned by the RAN on 1 July 1941. Her forward and aft masts had been removed to provide for the fitting of the 12-pounder and Oerlikon guns and give the guns a clear arc of fire. Her first mission with the RAN was as an Examination ship for Port Kembla. I believe she began her first task as a Store Ship leaving Sydney in November 1943 for duties north of Australia and in the New Guinea theatre.

When I joined her, HMAS *Gerard* was on her way back to New Guinea after a major refit in Sydney. It had four Lieutenants, with the Commanding Officer being a Royal Navy Officer. I think the First Lieutenant was a New Zealander by birth; the other two were Australians. All were Reserve Officers, not permanent Navy. From memory the total number of crew was eighteen. I can't remember if the Coxswain was a Petty Officer or Leading Seaman. All other sailors were Able Rates who had been in the Navy for some considerable time.

Mess Deck

I was met on the ship's upper deck by a member of the crew who helped me, my bag and hammock to reach the Mess Deck. There was a wide metal ladder leading from the deck to the mess deck below. I can't remember any handrails on either side.

There were several bunks against each of the bulkheads and at the forward end of the mess deck space. On the deck area was a table with bench seating on either side. There may have been other seating or small tables in this area that I don't remember. I was told I'd have to use my hammock as bedding and shown an empty bunk and a locker for my goods and chattels.

I then put my hammock on the bunk and arranged my bedding. After that, I put what I required into the locker and found out where to store my sea and overnight bags.

I was introduced to those sailors in the mess deck and later the rest of the crew when they came back from shore leave.

Besides me joining for passage, there was another passenger, a Leading Cook, who I found out was a Chef in a top hotel in Melbourne, before joining up. He worked with the Cook and provided extra expertise in the galley. I found the meals generally good and no reason for complaints about the food. Unfortunately, the 12-pounder was over the galley, and although not fired during my time on board, no doubt it upset the cook and his cooking whenever it did fire.

Officers Mess

The Wardroom (Officers' Mess) was reached through a hatchway off the upper deck and was under the Oerlikon, AA (Anti-Aircraft gun). It was a cockpit-type compartment with a table and seating for the Officers.

Hatch

On the upper deck there was a main hatch opening to the hold below with a 12" high railing around each side and covered by a hatch cover and tarpaulin. A derrick rig, attached to the mast, was used to load, and unload stores and other items to and from the hold.

Ship's Routine.

When in harbour, the Ship's Company was employed cleaning the ship and chipping away and painting any rust et cetera. If there were stores to be loaded, then there would be someone put in charge of the winch, someone to take charge of the lifting of any cargo, and the rest employed either in the hold or on the wharf to manhandle the cargo. There were breaks for morning and afternoon tea and lunch.

The Ship's Company was split up into three watches, with the Leading Seaman in charge of one watch, and I think it was a Senior Able Seaman in charge of each of the other two watches. Each watch provided the Helmsman, two Lookouts and some extra personnel when at sea. I seem to remember we split the period between 4 pm and 8 pm into two-hour watches (Dog Watches) which allowed the personnel to be rotated each day, so you did not do the same watch each day.

The Helmsman was rotated with the lookouts after each period of an hour.

Other comments

It didn't take long for me to pick up that the First Lieutenant was not the most popular person as far as the Ship's Company were concerned. Initially, I couldn't find any reason for such an attitude until I had been on the ship for some time. The captain appeared to be moderately strict.

Sentry Duties.

When the ship was alongside, a sailor was posted on the wharf who was armed with a revolver to ensure no one got on board who shouldn't.

On the afternoon, the day before we were to leave the CSR wharf in Brisbane, the sentry on duty called out to those below on the ship, ***"Fellows, I need a hand up here urgently!"*** Everyone raced up the ladder and found a group of civilian workers from the CSR approaching the gangway with the intention of stealing the fresh bread that had just been delivered from HMAS *Moreton*, for the first few days of our voyage north. The sentry had his gun out and stated to the approaching workers that he was prepared to fire if they came any closer.

Appreciating the situation, the Oerlikon Gun crew manned their gun, loaded a live magazine, and aimed it at the advancing group, advising the workers that they were prepared to fire also. With the rest of the ship's crew standing on either side of the bread stack, the workers decided the gunners were dinkum and backed off. As far as I can remember, there were no officers on board at the time.

The only casualty was me. In racing up the ladder that had no handrails, which was very wet, I slipped halfway up and finished at the bottom of the stairs with a twisted ankle. I made the top eventually. After the incident above, the Coxswain treated the broken skin and bandaged up the ankle. I still have trouble with this ankle today, 77 or more years later, even though it has been operated on to remove bone fragments. The incident result you could say was, "Welcome to Active Service."

Departure for Brisbane.

Finally, we sailed from Brisbane heading for Townsville, Cairns, Thursday Island, and then it would be on to New Guinea. The first few days were pleasant, with the ship rolling a bit. However, when the weather changed and the sea got quite rough, the ship rolled and pitched quite a lot, and I was seasick.

I was expected to keep working, and I made frequent dashes to the ship's side to throw up. The Leading Cook, a passenger with me, saw my predicament and produced a Swallows Biscuit tin with a flip lid and cord to hang around my neck. This helped. Before I left the upper deck to go below to the mess, I would clean the tin with salt water. The sea sickness soon passed, and I kept the tin ready just in case.

The Wheel House

The Wheelhouse was below the Bridge. There was a magnetic compass to steer by, and this had a repeat above the front window. The wheel was quite large, about four feet or so. However, it was attached to the rear bulkhead, and you had to stand in front of the wheel and move with your hands behind your back or stand to one side.

There appeared to be no reduction gear in the cables running from the rudder to the steering wheel and, in a seaway, it was often hard to keep the wheel from spinning out of one's hands when the rudder came out of the water and was hit by a wave.

On one occasion, when the OOW (Officer of Watch) called out a change of course he got no answer from the helmsman. One of the lookouts was sent to see what was wrong and found the helmsman unconscious. He apparently had been standing in front of the wheel, with hands behind him, and been thrown against the bulkhead when a large wave hit the rudder and the ship pitched and rolled. From then on, I always stood to the side of the wheel.

On one occasion, and the only occasion ever, I made the mistake of following the Lubbers Line, which caused the ship to veer off course. As we were heading for a reef, the OOW realised something was wrong and called out to me, "What the ??XX @@ do you think you are doing!" I quickly realised what I had done and corrected the course. A lookout was sent down to watch me for the rest of the watch.

Sugar

During the ship's voyage up the coast, a signal (radio message) was received saying that the number of bags of sugar had disappeared from the CSR store and, as we were the only ship berthed there, it appeared that the ship was somehow responsible for the sugar's disappearance. Lower deck was cleared, and all the Ship's Company were mustered on the upper deck. The officers then began a thorough search of the ship. No sugar was found during the search. A signal was sent stating that the search had been done and no sugar had been found on board. More about the sugar a little bit later.

Gladstone

The ship's engine decided to play up and we were forced to reduce speed and proceed to the port of Gladstone, Queensland. The berthing alongside proved to be a difficult one, due to the fast, ebbing tide. We managed to get a line onto the jetty. Unfortunately, the engine could not provide enough power to stem the tide. In paying out the headline, one of the sailors on the forecastle had his leg caught in a loop and was being pulled towards the bow quite quickly. Fortunately, another sailor saw what was happening and, pulling out his sailmaker's knife, cut the headline, thereby saving the sailor.

This caused the ship to move backward with the tide, and it was necessary to let the anchor go to prevent us from being swept out of the harbour. Eventually, as the tide changed, we were able to get alongside and secure the ship in the slack water before the incoming tide could stop us from securing it to the wharf.

The lesson I learned from this incident was to make sure I had a sharp knife with me when handling lines. When the opportunity arose, I acquired a sailmaker's knife.

Stay in Gladstone

We were to stay in Gladstone for some time whilst the spare parts were flown up from the south. During this time, the Leading Seaman, who acted as a Buffer in charge of the seamen, happened upon a girl whose father was a local Baker. This Leading Seaman had trained as a baker and pastry cook prior to joining the Navy. He asked the girl's father if he could help in the bakery to keep his hand in. This offer was taken up and he would spend time in the bakehouse. During this time, the leading seaman found the baker was having problems getting sugar.

I'm not sure of the details, but somehow, the ship acquired some bags of flour for what I believe was an exchange for sugar. I wasn't privy to the payment details. You do not have to be a genius to realise where the sugar had come from. How it was not found by the Officers doing the searching after leaving Brisbane is a mystery. I came to learn later in my service career, of the ability of sailors to conceal things they didn't want found.

What I do know is that after we left Gladstone, every time you went on watch during the night and made a cup of hot Kai (chocolate) in the galley you would find some pastries in the oven.

Beer Embarkation

On the afternoon before we left Gladstone, several crates of beer were delivered to the ship side. Here, I was to learn something more about sailors and beer.

Opening the crates on the wharf, we found each bottle was wrapped in a straw protector. They were large 26oz bottles. To load the beer, there was a small team on the jetty and a line of sailors on the upper deck to the door of the entrance to the Wardroom. When the straw protector had been removed, two bottles were handed to the first sailor in the line and passed along the line by hand to the Wardroom entrance where an officer was making a note of the number of bottles being passed into the Wardroom for storage under the deck.

I was one of the sailors on the wharf opening the crates and removing the straw protectors. I noticed that when the bottles reached the last sailor in the line, at the door to the Wardroom, he would show the two bottles to the officer, who looked down to mark them on his clipboard, and the sailor would pass one into the Wardroom and the other to a person lying on the top of the Wardroom who passed it back to someone behind him, unknown to the Supervising Officer. It didn't happen every time, only occasionally.

Occasionally, a bottle would slip out of the hand of the sailor on the wharf and smash (accidentally, of course). I noticed that the tops of the smashed bottles were placed on the edge of the wharf and, by the time we had finished unloading, there was something like twenty bottle tops from broken bottles, all with tops firmly on. I don't think from memory that twenty bottles were broken, and someone must have made up the numbers with old tops. Most of those tops had mysteriously appeared in the line. They were checked by the officer at the end of their unloading. Of course, the remains of the broken bottles had been placed in a dustbin with the straw protectors. The crates were broken down for easy transport back from whence they had come. No need to guess where the bottles finished up.

Aftermath

Sometime after we sailed from Gladstone, the officer responsible for the beer came into the Mess Deck and stated he required twenty shillings for the bottles that had not arrived in the Wardroom. He was heckled and told that no beer had been taken. He said he would be back in one hour to pick up the twenty shillings. Should there be no twenty shillings he would have to tell the captain that there had been pilfering. One hour later, he returned, and the twenty shillings were on the table. As I did not drink, one of the other sailors put in the extra shilling needed. An amicable solution.

Fishing

Sailing up the coast of Queensland for Townsville, I found it remarkably interesting to see the Barrier Reef for the first time. Some of the crew set up fishing lines and the fish caught made a welcome addition to the diet.

Air Bedding

On one occasion, whilst at sea on a fine day, all the crew had to air bedding by taking their bedclothes onto the upper deck and spreading them out in the sunshine or just securing them over the guard rails.

Townsville, Cairns, and Thursday Island

The ship called first into Townsville and later Cairns, where the ship unloaded stores and equipment and loaded other items for New Guinea. At Thursday Island, we refuelled for the trip to Port Moresby. I can't remember if we landed any stores.

Thursday Island to Port Moresby

During this section of the voyage, the ship would anchor at night in the lee of an island as there was a possible submarine in the area. Also, the engine played up and it was necessary to anchor to affect repairs.

Lack of a Relief

When acting as helmsman one night, I was not relieved by anyone at the change of the watch. When the OOW asked who was on the wheel, he realised that I was not in his watch. I was relieved by one of the lookouts, and the Able Seaman in charge of the new watch took me to the galley, where he made a steaming hot cup of Kai. I accompanied him to the mess deck where he shook my relief awake. The relief told him to get lost. My escort then placed the Kai in his hand and said, "I'll see you on the Bridge." I must admit that I smiled as the sailor struggled to get out of the bedclothes and upper bunk without spilling any of the hot Kai on himself or the bedclothes. I don't think he was ever late at relieving anyone after that.

Port Moresby

After our stop/start voyage from Thursday Island, we arrived at the entrance to Port Moresby and answered the challenge from the Guard Ship. However, 'Gerard's codes were out of date, and we were led into the harbour under escort. They thought we were pulling a Japanese repeat of the Australian Z Force successful attack on Singapore. The problem was sorted out and we began discharging our cargo using the ship's derrick.

During the unloading, the First Lieutenant decided to check on the crew in the hold. As he was looking down into the hold, the block of the derrick missed him by inches as it swung out over the hold. He accused the derrick operator of trying to kill him. They assured him it was an accident as the hook had slipped out of somebody's hands.

I found a few nights later when I went to the First Lieutenant's cabin to wake him for his turn as OOW, he obviously had a mental problem. He did not respond to my knock and call from the outside of the cabin, so I entered the cabin and called again. There was no response, so I pulled on the bedclothes and called again to find myself with a revolver in my face.

Moresby to Madang

After unloading and taking on more stores, we sailed for Milne Bay. Here we unloaded some stores and loaded others before proceeding further. From Milne Bay, 'Gerard' sailed further around the coast until we reached Madang. Here I disembarked. I seem to recall it was more than thirty days since I joined the ship in Brisbane. So much for a Category 2 flight from Brisbane to New Guinea. So, with extra insights into the ways of sailors gained whilst aboard 'Gerard' I stepped ashore with my bag and hammock to a new adventure in HMAS *Madang*. Here I was to wait for another ship to take me further north to Moratai.

Chapter 7

HMAS *Madang*

18 June 1945 to 5 July 1945

Introduction

Madang is in New Guinea, now known as Papua New Guinea. Madang is located on the east coast as shown in the map below. At the time I joined, it had been retaken from the Japanese and established as a Royal Australian Naval Base to support ships, especially small ships, operating in that area.

HMAS *Gerard* secured alongside the wharf. On landing, I was taken to the Regulating Office with my bag and hammock. I was given a Station Card and taken to a tent. (There was no other accommodation). There was a Headquarters building.

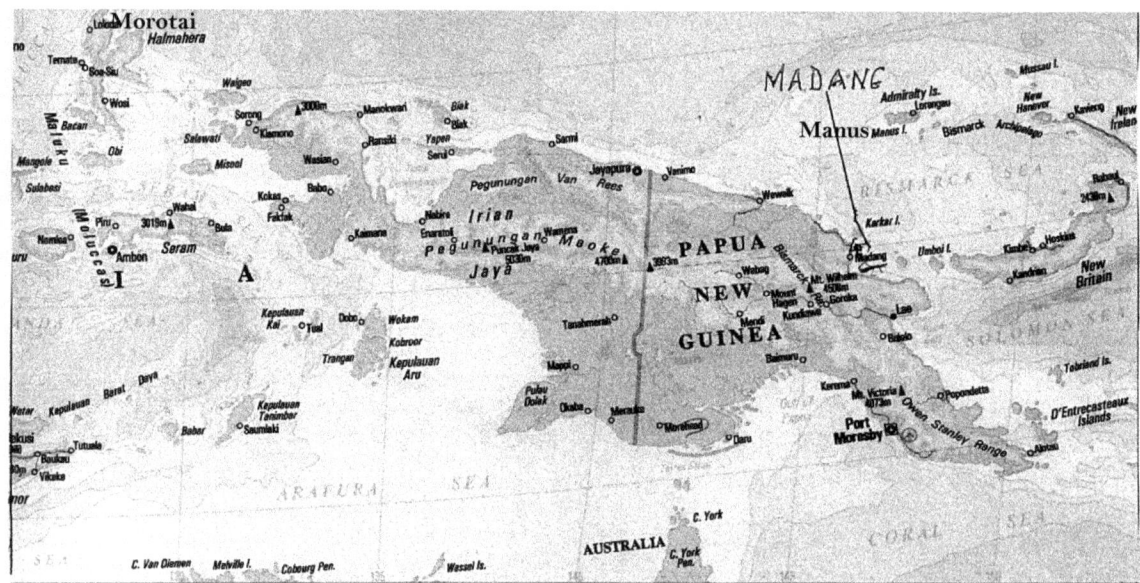

I found my tent mates very amiable and was introduced to Paw Paw, which they had picked from the nearby jungle. At the time I was still an Ordinary Seaman among all others who were Able Seamen or above.

Facilities

The facilities were basic. The Dining Hall was in a big marquee, the showers were in a makeshift bathroom and the toilets consisted of a deep trench with a timber plank with a few seats over the top. No privacy. I wasn't worried too much. I expected to be sent further north as soon as a ship going that way appeared.

Daily Tasks

After checking in at the Regulating Office, I was given the job of assisting the PO Electrician. Basically, I became his bag carrier and helped him with any task that he required me to do. It was interesting to watch him as he carried out his tasks. I believe I got the job because of being a radar operator.

Duty Watch

Besides helping clean up, etc, I found I was in a four- or five-man Guard maintaining security at a Store complex across the river running past the Base. The watches were arranged in the traditional Forenoon (8-12 am), Afternoon (12-4 pm), Combined Dog Watch (4 pm to 8 pm), Evening (8-12 pm), Midnight (Midnight to 4 am) and Morning 4-8 am).

Guard Duties

The Guards were required to march up and down in front of the Stores complex. We had to march with rifles at the slope and were spaced so that one guard was coming back, and the others marched towards him. This way, everyone's back was covered. You were expected to do this for up to four hours without a break.

This guard was needed because there were still Japanese in the jungle and locals who might try to break into the Stores complex.

When coming on watch, I would look on either side of the path to see if there was any rubbish or any other item that might make a noise if trodden on. I also surveyed the area to see if there were any fallen branches or anything else that would make a noise if trodden on. I had been taught to do this when serving in the Volunteer Defence Corps before I joined up.

Incident. When doing an evening period, there was a loud cracking noise as if someone had trodden on a dried-out branch of a tree. All the sentries challenged with the standard "HALT! WHO GOES THERE." There was no response to the challenges, and I challenged a second time.

As I had been taught in the VDC, I dropped my rifle to my hip and fired a slightly elevated warning shot in the direction of the sound when there was no reply.

There was a slight pause, and suddenly a figure emerged from behind a tree shouting "STOP FIRING, STOP FIRING. OFFICER OF THE GUARD, OFFICER OF THE GUARD." The voice was rather strained. He demanded to know who had fired the shot and I acknowledged that I had. Then he demanded to know why I had fired.

My reply was that I had been trained to fire an elevated shot in the direction of the sound when there was no reply to the second "Halt! Who Goes There." He ordered his escort to seize my rifle and escort me back to the Base.

Disciplinary Charges

There were no cells at the Base, and I was confined to my tent. Next morning, I was escorted to breakfast and later taken before the Executive Officer at his disciplinary table where I was charged with "having deliberately fired at the Officer of The Guard." I pleaded "NOT GUILTY."

The OOG vehemently stated that I had deliberately fired at him. When asked why I had fired, I simply said, "I had issued Two Halt Who Goes There" and as I had been trained when serving in the Volunteer Defence Corps before joining the Navy; that if there was no reply to the second challenge, a slightly elevated shot was to be fired in the direction of the sound. This is what I had done.

The OOG wanted to continue the argument. The XO stopped him and asked members of the guard individually what they had heard and seen. The OOG then stated that I had fired from the hip, and it was deliberate.

The XO asked why I had fired from the hip, and I explained that the old soldiers had taught me to put my pointer finger along the side of the gun and pull the trigger with my centre finger as this was quicker and more accurate than throwing the rifle onto the shoulder to fire quickly. They also said this was more appropriate in the jungle as the gun would not be on your shoulder but near your hip.

I recall that I thought the XO was a bit amused by the Guard Officer's situation.

XO found I was innocent and dismissed the case, much to the disgust of the OOG.

A short while after the case was dismissed, the OOG escort to the OOG sought me out and advised me that my shot had dislodged a part of a branch from the tree the OOG had been hiding behind and that it had fallen on the OOG. I felt very sorry for him as I put myself in his place.

I was removed from the guard's list.

VIP Guard

That incident did not stop me being selected to train in a VIP Guard. Some VIP was due to visit and each day we were trained for an hour or so at a time. We were drilled on all the correct moves. However, the poor Instructor was faced with a number of the guard suddenly putting their rifles on the ground and making for the heads. They were all suffering from dysentery. Fortunately, the VIP visit was cancelled at the last minute. Also, I was one of the unfortunates.

Departure

Shortly after this incident, HMAS *Broome* arrived for passage to HMAS *Platypus*, then stationed in Morotai further north. (see map)

Chapter 8

HMAS *Broome*

6 July 1945 to 20 July 1945

Dimensions	Displacement	Engine
56.8mx9.7mx270cm	733 Tons	
		4.642 diesels
	1025 Tons (Full Load)	

	Armament	
1x4" gun	3 Oelikeons	Machine guns
	Depth Charges	
	Crew	
	85	

Joining

I joined HMAS *Broome* and was allocated to a Seaman's Mess. I was shown a spot to sling my hammock. I was allocated to one of the Seaman's watches and this entailed duty as a Lookout (good for radar eyes), helmsman, watch on deck, and sea boat crew. I had no problem settling in and was made to feel one of the crew.

When not on watch, it was the usual chip, scrape and paint or clean mess decks and ablution facilities. If you were on the morning watch, you also had to pump fresh water into the holding tank above deck so there was enough water for the crew to have a wash, shower and/or wash clothes before breakfast.

Dawn and Dusk Action Stations

Each morning and afternoon, we went to Dawn and Dusk Action Stations. My station was in the Damage Control party between decks. On one or two occasions, there were unknown radar contacts. However, nothing came of these contacts.

Near Collision

During one of my watches as Lookout, there was a very heavy fog, and it was very hard to see the bow of the ship from the Bridge. During the watch, I heard the duty Radar Operator calling the range and bearing of a ship some distance away. I soon realised that the bearing was not changing, and the range was closing.

From my training, I knew the other ship and "Broome" were on a collision course. I knew that the captain and the Duty Officer Watch were on the Bridge listening to the radar reports. I realised the gravity of the situation and was wondering when we would take evasive action if the other ship did not alter course. I walked into the enclosed Bridge and asked the OOW if he realised the closing ship was on a collision course. He said he did. Eventually, we made a turn away just after the radar operator had lost contact with the radar ground wave.

Suddenly, there appeared alongside my side of the ship a ghostly steel shape towering above HMAS *Broome*. The distance would have been no more than twenty-five to thirty feet away. From the shape, it would have been a WWII Liberty Ship, and they sailed on probably never to know how close they were to a collision. *Broome* sailed on knowing what a close shave it had been.

Operation of Radar

During my time on HMAS *Broome*, I convinced the Leading Seaman in charge of the Radar Operators to let me take a turn on the radar. I was able to complete twenty minutes of operating and reporting, which was the total amount of radar operating I was to do during World War II.

Light Relief

On one occasion during my time on HMAS *Broome*, the Sonar operator indicated he had a contact, and the ship was sent to Action Stations. With other members of the Damage Control party, I assembled in one of the mess decks. There was some tension throughout the ship as the contact could have been an enemy submarine.

While trying to confirm the nature of the contact, a song came over the ship's broadcast system. Among the words were, "COME OUT WHEREVER YOU ARE." These words were said a few times. This relieved the tension somewhat. However, the captain was not amused and sent an officer to try and find the culprit and switch off the broadcast system. The culprit was never found. Such is Jack Tar's sense of humor.

Disembarkation

Eventually, 'Broome' arrived at Moratai, and I left for HMAS *Platypus*. *Broome* berthed on *Platypus* and I was able to transfer by gangway rather than by boat. From the time I had completed my Radar training I had served in HMAS *Moreton*, HMAS *Gerard*, HMAS *Madang* and HMAS *Broome*. I had spent a considerable amount of time as a lookout, as part of the watch on deck, sea boat crew, and a lot of time chipping, scraping, and painting ships, but no proper radar operator watchkeeping experience. It was then on to the next part of my wartime service.

Chapter 9

HMAS *Platypus*

21 July 1945 to 10 August 1945

Dimensions	Displacement	Engine
325'x44'x15'8"	3476 Tons	2 sets of Triple Expansion Reciprocating

Armament

Twin Screw 1 x 4.7 Gun

Joining.

HMAS *Platypus* was a Repair and Stores Ship for small craft operating out of Moratai in the North Maluku Islands. *See map below*. From time to time, it was re-stored from a supply ship, named *Wing Po* from memory.

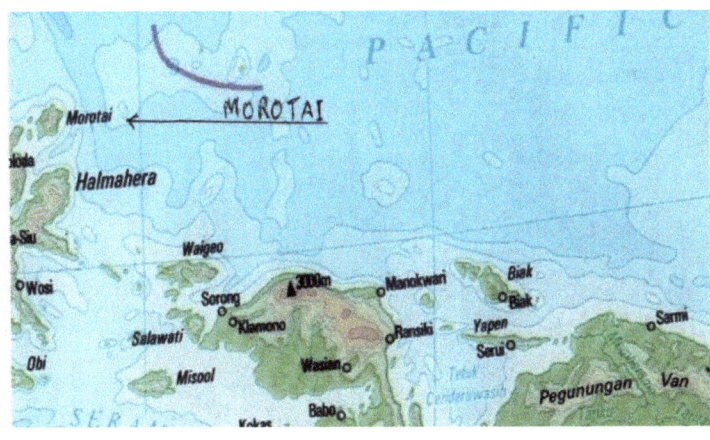

On arrival in Moratai Harbour, HMAS *Broome* came alongside HMAS *Platypus*. I was transferred to the *Platypus* via a gangway rather than by boat.

After reporting to the MAA Office, I was allocated to a Mess, shown my allocated locker and placed my hammock in the hammock bin. I was able to put some gear into the locker and have a look around the mess.

I had been allocated to Quarterdeck parts of the ship in the Seamen's Division. Besides the normal Dawn and Dusk Action Stations, it was the usual clean ship in the morning by scrubbing the Upper Deck and Mess Decks. The seamen would be employed in unloading and loading ships that came alongside to replenish the store stocks on board.

The war had moved further north and there was a relaxed atmosphere prevailing. However, there was still an alertness about what was happening around us.

Clean Ship

HMAS *Platypus* had a wooden quarterdeck. It was here that I first learnt to use a holy stone. A holy stone was an abrasive block with a hole to put a broom handle into. The use of holy stones scrubbed the wooden deck of the quarterdeck very clean. However, sailors disliked using them because they were harder to push around than using a scrubbing brush or mop.

Off Duty

The ship had upper deck sentries posted in case of swimmer attacks. Each afternoon, if there were no store parties or other requirements, the crew was allowed to relax. Sometimes, there was swimming over the side, with armed sentries posted. Each evening, there was usually a movie on the upper deck. I found a seat in an upper deck locker to view the movies.

This locker was used to store the holy stones. Other activities were playing cards, Mahjong, Dominos, Snakes and Ladders, or similar games. Reading, listening to music or writing home were other crew activities when off watch. Of an evening, many of the crew sat on the forecastle and listened to music instead of the movie.

Incident 1. On one occasion, after a major storing, the holy stone locker had been filled with Holy Stones. That night as I sat on the locker, some Able Seamen came and told me to find myself another place to see that night's movie. Being an Ordinary Seaman, I thought better than arguing and moved to another spot. During the movie, I occasionally heard a plop as if something had been dropped into the water. At the time, I didn't take much notice.

However, the next morning when the Chief Boatswain's Mate sent some sailors to get some holy stones out of the locker, they reported there were no holy stones in the locker when they unlocked it. The Chief Boatswain's Mate did not believe them and went to look for himself and found the locker empty. I then realised why I had been moved off the locker the night before and that the plops I had heard were the new holy stones being consigned to Davy Jones's locker.

Incident 2. On another occasion when storing ship, I was at the bottom of the ladder where various stores were being passed down from the upper deck to the storeroom lower down in the ship. On a couple of occasions, I was told to get off the ladder, and a wooden box with what turned out to be tinned fruit was let go at the top of the ladder and of course smashed open at the bottom. It is not hard to guess what happened to the tins and the wooden crate.

Upper Deck Sentry.

My next brush with my Superiors came whilst as Sentry. One night, I was employed as the sentry on top of the ship's bridge. My duty was to walk around the top of the bridge, keep an eye out for anything or anybody approaching the ship. In the middle of this area, on top of the bridge, was a structure that I had to walk around. As you can imagine, one got bored walking around with a Tommy gun at the ready during a four-hour watch.

Before I had left Sydney I had been taught to waltz, and with beautiful waltz music from the forecastle, I began to waltz using my gun as a partner, keeping my eyes on the area around the ship.

Suddenly, I heard a commotion and someone calling out, "What the hell is going on up there?" As I went to where the ladder to the top of the bridge was, there was a Commander stepping onto the top of the bridge. He was not happy and wanted to know who else was on top of the bridge with me. I stated that I was alone and was patrolling around the structure looking for anyone or anything approaching the ship. He was the Commander in charge of the operation of the various small ships used in the area.

He came around looking for someone else up there with me and found no one. In his frustration at not being able to ascertain what was going on, he told me that that there was a swimmer under one of the several boxes floating past the ship. He pointed to a particular box about 100 yards slightly ahead and to one side of the bow and said, "Japanese swimmer under that box." I immediately put the Tommy gun to my shoulder and fired several shots and hit the box. The crowd on the forecastle flattened themselves on the deck as the bullets flew over them.

The next minute, the Officer of the Watch appeared on top of the bridge, wanting to know what was going on. The Commander told the Officer of the Watch he was just testing the reaction of the sentry. He then left the platform and returned to his cabin. Unknown to me, the Commander's cabin was right underneath where I had been dancing in my hobnailed boots. Lesson: don't dance in hobnailed boots on top of a Commander's cabin.

Later in my service, he was at HMAS *Watson*, and I was tempted to go up and talk to him and tell him the truth about the cause of that incident, but I reneged.

Posting

Having been on *Platypus* for just over three weeks, it was time to move on. One day, I was summoned and told to assemble a steaming kit and secure my kitbag as it would be placed in a secure storage until I returned. When I asked what was going on, I was told I was going to HMAS *Bathurst*, which was short of a Radar Operator for a short time. As I wouldn't be away long, there was no need to take all my full kit. **Bad Decision**. I made a few inquiries of what I should take and assembled what I thought would see me through until I returned to HMAS *Platypus*. **Famous last thoughts.**

And so it was that I left HMAS *Platypus* in pouring rain to join HMAS *Bathurst*.

Chapter 10

HMAS *Bathurst*

11 August 1945 to 2 October 1945

HMAS Bathurst was the first of the 60 Corvettes built in Australia.

Dimensions	Draught	Engine
270m x 9.7m	56.80cm	

Joining

My boat trip from HMAS *Platypus* to HMAS *Bathurst* by the ship's boat was during an afternoon tropical storm. It was pouring rain during the trip. As I climbed up the ladder to board HMAS *Bathurst*, my Burberry (raincoat) was soaking wet with the white Blanco from my round sailor's hat was running down the side of my head and was all over the Burberry.

The ship's Coxswain was waiting for me to arrive on board and asked what specialist rate I was. My reply was, "Radar Operator."

His reply was, "You must have good eyes to be a radar operator.

My reply was that they were okay and were probably average.

He then said, "You would be a good Lookout." He followed up with, "You're masthead Lookout for leaving harbour. Hop to it! I'll look after your bag and hammock."

Welcome aboard, sailor.

Fortunately, having served on HMAS *Broome*, I knew the way to the masthead lookout and arrived to take over the glasses from the harbour lookout. He pointed out the best way to the bridge for when I was relieved. I reported to the Officer of the Watch (OOW), via the voice pipe, that I had taken over the lookout duties and the glasses were correct. *I was not a very happy chappie being soaked and cold in the exposed Crows-Nest.*

Departure Morotai

Very shortly after I took over as lookout, the ship sailed, and I began to report the various ships on the left and right of our track out of the harbour. Due to the rain squalls, visibility was reduced, and from time to time, it was difficult to see in the pouring rain. There were occasions when I was told off for not reporting a ship that I hadn't seen due to the rain.

The sea was rising as we left the harbour and, like all good Corvettes, began to pitch and roll forwards and backwards and from side to side. I remembered being told that Corvettes could roll on wet grass and I now appreciated why that comment was made, as I hung on grimly to the side of the Crows-Nest. My impression at the time was the tip of the mast would touch the top of the waves. Looking back, however, it wasn't rolling quite that severely. It didn't take long before I had an attack of Mel de Mer and was sick. Fortunately, I had the good sense to turn my back to the wind and the contents of my stomach blew away from me and the ship.

Of course, this distracted me from my lookout duties, and I continued to be shouted at up the voice pipe about why I was not reporting that ship or another. Eventually, this torture finished when Special Sea Duty men were fallen out, and the steaming lookout arrived and relieved me.

I made my way down to the bridge to report that I had been relieved and called out, "Lookout relieved and glasses correct," but it was not heard above the din of the Bridge. I kept repeating, "Lookout relieved and glasses correct," when suddenly the captain appeared and asked, "Where the hell did you come from?" Without thinking, dripping wet with blanco all over the side of my face and Burberry, Muggins me pointed up to the mast to the lookout position and said, "Up there, sir." He went ballistic and demanded, "OOW, remove this thing from my bridge." So chastised, I was shown to the ladder off the bridge by the OOW and made my way to the mess decks.

Mess Deck

I found the mess I was allocated to and recovered my steaming kitbag and hammock, still looking like a drowned rat. By this time, the ship had stopped rolling and pitching a lot and I was not seasick. My first concern was to get all the white stuff off my Burberry.

I made my way to the bathroom and found the freshwater on and was able to remove all the whiting off my Burberry. I also washed my face and hands, then made my way back to the mess and placed my few things into the vacant locker I was shown. When people began to sling their hammocks, I asked the Leading hand where there was a spare sling. The whole mess erupted in laughter, and I found out why soon after. The mess was overcrowded, and besides those in hammocks, people were sleeping on the top of ship side lockers, on the seat lockers below them, under the mess deck table, on the table and in the passageway. My patch was alongside the table in the passageway.

Aside. The reason for this was that Corvettes were designed for 60 or so crew and Bathurst had about 80 to 90 on board.

Laying out my hammock and bedding on the floor, I was looking for a good night's sleep. However, people going and coming off watch found it hard to avoid stepping on me. That was my first night's welcome to the mess.

Next morning, I had to pull my hammock and bedding out of the way of the passage and wait until there was a spare sling to roll up my hammock and bedding, secure my hammock and place it in the Hammock bin.

Duties

After breakfast, I was told I would be in one of the Seaman's Watches on Deck, and that meant I would take my turn as Lookout, Telegraphsman, Helmsman, and Watch on Deck, and I was to be the Bowman of the Whaler or sea boat if it was called away during my watch on deck.

I think it was just before or after sailing that we became aware that A Bombs had been dropped on Japan. That was greeted with a sense of satisfaction. I subsequently found out that the first bomb was dropped on Hiroshima on 6th August and on Nagasaki on 9th August.

Diverted to Subic Bay

On 16 August, two days after sailing, the ship received a radio message to proceed to Subic Bay instead of Zambornga. The Japanese had agreed to a surrender because of this bombing. From other sources I learnt that the date they agreed was the 15th August and that the Emperor of Japan signed the Document of Surrender on 2nd September 1945.

On the 20th of August, we arrived at Subic Bay to find that other minesweepers had arrived and that others would be arriving shortly. On the 24th and 25th, with other minesweepers, we exercised outside Subic Bay, returning to the harbour each night. On the 27th, Bathurst, with the other minesweepers, departed Subic Bay, heading for the reoccupation of Hong Kong.

Hong Kong

We rendezvoused with other minesweepers and became part of the British Pacific Fleet. We learnt that supporting the retaking of Hong Kong was the battleship HMS Anson and a number of Royal Naval cruisers, destroyers, submarines and other ships to support the landing. Our minesweeper group was to sweep into the approaches of Hong Kong harbour, clearing any mines that might be laid in the channel into the harbour.

On 29 August, the ship anchored off Tamkan Island after transiting a 36-mile channel that had been swept by HMA Ships Mildura, Bathurst, and Castlemaine north of the island.

On 30 August, *Bathurst*, and other minesweepers, formed two lines and began sweeping before dawn, HMAS *Bathurst* leading one line of minesweepers and HMAS *Ballarat*, the leader of the group, leading the other line of minesweepers. Everyone was very edgy not knowing whether the Japanese defenders would honour the ceasefire. There were reports of motor torpedo boats in a bay on the outside of Hong Kong Island and there were fears they may carry out a kamikaze type of attack.

As we approached the mouth of the harbour, I was the Port bridge Lookout and reported a flash of light 20° ahead and to port from high up on the hill on the left side of the harbour entrance. We waited for the sound of the shell passing overhead. It was finally assessed that the light was from a hooded car light. I think everyone breathed a large sigh of relief. At the end of our sweeping, we recovered our minesweeping gear. No mines had been swept as far as I remember.

We waited on one side of the channel and witnessed HMS Swiftsure heading into the harbour with a load of Royal Marines to secure the Naval base inside the harbour. Other ships following were HM Ships Euryalus, Prince Robert, two destroyers and two submarines, and finally, it was the turn of the minesweepers to enter the harbour and anchor.

The map shows some positions that will be noted in my comments shortly

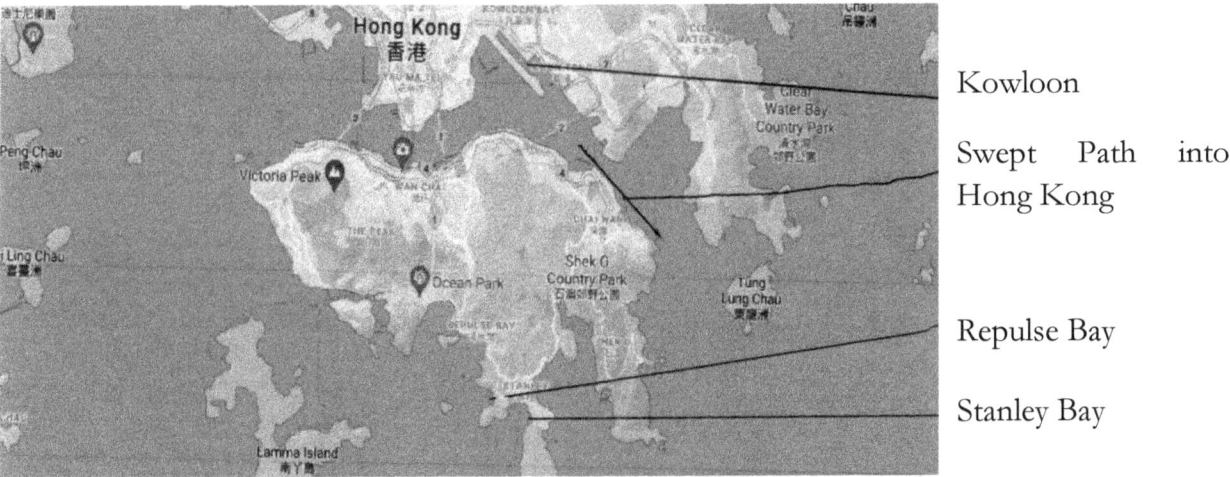

Kowloon

Swept Path into Hong Kong

Repulse Bay

Stanley Bay

On the 31st of August, I sailed back to Tamkan Island anchorage to lead other ships into Hong Kong harbour.

Kowloon

On 4th October, Bathurst was ordered to go to Kowloon, where there had been looting and rioting, and secure the Cosmopolitan Dockyard. We had people lying on the forecastle with rifles ready as we approached the landing. However, there was no resistance in the area and it was secured. Later, the same day, an RAF contingent took over. Over the next two nights we provided lighting of the area.

We returned to Anchorage in Hong Kong.

Our next task was to leave Hong Kong Harbour and proceed to, and to sweep, Stanley Bay. We sailed out of Hong Kong around to Stanley Bay.

Stanley Bay

We started sweeping on 8th October and, on completion of sweeping, we anchored close to the entrance to the Stanley Prison main entrance. This Prison had been used to intern the women whilst the men were interned in the Kowloon Prison.

Our motorboat was out of service, so it was necessary to use our 27-foot Whaler. I was the Bowman of the boat and as we touched the beach in front of the prison, I jumped out with the bow line and secured the boat. I was then ordered to go up and escort the internees to the boat. Other Corvettes of the group were also anchored close by and sending their motorboats to the beach towing their whalers.

I walked up the beach to the main gate and just before I reached it, I saw an elderly woman, accompanied by a much younger woman, coming out of the gate. I approached them saying I had been sent to escort them to the boat. They were a mother and daughter, and I can't remember which one of them was carrying a very small case. It would have been in the order of 200 mm x 130mm x 5-8mm wide. It was like the one I carried to my first school. It contained all their worldly possessions. I declined the offer of a Japanese cigarette, stating that I didn't smoke. We arrived at the Whaler boat and I, and others, helped them to get aboard.

Aside. I will comment further on these two ladies a bit later in this commentary.

I then returned to help other ladies board the boat. When the boat was full, we pulled (rowed) them out to the ship and helped them up the ladder to the upper deck. This routine was completed several times. I believe that we transferred about 234 ladies. Trucks also took some of the women back to Hong Kong. We sailed from Stanley to Junk Bay, where we transferred the women to the Empress of Australia.

Dockyard

On 14th September, Bathurst returned to Hong Kong Harbour and berthed at the Dockyard for a Boiler Clean. We were to remain alongside until the 19th. Short leave was granted, and it was possible to look around Hong Kong for the first time. I think it was this time that, as I wandered around, I came across an American Red Cross centre that was providing meals and some forms of entertainment. I went in and was able to have lunch and after, I began reading some of the papers that were there. A lady came up and asked me if I would like to join the quiz. I initially said I suppose it's all about America, and she said no, it was a general quiz. So, I went and participated in the quiz and after we went back to reading magazines. Suddenly the lady appeared and handed me a plate with some sort of pie on it. When I asked what this was for, she replied "You won the quiz." On the plate was a pumpkin pie, the prize for winning. I thanked her and shortly after left with my prize to return to the ship.

Aside. As I write this memoir, it is interesting to me to consider what we were taught up to and including year nine, the three R's.by way of Reading, Riting, Rithmetic and Spelling that I could go out and hold my own against much more highly educated people. Obviously, the University of hard knocks, as well as the religious instruction of right and wrong, has stood me in good stead. Perhaps it is something today's educators may like to think about that.

On 20th October, Bathurst sailed to dump depth charges at sea.

We eventually returned to Hong Kong before being sent to sweep Repulse Bay. On completion of sweeping, we helped clear a sunken log boom and its serrated wiring. Then, it was alongside in the Dock yard for a Boiler Clean.

The Stanley Prison Ladies

During one of my short leave days in Hong Kong, I was returning to the ship when I saw two ladies coming towards me on the same side of the road. I recognised them as the two I had helped at Stanley Bay. I waved as I approached them. They did not acknowledge the wave and immediately crossed to the other side of the road. I was a little disappointed and could not work out why they would want to avoid me. Maybe they had dropped back into the Colonial Ways of before the war. However, I just accepted it and went back to the ship.

Fact or Fiction

In 1972 or 1975, (I can't remember which) I was serving in HMAS *Melbourne* when we visited Hong Kong after a major exercise. On board was a great punter Kyran O'D, who found out that an English officer, Robby B, on exchange service, had never been to a race meeting. Kyran asked him if you like to go to the races in Hong Kong, and he said he would, so off they went.

I understand that at the racecourse, they both bought a race book, and Robby was asked to select a horse in each race. Kyran explained the ways to place a bet and left Robby to make his selection.

Robbie later told me that he had no idea which to pick, so he decided to use his wedding date, his wife's birth date, and the children's birth dates and pick a number out of the air.

During the meeting, Robbie got separated from Kyran. As I was finishing my work, I decided to have a shower and found Kyran in the shower alongside mine. He had lost all his money. When I asked where Robbie was, he said he didn't know as they had become separated.

Suddenly the shower doors opened, a head popped around the corner of the door asking if Kyan was there. When I said yes, Kyran poked his head out saying in a gruff voice "What do you want?" Robbie opened his shirt and out floated quite a few notes, falling onto the shower room floor. Robbie had picked the winner of every race and had over $5000 in his possession. Kyran was disgusted.

Later that night, Robbie said he was taking some people ashore for dinner and asked me to join him. I had a couple things to complete before I could go ashore, so I asked him where they would be, and he gave me the name of a restaurant that I knew from previous visits. I indicated I would join him as soon as I'd finished the work I had to do.

I proceeded ashore and found they weren't at the restaurant that he had named and did a square search of restaurants in the immediate vicinity, and they were not to be found so I returned on board.

The next morning, Robbie asked me why I hadn't come, and I said I had, but they weren't where he said they would be. He advised me that they had called into a hotel instead, where they made marvelous martinis. He couldn't remember the name of the hotel but said the bar's name was

The Captain's Bar and did I know where it was. I said yes, I knew it, and he invited me to accompany him that night to have a meal together. Whilst we were sitting at the bar enjoying our martinis, two women and a man walked past behind us speaking in very English voices. Robbie spun around and asked if they were English, and receiving a positive answer, asked them to join us for a drink as he'd had a lot of luck, and it would be his privilege to buy them one. Initially, they refused, but at his insistence, they agreed to have a drink with him. They proceeded to be seated while Robbie ordered the drinks, and we took them over and joined them.

Robbie then quizzed where they were born in England, and the reply was that they had all been born in Hong Kong. My ears pricked up, and when the conversation finished, I said to the two ladies and the man, "Were you in Hong Kong during the war?" and they indicated that they had been interned. I then said, "You ladies would have been in Stanley prison camp, and the man, you would have been in the Kowloon prison."

They sat bolt upright and asked, "How the hell would you know that?"

I then asked the women, "how did you return to Hong Kong from the prison?"

One lady said she went by truck, and the other said she went by an Australian ship.

I asked her, "What was the name of the ship?" and she said she couldn't quite remember.

I then asked, "How were you taken from the shore to the ship?"

She said, "We were rowed out to the ship and, on boarding, we were given a beautiful piece of soap."

I asked, "Could the ship's name be Bathurst?"

She acknowledged that is what it was.

I then asked her if she had anyone with her when she left the prison, and she said, "Yes, I accompanied my mother to the boat."

I asked, "Were you carrying a very small case," and indicated the size of 30cm x 20cm x 10cm wide. Her eyes nearly popped out, and she said, "Yes. How the heck would you know that?"

I then said, "I was the young sailor who met you and your mother and escorted you both to the boat." Stranger than Fiction???

I was to keep in touch with this lady by sending and receiving Christmas cards for several years. However, when I didn't receive any for two years, I realised that she had probably passed away.

Back to the Grind

After the boiler was cleaned, we went to sea to dump depth charges and generally carry out whatever was asked of us.

On 1 October we were sent to Mirs Bay for sweeping operations and then on the 6th we moved to Bias Bay for further mine sweeping before being recalled to Hong Kong on the 10th

Amoy and Swathow China

11 October, the minesweepers, including Bathurst, were sent to sweep the approaches to the ports of Amoy and Swatow on the Chinese coast. *(See Map below)* On the 15th, sweeping began to clear the entrance to Amoy and continued until the 29th. On the 30th, Bathurst left Amoy heading for Hong Kong via Swatow. I cannot remember the number of mines that Bathurst and other ships swept up.

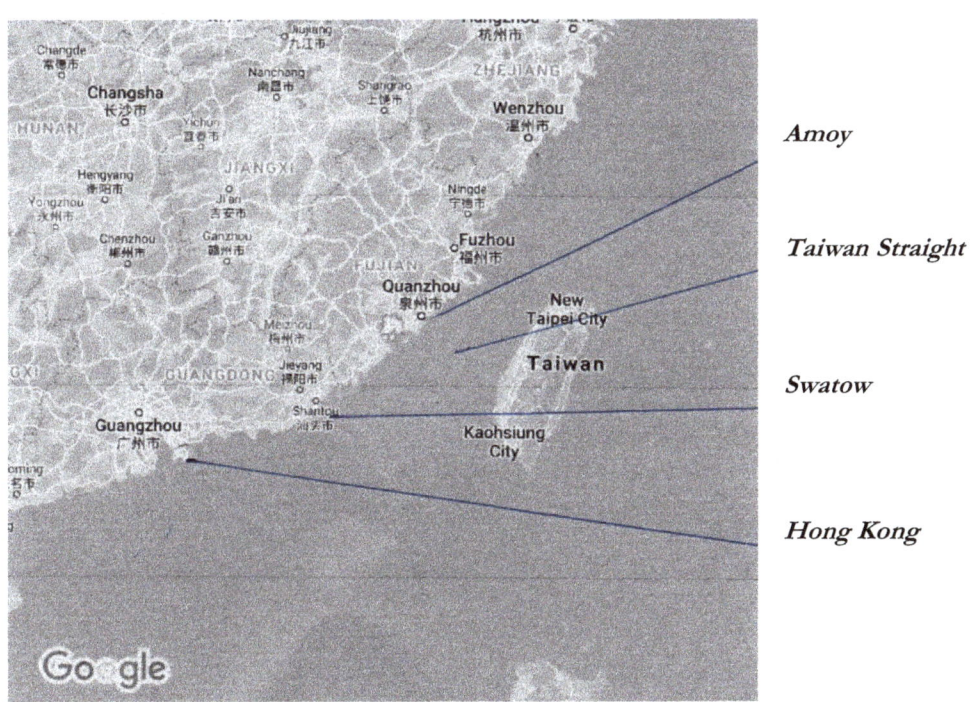

On the 31st, the ship left Swatow for Hong Kong, arriving there on 1 December. the ship loaded stores, supplies, and mail for those minesweeping at Amoy and Swathow. Then, the ships departed for Swathow on the afternoon of 2 November, arrived there in the forenoon of 3 November, and began to discharge cargo, stores, and mail to the ships there.

The ship sailed the same afternoon for Amoy, arriving there on 4 November. She discharged stores and mail there.

On 6th November, Bathurst recommenced minesweeping with the others in the group. At the end of the day, as they were returning to the harbour, HMAS *Ballarat* detonated an acoustic or magnetic mine, damaging her steering. Other ships went to her aid and towed her into the safe anchorage.

On 7th November, the ships sailed, minus *Ballarat*, to sweep the Formosa Strait. No mines were found so ships returned to anchor in Amoy. On the 11th, ships, less *Ballarat*, sailed for Hong Kong, arriving there on 12th November. the ship was restored and fueled for the trip back to Australia.

Homeward Bound

On 22 November, the ships left Hong Kong, heading for Morotai, where they arrived on the 23rd. Willie boy was required to back his bag and hammock and transfer back to HMAS *Platypus*. Disappointed was I that I would not be returning to Australia in HMAS *Bathurst*. However, my good God had something planned for me that was better than going back to Australia's east coast.

My time on *Bathurst* had widened my knowledge of seamanship, minesweeping, and living in confined spaces. I spent many hours as lookout or on the helm, being the telegraphs men, been bowman of the whaler as well as other ship husbandry duties. I had been part of those personnel cleaning out the showers and heads (toilets), and participated in Mess activities, such as preparing the vegetables for the mess meals. I felt more confident in myself, and prepared for the next part of my service.

I was taken back by boat to HMAS *Platypus*.

Chapter 11

HMAS Platypus 2nd Time

3 October, 1945 to 12 November, 1945

Joining

On arrival back on board HMAS *Platypus*, I was allocated to a mess and a watch. I made my way there to settle in and reclaim my sea bag and kit, which had been stowed while I had been away.

The next morning, I was in the mess when I heard a Petty Officer Regulator calling out, "Any West Australians here?" I said, "I am a Western Australian," and was then asked, "Do you want to go home via the West Coast." My answer was, "Yes, I would so like." He then said, "pack your bag and hammock and get to the gangway by such a such time for you are going home in *Fremantle*."

I quickly recovered my kitbag and cleaned out my locker and packed my bag ready for transfer. Then got my hammock out of the bin and made my way to the gangway to be transferred to HMAS *Fremantle* by boat.

Chapters 12, 12A & 12B

HMAS Fremantle

13 November 1945 to 24 January 1946

Includes HMAS Lonsdale - 25 January to 11 February 1946

& HMAS Leeuwin - 12 February to 14 February 1946

Dimensions	Displacement	Engine
186ft x 31ft		Triple Expansion
665 Tons/930 tons full load	8.86ft	2000hp

Armament		
1x4" Gun	2x20mm Oerlikons	1x40mm Bofors

Crew

85

Joining

Fremantle here I come. There was no tropical storm to soak me as the boat took me across to HMAS *Fremantle* from HMAS *Platypus*. As I came aboard the *Fremantle*, the Coxswain asked me, "What rate?" and I said, "Radar." He asked if I had any experience as a Helmsman. I replied, "Yes, in HMAS *Gerard, Broome,* and *Bathurst*." He then said, "You will be one of the Quartermasters for the trip home." I was happy with this, especially since I was still an Ordinary Seaman. Happier still when I found out that we would only be required to act as Quartermasters. This meant that I would be required to steer the ship during my time on watch and, during the morning watch, be required to pump water into the overhead tank.

When on watch, I would change tasks with the Telegraphsman who stood alongside me on the bridge. This gave him experience as a helmsman. When in harbour I knew I would be Gangway Sentry with the Bosun's Mate. (I had not received notice that I'd been promoted to Able Seman at that time.)

Voyage Home

On November 25th, the ship sailed from Moratai with the other Corvettes for Australia. On the 27th, *Fremantle* and *Burnie* were detached to proceed to Darwin, where the ships were to refuel and take on victualing stores. This was to be my first visit to Darwin, and I was looking forward to seeing this town that had been bombed by the Japanese.

I didn't know it then, but I would visit Darwin several times in my future life, including Navy Help Darwin, after Cyclone Tracy devastated the place on Christmas Day 1974. I would be HMAS *Melbourne's* Disaster Coordinator, providing sailors to help in the relief work.

Broome and Geraldton

From Darwin, ships headed west and then down along the coast to Broome where again the ships refuelled. Onwards and down the West Coast until we called into Geraldton, again for fuel and stores. A short period of liberty ashore was given and natives from that area and to the north were given long leave. I stayed on board. I did not know then that in later years, I would visit Geraldton every year for the official dedication and yearly Memorial Service for HMAS *Sydney 2*.

Plotting Exercise

There was another Ordinary Seaman radar on board, whose surname I think was Beasley or similar. The captain decided that the two radar operators should get some plotting practice. We were given a chart, a parallel ruler, a set of dividers, and pencils. The only place to lay out the chart was on the deck in a corner of the bridge.

HMAS *Fremantle* and HMAS *Gympie* began OOW manoeuvres and the two of us tried to plot the change of course continually receiving the radar range and bearing of HMAS *Gympie*, and our own 'Ship's' course changes, to plot on the chart. This was quite a challenge as the ships kept altering course at approximately 10-minute intervals. I must admit that it was not much of a plot. Neither of us had done any plotting since leaving RAN station 284.

Fremantle

The next port was Fremantle. I think the ship's alongside time at Fremantle was to be 0900 as there was to be a VIP welcome.

Engineers Breeze

As we came south, some of the lighthouses and navigation lights were being switched on. On one occasion, the OOW reported to the captain that a certain light had been raised (loom sighted). The captain came to the bridge and, after looking at the light, told the OOW that the name of the light was not correct and that it was one further down the coast towards Fremantle.

The captain, I believe, had been employed by the Harbour and Lights group in Fremantle before joining up in World War II and knew the various flashing and occulting patterns for each of the lights on the West Coast.

It appears that those in the engine room decided we could get home a bit quicker if they gave the throttle control a bit of a nudge. (Known by some as a stoker's breeze).

This stoker's breeze had put the ship some number of nautical miles ahead of where it should be. This resulted in the ship having to steam up and down outside Fremantle so that we could berth alongside at exactly 0900.

Entry into Fremantle

I was the Quartermaster approaching the berth in Fremantle harbour. I expected the ship's Coxswain to take over as we neared the actual entrance. However, he never took over until about 100 yards or less from alongside.

At the berth, VIPS and other dignitaries were waiting at the ship's berth and welcomed us home from the war very lustily. There were welcome home speeches, and eventually, leave was piped.

I caught the train from Fremantle and dropped in on my Aunt Nell Martin at 125 Seventh Avenue, Inglewood. I was also able to contact the girl next door, Elsa, and invited her to come and see the ship as the Ship's Company was able to show family and friends over the ship. During Elsa's visit I took a picture of her standing in front of the mast on her camera. I got a blast for not asking the OOW permission and drawing the transmitter keys so no transmissions were made that could have had far consequences. God looks after his own and Elsa and I suffered no ill effects.

Aside. That picture was to have a surprising effect some year or two later. Elsa was going out with a chap called Clem E, who she later married. During an afternoon, with friends in a café, the group began showing one another photos. Elsa produced the one of her in the mast of

HMAS *Fremantle*. Clem immediately said, "How did you get that?", and said he didn't know she knew any sailors. Elsa's reply to Clem was, "You wouldn't know him as he used to come down from Kalgoorlie and stay with his aunt in the house next door to mine." He insisted she tell him the name. When she said, "Bill Ritchie" Clem's jaw dropped wide open. He and I had joined on the same day and travelled east together and were in the same recruit class.

He was called Gandi because of his features. His other claim to fame was, initially, he had difficulty in marching properly and when he began to march his right arm would swing forward with is right leg instead of the left arm. I was to remain close friends with both Clem, Elsa, and family until they crossed the bar." (died)

Minesweeping off Rottnest

On the 12th of December HMAS *Fremantle* and HMAS *Burnie* proceeded to sea to sweep for some mines off Rottnest. Again, on the 13th, both ships swept an area to the south of Rottnest. On the 14th, *Fremantle* was employed in transferring Army personnel from the ship anchored out into Fremantle. On the 18th, the ships said farewell to Fremantle to sail for Adelaide.

An Aside. HMAS *Burnie* had been with Fremantle for most of the trip home. I did not know until much later that the captain of HMAS *Burnie* was the son of the lady I had stayed with in Cottesloe when recovering from my "Village Idiot" episode before joining the Navy.

From memory, the passage across the Great Australian Bight was pleasant enough and there is really nothing to say about this part of the voyage to pay off the ship in Melbourne. On the 23rd of December, HMAS *Fremantle* berthed in Port Adelaide and was to remain there for Christmas. *Fremantle* secured alongside. It turned out that I was to be the morning watch (4 am to 8 am) quartermaster on the gangway on Christmas Day.

Christmas Mass

So that I could go to Mass on Christmas morning I swapped with the quartermaster of the forenoon watch (8 am to 12 noon). During my watch, it got to something like 104 degrees Fahrenheit at the gangway, with no overhead cover, and I was glad to be relieved at midday so I could go below and get a nice cold drink.

Non-drinker

I opened the fridge and found no soft drinks, cold water, or beer, only a 26-ounce bottle.

The Ship's Company had received a beer issue for Christmas, and there was a bottle provided for me. As I had taken the pledge at my confirmation not to drink until I was 21, the bottle of beer was not for me. When I went to get some cold water out of the tap, I found it was very hot due to the water tank being exposed to the hot sun.

The duty Leading Seaman was sitting in the mess and asked me why I had not taken my bottle of beer out of the fridge. I explained why and said I'd have to go and make a cup of tea. However, he asked me if I drank hop beer, to which I said, "Yes, my father used to make it from time to time." Taking the bottle, the leading Seaman made a sign of the cross over the bottle and said, "It's now hop beer." My thirst got the better of me and I drank this bottle of (hop) beer, the first and only time I was to break my pledge before the age of twenty-one. Fortunately, my lunch had been set aside and I was able to have a very enjoyable Christmas lunch with a very cold drink.

After completing our fuelling, and taking on some fresh victuals, it was off to Melbourne and to pay off the ship. There was nothing special to report and *Fremantle* entered Port Phillip Bay and proceeded upriver to berth alongside the wharf almost under the Spencer Street Bridge in Melbourne.

Melbourne

The Ship's Company soon slotted into removing gear from the ship. I was able to re-establish contact with my first girlfriend, Betty E, and we went for an evening meal or two and the pictures.

Chapter 12A

25th January 1946 – 11th February 1946

HMAS *Lonsdale*

I left the ship and went to HMAS *Lonsdale*, where I worked sorting mail for the British Pacific Fleet. I was handed a rail ticket back to Western Australia. Up bag and hammock and entrain to Adelaide.

The Journey Home to WA. Having boarded the train in Melbourne it was a pleasant journey to Adelaide where I changed trains, and it was then on to Port Pirie where the then Trans Train was waiting. It was not unusual for the troops to slip across to the pub and buy some beer to be smuggled onto the train.

There were efforts to stop this, and one poor sod would be set up to walk onto the platform with a bottle in his hand. The OIC would chastise the perpetrator and then smash bottle on the side of the platform. However, whilst this pantomime was going others were busy on the other side of the train loading their beer and stowing it away for the journey west. Again, it showed how inventive military personnel can be in bending the rules.

I volunteered to go in a cattle truck so that I could swing my hammock across the corner of the truck instead of having to sleep on a very thin straw-filled mattress. Again, some of the soldiers in the cattle truck with me asked if they could try my hammock. It was a good laugh seeing them try to get into the hammock. After a while, I took pity on them and let it be known how to do it.

There was the usual stop for meals prepared by the galley attached to the train. We would line up and get whatever was on offer and go back and eat it in the cattle truck. There were regular stops to take on water for the engine.

Eventually, we arrived at Kalgoorlie, and I was able to slip off home and have a quick shower and see my mum before it was off in the Westland train to Perth. I think I sat up with others for this part of the journey. At Perth Station I was met by a driver and vehicle for travel to Fremantle and taken to HMAS *Leeuwin*.

Chapter 12B

12th February 1946 to 14th February 1946

HMAS Leeuwin.

I arrived at HMAS *Leeuwin* sometime after lunch. My draft-in routine consisted of visiting various offices and having them sign off on the draft-in form I had been given.

I started this routine the next morning. As I was crossing the parade ground, a member of the regulating staff caught up with me and handed me a train ticket to Sydney and told me to make sure I was on it. Having just come from Melbourne I was a bit confused as to why I was being sent back east to a place called HMAS *Watson*. No one at HMAS *Leeuwin* had heard of HMAS *Watson* at that time.

As I said, somewhat confused, I approached the Master at Arms (the CPO in charge of the regulating staff) and asked if he knew why I was going back to Sydney having just come from Melbourne. He had no idea why I was going to HMAS *Watson* and suggested that, as I was a 1944 entry, it would be some time before I would be demobbed.

He said, in view of this, I should go to Sydney and enjoy myself because after I left the Navy it would be some time before I could afford a holiday in Sydney. His statement then was that I would be doing about the same as what I would be doing in HMAS *Leeuwin*, sweeping the gutters, painting the curb etc. He also pointed out that I would have a sleeper compartment on the way to Kalgoorlie and to Port Pirie. So once again, it was up bag and hammock and hop on to the train.

Journey to Sydney

On arrival in Kalgoorlie, I shot home to see my mother and to pick up some fruit for the trip across the Nullarbor. It was a pleasant trip, and I was able to go to the dining car instead of the cookhouse on the troop trains. The various stops for water for the engine allowed me to have a better look around some of the stops. After changing trains at Port Pirie, and then Adelaide, it was on to Melbourne, another change of train and onto Albury on the border of New South Wales and Victoria. It was very cold at Albury, and I bought a pie and a cuppa coffee, hoping to warm myself up. However, they were barely warm, and I was glad to rejoin the new train from Albury to Sydney.

Arrival Sydney

The train arrived at Central Station, and I was met by a Leading Patrolman who took me out of the station to where a WRAN driver was waiting to take me to HMAS *Watson* in what was a large, covered truck. I threw my sea bag and hammock into the back of the truck. There was a large, black Great Dane in the back, and I was somewhat surprised to see him try and rape my hammock. His name was Horse and I came to know him well in the days to follow.

When I asked the driver where HMAS *Watson* was, she advised that it was at Watsons Bay. I then realised it was the RAN station 284 where I had done my initial radar training.

As we travelled from Central Station to Watsons Bay, the young WRAN had trouble changing gears as we went up and down the various hills en route. When I asked how long she had been driving, she indicated she had not long qualified. Eventually, we arrived at Watsons Bay and drove up the hill. HMAS Watson had been commissioned on May 4, 1945.

Chapter 13

HMAS *Watson* (1st Stint)

15 March 1946 to 28 July 1947

Includes HMAS Murchison 31 August – 1 December 1946

Training Centre
The above is a visual of South Head and Sydney Harbour 2018.

Introduction

HMAS *Watson* turned out to be RAN Station 284 where I had originally trained to be a Radar Operator. Here I was to draw a comparison between my original time of Radar training and what had happened since I first trained there. The above picture was taken in 2018, and the buildings on my arrival this time are not shown in this picture. They were further to the left of the picture above.

Post War Arrival

Driving into HMAS *Watson*, I noticed that some new buildings had been added. There was still the Administration building, B block and the Guardhouse. Other buildings turned out to be Senior Sailors onboard accommodation in single cabins and a dining and cooking area in another building. Below the Admin block were some other buildings which turned out to be the Sailors accommodation huts. I don't think the Action Information Training Centre Building, known as the AITC, had been built at this time.

When the truck stopped, I grabbed my bag and hammock and put them on the ground near the door into the Administration building. The Training Office, classrooms and cinema were in this building. I reported to the Training Office announcing my name was Ritchie and stating I just come off the train from Western Australia.

The Training Officer, who will remain nameless, said "You're late!" When I said, "Late for what?" his next words were, "Get into class." When I tried to say, "What class?" I was told to "Shut up and do what you are told!" After several attempts I gave up trying to ask my question.

Still protesting, I was led to a classroom to find several other sailors being instructed to become Radar Plot 2nd Class. I shut my bib and settled in and had to catch up with what had already been taught. The course length was to be eight weeks. The syllabus was to teach us in-depth the various radars, the use of plotting tables, relative velocity solving and the use of charts, air contact plotting, update us on the correct radio operating procedures and how to Instruct. I can't remember any man management training or instruction. You just picked that up by experience.

Decision Time

The seventh week of the course was made up of revising what we had been taught in preparation for the final examination the following week. During this seventh week, my mate Jack L, who had joined with me and had proposed we apply to be radar operators, rang me from Western Australia to say that he had received his discharge date. I mentioned this to the Class Instructor and said, "As he was an L and I was an R, my discharge date could not be far behind." All hell broke loose, and I was summoned by the Training Officer and asked why I had not told them I was a Rocky (Reservist for Hostilities only), so I said, "I tried to tell you when I first arrived, but you kept telling me to shut up and get into the class." No doubt remembering my attempts to speak on arrival, the next thing I was told, "You have 24 hours to make up your mind as to whether you wish to remain in the Navy or return to civilian life."

An Aside. As I was to learn later, during WW2, the system had mainly trained Reserve personnel to be radar operators and the push was now on to train Permanent Service personnel all the tricks of the trade and for some to remain as Instructors or be sent to sea. There were only about sixteen Permanent Navy persons who had been trained, that included a couple Reserves like me who transferred to the Permanent Navy. This meant Reserve sailors were being held back from discharge until Permanent sailors could replace them.

My Dilemma and Decision

I walked down to one end of the corridor, thinking about what it was that I wanted out of life. Go back to Kalgoorlie and mining, or whatever, or accept the option to serve the balance of twelve years in the Permanent Navy. I really had no idea about what I wanted to do. I certainly did not want to go back to mining. I was tossing up my options about what I would do back in WA when I reached the end of the corridor.

At the end was an office, occupied by the postman, Lex D, who was also responsible for the sale of cigarettes and tobacco against a card for such. From the good conduct stripes on his arm, I knew he was a long-serving sailor and had spent some years in the pre-war Navy. I asked Lex what it was like to be in the Permanent Navy, and he replied, "Well, you get three meals a day, have a bed to sleep in, you have your medical and health needs looked after, and they give you a bit of money to spend. Now the war is over nobody will be shooting at you."

That was good enough for me.

Knowing that I had always wanted to be a sailor from about the age of nine, and as I was having a good time in Sydney, going to various places like Picture Shows, the Anzac Buffet in Hyde Park, or the Catholic (CUSA) Club near Circular Quay, and some other places I can't remember the name of, meeting people of all persuasions, it did not take me long to decide I would stay in the Navy. I returned to the Training Office and said," Where do I sign?" My Service Records show that I signed to complete ten years and fifty-five days to complete a twelve-year engagement.

Entrance to Base.

The area of the Base was fenced. A Guard House was located on the southern side of and a short distance from the Administration block. Here a sentry checked personnel in or out. There was a rough, unmade rocky path that led down into Watson's Bay and the tram stop. You had to watch your step as you went up or down.

The other entrance was up closer to the harbour entrance and was the vehicle entrance.

Accommodation Block

The Senior Sailors' Accommodation was between the Administration Block and B Block, and Fibro built single cabins adjacent to the huts, with, I believe, showers and toilets.

The Sailors' Accommodation that had been added since I was at RAN Station 284 consisted of fibro-clad huts, where we slung our hammocks from cross beams that held up the roof. The floor covering was a type of linoleum. There were wooden lockers, about 3ft high, about 18 inches across and 15 to 20 inches deep along one wall of the hut. There were no wardrobes to hang anything in. One's total kit was required to be stowed in the small space of each locker. They had shelves with slatted doors, with a spacing between each of the slats. There was a simple hasp and staple provided for a lock. To ensure that no one could see into the locker it was necessary to provide towelling or a canvas screen on the inside of the door. The door also contained a metal hanger for a towel inside the locker. The tops of the locker provided a place to put items on whilst dressing.

The Toilets and Showers for Junior Sailors were in a separate block outside the accommodation huts. They were reached by a concrete path to the door of the hut. In winter, or, when raining, it was miserable going to and from these facilities. However, on a fine morning, with nothing but a towel around your hips, a toothbrush hanging out the side of your mouth, it was lovely to look down Sydney Harbour and realise what a magnificent view one had and that many would give anything to have a home in this spot. This was to be my onshore home when not at sea until I married.

I found myself teaching a Radar Plot 3 course, after the tests for RP2. Fortunately, I had studied quite hard during the course and was confident that I could pass on the knowledge I had to the students. It certainly kept me very busy and making sure that I had the proper notes for each day's lesson.

HMAS *Murchison*

Each RP3 class had to be taken to sea in HMAS *Murchison* to give them on-the-job training at sea. I found myself on loan to HMAS *Murchison*, a River Class Frigate: (Dimensions: 91.74m x 10.97m x Draft 3.6m), for training of RP Sailors, and the operation of Radar and Operations Room equipment at sea.

I was to be attached to HMAS *Murchison* from 3/8/1946 to 1/12/1946. I would take the class to the ship, oversee training, and then return to HMAS *Watson* with the class during this period. However, I normally slept on the ship.

HMAS Murchison

Aside. As I write these words I am smiling as I remember that my total operating time on a radar set before transferring to the Permanent Navy had been twenty minutes during World War II.

Sea Training

The first trip to sea as an RP2 started with a voyage in HMAS *Murchison* with a class of wanna-be RP3s. the ship was tied up at the Watsons Bay Jetty, so it wasn't far to go to board the ship.

The Chief Boatswain's Mate was at the gangway as I boarded and, noticing that I was an Able Seamen, said, "I require you on the forecastle as part of the Special Sea Duty Cable Party." My reply was, "Look, I'm the Instructor for this class. Can I first settle these trainees into their mess and their duties in the Operations Room." He agreed. By the time I had done this the ship was well on its way and was starting to pass through the heads out of Sydney Harbour. I had begun my supervising job at sea overseeing my Plot Class. Shortly after, the Sea watch relieved the Special Sea Duty Men.

The training cruise would either go down near the Gabo Island area, near the Victorian Border or sail north to Hervey Bay in Queensland. Usually, there would be a port visit for a weekend and then back to Sydney.

My job was making sure that the trainees on watch in the Operations Room put into practice what they had been taught ashore. Things like me instigating a plotting table malfunction and how to keep it going manually, practising their Relative Velocity, verifying the answers, and making sure they used the correct terminology on the radio and so on. It also meant keeping an eye on those operating the radar sets providing information to the plots. I was kept busy, and this included supervising the operation of the Mess the trainees had been allocated to.

Checking on each watch as it closed was demanding. However, I was learning a lot myself on how to run an Operations Room and provide the OOW and Captain with the information they sought from the plotters from time to time. I was also in charge of the Trainees' mess and had to make sure it was clean, and there was a Cook of the Rook to sort out the meal preparation and service and make sure the Mess was up to the cleanliness required.

When the ship returned to Watsons Bay and the class disembarked, I reported back to HMAS *Watson* with my assessment sheet. In making my report, I made it clear that I thought it was necessary to send a Leading Seaman in charge in the future because of my experience with the Chief Bosun's Mate. That fell on deaf ears – probably because there were no Leading Seaman RP2's available at that time.

Direct Order

On each occasion I boarded with a new class, I was met by the Chief Bosun's Mate and was told to report to the forecastle, and the result was as previously stated. However, on what was to be my final sea training trip, as soon as I got across the brow and was on board, the Chief Bosun's gave me a "Direct Order to get to forecastle immediately, and he would get the class settled into their mess and look after my gear." I protested but, being a Direct Order, I naturally obeyed. I then waited for what I knew would happen.

The ship was proceeding through Sydney Heads, and fog was limiting the visual range to about a mile or two. Naturally, the OOW called to the Operations room for the range, bearing, and course of several ships vaguely visible in the fog. Getting no reply, a sailor was sent from the Bridge to check the Operations room. He found no one had closed.

Shortly after, he returned to the Bridge, and piped on the broadcast system for, "Able Seamen Ritchie, report to the Bridge!" Leaving the forecastle, I reported to the Bridge. An angry captain wanted to know in no uncertain terms why there was no one in the Ops Room.

I explained that he would need to ask his Chief Boatswain's Mate why he had given me a direct order to report to the forecastle immediately I had stepped aboard and that he said would look after the class and settle them in." The Chief Boatswain's Mate was sent for and confirmed what I had said. I was then told to get the Operations room closed, pronto, and that I would hear more of this when I returned to HMAS *Watson*.

At the end of the training cruise, I returned to *Watson* and was put before a very angry Training Officer and asked to explain what I had been up to. I explained exactly what had been happening on each of the training cruisers and that on this last cruise, having received a direct order to go to the forecastle immediately, I could not see how I could avoid disobeying that order. I also made clear that I had reported this type of situation could arise in earlier cruise reports. I was dismissed and told to return to my training duties in the school. Future training cruisers were led by a Leading Seaman.

Play Time

It was not all work and no play during my time at HMAS *Watson*. Most of the Ship's Company tended to live and go ashore as they were either married, came from Sydney, or had overnight leave. From memory, I think it cost three pence (cents) to catch the tram into Sydney CBD.

It was not unknown that, after night rounds, for a couple or three of the duty watch to repair down into Watsons Bay and be joined by some of the local girls for a drink and slap and tickle, either in the park or concealed in the rock formations alongside the tramline running up from the Bay itself; that Lieutenant Commander, who took pleasure after lights out of mustering the Duty Watch. He was often accompanied by the large Great Dane, Horse.

The Quartermaster would go into the huts and make the appropriate pipe, and he would give a couple of extra pips to indicate that the said Officer and duty Petty Officer were watching the gangway or a hole in the fence or vice versa. When all were back and in pyjamas, one of the duty watches would then approach the Officer and his escort and tell him the Duty Watch was mustered.

The Officer would then demand to know where everyone had been as they were not in their hammocks. Some were in the latrines, others along the clifftop admiring the moon and or sea and the stars or some other interesting item. Of course, he didn't believe them but could do nothing as he could not prove they had not been on board.

I was learning the tricks of the matelot fraternity. The same officer was not unknown to invite the Sentry at the North Road gate to come and have a drink with him. He would leave the chap in his cabin, call the duty Petty Officer, and go with him to the gate and, of course, find no one on sentry duty. He would then charge the sailor, who he had seduced to leave his post to have a drink.

After the first occasion of this happening, an arrangement was for the sentry to unobtrusively use the telephone system to indicate to the Quartermaster that he was leaving his post.

A replacement was quickly roused and stood in for the absent sentry causing some confusion and no charge to be laid against the sentry then in the officer's cabin.

Girl Friend on Board

One person, who will remain nameless, had a girlfriend on board during the evening at some secluded place. On one occasion, he had his girlfriend sleeping in an enclosed space under a platform that held the projector in the cinema. He used to bring her meals and when all was quiet, she would go to the showers that were outside, separate from the sleeping huts.

On one occasion, one of my buddies, who ran a dhobying (laundry) firm with me, came home from a night ashore and decided to take a shower. There were showers on each side of the metal wall, and he was on one side, and he heard someone on the other side. He put his head around the end of the wall and got the shock of his life to see the girl showering.

Eventually, the fact the girl was being kept on board by the sailor became more widely known and she was shifted to a location in one of the old gun areas on the clifftop.

These areas were for stores, ammunition, and crew rest areas, used by the gun crews who had manned the guns placed along the clifftop during World War II. Finally, she was smuggled off the base in the Dry Cleaners van that came regularly to pick up and return dry cleaning for the Ship's Company.

Horse

It was not unknown for Horse to accompany someone going on shore leave into the city by tram. Horse would be put in the rear driver's compartment by whoever he was accompanying. If the conductor tried to get a fare from the sailor, Horse would bare his teeth, and the conductor would generally leave the pair alone. I can't recall if Horse ever bit anyone.

On 1/1/1947, I was promoted to the heady rank of Temporary **Acting Leading Seaman.** I had not, at that stage, been in the Navy three years for my first Good Conduct Badge.

Other Comments

I think it was during this time ashore that I visited the CUSA Club, located adjacent to the Ferry Wharf in the CBD. I became friendly with some of the girls, and one caught my eye and invited me home to meet her family. This became like a second home where I could go and relax.

The mother was a widow and always asked after I arrived if I would like a cuppa. There were four girls at home. An elder sister was a Religious Sister, and one of the two brothers was a Priest. It is interesting to reflect as I write this epistle that I keep in touch with this girl still and her remaining family. I had asked her to marry me at one time, and many years later, she told me "The No" was because she wanted a husband who would not be going away regularly.

Finally, my time at HMAS *Watson* came to an end when I was posted to HMAS *Bataan*, a Tribal Class Destroyer.

Chapter 14

HMAS *Bataan*

29 July 1947 to 30 September 1948

Dimensions	Draft	Displacement
115.1m x 11.1m	m	2116 Tons
	Engine	
	Parson Turbines	
	Armament	

Introduction

HMAS *Bataan* was a Tribal Class Destroyer commissioned in 1945. The destroyer was originally named *Chingilly* or *Kurnai* but was renamed prior to the launch in honour of the US stand during the Battle of Bataan. It paid off in 1954.

Aside. My mate Jack L, who joined with me and introduced me to Radar, was a member of the Commissioning crew.

Commissioned on 25 May 1945, it never really participated in WWII but was present in Tokyo Bay for the official Japanese Surrender. Subsequently, it made four deployments to the British Commonwealth Occupation Force and was deployed in Japanese waters. In 1950, whilst en route for her fifth Occupational Force deployment, she was diverted to serve in the Korean War as a Patrol Ship and Carrier Escort until 1951. A second Korean War tour was carried out in 1952.

Joining the Ship

On 28 July 1947, I joined HMAS *Bataan*, anchored off Garden Island, Sydney, New South Wales. On boarding the ship by boat from Garden Island, I was shown to one of the messes and informed I was to be the Leading Seaman in charge of that mess. I found an empty locker for my use, and taking my kit from my sea bag, I stowed it into the locker. My hammock was placed in a hammock storage area.

I can't remember the exact time I boarded the ship; it was probably in the afternoon as I can't remember meeting many of the people in the mess until the following morning.

Next morning as the people returned from shore leave, I noticed there was a three-badge-man (over 12 years' service), some two-badge men (over eight years' service) and, except for five ordinary Seaman, the rest of the sailors were one-badge men. (I think was three years' service at the time that later became four).

As a temporary, no badge, Leading Seaman, I realised I could have a problem because of the vast experience of Naval Service among the group.

Man, Management Begins

It didn't take long before I was put to the test. As my first breakfast on board was ending, and people were leaving the mess for their various parts of the ship, one of the two-badge men said, "Hooky, we need a new cook of the Rook roster." My answer was, "Okay, I'll sort that out." I had to do some fast thinking. (*Cook of the Rook was the sailor who prepared the vegetables for the meals and looked after keeping the mess area neat and tidy.*)

The last man to leave the mess was the three-badge man. I took a punt and said, "As I don't know any of the names of the people in the mess at this stage, could you help me out by making out a Cook of the Rook roster until I get to know everybody."

He said," No problem, Hooky." From then on, I never had to make out the Roster.

(**Hookey** was a term used to address a Leading Seaman. Leading Seaman's badge was an anchor he wore on his uniform.)

My experiences in Man Management had begun.

Besides my duties in supervising the Operations room as the senior Radar Plotter (RP), I also had other duties in my part of ship, which was the Quarterdeck.

Aside. The Seaman division in a ship is divided into four parts. The fore part of the ship is known as the **Forecastle,** the starboard side is the **Main Top,** the Port side is the **Fore top** and the after section is the **Quarterdeck**.

Washing Up

The duty Leading Seaman, of which I was one, oversaw the sailors responsible for the washing up of the American-style metal trays used as plates. This was a tedious duty and could be uncomfortable when there was a sea running, the trough for washing the dishes being in the open on the upper deck near the galley. It was not unknown for sailors doing the washing up to slip some of the metal trays over the side despite the best efforts to prevent it. This led to the Supply Officer being upset by having to provide extra trays when there were not enough for everyone to receive their meals.

My Abilities

It was not long before the Lieutenant TAS (*Torpedo and Anti-submarine*) made it clear that he had concerns about my abilities as a Leading Seaman. My lack of a length of Service stripe indicated I had not been in the Navy for three years and, therefore, would be lacking in experience as a seaman.

His background would have been promotion from the lower deck and, as a Lieutenant, would have had many, many years of service as a sailor and officer. He took every opportunity to inform me that I didn't know what I was doing.

I had realised after my promotion to Leading Seaman that my knowledge of practical seamanship was limited. The Lieutenant seemed to take great delight in pointing it out to me. No matter how hard I tried to do the right thing he would tell me that I was doing it all wrong, especially when coming alongside a wharf or leaving it.

Theft and Outcome.

> **'No room to swing a cat'**
> This is a very popular phrase, and is used today to describe a place that has very little space available, or is very cramped. The phrase dates from at least the 1600s, and was first recorded in Richard Kephale's Medela Pestilentiae (1665): 'They had not space enough to swing a cat in.'
> The 'cat' is believed to be the cat-o'-nine-tails, which was a whip with nine lashes which was popularly used to punish sailors in the Royal Navy.
> Below deck, there was no room to swing the whip, so the punishment was carried out on deck, which provided plenty of room to swing the cat.

During our first days at Recruit School as we were marking our names on our clothes, we were made very aware that to be found in the possession of somebody's gear was a serious offence and we would be severely punished. **Trust** in one's mess mates was essential in the close living found in a ship's mess deck.

Olden Day Navy Punishment, left.

On *Bataan*, I found out early what that could entail. One morning shortly after joining the ship, the pipe **"clear lower deck and muster on the upper deck"** was made. The Ship's Company was formed up in two lines from the bow to the quarter deck, down one side of the deck. Each was given or had a length of rope with a knot in the end, or a leather strap. A sailor, who had been charged with stealing, was led to the bow and then told to make his way to the stern through the two lines. As he ran, each sailor tried to make sure he felt the rope/leather strap.

By the time he arrived at the stern, where the captain was waiting at the Defaulters Table, he could hardly stand up and had to be supported. The charge was read, he pleaded guilty and was sentenced to 90 days Hard Labour in Holsworthy Detention Centre, which was run by the Army. Not a very nice place to be. He was then to be discharged. On discharge his Service Certificate would have the corner cut off to show he had been dishonourably discharged. Such was the attitude to theft in those days.

On September 1st, the ship moved from the buoy to alongside the HMAS *Warramunga*, which was berthed at the Cruiser wharf. the ship was made ready in all respects for sea and for operations as part of the Occupation Forces in Japan.

Passage to Japan

On Friday, the 6th of August 1947, HMAS *Bataan* departed Sydney with HMAS *Hobart* in company, heading north via Cairns, Madang, Manus, and Guam for fuel. The destination was Kure, Japan. The map shows the route from Sydney to Kure.

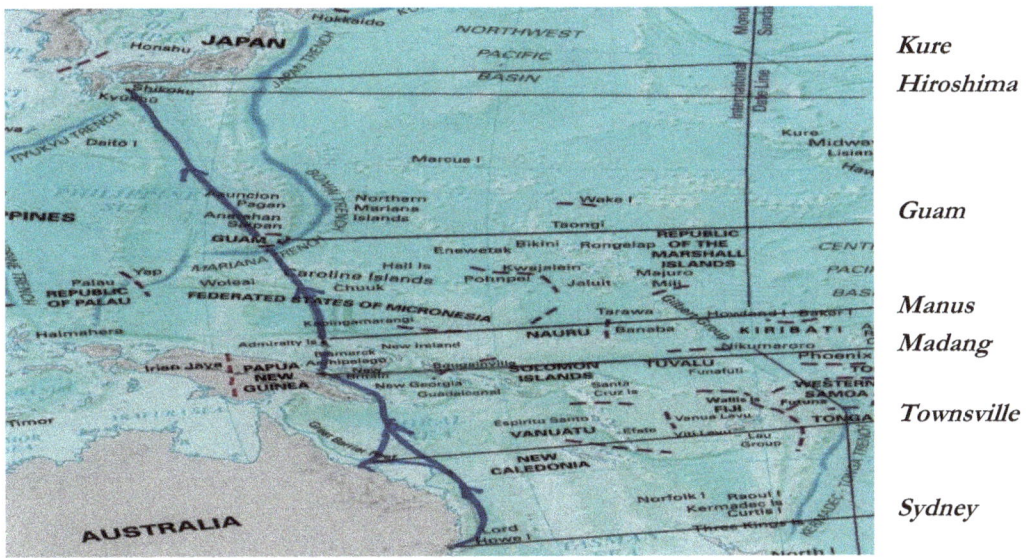

The above map shows the passage taken and ports visited

Unfortunately, on leaving Dreager Harbour, it was necessary to proceed to Manus Island's Seeadler harbour due to an evaporator breakdown in Dreger Harbour. Sea Repairs were affected in a short time, and it was onto Guam.

Crossing the Equator

As we crossed the equator, there were many uninitiated persons on board who had not crossed the equator before and had to attend King Neptune's crossing the line (equator) Court. King Neptune arrived with his Queen and Court officials, appropriately dressed. For people taken before him and the charge read, they were given a chance to plead, and some very humorous pleas resulted.

However, they were sinners no matter how good their plea, and the sentence resulted in the prisoner being covered in smelly substances and ducked in the swimming pool. This revelry reduced some of the tension that had been built up during the intensive training before and during the transit to Japan.

Training

During the passage, everyone was flat out preparing various crews and all organisations for the task ahead and carrying out various evolutions at evening quarters. I had been very busy making sure the Operations room crew was up to the mark.

We exercised all aspects of the duties we could expect to do when on patrol. *Bataan* was to be based in Kure, which was in the British Commonwealth area of responsibility.

Guam (11-14 August 1947)

I remember that the United States Navy looked after us, and we enjoyed their recreational facilities, which were open to our Ship's Company and provided free beer. Fuelling and recreation over, it was onwards to meet up with HMAS *Quickmatch* in the Inland Sea.

Arrival Japan.

Turnover. At 0500 on Monday, the 18th of August, the Bataan rendezvoused with HMAS *Quickmatch* off Mitsuhama in the Inland Sea (see map above) for turnover of operational data and mail. On completion, *Quickmatch* departed for Australia and *Bataan* proceeded to Kure through the Inland Sea.

Kure

Kure is located on the shores of Inland Sea on the Isle of Shikoku. It was a former Japanese Naval Base and had been heavily bombed. It was not very far from Hiroshima, where the first atomic bomb had been dropped during World War II. Kure was devastated, and it was interesting to see the tunnels behind the wharf where there were workshops etc. These tunnels and workshops allowed the Japanese to carry on maintaining their ships despite the air raids.

Each day, when alongside, we were allowed to go ashore in the afternoon if not on duty. There was no overnight leave. There were bars and places to eat, as well as steam baths and massage places. We were not allowed to visit Japanese homes or the like and certainly not allowed to go and have a look at Hiroshima. The Australian Army was in Kure, and the Royal

Australian Air Force was at Iwakuni, a relatively short distance away.

On arrival in Kure at 1000 on August 18th, Bataan was secured alongside the pontoon. the ship stayed in Kure until the 26th, during which time cleaning and touch-up painting of the ship were carried out. A Japanese working party proved extremely useful.

Short leave. For most sailors, and myself, the routine was to have some drinks, retire for a steam bath and a massage and then go and have something to eat. When it was time, we would return to the ship. Occasionally we would play sport.

During our time in Japan, we were paid in script, the money introduced by General Douglas MacArthur. It was used throughout Japan by the Occupation Forces. To obtain Japanese Yen I think we had to find a Japanese money man to do that.

In each of the bars, you could bet that a lot of local girls would join the group and ask to be supplied with a drink. We soon found out that all they wanted was an expensive cocktail which the sailors called a "sticky green". It was probably not alcoholic and only coloured water. It didn't take long for the sailors to tell the girls that, "they drank beer, and the girls would have to do with a beer." Most girls soon left and the ones who stayed were generally interested in learning more English.

There were Australian Army military police patrols, and they discouraged any close association with the local population.

I remember one night meeting up with one of these Army patrols on the way back to the ship. One of the patrolmen came from Kalgoorlie. We had a good old chat about our hometown and what he was doing and his outlook on the local area. He asked me about what we were doing; I gave him a basic description and that we would be sailing in a few days' time. (You can't go anywhere in the world without meeting someone from Kalgoorlie.)

Note. There are several ways I set out this period in *Bataan*. I have decided to give a detailed account with dates and places and what the ship was doing and what I, particularly. was up to.

Sasebo

Bataan arrived at Sasebo on the 28th of August before going on patrol for the first time. There was a large natural harbour. The Naval Section was at the southern end of the bay. *Bataan* secured to a buoy. However, there was no leave granted due to a mild outbreak of infantile paralysis. The map on the next page shows the places that will be mentioned in this epistle.

First Patrol

On the 29th of August, *Bataan* sailed for Sasebo for her first patrol. Any intercepts would be inspected as would any vessel heading for Japan. They would be searched for any contraband and, if found, they would be escorted into the harbour or dealt with at sea. This meant there was always a sea-boat crew and boarding party ready to man the ship's 27-foot whaler whilst we were on patrol. There were also many South Korean fishermen in the area, and they were not impressed by our presence in their fishing areas.

The map shows each place mentioned in this epistle.

Hiroshima

Kure

Turnover

Sasebo

Nagasaki

Kagoshima

Boarding Party

During one of our patrols, the Chief Boatswain's Mate somehow found out that I had never taken a whaler away from a ship at sea. I suddenly found myself as the coxswain of the whaler, powered by five oarsmen as explained earlier in this history.

I had experience as a coxswain of the lowering and hoisting of the whaler and taking it away in the harbour. However, it can be quite a different kettle of fish when there is a sea running. I had some misgivings that I wouldn't get it right when returning to the ship.

Fortunately, the sea was relatively smooth on my first trip away with a Boarding party. Slipping from the falls and the head rope caused no problem in getting clear of the ship. Coming alongside the vessel to be inspected and transferring the Boarding party went well and we were able to move a short distance off the vessel until the Boarding party was ready to return to the ship.

My return alongside and the hoisting of the boat went very well. My competency in boat handling increased, thanks to this exercise. I saw the TAS Gunner keeping an eye on my efforts. I think he was quite disappointed that I had not made a mess of this evolution.

During this patrol, we intercepted and inspected seven ships. The patrol ended on the 30th of August when HMAS *Narrani* arrived, and the ship handed over patrol documentation and charts and I think we received mail and some stores.

Sasebo

Bataan returned to Sasebo arriving at 1500, Sunday 31st of August, first storing and refuelling, then securing to a buoy. Now some comments on Sasebo.

Sasebo was one of the Japanese Naval bases used by the Americans. The Americans had converted one of the Japanese recreational facilities into a place where one could go and get a drink and a meal and some entertainment. I can't remember the name it was called but something like Casbah comes to mind. The other recreational places near, or close by, were the American PX or shopping area and some playing fields for their servicemen and any families on the Base. Sometimes we would play softball against an American team. Although different to cricket, we usually held our own.

Bataan was always allocated a buoy some considerable distance from the shore landing. Using the motorboat and towing the whaler took some time, and we were not able to land all the liberty men in a reasonable time. Fortunately, the American Small Boat section had large and not-so-large landing craft available, and we were able to obtain one of these to land and recover those going on shore leave.

Landing Craft

After the ship's motorboat, they were very powerful and fast and a joy to be the coxswain of. However, at night there was often reduced visibility due to fog or mists. The channel between *Bataan* and the landing pier was lined by ships on either side, moored fore and aft to buoys. If one was not careful, it was possible to run into a buoy or snag a line securing a ship to the buoy. Fortunately, I always had a good bowman who alerted me in time to avoid any hazard stop.

Shore Patrol

The American Navy had Service Police, or Shore Patrols, usually sailors, at the door of venues to check you going in and to make sure you took nothing out of the Casbah or venue. They could be quite rough if you looked like you were drunk or cheeky when being checked out. They had no hesitation in using their long batons, especially on their own people.

Bataan was required to provide a Shore Patrol each day, usually a Leading Seaman with a couple of Able Seamen, to assist. They often rode around in a jeep with an American Shore Patrol. Early on we convinced the Americans to let us deal with our own people so as not to start a brawl. As a rule, we were able to avoid any conflict with the American Shore Patrol people and I think they were grateful that we came to this arrangement.

However, on this visit. we only had one afternoon and night to go ashore.

During one of the times I oversaw the Australian Shore Patrol, we were taken to a women's prison. Here were cells full of disease-ridden women who had been 'Comfort Girls' for the Japanese Military. It was a very sad and depressing situation.

September 1947

Naval Exercise

On the 2nd of September *Bataan* sailed for a two-day exercise in which eleven Royal Naval ships and two British RFA's were engaged. The force was divided into red and blue forces. Red Force consisted of nine ships, including *Bataan*, and the Blue Force consisted of three.

Two serials consisted of submarine attacks. At night, it was shadowing exercises, and a single attack was made on Red Force while replenishing. Six Australian sailors were transferred by Breeches buoy method from our RFA Fort Sandusky.

As you can imagine, during these exercises, I spent a considerable time in the Operations Room making sure that my people were providing up-to-date information to the Command.

Aside. Looking back on the time I served in HMAS *Bataan*, I have come to realise that some of the things that happened in my later career, as far as experience was concerned, particularly in radar operation and managing an operations room, were due to what I quickly had to learn as a young acting leading Seaman in *Bataan*.

On completion of the Exercises, the ships proceeded to Kagoshima Wan and stored from Fort Beauharnais.

At 1700 on Friday the 5th of September, *Bataan* sailed for Yokohama, arriving there at 1010 on Sunday the 7th. the ship secured to Number 21 buoy in Yokohama outer harbour.

Yokohama

From the 7th to the 17th, *Bataan* remained in Yokohama. The US recreational facilities were available and there were the usual local bars.

The usual lot of girls appeared in the bars. Here again, the rule of **"we drink beer, you drink beer"** applied, and that certainly reduced the number of ladies with the group. They were used to the Americans who were paid much more than we were.

Again, it was possible to go to a bathhouse and have a steam bath and massage and see what the food was like in the local facilities and to look around the area and note the damage done by the bombing.

Typhoon

On the 14th of September, *Bataan* proceeded to sea with HMAS *Culgoa* because of an approaching typhoon and its usual heavy rain. Fortunately, the typhoon altered course and the ship was able to return to port on the 15th.

All good things come to an end, and on September 17th, *Bataan* proceeded to sea and headed for Kure.

Kure

Bataan arrived in Kure on the 19th of September and secured to the pontoon. the ship progressed gunnery and seamanship training until the 23rd, when the ship hoisted the flag of the C in C British Commonwealth Forces. *Bataan* then sailed to watch a firepower demonstration given by the RAAF on various targets. When *Bataan* got there, I think there was a remark, it was like "Henley on Sea" with all the spectators assembled along the target line and a short distance from it.

The demonstration commenced with a flypast of eighty-four aircraft. They then demonstrated their firepower. After the demonstration the captain entertained the General and his guest to lunch. Finally, the ship returned to Kure and disembarked the guests before sailing for Shanghai in the company with HMS *Gambia*.

Shanghai

At 1045 on September 26th, *Bataan* and HMS *Gambia* arrived in Shanghai, and *Bataan* was secured alongside HMS *Gambia* until the 30th.

HMS Gambia

The buzz (rumour) went around the ship that we were there for a Court of Enquiry. The Enquiry was to investigate the suspect activities of the Ship's Supply Officer the previous Christmas when the ship was in Shanghai.

One thing I do remember was there was plenty of opportunity for sport in both Kure and Shanghai during our visits. We also appreciated films led by our RNEC to the ship.

And so, another month had passed. My education in all aspects of my duties as a Quartermaster in harbour had been expanded. I had no problems in the mess.

Shanghai

Hong Kong

October 1947

Hong Kong

On the 2nd of October, the ship slipped from alongside *Gambia* and proceeded to Hong Kong. Pilots were used to transit the Yangten Estuary and the Whangpoo River because of the very strong tide and the many and varied craft using these waterways. The passage south was uneventful.

On the 5th of October, *Bataan* arrived in Hong Kong. As the ship approached the harbour, I slipped out of the Operations room onto the bridge wing and recalled my first entrance into Hong Kong at the end of WWII while serving in HMAS *Bathurst*. She was part of mine-sweeping operations clearing the entrance for the British Fleet to enter Hong Kong.

Bataan berthed on 'Cossack' at No 7 buoy. Off the dockyard, however, on the 7th, *Bataan* was ordered to sea with five Royal Naval ships due to an approaching typhoon. It was quite rough as you can imagine; fortunately, the typhoon veered away. That evening a Night Encounter exercise was conducted as the winds abated. the ship then returned to Hong Kong.

On arrival back in Hong Kong, *Bataan* secured to a buoy, and the ship reverted to extended notice for steam so that work would be carried out on our main steam lines. This required dockyard assistance, and the ship was delayed sailing until the 18th. The C in C British Pacific Fleet inspected the Ship's Company at Divisions at 1100 on the 16th of October.

China Fleet Club

One thing that comes to mind was the use of the China Fleet Club and the excellent meals at a reasonable cost that were available in the club. There were cabins for the Petty officers and

Chief Petty officers and dormitories for the Junior sailors. They were quite comfortable if one slept ashore. There were also billiard tables and a cinema. The Club was run by the British Pacific Fleet Central Canteens Committee. Female guests were allowed in the Club, and they were not necessarily the usual type of bar girl you found elsewhere.

For my part, I tended to go sightseeing in both Hong Kong and Kowloon and remember some of the places I visited back in 1945. I wasn't into just sitting and drinking.

It was not all beer and skittles. Training classes for Ordinary Seaman continued, and while in Hong Kong, 25 of 26 passed the test for Able Seaman.

The ship refueled and took on water before sailing at 1515 on October 18th, *Bataan*, headed for Sasebo. The passage was unpleasant due to steep seas and a strong headwind.

Sasebo

Bataan arrived at Sasebo at 0900 on Wednesday, the 22nd of October, and reported to CTU 96.5.2 for duty. *Bataan* remained in Sasebo until 1630 on the 30th, when it set sail for Kure.

The captain had left the ship in the hands of the XO who took command of the passage to Kure. On the way, the ship was diverted to Iwakuni to pick up the Flag Officer Commanding Australian Squadron. The captain also re-joined the ship here.

November 1947

Kure

The ship continued on to Kure and arrived at 1000 on Sunday, 2nd November.

It was to remain alongside the pontoon until 1500 on Friday, November 7th, when it sailed for Shanghai.

En route, one of the propellers had a problem, and after divers had looked into the problem, the ship continued at a reduced speed to Shanghai.

Shanghai

On November 10th, the *Bataan* was secured alongside HMAS *Australia* in Shanghai. Because of the strong current, divers could not work on the shafts.

HMAS Australia

During this stay, there was a strong sporting programme, and the entertainment was of its usual high standard. At 1330 on November 13th, *Bataan* sailed for Yokosuka to have the shafts looked at.

Informer

I think it was about this time that a Petty Officer joined *Bataan*. He took a great deal of interest in talking to various sailors about the deployment and their goings on ashore. This was unusual, and it didn't take long for people to wake up that he was out to trap people into revealing any unauthorised purchases or goings on. He was fed a lot of claptrap.

Yokosuka

HMS *Sussex* was met on the way, and both ships arrived in Yokosuka on the 22nd. *Bataan* secured to Piedmont Pier. *Sussex* divers were soon looking at and identifying the likely problem and correcting what they could.

HMA ships, *Arunta* and *Warramunga*, berthed on *Bataan* at 0140 on Monday 24th of November. At 0630, the three ships sailed for a two-day exercise with American and RN units. These consisted of RN ship towing USN and vis versa, getting used to USN manoeuvring signals before participating in a Night Encounter.

There was also an air attack and RN ships fuelled USN ships and vis versa. Finally, the exercise ended at 1545 on Wednesday, and the ships returned to Yokosuka.

My Duties

During all exercises, I was fully occupied seeing the Ops Room was on the ball and on passage I would keep a watch in charge of the Ops Room. Entering and leaving harbour I would be closed as a Special Sea Duty man in the Ops Room. If in Harbour in Japan, and leave was granted, I, with some of the crew, would take the opportunity to relax in a bathhouse with a massage and then go and find a bar and place to eat.

Homeward Bound

At 1000 on Thursday 27th of November *Bataan* sailed for Manus and Sydney.

December 1947

Between the 1st and 4th of December, *Bataan* was on passage to Manus. Rendezvous was made with HMA ships *Australia* and *Culgoa*, and the ships entered Seadler Harbour at 0604 on the 4th of December.

Bataan and *Culgoa* berthed on either side of *Australia*. After fuelling was completed, the ships proceeded, with *Bataan* and *Culgoa* taking station astern of *Australia*.

HMAS *Condamine* was sighted on the morning of 8th of December.

It was an uneventful passage to Sydney and *Bataan* proceeded *Australia* into harbour at 1159 on Wednesday, 10th of December, securing at No 2 buoy to obtain pratique. Twenty minutes later the ship slipped and proceeded to berth at Fitting Out Wharf, Woolloomooloo, where Customs Officials came on board. Customs Declaration forms had been filled in by the crew while en route to Sydney.

My Return to Sydney

Just before entering Sydney Harbour, I was sent for and told I would be the coxswain of the whaler taking the buoy jumpers to the buoy *Bataan* was to secure to. Again, this was something new for me to do.

The evolution involved the ship being underway as it dropped the boat, with the crew and buoy jumpers on board. The boat was pulled by a head rope, manned by personnel on board, so you did not need to put out oars. Once the boat's head rope was slipped, the boat shot forward and was steered until it was alongside the buoy.

The speed of the boat was such that you needed a method of stopping alongside the buoy without the use of the oars so the buoy jumpers could hop onto the buoy. How to stop the boat's momentum and get away before the ship's bow arrived at the buoy was something I was very concerned about. I asked one of the senior Leading Seaman to help me out. His advice was to take a full bucket of water, secure a line to the bucket and after thwart (seat) with enough line to drop the bucket over the stern of the boat as it arrives at the buoy.

This I did, and it worked a treat. As I was recovering the bucket and calling ordering ***"out oars and push off"***, I looked up to see the bow of the ship towering above my head and almost touching the buoy. I managed to get the boat away quickly; then it was a case of laying off waiting for the buoy jumpers to finish securing the ship to the buoy, collecting the buoy jumpers, and pulling (rowing) back alongside and the boat being hoisted.

My TAS Gunner did not appear on this occasion.

Captain Cook Dock

On Friday, December 12th, *Bataan* entered the Dock, followed by HMAS *Quiberon*, and would remain there until January 23rd.

Long Leave

I proceeded on my six weeks of annual leave on the 12th of December. This consisted of five days travelling time there and five days back, and six weeks in the West.

The journey home was Sydney, Albury, change of train to Melbourne, overnight Melbourne, then onto Port Pirie and finally, for a change having a sleeper on the Nullabor crossing on the Trans Train to Kalgoorlie. Also, I was able to have all meals in the dining car on the last section home. Being in uniform, some people talked to me asking what did and where I had been.

Home (Long Leave)

On arrival in Kalgoorlie, I grabbed my bag and walked up to the tram stop that would take me to within two streets of my home. My mum was a bit surprised to see me as I had not told her I was coming on leave and would be joining them for Christmas.

My usual way of using my leave was to spend up to two weeks in Kalgoorlie, go to Perth for two weeks or so, and return to Kalgoorlie for what was left of my leave.

As I have mentioned in an earlier chapter my mum and us children would go to Perth each year to spend Christmas at our Uncle Harry and Auntie Nell's place in Maylands. So, I joined the rest of the family on the trip to Perth.

While in Perth, I contacted old friends and my other uncles, aunts, and cousins. I also spent an occasional day at the beach with friends. I won't go into a blow-by-blow summary.

When I did return to Kalgoorlie, I prepared for the trip back to Sydney.

I cannot remember the date I left Kalgoorlie for Sydney, but I was back in time to be on *Bataan* being moved out of the Drydock on Thursday the 29th of January 1948.

Promotion to Leading Seaman

One thing I do remember, and have from my records, I had been promoted to Leading Seaman on the 1st of January 1948.

February 1948

The first few days of February was spent restoring, taking on fresh provisions, ammunition, and fuel for the coming voyage to Tasmania and New Zealand.

There had been some basic Command and Operations Room training at HMAS *Watson* during the period before sailing.

Joint RAN/USN Exercise

On the 4th of February, *Bataan* sailed in company with HMAS ships *Australia, Quickmatch, Shoalhaven, Murchison,* and *Culgoa* as the Australian Squadron, to exercise with the US Task Force 38, comprising US ships *Valley Forge*, destroyers *Kepler, Lawe Thomas* and *Wood*. These exercises continued until about noon on the 5th with the forces splitting, and the US Group heading off elsewhere.

HMAS *Quickmatch* developed a problem with her engines and was detached to proceed to Sydney. *Bataan* was also detached to follow *Quickmatch* and transfer ammunition to *Bataan* who would replace her for gunnery school firings out of Melbourne.

Plotting Exercises

As the ships sailed south, a series of competitive plotting exercises were organised between ships in company. A ship would be required to steer a course of their choosing before altering to another course for ten minutes; the other ship would be required to calculate the course of the other ship using the surface radar and a plotting table. This was the first time I had been required to supervise such an exercise. Initially, I used the normal plotting scale.

However, the Ship's Gunnery officer suggested I use another scale, and to use only the middle six or seven minutes of plots to calculate the course of the other ship(s). This little piece of advice allowed *Bataan* to be placed first in the competition.

Gunnery School Firings

On the 7th of February, *Bataan* proceeded independently and secured alongside Nelson's pier Williamtown. The following morning the ship sailed with gunnery classes embarked for sub calibre firings. On completion of night firing, the ship returned alongside Williamtown. The following day, the ship was at sea again for AA firings and on completion, returned to Melbourne, berthing at Inner East Station Pier, Melbourne.

On the 11th of February, *Bataan* slipped and rendezvoused with the Australian Squadron and carried out surface tracking exercises, and a shadowing attack was made on HMAS *Australia* by the destroyer flotilla.

On the 12th of February, *Murchison* re-joined the group, and in line abreast the Squadron headed for Hobart carrying out soundings as they sailed south.

Hobart

On the 13th of February, the Squadron arrived in Hobart and the entry was marred by a thick curtain of rain. *Bataan* secured to the inner South berth and ocean pier and the rest of the day was spent cleaning the ship. The Ship's Company participated in the Annual Fleet Regatta.

Regatta

The Regatta consisted of several sporting events such as pulling (rowing) races between whalers, big ships cutter crews, sailing races, athletics, cross-country running, wood chop, and cross saw cutting of timber.

After I had participated in the whaler pulling races, I went to watch the various other events. I was watching the wood chop when a fellow crew member from the ship approached me and asked if I would join him in the crosscut saw event, which was due to start. The person who was to be his mate had been kept on board as he was on duty watch. Against the odds, we won the event.

I was also asked to make up the numbers in the ship's cricket team. I was the last man in, and the situation was that we needed four runs to win with three balls remaining. The ship's PTI, (Physical Training Instructor) came down and said, "just tap the ball and run, I will get the rest."

I was prepared to tap and run until the ball stood up in front of me. I laid back and whacked the ball as hard as I could, and it was the longest distance I ever hit a cricket ball. It flew over the boundary and that was the end of the innings.

Bataan won the most events and was named "Cock of the Fleet." A large Rooster cut out was secured to the top of the ship's mast.

This led to numerous attempts by other ship crews trying to remove the Rooster and place it at the top of their ship's mast. *Bataan's* on-duty Quartermaster and Bo'sun's Mate had to be very vigilant to make sure nobody from other ships managed to get aboard. There were several attempts; all were repelled.

Hobart Delights

One of the special delights in Hobart was to have a meal of crayfish when on shore leave. There was a nice café in the main street that was well patronised. So, my love of crayfish and lobster began.

Also, when returning to the ship there were cray boats tied up to the wharf that *Bataan* was secured to. We were generally able to get a live cray from the cray boats. If there was a crew member on board the cray boat, he dug one out of the holding area for two shillings (20 cents) or, if no one was on board, we helped ourselves and left the money on the hatch.

Cooking Crayfish

In *Bataan*, there was a large vat adjacent to the galley door, and it contained very hot water. You would throw your cray into the vat, grab a long-handled scoop, and see if you could find a cray already cooked. There was always someone who threw their cray in and wandered off to bed.

An alternative was for someone to take a live cray into the mess and place it into the hammock of someone asleep. The reaction and language that came as the cray's feelers searched the sleeper's face were unprintable and usually a sight to behold. The cray would be knocked out of the hammock and slide across the floor and under the lockers. The next morning, the owner of the cray could be found searching for it.

Punishment

On one occasion, I was duty Quartermaster, and after completing my weekend duty, I washed my white shorts and shirts and hung them in the boiler uptake to dry. Shortly after hanging them up, I was told I was required to be in a VIP piping party in just over an hour. I grabbed a wet pair of shorts and a shirt and began ironing them dry in the mess deck in time for the piping party.

My friend, the TAS Gunner spotted me and had me charged with being in an improper place. I appeared before the Executive Officer and, despite explaining the situation that I had found myself in, I was found guilty and given two days' stoppage of leave. It was the only punishment I received in my entire career.

The ship sailed that day, so the basic effect on my leave was zero. I have a suspicion that the XO may have been aware of my position with the TAS Gunner, and knowing we were sailing, and it would have no effect on my actual leave, gave the verdict to get the TAS Gunner off my back. It worked for a while.

Our time in Hobart came to an end and it was then off to New Zealand.

New Zealand

Bataan departed Hobart on the 1st of March for New Zealand. Being my birthday, unknown to me, one of my senior radar plotters and go ashore mate, Alex D, had hidden a bottle of Scotch whiskey in a locker of the Operations Room to celebrate my birthday. Up until that time I had never imbibed much, certainly no whiskey.

The next morning, I found I could hardly lift my head off the pillow, and this lasted for three days; I was incapacitated and unable to do my duties. Fortunately, the weather was most unfriendly, so I was able to get away with not being in the Operations room. My people covered for me. I was not found to have been drunk on board. So, I really began my alcoholic drinking experiences. I had stuck to beer only for the past year since my 21st birthday, and, after the above experience, I stayed with a beer until I discovered the joys of drinking wine.

Dunedin

Bataan arrived in Dunedin at 0850 on Friday, the 5th of March. I will always remember the steep roads of this town. We were granted shore leave and were able to go to the dances and meet local girls. Of course, the pubs and clubs were also included in our activities and a game of rugby was not amiss. I got up for a dance or two, much to the sorrow of the girls I danced with. I was still in the learner dancer phase, except for the waltz.

Places Mentioned in this Epistle.

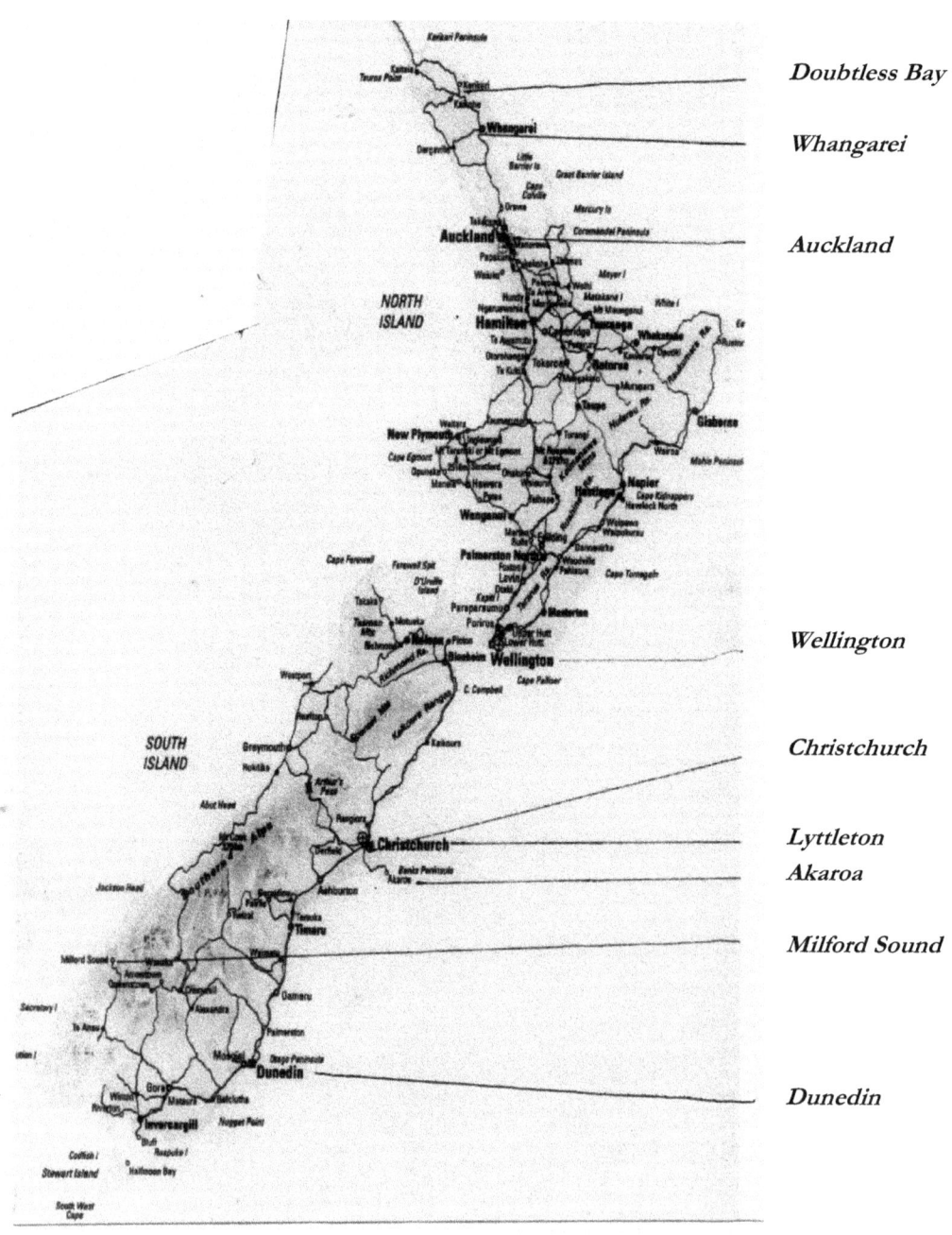

Dunedin

One thing I do remember, after an all-night party, I was making my way back to the ship and I came across the milkman and he offered to drive me back to the ship. I was very happy to accept, and on arrival at the ship, he was rewarded when he was rushed by sailors for a bottle of milk.

After a very pleasant stay, *Bataan* sailed for Lyttleton at 1430 on Tuesday the 9th of March.

Lyttleton

Arrived alongside Lyttleton at 0845, on Wednesday, the 10th of March. The activities at Lyttleton were much the same as for Dunedin without the all-night party and milkman. I had a look around, played Rugby and took part in whatever was going. Then it was onto Wellington at 1547 on the 15th.

Wellington

HMAS *Australia* led *Bataan* into Wellington at 0852 on the 16th. Known as 'Windy Wellington', it lived up to its name while on passage and as the ship berthed alongside. It was an interesting city to explore. Again, there was entertainment and sport. I also took a conducted tour that was very interesting. Finally at 1515, on the 22nd, *Bataan* sailed for Auckland.

While on passage HMNZN *Bellona* joined in surface tracking, sub-calibre firings at a target towed by *Bellona*, sea boat exercises, and some OOW training were all carried out on the way to Auckland.

Auckland

Bellona led *Australia* and *Bataan* into Auckland, and they stayed in the harbour until the 30th. Again, it was rest, play, and sightseeing. I was happy to look around and take a very interesting tour. By this time, I think most of the crew were looking forward to heading back to Sydney.

April 1948

Enroute Sydney.

After clearing the harbour, *Australia* and *Bellona* exercised fuelling, OOWs were exercised by the three ships until 1615 when *Bellona* parted company and the Australian ships proceeded north along the coast and then headed for Sydney.

On the 1st of April, while on passage from Auckland to Sydney, *Bataan* streamed a splash target for *Australia* to carry out sub-calibre firings. Following the recovery of the target, the *Bataan* worked up for a full power trial, and something like 32 knots were recorded. It was pleasing to note that the machinery behaved itself.

Bataan entered Sydney Harbour just before midnight on the 2nd of April, securing to No 1 buoy. Up until the 12th of April was spent preparing the ship for the Admiral's inspection. the ship was painted overall and cleaned up everywhere you can imagine.

Sea Training

On the 12th of April, the time came to slip from the buoy and follow the flagship, HMAS *Australia*, out of the harbor and onto Jervis Bay. During the transit to Jervis Bay a target was streamed by *Bataan* so the *Australia* could carry out sub-calibre firings. After recovering the target, surface tracking exercises and close-range weapons functioning trials were carried out. *Bataan* then proceeded into Jervis Bay independently.

Preparation for Inspection

Bataan anchored off Captain's Point at 1920hrs. The period to the 20th of April was spent in working up for inspection, including inspection of the ship and carrying out independent drills and gunnery exercises. Bad weather prevented the one day at sea allowed during this period.

The Minister for Navy, Mr Reardon, and Mrs Reardon walked around *Bataan* during the forenoon of Sunday the 18th.

Admiral's Inspection

On Tuesday, the 20th of April, the ship was inspected at Divisions, General Quarters and General Drills by the Flag Officer Commanding the Australian Squadron.

Admiral Inspecting Crew

Back to Sea

On completion of the Inspection, an HRS, the target, was passed to *Bataan* by *Australia* and was secured astern overnight.

At 0700 on the 21st of April, *Bataan* proceeded to sea, streaming the target as it went. Weather conditions were unsuitable for this type of target. The tow parted twice at the after-fair lead. Australia recovered the target.

At 1600 on Thursday, the 22nd of April, the ship weighed and proceeded in company with *Australia* toward Sydney. Planned exercises could not be carried out. On the morning of Friday, 23 April, close-range weapons functioning trials and long- and close-range weapons HA firings were carried out.

The weather was unsuitable for battle practice, and eventually, *Bataan* was able to proceed to Sydney Harbour at 1515, secured alongside the Fitting Out wharf at 1550.

Note. I spent a considerable time in the Ops Room during the above periods. However, once we entered the harbour, I was back on the Quartermaster roster. the ship dressed overall and was illuminated for Anzac Day 1948.

Change of Command

On the 26th of April, Captain JC Morrow, DSO, DSC, ADC, RAN relieved Captain WH Harrington DSO, RAN as Captain (D), 10th Destroyer Flotilla, and Lieutenant Commander NHS White RAN took over Command of HMAS *Bataan*

May 1948

Dockyard Assistance

All the month of May was spent in Dockyard hands or in the engraving graving dock.

Social Life

I was able to renew the few friends I had made in Sydney and visit my cousin Dora and family. One of the families that had made me feel very much at home was a mother, Mrs Miles, and her three daughters. Another sister was a nun, and a brother a priest. A second brother was working on the Trans Train Line.

From time to time, I took one of the girls, Anne, out to the pictures or for a meal or a dance. At one time later I had asked her to marry me, but she didn't want a husband who would always be going away for lengthy periods. We are still in contact over 75 years later.

Aside. After Retirement, when I visited Sydney each year, I would take the three girls out to lunch.

During this visit I found the second brother had come home and he casually asked me if I played tennis. I replied that I did, and he asked me if I would care to come and make up a second male so the girls he played with could play mixed doubles. I agreed to come on the next Wednesday.

Karma or Miracle. I will leave it up to the reader to decide.

The next Wednesday, the brother and I arrived at the tennis court, and as I was about to put on my tennis shoes, I looked up and saw a girl crossing at the other end of the court. I instantly said, "I am going to marry that girl." (exact words).

My friend said, "What? You don't even know her."

I replied, "I know that."

In December 1955, in London, under training to become an Officer, I did marry her. I believe someone provoked me at the tennis court to say what I did. We had fifty-seven delightful years together, but that is for later.

Change of Command

On the 27th of May, there was another Change of Command, and Commander AS Storey, RAN, relieved Lieutenant A S White, RAN., the temporary CO. During, I had been a Quartermaster for some of the period and worked in my part of ship and I think was still the Quarterdeck.

June 1948

Preparation for Sea

On the 8th of June, *Bataan* was moved to a buoy from the drydock to embark shores and provisions. I was busy ensuring the Ops Room was ready for sea and the Radars, etc, were working properly.

Custom Swoop

I think I may have mentioned this before. One way people obtained Japanese yen was to swap saccharin tablets for yen.

On the morning of our departure for *Bataan's* next tour of Japan, the ship was boarded by Custom Officers who began a search of the ship. It was interesting to note that some of these Officers made a beeline for a particular mess and went straight to a particular cupboard expecting to find a hoard of saccharine. To their surprise, the cupboard was empty. Soon after the Customs people left the ship and many of the crew breathed a deep sigh of relief, especially the members of that mess. No need to ask why.

What the Customs officers were looking for were bottles of Saccharin tablets the mess members had bought so they could be swapped for yen to buy Japanese goods and services, not available in the American or Australian facilities, where script only was accepted in British Commonwealth and American bases. It was not hard to work out that our over-friendly Petty Officer of the last time up in Japan had passed on the information to Customs. He never returned to the ship.

The mess members were surprised that nothing had been found. A very enterprising mess man had slipped all the bottles into a slop bucket and taken it ashore as soon as he heard Customs were on board.

On the same day, ten Lieutenants (P) (P for Pilots from the Fleet Air Arm) joined for sea experience in other than a Carrier. On the 15th of June, *Bataan* sailed for her next deployment in the Occupation of Japan Forces and headed first for Cairns.

The weather was not very kind. I think the embarked Pilots wished they had chosen a different occupation. These weather conditions prevented planned exercises from being carried out.

On the 16th of June, the weather had abated sufficiently to allow the embarked Lieutenants to practice bringing the ship alongside a drifting target.

Passage to Japan

Bataan arrived in Cairns on the 19th for fuel and water. Then it was on to Darwin. Two radars and the echo sounder became unserviceable, and it was necessary, with the discovery that one channel buoy light was not working as we transited across the top of Australia, for the ship to anchor for the night. During the night, the ship's staff were able to make repairs to the radars and echo sounder.

In addition, the ship's main refrigerator was giving trouble, and, on arrival at Darwin on the 24th of June, the ship's staff were able to remove the contents to a shore refrigerator whilst repairs were made.

July 1948

Sasebo

Bataan secured to a Typhoon buoy in Sasebo on the 6th of July. A Typhoon was affecting movements and it passed about 250 miles to the westward on the 7th of July. **A GREAT WELCOME BACK?** Then, on the 8th of July, it was on Patrol again.

On Patrol

The patrol was in the Tsushima Straight and lasted until the 11th of July when we returned to Sasebo. This was an uneventful patrol, and the opportunity was taken to carry out sub-calibre firings at a drifting target.

The time in Sasebo allowed the crew to renew their association with the Casbah. I enjoyed the bathhouse and massage as it relaxed the tension that had built up from the time since returning from leave. I had spent a lot of time ensuring my team were ready and up to the mark. Also making sure the newcomers to my mess settled in well.

Bataan repeated this patrol from the 14th to 17th inclusive, and the only event of interest with a failing gyro compass due to dirty mercury. This was cleaned up by the ship's staff.

Kure

At the end of the second patrol, the ship was ordered to Kure for seven days availability. A rest period, no, to sort out some problems. the ship arrived in Kure on Sunday the 18th and the shore staff were of great assistance.

The ship's engine room personnel worked on the boilers and engines, overhauling and correcting a few minor leaks in the steam lines. The opportunity was also taken to paint the ship.

Boiler Clean

A Boiler Clean was undertaken by the ship's engineering sailors whilst the seamen attended to removing rust and painting the ship's side and the superstructure. When we sailed for our next patrol, the Boilers had problems and we returned to Kure for a repeat clean.

At 1330 on the 25th of July, maintenance work was completed just after lunch. *Bataan* proceeded to sea to join CTG 96.5 in USS *Oakland*, and USS *Bass* (D) for exercises with the American Far Eastern Air Force. Close-range attacks by Mustangs were good training for my team and the other ship's teams.

However, the loss of one A 26, ten miles from the force marred the day. Search and rescue attempts were unsuccessful.

Bataan arrived in Yokosuka on the 27th. On the 28th, she went to sea for a three-day antisubmarine exercise with the submarine USS *Bugara*. This provided much-needed experience for Asdic operators. the ship returned to Yokosuka at 1545 on the 31st.

August 1948

During the visit, US Senior Sailors and enlisted men entertained Senior Sailors. Enlisted Men entertained their corresponding ranks from the RN and RAN in their Clubs, and this was greatly appreciated.

The Fleet Work exercises proved very valuable for the Officer of the Watches, especially our aircrew officers embarked for training. I was very busy in the operations room. After the debriefing, the ship proceeded to Tokyo on the 4th of August.

An invitation had been issued to Mrs McArthur, who had named the *Bataan*, and she came aboard the ship on Sunday, the 7th of August. She met all the Officers and the only crew member on board who was in the Commissioning crew, Leading Seaman Ham.

Yokosuka   Tateyama,   Tokyo Bay.

The American and British Communities entertained both officers and men. Then, at 0700 on Monday the 9th, *Bataan* proceeded to Yokosuka, arriving and departing for Sasebo and our next patrol. At 1230, *Bataan* arrived in Sasebo on the 11th only to find out fresh provisions from Kure had not arrived. They had been delayed en route.

Patrol

Bataan then proceeded to the patrol area. Eventually, the ship was informed that the provisions had arrived. the ship interrupted the patrol on the 13th to return to Sasebo and collect the provisions, particularly the fresh ones. *Bataan* resumed patrol until the 14th when the ship returned to Sasebo.

More A/S Exercises

These exercises were to last four days and were like those carried out earlier. Those on the first day were elementary. A material failure marred the ship's performance from the afternoon of the first day, and the problem was rectified to enable participation in the next days' exercises.

I was kept busy in the Ops Room during these exercises. All ships returned to harbour at the end of the exercises.

Reception. On the evening of our return to harbour, The Naval Base Sasebo and a US ship, whose name I have forgotten, entertained *Bataan's* Ship's Company to a dance at their Club. Despite the free beer, behaviour was exemplary, and there were no incidents.

On Patrol

At 0700 on the 21st of August, *Bataan* proceeded on patrol on the south-east coast of Tsushima and, in one bay, found a Japanese patrol vessel and three other ships that were inspected. Nothing was found.

Bataan was relieved and returned to Sasebo on the 22nd of August, and further fresh and dry provisions from Kure were embarked.

Yokosuka

Bataan sailed for Yokosuka at 0830 on Tuesday, August 24th, arriving alongside a maintenance berth to allow engineering maintenance to progress.

Exercises

Bataan sailed in company with USS *Oakland* and US Destroyers *Orleck*, *Bass* and *Craig* on the 31st of August, rendezvousing with British units at 0300 on the 1st of September.

September 1948

The exercises were to last until 0700 on the 2nd of September. However, an engine defect resulted in *Bataan* leaving the area and returning to Yokosuka.

Yokosuka

During berthing on the 1st, the remaining engine failed, and fortunately, the ship was able to secure to a buoy until it moved alongside.

Maintenance

Eight days were spent in intensive boiler cleaning and a self-refitting period. To speed up the boiler cleaning, the ship's crew was divided into two watches. This was completed by the 7th of September, and normal arrangements were resumed.

By Saturday, September 11th, enough work had been done to attempt a Basin Trial. This was attempted on Sunday, the 12th. It was not a success. Further repair work was undertaken and continued until the 22nd.

HMAS *Culgoa* arrived from Hong Kong and secured alongside *Bataan* on the 5th and transfer of Occupational Paperwork began. Later, motor cutters were exchanged.

I would have been a Quartermaster during this stay in Kure.

At 1130 on the 6th of September, *Bataan* cast off and proceeded to Manus, having completed its third duty in the Occupational Forces of Japan since I joined the ship in 1947.

During the passage to Manus, *Bataan* struck the edge of the typhoon, with rain squalls and winds gusting to about 50 knots in the afternoon and evening of the 10th. Apart from that, I remember the rest of the long journey being uneventful. No land or ships were sighted on the nine-day passage.

Manus

Bataan's arrival alongside in Manus was at 0800, on the 15th of September, with only 59.5 tons of fuel remaining.

On 16 September 1930, having fuel to capacity, *Bataan* cast off, intending to proceed to Auki, Florida Island in the Solomons. However, the Resident Commissioner requested that *Bataan* come directly to Honiara, and the ship's next port was changed.

Honiara

On arrival at Honiara on the 21st, it was found that the US *Coaster* was alongside the pier. *Bataan* was unable to secure astern him, as the pier was only 600 feet long. The US ship agreed to move up the pier, and *Bataan* berthed astern of it. From memory, *Bataan* had about 130 of her 377 feet hanging off the pier. The requirement for freshwater required the ship to do the best it could.

When the wind increased, during a Captain's dinner party on board, the ship moved away from the pier and the guests were taken to sea, where *Bataan* moored with two anchors. Later, the ship re-berthed and the guests were landed.

At 1700 on the 21st of September, *Bataan* cast off and proceeded to Brisbane for fuel.

Brisbane

At 2200 on the 25th of September, *Bataan* berthed at Newstead Wharf and took on fuel and water. The following day I remember HMA ships *Sydney* and *Culgoa* arrived. *Bataan* headed off to Sydney at 1400.

Sydney

The passage to Sydney was uneventful. On the 28th of September, at 0720, the ship was secured along Charter Bay pier for fuel. On completion of fuelling, *Bataan* berthed alongside HMAS *Barcoo* at Cruiser Wharf, Garden Island.

At 1500 on the 30th, *Bataan* moved berth again to the Farm Cove Destroyer *Trot*.

Departure from Ship

Records show that I posted out of the ship on September 30th, probably from the Cruiser wharf, where the vehicle to take me to HMAS *Watson* would have picked me up.

Summary

I had joined *Bataan* as a young, no badge and inexperienced Leading Seaman. Somehow, I managed (thanks to Karma) to gain considerable and valuable experience in the Operation Room and working with the Radars of the Ship. Fortunately (again, thanks to Karma), I managed to learn how to man manage, which was to stand me in good stead in the years ahead.

Chapter 15

HMAS *Watson* (2nd Stint)

1 October 1948 to 28 January 1949

Return to Shore

Official records are a bit hit and miss for when I left HMAS *Bataan* and returned to HMAS *Watson*. The above days are the best assessment.

Instructor

I was put to work instructing sailors to be Radar Plotters. The experience I had gained on HMAS *Bataan* paid off as I was now fully aware of what they would be required to do.

One thing I particularly remember from the actual plotting time is that when standing in front of the plot and looking at it, the right arm is on the right side of the plot. However, when standing at the back of the plot and facing it, the right arm is on the left of the plot.

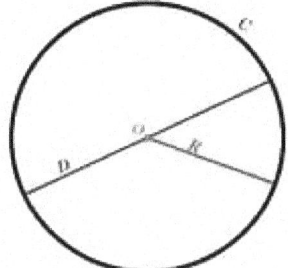

O70   290

090   270

105   255

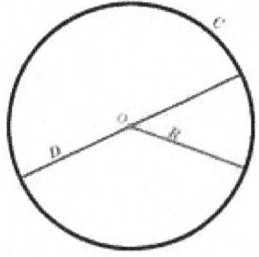

Front View Arm on Right   *Rear-view R/Arm on left.*

Training.

Before doing actual plotting, I would stand each student behind the plots and call out a bearing and watch as a student carefully looked for the bearing. I would then lessen the time between each bearing and it didn't take long to get them working quickly and automatically selecting the correct side.

From that point on they would be connected to the radar operator for live plotting. and plot his bearing and range from the ship. The next radar would be on the same bearing, but the range would have caged, giving the direction of the aircraft. By analyzing the distance between the plots over one or two minutes, the rough speed of the aircraft could be worked out.

Besides air plotting, I also taught how to use a radar display accurately on surface plots, radio reporting procedures, the General Plot, and any other snippets they should know about operating in an operation when in company and exercising.

Sport and Social Activities

I rejoined the HMAS *Watson* Rugby team and played tennis or went swimming at a local beach. I renewed my time with friends, my cousin Dora, and family. I attended several dances during my time ashore. I occasionally went for a meal at a restaurant, where I learnt about oysters and other seafood.

In general, I made the most of the time ashore. And often visited the Miles family.

Promotion

I was promoted to Acting Petty Officer RP2 on 1/10/1948 and undertook the Radar First Class course.

RP1 Course.

The Three Ps. Early on in this course "How to Instruct" was one of the subjects. I remember we were all in the classroom waiting for the instructor to arrive, when in walks a short officer, who we later learnt had been a Prisoner of War following the sinking of HMAS Perth, sunk in Sundra Straight during WWII. He had been the ship's Instructor Officer.

He never said a word. He walked up to the blackboard and drew three large Ps, one under the other in different colours. His first comment was "What these letters represent is the words you all you need to know about instructing." His next comment was "Can you tell me what each of the words the letters will form, first for the top letter." He then questioned the class on what was the first word that the top "P" began.

I am not sure what my classmates thought, but my reaction was "What's he up to?" We all tried to guess, and eventually, he completed the word "PREPARATION" without comment. He then moved onto the second letter "P" and again asked us to comment on what the word was. Again, none of the class came close and he completed the word "PRESENTATION."

We again tried to guess what the remaining word would be for this final "P". He then completed the word "PERSONALITY." His comment then "was to burn the words into our brain" for they were the very basis of successfully passing on information to a class or audience.

Time Spent. His next question was for us to give a percentage of time we should spend on each of these words when preparing any lecture or presentation. We gave our ideas, 50% and they were nowhere near the percentages he placed against each word. They were:

```
              PREPARATION        80%
              PRESENTATION       15%
              PERSONALITY         5%
```

The rest of the class time he spent expounding on the need for in-depth Preparation and indicating that we should use several aids to get the message across in our Presentation. He explained the whys and wherefores under the first two words, and under each heading he emphasised why this was essential. He also stated that we should never stand in front of an audience without detailed comments. For there would be times, we could lose track of what we wanted to say. His comment was that never to think it won't happen because of some distraction or questions being asked by the class as we made a presentation.

At this stage, it appeared that this lecture was coming to an end, and a member of the class asked about the word Personality. This reply was that some of us would just have the knack and become very good instructors. Others may not be so confident, and it would take longer to become very good Presenters. If we used what he had just explained, we all would be excellent Instructors.

He also commented that should you suddenly become ill and not be able to go on, someone should be able to replace you and use your notes to pick up where you left off, even if it meant they just had to read your notes to finish the lecture.

I guess the whole class appreciated what was taught that day, and in one lesson, our eyes were opened to the way to Prepare and Present in the future.

Note: Most of us had been instructing at some time or another and this was an eye-opener to us. However, I have rarely, if ever, got up to speak as an instructor or give a speech, and I have not used that formula to prepare.

In passing: Later, after I had become an officer and built our home in Ashfield, Sydney, I found the Schoolie lived just one street from me, and I took to picking him up and taking him to HMAS *Watson* by car. Tiger and I became good friends, and he was my mentor. He was a great character and certainly is mentioned in one of the books I have read, produced by one of the survivors.

Promotion.

Having passed the course, I was promoted to RP1. Also, during the period just past, I had been promoted to Acting Petty Officer. Upon completion of the course, I was sent on leave back to the West and was looking forward to some time in *Watson* to catch up with relatives on my return.

This was not to be.

I enjoyed my trip home for Christmas.

Posting.

On my return from leave, I found I had been posted to HMAS *Albatross*. When I inquired about what and where it was, nobody seemed to know much about it. I eventually found out it was the home of the reformed Australian Naval Fleet Air Arm, and it was in southern NSW near the town of Nowra.

So, on the 28th of January 1949, it was up bag and hammock and off to Central Railway and embark on a train for Bombardary, a short distance from Nowra, and much further from the Air Base.

Chapter 16

HMAS *Albatross*

29th January 1949 to 15th July 1949

Introduction

My Service Records for my time in *Bataan* and return to HMAS *Watson* are not correct. They show that I was drafted to HMAS *Watson*, accounts in HMAS *Kuttabul*, on 29 July 1947. However, that was the day I joined HMAS *Bataan*. They also show that my accounts were held by HMAS *Penguin* on 1/10/1947. That date probably reflects the transfer of books between Shore Establishments. However, I was on *Bataan* and was operating in the Occupation of Japan area.

It also shows I was drafted to HMAS *Albatross* on 29 January 1950. At that time, I would have been on the RP 1 Course. On completion, it would have left HMAS *Watson* for HMAS *Albatross*.

Draft

Shortly after finishing the course and I was taken to the Station for a train trip to a place called HMAS *Albatross*. Nobody in HMAS *Watson* knew much about it or where it was.

Now an Acting Petty Officer RP1 and wearing my sailor's round rig, with my bag containing all my worldly possessions, and my hammock, I arrived at Central Railway Station, Sydney, and was met by a Regulating Petty Officer. He handed me a rail ticket to Bombardary. He escorted me to the platform where the train was waiting.

From discussions on the way to the Platform, I gathered that Bombardary was near Nowra and south of Sydney, inland from Jervis Bay.

The train journey was interesting, as I had never travelled south of Sydney. I certainly knew where Jervis Bay was, as ships working up would anchor there from time to time during the workups.

On arrival at Bombardary, I was met by two sailors who helped put my bag and hammock in the back of their small truck. I sat in the cab with them as we headed for HMAS *Albatross*.

During the drive along the Princes Highway, we passed Nowra township and proceeded further south, where we turned right into Bru Road. The airfield was some distance from the highway. Approaching the base, I noticed a large hill with a 277-radar aerial standing proud.

Base in Foreground – Nowra Hill in background.

During the drive from Bombardary, I learnt that the airfield had been used by the Royal Navy in WWII. It was now the Royal Australian Naval Air Station (RANAS,) HMAS *Albatross*. Commissioning had taken place on 31 August 1948.

Base Entrance Firefly Aircraft

Royal Australian Naval Air Station

On arrival at the front gate of the Base, I was taken into the Regulating Office to complete my draft in documentation and receive my Station Card. I was then shown my cabin. The dining room and recreation facility were pointed out to me. I was then left to my own devices to settle in.

HMAS Albatross Petty Officers Mess

I unpacked my sea bag and then went to the Aircraft Control Tower to see where the Radar Plotters were located. My job was to supervise these plotters. Their duties were to provide radiocommunication with the aircraft once they left the immediate area of the airfield and there were radar displays to track the aircraft. However, during my time, these displays did not work due to a fault in the transmission line from the radar I had seen on my way in, located on Nowra Hill.

The other task the operators had was to assist aircraft find their way home in times of low visibility. They had to be taught to detect if an aircraft was flying toward or away from the Base.

This could be the case if the aircraft had a faulty compass. As I settled into my new life, I found two other Seaman Petty Officers, and we formed our own group among those of the Aviation Branch.

A View of the Base
Runways and Hangars are off the picture to the right

HMAS Sydney and Carrier Air Group

At this time, the Carrier Air Group (CAG) embarked on HMAS *Sydney*, was still on its way from the United Kingdom.

Sports

The formation of a rugby team was proceeding. However, the local competition played Rugby League, not Rugby Union. This meant having to learn some new rules. From memory, the teams the Base played were from towns between Kiama and Nowra. It was interesting playing League instead of Union, and I quickly adapted to the rules. I tended to play on the wing.

I was also able to play tennis from time to time. I also played hockey.

Other Activities

Leave was given each day when not in the duty watch. To get to Nowra, you either caught the bus taking the married people into town straight after work and then would have to get a taxi or hope you could cadge a lift from someone who had a car and lived on the Base. Not many sailors owned cars in those days and the price of the taxi fare home meant you couldn't go to town that often.

Alternatively, you could acquire a pushbike and ride to and from Nowra, so I could go to town to buy things not available on the Base. Also, to meet local girls at the local dance night, I purchased a push bike, and this gave me some freedom to meet local people.

I met several lovely girls. After a Rugby game in Gerringong, a seaside town between Nowra and Kiama, one girl invited me to meet her family, and as a result, I sometimes stayed for the weekend in Gerringong at the aunt's place where the girl also resided. It was a platonic relationship. To get back to the Base, I would catch a regular bus from Gerringong to Nowra and catch the Base's bus. This also allowed me to go to Mass each Sunday.

As a regular at the dances in Nowra, on one occasion, I danced often with a very attractive lass who lived on the airfield side of Nowra. She drove her father's car to the dances. She was able to take me to where I had hidden my bike in the bush on the outskirts of town. We made arrangements that I could leave my bike at her place when going to the next dance. I could also meet her parents before going to the next dance.

Uniform or Civilian Clothes

On the next dance night, I rode to her place and met the parents. In those days, we had to wear our uniform when going ashore. The parents made me quite welcome. Just as we were leaving to go to the dance, the father asked me if I would like to put on a civilian jacket in place of my uniform jacket. He suggested that he would prefer his daughter not to be seen with a sailor. I indicated that I understood his concern but that I was very proud of my uniform and my service in WWII. I declined the offer and said my farewell.

I was somewhat upset and felt insulted by the request. As I headed into town on foot, the girl drove up behind me and apologised. She asked me to get in and said she would drive me to the dance and bring me back afterwards. Although I was upset, I agreed. I think I had one or two dances with her that night. On the way home, she agreed that, because of her father's concern, we should not see one another again except at the dance. At the time, there were very few sailors in the area. I don't think the father realised that very shortly there would be over 480 Navy personnel coming to *Albatross* and many were married, would live in the Nowra area with their wives and children, and many would be single men living in the town.

Administration 101

One day I was called to see the Master at Arms (MAA) in the Regulating Office. This was a bit unusual, and I had no idea what I might have done, or my sailors had done, that required me to talk to the MAA.

When I entered his office, he told me to sit down. Then he told me that I had been seconded to work in his office and to be responsible for compiling the Draft In routine for the Carrier Air Group Personnel who would shortly arrive in Jervis Bay. They would be disembarking there and travelling by bus and truck to the Air Station. He gave me a sheaf of papers that listed the names of the personnel who would be arriving and told me to get cracking.

First Experience in the Administration Field.

I was given a desk and chair in the main office and set about preparing 400 or so Station Cards, printing by hand the Christian and Surname, official numbers, and I believe, the accommodation details for each person who was not an officer.

From memory, the lists gave the names of the personnel in each of the Squadrons, 805 and 808 (Sea Fury), 816 (Firefly), the Head Quarters staff and the Odds & Sods who made up the CAG. I arranged the cards in alphabetical order by rank and/or specialisation and by Squadron.

It was a time-consuming task, with an occasional break to check my radar plotters. Eventually, all was completed, and I sat back, pleased with myself. You could feel the excitement growing as the date and time of *Sydney's* arrival became known.

Arrival of CAG

HMAS *Sydney* was commissioned on 16/12/1948 in England and, after work up, sailed for Australia, arriving and anchoring in Jervis Bay in May 1949. HMAS *Sydney* began disembarking aircraft and personnel at Jervis Bay at this time.

Drafting In

Assisted by the Master at Arms staff, each group of personnel arriving was fallen in outside the guardhouse and issued their station card. They were then led to their accommodation so they could settle in.

The only hiccups were that we were not told that some of the personnel from a particular Squadron or Group had been held back to clean up on the ship.

HMAS Sydney en route to Australia
Aircraft on Deck

Once this was sorted out, handing out of station cards to a group went very smoothly. At the end of all this, the Master at Arms congratulated me on my efforts, and I was released to go back to the tower and supervise my operators. So ended my first real experience in Administration.

Shortly after finishing the draft-in routine, the first of the aircraft from HMAS *Sydney* was towed into the Base and aircraft continued to arrive throughout the rest of the day and the next.

Galley Raid

The morning after the Air Group arrived, several ex-RN Chiefs were severely chastised for breaking into the galley late at night after the bar had closed. There was a tendency at this time, and later when I served with the Royal Navy, for RN personnel to consider us as the Royal Amateur Navy. The two other Seaman Petty Officers and I made it clear we were not impressed by the conduct of the Chiefs, nor was the Supply Officer.

Flying Commences

Soon, the first aircraft were flying, and after a while, the Radar Plotters were offered a seat in the Fireflies. We all took advantage of the offer to familiarise ourselves with the aircraft. We were all given a sick bag in case we were air-sick.

You don't have to be a mind reader to know that the pilots went to great efforts to ensure that no one came back without being sick. Initially, the aerobatics were fun but that changed as the pilot threw the aircraft this way and that.

When I landed, I told the ground crew for that aircraft that I would clean up the mess I had made. They said, it's ok, PO (Petty Officer) they would do it. I took the offer up and thanked them as I was not feeling that well.

When Flying Commenced

The radar operators put their training to work communicating with the aircraft. From time to time the aircraft would request a homing. Initially, the pilots did not pull any tricks. Eventually, they began to test the operators and would tell the operator they were flying in a southerly direction when, in fact, they were flying a northerly course. This simulated compass failure. The operators had been trained to pick this problem up by the fact that the white line dictating the bearing of the aircraft would be moving left to right instead of right to left.

As far as I was concerned the radar operators were using the right procedures when communicating with the aircraft and were able to home aircraft without much fuss or confusion.

Family Death

During my time at *Albatross*, the MAA received a telephone call advising that Mum had died and that this message had come from my cousin, Dora, who lived in Sydney. I initially thought she was talking about my own mother and, when I rang her, I found out that it was her mother not mine. Her mother had married George Proud. Dora had married Ted Edmunds and had two sons, George and Donald. They lived in the suburb of Kingsford in Sydney, and as stated earlier in my story I regularly visited them when in Sydney.

On Draft again

In July 1949, I was told it was time for me to pack my bag and hammock and move on as I had been posted to HMAS *Sydney*, then maintaining in Sydney's Naval Dockyard at Garden Island, and giving leave to the personnel who had brought *Sydney* back from England.

On about 15 July 1949, still an acting Petty Officer, I left the Nowra area by train for Sydney and bid farewell to the Air Group for the time being.

Aside. I was not to foresee that my posting to HMAS *Sydney* would be the first of seven times I would serve on a carrier from 1949. 1975. Two I was to serve in twice, and one three times, the rest once.

Chapter 17

HMAS *Sydney*

16 July 1949 to 26 October 1952

Dimensions	Displacement	Engine
696ft x 90ft	25 ft	Curtis Turbo

Armament	Radars	
40mm Bofors x 8 Single and 12 Twin	2x277Q. 1x293M. 1x960	

	Aircraft	
805 Squadron Sea Fury	817 Squadron Fairy Firefly	

Introduction

HMAS Sydney was one of six Majestic Class Aircraft Carriers. She was built in HM Dockyard, Devonport, England. At her launching on the 30th of September 1944, by a Mrs Duncan Sandys. She was named HMS *Terrible*. The construction was stopped at the end of World War 2.

The Ship was commissioned into the Royal Australian Navy on the 16th of December 1948 as HMAS Sydney. She was the third ship so named in the Royal Australian Navy and was the first flattop to be operated by the RAN. The Commissioning Lady was Mrs J A Beasley, wife of the then Australian High Commissioner to the UK. Subsequently, she was accepted into service on the 5th of February 1949, under the command of Captain R.R. Dowling, DSO.RAN.

Joining HMAS *Sydney*

On arrival at Sydney Central Railway Station, I was met by a member of the Regulating staff and a driver who was to take me to Garden Island Dockyard where *Sydney* was berthed.

At the ship's side, I unloaded my goods and chattels and proceeded up the gangway, reporting to the Officer of the Watch. I was taken to the Regulating Office to complete the paperwork and obtain my Station Card. I was then shown to the Petty Officers Mess, M24, which was located on the Port side, about midships and one deck below the upper deck. On entering the mess, I was made welcome and shown an empty locker in which to store my gear. I think all Seaman Branch Petty Officers, including a Physical Training Instructor, and some Petty Officer Cooks and Stewards and some members of the Supply Branch, comprised the membership of this mess. There was a separate dining room and showers and toilets allocated for the members' use.

Second Captain of the Foretop

As the most junior Petty Officer Seaman, I was allocated to the Foretop division. My job was to supervise the sailors detailed to clean the below-decks area of Foretop responsibility. This was not an onerous task and generally involved making sure that the sailors cleaning their respective areas between Decks did their job properly.

The Foretop Division was also responsible for maintaining and cleaning the Port side of the Upper Deck, two whalers (boats), the berthing ropes and wires, gangways (Shipside ladder), and a Boat Boom.

Seamanship Knowledge

Realising that, from time to time, I would have to take charge of the Duty Watch in harbour and be called upon to be the Petty Officer in Charge of the Watch on Deck when at sea, I decided to approach the Captain of my top and explain that I had limited Seamanship experience and asked if each day, after I had got my sailors to work, I could come and pick his brains about why, how and when the daily tasks were being done in his part of the ship.

His name was Scrumpy T, and he was most helpful and explained basically in words of one syllable why he did this or that on a particular day of the week. He also explained simple things like the method he used for the removal of rust and the preparation of the deckhead and bulkhead for painting and such. (Scrumpy was the nickname he acquired whilst standing by the ship in England and related to his ability to drink rough cider, known as scrumpy.)

I made sure that I was present whenever he was lowering or hoisting a boat or putting out the port boom in harbour. When in harbour and being used, the ship's boats would secure to the boom. There was a line hanging down from the boom that the boat secured to and a ladder to climb on board or down to the moored boat.

He allowed me to take charge of the hoisting and lowering of the boat in harbour and the putting out of the boom. There came a time when other parts of ship were hoisting or lowering boats, or the gangway ladders and he would send me to witness these operations. Under his guiding hand, I grew in confidence that I would be able to demonstrate my competence in carrying out any of these evolutions.

Other Duties

As a Radar Specialist, I was employed in the Air Direction Room (ADR), in charge of the Air Plot. This involved ensuring the plotters on the Air Plot and the Radar Displays did their job properly and keeping the Officer in Charge informed of any new air contact. At night, I could oversee the ADR.

The Air Plotters would be behind a large perspect plot. This meant that what would be a bearing on the right-hand side when looking at the plot from the front, at the back it would be on the left-hand side. When at HMAS *Watson* instructing, I had developed a procedure that trained plotters not to have to think was it was left or right by firing bearings at them so they instinctively could hit the correct side and bearing without thinking. It took practice, and at the start of a watch, I would throw a few bearings etc at the plotters. In time they became quite expert at the task.

Note: This also helped when they had to work on a surface plot when they had to do things upside down.

Sometimes, I was used to assist one of the Fighter Control Officers, keep up the radar tracks on his rather large, flat radar display. The two controllers were both Lieutenants at the time.

As previously stated, at other times when the ship was transiting and not flying, I could be called upon to be the Duty Petty officer of the Watch on Deck or in the Upper Operation Room, overseeing the Subsurface and Surface plotting and exchanging information with ships in the company.

Leaving or Entering Harbour

On leaving or entering the harbour, the Second Captain of the top was required to ensure that scuttles and hatches below the upper deck, in his areas of responsibility, were properly closed and secured and report this to the Damage Control Office. By the time I had checked all the lower decks, it was generally necessary to crawl through the manhole in the centre of a hatch cover to return to the main deck. The hatch would have been closed whilst I was checking the area below. I would report my area was secure to the Damage Control Centre, and then proceed to my entering harbour station with my part of ship.

Petty Officer of the Guard.

I can't remember exactly how long after I joined the ship, I was detailed as Petty Officer of the Guard leaving and entering the harbour. I had no problem with carrying out the duty. However, I was still required to carry out my second Captain of the Top duty and that meant climbing through the hatch manholes in my best white or blue uniform as I climbed up to the main deck after checking the watertight integrity of the area below the main deck. No matter how hard one tried it was almost impossible not to get some dirt or grit off the uniform. This would lead to adverse comment by the Officer in Charge of the Guard. Not enough time was available to change between the checking and being required to be with the Guard, ready to be taken by lift to the Flight Deck.

In the Gunnery Department, there were two Gunnery Instructors (GI), one of which was a Petty Officer. I decided to approach the Gunnery Officer and ask if I could be relieved of the Guard duties by the Petty Officer (GI). I explained my problem as second Captain of the Top, in having to check the watertight integrity of the foretop part of ship. He listened whilst I explained why I was making this request, and he indicated for his writer to leave the office. In words of very specific syllables, I was told I would continue to be Guard Petty Officer until he decided to relieve me. By the time I left his office, I felt as if I had been severely slashed with a sabre. I continued to have problems with marks on my uniform due to not having time to properly clean them before marching on the Guard.

Eventually, when I was confirmed in the Petty Officer rank, I was relieved of my guard duty to take up the position of Petty Officer in charge of the Foretop Part of Ship.

Sailing

On the 25th of July 1949, nine days after joining the ship, it left the harbour to embark on the advance party of the Carrier Air Group (CAG) at Jervis Bay. However, the weather was such that the embarkation was delayed until the 29th.

On the 30th, 5 Sea Fury and 4 Fireflys were embarked, and the ship returned to harbour in Jervis Bay.

August 1949

Touch and Goes

On the 1st of August, *Sydney* proceeded to sea for flying training. the ship did not have an angled deck. On 3rd August, seven Sea Fury and eight Fireflys were embarked and DLPs.

Deck Landing Practice

Batsman at Work

The aircraft would enter the landing circuit and when directly astern of the ship they would be directed by a batsman.

Discs, called bats, in each extended hand, were used to indicate to the pilot the correction needed, left or right, up or down, to touch down on the deck correctly

During Touch and Goes, the aircraft's hook would not be down, so they would touch the deck and then gun the engine and take off again.

Eventually, the arrester wires and barrier would be raised, and the aircraft would land on deck. Occasionally, an aircraft would miss hooking onto an arrester wire and finish up running into the Barrier stretched across the deck.

Sea Furies over HMAS Sydney

Fairy Firefly

On the 8th of August serious practice as an Air Group commenced with Carrier Controlled Approaches using the ship's search radar. Interception training, where one aircraft would act as a target, and the other would be controlled from the ADR to intercept it. On one occasion, there was an attack on Nowra, with some Sea Furys defending the target area.

During this period, the opportunity was taken to fuel HMAS *Warramunga* using the trough method. *Warramunga* had been acting as plane guard.

On the 12th, the ship returned to Sydney to refuel. Weekend leave was granted on the 13th and 14th, and then it was back to sea to carry on the work. Finally, Sydney returned to Sydney with a Flyover the city before berthing alongside on the 23rd of August.

Open To Public

On the 28th, the ship was open to the public to show them this new addition to their Fleet, and over 5,000 people took the opportunity to come aboard and look around.

September 1949

Queensland and Manus Island

On the 1st of September, it was off to sea again for exercises off the Queensland coast and some of the islands further north. Interceptions, ground attacks, and the usual maintenance of readiness levels continued during this period, and the Upper and Lower plotting rooms were kept very busy. With ships in company, I was again involved in overseeing the plots in the ADR and, with the upper-level Operations Room, participated in various exercises with ships in company.

I won't give a daily blow-by-blow commentary on the exercises. Sufficient to say that when at sea, the various search and strike, shadowing, air interceptions, and other operational requirements were the order of the day to bring the Air Group and Ship up to a high standard of readiness. Exercises between ships were conducted to improve the efficiency of the Upper Operations room and the ADR.

Visits

During this trip away, the ship spent some time operating off the Queensland coast and passed through the Whitsunday passage, later arriving at Manus. After a short time in the area, the ship headed for Brisbane, berthing there on September 26th.

Something like eight hundred schoolchildren, twenty army and twenty Air Force Officers and twelve Naval architectural students visited the ship during our time in Brisbane. There was the opportunity for sports, and the ship's hockey team, cricket team and rifle team were able to compete against Army teams. Golfers were also able to have a game. I got to play Ruby.

October 1949

Then it was time to return to Sydney, arriving there on the 1st of October. Before entering the harbour, the aircraft were flown off. It had been a busy period, and all was falling into place as far as readiness was concerned.

My Activities

As mentioned above, I was either in the ADR supervising plotters or working in my part of ship or in charge of the watch on deck. I was certainly busy.

Promotion

On 1 October 1949, I was officially **promoted to Petty Officer RP1** from acting rank. This required me to change uniforms to what was known a Square Rig – a jacket and shirt and tie and straight legged trousers instead of Bell Bottoms. I had already arranged for the two uniforms in anticipation of this day and obtained a peaked cap with insignia of a Petty Officer. It also cost me a round of drinks at the pub.

Windsor Knot

I will mention here the aftermath of my dealings with the Gunnery Officer after I changed from my acting Petty Officer's rig to that of a Petty Officer and wearing a shirt, tie, and jacket.

For some reason, I was on the quarterdeck, sitting on one of the gratings over the bollards, when the Gunnery Officer came up and said that he noticed that I did my tie in a Windsor knot. I, after a poignant pause, acknowledged I did.

He noticed the pause and said, "I hope you're not still thinking about the incident in my office, for I forgot about it the moment you left my office."

I didn't acknowledge that he might be right and then showed him how to tie a Windsor knot. Many years later, he was to be my Captain on my final sea time on HMAS *Melbourne*.

In a book on his life, published in 2021, he mentions this incident.

New Zealand Squadron

On the 3rd of October, a New Zealand squadron, comprising HMNZS *Bellona* (cruiser) and frigates *Taupo*, *Kaniere*, *Tutire*, *Rotoiti* and *Pukan* entered Sydney Harbour.

Joint Exercises

On the 7th of October, HMAS *Sydney* departed Sydney with HMA Ships *Bataan*, *Shoalhaven*, and *Murchison* in company. They were joined by the New Zealand Squadron for exercises off Jervis Bay. Again, I will not give a blow-by-blow description of the exercises, but rest assured there were night encounters, interceptions, live firing on targets, Officer of The Watch (OOW) exercises, fuelling, towing and so on. These exercises finally ended when the ships headed for Westernport, Victoria, on 15th October.

In Transit

As the ships headed south, they encountered a Force 8 gale which made all the ships very uncomfortable as they rocked and rolled. At one stage, smaller ships were obliged to slow down because of this weather. This bad weather forced the ships to arrive in Westernport seven hours later than planned.

During the afternoon before arrival in Westernport, the deck hockey final was played on the flight deck between 816 Squadron officers who were able to defeat the Officers Steward team.

On Tuesday the 18th, over one hundred recruits under training at HMAS *Cerberus* were shown around the ship. Then, there was a golf match between Cerberus, the NZ squadron, and Sydney. Cerberus won.

The next day, there was a half day flying, witnessed by seventy-five cadet midshipmen, ten NZ officers and ten ex-RAAF observers who were undertaking Naval training to become members of the Fleet Air Arm. Fourteen Fireflys and one Sea Fury carried out attacks on a towed target and two of the Fireflys did a photographic run over the Naval Depot.

On Thursday, the 20th of October, all ships, except *Sydney* and *Warramunga*, sailed for Melbourne. *Sydney* embarked 50 RAAF officers and 6 Press representatives for the trip to Melbourne and to witness a flying display on the way. During this flying session, the opportunity was taken by eleven Fireflys and one Sea Fury to fly over Flinders Naval depot, Frankston, Melbourne, Point Cook and Geelong. One aircraft was catapulted, and another performed a rocket-assisted take-off. The 1000th deck landing in Australian waters was recorded at this time. At the end of flying, the ship proceeded to berth at Port Melbourne.

Melbourne Visit

The ship berthed at the outer west berth of Princess Pier. There were various VIP functions as you can imagine, and a ceremonial march through the city of Melbourne by 1,650 officers and men. There was a Navy Ball and organised visits by:

- RAN probationary pilots from Point Cook
- Army officers from Military HQ
- RAAF officers from an Air Weapons course with instructors
- St Johns Ambulance
- Ex-Servicemen from Heidelberg Repat Hospital.
- Boys from Frankston Legacy
- Society of Naval Wives
- Boy Scouts
- Air Cadets and,

- various Students from Boys and Girls schools.

There was free admittance to:
- Dances
- Ice Skating
- Bus Trips to Dandenong Range
- Derby and Melbourne Cup Hill Enclosure.

I took the opportunity to attend my first Melbourne Cup, which was to be my only Melbourne Cup.

As you can imagine, with all the visitors, one was often caught up in showing them around. However, I also took the opportunity to catch up with my Melbourne relatives and friends, most of whom I had met when I was in initial training so many years before.

November 1949

Back to Sea

On the 2nd of November, *Sydney* and ships in company sailed from Melbourne. During the passage to exit Port Philip Bay, the ships sailed in line astern. Unfortunately, bad weather on the way to Jervis Bay prevented any flying activity. After arriving in Jervis Bay on the 5th, 805 Squadron personnel and equipment were unloaded as the Sea Furys were undergoing inspections and corrections to a fault that had been found. In addition, six obsolete howitzers were landed for the Beecroft air gunnery range.

On Sunday the 6th of November, the Admiral inspected the Ship's Company at Divisions. Then it was back to sea on the 7th. During this period at sea, a RAAF Beaufighter towed a wing target for practice firings by *Sydney's* aircraft.

There was what could be called a major Air Defence Exercise (ADX) that involved HMAS *Australia* and HMNZS *Bellona* acting as radar pickets. Ten Fireflys were used to attack the carrier and several Sea Furys were used to defend the force. This tested the air defence, and the ability of the air controllers to intercept the incoming enemy.

There were Direction Finding exercises to detect a submarine transmitting, and this was followed by a night encounter exercise.

There was an occasion when an RAAF Catalina, acting as a Scout for fourteen Mustangs and three Mosquitoes RAAF, was sent to detect the ships and guide the RAAF aircraft to attack the ships. Other aircraft acted as decoys. In the event, all the attacking aircraft were engaged by the Sea Furys.

On the 11th, the weather had deteriorated and near midnight the ship sailed to Sydney whilst the New Zealand Squadron sailed for Hobart before returning to New Zealand. On arrival in Sydney on the 12th, *Sydney* berthed at the Fitting Out wharf. The first leave party left the ship on that day. I can't remember if I also proceeded on leave to the West at about that time. the ship also began a major maintenance period and, on the 24th of November, entered Captain Cook graving dock. the ship was to remain in the harbour until the eleventh of January 1950.

The other area of interest is that while the ship was in harbour, there were three children's parties. The first was for the naval wives and children of those who had died during the war. The second was for the ship company's wives and children, and the third was for the Officers' wives and children.

My Leave

I won't bore you with my travel to and from Western Australia and what I did on leave. Sufficient to say I would have spent some of it in Perth over Christmas with my mum, brother and sister and uncle and aunt in Maylands as well as time in Kalgoorlie. Western Australian Natives usually only got one leave period a year due to the time of four or five days travelling to and from by train from the east coast. I certainly would have been back in Sydney before the ship sailed. I think I became Captain of Maintop Division about this time.

January 1950

Back to the Grind

So began a new year. I had returned from leave before New Year's Day. the ship was out of the dock and finishing her maintenance. On the 9th of January, Commander V.A.T. Smith, DFC RAN joined as the incoming Executive Officer. I did not know then that he and I would become sparring partners later when I was in charge of, first, the Main Top part of Ship and, later, the Quarterdeck.

On the 11th, the ship carried out range and inclination exercises with HMAS *Bataan*, our escort. The weather was unsuitable for flying, so later that day, we anchored in Jervis Bay. The following day, because of the weather, the ship was cleaned after the maintenance.

On Friday the 13th, it was off to sea to embark aircraft, five Fireflys and six Sea Furys. The aircraft practised deck landings. A record of a hundred and sixteen landings was achieved on this day. On the 16th, the rest of the aircraft of the CAG embarked and deck landing continued to bring aircrews up to speed. On return to Jervis Bay, the ship practised mooring procedures. The next two days were back to sea for flight drills and interceptions and general working up of the Air Group and the ship's teams.

On the 20th there were exercises with the RAAF. Also, on the 21st, while anchored in Jervis Bay, the Royal Navy submarine *Telemachas* put on a display at various depths and passed very close to the ship, giving everyone an interesting view, particularly of the submarine at periscope depth.

During this period the Sea Furys worked with the Artillery Reconnaissance Gunnery Group at Holsworthy, near Ingleburn.

Barrier Crash

On the 23rd, during the aircraft's recovery, two accidents occurred. Two Sea Fury aircraft overshot the arrester wires and crashed into the crash barrier. Both were cleared quickly, allowing the rest of the aircraft to be recovered.

The 24th was the last day of the workup. Sea Furies carried out air-to-air firings against a wing target towed by an RAAF aircraft while the Fireflies exercised with the submarine using Sonar Buoys.

About midnight on January 24th, the ship sailed for Westernport. From memory, the sea was up a bit, so there was little or no flying en route.

On the 26th, ten Fireflies and six Sea Furies flew over Geelong and Flinders Naval Base. After recovering the aircraft, the ship anchored at Westernport.

Spectators from the naval base were embarked and taken to sea to witness flying activities. During the landing, one Firefly overshot the arrestor wires and hook, which caught in the crash barrier. The aircraft came to a stop just short of the forward lift, which was interesting for the spectators who landed later that day.

After two days operating from Westernport, the ship sailed on the morning of the 28th and, after rendezvous with HMAS *Bataan*, continued flying operations en route to Adelaide.

Adelaide

Approaching Adelaide, ten Sea Furies and eleven Fireflies were launched at 0800, Monday the 30th of January and flew over Adelaide. After recovering the aircraft, the ship proceeded to number 4 berth Outer Harbour, Adelaide.

February 1950

There were 19,00 visitors to the ship over the 3rd, 4th, and 5th of February.

There was a good social programme, and extra trains and buses were arranged with some price of fare concessions due to the distance from the CBD.

At 0900 on Monday, the 6th of February, the ship sailed for Port Melbourne.

Melbourne

On the 7th, a flying programme of deck landings and Flight Deck drills was successfully carried out and completed at 1430 in view of the ETA in Melbourne. the ship berthed alongside the east side of Princes Pier at 2006 hrs and, on the 8th, shifted berth to an anchorage where she remained until 1703 when she sailed for Hobart with HMAS *Bataan* in company.

On the afternoon of the 9th, Navigational exercises were carried out by both Sea Furies and Fireflies. Three replacement aircraft from Nowra landed on board during this period.

Hobart

On the 10th of February, twelve Fireflies and eleven Sea Furies flew over Hobart. Later in the day, the ship berthed alongside Princes Wharf. On the 11th, 12th, and 18th, the ship was open to visitors and over 11,000 looked over the ship.

Regatta

The 113th Hobart Regatta began on the 14th. In the Cutter pulling (rowing) races, *Sydney* won three and *Bataan* won one. Three sailing races were won by *Sydney*. The Trans-Derwent swim was won by a Naval Airman, and the 80-yard championship and relay races were won by *Bataan*.

On Thursday the 16th, a Fleet at Home was held on board in B hanger with about 500 guests, one of whom was His Excellency, the Governor of Tasmania.

On Sunday the 19th, His Excellency embarked for our trip to Wellington. Operation Pinwheel (using aircraft to turn the ship) was successfully used when leaving the pier without tugs and I remember a large crowd being on the pier to see us depart for New Zealand.

Milford Sound

On the afternoon of the 22nd, *Sydney* entered Milford Sound, the first aircraft carrier to do so. An aircraft had been launched prior to entry to take photos.

Milford Sound

After the aircraft that had been launched to take pictures was recovered, HMAS *Warramunga* came alongside and fuelled.

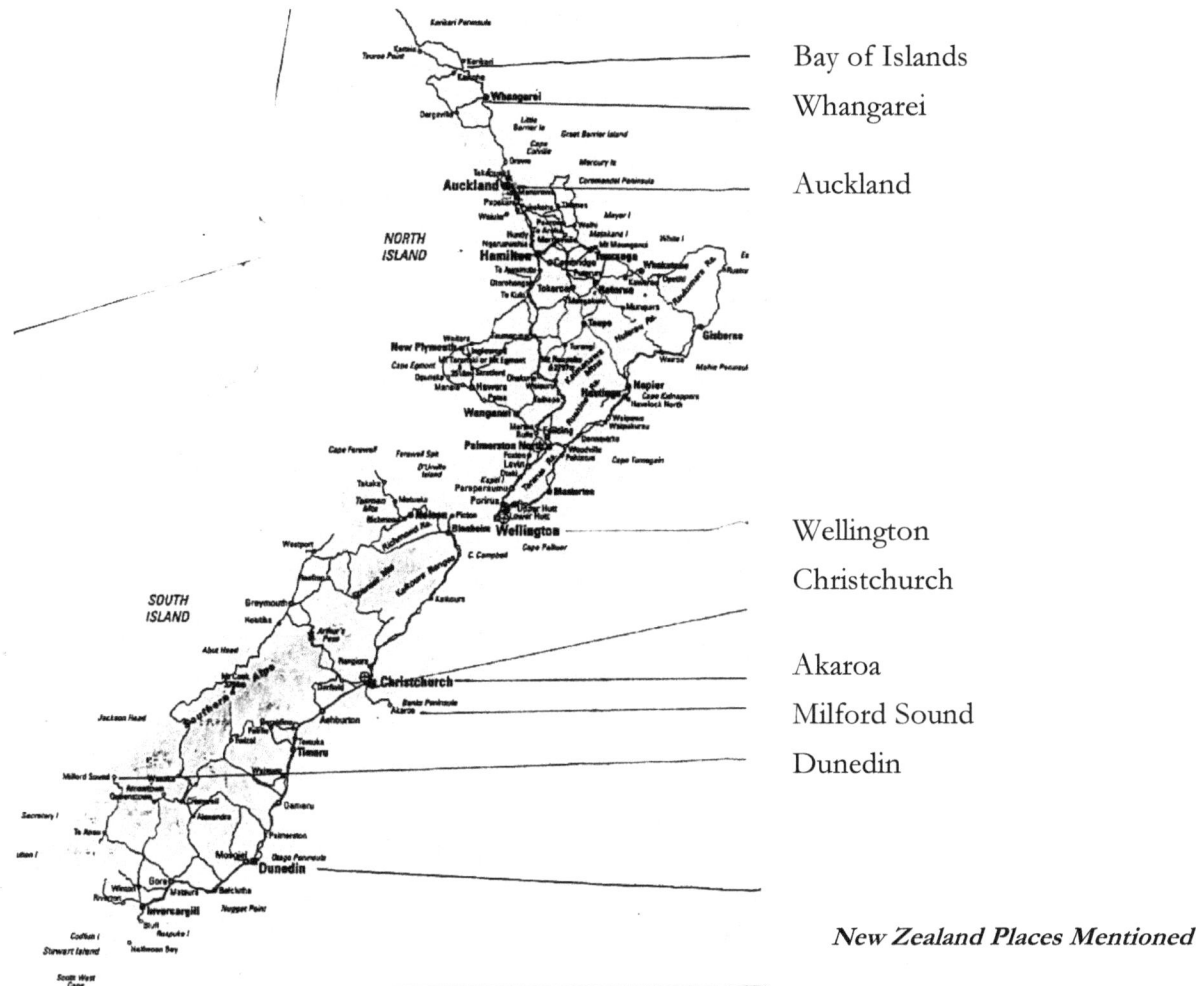

New Zealand Places Mentioned

Tactical Exercise

After leaving Milford Sound and en route to Wellington, on the 23rd and 24th, there was a large Tactical Exercise involving HMA ships *Sydney* and *Warramunga* and HMS *Telemachus* (submarine) as the White Force and HMA ships *Australia* and *Murchison* as the Black Force. Long-range searches and strikes were flown between 0800 and 1900, and during the day, there were twelve Fireflies and eleven Sea Furies available, which was a record for the ship. Later, when both forces had joined, there was a Submarine exercise involving HMS *Telemachus*, who had been sent ahead.

On completion of the exercises at 1648, ten Fireflies and ten Sea Furies were flown off for a flyover of Wellington, with six Sea Furies carrying acrobats over Wellington Harbour before landing back on.

Sydney entered Wellington Harbour at 0700 and berthed alongside Acta Quay at 0800.

In Port Activities

There were VIP officials calling on the Admiral or him calling on them. There were entertainment functions for VIPs and other guests conducted by the Officers. In addition, there were functions and tours arranged for the Ship's Company.

My Coming and Goings

During the visit to Wellington, I seem to remember that I played rugby and hockey. I also took part in a tour of the districts around Wellington and attended some dances and other functions that were arranged for us. Like everyone else, I think I was glad to be back in port for a while and not involved in exercises.

My at Sea Activities

Whilst Watch on Deck, or on Watch in the Air Direction Room, or supervising the Maintop Part of Ship, one was always on one's toes to make sure all ran smoothly. I found the Air Plotters had settled down nicely and could place a contact on the plot without having to think which way to go.

March 1950

Departure

I celebrated my 24th Birthday on the 1st of March. Like all good things, the time to depart came, and the ships sailed to participate in more exercises. On the 3rd of March, *Sydney* slipped from the pier. Operational Pinwheel, using the ship's aircraft, was used to leave the pier without tugs. Ships in company were HMA ships *Australia*, *Warramunga*, *Bataan*, and *Murchison*. HMS *Telemachus*, the submarine, had sailed earlier so that (ASW) exercises could be conducted as the ships were leaving.

At 1400, a Convoy exercise commenced with aircraft flying searches and strikes against the enemy, the New Zealand force of HMZN Ships Bellona, Taupo, Pukaki, and Tutira. The ship's aircraft found and attacked them. Later, there was a Night Encounter Counter exercise before the two groups merged.

The Australian Group was attacked by Mosquito Aircraft engaged by the Ship's Combat Air Patrol. *Sydney's* aircraft attacked the other group as it sailed south with considerable success. Later, there was a Night Encounter exercise.

The following day, the Australian and New Zealand groups joined together. Sydney's aircraft carried out navigation and target identification of selected pinpoints on the New Zealand mainland. Both groups then formed up for the entry into Akaroa Harbour, which is close to **Lyttleton.**

Petty Officers from the combined ships attended a dance organised by the Akaroa Rowing Club at the clubhouse. The ships remained in harbour on Sunday 5th. Organised recreation parties were not landed because of the small size of the town. However, a wet canteen was set up on the beach opposite the Townsite. I didn't bother to go ashore.

On Monday the 6th of March, the Group sailed for exercises, with the submarine attacking the ships as they sailed in a line. Later, height-finding exercises were carried out by three of the ships, whilst aircraft were employed in tactical reconnaissance and to exercise the gun crews of the group by dummy attacks. Exercises continued, and on the 10th, 11 Sea Furies flew over Christchurch whilst the Fireflies carried out A/S search and attack on the submarine using sonobuoys. Live firings were carried out by the aircraft on targets towed by *Sydney* and *Bellona*. Eventually, the exercises ended, and the Australian ships proceeded to Lyttleton for two days, which turned into three, due to very bad weather. Finally, on the 13th, the ship sailed for Auckland, exercising on the way.

Auckland

On the 16th of March, *Sydney* and the Australian ships came alongside in Auckland. There was quite a bit of pomp and ceremony following an 11-gun salute after we arrived. On Friday the 17th and on Saturday and Sunday, 120 sailors from the Australian Units were taken on tour to the thermal region of Rotorua. Similar arrangements were made for the Officers on Saturday and Sunday. I understand these tours were arranged by the Department of Interior and the Returned Soldiers Association and were much appreciated.

There were the usual dances and such to be enjoyed. The ship was open to visitors on Saturday the 18th, Sunday the 19th, and something like 12,000 came on board. On the 20th an athletics meeting was held between the RAN and RNZN personnel and the New Zealanders won easily.

On the 21st of March, HMA and HMNZ ships sailed for further exercises in the Bay of Islands area. HM Submarine *Telemachus* had sailed earlier and was waiting to carry out torpedo attacks on the force as we cleared the channel. After this exercise, the two groups separated and took up positions for the next phase of the exercises on the 22nd.

This exercise saw HMAS *Sydney* and Australian ships cover a landing of twenty Royal Marines from HMNZS *Bellona* on Sydney. Their mission was to destroy a radar station, which was defended by another twenty Royal Marines. The New Zealand ships were to prevent the escape by sea, and a night encounter exercise followed.

The next phase of the exercise of the following day was for torpedo firings by *Bellona*, *Warranmunga* and *Bataan*. Three Sea Furies were flown off to track the torpedoes so they could be recovered. A Navigation exercise was undertaken by a group of Fireflies, and six Sea Furies carried out a reconnaissance flight over the North Island.

Six of the fifteen aircraft airborne had landed when three and four arrestor wires became unserviceable. Due to the fuel situation, the remaining aircraft were diverted to Onerahi airfield. One Sea Fury was damaged in landing on the grass runway which was a little rough. The Air

Engineering Officer was flown off in the ship's Sea Otter to inspect the damage and assess if it could be repaired so the aircraft could be re-embarked. The next problem was that there was no 100-octane petrol available at Onerahi airfield, so it was necessary to have the required supply sent by road from Auckland. However, this could not reach the airfield before dusk, so the ship proceeded to Renowned Anchorage, Bay of Islands. Stores and Lorry and personnel required to repair the Sea Fury were sent by jeep and lorry.

The next day, the ship sailed to recover the aircraft except for the damaged Sea Fury and returned to the harbour. The aircrews, who had been marooned ashore overnight, reported that the people of Onerahi had shown them great hospitality.

That evening, a Fleet boxing tournament was held on the flight deck, attended by 200 officers and 1600 ratings. The New Zealand squadron was given the verdict; there was some discussion about that.

On Saturday, March 25th, the *Sydney* acted as a Flagship for the concurrently run Combined Fleet Regattas, one for the small ships and one for the *Sydney*, *Australia*, and *Bellona*. The New Zealanders won both regattas. Sunday, March 26th, was spent in harbour.

On Monday, the 27th of March, the ship proceeded to sea. The Commanding Officer of the Northern Military Districts embarked to witness flying. Six Fireflies were flown off on a reconnaissance exercise over the North Island whilst 6 Sea Furies gave an aerobatics display over Onerahi. One Firefly and the Sea Otter flew to the airfield to collect the maintenance ratings. Two other Sea Furies carried out height-finding exercises for *Warramunga*, *Bataan* and *Bellona*.

In the afternoon, eight Fireflies were a target for eight Sea Fury, Combat Air Patrol. (CAP) This was a Force Direction (Fighter Control) exercise for the Fleet. The Firefly and Sea Fury from Onerahi were recovered along with the other aircraft before returning to harbour.

During the forenoon of March 28th, the Fleet carried out a General Drill conducted by the Senior Officer of the New Zealand squadron. During these drills, the Flag Officer Commanding the Australian fleet walked around the ship, this forming part of his annual inspection, the remainder of which was to be carried out on the 1st and 2nd of April.

Disaster

Three Chief Petty Officers, a Petty Officer and the driver of the jeep and trailer, bringing back the maintenance personnel and equipment that repaired the damaged Sea Fury, were in an accident. The three Chief Petty Officers received serious injuries and later died. The Petty Officer was only slightly injured, and the driver was unhurt. No need to say how this was received on board and especially among the Air Group.

Later seven Fireflies took off for depth charge dropping and RP (Rocket Projectile firing exercises about 70 miles off the coast. Sea Furies gave an aerobatics display over the fleet.

During the aircraft's recovery, the 2000th landing since the ship arrived in Australia took place. The ship did not proceed to sea on the 30th. An on-board Inquiry was held into the vehicle accident ashore.

In the afternoon, the captain attended the funeral of two of the Chief Petty Officers killed. They were buried with full military honours at Russell, Bay of Islands. Many locals were present, and several wreaths and bunches of flowers were laid on the graves by local people. At the request of his wife, the third Chief was being taken back to Sydney for cremation on the 6th of April.

Departure New Zealand

On the evening of March 30th, the ship sailed for Jervis Bay and Sydney. The following day, the Ship's Company was fully employed in preparation for the Admiral's Inspection on April 1st.

Summary

The crews and exercises and time spent in New Zealand waters and ashore had been conducted with great success. The New Zealand Navy, civic bodies and individual New Zealand families had provided great friendship and hospitality.

Himself

I enjoyed myself during the time ashore dancing, participating in sporting activities, and enjoying the odd beer or two. The continual exercise further developed my oversight of my radar plotting team and my ability in general man management in my part of the ship. I was very happy within myself that I would be able to acquit myself well in the future.

April 1950

Admiral's Inspection

There are two parts to an Admiral's Inspection. One part is he inspects the ship's hangers, mess decks, offices, galleys, fight decks and storerooms on the main and lower decks. The second part is he inspects the Ship's Company at Divisions. The first part took place on the 1st of the month, followed by the second the following day. The ship was still at sea en route to Jervis Bay.

Disembarkation of CAG

Unfortunately, on the 3rd of May, the unsatisfactory weather forced the postponement of the launch of the aircraft for disembarkation to Nowra, so *Sydney* entered Jervis Bay to land aircraft stores and the damaged aircraft. Opportunity was taken to embark a damaged Sea Otter aircraft for return to the United States. The following morning, personnel of the Air Group were landed first thing before proceeding to sea to launch eleven Fireflies, eleven Sea Fury and the serviceable Sea Otter to NAS Nowra. On completion of the launch, the plane guard, HMAS

Warramunga, was ordered to proceed to Sydney whilst the ship returned to Jervis Bay to unload the remaining stores and luggage.

Sydney Town

At 2200, the ship departed Jervis Bay for Sydney, arriving at the Fitting Out wharf, Garden Island, at 0835 on Wednesday, the 5th of April. It was to remain here until 20 April, when the ship was moved into Captain Cook's dock. Dockyard work was to start on the 5th of May, when the dockyard took the ship in hand for making good any defects.

At 0930 on the 21st, the Admiral's Flag was transferred to HMAS *Australia*. On the 22nd of April, Captain Dowling was relieved by Captain ???.

May 1950

Long Leave

On the 6th of May, three weeks Long Leave began for the Ship's Company. However, being a Western Australian, I did not proceed on leave at this time as normally we would get six weeks leave plus travelling time once a year.

Visitors and Other Activities

On the 10th of May, 24 crippled children, accompanied by six nurses from the Royal Alexandra Hospital, visited the ship during the afternoon and the officers and men ensured they saw all that had to be seen in spite of their disabilities.

On Empire Day, officers and men from the ship delivered addresses on the value of Empire for the children of various public schools. In all cases, they were received with great enthusiasm.

The ship remained in the drydock until the 23rd of May when it was undocked and berthed at the Fitting Out Wharf. The Deck Landing Control Officers platform was repositioned. Other work being done was the providing of adequate escape hatches in the ship's side. Cleaning up all areas progressed in anticipation of the ship sailing for the United Kingdom in June.

On Sunday the 26th of May, there was a Memorial Service at St Andrews Cathedral arranged by the Naval Men's Association. Also, I remember that it was during this period that the Ship's Company was vaccinated and inoculated before the ship proceeded to the United Kingdom. I also seem to recall that somewhere about this time I had become the Petty Officer in charge of the Main Top division. (Starboard Side) and had relinquished my job as Petty Officer the Guard.

June 1950

Return to Operational Service

On the 1st of June, the ship returned to Operational Availability and the Ship's Company were employed and preparing for the voyage to the United Kingdom. This involved embarking stores, provisions, and a free freight for intermediate ports. On the 3rd of June, I remember three LCVPs being loaded. In the next few days, the ship was made ready to sail. The purpose of sailing to the UK was to pick up further aircraft of the 21st CAG Squadrons, 808 (Sea Fury) and 817 (Fireflies).

UK Bound.

Departure. On Wednesday, the 10th of June, the ship sailed from Sydney for Melbourne and a trial of two hours duration on 4/5ths full power was carried out on passage. I remember we ran into a fog on the Friday. Naturally, speed was reduced and using our surface radar we approached Hobson's Bay. However, the visibility was such that it was necessary to anchor. Just before lunch, the fog lifted and the ship was able to proceed and secured alongside Nelson's pier, Williamstown at about lunchtime.

It was while still alongside that the LCVPs were unloaded and the loading of stores for the UK, and a set of torpedo tubes, was carried out. Again, the fog had persisted and eventually, by mid-morning on 12th June, it had lifted enough for us to cast off and continue our journey to the UK.

Fremantle

It was typically bumpy as we rounded Cape Leeuwin on Friday. On arrival at Fremantle, we had to drop anchor in Gage Roads as the winds were something like force 7. The following morning, we were able to secure alongside North wharf in Fremantle Harbour.

Free freight was landed, and West Australians were granted 48 hrs leave. I took advantage of the leave but returned each night to sleep on board. I caught up with some old friends and some of my relatives. Meanwhile, those left on board continued to unload or load free freight and embarked provisions.

One thing I do remember very well about this visit was that the ship's rugby team distinguished themselves by holding the Western Australian state team to a 6-all draw. I was in the ship's team. One of my old Kalgoorlie girlfriends, then attending university in Perth, was in the spectators.

The ship sailed late in the morning of Tuesday the 20th of June and carried out a full power trial of two hours duration during the afternoon. Then it was, 'Aden in Africa, here we come'. (see map)

Suez   Red Sea   Aden

July 1950

Aden. On Tuesday the 4th of July, the ship entered Aden harbour and secured at No 1 fuelling berth. It was necessary to have an anchor and wires to three buoys. Privilege leave was granted to those who had not broken their leave over the previous six months. There were two groups, 0900 to 1200 and 1300 to 1600, and everyone behaved themselves when ashore.

Sydney departed Aden at 1730 on the same day and headed for Suez, which was reached at 0645 on Saturday the 6th of July, and entered the canal at 0730. Passage to Port Said was uneventful and the ship cleared Port Said at 2030 hrs and headed for Malta.

Gibraltar　　　　　　　　　　　　　　　　　　　　　　　　　　　　　　　　　　*Malta*

The weather was excellent during a passage to Malta and the custom of **'optional hands to bath'** was exercised daily during the dog watches.

Malta

At 0930 on the 12th of July, *Sydney* entered Grand Harbour, Malta, and secured to the Flag Ship buoys. (Fore and Aft) The Commander in Chief, Mediterranean, was absent elsewhere.

I am sure everyone enjoyed the ship's three-day stay as they explored this George Cross Island.

At 0930 on Saturday, the 15th of July, *Sydney* sailed from Malta having embarked 14 Officers 222 ratings for passage to England.

Note. I was not to know then that, a later time, after I was promoted to Officer, I would be based in Malta, with my wife Joan and baby son Anthony, whilst serving in HMS *Sheffield*, then the RN Flagship for the Mediterranean.

Possible Sinking Ship

A report of a white vessel about to sink some 80 miles north of the ship's course was received after leaving Malta. The reported location was reached about 1700 and a square search began. Half an hour later, a white mass was located and was assessed as being the reported vessel. The ship then resumed its course.

At about 1920 the same day, a Merchant Navy Captain, who had embarked at Fremantle, died on board and was buried at sea. Photographs of the ceremony were taken for forwarding to his widow and brothers.

Gibraltar

Sydney arrived at Gibraltar and secured to No 41 berth on Tuesday the 18th of July. I and others were able to go ashore and have a look around and ascend the peak for a good look over the area. Then it was back to sea on the morning of 20th. Passing up the coast of Spain and Portugal, USS *Midway* and escort of four destroyers were encountered in the Bay of Biscay; they were heading for Gibraltar. The passage through the Bay was calm, not like other passages through this area I was to undertake later in my career.

Map of UK and places referred to in the following commentary.

Lossiemouth

Edinburgh

Glasgow

Londonderry

Bangor

Belfast

Dublin

London

Portsmouth

Plymouth

Torbay

Portsmouth

On the 24th of July, *Sydney* secured alongside Pitch House Jetty, Portsmouth, at 0800. Just before entering harbour, sixteen aircraft of the two new squadrons flew over the ship. The passengers disembarked and then the planning for the ship's movements and the Work UP was begun.

During the week all passengers and free freight stores were landed. At the same time the embarkation and work up of the 21st CAG during the ship's stay in the United Kingdom was worked out and to send officers and men to the RN Home Schools in preparation for the embarkation of the 21st CAG Group we had come to collect.

The advantage of this was to give the students an ability to see, under instructional conditions, new equipment, knowledge of which did not exist in Australia except in book form.

Part of Ship

For me, the main task in harbour was to bring the Main Top Part of Ship back up to a high standard. I should have mentioned that the forward gangway to shore was in this area and there was a need to ensure the area was up to scratch.

The opportunity to paint the ship during this period in harbour was taken.

Like others in my Mess, we went ashore to sample the delights of the English pubs and their beer. I think I looked over the HMS *Victory*, a historical, ancient ship of the Royal Navy associated with Lord Nelson of the Battle of Trafalgar. It was interesting to see the conditions sailors of those days lived in and examine the guns and to look out the gun ports thinking of what it must've been like in action.

August 1950

Ship Open to Visitors

During the August Bank Holiday weekend, the ship was open to visitors from 1230 to 1800 on Saturday, Sunday, Monday, and Tuesday. Upwards of 15,000 people came aboard. In the absence of aircraft, a pictorial display of information concerning Australia was set up in the hangar. In addition, a cinema show was given at half hourly intervals showing aircraft operating from the ship as well as a film showing aspects of Australian life. These display items were lent by the Australian News and Information Bureau, Australia House.

I seem to remember during the Navy Day display there were four Australian girls who had come to Portsmouth at the invitation of some of our younger officers. They attended on board at the information bureau for the benefit of people who wished to know about conditions of life in Australia. They were billeted in the Duchess of Kent barracks during their stay.

Additional Crew

During our period alongside, the total of 150 re-entry recruits joined the Ship. 123 were seaman, 13 engine room and the remainder miscellaneous. These were ex Royal-Naval personnel who had been recruited into the RAN.

Back to Sea

Having been in harbour for over a month, and enjoyed the delights of Portsmouth, it was time to sail and, on the 28th of August, the *Sydney* left Portsmouth to embark the 21st CAG and work up. Enroute to Plymouth, *Sydney* exercised with two mosquito aircraft of the Royal Navy. The night was spent at sea and the ship secured to a buoy in Plymouth Sound on Tuesday, the 29th of August. The advance party from the 21st CAG was embarked in preparation for receiving the first aircraft of the group.

Deck Landing Practice

On the 30th, the ship sailed and was joined by HMS *Wilton*. 6 x Sea Fury and 1 x Firefly were embarked, and Deck Landing Practise (DLP) continued throughout the day. Unfortunately, heavy rain in the afternoon caused delays. The following day deck landings continued. A Firefly bounced on landing and despite the barrier carried on and trickled over the side. HMS *Wilton* recovered the pilot within three minutes of the accident.

September 1950

On 1st of September, DLPs continued in the western part of the English Channel and preliminary deck landing practice for the CAG was completed. Then it was time to disembark some of the pilots to fly the remaining aircraft of the 21st CAG on board the following day. On completion, the ship anchored **Torbay** and the remaining personnel of the Air Group were embarked in the Ship. 5 RAN Midshipmen joined during the evening.

On Sunday the 3rd, the opportunity was taken to carry out normal Sunday routine for the first time in many weeks. On the Monday it was back to sea with HMS *Rapid* joining as Plane Guard. At 1030, the Sea Furies carried out Fighter Direction exercises and Fireflies continued deck landing practice and Beacon exercises. As the weather deteriorated and all aircraft were recalled. Later in the day, it was possible to restart flying, however, the weather again closed in, and the aircraft were recalled and flying for the day was abandoned. *Sydney* then proceeded towards Scotland.

Scotland

During the rest of September, the Workup continued, however gales and low cloud often interrupted flying. I do not intend to give a blow-by-blow description of all the work up activities. There were occasional opportunities to go ashore, and I tended to stay on board unless it was something special like a weekend leave in **Edinburgh**. The gales and bad weather meant there was little work on the upper deck when flying was taking place.

When flying was taking place, my job was generally in the Air Direction Room supervising the plot or assisting the fighter controllers as necessary. On the 19th, the ship sailed for the Moray Firth. On 20th, 21st and 22nd, flying operations resumed in reasonably good weather and all types of exercises were carried out by the ship and aircraft. Friday 23rd, and 24th of September was employed embarking stores and pursuing recreational interests.

On Wednesday, 27th the ship anchored off **Lossiemouth**. When the ship sailed the weather was lousy and *Sydney* proceeded to gain the lee of the Irish coast and on the 27th flying was resumed.

I think it was on this day that the ship's Sea Otter was recovered from Lossiemouth. On the 29th, fuel was embarked from the RFA *Celerol*, and the damaged aircraft was disembarked by lighter. On completion, the ship proceeded from **Clyde** and the end of the month for the ship on its way to **Belfast.**

It had been a disappointing month especially with the Sea Furies and the limited flying experience for the pilots. Exceptional bad weather caused the loss of six flying days and interfered with the giving of leave. Despite all this the ship and Air Group were developing into a good team.

October 1950

Ireland

The ship arrived and anchored off Bangor, which is near Belfast, on the 1st of October. During the next two days there were preparations for a series of Anti-submarine Exercises with units of the Royal Navy. Forty officers and men were sent to the Joint Anti-submarine school for lectures and briefing on the forthcoming exercises that were to take place in the coming fortnight. I was among the forty.

Unfortunately, the exercise programme was frequently stopped by high winds, gales, and a heavy swell. This particularly impacted on *Sydney's* ability to provide the support outlined in the programme. On several occasions it was necessary to recover aircraft in difficult conditions and it was a credit to the pilots and their training that there were no accidents.

Bangor anchorage was used when not exercising. On the 13th of October, the ship proceeded to Belfast to embark aircraft that were to be taken to Australia. On the way, the eleven Sea Furies and the same number of Fireflies were flown off to two different airfields.

Glasgow

The following day, the ship sailed up the river Clyde and secured alongside the wharf in Glasgow. During the 3-day visit, the Victoria League and British Council provided various invitations to the Ship's Company. Unfortunately, not all invitations could be accepted due to the heavy workload placed in the Ship's Company. During the time alongside, 23 Fireflies and 32 Sea Furies were embarked, along with about 100 tons of air stores, for passage to Australia. On the afternoon of Wednesday the 18th of October, the ship sailed for Portsmouth. Our journey back to Australia had begun.

Portsmouth

Sydney arrived in Portsmouth on the 20th and the following day a Trafalgar Day service was held in HMS *Victory* and a wreath was laid where Lord Nelson fell.

From Monday 23rd to Wednesday 25th the embarkation of free freight, explosives, ammunition to complete the Ship's outfit, food stores, fresh provisions, naval stores, fuel, lubricating oil, and passengers were embarked. the ship sailed for Port Said on Thursday, the 26th of October.

Aside. As I look back on Portsmouth, I could not have foreseen that 5 years later, almost to the day, I would return for Officers Training in the Portsmouth area, my marriage would take place in London on the 17th of December 1955, that my first married home would be in Portsmouth, and I would drag my wife and son Tony to Chatham, Scotland and to Malta in the following two years. Then 3 years after returning home I would be back for an advanced Officers Course, with Portsmouth also my base, for the first of three years.

The Ship was enroute to Port Said as the month ended. Gibraltar was passed as we headed east into the Mediterranean towards Port Said. The voyage at this stage was comfortable.

November 1951

Medical Assistance. The passage was uneventful until the 2nd of November when the ship diverted to assist a US Tanker needing some medical aid. The following morning the ship's doctor was transferred by sea boat, and after treating the patient, our doctor returned back on-board and passage towards Port Said was resumed.

Port Said and Aden

After disembarking the pilot and equipment on Sunday the 5th, the ship proceeded into the Red Sea. The passage to Aden through the Red Sea was uneventful and there was the southerly breeze that helped cool the ship.

Sydney Homeward Bound

Aden

On Thursday the 9th of November the ship entered Aden harbour at 0700 and secured to the fuelling berth to top up with fuel. Privileged leave was given to half the Ship's Company for three hours (9 - 12) and the other half (1 - 3pm), it was my first chance to get a look around Aden. Having completed fuelling by 1700 (5pm) the ship sailed for Colombo. The weather was very good on passage.

Medical Assistance. The passage was uneventful until the 2nd of November, when on the evening of Friday the 10th, a call for medical advice was received from a British merchant ship. The Ship's Doctor provided medical advice by radio and, when the patient was found to be not improving from the treatment, the ship had to reverse course and headed back on our track until we rendezvoused with the merchant ship. The Senior and an assistant Doctor were transferred the next morning by boat. After examination and treatment of the patient, the doctors returned, and we resumed our passage to Columbo increasing speed to meet our previous expected time of arrival.

Colombo

Early on the 16th of November, the ship secured head and stern to buoys in Columbo harbour. Overnight leave was given in two watches. However, I seem to remember that most people preferred to come back on board. There was a game of soccer against the Royal Ceylon Naval Volunteers that they won, as did their Water Polo team. Their cricket team also won the match by one wicket. Cheap Bus Tours were arranged to Kandy, and I took the opportunity to go and have a look around.

Finally, on the morning of Saturday the 18th of November, *Sydney* sailed for Fremantle. The passage was quite uneventful in reasonably good weather, improving as we got further south. During the passage, the deck hockey and volleyball tournaments took place. Despite the cramped conditions, there was a successful concert staged on the 22nd, 23rd, and 24th of November. These activities helped the time pass rather quickly.

With the good weather and return to Australia there was a lot of scrubbing and cleaning to make sure we would be presentable on arrival in Fremantle. This kept me rather busy in the Part of Ship area.

Fremantle

After five months away, the Western Australian coast appeared on the afternoon of Monday the 27th of November; the ship berthed at north wharf Fremantle. Western Australian Long Leave liberty men were disembarked. This included me, and I spent a few days in Perth before going home to Kalgoorlie and catching up with Mum and Dad. After a couple weeks at home, I returned to Perth and caught up with relatives and friends who were all very interested in what I had been doing. I won't bore you with a blow-by-blow description of what I did, it is enough to say that I was glad to be able to relax and not worry about what was going on in the ship.

The ship embarked free freight whilst in Fremantle and sailed on Tuesday the 28th of November for Jervis Bay with calls at Adelaide and Melbourne.

Jervis Bay

The final act in *Sydney's* journey to the UK and back was the arrival of the ship in Jervis Bay on the 6th of December and the landing of the 65 aircraft, the air stores and personal baggage of the 21st CAG within 24 hours. After unloading, the ship to proceed to Sydney, arriving there on the forenoon of Friday, the 8th of December 1950.

January 1951

Leave

After spending my Christmas in Perth with the family, I returned to Kalgoorlie at the beginning of January, and after a few days at home, I caught the Trans train to Sydney, via Adelaide and Melbourne. I think I arrived back in Sydney and re-joined the ship about 13 January. It was not long out of dry dock and was berthed at Fitting out Wharf.

As you can imagine there was considerable amount of work to do in my Part of Ship to make it ship shape. *Sydney* was berthed with my part of ship against the wharf. There was a gangway in place for loading stores near the Main Top locker where the cleaning gear for use in the part of ship was stowed.

Sailors

As the day of sailing for a new work up period was approaching, there was a day when fresh food stores were loaded on. They came aboard up the gangway and would be taken into the hangar through a door that opened onto the upper deck. It happened that my Main Top locker was almost adjacent to the hangar door.

That night, as I was walking around the upper deck, checking on what was to be done the next day, I picked up the smell of something cooking. I knew it wasn't coming from ship's galleys and followed my nose that led me to my part of Ship locker, the door of which was closed.

As the smell was the strongest at this point, I opened the door of the locker and found that my locker-man was using an electric heater, placed flat on the deck, cooking a leg of ham in a kerosene tin. When I questioned him where he got the ham from, he admitted he had joined the queue that was taking in the stores, had picked up the leg of ham and, as the person checking what was coming aboard looked down at his pad to note the item, the sailor had walked into the locker instead of the hangar. At that stage, he had closed the door of the locker behind him.

The ham was almost cooked at that stage, and I directed him to switch off the heater and ditch the water in which it was being cooked. He removed the ham from the locker and hid it. Fortunately, there was a bit of a breeze, and the smell was soon gone.

Coil of Rope

I needed to replace the rope used for the cover of a particular item on the upper deck of my part of Ship as it was old, and I thought it could do with replacing. Unfortunately, the Ship's Bosun was not agreeable to the change. Using my 'locker-man' when loading cordage, he joined the line and, like the ham episode, I soon had a coil in the locker, and I was able to replace the old cordage. I then made sure the coil was hidden in another part of my responsibility where it would not be easily found. The Bosun searched the locker found nothing and went away disappointed.

Back to Sea (Work up 20th CAG)

On the 23rd of January, the advance party of the 20th CAG was embarked and on the following day we sailed for Deck Landing Practice for Sea Furies and Firefly aircrew of the 20th CAG. *Sydney* operated from Jervis Bay during these sessions and was there as the month ended.

Sydney continued the workup from Jervis Bay until the 16th when we returned to Sydney. The flying continued during the passage north and, unfortunately, a Firefly hit the fore mast and crashed into the sea. The observer escaped. However, the pilot was lost with the aircraft.

On arrival in Sydney, the ship secured to a buoy early on Saturday the 17th and ammunitioned. On completion, the ship was moved to the Fitting Out Wharf embarking stores and office gear of the Flag Officer Commanding Australian Fleet (FOCAF) and having the damage caused by the aircraft crash repaired.

On the 24th of February, the ship sailed for exercises and passage to Hobart where we arrived on the 28th of February and prepared for the Fleet Regatta that began on the 1st of March, my 25th birthday.

March 1951

The small ship section of the regatta was won by HMNZS *Hawea*, and the big ship section was won by HMAS *Sydney*. I was unable to celebrate my 25th birthday until the following day. With a couple of mates, we managed to demolish a few crayfish and a few bottles of ale. There was also a Ball that I attended and danced the night away.

On the 5th of March, the ship sailed, and a flyover of Hobart was carried out. Due to the unsatisfactory weather and swell conditions, flying operations were conducted from Storm Bay.

Exercises consisted of various tactical and flying operations with the ship anchoring most nights. One night, there was a bad storm and *Sydney* remained at sea for the night. Eventually *Sydney* returned to harbour on the 14th to fuel and then headed for Westernport.

Westernport

During our stay in Westernport there was a full program of social and sporting programs at Flinders Naval Depot. I participated in both areas unless I was Duty. Saying goodbye to Westernport, *Sydney* proceeded towards Adelaide, carrying out flying operations as weather and swell condition permitted.

On the 21st of March, 21 aircraft flew over Adelaide. After recovering the aircraft, the ship berthed at outer harbour and remained there until 28th. As Easter fell in this period, I was able to attend all the Easter Church Services.

Also, over the Saturday, Sunday, and Monday (24th, 25th, 26th March, the easter weekend), the ship was open to visitors, and it was estimated that 16,000 people visited.

Departure/Exercises

A gale stopped sailing on the 27th. On the 28th of March, the *Sydney* sailed and later was joined by HMAS *Tobruk* and passage was continued to Bass Straight. On the 29th the ship met up with the 1st Frigate Squadron for convoy exercises. The next day, little flying could be done due to bad weather. On the 30th, excellent weather allowed the best days flying of the whole cruise with participation in a variety of exercises.

On completion of the exercises, HMCS *Ontario* joined *Sydney* and HMAS *Australia* for passage to Jervis Bay. On the 31st of March, the ship anchored in Jervis Bay.

April 1951

To Sea

On the 2nd and 3rd of April, the ship continued to exercise off Jervis Bay with Task Force 75. On completion of the exercises on Tuesday the 3rd, the aircraft of the 20th CAG were flown off to RANAS *Nowra* and the next day personnel of that group and their baggage and air stores were landed. On completion, the ship sailed to Sydney and berthed at the Fitting Out wharf early in the morning of 5th April.

(Work Up 21st CAG)

The ship remained alongside until the 24th of April, sailing south to Jervis Bay, embarking 5 Sea Furies and 5 Fireflies of the 21st CAG enroute. The remainder of the day was spent doing DLPs that was somewhat hampered by the lack of wind. The ship remained at sea for the night. Next day, very favourable weather allowed continuation of the DLPs, and 132 deck landings were completed on this day. This was a record for the ship. Early in the evening, the ship anchored in Jervis Bay.

On Thursday the 26th of April, *Sydney* was at sea carrying out DLPs and on completion of the day's flying returned to Jervis Bay to embark the remainder of the 21st CAG's personnel luggage and stores. The remainder of the aircraft of the 21st CAG flew on-board on this day. On completion of the days' practices the ship returned to Jervis Bay and over the weekend of the 28th and 29th of April the ship remained at anchor, embarking remaining personnel and stores of the 21st CAG.

On Monday the 30th of April, the ship sailed for flying practices and remained at sea for the night.

May 1951

From the 1st to the 4th of May the work up for the 21st CAG continued. Unfortunately, on the 3rd, one of the Sea Fury aircraft crashed into the sea after a Rocket Assisted Take Off. I happened to be the Petty Officer of the Watch on Deck and was involved in getting the Sea Boat away. (27 foot Powered). Almost straight away after its launch, a pipe (announcement) was broadcast to launch the Lifeboat.

This was the same class of boat, and I hurried to the other side of the ship and had the boat turned out from its stowed position with a scratch crew jumping in. The first sailor in had taken up the position of coxswain of the boat. I didn't recognise him as of the seaman branch, so I asked what his rate was, and his reply was Cook. He admitted he had never coxswained a boat.

As I was about to grab one of the Leading Seaman I knew could coxswain a boat, the Executive Officer, who had just arrived and heard the conversation, ordered the sailor out of the boat, and directed me to jump in and take the boat away.

This I did and as soon as I had a full crew and a signalman, the Commander took control of lowering the boat. There was quite a sea running and fortunately I was able to give the order to slip, (let the boat go into the water on the top of a wave) and we got away safely.

A Dan Buoy had been dropped into the water at roughly the same time the aircraft had ditched. This became the starting point for the search. Both mine and other boat's crew were visually searching for wreckage. There was none. We continued searching, the state of the sea and swell was so high that, when in the trough, I could not see the ship which meant that the sea and swell was at least several metres from crest to the bottom of the trough.

We were going in the same direction as the sea and swell, and it was not too difficult. However, when we were over a mile or so from the ship, a light signal was received, as we topped a wave, recalling the boat.

I had been thinking about having to turn around to return to the ship and assessing how I was going to turn the boat 180 degrees without being swamped. I waited as the next wave was picking the boat up and, just before reaching the crest, used the Kitchener gear (direction and power tiller) and had the boat facing the right way as the wave fell away. My several prayers had been answered. It was slow trip back as you can imagine, and I had the crew making sure they were hanging on securely.

If I thought that was a problem, the coming alongside and hoisting the boat back on board provided a little drama I could have done without. I watched the waves rising and falling alongside the ship as I approached the falls. I had checked the disengaging gear was fully locked at my end and forward end and briefed the bowman to signal immediately his fall was locked on so I could engage my fall. We rode up a nice wave and, as it peaked and we were hooked on, I raised my hand to indicate it was OK to hoist, and shouted to **"hoist"**. Nothing happened and, as the wave fell away, the boat fell down a bit. I made sure the crew were all holding onto a lifeline and kept shouting **"hoist"**. I kept my eye on the next wave rapidly approaching and said a few very choice words as the boat slammed against the ship's side. I could see us all in the water if another hit as hard as that wave. Fortunately, my tirade worked and we just above wave height when the second wave slammed the ship's side.

Not long after securing the boat, I was sent for by the Executive Officer who had been responsible for hoisting the boat.

On reporting to his cabin, he asked for an explanation about my language. I apologised to him for my language and pointed out that I was highly concerned for the crew of the boat, as the next wave hitting the boat could smash it into the side of the ship, and we could all be in the water and, instead of looking for the airmen, he would be having to rescue five or six of the boat crew. He accepted my apology. I also made a comment that Officers should never take charge of hoisting or lowering a boat as they did not get the practice needed, and it should be left to the Chief or Petty Officer doing the task. He agreed. (Score a draw)

Sometime later, flying resumed and the work up continued. On the morning of the 4th of May, the Flag of the Flag Officer Commanding HM Australian Fleet was hoisted in the ship and, on return to Jervis Bay that afternoon, the Admiral himself embarked. Later in the evening, with HMAS *Anzac* as consort, we sailed for Port Lincoln.

Port Lincoln

During this passage, the workup was continued, and, because of the weather conditions, the ship anchored at Port Lincoln on Tuesday, the 8th of May.

The following week was spent at anchor at Port Lincoln, preparing for the Admiral's inspection and carrying out minor social engagements as circumstances allowed.

The program for the Annual Inspection of the ship to be carried out by the Admiral had to be altered the last moment due to rain persisting over two days. Inspection ended on Monday the 14th of May in the afternoon and, in company with HMAS *Anzac,* the ship departed for Jervis Bay via the Port Adelaide Anchorage.

The sudden departure from Port Lincoln and sending both South Australian and Western Australian personnel on leave from Adelaide was not explained to us. However, it was not too hard to realise something significant was happening with the ship's programme. *Sydney* and *Anzac* arrived at Port Adelaide anchorage early on Tuesday morning, 15th May, and disembarked Liberty men for South Australia and Western Australia. The South Australian Harbour Boards Tender landed these Liberty men.

Bud Rail Car

On landing in Adelaide, we WA Liberty men were taken into the city, and I cannot remember if we stayed overnight or went straight onto a train that took us to Port Pirie. Here, we boarded what was known as a Bud Railcar that was to take us to Kalgoorlie. This car had individual seats that were quite comfortable, and I think I was able to get a reasonable sleep during the passage to Kalgoorlie. The staff on the rail car were very attentive and looked after as well. I cannot remember if it was a one or a two-car set up.

Leave

All I carried onto the train was a travelling bag of hand luggage. On arrival at Kalgoorlie Station, I left the train as the rest of the group carried onto Perth.

I caught a passing tram to the nearest stop to my home. Home was only two streets away and a very surprised Mum welcomed me home like a long-lost sheep. I had a shower and then explained I was uninformed as to why I had been sent of leave early. My father was very surprised to see me and questioned me what I was up to. I informed him we had not been told but my wild guess was that we were off to Korea to relieve a British carrier.

I think the leave period was only for three weeks, so after a week at home I went to Perth and spent a week with my auntie and uncle. I caught up with some of my relatives and a few friends and, after a week, was back to Kalgoorlie to spend the last days of my leave with Mum and Dad. I think at that time my brother was away from Kalgoorlie and my sister was nursing in Northam.

June 1951

At the beginning of June, I was enjoying the last of my leave and, on the 6th or 7th or so, I was back on the train heading east. I seem to recall I had a sleeper, and meals were taken in the dining car of the normal Trans train as far as Port Pirie. Then it was the usual rail gauge change for the journey on to Adelaide and up to Albury, to change to the New South Wales rail gauge system and would have arrived back in Sydney on the 12th or 13th of the month.

During the rest of the month I had been away, the ship had been put into dry dock and was there when I arrived back. It was moved to the Fitting Out Wharf before the end of June, and you can imagine the effort was being put in to bring the ship back up to the high standard it had before this docking and to prepare for the task ahead of us. My tasks, at that time, was concentrating on the state of the Main Top Part of Ship, making sure that all the rust that could be removed had been, and all the other things such as lines and fittings were working.

I visited all my friends, particularly my cousin Dora and her family.

July 1951

Degaussing

On Monday, the 4th of July, the ship moved to a buoy and degaussing was carried out until the 9th. This process reduces the magnetic signature of the ship to help against magnetic mines. The preparation of making the ship ready for sea also continued whilst at the buoy.

Workup

On Tuesday the 10th of July, *Sydney* sailed for Jervis Bay and arrived there later that day. The remainder of the week was spent calibrating MF (Medium Frequency) and HF (High Frequency) DF (Direction Finding) sets at the anchorage and calibrating the VHF (Very High Frequency) (DF) and Radar 960 Search Radar at sea. On the 12th of July, a full power trial and general working up drills were carried out, including the fuelling of HMAS *Anzac* at sea.

Then began the DLP phase of working up the Sea Fury Squadron and, by the 19th, this was completed. Unfortunately, one Sea Fury's aircraft crashed into the sea during recovery. The Pilot was recovered by the attending destroyer.

Aside. I was not to know then that the pilot would be my Commanding Officer when I was serving as the Operations Officer of HMAS *Stuart* many, many years later.

On Monday and Tuesday, 23rd and 24th, preliminary working up practices were carried out and on the latter date 5 Fireflys were embarked for deck landing practice and later in the month the full outfit of both Squadrons were embarked and flying continued until the 28th of July with aircraft operating with permanent deck parking.

Anti-Aircraft Practise

On Monday the 30th of July, normal flying practice was carried out and, in the afternoon, a close-range anti-aircraft firing exercise was carried out by the ship at a sleeve target towed by a RAAF *Beaufighter*. On completion, the ship sailed for Newcastle area to allow practice bombing on the Bird Island range. The weather on the way was unsatisfactory for flying.

August 1951

The unsatisfactory weather continued on the 1st of August and the ship returned to Sydney securing alongside Fitting Out Wharf on the afternoon of that day. The remainder of the week with taken up in embarking fuel, and Naval and Victualling stores.

FOCAF re-joined the ship on the 6th of August and later that day the ship sailed for the Harvey Bay area with HMAS *Tobruk* in company. During the rest of the week following, flying practices were carried out using Bird Island and Morna Point ranges on the 7th and 8th using the ship's resources. Then on Thursday and Friday, 9th and 10th, Fairfax Island Range was used. We anchored in Bustard Bay on the 9th and 10th on completion of the days flying. These activities continued until the 16th of August, when the ship headed south to Sydney continuing to fly on the way.

Sydney

On arrival in Sydney on the 17th, the ship went straight into Captain Cook Dock remaining there until Tuesday the 28th of August. The Minister for Navy and FOCAF visited the ship before we sailed on the 31st for Japan via Manus. Close range A/A firings were carried out on a sleeve target towed by a RAAF *Beaufighter* as we sailed up the New South Wales coast. Finally, we were on our way to the Korean War.

Rabaul Visit

Flying continued as *Sydney* proceeded north until on the 4th when weather prevented flying. As a result of a message from headquarters in Canberra, the ship was diverted to Rabaul to show off the ship and provide a flying demonstration. This was done to meet a request by the people of Rabaul.

Manus Visit

On completion, *Sydney* sailed on towards Manus, continuing our flying operations until entering Seadler harbour and fuelling. The weekend of the 8th and 9th was spent in harbour with recreational and social activities despite the heat.

The ship was open to visitors, for some children of the settlement, members of the Royal Papuan Constabulary and nineteen Recruit Seaman of the new Guinea division of the Royal Australian Navy. The ship sailed for Yokosuka on Monday 10th of September.

Japan

Flying operations continued as we approached Japan and, unfortunately, one Sea Fury was lost due to engine failure. The pilot was recovered by the ship's Sea boat.

On Saturday the 15th of September, there was no flying to enable aircraft maintenance and to refuel HMAS *Tobruk*. Normal routine was exercised from pm on the 17th to daylight on 19th of September. Because of a typhoon near the Philippines that could easily menace southern Japan, the ship arrived at Yokosuka two days early and refuelled, just in case it was necessary to put to sea. The weather was lousy and the planned A/A shoot before arriving had to be cancelled. The ship was to be Depermed whilst in port, but that did not happen.

On anchoring, a comical note was struck by the appearance of an LCP alongside with the US Navy Squeegee Band and half a dozen Geisha girls who put on a turn for the benefit of the Ship's Company. During the next six days we were able to enjoy the delights of Yokosuka and Tokyo. On the 25th of September, we sailed to Kure.

Kure

The ship arrived at Kure on the 27th, berthing alongside the wharf with HMS *Glory*, whom we were to relieve, on the other side of the pontoon. The ship immediately took over the duties from HMS *Glory* and transferred aircraft and items of equipment. HMS *Unicorn*, the Flag Ship, and HMS *Alert* arrived the next day. A turnover of information concerning our future duties took place, and on Sunday the 30th of September, the C-in-C Far East visited the ship and inspected the Ship's Company at Divisions.

All too soon it was off to the west coast of Korea, and *Sydney*'s aircraft began seeking targets as necessary. These included troop concentrations, stores or buildings, train lines, inshore boats and so on.

Manning

Whilst in the operational area, the ship would have been in two watches. The period between 2000 and 0800 the following morning was split into two, 6 hours watches. In that way personnel were able to get some sleep before or after being on night watch.

My job continued to oversee the Air Plot in the Air Defence Room (ADR), making sure that the plotters, behind the plot, continued to provide accurate information on any aircraft detected. At times, I continued to act as a plotter for one of the Air Controllers and this was interesting. I was not to know that I would be trained as an Air Controller later in my career.

During the evening watches I oversaw the ADR and made sure that the people on the radar displays associated with Aircraft Detection were on the ball all the time, just in case an air attack on the Task Group occurred. Fortunately, no such attacks were launched against us. From time to time, a US reconnaissance aircraft would call up with an enemy report. Usually, I would have to call the Boss, who slept in the ADR, so he could take any messages. They would usually be encoded, and I was in the habit of listening and copying the code to make sure there were no mistakes. This was appreciated by the Boss.

During the day, when not on watch, I would be attending to my Part of Ship. Weather, of course, often meant not much could be done to keep the areas up to scratch.

The first patrol was in two parts, the 4th to 13th October, and the 17th to 27th. Initially, this first patrol involved transferring to the east coast for a special operation on the 10/11th of October. The patrol had begun on the West Coast of Korea and the ship returned to the West patrol area after the 11th. Four days later, the ship's aircraft attacked troop concentrations and suspected store dumps.

During this period the ship created a Light Fleet Carrier record number of aircraft launches and recoveries.

USS New Jersey passing astern of Sydney

Besides the aircraft strafing and bombing the targets, the Battleship USS *New Jersey* was provided with a *Sydney* spotter aircraft to call the fall of shot of her bombardment. The aircraft that was spotting for the USS *New Jersey* were complemented on their bombardment spotting. Finally, it was back to Sasebo where we arrived on the 14th to fuel and replenish our stores.

Typhoon Ruth

On 13 October 1951 a Typhoon had formed south of Japan, and while lying at anchor in Sasebo on the 14th, the ship received a warning of the approach of Typhoon Ruth. In view of the restricted and crowded nature of the anchorage, *Sydney* and other large ships were ordered to sea. On the 14th *Sydney* experienced the most intense phase of the Typhoon from 5 pm to midnight.

Sea Furies on Flight D

Damage. One Firefly aircraft, a 16-ft motor dinghy and a forklift truck washed overboard from the flight deck along with other stores and equipment. Aircraft at the after end of the flight deck were damaged. There were no major injuries to the Ship's Company despite the sea state and swell, the wind and rain conditions making the ship rock and roll and pitch.

I remember that night. I was going on a night watch and smelt aircraft fuel fumes leaking from where an aircraft that had broken free and the main part was lying over the side of the flight deck with some part in the gun sponson. I appreciated the risk, particularly as the Aircraft fumes appeared to be heading towards the boiler room fan intakes. Fortunately, these intakes were quickly closed, and the risk of fire and/or explosion was averted.

Flight Deck Forward *Looking at Bridge*

Sydney returned to Sasebo Harbour and completed storing and fuelling and the Ship's Company enjoyed the pleasures of Sasebo and its Casbah or the USN recreational facilities. On Wednesday the 17th of October, the ship sailed for the second part of the First Patrol and recommenced flying on the 18th.

I won't comment on specific operations during this period, sufficient to say that attacks against troops, junks, tunnels, transport etc. continued unless weather conditions were unsatisfactory.

On the 25th, a Sea Fury was hit and had to ditch. Fortunately, the pilot was picked up by a Dumbo aircraft (Seaplane).

Loan Helicopter

On the 26th of October, five Fireflies were attacking a tunnel and encountered intense light flak. One was hit and brought down and landed in a Paddy Field. The ship's helicopter, on loan from the USN and manned by an American pilot, took off and, although almost at the end of its range and with night approaching, managed to rescue the Pilot and his Observer.

To keep the enemy away from where the two were hiding, both Fireflies and Sea Furies strafed any moving troops. When the helicopter landed close to the pair, one enemy soldier was shot by one of the crew using an Owen gun. The helicopter had to fly to a friendly landing area and managed to get there at last light. This was beyond everybody's expectation.

The recovered aircrew were flown back to the ship the next day. The ship's Guardian Angel had been hard at work that's for sure.

An Aside. Many years later when attending a Fleet Air Arm Reunion at HMAS *Albatross* I was visiting the Fleet Air Arm Museum and came across a picture of the Pilot and Observer running towards helicopter at the end of one of the aisles. As I was looking at it, the Archivist came along with a lady and showed her the picture. He asked me to move away so the wife could view it. I advised him I had been working for one of the air controllers who was heavily engaged in his recovery on that day. However, he didn't want to know.

During this first patrol, mention should be made of the great work being done by the Flight Deck team and the Photographic Section having to deal with four photographic missions each day, producing over 7,000 prints daily. Many of these were produced within 50 minutes and used for briefings of later events. In this period, 427 landings were carried out with only one accident when an aircraft landed without a hook. Then it was off to Kure, arriving there on 28th.

An Aside. Cold Weather Gear. During this first patrol it had been very cold. Before the next patrol one of the members of my mess was seen pulling on two pair of nylon stockings using an elastic arrangement to keep them up. He put heavy socks over them. As you can imagine, he was subject to a lot of friendly banter. His answer was, "They keep me warm, and I do not care how it looks, at least I don't feel the cold so much."

Several of us saw the wisdom of his comments and promptly went, whilst in Sasebo, and bought ourselves stockings. I found his explanation was correct and we didn't have the near frozen feet of the previous periods at sea. It is said that sailors do sometimes think outside the square when it was needed.

November 1951

Second Patrol

The Second Patrol was from 5th to 13th and from the 19th to 29th of November. *Sydney* left Kure on the 3rd of November heading for the West Coast patrol. HMCS *Athabascan* joined enroute. Next morning HMCS *Cayuga* joined from Sasebo and the group took part in AA firing practice at the sleeve target as we sailed towards the Patrol area.

On the 5th of November, flying operations recommenced and HMCS *Sioux*, USS *Hanna* and USS *Collett* joined the screen. HMS *Belfast* closed the ship during flying off to the second event of the day. Shortly after the Flag Officer Second-in-Command, Far East Station and his Staff were embarked. HMS *Belfast* departed, taking with her HMCS *Athabascan*.

On this day our first casualty occurred when an aircraft failed to pull out of a strafing dive whilst attacking enemy transports.

On completion of operations on this day, *Sydney* and screen proceeded to Sasebo carrying out an AA shoot on a towed target on the way. I had the usual run ashore to the drinking house after the ship secured to a buoy on arrival in Sasebo on the 14th.

Sydney left Sasebo on the 18th, and on the 20th saw the start of two days of excellent flying weather enroute to the West Coast of Korea. Foul weather, sleet, snow, and low visibility prevented operations later; the wind was Force 10 with gusts to Force 12. No rest for the wicked.

The weather had abated sufficiently to rebegin operations, and on the 27th and 28th, the enemy realised our ship had not gone away. It was then time to depart for Kure, and the ship arrived at Kure on the 30th of November.

Annexes. I have attached two Annexes to his Chapter which show the daily Debriefing Report for 10th and 21st of November which give some idea of what was going on and the Aircraft usage.

Action Information Organisation (Ops Rooms)

The following comment was made by the Commanding Officer in his Monthly Report of Proceedings for November 1951.

> *The Action Information Organization has been fully engaged in all its aspects since commencement of operations on the 5th of October 1951. No fewer than 236 interceptions have been made, all being identified as friendly. ND Officers have rapidly become efficient in this art and a "miss" was a rare occurrence. In addition to interceptions, and its normal routine work vectoring aircraft to the target area, homing, height determination, interrogation, and classification of all tracks, the AIO played a major part in the rescue of the Firefly crew from behind enemy lines on 26th October. The accurate vectoring of the helicopter and the CAP to the rescue scene and from there to Kimpo airstrip, the co-ordination of all information, in fact the direction of the rescue, saved many precious minutes in the all-important time before dusk.*

> *The radar, and particularly the Type 960 (Long Range Air)), has performed admirably. Communications have, except on those odd occasions, been very good. Excellent two-way communication was held at 160 miles with a Sea Fury orbiting at 14,000 feet above the ditched aircraft.*

> *The Surface side of the AIO has not had so many opportunities to prove its worth. However, the information derived from the GOP (General Operations Plot) has been of great value to the Command. An important function of this Operation Room, in connection with the air operations, has been the sorting and filing of a great number of signals.*

The detailed pre- and other AIO training during deployment to Korea has stood the test of time, as reflected in the CO's comments about the AIO team.

Miracle???

An Aside. The simple act of buying Christmas cards for the friends I had in my address book was, at a future date, to change my life dramatically, as will be explained later in this epistle.

It wasn't always easy to work in the crowded mess deck. Knowing I had to complete and post these cards very quickly to ensure they were in the post to Australia in time for the delivery before Christmas, I decided I would write them up during the quiet period of the 8 pm to 2 am watch when in the ADR and there was no air activity. This was so they could be posted in the coming port visit.

I had checked my address book before I bought the number of cards. I needed to match the names in my address book. I had rechecked to ensure I had not left anyone out. When I finished making comments in each card and addressing envelopes, I found I had one card left.

I rechecked the address book and the cards completed aligned with the number of addresses. There was one spare card. I re-counted the cards I had filled in and that was the number I had bought. The extra was an additional one that had somehow got into the ones bought. I put the spare card to one side and waited for an aircraft to send a coded report on enemy positions for our briefings the next morning. The time was sometime well after midnight.

After taking the aircraft's message with my Boss, I had my mind in neutral. I suddenly had a vision of Joan H, one of the girls I played tennis with when in Sydney. She was very attractive and appeared to be quite talented and efficient in arranging the tennis games et cetera. I had taken her to a dance and dinner or two since I met her.

However, being at sea most of the time, I sometimes didn't get a chance to see her. I didn't have the number of her house although I knew the street name. I did remember she worked for the Confectionery Union and, oddly enough, had bumped into her doing her job in a shop I usually bought my chocolates for my cousin Dora. I also knew that she worked out of the Trades Hall in Sydney. I decided to send her this last card. I found the Trades Hall address in the Sydney telephone book in the mess. I will comment on what happened with that card later.

December 1951

Third Patrol

Sydney remained in Sasebo until the 5th of December, when it sailed for its third patrol, which lasted until the 18th of December. On the 7th, HMAS *Tobruk* joined the screen, and operations recommenced. Unfortunately, a Sea Fury was hit by flak and the pilot was forced to eject. His body was recovered by helicopter. He was buried at sea with full Naval Honours. It appears that he was killed when he hit the tail of plane as he left the aircraft.

One other Sea Fury had to land ashore with wheels up due the damage caused by flak.

A Firefly was hit by flak on the last event of the day and landed on a beach. The crew were picked up by a shore-based helicopter. Later they and the Sea Fury pilot were collected by HMAS *Tobruk* and to returned to *Sydney*.

On the 13th, the weather deteriorated, however, a full flying programme was achieved. One Sea Fury was shot down during the forenoon; the pilot had bailed out okay and was recovered by a shore-based helicopter, known as Pedro Fox.

After one of the Storms

In the afternoon, a second Sea Fury was hit. The Pilot bailed out and landed unhurt in shallow water. A friendly junk picked him up. Later, *Tobruk* picked these aircrew up from shore, but very severe weather on the 14th and 15th delayed the pilots return to the ship. On completion of operations on 17th, *Sydney* left the area and proceeded to Kure. During the passage, a close-range AA firing took place against a towed target. The ship arrived in Kure just before midday on the 19th.

Christmas 1951

It was nice to be away from the Operational area for Christmas. It didn't take long before my routine of going ashore for a few drinks with mates, a steam bath with a massage and then a nice lunch before more drink was over.

The box on the picture below shows:

    Sorties Flown   2386

    Bombs Dropped   1162

    Rockets Fired.   8655

    20mm Fired   571,218

    Record   89 Sorties in one day.

As is the custom, the Officers served the meal to the Junior Sailors. There was a beer issue I seem to recall.

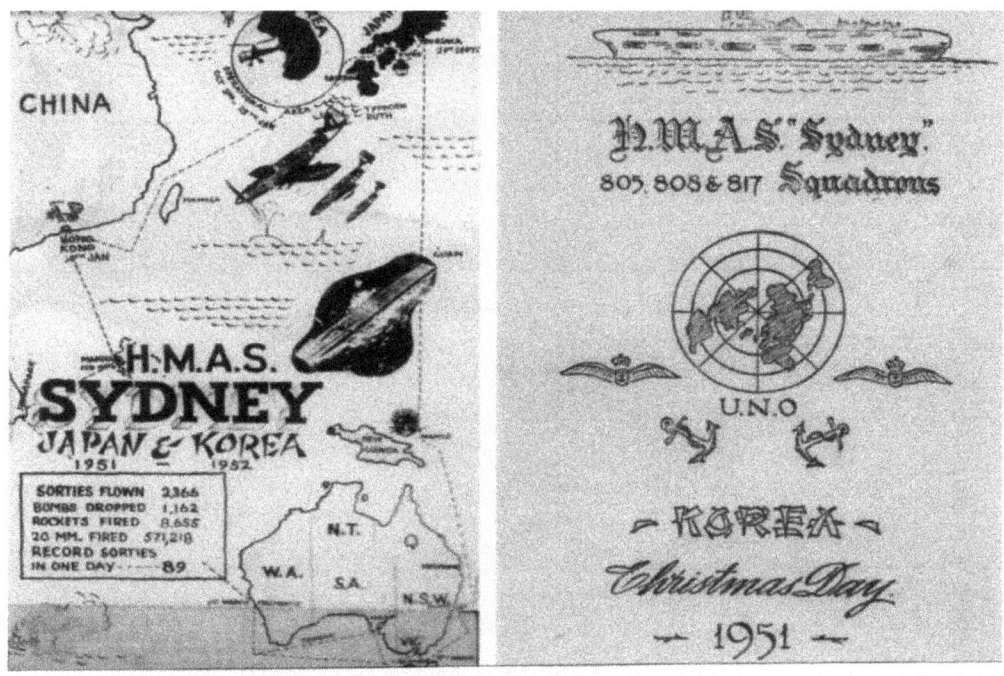

Christmas Menu Cover Pages

Next Patrol

The ship sailed from Kure on December 27th and began flying in the operational area on the 29th. For a time, the ship provided a CAP over a convoy as it passed through the area. We also provided fire support for evacuating friendly ground troops on an invaded island. Ninety of them were saved.

Christmas Parcels

Each crew member was given a Christmas parcel sent by a Charity I forget the name of. These contained scarves, gloves, tinned food, and other goodies I can't remember. We were well fed except for some confectionery items. I didn't use any of the other items.

I was very appreciative of having a **Catholic Chaplain** on board for the trip. Unless he was visiting the ships-in-company, he said Mass in the Chapel each day. When not on duty, I tried to attend. Being able to go to Mass on Christmas Day was a bonus.

The Chaplain had previously put out the word that any extra clothing, or goods, that people could spare, he would take for the children in an orphanage at Hiro. I seem to remember it was on the road to Hiroshima. On Boxing Day, I think it was, he again made an appeal and said the items could be left in his cabin.

I was dropping my contribution to his cabin when the Chaplain asked me to step in. He made the comment that he had noticed sailors walking past with bags but not stopping. I realised, almost immediately, that the sailors did not wish him to know who gave the items. I suggested he take his chair, something to read and sit in the gun sponson just outside his cabin and see what happened. I knew that he would be able to see those coming to his cabin from where he was sitting.

He later told me that he had no sooner sat down in the sponson when a sailor appeared with a bag and emptied the contents onto his bunk. Shortly after, more and more sailors arrived and tipped out their bags in his cabin. In the end,, he could hardly get into his cabin. You can imagine his delight. He had to make several trips in the ship's jeep to deliver the goods to the orphanage.

On the morning of sailing, the Padre took the last load to the orphanage. The captain did not appreciate the fact that the Jeep had not returned by the time the ship was to depart.

Finally, the Captain ordered the lines to be cast off, and just about the time he gave the engine orders to move the ship, the Jeep appeared on the wharf. The ship's crane was immediately swung over the side with the vehicle slings and the jeep was still being hauled aboard as the ship moved away from the wharf.

January 1952

Conditions on the 2nd of January were very uncomfortable but flying continued. On this day, another Sea Fury was lost when he became separated from his leader. A thorough search by Firefly aircraft and ships failed to find any trace of the aircraft or pilot. Weather was a problem at this time of the year. However, *Sydney* was able to keep operating. One pilot was wounded and was able to return and land on the ship.

An Aside. I made a comment about this Officer earlier.

Many years later, this last pilot mentioned was the Commanding Officer of HMAS *Stuart*. He specifically asked for me to be his Operations Officer. I didn't know that at that time.

There were no air operations on the 5th and 6th due to low cloud, snow showers and poor visibility. However, the type 960 search radar detected a single aircraft at 160 miles at 40,000ft. This worked out to be over the east coast of Korea.

On the 7th, the ship left the operating area heading for Kure where it arrived on the 9th of January. The ship was to remain in Kure until it sailed on Tuesday 15th of January for its final operations on the West Coast.

Presents for Ship's Company Children

Before leaving Kure for our last patrol, a small Committee was formed to go ashore and buy presents for Ship's Company members' children. For some reason, Muggins was put in charge of this buying expedition. Armed with a list of names and ages, we proceeded ashore to what appeared to be the best children's gift shop in Kure. Some of my assistants were married and had children and that helped.

Fortunately, the shop owner understood what we were about and was most helpful in suggesting gifts for boys or girls of various ages. When finished, the owner assured us that he would have all the gifts alongside the ship before it sailed. He was paid for what we had selected. For some reason, I trusted him.

He did not let me down, arriving with a large crate on the morning of the ship's departure. Later, when we began the task of wrapping and putting names on each gift, we found that the owner had included several extra gifts for every age group. I assumed it was in case some of the gifts were damaged.

An Aside. This trust, which I placed in the man, confirmed what my father had told me when he found out I was going to Japan for the first time. He said that his experience, working with Japanese people in the north-west of Western Australia before the war, was that they were very trustworthy. In all the visits I made to Japan, both in the service and as a tourist, I always felt that trust.

Homeward Bound

On the 25th of January 1952, *Sydney* completed her seventh and last patrol and headed for Sasebo to refuel and take on stores. On the 27th of January, the ship sailed from Sasebo, heading for Hong Kong for maintenance and to repaint the ship using the Chinese side parties to assist with painting. They were very good at their job. Meal leftovers were given to them as well as the funds for work done.

All the patrolling we had done, without being able to really do much about the look after the ship at sea needed to be rectified.

Hong Kong

Before entering Hong Kong on January 30th, six Fireflies were transferred by air to HMS *Glory*, which was replacing us on the Korean Patrol. Later, other aircraft and stores were transferred to HMS *Unicorn* while at a buoy in HK harbour.

For the first time, everyone could relax and enjoy the delights of Hong Kong. I went to my favourite Bath House and Massage Parlour, and then I socialised with mates or Hong Kong friends in the China Fleet Club or other bars. No, I didn't get too familiar with any girls.

I remember a Rugby match against a Royal Air Force team, in which we won 37 points to nil. I usually played on the wing or as a breakaway.

The Ship's Company was told that we were to meet up with the Royal Yacht, which was carrying Princess Elizabeth and Prince Phillip on their way to Australia, after leaving Singapore. However, King George VI died suddenly, and the Princess had to return to England to ascend the Throne.

Executive Officer (XO) and Himself

I was still the Captain of the Maintop (Starboard part of the upper deck). We now come to my second episode with the Executive Officer.

I knew that the Top would have to be more than up to scratch if we were to escort Princess Elizabeth and, on return to Australian Ports, my Top would be the side alongside the wharf and would have gangways from the wharf to the ship. Traffic to and from the ship would make it a bit difficult for maintenance. I made sure that, instead of the normal chipping away the rust, it would be scraped and burnished before applying the usual paint undercoat. This, of course, took longer than usual.

A completion day was given to each part of ship. To make sure there was minimum traffic through my part of the ship, I roped off access to the areas my people were preparing for painting. As the completion day approached, the XO was becoming alarmed that I would not finish the painting by the completion date. I promised him that it would be finished in time and offered to be rated back to Leading Seaman if it was not.

I also said I hoped my team could be given a make and mend day (Afternoon off) when back in Sydney. Came the day before completion day, it appeared that there was no way I would have the painting completed, and I was again threatened by the XO with the most dire consequences for my future.

Shortly after commencing work on completion day, the XO had to fight his way through extra roping off that I had put there the previous night. He appeared very upset when he confronted me, stating that I was impossible and that he would disrate me.

I suggested that he look around and he found that the top had been completely painted overnight, except for the cutting in area between the bottom of bulkhead and the deck. When he looked around everything was gleaming with new paint. The look on his face can only be imagined.

With a snort, he left my part of the ship without asking how I had been able to do the whole area in one night. I would have told him that one of my Able Seamen had been a spray painter before entering the Navy and had asked if he could use that skill. He promised me that he could do it in one night, and he did.

February 1952

Singapore

Sydney sailed for Singapore on Saturday, the 9th of February, after remaining in Harbour for the Royal Proclamation of the secession of Queen Elizabeth. The flight deck was covered in RAF Spitfires and Vampires for passage to Singapore. They could not be stowed in the Hangars. *Sydney* arrived in Singapore on the 13th of February.

Unloading of the RAF aircraft went ahead and ammunition for Australia was loaded from lighters at the same time. Later the ship went alongside a wharf. On the 15th of February, the ship sailed for Fremantle.

Fremantle

From Singapore, we proceeded to Fremantle, arriving on the 22nd of February. There, we found there were no tugs available to assist the ship in berthing alongside. This was due to a Waterside Workers strike. We entered Fremantle harbour, and aircraft were used to turn the ship.

We berthed with no difficulty. Local sailors provided the gangways, and the ship's facilities were used to lift the gangways into the ship.

After three days in Fremantle, the ship proceeded to Adelaide, then Melbourne and finally entered Jervis Bay to land the Carrier Air Group, having flown off the aircraft that were serviceable. The ship finally arrived in Sydney on the 5th of March.

Long Leave

All Western Australians were sent on Long Leave. Later, on the journey to Sydney, South Australians and Victorians would be landed for Long Leave.

I think I spent a few days in Perth, and then it was off to Kalgoorlie. I was able to surprise Mum and later Dad. I can't remember whether the leave period was three or six weeks. However long it was, I thoroughly enjoyed being away from the ship.

March 1952

I was able to celebrate my 26th birthday at home and a birthday at home was a something that was never to happen again again in WA until 1977.

Return to Ship

The time came to return to Sydney and take the usual Trans Train to South Australia, then via Adelaide, Melbourne, and finally the NSW Railway at Albury. I cannot remember the date of my re-joining *Sydney*, but it would have been late March or early April.

Sometime after arriving back, I found my Part of Ship was changed to be Captain of the Quarter Deck.

Captain of the Quarterdeck

The Captain of the Quarterdeck, who was normally the second senior seaman Petty Officer, was switched to the Fore Castle part of Ship due to a family or sickness problem of the previous Captain of Forecastle. I was suddenly switched to be the Captain of the Quarterdeck part of ship although there were Seaman Petty Officers senior to me.

Each morning the Seaman Division personnel would assemble on the Forecastle where the XO would brief us on the requirements for that day or the future.

On my first morning of overseeing the Quarterdeck Part of Ship, my Divisional Officer said that, as I didn't know any of the names of the people and what they did, he would detail them for the day's work. That made sense to me. However, in the following days, he continued to do this. I didn't say anything at the time.

One day, I was summonsed to his cabin.

"Where have you been?" he asked.

"I've been in my mess reading a book."

He said, "It must be a very interesting book," to which I replied, "It was."

He then said, "I thought you were supposed to be the Captain of the Top."

I said, "So did I. However, if you want to continue detailing them off each day, I am happy to let you do it."

"Oh, I see," he said, having got the implied message. He then proceeded to start giving me a list of tasks that the XO wanted completed. I pulled out my notebook, and after stating several items, he looked at me as I didn't appear to be writing anything in the book. Then he said, "Are you taking note of what I'm saying?" to which I replied, "I'm just ticking them off from the list I have in my book."

He said, "How come?"

My reply was, "Whilst I may not have appeared to be taking much interest in the quarterdeck, I have been noting what is required so that when I was allowed to do my proper duty as Captain of the Top, I would be ready."

He said, "Fair enough. It is now over to you."

Shortly after this, we were preparing to sail from Jervis Bay. One of the tasks was to raise and stow the after-gangway ladder on the starboard side. This ladder was used by officers to go ashore in a boat. My officer said, "How long do you think it will take for you to raise this ladder?"

My reply: "How long does it normally take?"

"15 or 16 minutes."

"OK then … it will be stowed in 15 minutes," I replied.

He said: "No way. I wouldn't bet on that."

My comment was: "If you want to bet, and I couldn't do it, then I will give you a bottle of beer from my next beer issue."

He said, "You are on," and disappeared down a ladder into the Wardroom.

The sailors who were preparing to raise the ladder had listened to the small pantomime. I think they thought I would be giving them specific instructions. My comments were, "Why are you all standing around? Haven't you raised the ladder before? You don't need me to tell you what to do."

I was knocking on the door of the Wardroom after 15 minutes asking to speak to my Divisional Officer. When he came to the door, I told him the ladder was closed stowed. He didn't believe it. He then rushed up to the gangway space to find the ladder close stowed. That night, my lockerman knocked on the door of my mess and said, "PO, there is a bottle of beer in the part of ship locker for you." I shared it with the lockerman.

Mess Dinner

A short time after arriving in Sydney, some members of my mess discussed that several of their wives were very interested in coming on board and seeing where they had lived. I was minding my own business when approached by several of the mess members and asked if I would approach the XO and see if they could bring their wives on for a dinner in the actual mess.

Eventually, I agreed and went to the XO's cabin with the request. I explained why I was making the request on behalf of my mess members and, eventually, he said yes, with the following qualifications: **the ladies had to be taken to the mess by a route that did not pass through an occupied mess.** Thanking him, I took the news to my messmates.

I had been on the ship for a long time, and my messmates asked me to see if it was possible to reach the mess without going through an occupied mess. Fortunately, the ship's gangway was adjacent to the Main Top locker and alongside it was a door to the hangar. There were no aircraft on board, and as I looked at each of the exits on the other side of the hangar one door opened into a passage or space that had a ladder going up to one of the air groups' messes on the deck above. I knew that on the other side of this mess was a ladder that took one down to the hangar deck where there was a hatch, with a ladder, leading to the door of our mess (M 24).

A day or so later, I went to the XO's cabin and confirmed that his instruction of **not to go through an occupied mess was possible and asked again if we could hold the dinner.** I then told him that there was a way to reach the mess without going through an occupied mess. He didn't believe me.

He jumped up, reached for his hat, and said show me. As we walked through the unoccupied Air Group mess, he said "This is a mess you must go through."

I drew his attention to his words, "occupied mess." I then discussed with him how we were going to organise the meal and asked for permission to serve a sherry to the ladies and a beer for the men, ensuring him that no one would drink too much, particularly as they had their wives or girlfriends with them.

When I returned to the mess, they were happy. I informed them that their wives were not to wear high heels and that low-heeled walking shoes were the order of the day.

I admire the XO for agreeing to allow the dinner to proceed with the extra drinks. A good time was had by all. I cannot recall or have heard of such a dinner being held in a Ship's Petty Officers' mess in the RAN.

Normally, on Christmas Day people can have family join them for lunch in the dining areas.

Royal Naval Sailors

Several ex-RN sailors had transferred to the Australian Navy and joined the ship in England. The seamen personnel were split equally between each part of the ship. Some of them were veterans from WWII, and all appeared to have a chip on their shoulder that they were from the Navy coming to help the Royal Amateur Navy.

One night in the mess, the other Captains of the Top were complaining about the attitude of these new arrivals. Suddenly I had a thought bubble. To their surprise, I said I would exchange my Australian sailors for the ex-RN sailors on a one-for-one basis. However, as the Radar Plot rates were divided between each part of the ship, I would have to keep those Australians in the Quarterdeck section. They thought that I was mad and so the exchange took place.

The first morning, the ex-RN sailors started work on the Quarterdeck; I lined up the whole team and spelt out that they were going to show the other parts of the ship how good they were. Each was going to be allocated a passageway or space as their own personal responsibility, and they would normally be required to work only in that space unless I needed them to help somewhere else. I emphasised there were to be no more references to their Royal Naval experience and that they and the Australians in my team had to be just that: they were a team in the Royal Australian Navy.

One afternoon after work, I was walking around the part of the ship when I found a stoker scrubbing one of the passageways. When asked what he thought he was doing, he said, "That bloke,", pointing to the sailor responsible for the space, "… he made me clean up the oil that I'd spilt."

My comment, "Good."

The VIP Cocktail Party

I was informed that a rather large VIP Cocktail Party was to be held on the Quarterdeck. As you can imagine, the pressure was on to keep the space spick-and-span. As was my way of allocating work, I started with what would take the longest and worked through until I had completed all necessary tasks.

I decided to take off the small brass plates that had an accumulation of dirt and grime etc. especially around the heads of the screws holding them in place on the bulkhead. These plates indicated what a particular cable or item was about. One of the ex-RN sailors, who was completely useless at any job he was given, asked me if he could polish the brass. When I asked why, he said that he had worked in a brass factory before joining the Navy. His job was to polish the finished product. I was doubtful but took a punt and went and spoke to the Chief Tiffy and asked if we could use the buffing machine in his workshop. He agreed after watching the young sailor doing his stuff. So, we had highly polished brass work which was covered in clear lacquer and much easier to wipe over.

XO Painter

With only one job to tick off in my book, I walked onto the quarterdeck and saw the XO in uniform, outside the guardrails, with a paintbrush in hand, painting the quarter light; that was the last job on my list. You can imagine the reaction when I said, "Able Seaman XO name, you are outside the guardrail without a lifeline, and what are you doing?"

He snorted and when he had finished, I followed up with, "Thanks for completing the last task in my notebook, and by the way, where did you get the paint from?" I won't quote the explosive reply. It did contain the words along the lines I was impossible, and he had drawn the paint himself from the paint locker, which happened to be at the other end of the ship. I went to take the paint from him so I could return it. However, he insisted on taking it all the way back to the other end of the ship to the Paint Locker.

I understand the Cocktail party was quite a success.

My Departure from HMAS *Sydney*

Having been in ship since the 16th of July 1949, I was posted back to HMAS *Watson* to undertake the Plot and Radar Instructor (PRI) course leaving the ship on the 26th of October, 1952.

I had spent 946 days (2.7 years) in the ship and was glad to be going ashore for a while. No doubt the XO was glad to see the back of me, although I think he also left at about the same time. We were never to serve together again.

Summary of My Service Aboard

As an under-experienced seaman A/PO, when I joined HMAS *Sydney*, I was leaving as a very able PO in both Seamanship and the Radar Specialisation. The experiences I had gained would prove to be very useful in the years ahead.

Chapter 18

HMAS *Watson* (3rd Stint)

27 October 1952 to 31 August 1953

Return to Navigation and Direction School

Re-joining *Watson*, it was nice to be back in a cabin on my own. To wake up each morning and, as one proceeded to the showers with toothbrush in mouth and a towel around the waist, to be able to pause and look down Sydney Harbour, a million-dollar view available to us lowly seafaring types.

Looking Down Sydney Harbour

It was nice to renew old acquaintances and new ones. I found out I would soon be undertaking the Plot and Radar Instructor Course. (PRI)

Initially, I was employed instructing until the beginning of the (PRI) course. This course was the highest level of training for the then Chief Petty Officers and Petty Officer of the Action Information System. In later years the Bosun PR Rank was replaced by Warrant Officer Rank like the Army Warrant Officer.

Plot and Radar Course

I won't bore you with the details and participation in the course. Enough to say we went deeper into the various aspects of plotting, radar types and operating and reporting, radio procedure and navigation and some man management. We were also to give presentations to the class to show that we were capable of instructing ranks below us. Almost all the class had come up through the Branch about the same time or a little after me. I can't remember exactly where I finished but it was near the top.

That Mind of Mine

During a break in the course, I was relaxing over a coffee in the instructor's office and, out of nowhere, my mind turned to Joan Hanna and whether she had received my Christmas card. I had known her long enough to know she would have sent me back a note if she had received it.

I found the telephone number for the Confectioner Union and rang. The call was answered by a gruff-voiced man. I asked to speak to Joan. He then demanded to know who I was and what I did. I gave him my name and told him I was a sailor who had not long returned from Korea. I indicated that I only wanted to ask Joan if she had received my Christmas card.

His next comment was, "She got it last week."

I think my next comment was, "I didn't know it took so long for a letter from Korea to reach its destination in Australia."

He then advised me that Joan had been overseas for a year and had only just got back. His comment was, "She will be in the office next week, so give her a ring then."

I later found out that the man was her uncle, Reg Jackson, and a member of the New South Wales Parliament.

I then started taking Joan out to dinner or to a picture show. On the occasions it was a picture show, on the way to her home, we would grab some fish and chips or some prawns and oysters or something other to eat. We seemed to enjoy one another's company at the tennis and attended numerous dances and other events.

To Be or Not to Be

I was returning to the CBD by train one night when I got the feeling that someone was watching me. Looking around, I noticed a woman smiling at me. She was sitting in the same seat on the opposite side of the aisle. Initially, I thought I must have met her somewhere; however, I could not place where or when and thought *Maybe she is trying to pick me up*.

She kept smiling at me even when we were getting off the train at Wynyard Station. I decided to give her the slip by not going out the main exit. I thought I had lost her until I stepped onto the escalator to get to the exit above. Behold, she was right behind me. We got to the top of the escalator, and I turned and asked her if we had met previously. She said no and she asked if I was from interstate. I said, "Yes, I'm from Western Australia."

She said, "I thought you might be and I wondered if you had anywhere to go while in Sydney."

I thanked her for her concern and was about to walk away when she gave me a telephone number and said, "If you ever want to come out to lunch, you could come and join my elderly mother and myself."

I thanked her, tucked the card into the top pocket of my jacket, and proceeded on my way.

I had forgotten all about this incident until one weekend when I was Duty Petty Officer. I found the card in the pocket of my uniform jacket. I put the card aside but, my mind kept niggling me, so I decided to give the lady a ring.

She said she was delighted to hear from me and that her sister and brother-in-law would be down for the next weekend, and I was very welcome to come for lunch. Curious, I took up the offer but said I probably couldn't get there before one or one-thirty as I would be playing hockey in the morning. She said that would be alright as they didn't intend to have lunch until about 2 pm.

The lady and her mother were very nice to me, as were the sister and her husband. I found out that the brother-in-law and sister owned a shop at Pearl Beach to the north of Sydney. Over time, I found out that the woman's late husband had worked in the newspaper area and that she had been left a typewriter business that also sold calculators.

I also ascertained that the lady who had invited me was a painter who, on weekends, would take her mother with her to sit with her as she painted. And so, a friendship developed that lasted until I sailed for England to qualify as an Officer. After her mother's death, it appears she remarried and moved to Victoria.

Car Driver

Following several visits, I was asked if I drove a car. I said I had a license but not much practice because I didn't own a car – didn't basically need one because of the tram and bus services and being at sea for long periods. She then asked if I would like to get some practice driving in Sydney.

She was looking for a way for her mother not to have to sit nearby while she painted. She thought I might like to drive the mother around while she painted. I agreed. It certainly prepared me for driving in a major city, and I was very thankful for this opportunity to improve my driving skills. Her mother, although quite old, had her wits about her and was good company, and we often recounted stories from our lives.

Painter Bill

During one of my visits, the lady appeared to be down in the dumps. I found out that she had received a quote to paint the gutters and eaves around her house. It was exorbitant. I looked around and saw she had a ladder that could reach the eaves and gutters without much of a problem. I suggested that I return her hospitality by undertaking the painting to be done. She agreed that I could do it piecemeal during my visits when I was not on duty. She purchased all the paints and brushes etc.

One day, I was painting a section when the mother appeared at the bottom of the ladder and asked me what I was thinking about as I painted. My reply was that I had put my mind into neutral and was not thinking about anything except where I was putting the paint. I'm not sure what she expected me to say, but I think she was unimpressed that I was not thinking of something useful.

Higher Education Test (H E.T.)

It was about this time that my Divisional Officer, an RN Officer on exchange, sent for me and said he wanted to discuss my future. He said he'd noted I had passed two or so Higher Education Tests that were needed if I wanted to qualify as an Officer. I made it clear I was not looking to become an Officer and was quite happy where I was in the pecking order.

We then discussed why I didn't want to be an Officer and my answer was I was at the top of my branch as a PRI and would no doubt be promoted to Chief Petty Officer in the not-too-distant future. I indicated that becoming an Officer was of no interest to me. After further discussion, he pointed out that he'd encountered a couple of people who he was responsible for in the Royal Navy who had a similar disposition toward our promotion. He suggested they undertake the practical test for what was known as the Bosun rank, which was recognised as Officer status. After much to and froing, he pointed out that passing the exam would not mean I would be selected for Officer training as I still had some educational exams to pass. To close the conversation, I said, "OK, I will take the practical exam.'

In my mind then, I thought I would get everyone off my back and fail the exam.

I WAS NOT TO KNOW A MUCH HIGHER AUTHORITY HAD OTHER IDEAS.

Practical Exam

On the appointed day, I fronted for a series of practical tests, which involved Parade Ground, Seamanship in several forms, Sailing and Power Boat Coxswain.

Parade Ground

I was first cab off the rank and reported to the Lieutenant Examiner, an old and bold from the Lower Deck. There was a small squad of personnel, with rifles at their side. He explained that he wanted me to take charge of the squad and that they had been trained and move them from their present position to another some distance away. When the squad arrived at the new position, he wanted the squad to be facing him with the present left-hand man of the front rank at the right-hand of the front rank in the new position.

I realised what he was asking me to do. I knew that it was one of the hardest exercises to get right with a trained squad.

I then marched to where the squad was and called them to attention, which they did without any hitch. I then said, "Slope Arms!" and rifles went in all directions to get them on the shoulder.

The squad had never been taught anything about rifle drill. The perfect Awkward Squad.

I tried not to show my disgust at myself for falling into the trap. So, I grabbed a rifle from one of the men and had them slope arms following me. The Examiner tried to interrupt, and I told him to let me complete his instructions and fail me if he must.

I also knew the squad could never do what he wanted as far as moving from one position to another and it would be a complete disaster to even attempt it. I also realised that to complete his instruction about the right-hand and left-hand man, I would have to do some basically simple movements of the squad. This basically meant marching to the nominated spot and requiring each rank to follow some basic instructions they understood and surprise, surprise, the Left-hand man was at the Right-hand end as required. The Examiner was shouting at me that I had not done what he wanted. I pointed out that his instruction was to move them from A to B and have them facing him with the left-hand man at the right-hand end.

Just then, a voice called out some words I don't remember, along the lines of, "Guns, he has carried out your Instruction." The voice was that of the President of the Examination Board who had watched the Pantomime. It just so happened that he was my Boss in the Training school.

Seamanship

As a practical Seaman with a lot of sea time, it was hard to make a mistake in tying a knot or answering specific questions. Also, by this time I had decided to not make any mistakes.

Boat work Examination

Sailing. The examiner for boat work, both sailing and power boat, was the Parade Ground Examiner.

I had to man a whaleboat with five oarsmen and myself as coxswain and sail out around the Balmoral Bay. I was aware that the wind often comes in from the east and, when sailing, you could keep the little pennant at the top of the mast at the same angle to the boat and find yourself doing a circle. As I was obeying the examiner's instructions to sail towards a particular point on the shore, he threw a life buoy over the side and told me to recover that life buoy.

With the wind that was blowing, I realised that I'd have to be very exact in sailing to the life buoy and stopping alongside to pick it up and even then, the wind, as it was, could play tricks and cause me to miss. I called the Bowman and told him I was going to keep sailing straight alongside the buoy, and he was to put his arm through the buoy and pull it in. I indicated he would be in the water with the buoy if he didn't put his arm through and bring it into the boat.

To the Examiner's surprise, I didn't stop as I approached the buoy, and the Bowman did what he was asked to do, and the buoy was recovered. The Examiner exploded and said I didn't do what he told me to do. I pointed out that what he had told me was to recover the buoy and I had done that. If that was not what he wanted me to do, then explain exactly how he wanted me to pick it up. By this time, he had had enough of me and told me to take him back alongside, which I did.

Powerboat

The Examiner decided not to come with me in the Powerboat. He gave me instructions to man the boat, which was then tied to the boom. His Instructions were to let go of the boom, proceed out into the Bay, and then return alongside. This I did as I had been instructed many years before and had done many, many times since.

I climbed down the ladder into the boat, had the stoker start up the engines, and, as I had been taught, had the Bowman let go of the security line and ladder and then backed away until the bow was clear of the end of the boom when I moved ahead and out into the Bay. I then brought the boat back alongside and was accused of not leaving the boom properly. The Examiner said I should have gone straight ahead.

Remember, this was around 1953/54, and I pointed out that because people had gone through the boom, there was considerable damage to the superstructure of the boat with a couple of dolphins missing. I pointed out that there was about £5,000 or more damage to the boat, and it would have to be taken out of service for a considerable time to effect repairs. I informed him that I had always been trained to back away from the ladder and lizard and make sure I went around the end of the boom so I did not damage the boat by fouling the ladder or securing the line.

Practical Test Results

I passed in all subjects undertaken.

Christmas Leave 1952

West Australian sailors were only given leave once a year instead of the two three-week periods that applied to sailors from the East. The reason was that it took five days each way to reach Perth.

As mentioned previously, the journey meant travelling by train from Sydney to Melbourne, to Adelaide, to Kalgoorlie, and on to Perth. We were seated eight to a compartment from Sydney to Port Pirie, where one would join what was then known as the Trans Train with sleeper accommodation to Perth. I was always able to get off at Kalgoorlie and save two days of travelling time.

I think I spent Christmas in Perth at my uncle and aunt's place in Inglewood. As my leave was coming to an end, I returned to Kalgoorlie for a few days before catching the train back east.

I also continued to take Joan out and I think it might have been about this time that I asked for her hand in marriage. She thanked me and said she was not yet ready to be married.

During this time at *Watson*, I was either employed instructing or in office administration.

Chief Petty Officer

I was promoted to CPO PRI on the 31st of March 1953, almost nine years since my enlistment. I continued the training of Radar Plot sailors until 16 August 1953 when it was another draft to HMAS *Sydney*.

Initially, I was posted to rejoin HMAS *Sydney*. However, when HMAS *Vengeance* was found to be unfit for service in Korean waters, I was switched to join HMAS *Vengeance*. I had spent almost nine and a half months ashore.

So once more it was up bag and hammock and be taken to HMAS *Vengeance*, then at Garden Island Dockyard.

Chapter 19

HMAS *Vengeance*

1 September 1953 to 5 August 1955

Dimensions	Draught	Engine
695ft x 80ft	21.6ft	Parsons Turbo
Armament		**Radars**
40mm Bofors x 12 and 32 x20 mm AA Guns.		2x277Q. 1x293M. 1x79
	Squadrons	
	808 Seafury 817 Firefly	

Introduction

HMS *Vengeance* was a Colossus Class Aircraft Carrier commissioned into the Royal Navy on 15 January 1945. After her workup in the Mediterranean, she operated in the East Indies fleet and then the British Pacific Fleet during World War 2. I seem to remember her in Hong Kong at some stage while serving in HMAS *Bathurst*. After the war she continued to serve in the British Home Fleet in the Mediterranean, off Africa, and conducting endurance trials in the Arctic. In September 1952, she commenced a refit in preparation for her Australian service.

RAN Commissioning

HMAS *Vengeance* was commissioned on 13 November 1952, on Loan, to the RAN at Devonport, England. She sailed from England to Australia in January 1953 under the Command of Captain Henry M Burrell RAN. She arrived in Sydney on 11 March 1953.

She began a three-month refit, and it was the initial intention that, on completion of a workup after the refit, she would see service in Korea. However, this was changed at the end of July, to HMAS *Sydney* replacing her in the Korean duty.

Prior to this point, I had received information that I would be posted to HMAS *Sydney*. However, this was later changed to me joining HMAS *Vengeance*.

Joining HMAS Vengeance

I joined HMAS *Vengeance* on 17 August 1953. I cannot remember if I joined before or after lunch. I would have been shown my mess and an empty locker to put my gear into. I would have completed my draft in routine and received my station card.

First Morning Aboard

Next morning, I made my way to the Chief's Dining hall. On entering, I saw some of the Chief Radio Mechanics I knew and was going to sit with them, when they indicated the Seaman Chiefs sat at the top table. They indicated where the President of the Mess was, his name and where he was sitting at the top table.

I made my way to the table and introduced myself to the President, who told me I was to sit with the Maintainers at the other table. I can only surmise that he never had anything to do with a Chief Plot and Radar Instructor to know we were Seaman first and Radar second. I duly made my way to the table indicated and had my breakfast.

Workup Exercises

On the 14th of September, *Vengeance*, with HMAS *Arunta* in company, sailed for Jervis Bay. Shortly after leaving harbour, a Sea Fury and a Firefly were embarked to exercise Flight Deck Drills.

I had made sure that the Radar personnel knew their jobs and had plenty of repetitive practise at plotting and the correct use of the radio and radio procedures.

Whilst en route to Jervis Bay, functioning trials of close-range weapons were carried out in the Dog Watches (1st DW 4 pm to 6 pm. 2nd DW 6 pm to 8 pm). Other exercises with the *Arunta* were also carried out before anchoring in Jervis Bay at 2130 (9.30 pm). The submarine HMS *Telemachus* was also in Jervis Bay under the control of RANAS *Nowra*. (HMAS *Albatross*)

When on duty in the Upper Ops Room, I always had one of my radar plotters listening to the manoeuvring frequency. I had a copy of the Signal Book, used by the signalmen, to report the manoeuvring orders to the Command (Captain and Officer of the Watch) This allowed those in the Ops room to be abreast of what was happening to the ships accompanying us. The manoeuvring messages to other ships are usually "execute to follow" or "immediate execute".

I am not sure if it was in this first period at sea or shortly after that the following incident took place.

During a period of manoeuvring exercises, my operator told me what the next order was to be. It was an immediate execute message and he read the meaning from the signal book. At the same time, I was listening at the voice pipe to the Bridge and heard the Signalman on the bridge telling the Command something different. Realising that the Signalman operator on the bridge or my radar operator had made a mistake, I rushed up to the Bridge and whispered into the ear of Chief Yeoman (Signalman) telling him to ask for a repeat of the order as I suspected his Signalman had got it wrong. He asked me how I knew that, and I replied, that in the Ops room I kept a listening watch on the manoeuvring frequency and a signal book. He immediately had his signalman request a repeat and the reply came back indicating that the signalman had been incorrect.

It turned out that the Chief Yeoman was the President of my mess. I had not recognised him initially when I went onto the Bridge, didn't expect any thanks, and got none.

Mess Table Seating Review

Next morning, I had started my breakfast when the Chief Butcher came to where I was sitting and told me that the President was inviting me to come and join him at the top table. As I was halfway through my breakfast, I replied to the President that I would join him at future meals. From then on, the Chief Yeoman and I became very good friends and often went ashore together.

During our runs ashore, the Chief Yeoman would be prepared to buy me a drink but would not let anyone pay for his. He told me that during his long service in the Navy, he had found that when drinking with a group, there was always someone who seemed to be absent when it was time for them to buy for the group. By purchasing his own drink, he was beholden to no one. From then on, we each paid for our own drink when we were together.

I had found that the other mess members were sociable, and we all got on well together.

Work Up

The workup consisted of touch-and-goes to requalify the pilots for deck landing. Nine Sea Furies of 808 Squadron and nine Fireflies were embarked on 17 September. In addition, during these operations, Radar Calibrations were carried out, and other plotting exercises were conducted to get the Ops Room Teams up to scratch. So, my days were busy making sure that all personnel were up to speed.

During the workup, we proceeded up the coast to operate off the Queensland Coast. Here, we transferred a shore party that had landed in Bundaberg to service aircraft that had to land ashore instead of on the ship.

Such Exercises as Aircraft Navex, Flight Drills and A/S Air Patrols were carried out. On one occasion, nine Sea Furies from HMAS *Sydney*, operating about 200 miles to the south, were detected at 25 miles flying on the deck (close to the wave tops). However, as *Vengeance* was refuelling HMAS *Quadrant*, no aircraft could be launched to intercept. Pity we didn't have CAP airborne to intercept them.

One interesting exercise that had not been done in my time in Sydney was the regular streaming of paravanes by *Vengeance*. Hadn't seen this done since my time in Minesweepers during and just after WWII.

Fly Over Brisbane

On September 29th, thirteen *Vengeance* aircraft rendezvoused with twenty-seven from HMAS *Sydney* over Caloundra and flew over Brisbane.

Towing Exercise.

On completion of flying on the 30th of September, HMAS *Quadrant* was ordered to stop, and *Vengeance* manoeuvred to take her in tow. When half a cable apart, a coston gun line was passed by Helo and towing lines passed. The tow was carried out at various speeds up to 9 knots.

October 1953

As the month of October began, the ship was operating in Hervey Bay, QLD. *Quadrant* was Plane Guard. On completion of the day's flying, HMAS *Quadrant* was refuelled and dispatched to Sydney. *Vengeance* headed for Caloundra. A pilot was embarked at 0250(L) and the ship proceeded towards Brisbane. A pall of bushfire smoke covered the area. The ship berthed at BHP Wharf, Hamilton Reach at 0714(L) on 2nd October, remaining alongside until 5th October.

I took the opportunity to visit friends of the lady who had befriended me in Sydney. They made me very welcome. They had a business that made straw brooms, and the son gave me some idea of what the business was. They took me to their Holiday home at Surfers Paradise.

The house was on the beach front. I was able to relax by swimming and basically doing nothing.

I was pleased with the break as it had been a busy time for me, with some different radar types to *Sydney* and getting to know my messmates and the personnel under me.

They had a daughter, Claire, and I was quite attracted to her, and we went out to see the sights of this area.

Back to Sea

When the ship departed Brisbane on October 5th, it proceeded south for Tasmania. Once again, I was in one or the other Operations Rooms, making sure all was well and that the radar operators on the displays were concentrating. The reason for heading south was to take up a position between Tasmania and New Zealand and act as a Safety ship for the aircraft participating in the London to Christchurch Air Race.

Sea-boats were exercised during the passage recovering life buoys. HMAS *Bataan* re-joined as Guard ship for flying operations at 0600 on 7 October. Flying consisted of rocketry, strafing and A/S Patrols. On completion, HMAS *Bataan* was refuelled. Strong southerly winds with squalls and rain marred flying as we headed for our Plane Guard Station for the London Christchurch Air Race. On the 9th, as we approached the Guard Station, flying resumed with rocketry and A/S Patrols.

In the evening, the Operations Rooms were placed in two watches and watch set on voice, D/F and Beacon Frequencies. All Radar operators were on high alert for aircraft contact. I made sure I was in the Lower Ops Room (Air Plot and Air Control)

London to Christchurch Air Race

Vengeance was required to be in a position be able to render assistance, if required, to aircraft participating in this race. For me, it meant putting the radar operators into two watches and making sure that the people manning the air radar detectors were on the ball and did not miss any radar contacts that came within the range of the radars.

At 0328(L) on the 10th of October, radar contact was made with an RAF Canberra aircraft, and voice communications were established; later, contact with two other *Canberra* aircraft, one flown by a RAAF pilot and the other by an RAF pilot, was made.

Vengeance's aircraft were on standby to be launched in case any of the Air Race aircraft had a problem before reaching the NZ area. When it was reported the three-race aircraft had landed safely, *Vengeance* aircraft were stood down.

At 1448(L), a *Canberra* aircraft was detected 50 miles to the westward. He was flying at 40,000ft and his speed was estimated to be 528 knots. At 1824(L) the leading aircraft in the transport section, a Viscount was detected at 45 miles to the north-east.

One other, a KLM DC.6 aircraft, the last in the race, was due to leave Brisbane shortly after midnight and a decision was made to start back towards Jervis Bay whilst still in position to render assistance.

Cyclone

At this time, a cyclone was approaching from the southwestern Tasman area and intensified into a gale. It quickly became a heavy storm that made conditions quite unpleasant with heavy seas and wind moving the ship heavily. Our escort, HMAS *Bataan* suffered quite a bit and required Dockyard assistance so was detached for Sydney, whilst *Vengeance* carried on to Jervis Bay.

Jervis Bay

On arrival in Jervis Bay on the 13th of October, the helicopter was flown off to bring pilots on board for deck landing practice. This practice was carried out in Jervis Bay because of the considerable sea and swell outside of the Bay. My lower operations room crew had returned to normal watches, and things were a bit more relaxed than when they were in two watches. Also, being in a Bay, the surrounding land mass cluttered the radar displays.

Whilst operating in Jervis Bay, the opportunity arose to spend some time at the Joint Anti-Submarine School at HMAS *Albatross* and undertake a course in A/S operations with the Captain and several ND Officers. It updated my knowledge on the subject.

From the 13th until the 24th of October, the ship exercised off Jervis Bay, carrying out exercises with the submarine, and other flying exercises, though I won't go into all the exercises. I was kept busy making sure that personnel were on top of the jobs in both plotting and detecting. On the 19th, the ship's Sea Furies flew over HMAS *Sydney* with HMAS *Bataan* in company, who were some 15 miles to the north en route to Korea. Thoughts did cross my mind that I could have been on *Sydney* instead of *Vengeance* if my original posting had not been cancelled.

An opportunity was taken to clean up the ship and the ship's side prior to returning to Sydney on the 21st of October to prepare for a Trafalgar Day Exhibition and for the Trafalgar Day ceremonies on the 24th of October. I smiled at the thought of not being in the Guard.

Trafalgar Day Exhibition

I cannot remember my task during this Exhibition; however, I would have been involved in escorting or supervising someone or other or supervising one of the displays. A brief outline of displays is as follows:

Hangar: in the hangar there was a display of airframes, engines and firefighting equipment safety equipment, radio, and electronics demonstrations.

The Flight Deck was rigged for the occasion.

Captain Cook dock and displays in marquees on Garden Island.

The Ships Open to visitors, and some 7000 visited HMAS *Vengeance*, with over 42,000 visiting the dockyard.

The Ship's Helicopter carried out a number of lifesaving displays.

The submarine Telemachus dived and surfaced in the dry dock.

The afternoon was very successful in showing off the ships and facilities.

Sea Again

On the 26th of October, *Vengeance* sailed. This time, however, it was a screened departure with two submarines waiting outside to attack the group. The Group was HMAS ships *Quadrant*, *Anzac*, and *Hawkesbury* as screen, with the Flag Ship HMAS *Australia* and HMAS *Vengeance* as the Main Body being protected by the escorts. For this period, I spent my time in the Upper Operations Room co-ordinating the information required by the Command.

After the departure exercise, two Fireflies were launched to help locate and assist in tracking and attacking the submarines. Later in the afternoon, the group was split in two and sailed one northward and one southward before turning when dark to carry out a NEX (Night Encounter Exercise). Again, it was necessary to be in the Upper Ops Room and make sure the right information was being passed to the Command on the Bridge.

On the 27th, flying and other exercises continued as we headed south for Port Phillip Bay, which was entered in the early morning of 8th October. I was closed for the entry into Port Phillip Bay and the ship berthed alongside the pier in Port Melbourne.

After entry to Port Phillip Bay, five Sea Furies and six Fireflies were launched for the flyover of Melbourne. They were recovered as we headed for our berth at Outer West Princes Pier astern of HMAS *Australia*.

Melbourne

The ship remained in Melbourne until 6 November. I took the opportunity to renew my friendship with the Bell family, who made me most welcome, and to get in touch with the family who used to put us up for the weekend leaves during our initial training at HMAS *Cerberus*. I also took the occasion to attend the Melbourne Cup.

I cannot recall if I was required to be on board during the ship's open-to-visitors period on November 1st and 3rd, when over ten thousand visitors came on board.

I do remember, however, that the helicopter carried out a winching display for the Press on November 2nd off Princess Pier.

Departure from Melbourne

Before departing on 6th November, the flag of the Flag Officer Commanding HM Australian Fleet was transferred to HMAS *Vengeance* for the duration of the Antisubmarine Exercises that were to be carried out over the next few days.

Perhaps it is pertinent to note the ships involved were HMA ships *Australia*, *Vengeance*, *Anzac*, *Quadrant*, *Hawkesbury*, *Condamine*, *Wagga*, *Cootamundra*, HM Submarines *Telemachus*, and *Tactician*.

Also participating in these exercises were six shore-based aircraft (RAAF) and five shore based Naval aircraft.

With all that Naval hardware involved I was kept busy in either the upper or lower operations rooms making sure that all my team were on the ball. Moving between the two rooms was sometimes tedious but had to be done.

Finally, these Joint Antisubmarine Exercises ended at 0800 on the 9th of November.

Having arrived off the entrance to Jervis Bay, the aircraft of both squadrons on board were disembarked, and I remember that the catapulting was photographed from the helicopter.

After anchoring in Jervis Bay, ground personnel, stores, and equipment of the two embarked squadrons were disembarked.

On the evening of 10th of November, the ship sailed from Jervis Bay berthing at the Fitting Out Wharf in Sydney the following morning. At midday on the 11th of November, the ship reverted to 48 hours' notice of steam, self-refit and leave.

During this period, I would have played tennis, cricket, deck hockey and rifle shooting when they were available.

Leave

I cannot recall the dates I took leave. I was very happy to be taking a break after the intensity of the past month's exercises, etc. However, I then embarked on the normal routine of taking the train to Melbourne, Adelaide, and on to Kalgoorlie, and I think at that stage I might have had a sleeper during the Adelaide to Kalgoorlie section. I would have left the train in Kalgoorlie and caught the tram home to be welcomed by my mother.

It was my usual Kalgoorlie for two weeks, Perth for two or so weeks and then back to Kalgoorlie for the remaining leave before embarking on the return train trip. I can't remember if I went into the bush with Uncle Harry during this leave.

December 1953

The ship was either alongside or in Captain Cook Dry Dock all of December. I would have arrived back sometime in late December. I have no idea where I spent Christmas Day or New Year's Eve. My mind is completely blank on this period.

I do remember that in the New Year we would be escorting the *Gothic* with the Queen and Prince Phillip embarked.

January 1954

On 7 January, the ship proceeded to sea and proceeded to Jervis Bay rendezvousing with HMAS *Arunta*. There were screening exercises between the two ships, and that meant that I was in the upper Ops room keeping an eye on things. Later, *Anzac* was detached to return to Sydney and *Vengeance* proceeded to anchor in Jervis Bay about dusk.

From the 8th to 10th January, the ship remained in Jervis Bay, preparing the ship side for painting later in the month. I remember the Outline Illumination Lights being rigged and tested.

When available I trained my people in voice procedures and plotting to get them up to speed for the days ahead.

From the 11th to the 20th of January, the two squadrons re-embarked, and after a series of practice landings, they were back in all sorts of air exercises and manoeuvring in preparation for the days ahead. The ship returned to Sydney on the 22nd of January.

From the 22nd to the 26th, the ship was painted overall and replenished with oil fuel, stores, and ammunition.

The ship sailed on 27th, with *Anzac* as plane guard, and flying recommenced with emphasise on the type of flying that would be required when the ship met up with the Royal Yacht. I remember conditions were not ideal, but the pilots did well in coping with difficult flying conditions.

Vengeance and *Anzac* returned to Sydney on completion of flying on the 29th of January securing to No 4 Buoy about noon. HMAS *Albatross* Blue Jacket Band joined.

At 1500, *Australia*, the Flagship led Anzac, Quadrant, and Vengeance out of harbour and headed south-east. Later, they rehearsed the joining procedure for the rendezvous with the Royal yacht, HMAS *Condamine*, which acted as the Royal Yacht.

I was very pleased to see that the training given to my plotters and other people in the operations room worked very well.

The weather conditions were very foul, with low visibility, drizzling rain, gale-force winds, and a heavy persistent swell. These conditions meant the plotters had to be at the top of their game to ensure that the position of the ships in the company was accurately plotted.

The month ended with the ships proceeding to take over as escort of the Royal yacht with the Queen on board.

February – April 1954

Royal Escort Duties

At 0900 on February 1st, a radar contact at 25 miles was identified as *Gothic*, the Royal Yacht. About 1030, the Australian ships turned to form an escort for the Queen. Unfortunately, the weather conditions prevented any flying. As the Australian ships formed the previous Escort, HMNZS *Black Prince*, hauled away its task completed.

Between February and April 1954, *Vengeance* was employed on Royal Escort duties and was one of several warships escorting Her Majesty Queen Elizabeth II and His Royal Highness the Duke of Edinburgh. HMAS ships *Anzac* and *Bataan* were part of the Royal Escort to SS *Gothic*, with the Royal Party embarked, remained in company until the tour reached the Cocos Islands on her way home.

HMAS Australia

SS Gothic

HMAS Vengeance

During the time in company with the Royal party, the Shipwright Officer marked out on the flight deck the Queen's signature. See picture below.

Her Majesty is reported to have commented that it was 'a most original forgery'.

HMAS Bataan Collision

During a replenishment operation, carried out after leaving Cocos Islands, and in deteriorating weather, HMAS *Bataan* was damaged in a collision with *Vengeance*. I felt for my old ship, the *Bataan*. Unfortunately, *Bataan* was drawn into the collision, being sucked into the side of *Vengeance* due to the weather that caused her to get to close.

Port Visits

Following the completion of Royal Escort Duty, *Vengeance* visited Manus Island and Rabual, before returning to Sydney in May 1954. During this time and on Royal Escort Duties the ship had continued to operate aircraft as the weather permitted.

However, *Vengeance's* time as an Operational Carrier was ending and the ship was informed that it would take over New Entry Sea training from HMAS *Australia*.

July 1954

Fleet Training Ship

Vengeance commenced service as a Fleet Training Ship, in July 1954, taking over from HMAS *Australia*. Besides Permanent Service Trainees, National Service Trainees were also embarked.

All aircraft and their stores were transferred ashore, and a Chief Gunnery Instructor (Reg) and I were seconded to the Training Organisation that was established on board. We worked from an office at the end of the Hangar. My job was to look after the paperwork for the various classes, subject, timing, and instructor, and for the training activities that were to be undertaken. My colleague, Reg, tended to look after all the Parade Ground drills and for the training of the Guard used when leaving and entering the harbour.

Training Classes

Our main activity was to embark student recruits from HMAS *Cerberus*. To embark the Classes, the ship sailed up to the entrance of the Creek known as Han's Inlet that led to HMAS *Cerberus*. It was not unusual to be taking up to 400 trainees up one side of the ship whilst discharging a similar number down the other side of the ship using the boats that brought trainees from shore. Sometimes, we entered Port Phillip Bay to discharge some, or all, of the trainees to a beach to be bused back to HMAS *Cerberus*.

Boating Accident

On one occasion, one of the ship's boats was taking the recruit class to land on a beach in Port Phillip Bay so they could return by bus to HMAS *Cerberus*. Just before beginning the approach to the beach, the boat broached and put everyone into the water. You can imagine the panic. I cannot recall if any of the Recruits were wearing lifejackets when they went into the water. I can't remember if any of the trainees were drowned. However, one of my future Commanding Officers in later life jumped into a boat and then the water and helped save some of the recruits.

Reg's (my fellow Training Chief) father had been a Gunnery Instructor and Reg followed in his footsteps. On one occasion, I recall a recruit entering the forward part of the hangar. Reg spotted him and ordered him to stop. The poor chap stopped dead in his tracks, as if hit by a bat, at the sound of Reg's very loud voice coming out of nowhere. Reg was at the other end of the hangar at the time, such was the power of Command of the Gunnery Instructor.

One of the training areas we spent time in was the Great Barrier Reef because of the suitable weather for boat work and the like.

The ship's rifle team, of which I was a member, managed to set up a rifle range on one of the uninhabited islands in the Barrier Reef. We would go ashore and place the red warning flags and make sure that it was clear for us to fire in the range area we had prepared. Before firing commenced, we would go down and prise oysters off the rocks, open them, and after each shot would swallow an oyster. In addition, some of us would prise the extra oysters off and fill up glass jars and take them back to share with messmates.

Brisbane

From time to time, the ship would sail to Brisbane, and shore leave would be granted for the weekend, especially the Brisbane natives. I would ring the people I had stayed with earlier, and we would go to Surfers Paradise for the weekend. From time to time, I bought them oysters and they appreciated my gift very much.

Later visits also saw me invited to stay for the weekend with them at Surfers Paradise. I think I have already mentioned their holiday house was right on the beachfront, and I was able to enjoy a lot of swimming and looking around Surfers Paradise and the adjacent areas where they would take me for a picnic or similar. I became interested in their Straw-broom-making business and its operation, and it made me think about what I would do when my Navy time was up in a couple of years in 1956. I also got the impression they liked me and would be prepared to help me settle into civilian life.

Their daughter Clare and I became quite friendly, and we would go the pictures, or a dance and I fell under her spell. I think the family were happy for her. Eventually, we became engaged.

Bringing Home RAAF No.77 Squadron

On 27 October 1954, *Vengeance* sailed from Sydney for Japan to embark aircraft, personnel and equipment of No 77 Squadron, Royal Australian Air Force, and return them to Australia.

The trainees on board were delighted to be going abroad during their time on the ship. You can imagine the excitement of going ashore in Japan and seeing the sights.

However, this trip did not stop the fairly intense training they were getting, particularly in the operating and daily workings in their parts of ship, for the engine room, or the stores or wherever.

As you would expect, those who had been to the Far East in the past tended to embellish their stories of their time there. The eager ears listened with great intent to some of the fabricated stories and no doubt visualised all sorts of details that were nowhere near the truth.

As we approached the Equator, preparations were made for the visit by King Neptune and his staff.

King Neptune and His Court

Eventually everything was in place by the appointed day for the visit.

The King and his Court appeared from nowhere and made their way along the deck to where his chair had been set up. Once the King and his Court had been seated one of his team read the proclamation on the previous page.

After the Proclamation, there were other announcements of those who had to front the King to respond to the charges that were laid against them. Some of the Ship's Company, who had already crossed the line before, were summoned and there was usually some good old-fashioned banter until the King pronounced guilty, and the person before him was led away for his punishment to be carried out.

They were usually smeared with a filthy, smelly substance and then tossed into the campus pool which had been set up near the King's throne. Of course, there was a lot of bantering coming.

Each victim received a copy of the King's proclamation below.

Then it was on to Japan

Japan

On arrival in Japanese waters the ship proceeded to Iwakani where 77 Squadron was based. *Vengeance* embarked 77 Squadron and their planes and equipment and stores before heading for Yokosuka.

Yokosuka

For those who had not visited Japan before, the introduction to Japanese bars was interesting to watch.

Using the same procedure we had used in HMAS *Bataan* and HMAS *Sydney*, where the girls were told we drink beer, they drink beer, this soon sorted out the girls who were only interested in having us buying them expensive sticky green drinks at an inflated price. They soon realised Australian Sailors were not as well paid as the Americans who were based in Yokosuka.

The ship arrived back in Sydney on 3 December 1954. It was again time to leave back to the West.

Annual Leave

With my engagement, I thought it opportune for Claire to meet my parents. She accompanied me on my Christmas leave in 1954 to meet my family. They liked her, and I gave her a tour of Kalgoorlie and Boulder and showed her where I used to work. We spent Christmas as usual, at my uncle and aunt's place in Inglewood. I showed her around Perth and the beaches and the city. All seemed to be going quite well.

After Christmas she returned home whilst I re-joined the ship and continued New Entry training.

1955

Breaking of Engagement

After Christmas 1954, on what was to be my last visit to the Brisbane family, I was staying with them as usual. I knew that, from time to time, my girl was subject to migraine attacks. Generally, she retired until the attack had passed and was then her normal self.

At the end of this visit, my girl told me, in no uncertain terms, that the engagement was off, and she had no desire to marry me. I asked if I had done something wrong to upset her and received no reply. I knew that I had been very careful in my dealings with her as far as advances etc. was concerned. I was both surprised and taken aback and said if that was the case I accepted and left it to her to sort out, with her friends, what was to happen to the various presents she had received. She gave me the ring back. Before the ship sailed, I wrote a letter formally accepting the breaking of the engagement and another to the parents thanking them for their hospitality.

I subsequently received a letter saying she had made a mistake. I replied that I was not prepared to go on with the engagement that she had broken.

Naturally my Sydney Lady, and her mum, who had introduced me to the family, were very disappointed.

Resume Training Duties

In February 1955, *Vengeance* completed a three-month refit. Returning from Christmas leave I bumped into Joan Hanna, and we resumed our friendship, going to dances, having a meal in the city or at her home and generally getting re-acquainted.

On completion of the refit, *Vengeance* resumed her training duties until late April. At this time the ship was prepared for return to the Royal Navy. I was also informed I had been selected for the Bosun Plot and Radar course in England. I decided I may as well give it a go.

Second Engagement

Vengeance was due to sail for England on 16 June 1955. I had taken Joan to the pictures about five or six days before sailing. She had congratulated me on being selected for Officer training. On the way home from the pictures, we picked up a bundle of prawns and oysters. When I started to peel the prawns as normal, she told me she would do that and for me to go and sit in the adjacent dining room.

I was a bit surprised and, while sitting waiting for the prawns to be all peeled, out of nowhere I thought, *maybe if she's peeling the prawns for me tonight, will she be prepared for a proposal of marriage?* I didn't spring this on her until I was about to leave when I pointed out that we seemed to get along very well together and that I realised I loved her; we had many of the same interests and religious outlook. I again emphasised I could be away for at least one year and possibly three. I then proposed and was perhaps a little surprised when she accepted.

I pointed out that it was not possible to get a special license within five days and she replied she was happy to come to England and be married there. She pointed out that her sister could come and be her bridesmaid. We then agreed it was up to me to arrange the place and time for the marriage to take place, preferably in London where she had some friends she would stay with until she was married.

I formally asked her parents for her hand in marriage. We went together the next day and I put a ring on her finger. We both went to the Church in Haymarket to say thank you for bringing us together. Those last few days were hectic as you could imagine.

Passage to England

On 16 June, *Vengeance* sailed from Sydney with almost 1000 Officers and Sailors who were to commission HMAS *Melbourne 2*. It was a long passage, visiting Singapore followed by Columbo, Aden, Port Said and Malta, arriving at Devonport on 13 August 1955. From Devonport, the ship sailed to Portsmouth where I disembarked.

Sunday Transfer Ashore

I think it was the 6th of August when a small Royal Naval truck, manned by two sailors, arrived alongside to take me to HMS *Dryad*. I put my bag and hammock, my wooden gun box, containing 2 x Lee Enfield, 303 rifles, my rifle bag with telescope, tripod, and cleaning gear in the back of the truck and joined the driver and mate in the front seat.

The look on the sailor's faces was one of 'who is this guy coming ashore with rifles' et cetera. On the way to HMS *Dryad*, we drove along the top of Portsmouth Hill passing one of the old forts being used for training. Later, I was to spend time at one of these forts learning about, and familiarising myself, with the different types of Radar that the Australian Navy did not have.

The sailors were not very talkative. I was able to take in some of the scenery on the route and overlooking Portsmouth harbour. Eventually we arrived at HMS *Dryad* and so began my three-year stint with the Royal Navy.

Chapter 20

HMS *Dryad*

6 August 1955 to 17 December 1956

Introduction

HMS *Dryad* was situated in Southwick House estate, to the north of Portsmouth. The 1944 D-Day Landing HQ was in Southwick House. A picture of the House and Map are shown below.

Southwick House

D-Day Wall Map June 1944 Southwick House

The buildings on the estate were used to train Radar Operators and Plotters. This is where I was to be trained as a Bosun and Plot and Radar Officer.

Besides instruction at HMS *Dryad*, the Course would entail training at other Specialist schools in the Portsmouth area and elsewhere. One thing of note was the use of the horse stalls in the Stable to set up plotting rooms with tables as used in an Operations Room. In HMAS *Watson* the Action Information Training Centre was an exact copy, as I think I have mentioned previously.

Posting In

I left HMAS *Vengeance* at Portsmouth on a Sunday afternoon. A small truck had arrived with two sailors. As I mentioned in the last chapter ending, I don't know what they thought as they loaded my Hammock, Kit Bag, go ashore bag with odds and ends, my wooden Rifle Case holding two .303 rifles and my Rifle bag containing telescope and my cleaning gear.

When everything was loaded, I sat between the two sailors and was driven from the Dockyard to HMS Dryad. Initially, the truck travelled on the road to London until we reached the top of Portsmouth Hill, running east-west. Here, we turned left and drove along the top, giving an overview of Portsmouth and its Harbour. We passed a fort on the way, and I was told it, and another, were used for training.

On arrival and being checked in at the Regulating Office, I surrendered my rifle gear for security reasons; my kit was unloaded at the Chief Petty Officers Accommodation Block, and I was shown my sleeping quarters. All the other Chiefs were living ashore, I was told.

I was shown where the Dining Room and CPOs Recreation area was and the time of the evening meal. I spent the rest of the afternoon unpacking, storing my clothes and acquainting myself where the bathrooms, etc, were.

My First RN Meal

At the appointed time I went to the Dining Room and there was nobody there. After a short wait I made myself a cuppa, found the toaster and made myself a small snack and went back to my cabin. There was no one in the Chiefs recreational room and I had a game of snooker and went back to my room and arranged it as I wanted it to be.

Breakfast

After a shower and shave I went to the Chiefs Dining Room and found several Chiefs having breakfast. I introduced myself and they responded and made me feel welcome to join them. The President of the Mess came and introduced himself and asked if I had settled in OK and if I had any problems to seek him out. He advised me of the lunch arrangements and also my evening meals from then on.

The Daily Tot of Rum

Some day or two later he sought me out and said, "You have not been drinking your tot."

A tot was a rum issue that Chief Petty officers and Petty officers received neat, as opposed to the sailors whose tot was watered down. That night I found that there were three tots in a bottle, so I transferred them to my own bottle after having a couple of sips.

The RAN did not adopt this Royal Navy custom when it was formed.

Training Office

After Colours at 8 am, I found the Training Office. The Training Officer advised that my course would not be starting for some time and asked if there was anything I would like to do prior to the course starting. I said I would like to get up to date on their radars and to watch the training of plotters and operators to see if there were any differences to the way we trained people.

I was told to make myself at home. I was shown how to order transport to where the live radars were and then left to my own devices.

Pre-Course

I decided that I would stay at *Dryad* for the first few days and acquaint myself with their plotting training. I discovered that there was little difference between what I was observing and the way we trained in Australia. There were Wren RPs working at the plotting tables. They wore the same square neck tops as sailors. When a Wren leaned over the surface plotting table to plot a contact, it was quite a distraction, I'm sure, for the sailors working on the other side of the table, not to see the breasts of the girls as they were in full view.

I found that their Radio Operator training was the same as ours. After a couple of days, I took transport to where the radar sets were located at a second fort on the top of Portsmouth Hill. This was some miles from *Dryad* and I enjoyed looking out over Portsmouth each morning. Here I was able to learn about those radars, which were quite different to those I had operated in Australia. This experience was to stand me in good stead later when on course and at sea afterwards.

Petty Officers Recreation Area

It was not long after I joined *Dryad* that a Petty Officer came up to me and said, "Chief, seeing you are the only Chief living on board, you are welcome to come into our area and join us each night if you'd like some company." I thanked him and accepted the offer and, when not studying, I would go in and enjoy a game of snooker or darts or just have a drink with them.

I found that, besides the Petty officers, there were civilians, known as Wardroom Attendants (WRA) (previous CPOs, POs, or ex-Sailors). These people were employed as Stewards in the Wardroom at Table or in looking after the cabins.

I came to enjoy the company and, whenever I had some rum tots saved up, I would take them in and invite anyone who wanted to have what was called "sippers." This little tipple was to be rewarded later in my career.

Sunday Mass

As my first Sunday ashore approached, I inquired if there was a Mass celebrated on board. The answer was no. I was told the nearest Catholic Church was in a suburb called Cosham, at the foot of Portsmouth Hill. I was given the Mass times and found out about a bus and its timetable that came past the front gate of the base. This allowed me to attend Mass every Sunday.

One day, whilst in the Petty Officers recreation area, one of them approached me and said, "Chief, I noticed you at Mass on Sunday. If I am on board from now on, I will take you and bring you back from Mass each Sunday." So began a relationship that was to last until the Petty Officer, Eric W, died in Canada many, many years later.

New Car

During the period before starting the course, I purchased a new car, the Hillman Minx sedan. I was able to use my International Driver's license for the first year in England. With Eric as supervisor, I learnt all about entering and leaving roundabouts and, for the first time, had the left and right turn indicators to get used to.

Skittles

From time to time, the Petty Officers would leave the base and visit a Pub and introduced me to what I called Skittles. The wooden balls used were so well worn that they no longer ran true to the skittles.

Cricket

The Petty Officers asked me to fill in a place in their team that was to play the Officers. There were several Australian Officers in the Officers' teams. When one of them came in and saw me standing there, he said, "Ritchie, if you don't move, I am going to drive the ball straight through you." He drove a ball straight at me and, having caught it, I said, "Thanks, you are out." He was furious. I was not to know that later in my career he was to be my Boss at HMAS *Watson* and didn't make my life easy.

Wedding Planning

During of our conversations, I mentioned to Eric that I intended to be married in London in December. He promptly told me he was a professional Best Man and had acted as such on quite a few times. He also stated that if I didn't have one, he would be happy to act as my best man. I accepted his offer and told him I would be getting married in December. He said there was a suitable church in London, St James, Spanish Place. So, on the next weekend he took me to London in his car. I approached the Priest in Charge, and the date was set for the 17th of

December at 10 am. He also agreed that the Catholic Padre, who had been on *Vengeance* with me, could conduct the ceremony.

My next task was to find out from the Birth, Death, and Marriage Registrar for that area of London, what were the residential requirements. This was three weeks. I didn't mention it to him that I would be on course in Portsmouth during the lead up to the agreed date. However, as Kalgoorlie Kid, I devised a way to meet the requirement.

I had been staying at a Service Hostel not far from the church. I used to book a room for the weekend. I approached the manager and asked if I could have a room for three weeks as I was going to be married just around the corner. I paid him in advance and explained that I would not be using the room during weekdays if he needed to use it. I told him I would be leaving a suitcase in the cloakroom. He agreed. So, officially, I was a resident of London for the required three weeks.

Reception

I had noticed a nice-looking hotel about a block and half from the church. I approached the Functions Manager, and he showed me a side room that was just about the right size for the number of guests I expected. I explained we were getting married in St James just up the road on 17 December. He said he had no problem with that date in providing the room for us for the Wedding Feast.

I sat with him and discussed menus, and there was one he suggested that I thought would be most suitable for the situation, and my pocket. Then it was on to suggesting the liquid refreshments.

When I mentioned we would have Champagne, he said I couldn't afford it, and that he would look after a suitable wine to go with the meal and any beers and soft drinks that might be required. I made a deposit, and from then on, I made sure I didn't spend anything unnecessarily.

Joan's Pre-Marriage Accommodation

Joan had arranged for her sister and herself to stay with friends she had made during her European tour previously. She had also told me that the person giving her away would be the Agent General for New South Wales and she would inform any of her guests of date and time.

I later issued invitations to my classmates and their wives, and all preparations were now complete.

The Officer Course Commences

I can't remember the actual date the course started; I think it was sometime in November. After an initial period at HMS *Dryad*, the first place visited was Whale Island, the home of Parade Ground Drill, Gunnery, and the like training, where we were to be put through our paces doing squad and rifle drill and various lectures on all aspects of Gunnery and missiles.

Whale Island

Whale Island in Portsmouth was close to the centre of Portsmouth, and the Base was on an island, reached by a bridge.

The day normally began with a Parade and Inspection of the various groups under training, like our class, by a Senior Officer from the School. It normally was under a very large shelter or shed to start with. After this, the parade would be marched off and would have to pass a saluting platform.

If the Reviewing Officer thought a group was not marching correctly, they would be made to go around again. Those who passed the test would then have to complete a circuit around the main Administration Buildings. There were about eight gun or similar positions, equally spaced around the circuit. The classes would double march up to the position where a Gunnery instructor would take charge and march the group back and forth until he was satisfied with the drill. Then, it would be a double march to the next position. There were usually classes going both ways around the circuit.

One of our classmates had previously served at Whale Island. After a day or so of going around the circuit and having passed the first gun position, he suddenly led us into a small open-air passage between two buildings. The class was far enough off the route not to be noticed. Those who smoked had a cigarette, and then we marched out and back the way the class had come. Instead of doing eight back-and-forth, we did two. No one noticed.

A Beasty on Parade

A Sub Lieutenants Class was about to pass out (complete training) and, after the normal morning Parade and inspection, they marched off to do the circuits. As they left the end of the covered Parade buildings, one of the classmates led an elephant from behind the shed and moved to the rear of the group as they marched past.

The Officer reviewing the march past obviously saw the humour of the occasion and ordered the class to repeat the circuit again. As you can imagine, the other classes laughed a lot. The elephant was from a circus nearby, and the Sub-Lts had got the owner to lend them the elephant.

At the time the elephant was brought on the base, the tide on the causeway alongside the bridge, normally used to enter the base, was at Low Water. The sentry on the entrance had rung the Duty Officer and reported an elephant approaching the Base. The Duty Officer thought it was a joke and ignored the call.

Motor Car Parking

Somehow, Commander Supply upset the Subs on course. After he had retired for the night, they moved his small car from the parking lot upstairs to outside and right up to the door of his cabin on the first floor. You can imagine his reaction the next morning. However, nobody saw anyone taking the car up.

These two events are just some of the interesting actions by Sub Lieutenants and others got up to.

After completing the Whale Island section of our course, it was time to break for Christmas and head off to London with Eric to be married.

After Joan and her sister's arrival in London, I did not have the opportunity to catch up with her. I had posted all the details of the wedding arrangements to where she would be staying and talked to her on the phone. The first time I saw her in London, was as she walked down the aisle.

Our Marriage

Eric joined me at the hostel I stayed at, and we drove my car and parked it outside the hotel where the reception was to be held. It had been snowing but was basically clear as we walked to the church. As we approached the church, we noticed there was a red carpet laid to the approaches and a canopy over the entrance path. I didn't think it was for this Australian pair. It turned out to be for some VIP's wedding later in the day.

The Church

St James. Spanish Place, London

Note: St James was the Catholic Church used by Catholic Nobility and VIPS.

The Church was magnificent. The Australian Padre conducted the service, and we signed the appropriate forms on the Altar.

The Chaplain then led us into the Sacristy where we had to participate in a **Civil Marriage Service** because the Padre was not licensed to conduct a marriage in England.

The Registrar of BDM's was there to supervise the ceremony and allowed the Padre to conduct the Civil Service although the Registrar signed the documentation.

We walked down the aisle to be greeted by many compliments and comments and well wishes for a happy marriage.

Finally, I was married to my wonderful partner, and we didn't know it then, but it was to last 57 years.

Leaving the church, we didn't worry about any transport and walked the short distance to the Hotel. When we arrived, we had pictures taken alongside the car and in the Dining Hall Room.

The guests also wanted to get pictures of us, so we stood by the car that was covered in snow. Once everyone had taken their pictures, it was moving into the Dining Room and getting on with the luncheon.

Everyone enjoyed the lunch and the drinks provided. Towards the end of the lunch, the Agent General asked where I had got the wine from. I explained that the Functions Manager had agreed to select a suitable wine and was glad that he enjoyed it as I had. I then learnt the Agent General would like to obtain some of the wine, so I asked the Steward attending us to ask the Functions Manager to come in. I introduced him to the Agent General and he sorted out the purchase.

Eventually, the lunch finished, and Joan went off to get changed for our trip to the south-west of England. I had arranged for her bags to be put in the car and everyone came out to say farewell. I thanked Eric for his help.

Honeymoon

Joan's friends had organised with one of their friends for us to rent her holiday cottage. As we drove off there was the usual bits and pieces bouncing along the road and a sign across the back saying JUST MARRIED. Once we were around the corner, I was able to remove the bits and pieces and the sign and navigate our way out of London.

It was an uneventful road trip and we both spent the time relaxing and enjoying one another's company. We were able to locate the holiday home and the key and settled in. Initially, we had enough shillings to keep the gas fire going until it was bedtime.

Fortunately, the bed had plenty of covering and we slept holding one another closely. I was exhausted from the course and finally able to relax now the ceremony was over. We both slept like a log, enjoying being able to sleep in and not having to worry about anything.

The next morning, we went for a stroll around the village where the holiday home was located. We found somewhere to obtain a handful of shillings so we could boil the kettle and turn on the heater.

For the rest of our stay, we toured the area and visited Yeovil until, on the morning of Christmas Eve, we returned to an area just outside London to stay with Eric's parents and enjoy Christmas Day with them.

Eric's Father

Eric's father had been in the Royal Navy and had in fact been part of the crew bringing one of the first RAN ships out from England. On retirement, he had become a Confidential Courier taking correspondence around various facilities in London.

He had received three turkeys from people he called on, and for the first time, I enjoyed roast turkey. However, by the end of our stay, with various meals of turkey and finally turkey soup, I had exceeded my preference for turkey.

The family made us most welcome, and we felt like part of the family. It was a most satisfying and relaxing break from the Course.

First Home

Part of the preparation for our marriage was seeking out a suitable house for Joan and myself to live in whilst on course and if necessary after I qualified.

I had consulted a couple of agents and accepted what had been a Granny Flat attached to a two-storey house in Widly Close; I think was the name of the street. It was located on the top of Portsmouth Hill. The owners of the property, who lived in the Main House, made us very welcome.

Knowing that I would be going to other training establishments around and outside Portsmouth, Joan asked if I would mind her taking her sister to the Continent. I must say that I had expected this and agreed that they could go.

Return to Training Course

All too soon it was time to return to my Officers training course. The following establishments visited were in the Portsmouth area.

HMS *Vernon*

HMS *Vernon* was the Antisubmarine Warfare and Diving School. The most significant aspect of attending this establishment was the diving component. The first exercise was to go inside a Compression Chamber to establish the level of pressure we could stand. I found I had a problem with my ears and was unable to go to any significant depth.

We were taken to Horsey Lake and introduced to being dressed in a wet suit and using a snorkel. Being January, the water was extremely cold. One of the exercises was to swim, using the snorkel, about a quarter of a mile up this lake, land on the opposite side, and then run back to opposite where we had entered the water and swim across. As we got out of the water it was freezing. There was a normal-sized bath filled with fresh cold water; some used this to get a little warm before taking off their wetsuits. I only wanted to get out of the wetsuit, towel myself down and get into some warm clothes.

We were also trained in the use and wearing of deep-sea diving equipment. However, because of my ear problem, I was unable to descend to any depth.

Soon, the torture of swimming in icy water was over and we returned to *Vernon* for the next part of our training.

Problem. Because I had not been able to do all of what was required, I was told that I would have to come back and qualify in diving because of my cold. When I asked what cold, I was told the one that prevented me from swimming deep and using the deep-sea diving equipment. I pointed out that I did not have a cold and the problem was my ears. When they wanted to continue arguing, I asked if I could use a phone to call the Naval Attaché, in London. I was referred to the sickbay, and the matter was resolved that because it was a pressure problem in my ears, I would not have to come back and do the course again.

We were then instructed in the various aspects of Anti- Submarine Warfare, undertook the necessary exams, and finally left HMS *Vernon*.

HMS *Mercury*

HMS *Mercury* was where Communications and Electronic Warfare (EW) Instruction took place. We received advanced training in EW usage as well as being updated on all the latest Communications systems. After more exams, it was onto the next School.

I was able to be home with Joan after she returned from the Continent with her sister. Eventually, her sister sailed for home.

New House

Our lease of the Granny Flat was coming up for renewal when we noticed an Australian style Bungalow, at the end of the street we lived in, was up for lease. We quickly made an offer, and it was accepted. We were able to move our goods and chattels without the need of a removalist.

Unfortunately, I have mislaid a picture of this house,

HMS Mercury

HMS *Mercury* was the communication training centre located on the outskirts of Portsmouth. Here we were instructed in the various aspects of communication and the use of codes. More Exams and I can't think of anything else to say of my time at *Mercury*. It was nose down and trying to pick questions we would be asked in a three-hour exam.

Joan's Pregnancy

To our great joint joy, Joan became pregnant. After a while she had a few problems with the pregnancy and the wife of one of my contemporaries, (Len P), who had done the same course as me one year earlier, insisted we move in with her and she would care for Joan, because she knew the pressures I would be undergoing from what her husband had been through.

Betty knew that I would be absent from the area from time to time and Joan should not be alone. We were more than happy with this arrangement.

Each night, after dinner, Betty would insist on me studying in the dining room for about two hours. She would bring me a hot drink after about an hour. You can imagine how much I appreciated this for I was able to review that day's instruction and any other area I felt I needed to review.

NBCD School

I think we returned to HMS *Dryad* after *Mercury*. At some time, we went to the Nuclear Biological Chemical and Damage Control School. (NBCD) for training in Firefighting, Damage Control and practical exercises for things that could happen in simulated ship situations of firefighting, flooding, and other incidents that could occur in the structure of a ship, so we practised and were tested on all likely types of incidents that had arisen in ships. We also underwent instruction on Nuclear, Biological and Chemical warfare.

These exercises exercised the mind and proved exhausting.

Finally, more exams and comments on the practical exercises we had carried out.

Then it was training at centres outside Portsmouth.

HMS *Harrier*

The next part of our training was carried out at HMS *Harrier*. *Harrier* was the RN School of Aircraft Direction, Royal Navy School of Meteorology, and a RN Radar Plotting Training School. I seem to remember that we spent up to five days or more learning about the various requirements in each of these areas.

On our first night, there was an incident in our dormitory.

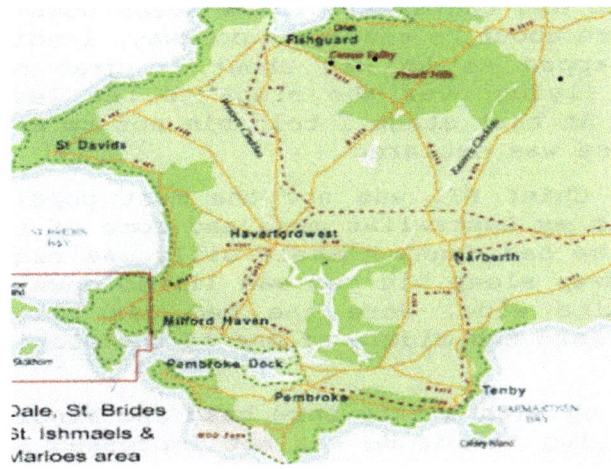

Incident

There were some incidents in the dormitory where we slept.

On the first night, my Australian classmate and I went to get into our beds to find someone had short-sheeted our beds. There were laughs all round as we remade them.

HMS Harrier

The next night, I decided to return the compliment, and I adjusted several beds so that when the occupant went to hop into the bed, it would collapse. I included my own bed in this little exercise, I especially avoided doing the Chief Physical Trainer's (PTI) bed, as he apparently had been the instigator of the short sheeting of our beds.

I made sure that my bed collapsed first. There was a great laugh all round at my predicament with some amusement as the rest of the beds collapsed. I then accused the PTI of being responsible.

He eventually woke up that I had done it and headed for me saying he was going to knock my block off. I took off down the corridor with him racing after me. As we neared the end of the room, I saw there were three steps down to another level. Just as I was about to reach the doorway, I sidestepped as he was about to grab me. Suddenly there was a PTI flying over the steps to the level below. Not a happy chappy. At that stage, I told him not to mess with Australians, and a truce was declared.

Final Note on PTI

The other Chiefs seemed to not have a good opinion of their PTI. They asked my Australian mate and me if we would help them take the PTI, heavily asleep from drinking, and put him out on one of the playing fields. A group of us hoisted the bed up, tilted it through the doorway without spilling the PTI out, and set it in the middle of one of the playing fields.

The two of us Australians never had any further problems with the PTI.

Meteorology

Meteorology instruction was over two days, after which we were given an exam on what we had covered. I was surprised when the Senior Officer in charge of the school told us that we would have to redo the exam because there was something wrong with the results.

When I asked for an explanation, I received none. I asked again as I suspected that, because of the way we revised each lecture each day, and we had only had two days instruction the results were so very high that they suspected we had cheated.

I challenged the Officer to confirm that he thought we had cheated. I pointed out if that was the case, the class was being accused of cheating. I also stated that I had never cheated in my life. I then asked could he explain how it could have happened as each of us sat at a separate desk, at least a metre or more apart, and there was an Invigilator walking round the room throughout the whole exam. I pointed out that he could not have been doing his job if they suspected we were cheating.

When it was obvious that I was not going to get an answer, I asked if I could make a telephone call to Australia House in London because I felt that I, and my classmates, were being accused of cheating and I knew this was not so. As a result of little confrontation, we were told we would not be required to come back and repeat the training.

Each of the other subjects we were trained in at *Harrier* were passed without any comment on the exam results.

The Kete Pub

After a hard day's training, it was not uncommon for some of us to walk down to the local pub. It was very traditional in their English way of pubs, and we were quite often able to converse with the locals who were very interested in us two Australians. We were also able to get to know some of the other personnel from *Harrier* and among them were a few WRENS (female sailors on the Radar Plot branch) who we had worked with during some of our practical training in the Operations room.

They showed us the quickest way back to the Base was through a few fields of wheat or similar cereal. The stalks had been cut in the field, and all these clumps were waiting to be put into bales. As you passed some of these clumps you might hear a giggle or two from a couple enjoying themselves.

When we arrived at the fence around the base, there was a gate you could go through if it had not been locked. On one occasion, we arrived when the gate had been locked, and the girls showed us another way in if it happened to us again.

Tennis

On occasions after work, two of us would play tennis. Sometimes WRENS would be playing, and we would play mixed doubles.

Squash

On one afternoon break, one of my English classmates asked if I played squash. My answer was no; I had never played. He invited me to have a hit-up. So began my first and only time on a Squash court.

We hit the ball around for about 15 or 20 minutes and he asked if I would like to have a game, to which I agreed. I found it interesting and appeared to be doing the right thing. When we stopped, I was accused of lying about not playing. I again stated that until that day I had never had a squash racquet in my hand and never been on a squash court.

Many years later, when reflecting on my school days at CBC, I suddenly realised why I always seemed to be in the right place on the Squash Court, to return and play the ball, was because I had played so many games of handball at school.

Farewell

On the night before we left *Harrier*, we invited those in the Chief and Petty Officers Mess and the Officers who had been involved in our training to farewell drinks. As you can imagine, there were seven or eight neat tots a day saved, and we had a large dispenser in which the rum had been saved.

When we invited the Officers, we did not know that they were having a formal Dining Night. By the time they left our mess they were in a somewhat inebriated state as they normally didn't get a rum issue. I am sure the Formal Dinner would have been a very interesting event knowing just what inebriated Officers can get up to. I noticed a few very sore heads as the Officers assembled to see us off.

Next morning, with our bags and hammocks packed, we were taken to the station to return to HMS *Dryad* to complete our course and receive an assessment of our training over the past year.

My total results over the year resulted in an 89% mark and the rest of the class were in the range 79%-82%. I was very pleased to top the course and felt very rewarded for all the study I had done.

Dryad

Back at *Dryad*, I think the Training Staff found the *Harrier* results very satisfying and congratulated us.

After more training, the class undertook practical and written examinations, and the course finally came to an end.

During the resumption of our course, the class was congratulated on a job well done. We had all passed the course, and we would be promoted to Sub Lieutenant Bosun Plot and Radar.

We were then sent off on short leave to get measured for our new Officer uniforms and other kit. In my case, I had to hand in my bag and hammock and obtain a Tink for my goods and chattels.

While being measured for a couple of suits at Gieves in Portsmouth, I purchased a second-hand sword and sword belt, which I still have today.

Knife Fork and Spoon Course

After being kitted out, we had to undertake a course of instruction in the way of Officers Messes, and we were instructed on Formal Dinner procedures.

We Australians were taught about the issue of rum. We also were shown, or instructed, on the many ways the people involved in drawing the rum each day could cheat.

First Wardroom Breakfast

We had breakfast in the HMS *Victory* mess in Portsmouth. I remember the first morning we went to breakfast, we were somewhat excited to be waited on and naturally were interested in what the others had been doing since we last had been together on course. Across the table from us was a more senior officer, a Commander I think, reading a newspaper. He lowered the newspaper and peered at us over glasses at the tip of his nose. The gaze told us to be silent.

Posting as an Officer

When Sailors are moved to a ship or base it is called **a Draft.** When Officers move it is called **a Posting.**

All of us were naturally looking forward to our first Posting as an Officer. I found myself posted to HMS *Tumult*, based at Portland in Devon, and I was to join the ship on the 17th of December (1956), my first wedding anniversary. Not the best of outcomes, especially with Joan pregnant.

All the other class members were to join their ships after Christmas. I requested that consideration be given to joining after Christmas, particularly as my wife was having some difficulty in her pregnancy and that I would like to spend the first Christmas since we married together. This request was denied; I was told to get on with it.

Bill was not a Happy Chappy, I can tell you.

However, as I now reflect, it was professionally the best thing that could have happened. I was to quickly learn the whys and wherefores of living in a Ship's Officers' Mess and some of the ways required to entertain visitors.

So, after a very short leave, my destination was Portland and HMS *Tumult*.

Chapter 21

HMS *Tumult*

18 December 1956 to 16 June 1957

	Dimensions	Displacement	Engine
Length -	359ft 9"	1710 tons	
Beam	35ft 8"		
Draught -	???		
		Armament	
		3 x 4" guns	

HMS *Tumult* was commissioned on the 2nd of April 1943 and saw service during WWII. After the war it was employed training ASDIC (Anti-Submarine Detector operators) off the Southern coast of England.

Joining

I took the train from Portsmouth to Yeovil. (I'm not sure if this was the station I left the train.)

The weather reflected my mood as it was drizzling rain. Two sailors from HMS *Tumult* were waiting at the station with a small van and helped put my gear into the back. I sat with the two in the front asking questions about some of the properties we passed on the way.

We passed a high-fenced property and, on enquiring, were told it was owned by a retired Admiral named Earnly, Earn Drax. (I am not sure if this is the correct spelling.) I did not know then that he had a son, and I would serve with him in HMS *Sheffield* after I completed my six months in *Tumult*.

Welcome Aboard

We drove down the wharf at Portland and I got my first glimpse of HMS *Tumult*, a destroyer modified to act as an Anti- Submarine Warfare Training ship.

As the sailors were taking my trunk and bags onto the ship, I was greeted by the Duty Officer, a young Sub Lieutenant Supply. He advised me that all the other Officers were ashore, Christmas shopping. He led me down to the cabin I had been allocated with the sailors following with my gear. They managed to let my trunk slip down the ladder, and Bill was not impressed.

The Sub Lieutenant suggested I settle into the cabin and come up to the Wardroom after I had unpacked.

The Cabin

On entering the cabin, I found that there were two bunks against each side wall, a writing desk under the bunks and a few drawers under the writing desk. There was a small cupboard at the end of each bunk for hanging one's uniforms.

I worked out the bunk my cabin mate was sleeping in and then proceeded to move from my bunk and drawers a whole series of photographic equipment, and other items in the drawers, over onto the other bunk. I also found a few empty Gin bottles on my side of the cabin, and proceeded to put these on the other bunk.

Cabin Mate

It was getting late when my cabin mate arrived back from his Christmas shopping and introduced himself. He was a bit older than me and somewhat overweight.

He directed me to the Officers bathroom for our area, and after showering, I returned to the cabin, and because of the late hour, I dressed in my evening attire. As I was putting on my soft evening shirt, my cabin mate stated that the captain, being a Lieutenant Commander, ate with the Officers, and required his officers to wear the formal dress shirt. I should have been a wake-up to him setting me up.

Wardroom

By the time I reached the Wardroom, the Officers were at table, the captain at its head, with the Executive Officer alongside him. I introduced myself and was invited to sit down. There were two empty chairs and enquired about which one I should sit in. I was standing alongside one of several chairs up from the end of the table. The Executive Officer, who was the President of the Mess, indicated that I should sit at the one I was standing alongside.

I had hardly taken my seat before my cabin mate entered the Wardroom and walking up behind me, said in a very plummy English voice, "Auuuustralian you are in my seat."

Everyone at the table stopped talking. I looked at the President and seeing no response that he had told me to sit there, I stood up and said "Sorry, I didn't realise it was your seat." There was an audible sigh from around the table and I moved to the seat at the end of the table.

After that everyone introduced themselves and what their position was in the ship. When the meal ended, I was asked to join the Captain and Executive Officer for a drink and to meet each of the Officers. I didn't stay long, took my leave, and returned to the cabin to prepare for bed.

My cabin mate returned somewhat later, obviously having had quite a few drinks. I got up and confronted him about giving me the wrong information on dressing for dinner and the chair incident, indicating that the President had told me to take that seat. I also informed him, in no uncertain terms, to get rid of the gin bottles or I would be forced to inform the XO of his drinking in the cabin. I made clear to him that he would be worse for wear if he thought of embarrassing me again.

Daily Routine

Each day the ship proceeded to sea, to work with a submarine. A class of Anti-Submarine (ASDIC) sailors were being trained in detecting and tracking a submarine. My leaving harbour, and at sea station was on the bridge. Whilst at sea, I was expected to help keep the position of the ship up to date by fixing its position and to keep a lookout for any problems that the TAS Training Officer may not be aware of.

Eventually, we stopped training, and the ship was berthed alongside, preparing for Christmas. The captain was to have his quite heavily pregnant wife on board for Christmas day.

Christmas Day

Christmas festivities were interrupted by a gale, and a decision was made to remain alongside. Extra berthing lines were secured to the wharf. At one stage, it was suggested we take out the section of the anchor cable and use it to keep the ship alongside. Eventually, common sense prevailed, and the captain's wife was led down the moving gangway onto the wharf, and preparations were made to go and anchor in the harbour.

The Ships Company was summoned to leave Ship stations' (leaving the wharf), and I was told to go to the Bridge and select and plan for anchoring. I was very concerned as I tried to make out where all the other ships in the harbour were and where the best spot to anchor would be without fouling another ship. It was raining heavily, it was growing dark, and visibility was poor, and I realised I was a bit out of my depth. Fortunately, the Squadron Navigator lived on-board and took over the task, with me looking on at what he did.

I can't remember how long we stayed at anchor, but I think it was a day or so before we got back alongside.

Executive Officer's Parties

In the first few days on board, I became aware that the Executive Officer (XO) was a player and stayer when it came to parties on board. I also found out his idea of a party, with partners on board, would see everyone get their preferred drink and mixes and select a suitable place on the lounge-type seating. The globes would be removed, and the only light was that coming through the port holes. However, on several occasions, the captain had returned on board and found the place in darkness when he entered the Wardroom. This did not stop the XO having his parties.

The reason this situation arose was that the Quartermaster was unable to see the captain approaching the ship until he came into view about 50 or so metres from the gangway. By the time the Quartermaster rushed to the Wardroom and alerted the XO and Duty Officer, the Captain tended to be only a short distance behind the Quartermaster and there was no time to have the lights back working.

Came the day of my first duty. Being under training, I was very anxious to make sure I had a plan to avoid this situation. Having spent a lot of time as a Quartermaster in harbour, in various ships as a sailor, I went and stood where the Quartermaster usually stood. As I looked around, I noticed the most forward port hole in the Wardroom was almost at my shoulder. I went back into the Wardroom undid the holding lugs and opened the Port Hole. I checked again from the position the Quartermaster stood and realised I had a solution.

The solution was for the Quartermaster to push the unsecured porthole open and give two pips on his Bosun's Pipe. He was so briefed that he stood by the gangway with his Bosun's Mate and greeted the captain. Except for the Quartermaster, no one else knew what I was up to.

I was sitting in a chair in the Wardroom in the semi-dark when there were two pips. I grabbed my hat and headed for the door of the Wardroom. The XO asked, "What was those two pips?" and my reply as I reached the door was, "The captain was about to come aboard."

I was at the gangway when the captain was halfway up and met him with, "Good evening, sir," and saluted, and then asked if he had enjoyed his evening with his friend, the Commodore of the Base. I managed to delay him a few more minutes with a comment about the weather and that all was quiet on board.

He asked if the XO was on board and I replied, "Yes and he has a few friends on board." The captain then said, "Well, I think I'll have drink before turning in."

With heart in my mouth and pumping, he knocked on the door of the Wardroom and opened the door to find all lights on and those present playing Charades.

The next morning, after we had sailed, I was summoned from the Bridge to the XO's cabin to find him turned in after seeing the ship safely on its way to sea. His question: "What were the two pips about?" I explained what I had arranged with the Quartermaster to alert me by the two pips so I would have time to get the Wardroom ready for the captain as he came aboard.

I also added that *they* had sent their prisoners to Australia, and we had learnt a lot from them. I also commented that, because I was under training, I didn't wish to have any marks against me. The XO and his parties were never found wanting after that.

Rum Issue

As the Duty Officer, one of my duties was to go down to a lower storage area with a Supply sailor and his assistant and another sailor, known as the Tankie. My job was to make sure that the drawing of the rum and pouring it into a receptible was done correctly and that the two sailors were not cheating.

I looked for all the ways we had been shown when doing the knife, fork and spoon course at the end of our training. The procedure was to use a measured small receptacle that took exactly one tot. A fingertip inside the rim of the receptacle was one way of short-changing the amount.

With over a hundred plus crew, this became a reasonable amount for the sailors involved and they could then come back unaccompanied by an Officer and have an extra one or two tots of neat rum.

The way the sailors looked at one another from time to time made my instincts, from my experiences of handling sailors before becoming an Officer, kick in, and I realised that they were probably cheating and taking advantage of my limited knowledge of the drawing the rum issue.

Having carefully counted each tot, the Tankie said, "That's it, sir," then proceeded to put the plug back in the rum barrel. You can imagine their surprise when I told them to pour everything back into the barrel and do it properly this time. The look on their faces told me that they had been cheating. (They normally covered the shortfall by adding a little extra water when the Rum was broken down for serving to sailors.

Repeating the exercise, they showed me every full measure before putting it into the receptacle. This caused the rum issue to the Ship's Company to be delayed, a mortal sin to the sailors waiting in the upper levels for their tot. The remarks made to the Tankie and his mates for being late cannot be printed. They blamed 'that Australian Officer' for the delay.

Later, I was sent for by the Executive Officer to explain what had happened. My reply was that my time on the lower deck had given me a sixth sense of when sailors may be cheating, and I was sure they were taking me on, knowing it was my first time witnessing the drawing of rum. From memory, another officer was chosen to supervise drawing of rum each day. This did not worry me that all.

Lunch Time Rounds

In most small ships at the time, there was no separate Dining Hall. There were tables in each mess where the duty Messman would bring the food from the galley to the mess and serve it. The Messman would have prepared vegetables to go with the meat or fish.

The Duty Officer would do rounds of the Mess Decks at lunch time and would ask each Mess if there were any complaints about the meal. Complaints could be "Not fit to eat," or "Not enough to eat."

I automatically did these rounds when I was on duty. I didn't ask if I had to, I just did it. I can't remember how many duties I had done when, on one occasion, I walked into a mess and the sailors were all sitting on the top of lockers and other seating. Alarm bells rang that something was about to happen. I asked the question about any complaints and not a word until I was about to leave the mess, when a voice piped up.

"Sir, I have a complaint."

My reply was, "You may complain that the food was not fit to eat or there was not enough."

The answer, "Not Enough."

My reply was, "Well, you better have a go at your Duty Mess Cook and tell him to make sure there are more vegetables peeled."

The Mess roared with laughter and said "Good on you, sir."

Lunch Time Drinks

From time to time, it was the practise for a one ship alongside to fly what was known as the "Gin Pennant." This meant they were inviting Officers from other ships alongside to come on board for a lunch time drink.

On arrival at that ship's gangway, you would be welcomed aboard by the Duty Officer and led to the Wardroom by a sailor. Here, you would be welcomed into the Wardroom and be engaged in conversation by a member of the Mess. Initially, during the first few of these drinkies, I was asked about the RAN by some of the hosts. Sometimes it seemed ages before a steward would ask you what you would like to drink. Most seemed to drink Brandy and Dry, Whisky and Soda, or Gin and Tonic. I began trying each of these spirit drinks and found I liked a gin and tonic with ice and lemon.

HMS *Tumult's* Luncheon Drinks

I happened to be the Duty Officer the first time one of these lunch drinkies was held on the ship after I arrived on board.

Before anyone arrived, I was in the Wardroom and noticed the XO supervising the pouring of alcohol of one sort or another into lines of glasses set up adjacent to the doorway. Mixes were on the table alongside of them.

As the guests arrived, they would be welcomed by the XO and asked what they would like to drink. The Stewards would then add mixes and hand the glass to the visitor who would then be greeted by a member of the Wardroom and moved away from the entrance area. I was most impressed.

Being Duty I could not drink. However, me standing there without a glass caught the XO's eye and before I knew it, he handed me a glass of tonic water with lemon and ice. From that day until I left the Navy, I used this procedure if I was duty and there was Cocktail party. A couple of times, overzealous Officers accused me of drinking on Duty. However, when invited to taste the drink they were disappointed to find no alcohol in it.

Visit To France

During a break in classes, the ship visited a port in France. I soon observed that the reason was to replenish with French wines, especially Champagne. Unfortunately, I can't remember the name of the French Port, but it was somewhere near a major wine growing area. I noted that some of the Officers had placed bags in the transport taking us to the American Consul to France who had invited the Officers to his home for a luncheon. The Consul was an American and his wife was French and a lovely hostess. The house was a magnificent Chateau with beautiful gardens.

We were greeted with Champagne on arrival and kept topped up. We were treated to a delightful lunch. I had a great time as both the Consul and wife were very interested in an Australian serving on a British ship.

When we returned to the ship and were boarding, I became aware of clinking of bottles in the bags. I was to learn later that the American had swopped top champagne for rum. (At no cost to either side.)

Birth of a Son

I can't remember exactly where the ship was when I received information that I had a son – Anthony. He was born on the 18th of April 1957. I was able to get to see Joan whilst she was still in hospital. I was not very happy that I could not be there to help when she came out of hospital.

Chatham

I can't remember how long after I joined that the ship went back to Chatham (its Home Port). Reason for this was to undergo a short maintenance period. On the way, the ship visited Portsmouth to discharge the training class. The captain took the opportunity to invite all the Officers to come to his property on the outside of Portsmouth for an informal meal. Apparently, he grew Brussel Sprouts and the first of the crop had just been harvested.

It was rather an informal meal with people standing around and being given a plate with meat and veg that included some Brussel Sprouts. I found I did not like them. I was about to leave them on my plate when the XO advised me to eat them as they were the captain's pride and joy, and my rejection would be noted. So, I consumed those on my plate.

I was able to visit Joan and my new son during this visit to Portsmouth.

Return to Portland

Just before we left Chatham to return to Portland, the XO instructed me to go to London by train and collect some bamboo poles from a particular store. When I arrived at the store, I found they were about 7 or 8 feet in length and several inches in diameter. The store drove me back to the station, and I had to juggle these poles all the way back to Chatham, standing in the entrance to the carriage.

The driver of the ship's truck and his mate took charge of the poles at the Chatham Station and unloaded them onto the ship on arrival alongside. My curiosity and what the poles were for was answered when I found they were being split in half and used on the front of the bar in the Wardroom. Later, a suitable cover was placed as the roof over the bar, and it looked very tropical. It was the only bar in any of the ships at Portland. It had a small keg on the counter that served beer.

The result was enough to take away my dark thoughts.

May 1957

At the beginning of May, we continued training ASDIC operators, and my time on the Bridge resulted in a "Certificate of Competency" for my duties on the Bridge being awarded. This meant I would soon be posted to another ship to gain a "Bridge Officer of the Watch Qualification."

Shortly after I received notification that I was posted to HMS *Sheffield*, the coming out of an extended refit and due to recommission. I then found out HMS *Sheffield* was in Chatham, and it just happened HMS *Tumult* was returning there to undertake a refit.

Chatham

On arrival in Chatham, *Tumult's* berth was some distance from HMS *Sheffield*. The XO sent for me and suggested that, to make a good impression, I should plan to join HMS *Sheffield* on the appointed day at 0900 (9 am) and should be wearing my medals and sword. I knew this was a custom followed by Officers of the RN.

To ensure I arrived exactly at 0900, I spent several mornings working out the timing and arranged with one of the Dockyard maties not to open a particular pontoon until I and those pulling ++++.

On the appointed day, I marched to HMS *Sheffield* wearing sword and medals, with two sailors pushing the barrow with my gear trailing behind. All the pontoons remained closed, and I passed a liquid present to the pontoon man for his assistance.

I was not to know what was to follow my joining in sword and medals.

Officers Certificate

17 December to 21 May 1957

To my entire satisfaction.

He has put in all he's got into his work and into the ship and has been a first-class asset in every way.

21 May to 17 June 1957

To my entire satisfaction.

A most likeable and loyal officer with a good sense of responsibility and humour. He should do very well

Chapter 22

HMS *Sheffield*

17th June 1957 to 9th February 1959

Dimensions	Displacement	Engine
Length 180.14m		
Beam 18.80M	1350 tons	
Draught 6.55M		

Armament

12 x 6"   3 x QF 4"   4 x 3 Pounder   8 x QF 2 Pounder

Plus 6 21" Torpedo Tubes

The Ship

The *Sheffield* was commissioned 25th of August 1937. Her nickname was *Shiny Sheff* because all her fittings were constructed from stainless steel instead of the more traditional brass. This was an attempt to reduce the amount of cleaning required on the part of the crew.

A prototype radar system was placed into service in August 1938 on the *Sheffield*. It was the 1st vessel in the Royal Navy to be so equipped.

During World War II *Sheffield* saw service in Norway and Spartivento in 1940, in the Atlantic 1941-43, Bismarck Action 1941, Mediterranean & Malta convoys 1941, Artic 1941-43, Nth Africa & Barents Sea 1942, Biscay 1943, Salerno & Nth Cape 1943.

During the Bismarck action in 1941, she was attacked by friendly aircraft, who in the conditions thought she was *Bismarck*. Eleven torpedos were dropped against her and skillful ship handling and defects in the torpedo firing systems saw her escape unscathed.

This was the ship I was to join on the 21st May 1957. At the time of my joining, she was completing a prolonged refit prior to recommissioning. She was berthed at Chatham dockyard on the banks of the river Medway.

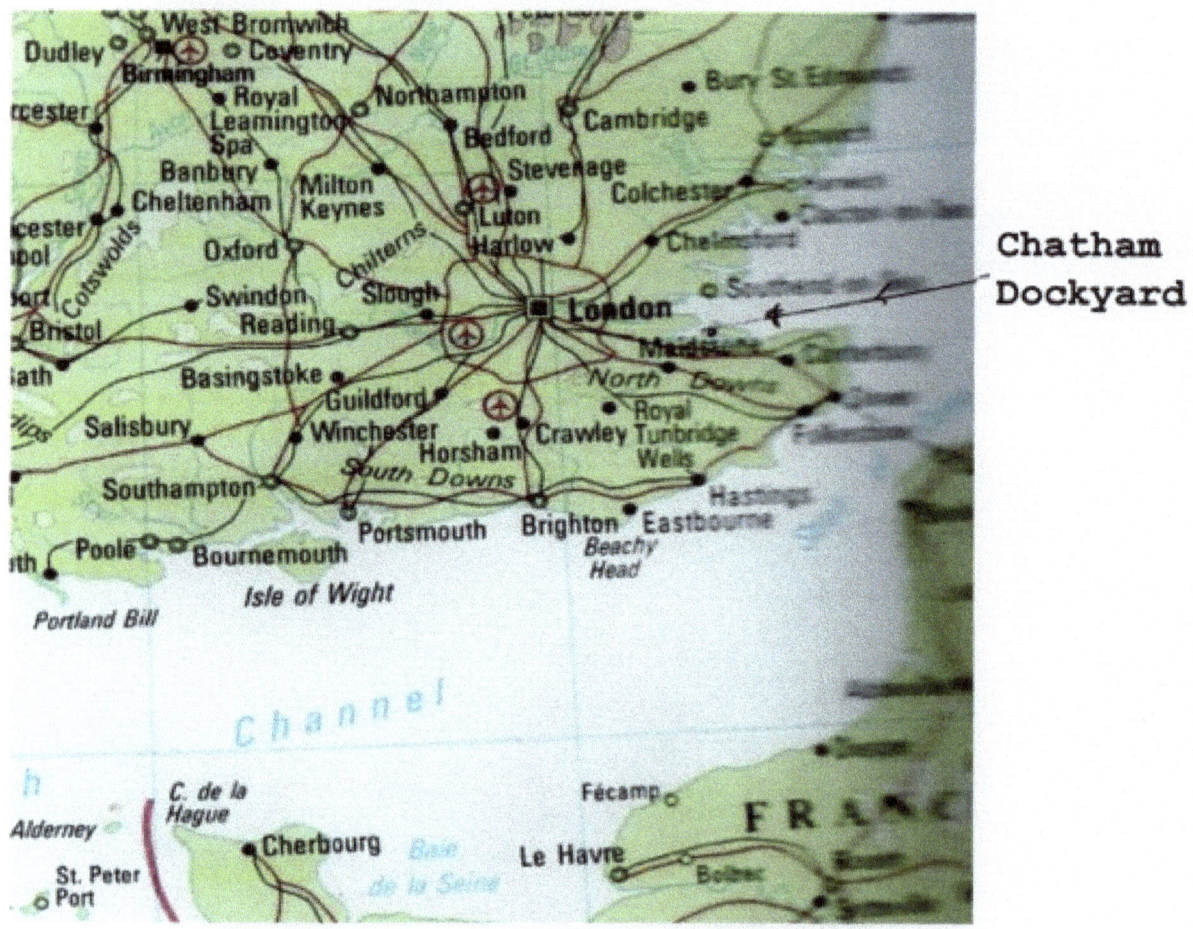

Joining HMS *Sheffield*

Prior to joining the ship, I had walked from where HMS *Tumult* was berthed to where HMS *Sheffield* was berthed, using the shortest distance, and timed how long it took. The only thing that could upset my timing was that there was a caisson that opened the passage between two areas for boats to pass. Fortunately, having explained what I was doing, the person in charge of opening the caisson agreed to make sure that the caisson was open on the day and time, I would be walking from *Tumult* to *Sheffield*.

On the 25 May 1957 I left HMS *Tumult*, dressed in my No 1 Uniform, with Sword and Medals, leading two sailors pulling a handcart that contained my tin trunk, rifles container and my other goods and chattels. The caisson was closed as arranged and, as I passed the man in charge of the opening, I passed to him a liquid gift.

As I approached HMS *Sheffield*, I noticed there was a scurry of activity around the gangway. On arrival, I proceeded up the gangway saluting the flag on the stern in accordance with the custom as the bell was struck for 0900. I asked for permission to come aboard. A young Royal Marine Officer greeted me. I gave my name to him and that I was joining the ship.

No sooner had I done this when the Executive Officer, a Commander, who turned out to have been the Officer in Charge of Gunnery and Parade training whilst at Whale Island appeared. He said in a rather terse voice, "Oh it's only you, Ritchie. Get rid of all that wangle dangle (meaning my Sword and Medals) and get yourself a cup of coffee. I will see you later."

The Royal Marine Officer on the gangway then whispered in my ear that he thought I was the Officer of the Guard doing his rounds and that he had rushed into tell XO just as he had cut the top off his boiled egg. Hence the terse welcome by said XO. I found out later it was the Royal Marine Officer's first duty as Officer of the Watch on the gangway.

I was escorted to the Officers' accommodation area and shown my cabin. This had a single bunk in it, with a writing desk and draws under it. My trunk and other gear were there. My rifles had been taken to the ship's armoury for security. I began unpacking and was soon summonsed to the XO's cabin.

Executive Officers Briefing

He then told me that I would be the assistant to the Direction Officer who oversaw the operation room. I would also be taking my place in the Seaman Officer of the Watch Roster. I was not that impressed when told this as almost all the other of Officers of my Branch tended to be employed as Officer of the Day because they were older than the other officers who kept watch on the gangway and did not do as many duties.

The XO must've seen my expression and said it was my fault for doing my course at a later age than most Seaman OOW. I knew I would be acting as the second Officer of the Watch on the Bridge, when at sea, so was able to gain my Seaman's Watch Keeping ticket that would allow me to be a first OOW on the bridge of any Navy ship I was posted to.

He then told me to 'carry on' and, as I reached the door, he told me to come back and sit down. He then said, "That's all that Radar nonsense and you will be the ship's Bosun." That came as no surprise as I knew that other Sub Lieutenants of my branch were so employed.

Before I was dismissed, he then stated that I had eleven days to prepare and update the Ship's Evolution Book. When I asked where I would find the existing one, he told me that it had been misplaced and I was to prepare a new booklet.

I then returned to my cabin to continue unpacking.

I finished unpacking and changed into my working uniform. Soon it was lunchtime and I proceeded to the Wardroom for a pre-lunch drink and to introduce myself to the other Officers who were there. When completed I made my way to the Bosun's Store where the sailors who were to work for me would be, and made myself known. I made sure they understood I would expect them to do their job properly. If they had a problem, whatever that may be, I was their Divisional Officer and would try to get a satisfactory outcome for them.

The Ship's Evolution Book

So began my life as the Bosun of the ship and the scratching of my head as to how I would put the booklet together in such a short time. I had considerable experience as a Petty Officer doing most Evolutions. I drew the standard reference book on the subject and began setting out a draft layout. Realising the time I had been given was rather short, I decided to approach the Master Attendant of the Dockyard, who was a professional Seaman Bosun, who had recently been promoted to Commander, when the new structure of the Special Duties list came into being. I explained my predicament and he referred me to the Bosun of the Yard, a newly promoted Lieutenant but very experienced.

I invited this Officer to lunch on board *Sheffield* and made sure he had plenty to drink. I had explained that what I really wanted was the layout usually found in a Ship's Evolution Booklet and not the copying of some other ship's book.

He suggested we talk to the Bosun of another Cruiser, then maintaining in the dockyard. This Bosun was prepared to lend me his evolution book for a day, so I could get what I needed.

I must admit that I played on the fact that I was Radar, which suggested I may not have all the knowledge of seamanship that Seaman Bosun's had.

Now armed with a standard evolutional book layout I walked round the HMS *Sheffield* making notes of where the various securing points and other fittings were located. So armed, I was able to complete the book within eleven days. I was not to know then but found out later, when I was about to leave the ship, that I had gained a few brownie points for my effort. I will refer to this again as my time in *Sheffield* comes to an end.

Duty Officer

It didn't take long before I found myself as Officer of the Watch on the gangway where I oversaw the gangway staff and required to make sure that all people coming and going on board were greeted with the proper formalities. Also, to ensure that the Quartermaster (QM), or his offsider the Boatswain's Mate (BM,) made the routine pipes and the striking of the bell on time every hour. The usual length of a watch was four hours. Sometimes, the watch passed quickly and at other times dawdled along. The main thing for me was to make sure that everything ran smoothly, and here the many hours I had spent as a Quartermaster helped.

Knowing we were to have a Flag Officer on board meant everything had to be first class. I instructed my QM and BM that if they wanted to have a smoke or grab a cup of coffee, they were to ask me first, and were not to smoke or drink the coffee on the quarterdeck. They were to go inside the superstructure and be prepared to come out onto the quarterdeck should something happen that required their presence. Initially, I don't think they were particularly happy, but as time went by they realised why I was so insistent on the procedure I had set down. They came to realise that when on watch with me there were no hassles as sometimes occurred with other OOW.

As a refit was coming to an end, every effort was made to see the ship was spick-and-span. One of the activities was every morning the ship's company was put to work cleaning the various compartments. Groups of sailors were responsible for a particular compartment, and deciding on its size, one or two or more were employed to clean it.

The after turret was the responsibility of the Royal Marines embarked and they made a point of ensuring their gun was very, very, clean.

Family Removal

One of the things I had found out was that after commissioning, the ship would be sailing to operate out of Rosyth in Scotland. It was off to Portsmouth on a particular weekend as it would give me an opportunity to discuss where Joan was to live when the ship left Chatham.

We agreed that she and Anthony would come to Chatham in the interim and we would search for a suitable place for her to stay near the dockyard in Rosyth. I had already sounded out a nice boarding house near the dockyard in Chatham. Except when on duty, I was able to go home every night and get to know my son Anthony.

Asking around the ship, I learnt of a pub, literally under the Fifth of Fourth bridge, that would be suitable. Although it was across the Bay from Rosyth Dockyard, it was possible to be taken across by boat and land near the pub. We made a booking for the likely dates that Joan would arrive in that area.

The Commissioning

I have failed to mention before that the captain was a Royal New Zealand Naval Officer whose career began as a midshipman in the RAN. Unfortunately, he was one of the midshipmen who was made redundant when there was a reduction of the number of midshipmen under training in the RAN due to the financial position due to the GREAT DEPRESSION. He had continued association with the sea in the Merchant Navy. He had joined the fledgling Royal New Zealand Navy around the time it was being formed.

Note. You will no doubt recall that during my initial training I referred to Catholics falling out during Divisions when the Prayer section was about to start.

The XO, with the help of other Senior Officers and the Padre, prepared the Commissioning Ceremony, and all the details associated with a Commissioning. They submitted their plan to the captain.

To the dismay of the XO, and others, he amended the plan so that he, and not a Bishop, would lead the Ceremony. It turns out he was a Roman Catholic and insisted that no member of his Ship's Company would fall out from a Service or Parade. This situation was not greeted with any enthusiasm by the Royal Naval Officers. However, the Captain's will prevailed.

This was to be the first Ecumenical Service I was to attend.

After the formal Ceremony of Commissioning, the guests attended a Reception on board. We had been able to arrange a babysitter for Anthony and Joan attended the Service and Reception.

Cat the Anchor

Finally, *Sheffield* was once again a member of the Royal Navy's seagoing fleet. Completing the storing and fuelling of the ship, the ship ammunitioned at a buoy. Here, my first test as Bosun occurred and that was going to secure to a buoy. This meant the starboard anchor and a length of cable had to be moved from the normal secured position in the hawse pipe and moved and secured to a position on the ship's side known as the Cathead. The reason was that the cable, minus the anchor, was needed to secure the buoy. It was called "catting the anchor."

I had never seen this done and had made sure I swatted up on what was to happen. In the event, all went well because the sailors on the forecastle had done it all before, and I invited them to get on with it rather than tell them what to do. Also, I made sure that a few marks (paint) were placed on the cable so that every time we had to do this evolution I knew exactly where to place the securing slips on the cable attached to the anchor.

Off to Scotland

It was time to farewell Joan and Anthony. Joan once again packed up, and with baby Anthony, caught the train to Edinburgh. From there she made her way to the hotel.

The ship let go of all lines and proceeded for Work Up off Scotland. I don't have the date we sailed.

Leaving Harbour Station

When leaving the harbour, my duty was to oversee the operation of the forecastle section on the cable deck and its anchors and securing lines. Although I had spent time on the cable deck in HMAS Murchison, this was the first time I had to supervise what was going on.

The ship sailed up the coast through the English Channel, carrying out various internal and other exercises needed to bring it up to the normal requirements of a naval vessel.

Eventually, *Sheffield* arrived at Rosyth and, by courtesy of using the ship's boat, I was taken across to a rocky outcrop adjacent to the Hotel, where I was able to jump off the ship's boat onto the rocks and make my way to the Hotel.

Time at the Hotel

I was delighted to be united with Joan and Anthony. Having settled Anthony for the night we proceeded to the dining room and ordered our drinks and meal. I caught up with all that had happened to Joan since she left Chatham and how Anthony had begun teething.

No one else was in the dining room, and I remarked to Joan, "Aren't there any others living in the hotel besides you?" She supplied the information that there were a few Diamond Drillers living in the hotel and that they took their meals in the kitchen. Anthony and Joan also had been taking their meals in the kitchen until that night. Joan said that because I was an Officer, the management had thought it appropriate for us to eat in the dining room. I found the room quite cold.

After dinner, we went into the front bar of the hotel where I met the landlady. After a drink or two, I indicated to her that I was quite happy to join the others for my meals in the kitchen. I think she was surprised but indicated she was quite happy for me to be fed in the kitchen. I also found out that her husband, who was the Chef and bottle washer, had been a Chief Petty Officer Cook in the Royal Navy. Later I was to learn he was a teetotaller, unlike his wife.

A boat came over early the next morning and I had breakfast on board.

The next night, I met the Diamond Drillers. They were happy group of chappies and quickly made welcome and at ease with this Officer sharing the table with them. They liked a drink or two of Irish Whiskey.

There was a very large cooking range, and it warmed the whole kitchen. The range also heated the water for the rooms. It was a very pleasant place to be, and Anthony was not subjected to the cold dining room. He would crawl around the floor while we ate. The only problem was that he was teething and that troubled him somewhat.

The Chef indicated that they gave their children a spoonful of whiskey to ease the pain. So, taking their advice, some whiskey was poured into a teaspoon and tried to get him to take it. When he did it was promptly spat out, so we had to try other remedies to help him with the pain.

We spent time looking around the area during the weekend, and all too soon, the weekend ended, and the ship's boat came back and picked me up from the rocks. While the ship was alongside, I was able to go to the hotel each night using the ship's boat.

Alas, it was all over too soon, and the ship sailed for the North Sea to participate in an exercise with other RN and United States of America's (USN) ships.

Remember, it was the Cold War period. The exercises were for cooperation between RN and USN forces.

Besides my duty as second Officer of the Watch on the Bridge, I mainly watched in the Operations Room, supervising the Radar Plotters. I cannot recall how close to the Arctic Circle we sailed, but it was not far away. From time to time, our presence in these waters triggered a response by Russian aircraft, who were detected, no doubt checking what we were up to. I don't think it is hard to imagine the rough state of the sea.

Refuelling American Destroyer

As the Exercises were coming to a close there was an urgent need to fuel a USN destroyer who was low on fuel with no other ship close enough to help. *Sheffield* was detailed to do the job and proceeded at best speed to give aid.

During the transit, the fuelling equipment was made ready. This consisted of erecting a pole, which had four stays to keep it upright. The ship's crane had a wireline to which several troughs were hung. These troughs carried the fuel hose along the line that ran between the two ships.

I won't go into any other detail except to say that the sea and swell were such that the normal operating distance of 80 feet between the ships was going to be hazardous, and some adjustment had to be made to the rigging of the fuel line.

I was asked, as the Bosun, to work out a way of extending the oil fuel hose. My suggestion that an extra trough to support another twenty feet of hose which would allow a small extra distance of hose between the two ships. This extra hose should be enough to avoid the ships colliding. To control this extra trough as the ships came closer or further apart, this meant using manpower to control the trough so it did not drop into the water.

In a refuelling, the supplying ship steers a steady course and speed whilst the ship receiving the fuel adjusts its speed and course to keep clear, the normal eighty feet was insufficient in the prevailing conditions to ensure the Destroyer would not have too much difficulty in avoiding a collision because of the sea state.

The Destroyer completed the fuelling without incident and was sent on her way. The fuelling personnel in *Sheffield*, especially the crane driver and those controlling line to the outer trough, did an excellent job in what were quite difficult conditions.

Soon after, the exercise ended, and we headed for Rosyth.

Return to Rosyth

After the Exercise was over, I think the whole ship's company was looking forward to being in Harbour due to the rock 'n' roll of the ship in the North Sea. By this time, I had been on *Sheffield* roughly six months.

Change of Operating Area

Out of the blue came the order to relocate to the Mediterranean area of operations and that we would be the Flagship for the area and required to carry the Rear Admiral in Charge of that area of Operations. The ship was to be based in Malta. As I mentioned, the Cold War in Europe was in full swing, and one of our jobs would be to stop any Russian ships trying to break out from their bases in the Black Sea.

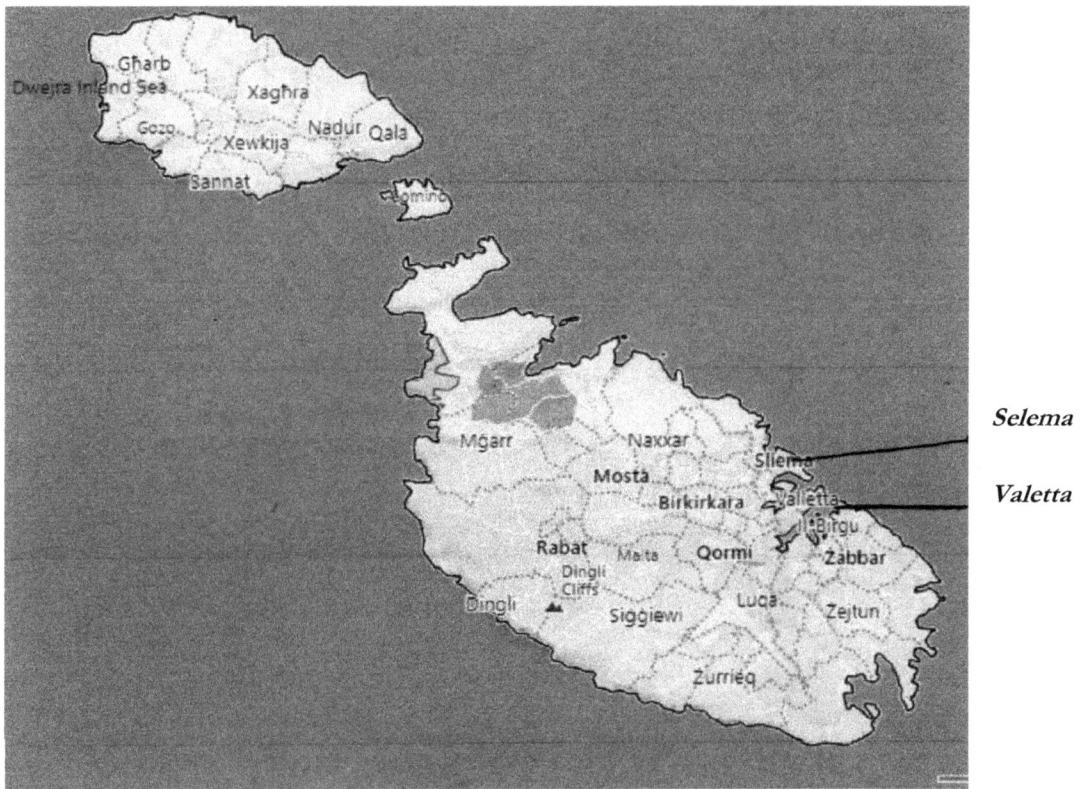

Camp Follower

The ship's move to Malta meant that Joan and baby Anthony would move to Malta for what turned out to be a year. We were able to obtain a rental in the old Maltese two-storey home. It was owned by two spinsters, and they occupied the top floor while we had the bottom floor.

It contained a double lock and one had to be careful when returning home, especially after a night out, as to whether it required one turn of the key or two. If you got the sequence wrong, it often took some time to get it right.

Our section contained the usual furnishings and a kerosene refrigerator. There were two doors at the entrance. The outer door was of heavy construction and designed, no doubt, to stop Raiders. The inner door only needed one turn of the key. This home was in Selema, not a great distance from Grand Harbour, and I could walk to get to work. During one of the official entertaining functions on board, a fellow Officer and his wife introduced us to a couple who were visiting them from Istanbul, and we were to meet them again when the ship visited that city.

On one occasion I came home to find that Anthony had put his hand around the back of the frig and placed his hands into the kerosene at the back. Some had got onto his sleeve and was creating severe pain and a nasty rash. We didn't know of any doctor close by, so we took him to the Royal Naval Hospital on the other side of Grand Harbour where he was attended to. I think he learned his lesson and never did it again.

Ship Operations

Basically, the ship operated throughout the Med from Gibraltar to Israel visiting various ports and being involved in exercises from time to time. On one occasion the ship was sent out to the Persian Gulf. Malta was the Home Port. I think we only expected to be away for about 100 days during our deployment and as Flag Ship. I think it turned out to be the other way round.

Spain

I will begin with a visit to Spain. The ship visited Barcelona, and from there, it was possible to explore further parts of Spain.

As always, we arranged a Reception on Board, and one for us was held ashore. I found the Spanish people made me quite welcome, and I had no complaints about the treatment I received from the various identities I met.

Lourdes

Barcelona

Rome

Naples

Gibraltar

I found it a very interesting place and enjoyed their food and wines. Not only were we able to walk around the city but we were also able to do some tours that gave us an idea of what the Spanish countryside was like. The Churches and Cathedral were impressive. I was able to visit Lourdes and see the Grotto and spring where the Blessed Virgin had appeared to Bernadette. This was where many are healed of their Human and spiritual afflictions.

Then it was time to sail and get on with our duties.

Italy

The place visited after exercises was Naples and I was able to get some leave to visit Rome. The Basilica was an eye-opener, as were the Fountain and the Colosseum.

It must have been New Year's Eve when we were in Rome with a couple of other officers from the ship, and we were warned not to be on the street at midnight as people threw out their old crockery and we could be hit. The other RN officers with me decided we should find a place to eat. Luckily, we found one just as it was about to close. When the owner found out I was an Australian, the offhanded way we were being served suddenly changed, and we are made most welcome. He changed the wine we were drinking to what he and his family and guests were drinking and we had a most enjoyable time.

Exercising

At some stage, we participated in exercises working with a group of five or six destroyers and a Fleet Auxiliary tanker and store ship. During one exercise we were to be a Russian cruiser trying to break out and six destroyers were deployed to intercept us.

Our Electronic Warfare (EW) team had found the destroyers' operating frequency, and I had an operator in the Ops room listening in on their operating channel. I was also able to watch on the radar the line of destroyers moving into position to launch a multi-ship attack on *Sheffield*.

I guessed roughly where they would turn towards *Sheffield* from line ahead to line abreast, and so provided multiple targets for us to defend against. The captain was standing beside me at the radar display, and I asked him if I could use the destroyers' operating frequency to interrupt their attack.

The captain said, "You better ask the Admiral." At that moment, the Admiral stepped through the Operations Room door and asked, "What's the problem?"

I explained to the Admiral what I wanted to do, and he said, "There was no Electronic warfare requirement in the exercise orders."

In my best imitation of Russian-speaking English, I said, "I am a Russian Cruiser and do not have a copy of the English orders." He understood my point and said, "Go for it."

I had already consulted the signal book for an appropriate order. I appreciated that the destroyers would be expecting an immediate execute order to turn towards *Sheffield*. Having been told they were an excellent destroyer group I was sure they would obey without question. I told the English radioman to give the order of an immediate turn away from *Sheffield*. I guessed correctly that none of them would confirm the order with the destroyer leader. My guess was correct and all but the leader turned away, allowing *Sheffield* to close within gun range so that we were able to use our greater range to engage each destroyer separately. This is what a Russian Cruiser would have done.

The Debriefing

The sequel to this incident occurred at the Debriefing. As the Admiral began his opening address, a very distinguished-looking Captain with lots of WWII medals stood up and made a comment along the lines that he wanted to make a complaint that nothing in the exercise orders had said that the ships would be subject to Electronic Warfare. The Admiral told the captain to sit down and called on me to inform the assembled group what I had said to him in the Operations Room. Again, using my best imitation of a Russian-speaking English, I repeated what I had said to the Admiral. When the Captain again stood up and was about to speak, the Admiral told him to sit down so he could get on with the debriefing.

When the debriefing came to an end, the Senior Officers went one way, and we Juniors went out through the rear door. As I headed for the door, a companion gave me a nudge and said, "I think someone is coming to talk to you," so I turned around and found what I thought was an angry Captain coming towards me. He opened by saying, "Are you Ritchie?" and noted that I was an Australian by the small badgers at the top of my coat sleeves. I think I was waiting for an adverse comment. He, however, said, "I wish to thank you for a lesson I was given today and that I should have been prepared for what occurred." I was quite surprised, and pleased, that a lowly Australian Sub Lieutenant had received such a compliment from a very experienced and distinguished Royal Naval Captain. So, on that day, I really enjoyed the lunch provided.

Transport of Royal Marines

One of the tasks that *Sheffield* was required to undertake was to embark on a group of Royal Marines and take them out to Bahrain. This meant transiting the Suez Canal, proceeding through the Red Sea to the Persian Gulf, and disembarking the Marines at Bahrain as required. The ship's stay in Bahrain was not long, and we proceeded to Muscat, a port for Oman.

Oman is as shown on the map on page 264, as is the Gulf of Oman and Muscat.

At Muscat we anchored in the port area and were given short, shore leave to explore the town.

I was invited to participate in a rifle competition with some local military personnel. I hadn't used my rifles for a long time, so I welcomed the chance to be a member of the ship's team. The result was a win for the ship. I thought the soldiers would win because everyone in Muscat appeared to be carrying a rifle of some sort.

While in Muscat, the ship received information that two ships had collided and that HMS *Bulwark* was on its way to provide aid. The crew of one ship, named *Melika*, had abandoned ship. After the collision, this ship steamed without anybody on board until the water, feeding the boilers, ran out and the boilers automatically shut down.

HMS *Bulwark* took *Melaka* in tow and headed for Muscat. On arrival, *Melika* was anchored not far from *Sheffield*. Melika had a list. Our Captain went aboard and, with his knowledge of Merchant ships, had the ship righted.

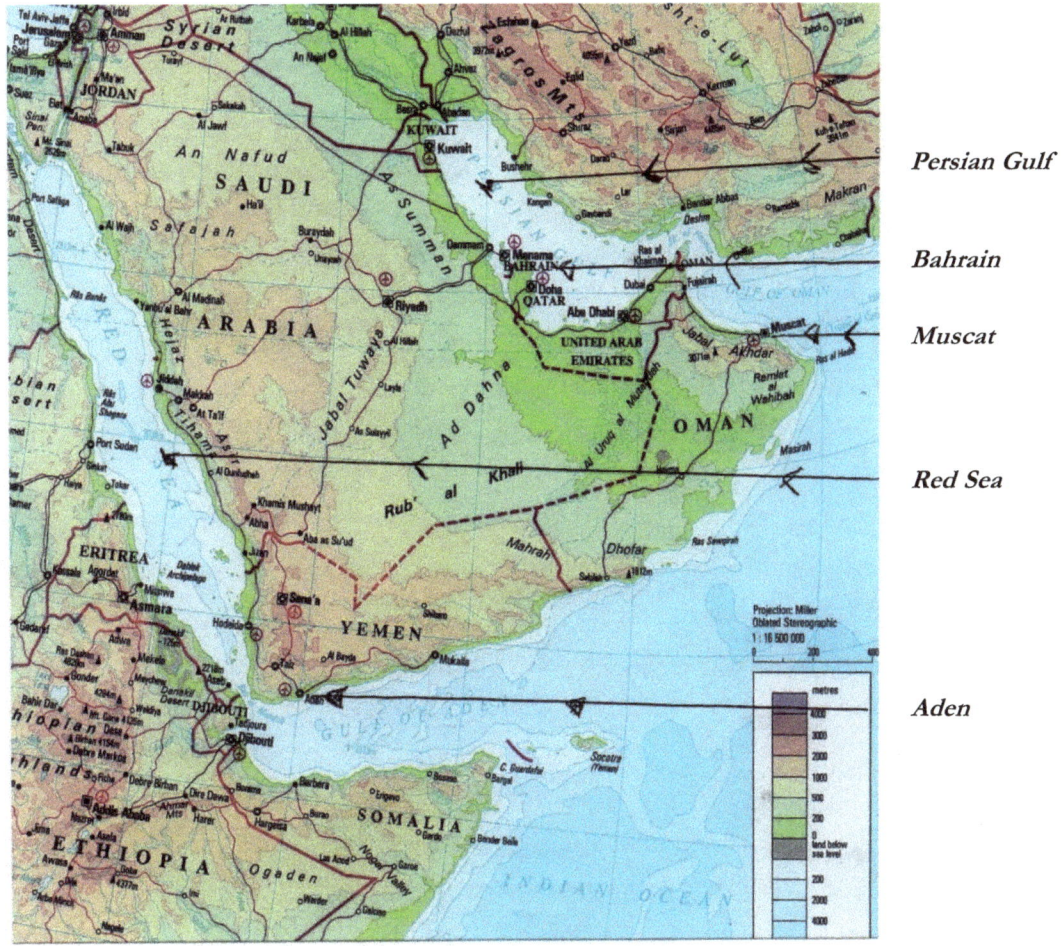

A signal was received ordering *Sheffield* to tow *Melaka* to Italy. Planning began for this long tow through the Suez Canal.

The Proposed Tow

The first thing required was to go aboard *Melika* and check the securing points on the ship for the tow and if there would be a requirement to send extra manpower to help those already on board.

I was surprised to find that the Officer in charge of Melika was an Australian Lieutenant named Donald W. (known as Weary). The year was 1958 and neither of us was to know that he would be my third boss later when based in Canberra in the Directorate of User Requirements (DUR) in 1970/71. Weary told me that they'd had problems with the tow parting several times during the passage to Muscat. He advised that this had resulted because of the chafing of the tow line as it passed in over the fairlead in HMS *Bulwark*.

A small committee was formed back on *Sheffield*, comprising the XO, Shipwright Officer, the Engineer and maybe one other officers and myself, as Boatswain, to discuss the tow and consider how to avoid the tow parting, and the recovery of the tow should it part. I was asked for my opinion and suggested that we bring a section of the anchor cable from the forecastle to the quarterdeck so that the chafing on the cable on *Sheffield's* fairlead should reduce the chance of the tow parting. This would require quite a few sailors to manhandle the cable from the forecastle to the quarterdeck.

Unfortunately, there was no direct route on the upper deck from the forecastle because the ship's bridge structure went out to both sides of the ship and blocked the way. This meant that, to get the chain cable from forward to aft, it would be necessary to take it down one deck along the passage and then up to the forecastle. This would be a major task but not impossible.

However, the Committee thought this was not feasible and was too much of a task to undertake. I then suggested we place the largest thickness of the wood on board across the fairlead to reduce the chafing on the tow wire. In the end, it was an interesting exercise to think about.

Someone with common sense back at Headquarters arranged for an Oceangoing tug to undertake the task. My heart beat a little slower when the ship was so advised because I expected to lose quite a lot of sleep during such a tow.

Finally, we sailed from Muscat heading back to the Med. About this time, I think, we were advised that we would now be making a courtesy visit to Istanbul. A planned one had to be cancelled to take the Marines to Bahrain.

Gallipoli and Istanbul.

Istanbul

Gallipoli

Cyprus

Suez Canal

As mentioned earlier, the friendly couple we had met in Malta, who lived there, arranged to meet Joan at the airport and take her our booked accommodation.

After returning through the Suez Canal, *Sheffield* headed for the Aegean Sea and up past Lemos Island, where my father had been a medic after a short stint on the Anzac Beach during the ANZAC landings in 1915. As we sailed past the Gallipoli Peninsular, I was looking at the beaches and hills and recalling what I had read about that campaign. The captain's voice called down to me on the Bridge saying, "Nobody else seems to appreciate what you and I are looking at."

Istanbul

It was quite rough as *Sheffield* anchored off Istanbul. It was decided that leave would not be granted to the Ship's Company until the weather improved. However, those with wives in town were permitted to take the risk of being hurt or otherwise when landing at the jetty. All such took the chance, and although getting off the ship's boat was dicey, we all made it.

It was only a short walk up a hill to the Hotel that Joan and I had booked. When I got there, Joan had not booked in, and there was a message to ring the couple from Istanbul we had met in Malta.

Istanbul

Gallipoli

Cyprus

Nearly Lost a Wife

I made the phone call and learnt that Joan and Anthony were presently staying with them. It was a long story, and they would relate it to me after I reached their unit. They gave me the address, and, with the officer friend of the couple, grabbed a taxi and gave him directions. However, in the rain and not understanding much English, it took the taxi driver some time to get to the units we were looking for. I was so delighted to see everyone. Then they told me the saga of how I nearly didn't have a wife and son.

The Saga

The saga began when the couple living in Istanbul decided to delay their departure for the airport for a short while because the plane from Malta was always late. However, the plane that Joan was on had arrived early, and with no one to meet her Joan caught the airport bus to the hotel we had booked.

On arrival at the hotel, she was told there was no booking for her, and they offered to arrange a hotel.

A taxi took them to a seedy part of the city and dropped her, Anthony, and the luggage at the door. Joan introduced herself and they confirmed the hotel had rung them. When she arrived there, she signed the register, had her passport taken, and was shown upstairs.

Meanwhile, the Istanbul couple, Jim and his wife arrived at the hotel Joan was in and asked to see Joan. He was told she was not there. Jim noticed her name in the register and demanded that Joan and son be brought down to see them. After an argument, and a threat to call the police, this was done, and Jim retrieved the passport and her cases and with his wife took them to his place.

Apparently, if Jim had not arrived as quickly as he did, and his ability to converse in Turkish, we may never have seen Joan and Anthony again.

The remainder of our stay was spent sightseeing and occasionally going out to dinner; the hotel arranged for a babysitter to look after Anthony when we went out at night. We enjoyed taking a tour around the area. Then it was time for the ship to leave and for Joan to pack up and return to Malta. (Life can be exciting, can't it?)

Israel

HMS *Sheffield* was the first British warship to visit Israel after its war disputes with Egypt. The ship berthed in Tel Aviv. As usual, there was an official reception for the VIPs and military hierarchy and a return reception ashore.

Leave was given and three of us officers decided to try and get to Jerusalem. We approached the bus company and were told that all the tickets had been sold for that day. Whilst we were standing trying to decide what we would do, an American standing nearby said, "What's up Limeys?"

To which I replied, "Gentleman, I am not a Limey. I'm an Australian," and answered his question saying, "We are having a problem getting seats on the bus to Jerusalem. All buses are full, and we are trying to work out what we should do as we are only in port for a few days."

To our surprise he invited us to join him in the minibus he had hired that was driven by a tourist guide. We accepted his offer. He refused to accept any cash. It turns out the driver had been a senior officer in the Israeli Army and had an excellent knowledge of the tourist spots. I won't go into all the bits and pieces except to say that we walked part of the Way of the Cross, visited Mount Calvary and the Temple, the place of the Last Supper, and generally saw other places like the Wailing Wall.

At one of our stops in Jerusalem, we found a street with a barbed wire fence down it. Our guide said to look up, and what we saw were rifles pointing out towards the other side of the street. These were the Arab marksmen in this section of the city. When we looked up at the other side of the street, we found there were Israeli rifles pointing across the street.

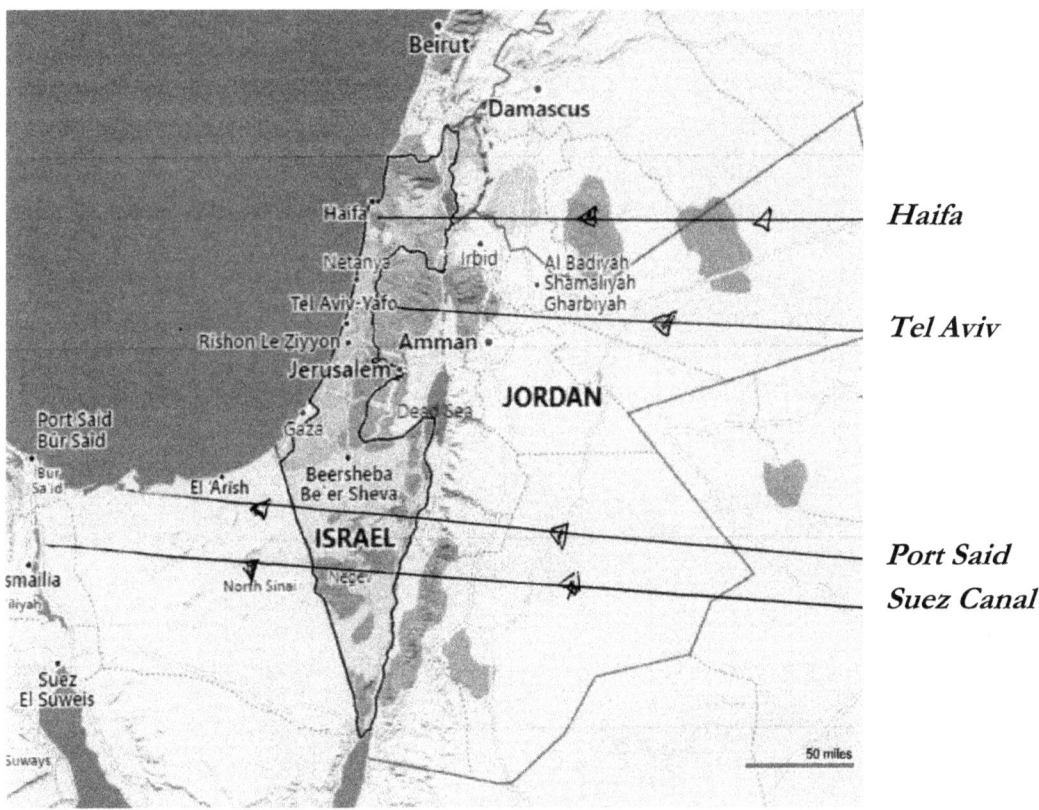

Mayoral Lunch

Our American host told us that we would be going to have lunch in Jericho. This turned out to be a meal with the local Mayor of that town. He must have noticed me looking at him several times. He asked if there was something wrong.

I said, "I am wondering how an Arab is Mayor of an Israel town."

He burst out laughing and said, "We Arabs hold many positions within Israel and there are no problems between us Arabs living in Israel."

You learn something every day.

After lunch, our host took us back to the bus station in Jerusalem, and we were able to return to Tel Aviv.

Kibbutz

One of the people we met at an official reception on board was a pilot flying for the Israeli airlines. It turns out he had been trained as a Gunnery Officer at Whale Island. He invited us to visit a Kibbutz for an evening of entertainment. Here we met several Israeli army men and women who entertained us with singing and dancing. This was excellent. In addition, they plied us with brandy and pieces of orange to suck after sipping the brandy. It really was a beautiful evening.

Eventually the time came for the ship to sail and continue our patrol of the Mediterranean and, from time-to-time, return to Malta.

Cyprus

On one occasion, we were sent to Cyprus, where the Greeks and people of Cyprus were in dispute over the island. I seem to recall that the Greeks had one part of the island and the Cypriots the rest. The ship's job was to be ready to intervene should there be trouble. The port the ship visited was Famagusta.

I cannot remember exactly where a yacht club or similar was. Here was a nice place to swim, a nice bar, and an eating place. It had a pontoon lying off the beach for people to swim out to. One thing we became aware of was that there were members of Eorka working in the area, and they may be the person serving you in the yacht club.

One day, the XO came to me and told me to go and resecure the pontoon as it had broken its mooring. I managed to secure the pontoon and made sure that I had secured the bolt of the shackle with wire. The next day, the XO sent for me and said, "I thought I told you to secure the pontoon ashore."

I replied. "I did secure it and wired the shackle so the pin could not come loose."

I was sent ashore again, to secure it again. I made sure there was a double wiring securing the pin. The next morning, it was unsecured and obvious to me that someone was having us on. Fortunately, *Sheffield* sailed before midday the next day and I didn't have to go to it a third time.

Eventually, the ship's period of duty in the Mediterranean came to an end. Joan packed up and flew back to England and awaited my return. On *Sheffield's* return to England, it berthed in Chatham.

My exchange service with the Royal Navy came to an end on 11th February 1959. However, my service records were held in Australia House I think and may show different dates.

I had packed my tin trunk and other goods and chattels, including rifles, and travelled to London where we stayed in a hostel until it was time to board the ship. Our heavy baggage was embarked before we were to board.

OFFICERS CERTIFICATE

TO MY ENTIRE SATISFACTION

AN ABLE OFFICER, ENERGETIC OFFICER AND SMART WITH A CHEERFUL, CONFIDENT MANNER.

Chapter 23

Homeward Bound and A New Home

11 February 1959

Departure England and New Home

On the 10th of February 1959, the day before our embarkation for home, saw me take our car and heavy baggage to the wharf where the ship home was berthed. That done, it was time to relax and enjoy our last meal in England for this posting.

SS Oriana

The voyage home was pleasant, and we enjoyed having our breakfast and dinner in the Dining Room. Our companions at dinner were easy to get on with and good company. I usually spent time in the gym, walking around the upper deck and swimming in the pool. Joan sometimes joined me in the pool and on the walks. Anthony was usually in the ship's nursery except for meals, and occasionally, we would have him with us on the upper deck.

Arrival Sydney

Joan's parents met us and took us to their home. The next day, I retrieved the heavy baggage and car. Then, it was time to register the car and my Australian driving license.

The homecoming get-together with family was very pleasant, and everyone enjoyed seeing and cuddling Anthony. After a few days, it was time to look for a rental to live in, close to HMAS *Watson* before I had to report for duty. I will leave joining HMAS *Watson* for the time being.

Finding a Home Rental

I was able to find an Estate Agent who had a property to rent in Watsons Bay and brought Joan out to ensure she was happy with the house and furnishings etc.

The Rental at Watsons Bay was most convenient as far as work was concerned. It was within walking distance of HMAS *Watson*, had a small shopping centre, a church close by and a good public transport system to the CBD.

However, we soon started to think of having our own home. Like many other things in my life, our finding of a suitably located place was unexpected.

Permanent Home

During a visit to one of Joan's friends in John Street, Ashfield, (Sydney eastern suburbs), I noticed that four houses were being built on a block of land on the opposite side of the road. The area of this building activity had been part of a large estate that had been used by an Overseas Consul and was then occupied and owned by an aging doctor.

I contacted the agent and applied for the corner house. This was accepted. The next step was to get the Defence Housing loan. This was approved. I didn't know until later that one of my old girl friends was also there applying for a loan.

Joan's mother gave us the name of a local Bank Manager and he was managing the same Bank our funds were in. He agreed to a loan, and everything appeared to be all set.

The location was in a suburb adjacent to Joan's parents and close to schooling and the church as well as the railway station. Also, the Naval Wife, (Betty P), who had looked after Joan during her pregnancy in England, lived in the same suburb about four streets away. Everything seemed fine.

Out of the blue, the agent rang and advised me that the house had been withdrawn from the market. It turned out that a higher bid had been placed. I was disappointed, of course. However, a few days later, I asked if the house next door was available and gave the agent my offer. The house had three bedrooms and a nice-sized backyard. This was to become our first house, 21A John Street, Ashfield.

Chippy Chappie

One afternoon, while driving home from *Watson*, I drove past a school in the eastern suburbs that was advertising that an evening class in Woodwork was about to start. I applied and was accepted. So began my training to be a Chippy Chappy.

My aim was to build a dining table and chairs as I had exhausted most of our funds in purchasing a bed and mattress for our son and a double mattress for ourselves, plus the necessary pots and pans, etc.

Eventually, when the house was completed, we were able to move in. There was a nook in the kitchen, so I promptly made a table and seating with storage space under it. This allowed us to have a place to eat our meals. We set up a room for our son and for ourselves. We had a dressing table and a double mattress on the floor. The built-in wardrobe in our bedroom did not have any doors.

Each week, I continued to travel to the school and be guided by the instructor. In due course, a table and six chairs with padded seats were completed. In the meantime, a section of the lounge/dining room had been selected for the dining area, and I laid parquet flooring in this area.

Kalgoorlie Friend Visit

You can imagine the lounge area with timber, tools, carpentry horses and other items all over the place.

One weekend, there was a knock on the door at 10 am, and behold, it was the Cub Mistress from Kalgoorlie, who I had worked with when in the Boy Scouts all those years ago. Someone who knew me had given her my address.

I excused the mess, and Joan and I entertained her and her husband with a nice cup of tea and treats at the dining table. We exchanged pleasantries etc. about old times and what I was up to. After they left, I promised Joan that within five years she would have everything. In fact, it was very much less than that. The house was fully furnished and carpeted in a couple or so years.

During this period, I continued to travel to school. Having basically done all I could inside, my next task was to sort out the front and back gardens.

Front Yard

The front fence line was a metre-high brick wall that provided a level lawn between the street and the house's front garden bed. The lawn area was a small distance below the top of the brick wall. There was a sloping concrete driveway on the left-hand side of the lawn, going right up alongside the house and part-way up the embankment at the back of the house. The driveway on the left-hand side facing the house was sloped, and a brick section prevented the lawn from slipping into the driveway. The area the houses were built on had been a vegetable and fruit garden originally, and old roots and leftover foliage were about a metre below the top of the lawn.

Lawn Preparation

Before I could get a lawn laid in the front yard, I had to remove all traces of Blackberry bushes that had been part of the garden of the original estate. This meant sometimes digging down anything up to a metre or more to remove their roots. Passersby thought I was preparing for a swimming pool.

Eventually, I was able to plant a lawn and put some flowers in beds in front of the house and one side fence line. Then it was time for the backyard.

Back Yard

The backyard was quite level until some distance from the back of the house. As previously stated, the area for the back lawn was a little over a metre above the concrete area at the back of the house. I obtained square concrete slabs and adjusted the face of the slope, so it was vertical.

A wall was built at the base of the slope, the first line about a metre from the slope and faced with slabs to form a level area for a garden. At one point, a set of concrete steps was set into it. A second wall was run parallel, about halfway between the lower wall and where a second-level garden across the back of the block. I faced the edge of the lawn with another concrete wall, so the edge of the back lawn was vertical.

The concrete area at the back of the house provided a wide space for my son to play in. A rotary clothesline was set up on the upper level.

Note. Much later, and after a second tour of England for an advanced component of my qualifications, and the growing up of the children and a fourth child arriving, an extension of the house was undertaken to provide a fourth bedroom and a large recreation playroom. This took away a lot of this concrete area. Joan's sister's husband designed and organised the extension and later the design of a garage which he built, with me as his offsider.

Master Bedroom

Eventually a double bed was purchased with the rest of the furniture for the master bedroom. I can't remember if my brother-in-law Barry, or I fitted the sliding doors to the wardrobe.

A Daughter

Joan became pregnant again and we were rewarded with a daughter, Anne, to join Anthony.

Departure for England.

The family was to enjoy this home until the end of 1962 when the family sailed for England. The home was let during our absence abroad for three years.

21A John Street, Ashfield

Chapter 24

HMAS A *Watson*

22 April 1959 to 28 March 1962

Wardroom Admin JR Accom. Tactical Trainer Posting In.

Returning from England, after qualifying as an officer and two years on exchange with the Royal Navy in HMS *Tumult* and HMS *Sheffield*, I joined HMAS *Watson* on the 22nd of April 1959. My job was the Officer in Charge of the Action Information Training Centre (AITC) that had been erected during my absence overseas.

My Job

As the Officer in Charge of the Action Information Training Centre (AITC), I was responsible for practical training in Surface, Sub-surface and Air Control and Plotting. The practical training took place on the ground floor. On the upper floor was my office, and the Controlling Stations for students were on the ground floor.

This building was an exact replica of the stables that had been converted for training purposes at HMS *Dryad*. The horse stalls had been modified to provide a space where surface/subsurface plotting tables, as used ships, had been installed, and the largest area was set up with the Air plotting and Air control equipment.

My deputy was a CPO PRI who was a friend and had grown up with me in the branch before I went to England. His first question was, "What do I call you?"

My reply was, "What did you call the last OIC?"

He said, "Boss or sir."

"Then that is what you call me," said I.

Later I took him aside and told him that once we were outside the fence around the Base, I was Bill, unless there were Junior Sailors or Officers present.

The building was placed very close to the edge of the vertical cliffs, and outside one end of the building was a flag mast where the Australian National Flag was flown during the daylight hours. This flag was to become the bane of my life.

The other training facilities in the Navigation and Direction school were basically the same as when I arrived back in 1946.

Ship's Company Accommodation

However, there had been a transformation in the facilities available for the Senior and Junior sailors. They were accommodated in new brick buildings closer to the harbour. There was also a new Administration Building between the Wardroom and the other accommodation for the Sailors. It was at the top of the road that led into the base.

Below the Senior and Junior Sailors accommodation area, and closer to the harbour, was the Tactical Trainer Building, and next door was the Torpedo Anti-submarine Training School that had been moved from Rushcutters Bay.

Tactical Trainer

At the northern end of *Watson*, nearer to the beaches just inside the entrance to Sydney Harbour, a new Tactical Training building (TTB) had been built to conduct more advanced, higher-level training for Ships Operations Room Officers and their crew.

When there was a ship's team working up in the Tactical Trainer, I would try and make myself available to man one of the training areas used to support that ship's team. In other words, to provide the information chat an escort would be using in support of the ship in question. This meant continuing to interpret messages in the Signal book and increasing my knowledge for when I was next in a ship's operation room.

This training was to stand me in good stead in the years ahead. It supplemented the knowledge I already had and had used whilst serving in HMS *Sheffield*.

Cookery School

The original kitchen/dining room building located at the southern end of the Base had been converted into a Cookery school. It was not far from the AITC and, from time to time, I would be an invited to participant and pass judgement on the meal being prepared by those cooks who were passing out on the school.

AIO Staffing

During my first set of exercises in the AITC, there was a shortfall of personnel to man the lower-level plots. When I asked why the extra WRANS on the top floor were not being used, I was told that the previous OIC had found when male and females working alongside one another in the lower level, they could be found holding hands and snuggling up to one another, and not concentrating on the job they were supposed to be doing.

I mustered the AITC crew outside my office and read the Riot Act. I made the point that we were there to train Radar Plotters so that when they went to sea, they were up to the mark. I pointed out that, from then on, male and female would work where necessary. I then asked if they had any questions. They acknowledged that what I was talking about was unacceptable.

Before talking to them, I had slipped a steel ruler up my coat sleeve and said if I caught anyone holding hands, etc., they would get a rap over the knuckles. They all said they understood the penalty.

The horse stalls had a small platform on the outer side, and it was possible to stand on it and look over the low wall and see the plotters at work. They would have their backs to you.

All went well for three weeks before I caught a pair holding hands, giggling, etc. A light rap on the knuckles caused them to fly apart. They looked around to see me scowling.

Later, I summoned the pair to my office, and they had no complaint and apologised. I never had to use the ruler again.

Officers in Charge

My first Officer in Charge of the ND school was a Lieutenant Commander, RN. He occasionally called me into the office to check out how I was going and to introduce me to the way I should prepare reports and letters. I found these talks helpful, and I still set down the main points of what I want to write about when preparing a presentation or letter.

This officer was relieved by an RAN officer, who happened to be the officer who, when playing cricket in HMS *Dryad* for the Petty Officers team against the officers, was going to drive the ball straight through me. When he tried a hard slog, I caught it, much to his displeasure. He was to become the bain of my life because of the Australian National Flag that flew alongside the AITC building.

I would get a very short telephone call stating, "The flag is fouled. Fix it!"

Quite often this would occur during a major training exercise. So, with no sailors or WRANS available, I personally would have to go and reset the flag. Not a happy chappy, as it took me away from supervising what was going on. This pantomime was to continue, sometimes several times a day, on an almost daily basis, until the officer was finally posted out.

Duty Officer

Eventually my turn as Duty Officer came up. Knowing that there were several Chiefs and Petty Officers still around who knew of my old drinking habits, I realised they would expect me to have a drink during my rounds to check the bars were closed.

Just after bar closing time of 2300 (11 pm), I arrived at their Mess and, with the bar still open, asked why it had not been closed. They smiled and I was invited in for a drink. I insisted the bar be closed NOW.

During this exchange with the person in charge, a very small drunken CPO from a Submarine based at HMAS *Penguin* came up and said, "You can't close the bar."

I said, "Want to bet?"

He wanted to go on about it. I told him he was heading for a sleep in the cells if he didn't go away. His reply was, "You can't put me in the cells."

One of those in the mess grabbed him and took him away. They closed the bar and returned the keys.

The next morning, I asked for the President of the Mess to see me. I explained I was still under training, and could he advise his Duty people that when I was Duty the bar closed at 2300 – and it did for the remainder of my time in Watson.

The Thief.

One night a Leading Seaman came back to his cubicle on the upper floor of the accommodation block and noticed a light on in the adjacent cubicle. He knew there was no one living there, so he quietly went to the door and looked in and there was a sailor, with his back to him, standing in front of an open locker surveying all the goodies he had stolen. The Leader quietly roused his cubicle mate, and together, they grabbed the thief and brought him up to the Guard House, where he was put in a cell.

I thanked the Leader and his mate for their actions. I enquired if the thief had fallen on any of the steps from the upper floor. The answer was no.

The next morning, the leader came up to me and asked why I had asked about the thief falling on any of the stairs. I explained that, in my day, he would have fallen down every one of the steps.

Harbour the Plotting Exercises

Before I took over the OIC of the AITC, an arrangement was made for Radio Procedure exercises to take place when requested by a ship alongside the dockyard in Sydney and HMAS *Watson*.

I realised that HMAS *Watson* had the capacity to conduct basic plotting exercises between the ships alongside the dockyard or even when they were sailing out of the harbour on their way to sea exercises. I also saw that it could be a good tool when ships at sea were transiting from one place to another and not participating in an exercise to be able to use such exercises to keep their plotting up to speed.

I collected all the setting up and other information that was used in the AITC and set it out into a book that became known as the Harbour Exercise Plotting Book. The book went on to be used for many years until it was overtaken by more efficient computer and digital systems available.

The Wardroom

The old Wardroom was still being used at this time. Sometimes at lunchtime I would take a drink and stand on the small veranda that stood out from the building and look at where my old cabin as a Chief/Petty Officer had been. I smiled as I remembered two of us removing a lady from the cabin next to mine, in a hammock mattress cover, for transport from the Base in the Drycleaners van. I also recalled how I would remove the bottles of Muskat wine from my cabin to the bar area whenever there were Captain's rounds.

When I first joined the Wardroom as an officer, there was another Special Duties Officer, a Communications specialist, who was the Wine Caterer responsible for the operation of the bar in the Mess. I cannot recall how I came to relieve him in the job, probably his posting from *Watson*. Having been the Bar manager in the old Chief and Petty Officer mess, I was quite happy to take over.

I can't remember the date – it was certainly nearing Christmas when, during a stocktake, it became obvious that a bottle of gin or three was missing. The Petty Officer who looked after the bar said that was not the first time this had happened.

There was only one living-in officer, a Commander, who I knew drank only brandy. I spoke to him, asking if he had noticed any of the stewards drinking whilst he was in the bar after hours. The reply was no.

I obtained the stewards' duty rosters over a period, and it was evident that the bottles went missing when one of the stewards was on duty. With the Christmas drinks for staff coming up in a few days, I decided not to do anything or ask any further questions until that function.

To Catch a Thief

On the day of the Christmas function, the staff were told they could have any type of drink they wanted. Because there was champagne and wines and beer, as I suspected only one steward asked if he could have a gin and tonic. I advised the people behind the bar to keep him supplied. When the function came to an end, this steward was very drunk.

As this steward would be passing the Administration building where the Master at Arms and his Regulating Staff and cells were, I rang the Master of Arms and alerted him to a very drunk steward who would be passing by shortly. The steward was taken into custody and charged with being Drunk on Board. I also arranged for the Master at Arms to contact his opposite number where this steward had been before his posting to HMAS *Watson*.

The result of this enquiry was that he had been suspected of removing liquor from the Officers' mess and had been posted to *Watson*. The Master at Arms and I were most unhappy that they had never thought to tell us of their suspicions.

Subsequently, he was seen as a Defaulter by the Captain, found guilty and sent to

Holdsworthy Military Detention Centre for ninety days hard labour. I can assure you that it would have been hard labour under the Military Police. On completion of his sentence, he was dishonourably discharged from the Navy.

The School Master

You may recall that earlier, immediately after I returned from World War II, the Schoolmaster (then known as an Instructor Officer) from HMAS *Perth 1,* who had been a POW for three years, taught us the basics of Instructing during my Radar Plot 2 course.

I found out that this officer lived on the next street to my home in Ashfield. He would catch a train and bus to *Watson* each day. To assist him in avoiding the steps at the railway stations and the walk up from the bus at Watsons Bay, I offered to drive him to work with me. He accepted the offer, and if he was still at *Watson* at the end of the day, I'd drive him home.

Sometimes, his work required him to be at HMAS *Kuttabul* near the Dockyard, and I would drive past, picking him up as it was not much of a diversion from the normal route home.

On occasion, he would ask to be dropped off at HMAS *Kuttabul* as he would be working there. There were other occasions when he would ring up before work ended and tell me not to pick him up from *Kuttabul*. I had a pretty good idea that on those occasions, he had met up with someone, was no doubt enjoying a tipple or three, and would be there for some time.

He was a real character and is mentioned in the book *Behind Bamboo* as someone who would sneak out under the wire of the prison camp to obtain food.

Before I left for England, he advised me he was looking forward to retirement and was planning to buy a home unit and make sure it had the rooms and all the facilities that he specifically wanted. I can't recall whether his wife died just before I left for, or just after we sailed for, England. What I do know is that he also died within about a year of his wife. This was while I was away in England. He was sadly missed by many and was a real character of the old order.

Chapel

During my time at *Watson*, it was decided to build a chapel on a site just north of the Administration Building. It was to be available for use by the various denominations. The Foundation Stone was laid on the 30th of April 1960.

It was to be available for all types of Service: weddings, funerals etc. and visits by the public. As I write this (in April 2022) the visits are no longer allowed, possibly due to the Virus.

I was fortunate to be at *Watson* for the Official Dedication and Opening. One of my tasks on that day was to escort guests from the car park, up the hill to the church. Then my past came back to haunt me. Whilst escorting a very elderly lady, she looked at me and said, "I know you," and, of course, I asked her how he knew me. She said, "Your name is Billy Ritchie and you used to come to my place with my daughter and her friends after you had all been swimming at Camp Cove Beach."

This beach was at the end of the road that passed the entrance to HMAS *Watson*. Her comment brought back memories of those times long ago when I was basically an Able Seaman. Her daughter had married and was now living somewhere else in New South Wales. We continued our conversation until I led her to a seat in the chapel.

The Chapel entrance

Below: An inside view of the Chapel. The window behind the altar gives views over the approaches to Sydney Harbour. North Head can be seen in the middle of the window.

AJAS Course

During my time in *Watson,* I was sent to HMAS *Albatross* to undertake an Australian Joint Anti-Submarine Course. It was interesting to be on a course with Air Force Officers and to participate in the various discussions. The many exercises on various ships conducting A/S exercises gave me a bit of an advantage.

The CO of the School, now a Commander, had been in HMAS *Vengeance* when I was there. His wife came from Kalgoorlie. He was very interested in showing a map of the Goldfields and discussing how he had been lucky to be put onto buying shares that had made him quite rich.

He was to my second Boss many years later when, as a Commodore, he became the Commanding Officer of HMAS *Stirling* after it had been commissioned.

Finally

I was selected to Undertake a Navigators Long Course in England in 1962. However, due to the earlier start date, the course was changed to what was then known as the Direction Officer course. This course was really an advanced Plot and Radar Course, with the main addition of training as an Aircraft Fighter Controller.

My appointment at HMAS *Watson* ended on 28 March 1962. So, I packed my bags and hammocks and sailed for England via the Panama Canal with my wife, Joan, and two children, Anthony and Anne.

Chapter 25

HMS *Dryad*

11 April 1962 to 21 December 1962

Introduction

Being selected to undertake a Navigation Course came as somewhat of a surprise, but I was pleased my Superiors must've thought that he could handle Navigation Officer's position in a ship. However, before I could leave for England, the position on the course was taken by a General List Officer (Naval College) who happened to be in England at the time.

My posting to England was changed because the Navigation course was starting before I could reach England. I was selected to undertake the Navigation and Direction Officers course. This was for Officers in charge of Operation Rooms and who carried out Fighter Control Duties. I had no problem in accepting the change as it would expand my considerable knowledge of being in overall charge of an Operations Room. As a sailor, and in my few years as an officer, I had a lot of time in this environment.

To England

With Joan and the two children, we embarked in Sydney in a Dutch ship and sailed for England via the Panama Canal. We visited Fiji and Hawaii, particularly. Son Tony and Joan enjoyed seeing the new places. Anne, who was only two, enjoyed the creche.

We also visited Fort Lauderdale, near Miami, before heading directly to England. After disembarking, we proceeded to Portsmouth, staying in a Guest House until we were able to obtain a lease of a two-storey house near Havant. This was very near the end of the Portsdown Hill Road that led to HMS *Dryad*. The back fence was alongside the road from Portsmouth to Havant. There were bus services going along this road.

The priority, before starting the course, was to get a new car. We took a trip to London and caught up with Joan's friends and I was able to get to the Hillman Minx establishment, who sold me my previous car, and buy another Minx.

On the other side of the road to our back fence was a very convenient shop that provided fresh bread, and next door was a butcher and a small Deli. The only problem was it was a bit of a walk along our street to get to the main road and then cross it.

Happily, settled in, it was time to report to HMS *Dryad* and I joined on the 11th of April 1962.

HMS *Dryad*

I do not intend to set out a great deal on each of the courses as in previous Chapters, rather to give an overview of what the subject of each part of the Course was.

I found there was a daily Naval Bus service that allowed me to travel to and from *Dryad* each day. This allowed Joan to have the car.

The Course included carrying out OOW duties in the Solent. Other studies were concerning Advanced Warfare Training. The course also involved taking charge of an Operation Room during intensive radar and plotting exercises. Advanced Electronic Warfare training was included.

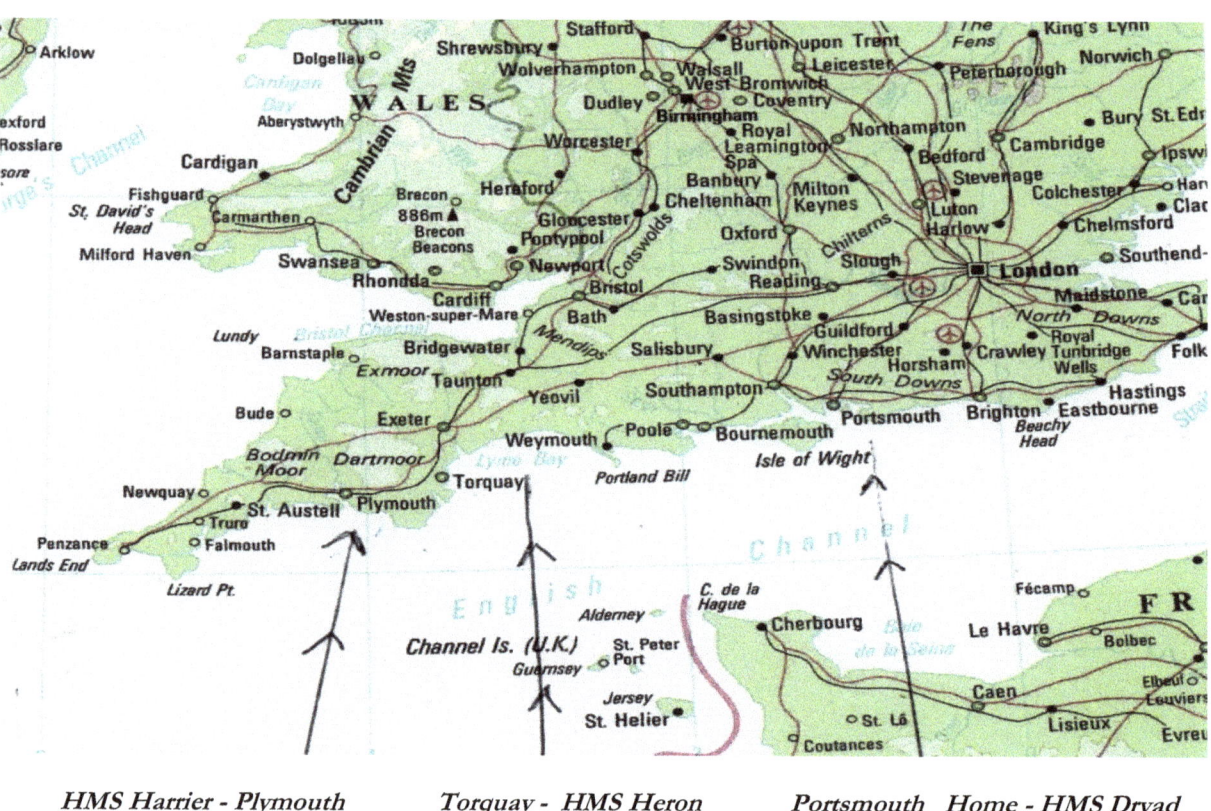

HMS Harrier - Plymouth   Torquay - HMS Heron   Portsmouth   Home - HMS Dryad

The most interesting part was the return to HMS *Harrier* for detailed Air Defence instruction and the basics of controlling fighters. The class was later to go to HMS *Heron*, near Yeovilton in south-west England for practical Aircraft Control training.

HMS Heron

At HMS *Heron* we were given basic instruction in the radio procedures and control instructions given to pilots. We were allowed to practice intercepting one fighter with another.

One of the tests was that, as an aircraft you were controlling was approaching the airfield and was about to line up and land, another aircraft behind him would declare an emergency and the expectation was that the aircraft with the emergency would have priority and be required to land first. Both aircraft would already have reported they were low on fuel. This required the controller of the lead aircraft to have to decide on what to do with his aircraft. The usual comment would be to abort the first aircraft's landing and turn him to go around again so the aircraft with the problem could land first.

When this happened to me, I realised that if I turned my aircraft away from landing with low fuel, and the problem aircraft crashed on landing, then my aircraft could be left up the creek if he ran out of fuel. I checked with the pilot his fuel state and he replied it was very low.

In all my time at the Base, I had never seen or heard of an aircraft not landing safely. My decision was to continue to control my aircraft to land and pray he didn't mess it up.

Initially, the Instructor was not impressed as usually everyone turned their aircraft from landing to let the disabled aircraft land first. I had not followed what he thought was the correct procedure. I carefully explained my logic and said that, if he had not reported he was very low on fuel, I would have done what he expected. He eventually agreed.

I was not to know that, later in my career, I would spend a very happy year at HMS *Heron* as the Fighter Controller for 890 Sea Vixen Squadron, with the family in a nice married quarter.

The course returned to HMS *Dryad* for final examinations and assessment. Then it was some leave for Christmas before travelling to Plymouth for a year in HMS *Ark Royal*.

I do not have actual marks for the course, but it was again near the top of the class. On completion of the course, we were sent on Leave, having been given our next posting. A classmate and I were posted to HMS *Ark Royal*.

New Arrival

It was during this time, son Peter was born, in October.

OFFICER'S CERTIFICATE COMMENTS

"HAS CONDUCTED HIMSELF VERY SATISFACTORY INDEED.

HE HAS NOW QUALIFIED IN DIRECTION OFFICER DUTIES AND WAS A GREAT ASSET TO THE WHOLE COURSE, USING FULL AND VERY CONSIDERABLE EXPERIENCE AND SOUND COMMON SENSE. I PREDICT A GREAT FUTURE FOR THIS OFFICER,"

My official date of leaving HMS *Dryad* is recorded as the 21st of December 1962.

With a classmate, we were to join with HMS *Ark Royal* in Plymouth on the 7 January 1963. The classmate and I agreed we would drive to Plymouth in my car.

On this occasion of completing a course, I was able to have Christmas with the family and enjoy Christmas morning and presents.

On January the 7th of January, I picked up my classmate and we took off for Plymouth after a heavy snowstorm.

Officer's Certificate

BRITISH ISLES - PHYSICAL AND POLITICAL

Chapter 26

HMS *Ark Royal*

7 January 1963 to 18 December 1963

The Ship

HMS *Ark Royal* was an Audacious Class Carrier. At the time of my posting, she was completing a refit in Devonport Dockyard, southern England.

Dimensions		Displacement	Engine
Dimensions	245m X 52m	53950 Tons	
Draft	10m		

Aircraft	
Sea Vixens	Scimitars

Joining HMS *Ark Royal*

I received my posting to HMS *Ark Royal* on the standard format that the Royal Navy used. It read as follows:

> *To Lieutenant W G Ritchie RAN*
>
> *THE Lords Commissioners of the Admiralty hereby appoint you "Lieutenant (SD)(D) of Her Majesty's Ship ARK ROYAL (D) additional for two years exchange service in the Royal Navy with LT (SD) (PR) D H Iles and direct you to report on board that Ship at Devonport on 7/1/1963. Your appointment is to take effect from that date* and vice Lt Cdr Whitaker (X) on a date to be reported.*

All this meant that I was to travel from Portsmouth to Devonport and join the ship on the 7 January 1963. I was to relieve Lieutenant Commander Whittaker (X is for Executive Branch).

Drive to Devonport

All too soon it was time to leave the family and head for Devonport. One of the other officers who had qualified with me as a Direction Officer, was also appointed to *Ark Royal*. We had become quite good friends. He was the one I played squash with during the course we had recently finished.

After consulting Joan, I had decided I would drive from Portsmouth to Devonport with my luggage and offered to take my classmate with me for company.

It had been snowing, and while a little apprehensive, I appreciated that I would have to be careful and ensure I maintained a very alert observation of the road ahead. I was completely unaware of how heavy the snowfall had been along the way. I picked up my officer mate and so began what was to be an interesting drive.

It had stopped snowing and snow ploughs had cleared the roads. I encountered no ice on the roads. However, just after passing into Devon, it was obvious the snowfall in this area had been very heavy. The snow plough had been able only go so far by the time we came up to it.

Eventually, we were stopped by workmen. The snow in front and at either side of the road had formed a wall about two metres-plus in height. I was told the road was completely blocked and we would have to wait until it was cleared. When I asked how long it would take to clear the road the answer was "Don't know." I certainly wasn't impressed with this news. We were asked to move the car back some distance from where the blockage was.

Side Track

Both of us were debating what we should do and how we could contact the ship to say we would be late on joining. (No mobiles then). Suddenly, a lorry appeared, a milk truck, and turned left off the highway and disappeared down a side road. I took a punt and decided to follow him. The road appeared to be in use and there was little or no snow on the track itself. However, the trucks had worn rather deep ruts and left a mound in the middle of the road. I found by putting one wheel on the mound and the other on the side of the road we could follow the truck.

We passed the truck picking up milk. Fortunately, track we were on continued and eventually reached the highway on the other side of the blockage. We were able to continue the Devonport. When we reached Exeter, we sought some advice as to what the road was like between there and Plymouth. We were advised there were several icy spots on the road and, as we would be going downhill for much of the way, we would have to be very careful in those sections. Generally, the advice was the road was open and we should be able to reach Plymouth.

There were no hitches from then on and finally, as it was getting dark, we arrived in Devonport and checked into the dockyard, then drove up alongside HMS *Ark Royal*. Sailors were sent down the gangway to carry our goods and chattels on board ship and down to our cabin. Both of us were to share the same cabin. I parked the car as directed. We tossed a coin to see who would have the bottom bunk. I lost. Fortunately, there was enough space above the bunk to allow me to sit up when required.

After a quick shower, and changing into our Mess Undress – bow tie stuff – we made our way to the Wardroom and introduced ourselves to those Officers who were having a drink and later a meal. After dinner, being rather tired, I excused myself and returned to the cabin to complete unpacking and, on completion of unpacking, climbed into the bunk and soon fell asleep.

Familiarisation with the Ship

After breakfast the next morning, I was interviewed by the Commander (Executive Officer) (XO)) and informed I would keep First Officer of the Watch duties in harbour and on the Bridge at sea when not required in the operation's (Air Defence Room (ADR). I had expected to be an Officer of the Day where you did not keep Bridge watches because of my age. I accepted the decision.

Note. It is interesting to note here that I was made a first Officer of the Watch. I had not been to sea since early 1959. I will make another remark about becoming a First Officer of Watch when I joined HMAS *Melbourne* on my return to Australia.

At the completion of this briefing, I was free to walk around to familiarise myself with the layout of the various boats and booms as well as to have a look in on the ADR and Upper Ops Room.

Not too long after this, I received my copy of the Officer of the Watch duty roster. I made sure where all the bits and pieces were on the Quarterdeck for duty in Harbour and checked out the Bridge. The Admiral, whose cabin was immediately below the Quarterdeck, usually made his way up on the Quarterdeck through a hatch in the middle of that area.

During my first harbour OOW duty on the Quarterdeck, I noticed the Quartermaster and bosun mate were smoking and having a cup of coffee at their position on the Quarterdeck. With the Admiral living on board, and the hatch and stairs to his quarters in the middle of the quarterdeck, I was not impressed and appreciated that should the Admiral appear unexpectedly, there could be a problem from their slack attitude to the job they were supposed to be doing.

I advised them that I had no problem with them having a coffee and/or a cigarette if they asked my permission, but not on the Quarterdeck itself. I explained the reason, besides the long tradition of the Quarterdeck being hallowed ground, and especially because the Admiral could suddenly appear unannounced, and there was also the possibility of them having to Man the Ship's side to greet someone important, coming aboard or going ashore, at very short notice. I also made it clear a part of their duties was to keep a watch on the wharf and area surrounding the ship. I made sure that they, and the other Quartermasters and Bosun Mates who worked with me, got the message.

It didn't take them long to wake up that, whilst I was from the RAN, I really knew what a high standard was required in a Flagship. I also suggested to them that when they came on watch they should make sure that everything was in place and that they should walk around the Quarterdeck to make sure that there was nothing lying around that shouldn't be there.

Slowly, the Quarterdeck was cleared of all the unwanted items and came up to the standard required of a Flagship, especially when I was on watch. From time to time, when coming on watch, and to keep the staff on their toes, I would visit the cleaning locker and pull flexible strands out of a mop. On my first walk around to make sure that everything was Tiddly Boo (clean), I would drop a mop shred here and there over the guard rail. A short time later I would again walk around and rediscover the strands. I would then call in a loud voice pointing "Irish Pennant." You can imagine the curse (under the breath) of the Leading Seaman, Quartermaster.

One afternoon, I was sitting in a small hotel bar when one of the Leading Seaman Quartermaster's came up and asked if he could put a question to me. I said 'yes if I could buy him a drink.' He then explained that, when he knew I was to be the Officer of the Watch, he went around that Quarterdeck and made sure there was nothing astray. He was always surprised that, somehow, he had missed strands from the mop. He apologised for not being more thorough. I then explained to him that I knew he had missed nothing, that I was the one who dropped the strands to keep them on their toes. I asked him if he had any problems being on watch with me. His answer was: No, he was very happy to be on watch with me for there never seemed to be any problems as there were sometimes with other OOWs. I told him there would be no more strands if he kept up a standard I had set.

February 1963

To Sea for Work Up

On the 4th of February 1963, *Ark Royal* slipped from her berth in Devonport and proceeded into the English Channel to make its way to the open sea. I am not sure of the circumstances, except that, having entered the channel and about to let the tug lines go, it was found that one engine was doing the reverse of what the telegraph to the engine room had signalled. It was found one engine telegraph, from the Bridge to Engine Room, had been rewired back to front.

Fortunately, the engines were immediately stopped, and luckily, the ship did not go aground in the narrow channel.

Eventually all was well, and we made our way to sea into the English Channel heading for the Lyme Bay Exercise Area.

Bridge Watchkeeper

My first Bridge OOW duty, at sea for nearly four years, was as the first OOW in charge of this 53,000-ton monster, charging up the English Channel, with ships to the left and right, going whichever way, and fishing and small craft all over the place. It was to be almost intense watch I have ever carried out as the First Officer of the Watch at sea. I was very pleased, and relieved, when the morning watch OOW took over the reins.

From February 4th to 9th, the ship conducted Deck Trials for the Buccaneer and VSTOL (Vertical Take Off and Landing Experimental trials). See the map below for the location of Lyme Bay.

From memory, this was the first time a VSTOL aircraft had landed on a carrier.

Lyme Bay   *Portsmouth*

After the trials, *Ark Royal* returned to Lyme Bay and anchored until the 12th when it headed for Portsmouth.

At Portsmouth I was able to spend a few nights at home with the family before the ship sailed back to Lyme Bay to Devonport, embarking the Air Group, including 890 Squadron. I was not to know that I would be closely associated with this Squadron much later.

Air Group Work Up

Deck Landing by the aircraft allocated to the ship was carried out between the 24th and the 26th of February. *Ark Royal* returned to Devonport on the 29th.

March 1963

I celebrated my 37th birthday in harbour and was able to have a drink with some other officers who found out it was my birthday.

We were back at sea for Flying Exercises and to compete in Exercise Dawn Breeze. After the Exercise, we returned to Devonport on the 16th of March to refuel, restore, etc. The aircraft had returned to their shore bases to be readied for our deployment.

During these periods at sea, I was able to get used to the English radar displays and the air radars. I was involved in carrying out air intercept exercises and the like and generally gained a lot of confidence in my ability. I also attended briefing and debriefing sessions for aircrew and got to know members of 890 Squadron, whom I would be Controlling.

Deployment

Sailing from Devonport on the 19th, the ship headed for Gibraltar, where, on arrival on the 21st of March, it entered Dry Dock until the 2nd of May.

During this period, I was able to explore Gibraltar and the adjacent Spanish town, where some of the crew went for Spanish-type meals and drinking, of course.

May 1963

Departing Gibraltar on the 3rd of May, the ship headed for the Suez Canal. A service was held over the Grave of the third HMS *Royal* shortly after sailing, and the next day, we re-embarked the ship's Air Group off the Balearic Islands. Then, it was on to Malta for a short stopover. On the 10th of May, the ship transited the Suez Canal and arrived Aden on the 13th of May for refuelling etc.

Sailing From Aden on the 14th of May the ship spent the next five days in this exercise area. On completion of Brown Trout, the ship used Aden as a base and spent until the 2nd of June exercising in this area.

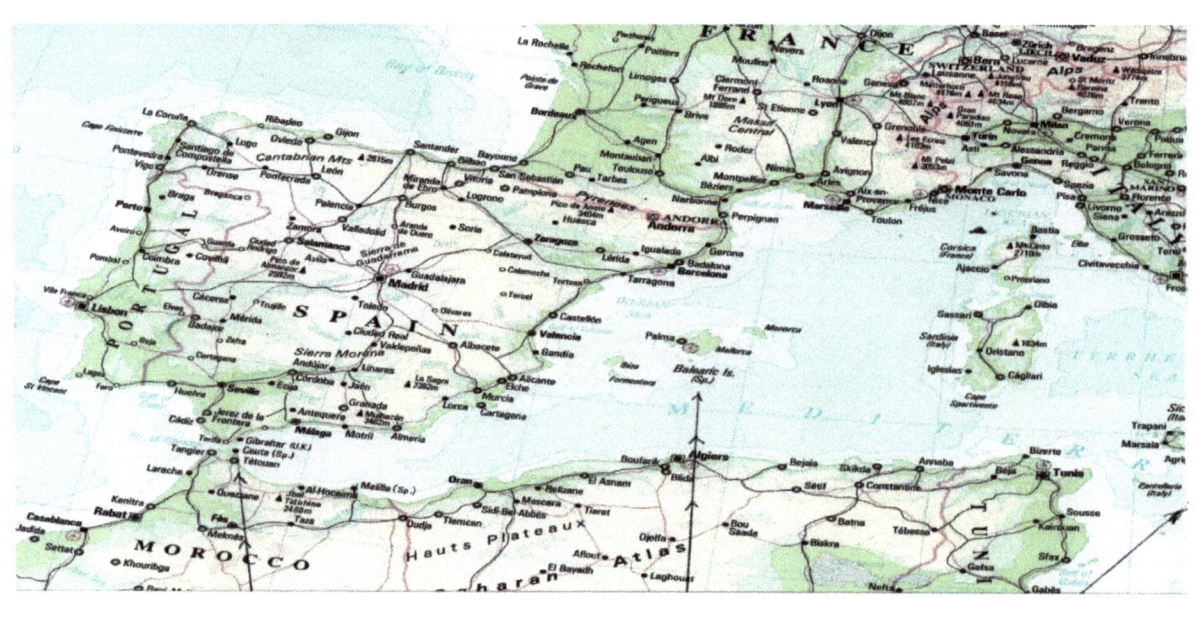

Gibraltar   *Balaeric Island*   *Malta*

Aden

Mombasa

Zanzibar
Dar es Salaam

June 1963

On the 3rd of June, all exercises ceased, and it was off to Mombasa for Rest and Recreation.

Mombasa

The ship arrived at Mombasa on the 7th of June. Here, I was able to go on a Safari with a couple of English officers and stayed two or three nights or so in a game park. We visited Mt Kilimanjaro but did not have time to climb it.

On the way back to Mombasa, we drove through several villages, and it was very apparent that not many visitors of our ilk came this way. We kept a good lookout for any trouble and arrived back in Mombasa without incident.

Back in Mombasa we attended several Receptions and meals with the local community and enjoyed the discussions that took place. They wanted to know about an Australian serving in the Royal Navy. However, my impression was the British Raj attitude still prevailed.

Zanzibar

I am not sure if it was this visit to Mombasa or a later one in October that the ship went to Zanzibar. I will comment on the visit there now.

During a break in flying, *Ark Royal* proceeded to Zanzibar to remove the British Protectorate and celebrate their Independence. The town was not large, and it was decided that, instead of being let loose in town, the ship's crew would use an island that had been a Quarantine Station and a Prison.

Island Supervisor

The Overseer's house remained. It was on stilts and had a veranda all round. The house was to provide overnight accommodation for the team overseeing the night ashore for the sailors. The prison area had a high wall about six metres high on the edge of the land above the sea. Rocks right under the wall were less than a metre below the water line. Could be fatal if you fell off the top of the wall.

The Island Recreation

The ship's Sports Officer oversaw setting up the arrangements and it was agreed that personnel could sleep on the island overnight if not on duty. The Sports Officer obtained approval for beer to be sold in unopened cans. A ship's whaler was provided as a safety boat in case someone got into trouble swimming.

I agreed to take over the first (afternoon) duty after the Sports Officer had set it up. So, several hours after the sailors had flocked to the island I arrived and relieved the Sports Officer. I had two young Air Crew Officers to assist me.

Bar Closure

I hadn't been on the island long before I realised almost everyone was drunk. I was watching the sale of the beer and noticed that sailors were staggering away with an armful of beer. I followed one chap, and he was burying the cans in the sand and returning for more. As this appeared to be happening by quite a few sailors, I closed the bar much to the protests of those wanting more beer. Fortunately, the Duty Petty Officer was a PTI, and sober, and handled the protests OK.

Man Overboard

As I walked around to survey the total scene, a sailor rushed up and told me a chap had fallen off the top of the Prison Wall into the water. I had all sorts of thoughts of him hitting the rocks. I sent the sailor to tell the boat coxswain to bring the whaler round to the wall side of the prison as there was a man in the water.

This sailor reappeared shortly after to say the whaler was unavailable as it had been sunk. Someone had pulled the plug out, and it had filled with water. I hurried to a place outside the wall and could see the sailor foundering and shouting that he couldn't swim.

The bank alongside the prison was vertical and well over a metre above the water level, so I sent the sailor back to get the bow line from the whaler. However, fortunately, a relatively sober sailor said, "Sir, would my hammock lashing be of any help?" I grabbed it off him and sat several quite drunk sailors down one behind the other, and put the rope in their hands and made them do a couple of practise heave in and change their hand position for the next heave in. Saying a prayer, I stripped off, climbed down and swam out to where the sailor was floundering.

I swam him back to where the rope was and tied it around his waist. I then got the sailors to heave etc. I helped the sailor up the face of the seawall. Unfortunately, he couldn't pull himself up the line or keep himself off the wall and suffered a few cuts from coral. I basically had to push him up each time the sailors heaved. Finally, I got him up onto level land and he just lay there. Some of his mates came and got him. I checked he was okay to go with them. I didn't ask him why he climbed onto the top of the wall; it was pointless.

Back to the Bar Closure

Having dried myself and put my shirt and shorts back on, I was relaxing on the house veranda when I saw a sailor demanding the POPTI open the bar. In his drunken state, he wouldn't go away. I heard the PTI say, "You will have to talk to the Aussie Officer up there on the veranda." The sailor headed for the stairs up to where I was sitting.

When he reached the bottom of the steps, the PTI stopped him and said something I didn't hear. I found out later the PTI had warned him that he was sure I would listen to his request politely. However, when he stated he wasn't ready to open the bar just yet and you, the sailor, wanted to argue about it, don't be surprised if he found himself at the foot of the stairs.

The sailor started up the stairs but, after about three steps, he decided it wasn't worth the risk.

Sequel. I was first Officer of the Watch. Shortly after leaving Zanzibar, the Captain took me to one side of the bridge and said, "I hear you had to punch a sailor, who was demanding the Bar be opened, and he fell down the stairs."

My reply was, "Sorry, your informant is wrong. The only punch I have ever thrown in my life was as a 12 or 13-year-old when I was bailed by kids from a rival school in a laneway. They had a boy bigger than me, who may have been being inducted into their gang, who kept pushing me with his hand. I pulled my hand way behind me and let fly and bloodied his nose, blood going everywhere. I jumped back into a boxing crouch and said 'who's next?' They scattered, and thereafter, they always were happy to ask me how I was if we passed in the street."

The captain accepted my explanation.

Mombasa

After a few more days in Mombasa, after leaving Zanzibar, *Ark Royal* headed for West Malaysia. En route, an Operation Readiness Inspection (ORI) was carried out. The ship anchored at Langkawi on the 7th of July. On the 8th and 9th, I participated in Exercise Birdbarge. I recall that the opposition included RAAF aircraft stationed at Butterworth. On completion, *Ark Royal* proceeded to Singapore. The ship remained in Singapore from the 11th to the 25th of July. The time in Singapore allowed me to catch up with some old friends and also to sample the delights of places I had visited previously.

The ship sailed for Exercise Forex 63 and anchored in Pulao Tio Mann, East Malaysia. From July 28th to August 3rd, the ship continued to Exercise off Singapore.

August 1963

Lost Aircraft

On the 29th or 30th of August, I was controlling a Sea Vixen piloted by Lieutenant Dunbar Dempsey, who reported he had a serious engine problem and needed to land ashore. He set course and I watched as he flew towards the coast. He changed radio frequencies to that of the airport. I continued to track the aircraft by radar until his radar contact merged with land. I had noted where he had crossed the coast.

I went to get a coffee and, on returning to the Ops Room, was informed that the Control Tower had lost radio contact. I immediately sat at my display and picked up the shoreline features where I had seen the aircraft cross the coast.

I then noticed a radar contact moving parallel with the coast and guessed it was a search aircraft. I managed to contact this aircraft and directed him to where I was confident the aircraft had crossed the coast. When the search aircraft arrived at the location, there, on the beach, were two personnel waving. It was the Pilot and his Observer. They had ejected as they crossed the coast, one landing at one end of the beach and the other at the other end.

They were pleased to buy me a drink when they came back on board.

September 1963

Hong Kong

The ship departed the Exercise area off Singapore, headed for Hong Kong, and anchored in Junk Bay. At the end of a two-day exercise period, the ship departed the Hong Kong area, arriving in Singapore on September 20th. It then departed Singapore for a Flyex off Butterworth. From there, it was onto the Gulf of Oman.

October 1963

Khor al Fakkan

Khor al Fakkan is today one of the world's leading container ports. It provided a shorebreak before another exercise in the Persian Gulf.

From Khor al Fakkan the ship sailed into the Persian Gulf and participated in Exercise Biltong. I can't remember much about this exercise. Being in the Persian Gulf created land masses on the radar.

On completion of our involvement in Exercise Biltong, the ship headed for Mombasa.

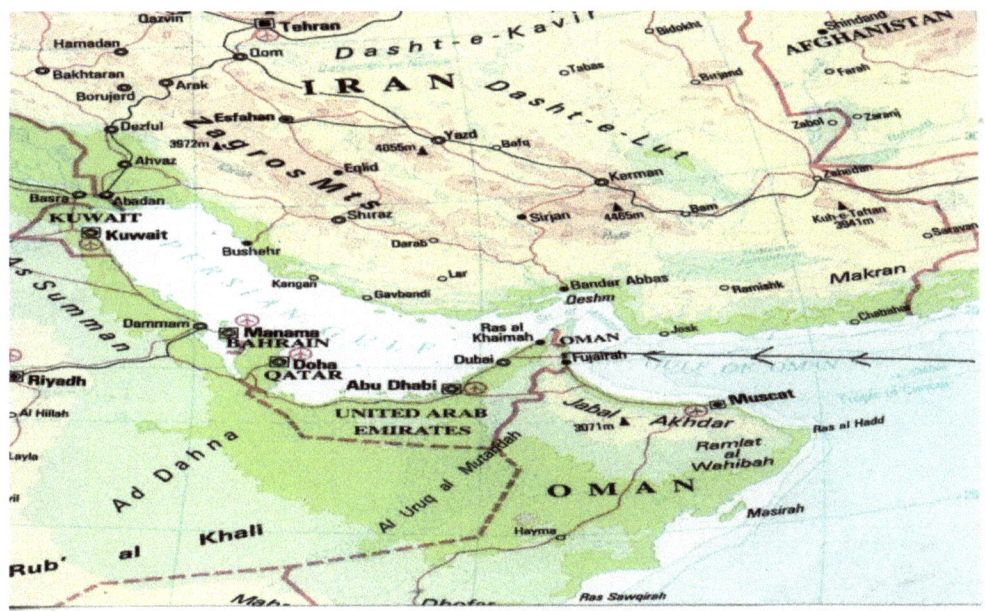

Khor al Fakkan at entrance to Persian Gulf.

Mombasa

Ark Royal arrived in Mombasa on the 18th of October and gave me the opportunity to visit a different game park, visit Nairobi, and be entertained in one of the Clubs.

December 1963

Finally, on December 1st, 1963, the ship headed for home via the Suez Canal. At Aden, three RN officers and I were flown to England, landing in London on Christmas Eve. We were to join HMS *Hermes* with 890 Squadron after Christmas to participate in an exercise whose name escapes me.

London Airport

After landing at London airport, we made our way to the exit gate. The three RN officers passed through okay, but my Australian Passport presented a problem, and I was directed to the back of a large queue of non-English passengers.

However, the RN officers finally convinced the gatekeeper I was serving in the Royal Navy, although an Australian, and I was allowed through. This delay caused us to miss the last train to Portsmouth, so we had to wait until after 4 am for the next train.

I had warned Joan I was sending her a Christmas present and hoped it would be delivered on Christmas Eve or Christmas morning. I knocked on the door about 5:30 am, and a very sleepy girl answered the door. I said, "Your Christmas present." She couldn't believe it was me. I was so tired, and Joan and I returned to bed to be woken by excited children wondering who the strange, bearded man was in bed with Mum. Once they realised it was me, they were all over me.

So, my time in *Ark Royal* had ended, and I was able to spend Christmas and a few days at home before joining HMS *Hermes*. There, I was to be used as an air controller for the 890 Squadron during a short exercise period during their workup before I came ashore to take up my next appointment.

HMS *Hermes*

HMS *Hermes* was to participate in an exercise off the south coast of England and 890 had been allocated to provide Air Defence for the ship and her escorts.

I can't recall where I joined the *Hermes* or what happened during the exercise. I would have controlled 890 most of the time during the exercise. It wasn't much different to being in *Ark Royal*.

Next Appointment

My next appointment required me to report to 890 Sea Vixen Squadron at HMS *Heron* as their Air Controller. I had also found out a married quarter, basically on the Base, had been allocated for our use. So, on return ashore, we gave up our lease in Portsmouth, and headed for Yeovilton and another two-storey home.

I will leave it to your imagination the packing up our goods and chattels, arranging a removalist for the heavy stuff and then, with the children and Joan, I drove to HMS *Heron* near Yeovilton and reported to the 890 Admi Office.

See the next chapter for time with 890 Squadron.

Officers Certificate

To my great satisfaction.

Ritchie is a first-class Officer and fine advertisement for the R.A.N. He has been of the greatest value in Ark Royal and I shall be sorry to lose him.

Chapter 27

890 Squadron

30 December 1963 to 18 December 1964

Introduction

890 Squadron aircraft were Sea Vixen and based at HMS *Heron,* Yeovilton in Somerset, England. It is north of Yeovil.

Yeovilton

Aerial View

Joining

My official date of joining was 30 December 1963. That was the day I joined the Squadron. However, in fact I went to HMS *Hermes*, attached to 890, for an exercise before arriving at HMS *Heron*, the Air Base and home to the Naval Aviation Museum. I can't remember where I embarked in *Hermes*.

Immediately after the exercise, I moved the family to Yeovilton and the married quarter basically on the Base.

Married Quarters

Our Married Quarter was a two-storey home and the family quickly settled in once the move from Portsmouth was complete. There was a small English pub not far from the Base where they served excellent meals.

Our settling in proceeded smoothly, and we were made very welcome by the neighbours.

The Squadron

The Squadron had its own building and Hangar on the Base. Whilst I knew most of the aircrew, there were some I had not met. I attended the briefings of the aircrew. The Squadrons aircraft was the Sea Vixen. See details below.

Sea Vixen

Sea Vixen

The de Havilland DH.110 Sea Vixen was a British twin-engine, twin boom-tailed, two-seat, carrier-based fleet air-defence fighter flown by the Royal Navy's Fleet Air Arm during the 1950s through to the early 1970s. The Sea Vixen was designed by the de Havilland Aircraft Company during the late 1940s at its Hatfield aircraft factory in Hertfordshire, developed from the company's earlier first generation jet fighters. It was later called the Hawker Siddeley Sea Vixen after de Havilland was absorbed by the Hawker Siddeley Corporation in 1960.

The Sea Vixen had the distinction of being the first British two-seat combat aircraft to achieve supersonic speed, albeit not in level flight. Operating from British aircraft carriers, it was used in combat over Tanganyika and over Yemen during the Aden Emergency. In 1972, the Sea Vixen was phased out in favour of the American-made McDonnell Douglas Phantom FG.1 interceptor. There have been no flying Sea Vixens since 2017.

My Job

My job in the Squadron was to conduct Fighter intercepts, usually controlling one aircraft to intercept the other. I was to be available every day except weekends when the aircraft would be maintained.

Initially, the aircrew would take off and do self-intercepts without my help. However, several times they missed one another, and I would inform the aircraft where the other was. They soon started using me to control them. I am not sure that there had been an air controller posted to the Squadron before me.

After they accepted me, my usual day was spent controlling intercepts as required. I would attend the aircrew briefing and establish Radio Contact once they left the circuit. I became attuned to the personalities of pilots and observers, and they soon accepted me as part of the team.

Soon after we arrived, Joan and I were invited to a social gathering at the home of one of the pilots. We were able to meet the wives and girlfriends of the team, which assisted Joan in making new friends and the children in meeting and playing with other children in the married quarters area.

The Pub

On Friday afternoons, there was generally no flying, and at lunchtime, it was not unusual to gather at the local pub for lunch. The meals were very good. On occasions, Joan and the children would accompany me.

On other Fridays, a group would visit a nearby pub with a skittle alley. It was always fun playing skittles with worn balls that didn't always go where you wanted them to.

V Bomber

It was still during the Cold War. From time to time the V Bomber force would do a practice emergency dispersal, and HMS *Heron* was one of the locations for a V Bomber to disperse to. On my first time of being able to walk around the aircraft I was able to make a few mental notes. We were not allowed to go on board.

That night in the Mess, the V Bomber CO was complaining that they could not get fully qualified as the RAF Fighters were all engaged in ground attack training. The 890 pilots said they could perhaps help and provide intercept training if that was satisfactory.

It was agreed that the V Bomber would telephone before takeoff and give his approximate time of returning over the West Coast from his patrol and his Identification code, as there were airways to be avoided.

First Intercept

I was manning the radar display when I picked up the Bomber and began the intercept. The Bomber came down to the normal height the Squadron exercised at. I was able to get the fighters in behind okay but, having detected the fighters, the bomber was able to turn inside the fighter turning circle and they could not lock on their missile control system. So, it was Bomber 1 and Fighters 0. The Bomber then proceeded to his Base and the fighters landed at *Heron*. I attended the debrief of the aircrew and listened to their reports.

After the debrief I went away and thought how it would be possible to get in behind the Bomber without detecting the fighters. This required me to recall my inspection of the Vulcan when it had landed at HMS *Heron*. From this recall and my interest in electronic warfare, I began the process of elimination until I thought I had a solution.

Second Intercept

I can't remember the time frame for when the Bomber CO said he would be coming back and would like to have another practice. I won't reveal here what procedure I devised. Enough to say, I was able to get the two fighters in behind the Bomber and his first clue they were there was when his alarm went off in the cockpit when the fighters locked on their fire control systems. Fighters 1 Bomber 0.

The fighters flew alongside the V Bomber before breaking away and landing. Shortly after, I learnt the V Bomber radioed he had an emergency and needed to land. I immediately thought something had gone wrong with the plane. However, a pantomime was to follow.

Pantomime

I attended the pilots' debrief and, grabbing a cup of coffee, retired to my corner chair and began reading a book. Suddenly, the door of the Briefing Room was violently thrown open, and in came an RAF Group Captain and some of his crew. As he opened the door, he shouted in a very angry voice, asking who the pilots who had intercepted him were.

The two pilots acknowledged they were the ones.

The Group Captain in a demanding and angry voice asked, "How did you get in behind me without me knowing?"

The pilots answered, "Don't know."

The Group Captain blew his top and insisted they tell him.

They again said, "Don't know" and then added, "Ask him," pointing to me.

As he headed towards me, he must have seen my Australia flashes on my coat and said in a disparaging voice, "Australian, eh?"

I acknowledged his comment.

Still very aggressive, he demanded, "Tell me how you got the two aircraft behind me."

My reply was, "That's my secret." He exploded again, demanding he be told.

This little scene continued for some minutes with him demanding and me refusing. Eventually, he woke up that his aggressive and demanding manner was not getting him anywhere and he was almost on his knees pleading to be told.

I also made a comment that 'you English had sent all your convicts to Australia, and we had learnt a few deception tricks.' That did not impress him, and he gave a snort.

Eventually, I relented and pointed out that I had thought about the first time and realised there was a way to deprive him of where the fighters were. Using that information, I developed a counter plan and it worked. I think he realised he may have a weak link in their countermeasures. He then turned and stormed out of the room – no thanks or any other comment.

For the first and only time in my career, I failed to stand up when addressing a Senior Officer. I have thought about his manner and have assumed that his unsuccessful evasion may have prevented him from getting fully qualified; however, that is mere conjecture on my part. It is interesting to note that he never came back, and neither did other V Bombers who had participated in Intercepts.

Recreation

With the family, we explored various villages and the countryside around Yeovilton. I was free every weekend, and quite often, we went into Yeovil for our main shopping and always on Sunday to attend Mass.

Some Fridays I would join some of the aircrew and visit the local pub and try and get used to English beer and enjoy a very nice lunch. As mentioned previously, there were occasions when Joan and the family also accompanied me to the pub for a meal.

Very occasionally, I would go with some aircrew to a neighbouring village and play Skittles. Otherwise, I spent as much time with the family as possible.

Air Museum

There was a museum that exhibited artefacts depicting Naval Air history. It was interesting to study the way the RN Fleet Air Arm had developed from its earliest days.

I had made a replica of an old RN warship of the sail-age and donated it to the museum.

Chaplin

The Catholic church in Yeovil provided one of their priests to act as Chaplain to those on the Base.

Every Friday there would be a buffet lunch in the Wardroom. I noticed on one Friday that the Catholic Chaplin was also having lunch and was beside me in the queue. He was helping himself to various meat dishes. He saw me looking at him and said, "I love being Chaplain and one of the best things I am excused from avoiding meat on Fridays when I act as Chaplain." At that time, members of the Navy, and I assume other Defence Personnel, were excused from eating meat and fasting on Fridays.

Mess Dinner

At one Mess Dinner, the Admiral in Charge of the Royal Navy came to dinner, and he was to advise that the Fleet Air Arm would not be getting Phantom Aircraft at that stage. You can imagine the disappointment among the fighter aircrew when told that at the dinner.

When the Admiral got up and began to speak and mentioned there would be no Phantoms for the Navy, he looked up to see a mini cardboard phantom heading straight for him, spewing flames out the back. He ducked down under the top table level as did others at that table until the object had passed overhead. Someone then removed the object from the line passing above the Admiral's head.

In anticipation of a negative statement, some disappointed officers had rigged a thin fishing line from a corner of the room to pass over the VIP table and had made a cardboard model of a Phantom aircraft and put a kind of cracker in the tail. The cracker was one that flamed but didn't go off.

The Admiral was not that impressed, but I seem to recall that his comments were along the lines that he understood the disappointment. As far as I was aware no one was punished for this incident as, while everyone's eyes were fixed on the flying object, those responsible slipped back to their places unnoticed.

Christmas Drinks and Farewell

My time at HMS *Heron* and 890 Squadron was coming to an end in December 1964 and we were invited to a farewell/Christmas Party. Everyone expressed their regrets we were leaving and wished us well for the future back in Australia.

I have not made many comments on the family activities whilst at HMS *Heron*. I am sure they enjoyed their activities and fun.

Summary

My time with 890 Squadron made me a very efficient Fighter and Air Controller. In particular, it gave a year with my family every day and, as you guess, that was the best thing to come out of my posting to 890 Squadron. Packing up was completed then it was off to London to embark for the trip home.

Departure

The trip to London was to prepare for boarding a ship taking the family home. I was looking forward to being able spend some time away from Naval duties and being with the family.

AND SO ENDED MY CLOSE ASSOCIATION WITH THE ROYAL NAVY

Officers Certificate

To my entire satisfaction

A most proficient fighter direction officer and a hardworking and efficient officer.

Recommended for promotion to Lieutenant Commander.

Chapter 28

Returning Home

6 January to 14 February 1965

From the Naval Board about Returning Home

My official notification of the family's return to Australia stated I was to embark in *Iberia* on the 6th of January 1965 for 39 days Foreign Service leave to date 8th of January 1965 and to *Melbourne* on completion of leave. That meant the time on the *Iberia* would take up just over half or so of that leave and the rest would allow me to settle the family back into our home before having to report for Duty.

Preparation

We stayed in a Service-related Hostel in London with son Anthony, daughter Anne and baby Peter. After our arrival and settling in, one of my first jobs was to get the car to the wharf for passage to Australia. Having established the date and place to present the car and our heavy baggage, it was done without any fuss or problems.

Joan was able to contact her friends and we were able to telephone my Best Man's parents and say farewell.

Leaving London, where we had enjoyed ourselves, was a bit of a downer. However, the prospects of being back in Australia and enjoying the leave left was something to look forward to.

On the day of embarkation, we caught a taxi to the wharf area. When the taxi arrived, the driver just sat there and was most unhelpful and never even asked if we needed any help with our baggage. We placed it in the space alongside the driver and climbed in.

On arrival at the area outside the entrance to the wharf, we took our baggage off the taxi, and I paid the driver. He muttered something about Australians, and I guessed he was unhappy I had not tipped him.

We had to cross the road to reach the Dockyard gate. Joan went ahead with the baby and other children and some of the baggage whilst I picked up the remainder. Checking the road was clear, I began crossing and had reached about halfway across when I heard a car revving up and saw our taxi pulling away from where he had parked and heading straight at me at speed. I dropped the case I was pulling and swung the tennis racket I had above my head as if I was going to throw it at his windscreen. He thought the better of it and stopped a few yards from me. I then continued to complete the crossing. Some people, also crossing with me asked if I was alright. They realised that he was heading straight at me.

At the Dockyard gates, we were met by a man and trolley. He loaded our belongings onto the trolley and took our gear to a ship's gangway, where it was taken on board and delivered to our cabin.

Voyage Home

We had two cabins – Joan and me in one and next door, the three children. What Anthony and Anne did not realise was that this voyage would complete an around the world sea trip for them, except from Fremantle to Sydney.

The trip home was pleasant, with stops at Gibraltar, Port Said and passage through the Suez Canal, a stop at Aden and later Colombo. At each port, we looked around before disembarking in Fremantle.

I had planned that we would stay with my Mum and Dad so they could meet Joan and the children and then Trans Train to South Australia before travelling by car to Sydney.

Ship Activities

There was a playroom for the children and a nursery where we could leave Peter. We tended to take most of the meals in the Dining room. The children would be fed before the adults. Joan and I opted to have most of our meals at the first sitting as the children were looked after until after the first entertainment show for the night.

Some lunchtimes, we would use the lunchtime buffet. I used the gym and walked around the deck to keep my fitness up. I tended to avoid the deck games that were always available. Sometimes, Joan would join me in walking and swimming in the pool.

Fremantle

Our heavy baggage was to be off-loaded in Sydney. In Fremantle, the car was disembarked. The family had to wait to be called to disembark.

Whilst sitting in the lounge, I noticed a uniformed Naval Officer appear and speak to some of the people until someone pointed towards where we were sitting. It turned out he was looking for me. He asked if I was Ritchie and handed me an envelope. When opened, I found I was required to join HMAS *Melbourne*, in Sydney, and embark in eleven days, as the ship would be sailing for the Far East Strategic Reserve (FESR)on that day. I think that day was the 4th of January.

So, my Foreign leave was reduced, and my plans had to be changed.

I don't think I have to tell you some very nasty thoughts went through my mind. I was not a happy Chappy. It meant amending our stay in the West, driving the car to Kalgoorlie, spend a couple of days with my Mum and Dad then board the train to the east.

Kalgoorlie

We apologised to my uncle and aunt for the change of plans and made our way to Kalgoorlie and stayed with my mum and dad. I showed the family around Kalgoorlie and where I had worked in the mines. Then all too soon it was onto the Trans Train and off to Port Pirie.

Train Trip

On the day of departure from Kalgoorlie, we mustered at Kalgoorlie Station, watched the car being embarked and settled into the two cabins allocated. Anthony and Anne in a two berth and ourselves and Peter in the one next door.

The evening meal for the children was before the adults. All other meals were together. It was a pleasant trip, and my mind went back to my early days with a hammock.

On arrival at Port Pirie, we disembarked, collected the car and baggage, and headed for Sydney along the Murray River. Alex D, who had served with me in HMAS *Bataan*, lived in one of the towns along the way and we stopped for a break at their place before continuing eastwards.

Overnight Stay

The route I intended to take passed through a farming town where one of Joan's friends lived. We guessed everyone would know most, if not all, the other farmers in the area. So, we decided to drop in on the friend.

It happened to be a Sunday as we arrived in the town, and as we were passing a Catholic church, people were coming out and most making for shops across the road. I stopped and Joan got out and found out her friend was at the Mass. One person said she had seen the friend enter a particular shop. Joan went in and surprised the friend who invited us to come and spend the night with her family.

This gave the children a break from the confines of the car, and it was great for Joan and the friend to catch up. For the children, the animals on the farm were a bonus.

It was a pleasant break, and it was possible then to make Sydney the next day without stopping somewhere overnight.

Family Reunion

On arrival in Sydney, we drove to Joan's parents' home. You can imagine their joy at seeing the family and welcoming baby Peter into the fold as well as the other children who had grown somewhat over the three years away. I think we stayed the night.

I obtained the keys to our house and moved the family across the short distance from the parents' house the next morning. Then it was off shopping to restock the larder and fridge.

What I do remember is that I joined HMAS *Melbourne* berthed at Garden Island on the 15th of February. On the 24th of February, the ship sailed for duty in the Malaysia/Indonesian Confrontation.

Chapter 29

HMAS *Melbourne*

15 February 1965 to 7 October 1965

Dimensions		Displacement	Engine
Length	701ft	16,740ton Standard	One or two Gear Turbines
Beam	80ft 2ins	20,000(Full Load)	
Draught	25ft 5ins		

Flight Deck	Speed		Range
690ft 8ins	24knots	12,000 @ 14knts	1355 includes 347 CAG

Armament

Anti-aircraft guns

Machinery	Aircraft Normally Onboard	Helicopter
Single reduction 42000 25x40 mm Bofors	Sea Venom Fighter Aircraft, and Fairy Gannets ASW	Wessex Helicopters (ASW)

This Chapter

To provide the variety of readers of this epistle some idea of what the ship was up to, I will be laying out a more detailed account of the *Melbourne's* activities during my period aboard.

Joining

I dutifully repaired onboard HMAS *Melbourne* on the appointed day (15th of February) with my bags and other gear. However, I should mention the following incident that occurred before I joined.

HMAS Voyager Incident

Prior to my joining, HMAS *Melbourne* had been involved in a collision with HMAS *Voyager* at approximately 8.30 pm on Monday, 24 February 1964. I will not dwell on this incident except to say that *Voyager* was moving from a position in the screen ahead of *Melbourne* to its Plane Guard station astern of *Melbourne*. It was night, and the ships were darkened, with only navigation lights on. Unfortunately, Voyager turned across *Melbourne's* bow and was cut in two.

Three months later, on the 11th of May 1964, *Melbourne* was again working up then proceeded to the South-East Asian deployment.

On joining, I found the ship was completing a 10-day Self Maintenance period.

My Allocated Duties

Surprise, surprise! I landed the job as Laundry Officer. I also took up my duties as the Assistant Direction Officer in the Air Defence Room (ADR) and acted as Air Controller for the Sea Venom and Gannet aircraft.

Then, when not required, my other duties were as Second Officer of the Watch on the Bridge. I smiled inwardly thinking of my first duty as first OOW duties in the Royal Navy in charge of the much larger HMS *Ark Royal*, in the middle watch, on its first night at sea after a refit and steaming amid the traffic in the English Channel. Remember, I had been ashore for the better part of four years when I did my first watch on HMS *Ark Royal*. On joining HMAS *Melbourne*, it was only a little over a year since I had been at sea.

In the days before sailing, I familiarised myself with the ship and the Bridge. I can't remember where my cabin was, but I recall it being a single cabin. It was interesting to note the differences between the ships HMAS Sydney, HMAS Vengeance, and HMS Ark Royal during this familiarisation.

Visitors to Ship

On February 17th, 100 Japanese cadets from their training ship Umitaka visited the ship. I was not involved in showing them around.

Preparations for and Departure

On Monday, February 22nd, the ship was moved to a buoy to take on ammunition and freight for Singapore. Then, on Wednesday, the 24th, the ship sailed for deployment in the Far East Strategic Reserve (FESR), heading for Manus Island with HMAS *Parramatta* in company. Three Gannet aircraft of 816 Squadron landed on board once clear of the heads as the ship was heading north for Manus.

During the passage to Manus, I was either in the Laundry, in the Air Direction Room (ADR) in charge or on the Bridge as an OOW. The accent was on flying and that involved me in the Air Defence Room. There were various exercises, both with the other ships involved in replenishments or other inter-ship exercises.

The Ship's Company was also exercised to ensure that those who had recently joined were up to speed on their duties, especially concerning Defence and Action Stations as we were entering an Operational area. It should be noted that at this time, there was tension between Malaysia and Indonesia.

Officer of Watch (OOW) Duties

I cannot remember whether it was during my first watch or a later watch as Second Officer the Watch. I remember it was off the East Coast as we headed north. When I arrived on the Bridge, I found the First OOW was another Special Duties Lieutenant who had arrived on watch before me. He oversaw the Bridge and maintained the ship on the course set down on the chart by the Navigator.

From time to time, he would take the fixes (bearings) of landmarks on the land as the ship proceeded northwards. I noticed that the three bearing lines of each of his fixes went through an exact point and thought what an excellent fixer he must be. His fixes were on the track that had been pencilled in on the chart by the Navigator. I also took observations and found that mine made a very small triangle. My fixes were off to one side of the track on the chart. I carried out a second fix straight away and it was also like my first. When he next took a fix, his marking on the chart again showed all the bearings intersecting at a single point. Again, like the earlier ones, they were on the track. Mine, on the other hand, made a small triangle and was again off to one side. From my many years of bridge watch keeping, I began to suspect that he might be adjusting his fixes.

I eventually suggested to him that, if he liked, I would do the fixing while he looked after the course and speed and running of the ship and where it was going. He quickly agreed, and I was happy to take over the fixing.

During this watch, the captain approached me on the Bridge and said, "First Officer the Watch …"

My reply was, "I am not the First Officer of the Watch, sir. Victor is."

The captain was obviously surprised that I was not the First OOW. Shortly after I'd finished the watch, the Navigator sent for me and advised that I was now on the First OOW roster.

Note: The captain had been the Training Officer at HMAS *Watson* when I first reported there after WWII. Also, he was the first and only Officer to send me a congratulatory note when I qualified as a Bosun Plot and Radar, way back in 1956, during my time on exchange in the Royal Navy. He also was on exchange duties.

March 1965

On the First of March I celebrated my 39th birthday, working hard.

Manus

The ship arrived in Manus on March 3rd and, after refuelling, sailed for Singapore on March 4th.

A Cocktail Party was held on board for the VIPs and locals whilst in Manus.

During the transit to Singapore, the ship transferred to the Operation Control of the Commander Far East Fleet. (COMFEF). Things got interesting when a Gannet had a fire in its port engine. After some hair-raising moments, it managed to land on board. Weather conditions interfered with flying during the last three days of the transit.

Singapore

The ship arrived in Singapore and secured to a buoy on Friday the 12th of March before sailing on the 15th. The freighted ammunition was off-loaded by barge. During the time in Harbour, the ship set Operation Awkward (upper deck armed lookouts for enemy divers) with the ship's divers on standby to counter any enemy swimmers. Once again, I was in a Combat Zone.

FOTEX

This was an Annual Fleet Operational Exercise, and the ship sailed from Singapore on the 15th of March to participate in Exercise FOTEX 65 between the 15th and 25th of March. There were five stages, Assembly, Tactical, Awkward, General Drills and Briefings. *Melbourne* was the winner of the Carrier Division.

The second Tactical phase was more intense. It was during this phase that a Gannet crashed over the side. Two crewmen were recovered. Unfortunately, the pilot was not found during the four-and-a-half-hour search.

The final phase consisted of another Tactical exercise. This exercise saw me in the ADR most of the time either on watch, in charge or controlling aircraft.

Showpiece

On 27 March 1965, the ship contributed to Exercise SHOWPIECE, which was designed to impress on the political and military leaders of the region, and the continued strength and readiness of the British Far East Fleet. Somewhere I have a picture showing something like 14 ships participating in these exercises.

Washup and Short Leave (Singapore)

On the 29th of March, the ship returned to Singapore and berthed at the Stores wharf until the 2nd of April 1965.

A Wash up of the Exercises was held on the 31st of March. The Exercises had provided excellent training, and materially, the ship had done well. From time to time the ship had visited Singapore for fuel and stores. This allowed the Ship's Company to go ashore and enjoy themselves. In Singapore, there was a street called Boogey Street. It was a place where you could find very pretty girls serving drinks and/or providing company/pleasures. Some of these pretty girls were not quite what they appeared to be.

I tended not visit this area and was not interested in any female company. If I, with others, was in a bar and approached by girls we soon sorted them out, (the ones who were after your money) by stating if they wanted to drink with us, they drank beer and not sticky greens.

Surprises

As stated above, one of my duties in the ship was Laundry Officer. There were several young Ordinary Seaman trainees working there and it would have been their first time in the Far East. The trainees would not have acquired the knowledge that what they saw was not always the actual case.

One morning, when I went down to check out how the laundry was going, I found the Leading Seaman in charge had not arrived for work. The young sailors told me they'd seen him ashore with a very pretty girl the previous night.

As I was about to leave the Laundry, the Leading Seaman arrived and, by the look on his face, he was not a very happy chappy. I said to him, "How was your date last night? I hear you had a very pretty girl in tow."

He said, "I don't want talk about it."

This aroused my suspicions that the girl was not what she seemed to be.

All the junior trainees were full of ears as I talked to the Leading Seaman. I asked him what the girl was like. When his reply was again, "I don't want to talk about it," I replied, "Oh, I see. I guess you were very upset when your wandering hand encountered a toggle and two."

The look on his face confirmed what I had suspected, that the beautiful girl had been a male, beautifully made and attired as a female, and known as a Beanie Boy.

When I said this, the junior sailors woke up to what I was saying and burst out laughing. They had been warned about such people existing. The Leader was not impressed and scowled as he went about his business of supervising.

The ship also visited Hong Kong. As we entered the harbour, I looked up towards the point where I had seen and reported a flash of light back in 1945 as we approached the harbour. I have been to Hong Kong many times since 1945 and always looked up and smiled as I thought back to that event.

Cocktail Parties

In Singapore, there were Cocktail Parties that entertained local dignitaries and officers and wives/girlfriends of military personnel in the area. I was the Duty Officer on one of these occasions. Not OOW. To meet with some of the guests, I had long ago learnt, whilst in HMS *Tumult*, to have the stewards bring me a glass of tonic water with a piece of lemon in the glass. This gave the impression that I was drinking a gin and tonic and stopped people asking why I was not drinking if I didn't have a glass in my hand. This met the requirement that, as a Seaman Officer on duty, you didn't drink.

Lunch Invitation

During the Cocktail party, I talked to a man and his wife who provided the vessel's Victualing services. They were just about to leave when they asked if I would like to join them for lunch on the coming Sunday. They said they always went to a Curry House for Sunday lunch, and if I was free, they would like me to join them.

I took up the offer and duly arrived at the Curry House. As I was looking at the menu his wife made the statement that I should be aware that they made very hot curries and, if I were not used to such, to make sure I requested a basic level curry. This I did and found that it was quite hot but not beyond my ability to enjoy. The husband, on the other hand, ordered a very hot curry and shook a bottle, containing gin and peppers mixed, to make it even hotter. I didn't make any comment but wondered how long his stomach would last.

April 1965

Hong Kong

The ship left Singapore for Hong Kong on the 2nd of April and arrived for a 17-day maintenance period berthing alongside the north wharf Victoria Basin. Maintenance was steadily progressed, and Jenny's side party took on the painting of the ship's side. (Jenny was a Chinese lady who ran a small group of people who took on such tasks and was well-known to the Australian ships.)

There were numerous VIP visits and a Cocktail Party for HK VIPs and wives, as well as Naval and Military Senior Officers etc. As First Officer on the gangway it was often a busy time. In addition, there was the Laundry to look after, and to get ashore and buy up presents for the family, as we would be heading for Sydney once we left Hong Kong.

On the 21st of April, the ship sailed from Hong Kong to a serenade of fireworks from Jenny's side party and headed for Singapore with HMAS *Parramatta* in company.

The planned programme was interrupted when the ship was diverted to search for two ships of interest that were reputedly in the area. However, air searches on the 23rd and 24th of April located nothing.

During the passage, Aircrew Officers were transferred to HMAS *Parramatta*, and Parramatta Officers were transferred to *Melbourne* to familiarise themselves with the workings of each ship.

On the 25th of April (Anzac Day) Melbourne rendezvoused with HMS *London* off the West Coast of Malaysia and flying training in preparation for Annual Exercise SEAHORSE. It was conducted between 25th and 27th of April. On completion of exercising, the ship proceeded to Singapore.

The *Melbourne* entered Singapore and secured to a buoy on the 27th, moving alongside the Dockyard on the 30th.

May 1965

On the 3rd of May, *Melbourne* sailed for Manila and was joined by HMAS *Supply* and HMS *Corunna*. On Tuesday, the 4th of May, HMAS Yarra joined. Exercises were carried out en route, including day and night flying, which kept me busy in the Air Direction Room. HMAS Parramatta joined the force on the 6th of May, and on the 7th of May, the force entered Manila, proceeding to allocated berths in preparation for the SEATO Exercises.

After all ships had arrived in Manila and participated in various briefings, it was time for the Work Up.

SEAHORSE

The Exercise consisted of three phases:

Assembly	1 – 8 May
Work Up Phase	8 – 11 May
Convoy Phase	11 – 22 May

Work Up

Melbourne sailed on Monday, the 10th of May, and carried out flight operations, A/S exercises and Manoeuvring exercises. As you can imagine with Flying, and the other exercises, I was kept very busy mainly in the Air Defence Room.

All ships taking part in the Work Up joined the Underway Replenishment Group on Thursday, May 11th, and refuelled en route to Manila, anchoring at 1105.

That afternoon, on Tuesday afternoon, a Pre-sail Conference was held on the USS Bennington (Carrier). I attended this Conference along with others from the ship.

The map below shows the area of our exercising and the location of the various ports mentioned.

Bangkok

Singapore

Manila and Subic Bay

Convoy Phase

The Convoy Phase began with opposed departures from Manila on Wednesday the 12th of May and *Melbourne* proceeded to Manila Bay, where it stopped and provided Helo Support for the screen of the departing ships.

Passage Exercise Area

Melbourne then proceeded astern of the convoy until the convoy formed up for the passage to Bangkok. There were fourteen ships in *Melbourne's* group.

HMS *Victorious* and USS *Bennington* operated separately, providing air defence and anti-submarine support respectively.

Melbourne continued to support the convoy for the next ten days during the convoy's passage to Bangkok.

Sonar conditions were poor and unalerted attacks were few. At least five submarine contacts were made by Gannets using their A/S equipment.

Opposed replenishments occurred on the 14th, 17th, and 21st of May and a simulated nuclear attack on the 20th of May. The helicopters spent up to 18 hours per day on the screen. A Gannet was on Task during daylight hours, and each Sea Venom crew flew three sorties a day.

An active intertropical convergence zone added to the problems for the helicopters.

Surface Attack. Surface units had been detached from the group, forming an attack group, who attacked the convoy. From all the above, you can imagine how busy I was throughout this period overseeing the Air Defence Room and Air Controllers.

The training value was very high.

Cross Operation. On the 20th of May, one of USS Bennington's Douglas A4B aircraft successfully landed on *Melbourne*. Also, helicopters were exchanged between USS *Bennington* and *Melbourne*.

Exercise End.

On the 21st of May the exercise ended, and *Melbourne* launched two Venoms, Gannets and six Wessex who took part in a Seahorse flyover of Bangkok. After recovering the aircraft, the *Melbourne* anchored off Bang Saen near the head of the Gulf of Thailand on the 22nd of May remaining there until sailing on the 25th.

Exercise Summary

The exercise was considered to have been most valuable in furthering SEATO cooperation, in providing anti-submarine, air defence and replenishment training, and in highlighting the difficulties of passing a military convoy through an area subjected to different forms of attack.

Bangkok

To get to Bangkok, liberty men took a 40-minute boat ride, then a two-and-a-half hour bus ride. Leave was restricted by local curfew and only about 250 men were landed each day.

On the 25th of May, *Melbourne* weighed and proceeded to sea and refuelled HMAS *Parramatta* during the forenoon. HMS *Vampire* joined for the passage to Subic Bay.

Delayed Departure for Home

On this day, the captain addressed the Ship's Company and advised them that our planned return to Australia had been delayed and that the ship would be escorting HMAS *Sydney* to South

Vietnam. Before the speech, there had been rumours on the ship that a change was imminent.

Day flying was carried out on the 27th, and HMAS *Supply* joined and replenished both *Melbourne* and HMAS *Vampire* on the 28th.

Subic Bay

Melbourne arrived in Subic Bay on the 29th of May, secured to a buoy. The rainy season had arrived, but it did not deter the crew from proceeding ashore, with 700 landings each day.

Finally, it was time to sail, and on the 31st of May, *Melbourne* sailed, with HMA ships *Supply* and *Vampire* in company, to rendezvous with HMAS *Sydney* and escort her to Vietnam.

As the month ended, we were again at sea and flying was carried out. No rest for himself, who had been Officer of Watch in Harbour. Besides the exercises of all descriptions, I had been busy preparing for an Admiral's Inspection to be carried out on the way home.

June 1965

In early June, the ship joined HMAS Sydney (3) for four days during the Troop Carriers voyage to Vietnam. the ship went to Defence Stations on the 4th and an extra level of readiness was set for the passage to Vung Tu.

Sufficient to say it was a very busy time and I won't go into a blow-by-blow detail of the activities. The long periods of inactivity gave sailors a real appreciation of the monotony of Escort duties.

Detaching and Homeward Bound.

Came Tuesday the 8th of June, *Melbourne* and HMAS *Vampire* detached and headed for Manus and fuelled HMAS *Vampire* in lousy weather. Fortunately, I was not involved in the Replenishments anymore.

HMAS *Supply* rendezvoused on Thursday, the 10th of June. It was then time for *Melbourne* to refuel and get stores, mail and fresh provisions.

Admiral's Inspection

The Admiral began his Inspection on Friday, the 11th of June, progressing it during the passage to Manus.

Manus.

The ship anchored in Seadler Harbour on the 15th of June. Mail and a night at anchor were most welcome after sixteen days at sea.

On Wednesday the 16th, the Admiral inspected the Ship's Company at Divisions and afterwards expressed his satisfaction with the appearance of the sailors and the state of the ship. On completion, it was up anchors and set sail for Sydney. It would not be too hard to guess that I, and the ship's crew, were looking forward to the run home after four months of valuable training, especially for those who were at sea for the first time.

During the passage across the Coral, Sea, a sports programme was held on Saturday the 19th.

The day before the ship arrived in Sydney on the 22nd of March, Customs officials were flown on board by Wessex helicopters so that Custom clearances could be completed before entry.

Once the Custom clearances were over, five Gannets and three Sea Venoms were flown off to Nowra. Twelve Wessex Helicopters were also flown off just before entry into Sydney Harbour.

Sydney

Melbourne berthed at the Fitting Out Wharf at 10.10 am to be greeted by a large crowd of families and friends. Families were invited on board for morning tea.

The Ship remained alongside for the rest of the month, undergoing self-maintenance and granting ten days leave. I was very pleased to be home for a short while and catch up with the family.

July 1965

The ship was to remain alongside for all of July, carrying out Self-Maintenance and leaving. When not on leave, I did my turn as OOW on the gangway. At least I got home every night I was not OOW.

The only other noteworthy item was that three USN midshipmen joined for two months for sea training. They were sent to HMAS *Vendetta* and *Anzac* until the end of the month when they would re-join the *Melbourne*.

August 1965

On Monday, 2nd of August, the ship sailed for Jervis Bay for the initial workup. Emergency Stations, Leaving Ship stations, Sea Boats, Gun functioning trials and Deck landings drills were exercised during the passage south. HMA ships *Sydney, Supply* and *Anzac* were in company on leaving Sydney.

The aircraft operated from HMAS Albatross for day and night touch and go (non-arrestor landings and takeoffs) and then landings and catapult takeoffs, which saw three new Gannet pilots qualified for day deck landings and three Sea Venom pilots gain touch-and-go experience.

Visitors

On the 4th of August, a party of four officers, 43 midshipmen, and an ACT policeman from the RAN College at HMAS *Creswell* embarked by boat for a day at sea. The varied, full-day programme proved worthwhile and was enjoyed by all. At the end of the flight, the visitors landed by boat.

CAG Embarkation and Fleet Concentration.

On the 6th of August, six Gannets from 816 Squadron and ten Wessex from 817 Squadron were embarked and the ship anchored in Jervis Bay to embark the Squadron personnel, baggage, and stores. The following day the ship sailed for Hervey Bay for a Fleet Concentration period.

As usual, His Nibs was fully occupied with settling in the ADR personnel and keeping watches, overseeing aircraft controllers and plotters, and making sure the Laundry was settling down to efficient operations.

On some weekends, when anchored, some of the ship's personnel would land on the nearby island to swim and to fish ashore and from on board. The fishing was excellent.

Homeward Bound

In August, the ship headed for Sydney, continuing flying operations en route.

Sydney

The ship berthed at the Fitting Out Wharf, Garden Island on Thursday the 17th. The ship's Command Team (himself included) spent the rest of the day, and the one following, at HMAS *Watson*, participating in a series of A.S.S.T. (Anti-Submarine Tactical Training) exercises at HMAS *Watson*.

The seagoing part of this exercise took place when *Melbourne* sailed on Monday, the 23rd, until the 27th, when the ship returned to the Harbour and secured to No 2 buoy. A review of the Exercise was held onboard.

On Monday the 30th of August, the ship sailed for what was known as the Longex section of anti-submarine training that continued into September. HMAS *Anzac* and LRMP (Long Range Maritime) aircraft from the RAAF also participated in detecting and prosecuting the submarine.

September 1965

Aircraft Recovery

I think it was during this time a Gannet reported he had lost one of his two engines and was returning to the ship. He was, I recall, something like 100 kilometres away and the weather was steadily growing worse.

At the time there was no CCA (Carrier Controlled Approach Radar) fitted to *Melbourne*.

Because of the increasing clutter on the radar display, caused by the heavy clouds and rain, it was increasingly hard to track the aircraft. The Air Controller, who was talking to the Gannet, turned to me and said, "Boss, I am a bit out of my depth here and am not happy controlling."

I then took over and reset my Radar Display, as I had been taught way back in 1945, **(Focus, Centre, Calibrate),** and took over control of the aircraft. My experience came into play, and I was able to keep tracking the aircraft through the cloud and verified my plotting was accurate when the radar contacts reappeared from time to time. Over the last ten or so miles I could not get a radar contact and relied on my plotting skills. Eventually, the aircraft pilot reported he could see the ship (it was about a half to three-quarters of a mile or so). I was very happy when I heard the aircraft touch down safely.

You can imagine my reaction when the door of the ADR was flung open, and there was the pilot abusing all and sundry saying, "You didn't have me on the centreline." This meant he had to make a last-minute correction to be aligned with the centre of the flight deck.

I wagged my finger and asked him to come and have a look at the radar display I had to work on. I pointed out the blanket of interference I had tracked him through and got him to within sight of the ship without any radar contact as such. I pointed out the radars we had were not the most suitable for homing in such weather. By this time, the cloud interference on the radar was continuous and had extended out beyond ten miles. He left still in a huff. I can understand his anxiety for his own, and two aircrew's, health.

Homeward Bound

The time came to turn for home and return to Sydney and for the Ship's Company to be given some leave. We disembarked the aircraft off Jervis Bay, and they flew off to HMAS *Albatross* near Nowra, south of Sydney. The Air Group personnel were disembarked in Jervis Bay before the ship headed for Sydney.

I was able to get some leave and spend time with the family.

October 1965

Back to Sea

By October, we were back at sea participating in a Fleet Concentration Period.

I can't remember if a British Task Group was coming through the Jomar passage into the Coral Sea at this time for a visit to Sydney.

As part of the exercise, a RAAF Maritime Reconnaissance aircraft picked up the Task Group and reported its position, course, and speed. One of the ship's Gannets was sent up to continue tracking the British Group. On board, a flight of six Sea Venom crews were briefed and launched to carry out an attack on this Task Group.

I won't reveal the procedure, but suffice it to say that the Gannett provided a departure point for the Sea Venoms to travel to before attacking the task group. The Gannet then flew away from that point and kept providing long-range radar contact for the Task Group in a different direction from that from which the attack would come.

The attack aircraft would have descended whilst out of range of the Royal Naval Task Groups radar coverage. From the marker the ship's search aircraft had positioned, they would have travelled at very low level, (almost at the top of the waves) and carried out the attack.

It is very interesting to note the enemy contact report by the Task Group was that three aircraft had attacked and re-attacked the group. They do not seem to have realised that six aircraft had carried out the attack.

The ship participated in Exercise JUC 58, off Jervis Bay in late August and early September, before again escorting HMAS *Sydney* northwards off the Queensland coast towards New Guinea before detaching to Port Moresby, and later Rabual, and then the Solomon Islands. The ship returned to Jervis Bay on the 4th of October.

Summary

My practical experience in charge of the Air Direction Room, and controlling aircraft, had made me much more efficient in all aspects of my specialisation and, my experience as an Officer of the Watch on the Bridge and Gangway, had given me greater confidence in my abilities to cope.

Next Posting

Surprise, Surprise. On paper, my posting to *Melbourne* ended on the 7th of October 1965. My next appointment started on the 7th of October 1965 when I was required to join HMAS *Stuart*, refitting in Williamstown, near Melbourne, where it was converting from the IKARA Trials ship back to a Fleet unit.

I can't remember if I left HMAS *Melbourne* between the fourth and sixth of the month and proceeded to Melbourne by train.

And so ended nine months in HMAS *Melbourne*, immediately on my return from overseas, and here I was off to another ship.

OFFICER COMMENTS

"TO MY ENTIRE SATISFACTION"

Chapter 30

HMAS *Stuart*

7 October 1965 to 30 January 1967

Dimensions	Displacement	Engine
Length 112.5m	2700 Ton	Geared Steam Turbine
Beam 12.5m		
Draft 5.5m		

Armament	
Missiles	Torpedo
Sea Cat and Ikara	2 Triple Barrel

Max Speed	Complement
30Knots (2 Shafts)	234

HMAS Stuart was a type 12 Anti-Submarine Frigate and was the second ship to carry the name.

Joining

I joined HMAS *Stuart* on 7 October 1965. The ship was berthed alongside HMAS *Queensborough* at Williamstown dockyard, Melbourne, Victoria. Because of the work going on to convert HMAS *Stuart* from IKARA trials Ship to a Fleet unit we had to live on board HMAS *Queensborough*. That ship was out of commission/routine, and we were able to use the cabins and the Wardroom, and it was the Galley that cooked our meals. It was basic, however it provided food and lodging until the 'Stuart' was ready. I can't remember how many officers there were when I joined. It had no air conditioning working.

The Working Day

During the day, each of the officers would be working in their various areas in HMAS *Stuart*. At times, they may have to leave the dockyard or consult with dockyard officials. However, those officers living on board would usually be back in time to shower and have dinner, usually around 7 or 8 o'clock.

Evenings

Each evening after dinner, we played games of some sort. One of the favourites was playing darts. After a while, this developed into games where you threw the dart over your shoulder or bent down and threw it between your legs.

On other occasions we played cards, usually poker using matches as our stake. Then any variation to amuse us.

I also read a book or wrote letters when playing games bored me.

My Duties

My principal duties were to be running the Operations Room, supervising the Aircraft Controllers, and advising the captain as required. Also, to be the Officer the Watch on the Bridge at Sea or the Officer of the Day in Harbour, when available.

Surprise, surprise. I was also the Laundry Officer. Obviously, someone knew of my previous activities.

At this stage, my duties basically were to check out all the Operations Room equipment and ensure it was ready for the time the ship was to sail for Work up.

Leave

We had a duty Watch Bill, which meant the selected one would be responsible for both ships with a small Duty Watch to react to any incident involving the two ships, such as a fire or other incident.

I wasn't impressed that I was so far away from home and seem to remember on a couple of occasions I was able to get to Sydney for a weekend thanks to someone with a car.

I took the opportunity to visit a cousin of mine who lived in Williamstown, and, sometime during WWI, he would have served with my father in the Middle East. He made me welcome. My father appeared to be close to this cousin of mine.

On a couple of other occasions, I went up to Melbourne by train to visit my very first girlfriend, her husband, and her sister who lived next door. They made me very welcome. They lived in Brighton and lived very close to a tram stop. However, the distance from the Dockyard was considerable, and I was only able to visit a couple of times.

Command Team Training

From 2nd to 10th of December, Command Team Training took place in HMAS *Watson*. On the 11th there was a Naval Symposium at *Watson* as well. I was able to get home during this period.

I seem to recall I got home for Christmas.

January 1966

Return to HMAS Stuart

The Ship's Company moved back on board *Stuart* on 4th January 1966. It was nice to have air conditioning again. The refit was generally completed by the 10th of January, but the weapons systems still needed attention.

Finally, on the 29th of January, the ship slipped and proceeded into Port Phillip Bay and the forenoon was spent carrying out internal drills. In the afternoon, it was back alongside for ammunitioning.

After ammunitioning, it was back into the Bay to carry out runs on the measured mile. Then back alongside for training of the Landing Party by the Army and continuation of working on the weapons systems.

There was a chance for sport against HMAS *Cerberus* and HMAS *Anzac*.

February 1966

This month was spent alongside or in Port Phillip Bay. On one occasion, *Stuart* was docked to carry out healing trials. Work on the weapons systems and other areas continued apace.

March 1966

On the 1st of March I celebrated my 40th Birthday, again not home with the family.

From the 2nd to 4th, the ship sailed and carried on acceptance trials. On Tuesday the 8th of March, *Bataan* left Williamstown after having arrived there on the 2nd of August 1965, for Gunnery Acceptance trials, which turned out to be unsatisfactory.

After landing the Trials team, the ship proceeded to Sydney and conducted Electronic Warfare (EW) trials with HMAS *Watson* on the 10th, before entering Sydney Harbour and securing at Chowder Bay for fuel.

Two runs over the DG range proved that a full DG Ranging test would be necessary. On completion, the ship secured to No 3-buoy remaining there until the 14th.

Anti-Submarine (A/S) Trials and Exercises.

Initially, the ship worked with the HMS *Tabard* and a RAAF Maritime aircraft, firstly doing sonar acceptance trials and later anti-submarine training. A successful gunnery trial saw the gunnery system accepted. Electronic Warfare (EW) trials were also carried out with a Boeing 727 and a fuel replenishment from HMAS *Sydney* completed the programme and the ship returned to harbour to berth at Garden Island to embark equipment for further trials before sailing to Jervis Bay where it anchored at 7.15 pm.

The weekend was devoted to inter-part sport and all shore facilities were available. These activities continued until the 23rd of March, and ended on the day the ship secured to No 3 buoy, Sydney.

Stuart had finally ended the work up and was declared ready to rejoin the Fleet and prepare for our first overseas deployment.

An Aside. Marilyn Munro Picture

One of the officers had obtained a famous nude photo of this young lady on a large red rug. It was attached to the deckhead (ceiling) in the lounge area of the Wardroom. Our lounge chairs were of the type you could push back and lie back in.

It was always amusing to seat a guest or wife in one of these chairs and watch them push back and be gazing at the ceiling and finding they were looking at the picture. Re-actions varied from a quick return to upright and a light reddening of the face, being embarrassed or a good long look.

Most wives, who came to a function, would head for the chair, and have a good look again. Even guests who were embarrassed at the first look, also could be seen having a peep during a subsequent visit.

One of the officers, who will be nameless, was looking around a type of antiques shop when he came across a famed photo of another woman. Unbeknown to any of us, he substituted this picture for Marilyn's.

When the ship was in Sydney for the weekend, a Cocktail party was held in the Wardroom. One of the wives, who frequently gazed at Marilyn, sat in the chair and pushed it back and, with a look of horror, brought the chair suddenly to the upright position.

What she had seen was not Marilyn but a very ugly, very, very, very large-breasted woman, a most distressing sight. When we asked what was wrong, she pointed at the picture and wanted to know what that was. For those of us not in the know, we had a look, and soon, everybody was laughing, including the poor woman who had seen it first.

The ugly duckling was removed that night and Marilyn resumed her place of honour.

Finally Ready for Operations

On Thursday 24th of March, *Bataan* sailed from Sydney and joined the Flag ship HMAS *Melbourne*, and HMAS *Yarra*, and the group proceeded north. There were exercises involving the three ships, and I was kept busy either in the Operations Room or occasionally as OOW and, of course, supervising the Laundry.

Port Moresby Visit

On the evening of Sunday, the 27th, *Stuart* detached and proceeded to Port Moresby for its first overseas port visit. The weather resulted in several exercises being amended en route.

Upon anchoring in Port Moresby Harbour, the Deputy Naval Officer in Charge NG, LDCR Keith Graham, came aboard and accompanied the captain when he called on the Administrator New Guinea.

An Aside. Keith, a good friend, had been the Navigator during the "Ship's" trials of Ikara period. He was also responsible for me being in *Stuart*. He didn't know of my posting being straight after HMAS *Melbourne* leading to a prolonged period away from the family.

The PNG Army was most generous in supplying boats and transport, and particularly with hospitality and with sporting events and the various Army teams. The sporting events saw the PNG teams outclass those of *Stuart*.

There was no open to the General Public, but private visitors were allowed. Three parties of 100 Indigenous children were shown over the ship, no doubt a propaganda exercise to gain recruits for their Navy.

On the 31st of March, *Stuart* sailed for Sydney via Cairns. The crew had enjoyed their port visit to Port Moresby.

April 1966

Homeward Bound

The Cairns visit was short, arriving on 1 April. As soon as refuelling was complete, it was off to Sydney.

On the 3rd of April, there were prayers, and the captain addressed the crew of Security.

Sydney

On Tuesday, the 5th of April, the ship entered Sydney Harbour, berthing a Chowder Bay for fuel. On completion of fuelling, the ship moved to the No2 buoy for ammunition before coming alongside Garden Island, being shifted by tugs from the buoy.

On the 6th and 7th of April, tugs moved the ship to Dolphins in Rose Bay for Mortar Calibration.

Then it was leave over the Easter weekend and some time with family. One officer and twenty Sea Cadets joined on Friday the 8th and left on Sunday afternoon.

My Job

My job during all the trials and testing was seeing the Operations Room and Air controllers were on the job and efficient.

Trials and Tribulations

It was planned to sail from Sydney on the 12th of April. However, it was found that there was heavy contamination in the bottom of four of the fuel tanks. Cleaning efforts made during the day had little effect. The importance of Ikara Sea Trials programme saw *Stuart* sail for these trials before the tanks were cleaned. There was limited fuel/oil embarked.

From 12th to 23rd of April, testing and trialling and firing of Ikara, Compass Damping Unit testing, Sea Cat firings, AA tracking and firings, helicopter direction exercises, a surface shoot, bathythermograph calibrations and recovering lifebuoys, exercising swimmers and sea boat recovery were carried out with few hiccups.

The pumping out of contaminated fuel tanks in Sydney Harbour permitted the ship to carry more fuel and not return for fuel. After refuelling on the 21st of April, the ship sailed for Newcastle berthing at Merewether Wharf just before lunch on Friday 22nd of April.

There was a ship's Cocktail Party that night and the ship was open to visitors on Saturday, Sunday, and Monday afternoons. About fifteen hundred braved the heavy rain on Saturday and about two and a half thousand on the other two days.

Members of the Ship's Company were entertained in various RSL Clubs over the weekend. Matches of Rugby, Australian Rules, and Soccer were played in muddy conditions.

On the 25th of April, about 100 officers and men marched in the Anzac Day Parade. The captain laid a wreath at the Newcastle War Memorial.

After what had been a welcome break from trials and tribulations, it was back to sea on Tuesday, 26th of April. Air Interceptions were carried out using two Mirages from RAAF Williamtown. They gave an impressive display on completion of the exercise and two Sabres made attacks on the ship. This kept me on my toes as an air controller. On completion, it was off to Jervis Bay. En route, the weather was unsuitable for any exercises, and a bombardment and AA short had to be aborted.

On 27 April, *Stuart* proceeded to sea from Jervis Bay and carried out Helicopter direction exercises and mortar firing, returning to anchor in Jervis Bay in the late afternoon. The next day, the ship weighed and exercised an opposed departure, controlling four helicopters. Weather prevented the use of a submarine simulator, and the ship returned to Jervis Bay.

The next day, it was back to Sydney.

May 1966

Having returned to Sydney, maintenance began to prepare the ship for her visit to Hawaii for a Rim-Pac Exercise and to show off the Ikara to the USN. Also, mid-year leave was given, and I was able to finally get some time at home with the family, to carry out any maintenance of the house and gardens. There was also time to catch up with family and friends and live a normal suburban lifestyle.

However, it was not to last, and it was back to work to sail for Hawaii at the end of the month.

Deployment

Departing Sydney on the 30th of May 1966, *Stuart* proceeded east to Pearl Harbour, Hawaii, to demonstrate the IKARA.

Fiji

One of the ports *Stuart* called at on our way to Hawaii was Suva, Fiji. As we approached the harbour entrance, it was raining, and there were very low clouds obscuring landmarks that provided the fixing points for the Navigator to make sure he was in the entrance channel as there were reefs on either side of the entrance.

It is normal practice, on entering or leaving the harbour, for the Operations Room to have a Blind Pilotage team standing by in cases such as this. I personally took on the task of fixing the ship by radar. As soon as I took over, I made sure I focused, centred, and calibrated the radar display I was using. For a time, I was able to have ranging and bearing of landmarks and could give the Navigator some assistance. However, there came a time when the weather interference on the radar display was so great that I could see nothing of use. I reported to the captain, that I was not happy, and he stopped the ship. When eventually visibility improved, and we could proceed up the channel, it was found that dead ahead of where the ship had stopped was a reef that was on one side of the channel. I used to say that if the left side of my bum twitched it was time to back off and re-assess the situation. Thankfully, it worked on this occasion.

Cocktail Party

A Cocktail Party was held on board that night despite the heavy rain and it was surprising the number of umbrellas that appeared to shelter the visitors whilst on the upper deck until they reached the door into the ship's superstructure. As Baden Powell would have said to Boy Scouts and Guides, "BE PREPARED".

There was time to get a short look around Suva in the next three days before *Stuart* sailed on the 5th of June for Pago Pago, arriving there on the 6th of June. The apparent briefness of the passage was due to the extra day required to cross the International Dateline. The intention to immediately fuel was delayed as the Oil wharf man in charge did not start work until 8.30 am. In the event, the ship sailed at 1015 hrs for the long haul to Pearl Harbour.

King Neptune's Visit.

During the passage, King Neptune requested permission to come on board. When settled, he rebuked the ship for not having entered his domain during the past three years since it was commissioned. Then he dished out the usual hilarious punishments to the crew.

Samoa

I seem to recall that *Stuart* visited Samoa before arriving at Pearl Harbor. My recollections are very vague, although I remember it being a nice place to visit.

Pearl Harbour

This was my first visit to Pearl Harbour. I recalled the very interesting movies I had seen of the Japanese Attack in World War II, to look at USS Arizona, which had been sunk on that day. It had now been made into a Memorial. During our stay I and others visited the Memorial and found it very interesting.

Other interesting visits were to the famous beach and a tour around the island. We were also able to use the Officers Club and meet some of the local Navy families. We were also able to use their PX for some shopping. However, it was very expensive in the main shopping areas and beaches outside the Base. I took a tour around the main island, which was very interesting.

Back to Sea

All too soon, it was time to return to sea and participate in a major exercise being conducted by the Americans.

I would like to note here that besides excellent radar and sonar systems the ship had a first class, Electronic Countermeasure (ECM) System and team.

HMAS *Stuart* participation in this major exercise saw it as one of ships screening the main force. When the ECM team reported a contact on a particular bearing, the Air Controller, who had some USN helicopters under his control, directed them down the bearing to an estimated position the submarine was likely to have put up his periscope and sent out a ranging signal from his periscope radar to find out how far away the main body was and where the escorts were.

Submarine Contact

It didn't take long for the helicopters to make sonar contact and begin tracking the submarine. It also didn't take long before fixed-wing antisubmarine aircraft appeared on the scene to help track the submarine as it twisted and turned, hoping to lose the Helo and fixed-wing Trackers.

Before long, other Trackers called up and asked to join in so they could participate in the tracking of the submarine. It was at this stage that my Air Controller called me and said the situation was becoming beyond his experience because of the number of aircraft participating.

I took over from him, and when the next aircraft called on the radio asking for directions and which ship we were so he could depart on the right bearing, I said we were the funny green ship with the key on top. This was because our shipside colour was quite different from that on American ships and our LW02 aerial, on the top of its mast, looked like a key handle.

With the number of fixed-wing aircraft appearing, there was no way I could continue to have Positive control (that is, verbally directing each aircraft). I made a general request to the fixed-wing aircraft, asking who the senior aircraft was, and when he acknowledged, I asked if he was prepared to take charge of the fixed-wing aircraft, and he agreed. I was then able to assist any other aircraft that wanted to join the fun as well as keep the plot position of the submarine as reported by the helicopters.

Eventually, the helicopters reported that the submarine was surfacing. They reported what looked like blue smoke coming out of the conning tower, and a very upset submarine Captain wasn't happy that he needed fresh air for his crew and, in no uncertain words, told the aircraft to shove off as they had had their fun.

Captain's Query

When all settled back to normal, I grabbed a cup of coffee and went up to the Bridge wing to get some fresh air. The captain called me into the Bridge and asked how many aircraft I had under my control. I said I had 24 callsigns on the plot. He, being a pilot, who I had first met onboard HMAS *Sydney*, said it was impossible for me to control that many aircraft. I smiled before replying that when the fixed-wing aircraft kept joining in, I arranged that the senior fixed-wing pilot takeover as the positive controller and the helicopter senior was already controlling the helicopters. All I had to do was to sit back and watch on my radar that no problem was developing and continue plotting the Helo reported position. I can't remember him saying anything after that. I'm sure he realised I knew what I was doing as a Controller, and no words were necessary.

Ikara Firing

During this period at sea, *Stuart* was to demonstrate the Ikara missile system to the American Naval Officials. All the Submarine Safety Rules for firing torpedoes at a submarine had been set down.

On Thursday, the 16th of June, an American Admiral came aboard to observe the firing. The sonar conditions were poor, and the safety ship lost sonar contact with the submarine. In the event the firing was aborted.

On the following day, Friday, June 17th, two Ikara were fired at intervals of two minutes and ten seconds and ranges of 4300 yards and 4200 yards. The submarine reported that the torpedoes dropped close and appeared to attack, and post-run analysis confirmed that they had. After recovering the torpedos, *Stuart* returned to the Harbour.

On Monday, the 20th of June, *Stuart* proceeded to sea in company with US ships *Kearage*, *Phillip Kyes*, *Larsen*, *Evans*, *Renshaw* and *Perry* for phase 4 of Operations Readiness Evaluation (ORE). The concept was basically a Cold War that became hot.

The initial task of the escorts and shore-based aircraft was to locate and pin down the submarines (USS *Sabalo* and *Carbonero*) and to sink the submarines at the outbreak of war, in an area of 150 miles x 100 miles whilst protecting themselves and shipping passing through the area. This exercise continued until 1800 on the 21st, with all forces involved being annihilated several times.

The force steamed in company for the night for further weapons firing training when various torpedo types were fired. On completion *Stuart* returned and berthed in Pearl Harbour at 1850 on the 25th of July. Over 3300 miles had been sailed since leaving Pearl Harbour on the 13th.

In summary, all the ship's equipment worked extremely well during this period. The EW equipment surprised the USN and had considerable success. The ship's capabilities for helicopter and fixed-wing control (largely due to the ship's personnel) have caused much favourable comment. It has been a most interesting and valuable experience for all on board.

Self-Maintenance was carried out until the ship sailed from Pearl Harbour.

July 1966

Stuart remained in Pearl Harbour until the 9th of July, and during this period, the post Operational Readiness Evaluation was presented. It was not a particularly impressive debrief.

On the 1st of July, *Stuart* was berthed alongside a wharf and a farewell reception was held on board. That same night, USS *Kearsarge* held a dance on board, and some fifty of the Ship's Company attended.

Her Britannic Majesty's Consul held a reception for Officers of HMAS *Stuart* on the 8th of month, and USS *Benjamin Stoddert* gave a beach party for 150 of *Stuart's* Ship Company. *Stuart* had acted as host ship for USS *Stoddart* when that ship visited Sydney during Coral Sea Week. The hospitality was returned with a vengeance.

Himself

Although my first visits to Hawaii for such exercises, the standard of my Ops Room crew, air controllers and the EW team was excellent, and the pressure put on them during our workup had paid off.

My background and training as an officer also allowed me to fully participate in whatever entertainment was going and relaxed the mind from the pressures at sea. I was looking forward to the OOW duty on the way to Singapore.

Off To Far East Strategic Reserve (FESR)

On the 9th of July, *Stuart* sailed from Pearl Harbour and an AA shoot was successfully carried out and a drone shot down. A comment was made that no-one was sorry to leave as Honolulu proper was very expensive. However, the Chief's and Enlisted Men's clubs were excellent venues. So, next port Pago Pago.

Pago Pago

On Saturday, July 16th, Stuart berthed alongside Station Wharf. There was great hospitality, with buses and cars provided. A cable car crossed the harbour, and all these facilities were kept available.

On the 17th, the ship moved to the Oil Warf for refuelling and, upon completion, sailed for Suva. Except for a full power trial, the passage to Suva was not noteworthy.

Suva

We arrived in Suva on the morning of Wednesday, 20th of July, berthing on King's Wharf and, after fuelling, anchored in Suva Harbour.

Suva proved to be a popular port and model canoes were much sought after. Unfortunately, the cricket match was rained out, and the ship's rugby team was beaten by a RNZAF team.

On sailing, an AA tracking exercise was carried out with a RNZAF *Sunderland*. Then it was onwards to Manus. Heavy rain and swell were encountered for part of the passage.

Manus

On Thursday, July 28th, Stuart berthed alongside the HMAS Tarangau and refuelled. However, there was no mail waiting. Water polo, badminton, volleyball, and basketball were played during the afternoon, and the usual hospitality was provided.

On Friday afternoon, the ship sailed and carried out gunnery and Mortar Mk 10 practises to the North of the Island. Then, it returned to the harbour to pick up mail and stores before sailing for Singapore.

On passage, an inter-mess quiz championship proved popular. The Upper Deck Olympics occupied two afternoons of the weekend at sea and 5BX and circuit training were carried out each evening.

August 1966

On Wednesday, 3rd of August, *Stuart* secured alongside RFA *Eddyrock* in the Ligitan Channel on the north coast of Borneo and, after refuelling, headed for Singapore.

On Saturday, the 6th of August, *Stuart* berthed in Singapore Naval Base in the early afternoon. On Monday, HMAS *Parramatta* secured alongside *Stuart*. On the 14th of August *Stuart* sailed for its first stint as Duty Ship until the 19th of August when it returned alongside, this time berthing on HMS *Delight*. Basically, the rest of month was spent exercising practise programmes, and carrying out Duty Ship tasks.

The month ended with *Stuart* berthed in Singapore. It had been a good month where the various exercises, with consorts, that involved *Stuart* provided the ship and with units that she had not been involved with previously. The EW had worked very well during this period.

Himself had been fully employed overseeing the operations, either on watch or observing and providing advice as required.

September 1966

On the first of the month, the ship entered Singapore and secured alongside Singapore Naval Base. The next week was spent in routine maintenance and making good several steam leaks etc.

On Friday the 9th of September, *Stuart* sailed for the exercise area, and the following day ammunitioned from RFA Fort Rosalie and then anchored of Pulo Tiaman just after midday. Over the weekend, a beach BBQ was available and proved popular.

On Monday, the 12th, *Stuart* sailed for exercises, returning to anchor overnight. This continued until the 16th when *Stuart* entered Singapore and secured alongside HMS *Londerry*. The ship was shifted to a buoy on Saturday, 17th of September.

Stuart sailed on Sunday the 18th to rendezvous with HMS *Arethusa* on Monday the 19th. On completion of EW trials, the ship headed for Hong Kong.

On Friday the 23rd, *Stuart* joined units of the Far East Fleet and, after fuelling from RFA *Tidespring*, joined HM ships *Victorious, Leander, Cleopatra* and HMAS *Paramatta* for entry to Hong Kong, securing alongside Victoria Basin. From then until the end of the month I spent enjoying the pleasures of Hong Kong.

Hong Kong

There were two incidents involving me during a visit to Hong Kong.

The first of these incidents occurred in my laundry. One of their members, who was a very good musician had been invited to join the band in a particular bar in Wan Chai on the Island side of the harbour. The Laundry team insisted that I should come along and hear him. I agreed and, in due course, arrived at the bar on the ground floor and sat at the same table as my laundry crew. My chair was adjacent to the main passageway from the entrance to a stairway at the back of the bar, leading to another bar and servicing upstairs. It so happened that I observed the people going upstairs were Stokers from our ship, a get-together of the ship's engineering team.

Later, I observed a Naval Shore Patrol, accompanied by an Army Red Cap (military police), come into the bar, and proceed to the upstairs bar. Shortly after, they reappeared, and the two Navy Patrolmen had one of the ship's stokers between them and were heading for the main entrance door. I got up to find out what was going on and followed them towards the door. Just before they reached the door, I observed one of the patrolmen punching the stoker in the back.

Their prisoner reacted violently, and the patrolmen became, in my opinion, very heavy-handed with their prisoner. I asked one of the patrolmen what the problem was with the fellow and was told that he was drunk and they were taking him to the headquarters.

In the scuffle and wrestling match that had followed the punch-up, one of the prisoner's shoes came off and was lying on the footpath. I asked one of the patrolmen, if he would pick it up and take it with them. When that didn't happen, I picked it up myself and threw it in the paddy wagon.

Commodore's Office

Next day, the captain sent for me and said that he had to take me before the Commodore of the Naval Dockyard as a charge had been laid against me of giving a Naval Patrol sailor a direct order when they were placing their prisoner in the Paddy Wagon.

We duly fronted the Commodore. Those present were the sailor making the complaint, the Red Cap and, I'm not sure if there was anyone else, besides my Captain and myself.

The Commodore read the charge and asked what I had to say as I was out of order giving a Direct Order to the Patrolman when he was carrying out his duty. There was a big smirk on the Patrolman's face.

I explained to the Commodore that, as an officer from the sailor's ship, I was interested in the welfare of that sailor. As I followed the patrol and prisoner towards the door, I saw the patrolman punch the prisoner in the kidneys just before they reached the door. This naturally brought a reaction from the prisoner who, to that stage, in my opinion, was giving no problem.

I also stated that I believed that my Captain would back me up that I never used the words Direct Order, or that I particularly briefed any sailor or Petty Officer being promoted that they should never use the words Direct Order. The reason for this was that in my long experience, both in the RAN and whilst on periods of loan service with the Royal Navy, I had observed its misuse that, at times, led to wrongful convictions and sentencing due to a breakdown of other logical action.

Whilst the Commodore was digesting my comments, I asked if I could comment on something not related to my case, that I considered was relevant.

I explained that the Officer in Charge of the Naval Police and Patrolman had been at the RPC the ship had given whilst in Hong Kong. During a conversation, he implied laughingly how his patrolman sorted out little green men of the Welsh Regiment based in Hong Kong by provoking them to get a reaction so they could lock them up. I said I knew I couldn't prove what he had said, however, I was sure some of my ship's officers, who were in the group, would support me.

The Red Cap was asked if he could support the Patrolman's Statement and said he neither saw the punch or me giving a direct order.

My Captain stated he understood I went out of my way to make sure that those being promoted were well briefed never to use the words Direct Order. I was sent out of the room and, when recalled, the Commodore said that he was taking no further action.

I will comment later about the fallout of my comments above.

Second Incident

I was Officer the Watch as we left Hong Kong. As *Stuart* sailed to leave the harbour, several junks were crossing the harbour and I kept a close eye on each of them. However, one which appeared to be under power because of the lack of wind was going to come very close to us. We had the right-of-way because he was using power, and it appeared to me that he was not going to take avoiding action at all. It was my job to ensure we did not collide, so I altered course. However, the end of one of his sail poles touched one of the stanchions on our quarterdeck. The captain was told I was altering course because of the Junk coming too close. He observed what had been happening and made a report to the Commodore of the circumstances. There were no recriminations, as I suspect this had happened a number of times before when warships and other ships were moving down the harbour.

Final Singapore Visit

On their way south from Hong Kong *Stuart* stopped at Singapore to refuel and had a departure Party for those who had helped us during our visits in our time in the FESR.

Among the guests, I noticed the officer who had been in charge of the Naval Police and Patrolman in Hong Kong. His wife was with him. I went to welcome him, but he made it clear that he didn't want to talk to me as he had been moved from Hong Kong to Singapore. Obviously. the comments made when I fronted the Commodore in Hong Kong had been investigated and found to be correct.

Homeward Bound

During our passage southwards, we called into Manus Island and refuelled.

Arrival Sydney

The ship arrived back in Sydney on January 17, 1967. I spent 480 days on the ship and finally left for HMAS *Watson* on January 30, 1967.

Summary

Since arriving back in Australia in February 1965, I had spent 234 days in HMAS *Melbourne* and 480 days in HMAS *Stuart*. Altogether, 714 days or 1.9 years.

From my position as Operation Room Officer and OOW on the Bridge, and in Harbour from time to time, I had deepened my experience as an Officer and felt competent to undertake any task as such.

OFFICER COMMENTS

TO MY ENTIRE SATISFACTION

A CAPABLE AND HARDWORKING OFFICER

Chapter 31

HMAS *Watson*

31 January 1967 to 17 June 1968

HMAS Watson

Return to HMAS Watson

My appointment back to HMAS *Watson* was to start on the 30th of January 1967 for leave and, on completion, as AIO Trials Officer. I was basically a Staff Officer supervising Training and Trials. So, after almost two years since returning to Australia as a Direction Officer, I was to serve ashore at last. The prospect of really getting to know my family was great. I was looking forward to some shore time even if was not to last a full year.

Family, New Arrival & House Extension

I enjoyed my reunion with family and renewing old acquaintances around our home. There were matters that needed to be done around the house and, this was the time that my brother-in-law, Barry, designed and built an extension onto the back of the house that provided another bedroom onto the back of the house. This allowed Anthony who had been sharing with Peter to have his own room; it also allowed Walter, the new baby of the family, to share a room with Peter. The extension had a large rumpus room as well.

One of the things I enjoyed most during this posting was being home full-time with the family for the first time since we returned from England in early February 1965. (Two years before.) I was able to be with the family at home and catch up with any work that needed to be done on the house or gardens. The only requirement was for me to be Duty Officer from time to time. I was able to catch up with most of my old friends and, also Joan's friends.

Joining I-IYAS Watson

I drove across Sydney from my home in Ashfield (in the Western Suburbs) to HMAS *Watson* (in the Eastern Suburbs) to take up my posting as the Training Officer, ND, Navigation and Direction, ND Security and CB (Confidential Books) Officer, and ASIC (Anti-Submarine Course Officer). I had no problems with any of these tasks and was looking forward to being in the Training Role.

On the Job

Among the Instructors were several I'd grown up with as a Petty Officer or Chief Petty Officer in the radar branch; they knew the standards that I required from my previous time at HMAS *Watson* before going overseas to do my Direction Officer training.

Cookery School

Since my last posting to HMAS *Watson* in 1961, a Cookery School has operated in the old sailors' dining hall building. The Officer in Charge invited me to drop in for a coffee, which I did from time to time. Occasionally, I was invited to a meal prepared by the graduating class.

Sport

There was plenty of Base sport, including a .22 rifle range, as well as Tennis, Cricket in the local Navy Competition, Athletes, swimming, Volleyball, Ten Pin Bowling at Rushcutters Bay, Golf, Lawn Bowls, and Sailing.

I had given up sport and concentrated on running and an Exercise programme. Also, the physical work around the house kept me busy.

Leisure Activities

Except for shopping and visiting Joan's parents and sister and brother-in-law from time to time, we tended to take it easy. From time to time, we had friends come around and concentrated on sports for the children.

Every Sunday, we attended Mass in the nearby church that was opposite the children's School.

Promotion

On the 1 April 1967, I was promoted to Lieutenant Commander and reposted to HMAS *Watson* to continue the jobs outlined above. This meant a trip to the tailor to replace the two gold rings on my jackets with two and a half-sized rings of a Lieutenant Commander

Christmas

I was home for Christmas 1966 and 1967 and this allowed me to be more involved and I really enjoyed observing the children unwrap their presents.

January 1968 to June 1968

I recall that during this period there was a shortage of CPORP and PORP Instructors. Two PORPs awaiting discharge helped somewhat. The Communication staff were a great help in the areas of Fleet Work, Voice Procedures and EW (Electronic Warfare).

Mess Dinner

On the 17th of February, a Mess Dinner was held for the Chief of Naval Staff, Vice Admiral Sir Alan McNichol, during his farewell visit to HMAS *Watson*.

Birthday

On the 1st of March, I celebrated my 42nd Birthday with a family gathering. It was also a day for me to reflect on how lucky I was to have such a loving and devoted wife and in-laws; also, to reflect on how my family was growing up and doing well at school.

Visitors to I-DAS Watson

Something like 80 members of the Army Staff College came for a Familiarisation visit on the 19th of March.

Compassionate Leave

On 1 May 1968, I was granted seven days of Compassionate Leave. The reason for this leave was that Joan had miscarried the child she was carrying. You can imagine our great disappointment at this loss, and it was necessary to supervise the children while she was in hospital and then look after her when she came home. At the end of the seven days, I returned to HMAS *Watson* with a heavy heart. Each night I would come home and help Joan as needed.

Entertainment

From time to time, there would be a formal Cocktail or Dinner party at HMAS *Watson* and Joan and I would attend. We always enjoyed these functions although the long drive home afterwards was always a bit of a downer, and I was generally careful to not imbibe too much.

Posting

On June 17, 1968, I was posted additional to HPIAS Perth, which was returning from its first deployment to Vietnam. This transfer was to give me time to be briefed by the returning ship's Direction Officer in preparation for my posting to the ship on June 28, 1968.

Once again, it was off to sea and eventually to operations off North Vietnam. I was to be given information on the operations the ship would be required to carry out. It was called "*"Sea Dragon"* and operations were off the North Vietnam coast. The purpose of this operation was to prevent the passage of ammunition, guns and supplies south along the coast to support North Korean operations in and against South Korea.

Joining HMAS Perth

I flew north from Sydney to Manus Naval Base, known as HMAS *Tarangau*. I was able to look around the base and enjoy some good company among my fellow officers. *Perth* arrived for refuel ling.

THE SEA IS CALLING YOU AGAIN BILL

COMMANDING OFFICER'S COMMENTS

TO MY ENTIRE SATISFACTION

AN INDUSTRIOUS AND ENTHUSIASTIC

OFFICER WHO HAS DONE EXTREMELY

WELL IN ALL HIS DUTIES AND IS

RECOMMENDED FOR NAVAL STAFF

COURSE

Chapter 32

HMAS *Perth*

17 June 1968 to 26 May 1969

Dimensions			Displacement	Engine
Length	133.2	m	4850 Tonnes	
Beam	14.3	m		
Draught	20 m			

Armament

2x127mm(5in)   Ikara   Torpedos   Standard Surface to Air

Temporary Posting

To give me time to be briefed by the then Direction Officer of the HMAS *Perth*, I was flown to Manus Island at the beginning of May 1965 to greet the ship when it arrived for fuel on the 5th of May 1968. The purpose of this trip was to be briefed on the Vietnam operations in preparation for my posting to the ship on 17th of June 1968.

I had a couple of days in the Naval Base on Manus Island before HMAS *Perth* arrived. The Commanding Officer was an old shipmate and made me very welcome. There were others to join *Perth* for the trip to Sydney. On the night before the ship's arrival on the 5th of May 1968, there was a Wardroom Party and I admit that, unusually for me, I probably had too much to drink.

When the ship secured alongside I, and the others taking passage back to Australia, embarked and it was a bit crowded in the Wardroom.

Briefing

The Direction Officer of HMAS Perth had qualified as a Direction Officer on the same course as me, and we were good friends. He brought me up to date on the latest information of operating off Vietnam.

I was to be given information and briefed on the operations the ship may/would be called upon to carry out off the North Vietnam coast. These were known as "Operation Sea Dragon," and was divided into two sections known as North and South Sea Dragon. The purpose of these operations was to prevent the passage by sea of ammunition, guns and supplies south to support North Korean operations against South Korea. In addition, the ship would be required to provide interdiction gunfire against selected targets. These operations would use aircraft to spot the fall of shot from the ships.

Naval Blockade has been used successfully for centuries and had stopped the traffic along the North Vietnam coast. I was to later find out from some USN sources that the original blockade intention was changed when American politicians visited the ships on Operation Sea Dragon. When they found out that the ships only used their guns if they detected a vessel proceeding along the coast, these politicians wanted to know why the ships were not firing on a regular basis into North Vietnam. After they returned to America, the US Navy received instructions that they were to find targets in North Vietnam for the ships to fire at.

Unfortunately, as we left Manus there was quite a sea running and, combined with a completely new ship's movement and a belly full of alcohol I became a bit squeamish. At one stage I went up and stood on the wing on the bridge to let the wind blow over my face. The captain came out and made the comment, "Mal de Mer, eh, Ritchie." He wasn't far wrong. Fortunately, it didn't last too long.

Briefing continued

After my first briefing about Vietnam Operations, I concentrated on learning about the different American radars and their capabilities. The second was to be briefed on the USN radar displays and plotting arrangements in what was known in the United States Navy as CIC (Combat Information Centre.) This title was being used in the ships built in America rather than the traditional RAN name of Operations Room. Next, and my main requirement, was to understand the nature of the various missions the ship may be called upon to participate in, and how long the ship was on station off the Vietnam coast.

When I finished most of the briefings, I was able to wander around the ship and educate myself on its layout and where everything was.

Customs and other Medical Staff had joined the ship at Brisbane on the way home and all the necessary clearances had been given by the time the ship reached Sydney.

Sydney Arrival

The arrival in Sydney on the 10th of May was a delightful experience as I watched the ship's crew meet up with their families who were waiting on the wharf. Eventually I went ashore to prepare for my official joining later in June.

Dockyard and Ship's Staff Maintenance.

The ship had been put into full maintenance routine and Dockyard and ship's personnel worked on a complete overhaul of the engines, guns, missile system and so on. Long Leave was granted to those personnel who had been on the ship whilst it had been away. Some personnel were drafted to Shore Establishments, or to other ships undergoing full refits. Others, about 52%, were to remain in the ship for the second deployment.

For all the rest of May and until the 14th of June the Long Self Maintenance period continued.

Joining Ship

On 17th of June 1968, I joined HMAS *Perth* at Garden Island. It was at a buoy ammunitioning and the next day moved to Chowder Bay to refuel. On completion of fuelling, the ship proceeded to sea for a 10-day shakedown and setting to work period.

The task for me then was to set in place the training programme for my team so they were ready for whatever was thrown at them when operating off Vietnam.

Before launching into the details of my time in HMAS *Perth* I wish to advise that I will be using an abridged commentary of what it involved and the depth of things that happened during my time aboard.

Work Up

The preparation of my CIC personnel consisted of carrying out various plotting and voice procedure exercises every day when not participating in the programme prepared for our Work Up. My Radar Chief and I had known one another basically since we were Able Seaman together.

After he completed running an exercise, he would report to me and tell me if there had been any mistakes. I kept making them practice, practice, practice until they made no mistakes. Came the day when he reported to me with a big smile on his face; they had made no mistakes during that day's exercises. I said I was glad to hear that, and I required the team to do it all again the next day. He protested naturally, my comment was they could have fluked it and a second run on the morrow would prove how good they were. The next day he reported they had again made no mistakes with a smile even bigger than the one the day before.

Note. Later, in the deployment he was to make a comment referring to this incident.

Individual Medical Kit

There was a Naval Reserve Doctor attached to the ship during the Work Up. He had been a Medic in World War II and after the war qualified as a doctor. He gave a briefing on what he considered was the minimum of first aid items, each person should have on them. These were a white handkerchief, a lanyard, and a sharp knife as well as a bar or two of block chocolate. You can imagine he was soon asked why we would need these items on every person. (We also wore flak jackets when at Action Stations).

The doctor stated that, from his experience in World War II, he had found, when working with people who had been wounded, and could not be attended to by the medical team immediately, it required the wounded person, or those attending him, to use the white handkerchief, or lanyard, as a tourniquet to stem any bleeding.

When the medical team arrived, they could identify, if the colour on the handkerchief was bright red, the wound was bleeding. If a dark red, the bleeding had stopped, and the wound would be left alone for the time being. If bright red, it was necessary to stop the bleeding as quickly as possible. The reason for the sharp knife was that there were occasions when the medical team did not have a knife for one reason or another and the availability of a sharp knife on the person could be useful. The need for chocolate was if you had to abandon ship you had something to sustain you whilst in the water until you could be picked up.

During the doctor's briefing I discussed with him what I intended to do if one or more of my team was injured and all the equipment was still working. He agreed that the last place an injured person should be lying was in the CIC, particularly if he was in agony and his cries would be disturbing the people trying to do their job.

I briefed my team and told them if one of them was injured I would deal with their injuries as best I could, and he would be placed outside the CIC in the lobby and the medical team informed.

Jumping ahead a bit, we were fortunate that the ship was never hit, and I never had to take that action.

Aside. Many years later, I met up with one of my sailors who was working as a gardener at HMAS *Leeuwin* in Fremantle. He asked me if I would have removed him from the CIC if he had been injured as I had briefed them. My answer to him was yes, I would have.

Eventually, at the end of the work up, we were tested to see if we were Operationally Ready to return to Vietnam. We had worked very hard and had achieved the level required to be certified we were ready.

The rest of the time before departure was spent in storing, ammunitioning, and refuelling and spending time with family. Then it was time once again to say farewell.

September 1968

Departure for Vietnam Operations

Families were gathered on the wharf saying their farewells on Thursday 19th of September as the ship slipped and made its way out of the Sydney Harbour heading north for the ship's second tour of duty off Vietnam. During the passage north there was continuous training for the tasks ahead. We stopped at Manus Island to fuel. Operational Command of *Perth* was transferred to the Seventh Fleet whilst at Manus. On completion of fuelling, it was off to Subic Bay.

King Neptune

His Majesty King Neptune insisted on coming aboard during this passage and all called before him were duly dealt with.

Training

Training continued all the way to Subic Bay. Due to a typhoon further north, the winds were force 7 to 8 as the ship arrived at Subic Bay. Two tugs were used to berth alongside HMAS *Hobart*. *Hobart* departed for Australia on Monday the 30th of September.

The Direction Officer of *Hobart* had qualified as a Direction Officer on the same course as me and we were good friends. He brought me up to date on the latest information of operating off Vietnam.

Subic Bay Delights

It didn't take long for all on board to explore the facilities of the nearby Subic Bay town and get to know the drinking holes and where to get a good meal. It was a bit of a walk that most were happy to take to get off the ship for a few hours.

Some of the officers were golf tragics and invited me to join them in a round of golf. I went to the American PX and purchased a set of golf clubs and so began my learning process of how to play golf. As was to be expected my score was well above the others, but we enjoyed the outing. So, began my golf experience.

USN Support Staff

At the same time, we got to know the USN Engineering and Supply staff who supported the ship whilst alongside. When not working, we used the Naval Officers Club, especially the swimming pool. It was also used by American families.

Some families also invited some of the crew back to their homes from time to time.

Before we sailed for our first operational tour, we entertained the American officers and their wives. These officers were the people responsible for supporting us whilst alongside in Subic Bay. For the wives especially, this would have been a novel experience as they were served various forms of alcohol of their choice.

As I understand it USN ships are dry ships and do not "allow" alcohol to be served on board. It became a standard practice to have a party on board when back in Subic Bay.

On the 2nd of October, *Perth* sailed from Subic Bay for a two-week exercise programme and was put through the hoops on all aspects of various situations we might encounter.

I was a very busy boy in the CIC making sure everyone was up to scratch. I was pleased with the team and was confident they would not let me or the ship down.

October 1968

On the 5th of October, after refuelling and restoring, *Perth* sailed for the coast of South Vietnam to report to the Command for operations off Vietnam.

Vietnam

The ship arrived off the coast near Da Nang at 0500 on Monday, the 7th of October. Our Replenishment from USS *Chipola* ran smoothly, and we were surprised to learn we were their Champion for the shortest time engaging and disengaging as a DLG/DDG in her present deployment.

Our first firing on the 8th was to give Harassment and Interdiction (H&I) fire in support of the Third Marine Division. The ship was given nineteen targets over seven hours. I have set out the actual gunfire tasks and replenishments for the month in the table below.

It didn't take long before were sent north of the DMZ (Demilitarised Military Zone) to what was known as Northern Sea Dragon. On Wednesday, the 9th, *Perth* relieved USS *Berkeley* (a DDG) that had suffered a gun mount and computer casualty.

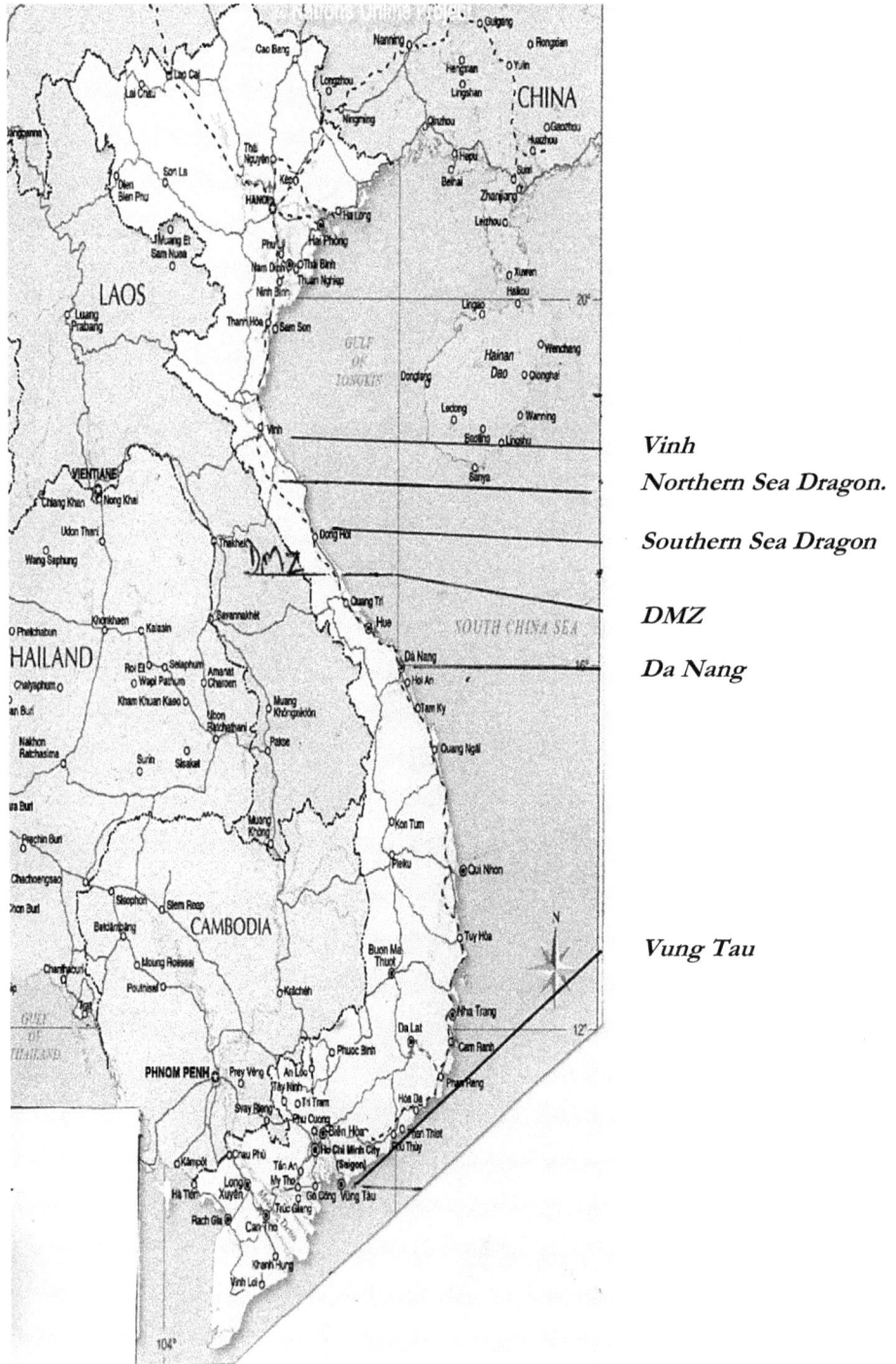

On joining USS *Berkeley*, documentation was handed over and *Perth* assumed the duties of CTU 77.1.1 in charge of Northern Sea Dragon. That night the Task Unit carried a Harassment mission on Water Borne Logistics craft.

That was not to last long, and on the following day we relieved USS *New Jersey*, a Battleship, in Southern Sea Dragon. In the early dawn of Thursday, the 10th *Perth* came alongside *New Jersey* and looking at its massive guns made one feel a little more secure. *Perth* then assumed the duties of CTU 77.1.2 whilst *New Jersey* went north to Northern Sea Dragon.

Sea Dragon Our Next Operation

There was no time to prepare our own firing plan for the next event and we used what had been given to us. The following is my recollection of events that followed.

Two spotting aircraft were detected and identified, and communications established in preparation for our first spotted bombardment on a vehicle parking area. We took up our position in accordance with the USS *New Jersey's* plan. The aircraft began reporting the map coordinates of the target. *Perth* fired ranging shots as directed by the aircraft. These shots were not observed by the aircraft. The ship fired a smoke-shell, and it was realised we needed to be closer to shore. We reversed our course and closed the range. This meant the ship was able to get our shots into the Vehicle Park. There were sixteen direct hits reported by the Spotters.

Shore Battery Fire

Just as we finished firing and were turning away from the coast, the Lookouts reported a shell had landed in the wake about a mile or so astern of our escort. The ship increased to full speed and laid down smoke and commenced zig zagging. However, the next shot from shore landed where we would have been if we had not turned. Shrapnel hit the side of the ship and our guns returned fire on the shore batteries.

Fortunately, the subsequent shore fire tended to hit the zag when the ship was on the zig and vis versa until we were out of range. Altogether a total of 30 rounds were observed to fall at varying distances from 10 to 100 yards from *Perth*.

Self-Inflicted Damage

The ship's guns fired at the shore batteries. However, when on a zig or zag (can't remember which), the forward gun arcs closed so the gun could not fire. As we changed course, and the arcs opened, the gun fired with the trajectory and blast almost along the ship's side. I was glad we were wearing flak jackets.

Initially, I thought we had been hit and, as I checked visually if any of my team were hurt, the Air Conditioning Ventilator, {close to nearly two metres in diameter and a third to half a metre in depth) dislodged from the deckhead and fell no more than a quarter of a metre behind my 17-year-old Air Plotter. He did not even know it was there as he was concentrating on his plotting, until we were out of range, and I told everyone to relax. He turned away from the Air Plot. His face went white as he saw what was behind him. I spoke to him on the phone and said to keep up what he had done, and we would all make it home.

When I had checked my crew after the blast went off, I also checked on the Lookouts by phone. I thought I had been a bit slow to check the lookouts.

Comment. From time to time I worried about that. However, when I was XO of HMAS *Stirling* many years later, I was visiting HMAS *Leeuwin*. As I walked to the main office a voice from a person doing some gardening said, "Hello, sir, remember me?" He had been in *Perth* Operations room behind me at the time of the above incident. He said, "I have always admired you for your reaction to the gun going off alongside of the ship and your instantaneous calling the Lookouts to see if they were okay."

I said, "I had always thought I had taken too long."

His reply was, "No, it was almost immediate that you reached for the phone whilst you were looking at the team." I thanked him as it relieved me of what I had thought was a slowness on my part.

Review of Shore Firing

Besides Harassment missions, another spotted mission was the destruction of a bridge.

Bridge Destruction

On the 15th, two A4s from USS *Intrepid* (CVS 11) provided the aircraft spotters for the destruction of a bridge. *Perth* shells bracketed the target but did not destroy it. The aircraft indicated they had bombs and dropped eight 500lb bombs, destroying the bridge.

Lesson. The use of Naval High Velocity muzzle guns and the inherent range spreads being used in this way against a point target showed that such targets should be dealt with effectively with aircraft as shown in the previous paragraph.

Note: The first week off Vietnam was exceedingly busy and was an appropriate baptism for those who had never been in action and under fire. The intensity was probably just right.

Although I have not mentioned what I was doing, I was in the CIC for all operations supervising and keeping a watch in CIC when not firing.

Danang Visit

We were programmed to stay in Sea Dragon until the 5th of November. Our new task was to provide missile cover for USS *New Jersey* in Northern I Corps supporting the Third Marine Division. This area was below the DMZ.

On the 27th, *Perth* joined USS *New Jersey*, who had formed a new Task Group, and was proceeding back to Sea Dragon for *New Jersey* to engage five targets twelve miles inland. However, the spotter aircraft could not locate four of the targets and only one was fired on.

Both ships returned to Northern I Corps on Monday, the 28th, and answered calls for fire by day and unspotted harassing missions by night. However, *Perth's* forward gun developed a defect.

Troublesome Gun

Perth was given a fifteen-hour standdown to transfer the after gun-mount's Recoil Cylinder to the forward gun mount. This meant that, unless we could complete an imminent bombardment assignment allocated to us before our looming R&R, we would have to return to Subic Bay for repair and maintenance and miss out on our R&R.

The Gunnery Maintenance staff suggested that the breach block of the after gun be transferred to the forward gun. It was a slim, desperate chance that, if it worked, we could complete the task allocated and have our R&R.

The heavy breach block was taken out of the rear gun and carried by a squad of sailors towards the front of the ship. However, due to the ship's design, where the superstructure went right out to the ship's side, it was necessary to pass the block down the hatch and carry it forward in the passageway until reaching a ladder to the forecastle. This was a most difficult task, a requirement requiring a lot of muscle and sweat to get the block to the forecastle and forward gun. To the credit of the maintenance team, they were able to complete the task and the ship sent a signal about one minute to midnight stating we were ready to carry out the assigned task. This *Perth* did and was able to proceed on our previously planned R&R.

Summary

The following is a summary of the types of firings and replenishments undertaken.

Air Spotted	18
Ground Spotted	5 * (two with Air Spotted)
Night Harassment	38
Day Harassment	2
Suppression	3
Counter Battery	<u>1</u>
	67

Replenishment Summary

FFO	5
FFO and Stores	1
Ammo and Stores	6
Turnover Material	5
	17

November 1968

Events of Interest

One item that should be mentioned here is that the ship's EW team was able to provide bearings of several enemy radar stations on the mainland. From these bearings we were able to ascertain the position of these radars and the times they would be switched on each day.

On one day we were completing a bombardment a little way up the coast from where one of these radar facilities had been located. This radar came on-air regularly at 8 o'clock each morning. In a coded message exchange, we found the spotting aircraft were carrying the right missiles to attack the frequency of the radar. We flew the aircraft parallel to the coast and just before 8 am they were turned towards the radar site. This they did and picked up the switching on of the radar and fired their missiles. Our EW team reported the enemy radar stopped operating at about the time the missiles would have reached the site. We assumed the aircraft weapons had hit the radar station and, as there were no further transmissions from that site, we were confident that we put the radar out of action.

Sometime later, however, the EW team detected a new radar position in a different locality and, on analysing the radar signature, it appeared to be the radar that we thought we had destroyed. I would have liked to have fired a couple of shells in the vicinity of this new station to let them know we knew we were on to them. However, the opportunity never arose where we could use the spotting aircraft to repeat their discomfort.

First Deployment Ends

On the 30th of November, *Perth* was able to transfer turnover material to USS *Joseph* and depart for Rest and Recreation in Subic and for Maintenance.

Engagement Summary November 1968.

The following is summary of the types of firings undertaken.

Air Spotted	14
Ground Spotted	
Night Harassment	11
Day Harassment	
Suppression	
Emergency Illumination	<u>1</u>
	<u>26</u>

Replenishment Summary

FFO	2
FFO and Stores	4
Stores	1
Turnover Material	<u>2</u>
	<u>9</u>

December 1968

Subic Bay

At the beginning of the month *Perth* was undergoing maintenance in Subic Bay. However frequent moves to let ships inside of *Perth* to sail was not a blessing.

However, on the 10th of December, *Perth* sailed for exercises with a submarine and the results were encouraging especially as the ship's team had been fully occupied with gunfire support. On completion of these exercises, it was back to Southern Vietnam.

Operations

Much like the previous month, the ship responded to calls for spotted and Harassment missions and a monthly summary is set out below.

Engagement Summary December 1968.

The following is summary of the types of firings undertaken.

Air Spotted	10
Ground Spotted	1
Night Harassment	14
Day Harassment	
Suppression	0
	25

Replenishment Summary

FFO	3
FFO and Stores	3
Stores	2
	8

Padre's Letter

Everyone on board looked forward to the arrival of mail. It was approaching the Christmas period when I received a letter from a Catholic Padre back in Sydney saying that he wanted to be with the Navy people serving, both at sea and ashore, operating in Vietnam for Christmas. However, it would require a message back from us to our authorities in Sydney asking for him to be able to come. The units he wished to visit were HMAS *Perth*, the RAN Helicopter flight operating with the Americans and the Clearance Diving team. I showed the letter to the captain, who was not a Catholic. We both knew the Padre very well. The captain told me to draw up a message requesting this particular Chaplain be sent to be on board at Christmas. So, it came to pass.

Christmas

On the 23rd Chaplain F Lyons joined the ship at Danang for the Christmas religious celebrations and was made most welcome.

He celebrated midnight Mass in the Wardroom, and on Christmas Day held a Combined Church Service for the crew. He celebrated Mass on the upper deck adjacent the missile launcher. His altar was the top of the structure used to observe the state of the missal on the launcher. This had a small flat area on the top of the structure. As a Catholic, I was very happy to be able to celebrate Mass and receive Communion on such a religious occasion, as were other Catholics on board.

During the serving of Communion, the Padre was suddenly confronted by the captain in the queue. The Padre to his credit gave the captain communion even though he knew he was not a Catholic.

Eventually the Padre was transferred to shore so he could visit the Helicopter and Diving sections ashore in Southern Vietnam.

Christmas Day Mess Decks Inspection

The traditional inspection of mess decks by the captain (youngest member of crew dressed as Captain) accompanied by the actual Captain (acing as a sailor) was carried out.

Perhaps the most appreciated Christmas present of all was a film of the families back home, produced by the Naval Photographic section, that was shown several times.

Another notable event was the bringing on board of some relatives of crew members serving in the Australian army at Nui Dat and Vung Tau. Two brothers of one sailor came aboard. Some Australian Naval Senior Officers serving ashore also came aboard.

At 1800 (6 pm) all visitors were landed, and the ship proceeded for operations, a Harassment mission that lasted from 2 pm to 10.20 pm.

Mail was collected from Vung Tau several times during the month.

Final Mission for Month.

Our final spotted mission for the month occurred on Thursday the 26th, about 25 miles south of Vung Tau. At 2 am on Friday 27th, the ship transferred documents to USS *Towers* (DDG) and *Perth* headed for Keelung in Taiwan for Rest and Recreation.

As we left the following messages were exchanged.

From HMAS Perth to CTU seven zero pt eight pt nine.

"The jolly green giant is at a loss
so we ask a query to the gunline boss
have yo a corps in excess of four
because we've done the lot for sure
Seadradon-the quartet and DMZEE
last night it was shootng in three
we're glad to go where needed most
we have our chums along the coast
a friendly bunch of in country guys
who call the fire and spot the flies
We are enjoying it all and are full of cheer
Merry Xmas and a Happy New Year

Reply

FM CTU Seven Zero pt Eight pt Nine to HMAS Perth

On the horizon there was a ship silhouettes
and as closer they came, the greener one gets
the Perth is always a welcome sight
for its really well known it can fight
and carry out my assignments whatever they be
from the tip of IV corps to the DMZ
in tense times as these it's refreshing to know
you've good Aussie friends from way down below.

Keelung

Keelung is on the top north-east coast of Taiwan as indicated on the map below. Tai-Pai is at about the same latitude and is in the centre of the island.

Perth secured alongside number three berth Keelung on Monday the 30th of December. It was time to relax.

With two other officers I decided to have a look around Keelung CBD and see if I could find any presents to take home.

The three of us came across bath house and massage parlour and I certainly enjoyed all my muscles being relaxed and I felt like a new man.

No, we didn't get too close to the staff.

Walking along the main street we came across a large bookstore, and I thought I would get a couple of books to read when not on watch. However, to our surprise every aisle and wall storage/display shelves were full of sexually explicit books. I had not seen anything like it in all my visits to the Far East.

January 1969

Taiwan

It didn't take long to find a bar eatery and enjoy a local meal as well as drinks. I could not find anything suitable as presents and we returned to the ship.

Taipei

Again, the three of us also visited Taipei and had an interesting local meal and drinks and observed the locals going about their business. However, nothing attracted my eye that would be suitable as presents for the family.

So began another year and the month of January was a bit different to the previous times in Sea Dragon or on the Gun Line.

Kaohsiung

On the 2nd of January the ship sailed for Kaohsiung on the lower west coast of Taiwan, arriving there the following morning and secured alongside the Number One Commercial Wharf.

The purpose of the visit was to use the facilities of the Repair Ship USS *Prairie*. In addition, the opportunity arose to re-provision from USS *Procyon* when it entered harbour. Fresh and dry provisions were transferred by LCM.

I did a run ashore with others and found a Bath House for a soak and massage. Otherwise, I spent most of my time on board either as duty officer, or ensuring the CIC was up to standard to resume operations. We left Kaohsiung on the morning of the 6th of January and headed for South Vietnam.

During the passage all sorts of exercises were carried out to ensure we were ready in all respects for our next stint on the Gun-Line.

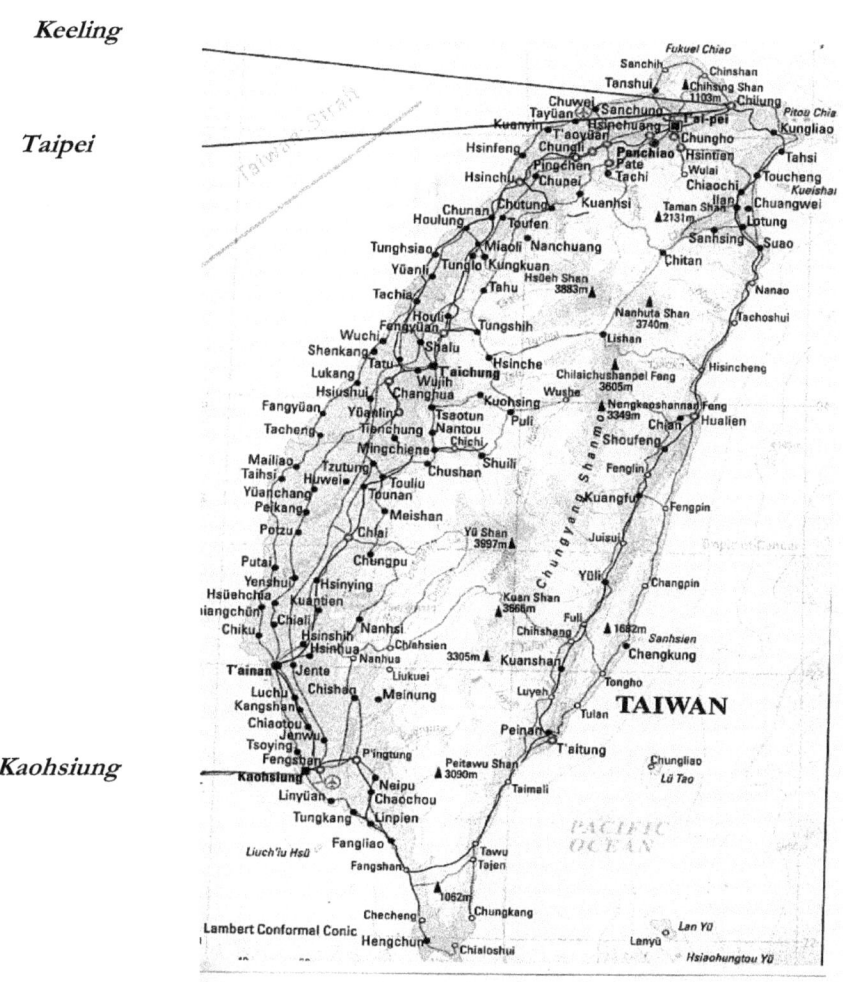

Gun Line

At 0600 (6 am), on Thursday the 9th, *Perth* relieved USS *Strauss* (DDG) in IV Corps and then proceeded to Vung Tau for a briefing by the Naval Gunfire Liaison Officer and collected 300 bags of welcome mail. It was not until the following day that the ship was required to carry out a spotted mission. And so, it was back to the grind.

At this time, off the coast of Vietnam, the ship fired its 5000th round. I should not have to tell that I was fully occupied in the CIC providing accurate and timely information to the Command as required.

During fuelling on the nineth, eight bags of sea mail were delivered from the tanker.

On the 17th our tour in IV Corps ended, and *Perth* proceeded to Yankee Station where she joined Task Group 70.4 comprising USS *Hornet*, and five escorts, US ships *Richard B Anderson*

(DD788), *Davidson* DE1045), *Lofberg* (DD758), *Ernest G Small* and *Shelton* (DD790)

The purpose of this group was to participate in an Anti-Submarine Warfare Exercise "BEACON LAMP 1/69" that began on Tuesday the 21st and ended on Saturday 25th.

I won't go into details of everything *Perth* was involved in. Of six submarine kills during the exercise three were initiated by visual aircraft detections, two by ECM interceptions and one by USS *Davidson's* sonar.

Perth took part in three of the actions and demonstrated the ability of combined air and surface operations to counter conventional submarines.

A visit by the Chief of Staff to COMASWGRU FIVE, and four officers, who came aboard *Perth* to discuss the Ikara system. They were very complimentary of *Perth's* performance in the exercise and in particular the EW Intercepts, it was clear that the training and experience of our EW Operators makes them vastly superior to their USN counterparts.

On detachment *Perth* headed north-west to return to the ASW training area at Yankee Station. Sunday the 26th was spent quietly on passage and on Monday 27th joined TG 77.9.2 for 18 hours of ASW and gunnery training.

Engagement Summary January 1969.

The following is summary of the types of firings undertaken.

Air Spotted	6
Ground Spotted	
Night Harassment	6
Day Harassment	
Suppression	
Counter Battery	0
	12

Replenishment Summary

FFO	4
FFO and Stores	3
Stores	4
	11

February 1969

Screen

The month began with *Perth* in charge of the screen around USS *Kittyhawk*. Also, on Saturday, the 1st, the Deputy Chief of Naval Staff and his Secretary came aboard. They were briefed on *Perth* activities, and afterwards walked around the ship and later they met officers in the Wardroom. They left the following day.

Weather and Relief

Weather during the first few days was lousy and the ship rolled heavily and at 2200 (10 pm) on the 5th, the ship was relieved and headed for Subic.

Subic

After ULQ6 checks *Perth* entered Subic on the 7th, securing alongside USS *Shelton* at 15.39 for an eleven-day maintenance period. The ship had only spent six days in harbour in the preceding two months, with and overall 82.7per cent underway since leaving Australia.

Holiday Accommodation

During the weekends, holiday accommodation was available at Grande Island, sailors paying 35 cents a day at the hotel and officers and CPO/POs paying three dollars per day for cottage accommodation. I can't remember staying at the cottages but probably spent one weekend there when not on duty.

Thirty-two sailors enjoyed a forty-eight-hour holiday with the Australian Community which was set up by the Australian Ambassador.

Sea Time

On the 19th of February, the ship sailed for one day of exercises outside of Subic. The purpose of this trip to sea was to check the Gunnery and Missiles systems, to carry out Interceptions and AA sleeve firings. The AA firings were most successful with 41 per cent TTBs and with three targets shot down.

We returned to harbour to drop off the repair yard personnel; it was then head for South Vietnam.

Downed Aircraft

A Navy F4 aircraft had ditched not too far from Subic when we were about 110 miles away and *Perth* was requested to return and aid. We reversed course and joined other units also searching. A fishing boat had seen the aircraft crash. There was no sign of the crew or aircraft, and *Perth* laid a dan buoy at 1000 on the location indicated by the fishermen. On being released, the ship resumed course for Vietnam.

En Route

In the afternoon, Damage Control Exercises were carried out the ship at Action Stations. All weapon systems, together with the Smoke Generator and 81mm mortar were tested. On Friday, the 21st a Pre Action-Calibration was carried out.

Gunline

Perth arrived on station at 0600, Saturday the 22nd, and was immediately directed to provide gunfire support. A spotter aircraft directed us to a position, but low cloud prevented aircraft spotting and we neutralised an area as directed. For the rest of the month, we supported Korean Marine Corps firing spotted and Harassment missions.

Engagement Summary February 1969.

The following is summary of the types of firings undertaken.

Air Spotted	7
Ground Spotted	
Night Harassment	7
Day Harassment	
Suppression	
Counter Battery	
Area Neutralization	<u>1</u>
	<u>15</u>

Replenishment Summary

FFO Stores	<u>4</u>
	<u>**8**</u>

March 1969

Hong Kong

On Thursday, the 18th of March, *Perth* arrived in Hong Kong and it was time to let our hair down. 48 hours leave was granted to each watch. General maintenance was required to bring the ship back to its usual best.

Suzie's Side Party were soon employed on cleaning and painting the ship's side. The general maintenance carried out on the upper deck and superstructure was to get rid of all the rust and stuff. On the 25th, the ship sailed for Subic Bay laden with Rabbits (presents) to hand over the weight to HMAS *Brisbane*.

Subic Bay

Perth arrived at Subic on the 27th. The following day there was great excitement when our relief HMAS *Brisbane* arrived, and the next two days details of the way ahead was carried out with a General Briefing followed by individual ones as required.

Transfer of Weight

On the 30th, the Weight was passed to HMAS *Brisbane*. HMAS *Perth's* involvement in the Vietnam War had come to an end and it was time to turn our mind to our home coming.

Engagement Summary March 1969.

The following is summary of the types of firings undertaken.

Air Spotted	12
Ground Spotted	2
Night Harassment	13
Day Harassment	
Suppression	0
	27

Replenishment Summary

FFO	4
Stores	6
	10

Perth, Here I Come

As the ship's Public Relations Officer, I disembarked at Subic for a flight from Manila to Fremantle where the ship would be visiting on the way home to Sydney. My job was to liaise with the Naval Commanding Officer Commanding (NOIC), Western Australia, on details and functions for the HMAS *Perth's* arrival at Fremantle on the way home to Sydney.

Farewell Messages

From Comseventh Fleet
To HMAS *Perth*

Sayonara

1. As you depart from the Seventh fleet I wish to personally thank you for a very <u>fine</u> job well done. Your <u>exemplary</u> performance as a NGFT, Sea Dragon and Escort Unit has been a source of pride and assurance to me for continuing the excellent working relationships of our Navies. You have also made an important contribution to the common cause of the free world forces in Asia. Well-done.

2. Best wishes for a smooth voyage back to Australia and for a happy reunion with family and friends and loved ones.

VDM WF Pringle

FROM. COMCRUDESGRUSEVENTHFLT
TO. HMAS *Perth*

Farewell

1. When one starts to view your ship's accomplishments during its second tour in Vietnam it is hard to remember that you are only one quote jolly green giant unquote. Your activities in all four corp areas, the DMZ and the commander of both Sea Dragon units have been as varied as could be possible. In every instance you have been cited for your excellent cooperation at short notice to recoveries of two crews from two downed aircraft and what the Secretary of State Rusk called your quote excellent cooperation at short notice to escorting of USS Dubuquve in the repatriation of NVN sailors. Your accurate NGFS has been not only to the training of your men but also their tenacity in repairing the troublesome 5.54 mount.

2. The combined efforts of the USN and RAN have resulted in considerable successes in Vietnam and provinces, a further basis for accomplishing future objectives we will have, as free nations of the world. My best wishes for smooth sailing on your homeward journey and joyous reunions when you get there. Rudden.

Fremantle

On arrival in Perth, I was met and taken to HMAS *Leeuwin* where I met the NOIC and basically told to go and enjoy myself as everything had been planned already.

I can't remember if I was billeted at *Leeuwin* or elsewhere. I certainly met up with my various aunts and uncles and a couple of other acquaintances and enjoyed being away from the ship.

Homeward Bound

Meanwhile at 0800 on the 31st of April, HMAS *Perth* sailed for Australia, calling at Singapore and Christmas Island en route. I understand a memorial service was held over the site of where HMAS *Perth 1* was sunk in WWII.

Arrival Fremantle

Perth arrived at Fairway Buoy at 0800 on the 12th of April and the NOCWA Liaison Officer, Custom Officers, and I, transferred from a boat. The ship then proceeded to 'H' Wharf Fremantle where there was a welcoming crowd, and interview at the Captain's Press Conference.

On the Sunday forenoon, a Memorial Service was held on board for the HMAS *Perth 1* survivors and families, about 80 people. They toured the ship after the Service. In the afternoon, the ship was open to visitors and 7,140 came aboard and were shown around.

Local Radio Station 6PR set up a caravan on the wharf and conducted daily broadcasts from alongside the ship whilst it was in Harbour. There was another ship open to visitors and something over 7,000 visited.

Ceremonial Entry to the City of Perth

263 Officers and Sailors marched through the City of Perth, exercising their right to enter the city. The Colour Guard marched with bayonets fixed.

Receptions

On completion of the parade, sailors attended a Reception in Anzac House and a Civic Reception for the Captain and Officers was held in Council House with lunch in the Council House Restaurant.

In the afternoon, the Fremantle Mayor hosted a Reception in his Council Chambers.

I seem to remember WA personnel were sent on leave before the ship sailed.

Departure Fremantle

Before departure, 13 Naval Reserve Ratings embarked to undergo thirteen days Annual Full-Time training.

On Tuesday, the 15th, the ship departed Fremantle for Sydney with three Custom Officers also embarked.

Holiday

Before arriving in Sydney, several of the officers in the Wardroom had discussed where they would take their family for a holiday. Someone indicated they were booking into a Defence Holiday Centre up in Queensland, not far from the New South Wales/Queensland border. Several other officers, including me, decided what a good idea that was, so I too booked into this Holiday Centre.

Arrival Sydney

On Sunday, the 20th, the *Perth* entered Sydney Harbour, stopping in Watsons Bay to pick up Customs Officers. It then proceeded to the Overseas Terminal and was greeted by a cheering crowd.

Joan greeted me at the foot of the gangway, and I was a very happy man to be back on home soil of Sydney.

Holiday

Joan had organised the family and it was not long before we were bound for Queensland by car. The Holiday Centre was ideally placed to allow us to visit the various attractions including a Currumbin Wildlife Park. Although each family and their children tended to go different ways, they seemed to mix well when at the Holiday Centre. All too soon the time for relaxing with family came to an end.

I returned to the ship after some leave and received a new Posting. I had anticipated being posted back to *Canberra*. However, to my dismay it was not to be.

Posting

My posting was to HMAS *Watson* as Officer in Charge of Navigation and Direction School and as AIO Trials Officer on Flag Officer Eastern Australia's Staff. I was not impressed and had already decided that I would again apply for the job at the Search and Rescue Centre in Canberra. The date of my posting was 26th May.

It was with some feeling I rang Joan and gave her the news. She, like me, was very disappointed and accepted that I would be applying for the Search and Rescue job.

Summary

As I look back these many years later, I believe that HMAS *Perth*, under Captain David Leach, was the best ship I ever served in. Certainly, the Operations Room Crew were among the best I ever had to supervise.

OFFICERS COMMENTS

"TO MY ENTIRE SATISFACTION.

A THOROUGH AND CAPABLE OFFICER WHO IS EXTREMELY RELIABLE AND LOYAL.

A CALM AND EFFECTIVE LEADER WHOSE ENTHUSIASTIC ZEAL CONTRIBUTED IN LARGE MEASURE TO PERTH'S PERFORMANCE IN VIETNAM."

Those comments softened the disappointment of my posting.

USN Meritorious Unit Commendation Award

After I had left the *Perth*, the following award was presented for her recent time in this deployment in the Vietnam Area.

On the 28th of August, the Ambassador of the United States of America, Mr Rice, presented the USN Meritorious Unit Commendation. The wording of the Commendation was along the lines of:

> *'Perth' contributed significantly to combat operations by conducting numerous successful fire missions against enemy installations and lines of communications.*

Chapter 33

HMAS *Watson*

26 May to 31 August 1969

Joining

After my holiday in Queensland, I reported to HMAS *Watson* where I was to be the Navigation and Direction School Training Officer.

It was nice to be back in familiar surroundings. I think, from memory, the Training Office was in the new ND School to the north end of the establishment. Today the 'RITCHIE' building.

Training Officer

I can't remember much of my time back at *Watson* but I would have checked from time to time of how people were going.

What I can remember is the "Uncle Bill" episode I was involved in in a training session and unbeknown to me a nephew was in the class. During a break, he came over and addressed me as Uncle Bill rather than by Sir. This was overheard by others and the class respectfully, in jest, referred to me as Uncle Bill for the duration of my involvement with them. This stuck for the next 20-odd years of the remainder of my time in the Navy, and even into retirement I was often referred to and became known as Uncle Bill.

What I did do was take the opportunity to participate in exercises with ship's teams in the training centre at the TAS (Torpedo Anti-Submarine) School. I would occupy one of the other escort cubicles and use my skills with the manoeuvring Signal Book to act as a support ship.

Visitors and Visitations

It was good to be able to visit friends or have them come round for a meal and as we were really starting to feel like a family again. Out of the blue I was posted to HMAS Melbourne then preparing for another stint in the Far East.

The worst of being good at your job and the lack of available Direction Officers.

Once again it was pack bag and whatever and join that ship.

OFF TO SEA AGAIN.

COMMANDING OFFICER'S COMMENTS

HAS CONDUCTED HIMSELF TO MY ENTIRE SATISFACTION. A KEEN, HARD WORKING AND EXPERIENCED DIRECTION OFFICR. 440

Chapter 34

HMAS *Melbourne*

1 September 1969 to 14 December 1970

*HMAS Melbourne
with aircraft ranged on Deck.*

Joining

HMAS Melbourne was in Sutherland Dock, Cockatoo Island, Sydney Harbour, when the time came for me to join on the 1st of September. I drove to the landing where there were boats ferrying Liberty men from the Mainland to the Island.

Mate of Upper Deck

On joining, I was informed I would be Mate of the Upper Deck. That basically put me In Charge of running the Seamanship Departments, the four Parts of Ship. This included all Seamanship Evolutions such as Replenishment at Sea (RAS), Jack Stay Transfers, Towing,

Lowering and Hoisting Boats, Anchoring, Ladders and Gangways, and the Maintenance and Cleanliness of the Four Parts of Ship.

My many years in Carriers, and previous time as a Petty Officer in Charge of the various Parts of Ship, and my later time as the Bosun in HMS *Sheffield* as a recently qualified officer, provided me with the background to supervise these areas efficiently.

Direction Officer

I was the Deputy to the Direction Officer and kept watches in Air Defence Room when there were flying operations, or exercises involving the Air Controllers or Air Plotting teams.

Officer of Watch and Duty Officer

At sea, I was required to act as First Officer of the Watch when at sea, when I was not required in either the ADR or attending to Replenishments and the like.

In Harbour, I was on the Lieutenant Commander's Duty Roster.

Goings On

To bring people up to date, I will briefly comment on why the ship was in Sutherland Dock getting a new Bow fitted. During her previous absence from Sydney, on Exercises in the Far East area of operations, the USS *Evans* had collided with *Melbourne* when repositioning to take up RESDES (Rescue Destroyer) astern and had been cut in two. *Melbourne* had damaged her bow and temporary repairs were made in Singapore so she could return to Sydney for a complete Bow replacement. It had been hoped the final fitting of the Bow would be complete relatively early in September 1969. The Bow had been completely fitted and the ship prepared to leave Sutherland Dock to embark some stores at the buoy, before proceeding to sea.

A Painters and Dockers Black Ban meant the ship could not be undocked and spent the rest of the month and early part of October in the Dock. This Black Ban was affecting the ship's programme.

October 1969

Un-Docking

The hierarchy decided to undock the ship using the ship's crew and some tugs that were not subject to the Ban.

On Saturday, the 11th of October, using uniform personnel to man the dockside lines, the assistance of the three small tugs, and 6 LCMs (Landing Craft) from HMAS *Sydney*, the ship began easing out of the Dock at 0715, slowly.

By 0830, the ship was out of the dock and proceeded to No 2 buoy, near Garden Island. Here the two bow anchors were secured to their cables and hove in. A small quantity of essential stores and pyrotechnics were taken on board. The Fleet Admiral addressed the Ship's Company before the ship departed at 1315 for Jervis Bay and anchored there for the night.

I would like to comment here on the great credit due to the Technical Department for bringing long idle machinery to Operational State at very short notice.

On the 14th of October, we embarked 1600 tons of fuel oil from HMAS *Supply* whilst at anchor. This relatively small amount was taken because it would have taken a long time to fill the double bottom tanks.

Checking Serviceability

On completion of fuelling, what are known as Moonlighting trials, Calibration runs, and Turning Trials were carried out. Wednesday, the 15th, Tracker aircraft carried out Mirror Landing trials with HMAS *Hobart* acting as RESDES. *Melbourne* entered Sydney harbour at 0615 on Thursday the 16th, to avoid any problems from the Unions. To the relief of all, the ship secured at Fitting Out Wharf, Garden Island without incident.

The Black Ban, by the Painters Dockers Union, remained until 17th when it was lifted. Catapult trials continued and Radar aerials were hoisted back into place. By the end of the month, nothing could now stop the ship from sailing in early November.

Work by Ship's Staff

The ship's staff undertook many tasks normally done by the dockyard. Savings resulted. For example: 'Stripping and repair of and auxiliary Feed Pump', that would normally take two months for the dockyard to successfully complete, was completed in two weeks. Repair of a 36" Ventilation Fan', normally took three weeks by the dockyard, was completed in 3½ days by ship's staff.

My job during this period was ensuring that the upper deck and all the bits and pieces were in place and clean. Except for when Duty, I was able to get home every night and at weekends when in Harbour.

October ended with the ship in Sydney Harbour alongside.

November 1969

Work Up

At 1010, on Monday the 3rd of November, the ship sailed for Working Up in the Jervis Bay Area. Bridal Trials and Deck Landing practice commenced on Tuesday the 4th continuing until Friday the 21st.

At 1800 on the 10th of November the ship rendezvoused with ships of the Combined Operations Training (COTP) group that had sailed from Sydney that morning. Night Fleet work was conducted until 0500. On the 11th, the ship replenished from HMAS *Supply*. Flying operations, including night flying, continued.

During times when the ship was flying, my job was 50% in the Air Direction Room and the remainder overseeing the Upper deck work, keeping an eye on the Upper Operations Room plotters, or getting some shut eye.

The priority of deck landing practice prevented *Melbourne* from participating in a very big part of the COTP. I seem to recall that a Nowra based Wessex helicopter was reported as ditching some eight or nine miles east off point perpendicular just before 5 pm on the 13th. All crew and passengers were recovered safely by HMAS *Vampire*. I think the helicopter had been doing a mail delivery. I can't recall what happened to the mail if it had not already been delivered.

Came the 14th of the month, the weather prevented any flying at sea and the following days flying was conducted inside Jervis Bay.

Night flying continued until the 21st when the ship rendezvoused with the Task Group that had just finished the Transit and Tactical phase of the COTP.

The ships involved in the Sydney Harbour entry were.

Australian	British	Canadian	New Zealand
Melbourne	London	St Croix	Blackpool
Hobart	Galatea	Qu'Appello	Taranaki
Vampire	Yarmouth	Saskatchewan	
Anzac	Tidereach		
Stalwart	Stromness Supply		

These ships provided the circular screen around HMAS *Melbourne*.

The Minister for Navy, the Honourable J Killen MP and the Chief of Naval staff Vice Admiral Sir Victor Smith, KBE, CB, the DSC, arrived by Tracker aircraft from Canberra. All three squadrons provide an air show for the visitors before the Fleet Commander was transferred to HMS *London*.

Fleet Entry

On the 22nd of November, led by HMAS *Melbourne*, the Group formed in column, carrying out a Ceremonial Fleet Entry into Sydney Harbour. I recall that *Melbourne* moved to one side of the line and allowed the ships to pass ceremonially. HMS *London*, which was carrying the Flag Officer, Second in Command Far East Fleet, Rear Admiral CT Lewin MBO DSC, fired a salute to the Australian Naval Board, which *Melbourne* returned.

On completion of the review, the *Melbourne* proceeded to the Fitting Out wharf and remained there all of December and until the 29th January 1970.

December 1969

Christmas Leave

I was able to take Christmas leave and enjoyed my time with the family. Meeting up with friends, after my time away, was also a great pleasure to see the children reacting to their presents.

Change of Command

On 8th January 1970, the Commanding Officer was relieved following the Enquiry into the USS *Evans* collision. Subsequently, he was exonerated of any failure on his part. However, the removal from the ship stalled his future promotions and he eventually left the service. This was a great loss as he was a very efficient officer.

January 1970

Command Team Training

During January 1970, I accompanied my Action Information Team, Plotters and Air Controllers to HMAS *Watson*, preparing them for the coming Sea Exercises that the ship would participate in. The following week, I, along with other members of the Command Team, attended HMAS *Nowra* lectures pertaining to Anti-submarine Warfare. During this month, when not absent undertaking training and back on board the ship, I was carrying out my Mate of the Upper Deck duties or Duty Officer.

I was able to be with the family on the weekends when not Duty.

Most of January 1970 was spent in harbour progressing self-maintenance, storing, fuelling, and preparing for the coming work up in preparations for departure from Australia for more service overseas.

Back to Sea

Before heading out of Sydney on 29th of January, the ship was cold moved to number 3 buoy, off Garden Island, and took on a load of Avgas for the coming Flying Operations off Jervis Bay. The next afternoon, one A4 Skyhawk and one S2E Tracker joined for Deck Landing practice. Lead aircraft were kept on board for handling and lifting trials.

On Saturday, the 31st of January, the ship proceeded to sea for Seamanship Drills, Evolutions that Ship Handling and passing a line between ships practice. These exercises kept me busy as you can imagine. 48 new entry Officer Cadets from HMAS *Creswell* came on board for the day.

February 1970

Day and night flying continued throughout the month of February and on 23rd, the ship's final battle problem was confined to AIO and NBCD ((Nuclear, Biological and Damage Control) training. In addition, the Skyhawks concurrently progressively armament serials whilst the 817 Detachment Helicopters carried out Anti-Submarine Air Control training with HMAS *Queensborough*.

Due to bad weather, there were times when the ship carried out flying operations in Jervis Bay. Later in the month, the Skyhawk and Tracker Squadrons embarked. Later the same day wreaths were dropped off Jervis Bay in memory of those who died in HMAS *Voyager*.

In addition to all the above there were continuing Seamanship, Gunnery, TAS and NBCD drills taking place as well as the odd RAS, which kept me on my toes.

The ship proceeded into Sydney Harbour on the 10th to embark the Skyhawk and Tracker Ground Parties, their Equipment, Stores etc.

Visitors

During this time in Sydney, the Director, Directing Staff and Students comprising the first course of the Joint Services Staff College visited the ship in preparation for JUC 76 LONGEX.

There were various other visitors including the Chief of Naval staff, Vice Admiral Sir Victor Smith, KBE, CB, DSC, the Commanding Officer of HMAS *Albatross*, (Captain, A.N. Dollard, DSC, RAN), Director of Naval Air Policy, (Captain G. Mc C Jude, RAN), Deputy Director of Naval Air Policy (Commander J. A. O'Farrell, RAN), and two members of the Group Pay Committee, Commander T.J. Holden, RAN and Mr Trist.

The following day the Commander, Far East Fleet, Vice Admiral A.D. Empson CB, RN arrived on board and witnessed flying operations before departing.

Return to Sydney

After night, *Jack Stay* approaches to the ship, in company with HMAS *Queensborough* and HMAS *Stuart*, entered harbour early on Friday, the 26th of February. During this period in Harbour, I was to get home each night unless I was Duty Officer.

March 1970

All too soon it was time to say goodbye to the family. On the 9th of March 1970, the ship sailed for another Far East deployment. HMAS *Derwent* accompanied *Melbourne* throughout the month.

Activities En route

The following day, Flying Operations recommenced, with RAAF Base Amberley available as a divergent airfield. During these operations the Trackers and Skyhawk aircraft participated in a Fly Past of the Gold Coast and the city of Brisbane.

During this day, the ship was stopped for a short Service whilst the Ashes of Petty Officer telegraphist Keith William Earl Oxley, and ex-Tingara Boy, was scattered.

Three days later we passed through the Jomard Passage, exiting the Coral Sea, and then HMAS *Derwent* was refuelled using the Abeam method.

Race Meeting

Following this fuelling in the morning, a race meeting was held with entries and spectators from *Derwent* attending, having been transferred by boat. A good time was had by all.

New Guinea

The following day, Trackers and Skyhawks conducted a flyover of the New Guinea towns of Lae and Finschhafen.

Early on Sunday, the 15th, the ship entered Seeadler Harbour, Manus Island. Fuel was taken from lighters and a Church service was held in the forenoon.

I recall that later, many the Ship's Company, who could be spared, landed for a Banyan (picnic) party, with transport provided by the resident Naval officer. In addition, the Ship's Band gave a recital at HMAS *Tarangau* in the evening which was well received.

The following morning, a triangular Sports Meeting, between a *Tarangau, Melbourne* and *Derwent*, was held ashore and the ship was open to visitors from 0900 to 1130 local time.

All things came to an end and, on Monday 16th, the ship sailed for Subic Bay in the Philippines. It was good weather from memory and flying and other evolutions were carried out during this period.

Philippines

During the forenoon of Friday, the 20th, the ship refuelled HMAS *Derwent* before entering the Bernadino Straight. The ship berthed at Leyte wharf, Subic Bay on Saturday the 21st and I remember there was some difficulty with local tugs and the pilot. I was standing in the wing on the Bridge when this drama was going on. The ship was finally secured, and the captain came out of the Bridge looking a bit harassed. I said to him, "It was always going to be okay, sir, because I said three Hail Marys to make sure." He said nothing.

Next day, with *Derwent* in company, we were joined by HM ships *Galatea* and *Lynx*, HMNZ *Taranaki* and HMAS *Duchess* and together entered Manila Harbour. *Melbourne* fired a national salute on behalf of the participating SEATO ships. A return salute was also fired.

The time in Manila was spent in doing harbour drills and exercises in preparation for the coming Sea Rover exercises. This included a briefing on the overall exercise. In addition, many Liberty men went ashore. Fortunately, the demonstrations that had been going on in the city did not interfere with the shore leave.

The ship's team played soccer, rugby, cricket against the NOMAD club and hockey against HMAS *Duchess*. The only win was against Duchess in the hockey.

Pre-Sea Rover Exercise Work Up

Finally, the ship sailed with USS *Matapori* and RFA *Tidespring* in company for the local exercise area for a six-day work up. This consisted of extensive flying, replenishment and other exercises that involved both the Operations rooms, Helicopter Anti-Submarine and Fighter control and Voice Procedure drills which kept me busy.

On the 30th of March, a sailor fell overboard from our flight deck and was speedily recovered by the ship's SAR (Search and Rescue) helicopter.

April 1970

On completion of the six-day work up, the ships spent one night in Manila Bay before proceeding on the 1st of April for an Opposed Departure which opened with the Transit phase of the Sea Rover exercise.

Sea Rover Exercise

As was to be expected there was intensive flying and replenishment exercises in dealing with Submarine Attacks which kept the Helos and Trackers busy. Air attacks kept the A4 Fighters also busy. My main role was in the ADR supervising the air plotting and reporting and the control of the fighter aircraft.

The other side of the coin was participating in the Replenishments and ensuring the parts of ship were not neglected.

The Thai and Philippine Navies provided units to participate in the exercise.

Thailand

The exercise ended on the 8th of April and *Melbourne* entered Sattahip Harbour for the debriefing phase of the Exercise. After this, the ship secured alongside Laem Long wharf. The flight deck was prepared, and rehearsal carried out for the Closing Ceremony the following day.

However, the Ceremony was disrupted by a heavy tropical rainstorm at the last moment. This meant moving the Ceremony ashore into a warehouse on the wharf.

There was no local leave given at Sattahip. However, several buses were organised to take officers and sailors to Bangkok for the day of arrival.

Melbourne sailed for Hong Kong on the 10th of April with *Derwent* in company.

Canberra Posting

It was about this time that I received information about my next posting. Instead of returning to HMAS *Watson* as OIC of the Navigation and Direction school, I would be taking up my first job at Fort Fumble (Navy Office) in Canberra. This would mean moving the family to Canberra and organising a place to live and arranging new schools for the children. I was to be the Deputy Director of User Requirements (DUR), whatever that was. Nobody in the ship seemed to know much about this Directorate. The date of the appointment was to be the 14th of December 1970.

Hong Kong

On Monday, the 13th of April, the ship berthed at North Arm, Victoria Harbour, and was to remain there for the rest of the month carrying out maintenance using shore parties.

A Fleet reception was held for 400 guests on the flight deck. On the completion, *Melbourne's* Band Beat Retreat.

On Anzac Day, *Melbourne* mounted a guard and band at the Hong Kong War Memorial for a simple wreath laying ceremony early in the morning.

May 1970

Japan Here We Come

On sailing from Hong Kong, rendezvous was made which HMA ships *Derwent* and *Duchess*. For most of the passage to Osaka the ship was required to use extra caution to proceed safely through the multitude of fishing vessels, particularly in the Taiwan Strait. There was one day of flying. Both *Derwent* and *Duchess* refuelled by the abeam method. I was involved, as always, with the preparation and supervision of these activities.

On Tuesday 5th, I remember the thick fog as the ship entered the Inland Sea of Japan. For me, it was the umpteenth time I had done so. Because of the fog I went to the Upper Operations Room to oversee those assisting the Bridge in Blind Pilotage. I checked they were doing their job. We finally anchored off the Osaka port breakwater where there were at least 100 other vessels waiting to enter the port.

With the partial lifting of the fog, you can imagine the rush for the channel through the breakwater. We had embarked a pilot and quarantine officials and finally berthed at No 1 Wharf Central Pier.

The purpose of the visit to Osaka was to be present at the Australian National day at Expo 70, attended by our Prime Minister. You can imagine the number of VIP visits by Japanese authorities and the return calls that had to be made by our Senior Officers.

There was a time when the ship had to close gangways late in the afternoon and early evening as a precaution against possible incidents. There was an approved labour demonstration that was scheduled to be held in the vicinity of our berth. From memory, there were no incidents involving the ship or its crew.

My Brother Harry

The firm my brother managed exported salt from Western Australia to Japan. He arranged for the Japanese company to provide a couple of guides around Osaka and some places inland. The two Japanese guides met me on the wharf. I arranged with them the time to pick me up.

They took me to a Japanese restaurant. I can't remember whether it was in Osaka or Kyoto. What I do remember are two things, one was they ordered steaks and suggested I also have one. It wasn't hard to work out that they had an expense account because such steaks cost a considerable amount in Japan, and it would be rare for them to buy such.

The second point was that when we sat at the table it was suggested I put my legs under the table instead of squatting. To my surprise the table was above a large hole in the floor that one could dangle one's legs whilst sitting at the table. In all my previous visits to Japan I had never encountered this in any of the places I had eaten. It followed that we would have Saki to drink. The waitress, who served us, was dressed in the traditional Japanese attire.

They also took me to do the rounds of the tourist attractions in Kyoto.

During the stay, the ship was open for public inspection during Thursday 7th, and from memory, over 2,600 people took the opportunity to have a look around. Perhaps the foggy and wet weather kept others away.

Kobe

On Saturday, the 9th, the ship proceeded to Kobe, only a short distance to the west of Osaka. There was the usual Welcoming Committee who came on board after arrival. That evening there was a Fleet reception on board for about 230-odd guests.

On the following day, the ship was open to visitors, and over 5,800 came aboard whilst a further 3,000 or more were turned away by the police to control the crowd on the pier.

Passage to Subic Bay

Finally, it was time to say goodbye to Japan and, at 0949 on Wednesday, the 9th of May, with *Derwent* and *Duchess* in company, *Melbourne* headed for Subic Bay. Flying operations resumed during the passage and I think there were three Skyhawks, three Trackers, flown off to NAS Cubi for deck Landing practice ashore. *Duchess* was refuelled during the passage.

Subic Bay

Melbourne entered Subic Bay on Sunday the 17th of May and proceeded to refuel from lighters. Later the same day we sailed for Singapore with *Duchess* in company. The following day, *Derwent* re-joined, and so we farewelled the Philippines.

Singapore

Day and night flying operations resumed daily whilst on passage to Singapore, and the aircraft that had been at NAS Cubi we embarked whilst on passage.

On Thursday, the 21st, *Melbourne* was joined by HMA ships *Supply, Stalwart, Parramatta, Stuart, Oxley, Teal, Ibis* and *Curlew*. The ships formed in column and proceeded towards Singapore. On entering harbour, *Melbourne* fired a salute to the Flag of the Commander Far East Fleet. The salute was returned. The ship secured at number seven berth in the Stores basin.

That evening a Fleet reception for over 400 guests was held on the flight deck and on completion *Melbourne's* Band Beat Retreat. During Fleet receptions, I was engaged with the visitors and often found some very interesting people to talk to and ensure they always had a drink in their hand.

There were three days of briefing for Exercise BERSATU PADU, before the ship departed on the 25th of May for the local exercise area, with *Parramatta* and *Derwent* in company. The first week of the Exercise work up included flying, screening, and replenishment exercises and this kept me busy in the Air Direction Room either in charge or supervising the air controllers or getting a chance to some air control myself. Other times, it is supervising the refuelling party, or I was checking on the upper Deck.

On the end of this week's exercises the ship arrived at PULAU TIOMAN on 29th and entered TELOK TEKOK, with HMAS *Supply* and RFA *Tidespring* carrying out a formation anchorage. An Operation Awkward (anti-enemy swimmer surveillance) of the ship was carried out in the evening. I recall that there was still conflict with Indonesia at this time. It was the third time I had been in this area during the Malaysia/Indonesian conflict and remember well the need for Operation Awkward whilst at a buoy or alongside.

Over the weekend Banyan and Barbecue parties were granted recreational leave ashore on PULA TIOMAN, until 1800 each day. And so, another month away from home came to an end.

June 1970

Resume exercise Bersatu Padu

On Monday, the 1st of June, *Melbourne* returned to sea for the work up phase of this exercise. There was day and night flying, and Gunnery and Replenishment exercises saw me busy either on the ADR or in the seamanship area.

On Friday, the 5th of June, led by HMS *Fife*, wearing the Flag of Flag Officer, Second in Command, Far East Fleet, *Melbourne* in company with thirty-seven other Commonwealth ships made a Ceremonial Entry into Singapore Naval base. The ship secured to a buoy. The entry also included a formation fly past in which four of the ship's Wessex helicopters took part.

Exercise Matlock

On Friday, the 12th of June, after embarking the Director of Joint Policy, Department of Defence, a Brigadier, the ship sailed for the Maritime portion of Besatu Padu, known as Matlock. There were a few semi-independent serials each covering a tactical period.

HMAS Supply was detached and HMA ships *Parramatta*, *Stuart* and *Derwent* joined *Melbourne* and proceeded to a position off the west coast of Malaysia. At this stage the ship was to provide close air support for the Amphibious forces ashore.

On Monday, the 15th, one of the tracker aircraft became overdue and a SAR alert was issued. Shortly after, information was received stating the aircraft had landed safely at RAF Changi.

Shortly after midnight the following day the ship provided support to the Underway Replenishment Group during the anti-submarine transit phase. Again, I was busy in the ADR.

Later that day, one of the screening Helos ditched and the aircrew were rescued uninjured. The ship proceeded to the ditched aircraft and safely recovered it. Helicopter flights were suspended until the 24th.

On completion of the transit phase, the ship proceeded to Pulau Tiaman for rest and recreation. The ship, with HMS *Bulwark* (an assault carrier) and HMAS *Stalwart*, entered the anchorage in formation. Again, recreational leave was granted until 1800 (6 pm).

On Saturday the 29th, in company with *Parramatta* and *Stuart*, the ship proceeded for the final part of exercise Matlock. This phase consisted of the escort of a joint amphibious task force in the face of surface, submarine, FPB (Fast Patrol Boat) and Air threats as well as Close Air support for ground forces after their landing. It was a hectic time for me.

On completion of Exercise Matlock on Thursday the 25th of June, the ship headed back to Singapore next morning to be joined by *Supply* and together entered Singapore Naval base before lunch.

During the month, I was involved in the following: two day, and three-night re-fuellings, light jackstay transfers. There have been two heaving line transfers and two lowering of boats and recovery.

July 1970

Homeward Bound

On 3rd of July, the ship proceeded to sea for the homeward passage to Sydney. As the ship left the port, she was reverse course, to transfer Stalwart's Medical Officer to HMAS *Melbourne*, for an appendectomy operation. When completed, the Medical Officer returned to *Stalwart* and we resumed our passage to Sydney.

Next day, *Derwent* joined and, on the 6th of July, was refuelled. Then with her in company we headed for Home. Due to the delay, arrival in Jervis Bay was amended the 14th of June. Those who would take leave in Darwin were transferred to the *Derwent* and she proceeded to that port, later re-joining *Supply* after the leave personnel had been landed.

Just after midnight on Tuesday the 7th of July, the ship went alongside *Supply* and refuelled with FFO. (Fuel Oil) used by the ship. *Supply* was then detached to take charge of *Stalwart* and *Derwent* who were to arrive off Sydney on the 15th after *Melbourne* had discharged the Air Group in Jervis Bay on the 14th.

Two Wessex helicopters conducted a fly past over Thursday Island and landed a sailor for long leave. Friday, the 10th, six helicopter sortie landed 17 North Queensland natives at Cairns. On Sunday 12th, anchored in Moreton Bay, and with the assistance of MV *Bellana*, the ship was able to land 87 Queensland Liberty men.

The ship entered Jervis Bay as planned on the 14th, and disembarked the Carrier Air Group squadrons stores, personnel, baggage, and rabbits to NAS *Nowra*. On completion of this exercise, the ship proceeded to sea to launch the Seahawk and Tracker squadrons for their landing at NAS *Nowra*.

Following the disembarkation of the CAG, the ship proceeded to Sydney, being joined by HMA ships *Supply*, *Stalwart*, and *Derwent* off Sydney heads. Forming into column, with *Melbourne* leading the ships entered Sydney Harbour and *Melbourne* secured to number two buoy. Some of the Ship's Company expressed their thoughts on the trip and arrival back in Sydney when interviewed on Garden Island by various TV stations.

A Tug strike prolonged the disembarkation of Liberty men by boat and the inconvenience caused to the families of the Ship's Company. The ship was able to move to the Fitting Out wharf on Thursday the 16th and so began a long self-maintenance and leave.

I remember that, towards the end of the month, the Joint Services course Staff visited the ship, and the Admiral addressed the group on the role and operation of the fleet.

Finally, the Captain reminded the Ship's Company of the need to be aware of the security requirements needed during the maintenance period.

I was able to take leave and enjoy the company of my family after so long away. I think most people would appreciate the long absences at sea meant I missed some of the growing up of my family.

August 1970

Self-Maintenance Period

The whole of August was spent alongside the Fitting Out Wharf on Garden Island dockyard. During this period, the Ship's Company were set on Long Leave, and I can't remember whether the family went to the West to see my mum and dad and relatives. Except for the occasional duty I was able to spend every night at home.

I do recall two ceremonies during the latter part of the month. The first of these was when the captain presented the Royal Australian Naval College Jubilee Year Graduate's Memorial Sword to Midshipman JF Smith, RAN.

The second ceremony was a presentation of the United States Meritorious Award to HMAS *Perth* by his Excellency, the United States Ambassador. I wear that award with pride in what we achieved in HMAS *Perth* while serving in Vietnam.

September 1970

SPN 35 Radar

It was during this maintenance period that this Carrier Controlled Approach (CCA) Radar was fitted. To allow proper calibration of the radar, the ship was cold moved to the Oil Wharf Garden Island. I was happy to see this radar being fitted as it took away from my department the need, in poor weather conditions, to get the aircraft to where they can see the Ship's Landing Assistance (Mirror) equipment. This radar was more accurate than the search radars used by my department.

The fitting of this radar to the ship meant there would be on board fully qualified Air Traffic Control (ATC) Officers to help the pilots to be correctly lined up for landing on board.

One aspect of the fitting of this radar that affected my Air controllers was that they were required to mark on their radar displays a position, known as the gate, when the hand-over of control of the aircraft returning to the ship was passed from the Air Controllers in the ADR to the ATC personnel.

Normally, with the time set for the first aircraft to touch down on the Carrier and intervals set for following aircraft, the personnel in the ADR had to work out and get the aircraft to the gate at a set time. My time in HMS *Ark Royal* and HMS *Hermes* provided me with the experience to teach my Aircraft Controllers how to achieve this.

Presentation of USS Naval Citation

On the same day as the calibration of SPN 35 was conducted, the captain presented Chief Yeoman BJ Daniels, with a Naval Citation, awarded by the Commander of the United States

Pacific Fleet, for initiative, leadership, and devotion to duty during the rescue operations following the ship's collision with the USS *Frank E Evans*.

Workup

The maintenance period and long leave completed it was time to ready the ship for the coming work up. On 8th of September, the ship moved to No 2 buoy off Garden Island and began taking on Avgas. The following day the ship ammunitioned and on completion sailed for the Sydney/Jervis Bay exercise area to begin the work up.

The advance party of the SAR flight was carried out in four sorties by Iroquois helicopters as the 817 aircraft were not available due to an unserviceability.

One Skyhawk and one Tracker aircraft carried out touch and go landing practice before being recovered on board. Deck handling trials were carried out. That night the ship anchored in Jervis Bay, off Huskisson. Two Wessex SAR aircraft were embarked and later the ship flew off the two fixed-wing aircraft before re-anchoring.

Over the weekend the Ship's Company were instructed in the use of life-saving equipment, and helicopter dry and wet winching drills were demonstrated.

Further flying operations, as well as Communications, Gunnery, NBCD, AIO and Seamanship training. Despite the periods of bad weather, all the frontline pilots, except for one, were day qualified. Additionally, two Skyhawk and five Tracker pilots qualified for night operations.

As you can imagine I was kept busy with these exercises and quite happy when we returned to Sydney on Thursday, the 17th, so that the defective mirror landing aid could repaired by dockyard. This gave me a weekend at home.

After the weekend, it was back to Jervis Bay with the ship carrying out heeling trials, beginning with 15° to port. Later, the ship was heeled 15° to starboard before being brought upright.

Completing this work up period, the ship returned to Sydney for a Shop Window where Federal, New South Wales Parliament Officers, Sydney business organisations and foreign service attaches were embarked for a day at sea.

The ship demonstrated flying, manoeuvring, and antisubmarine warfare exercises. It was unfortunate that there were no arrested landings to show the guests due to a catapult fault. On completion of Shop Window, the ship returned to Sydney Harbour securing to number two buoy to discharge the guests.

I do not know what attraction the *Melbourne* had that caused ships to run into her. Whilst at the buoy, on the last day of the month, the Manly Ferry, SS *Steyne* decided to run into the stern of Melbourne. Whilst in harbour the Admiral in Charge of the Fleet came aboard and inspected the Ship's Company at divisions. I seem to remember that before sailing a Royal Naval Vice Admiral, Flag Officer Commanding Her Majesty Submarines, was entertained on board by the

Chief of Staff to FOCAF.

October 1970

Final Three Days of Work Up

On the 13th of October the ship sailed for the final days of the Carrier Air Group work up. Unfortunately, the weather and intermittent serviceability of the SPN 35 prevented some Skyhawk pilots being qualified. Then it was time to return to Sydney for some self-maintenance, before proceeding for Exercise Swan Lake.

Complaint Against Me

As the ship left Jervis Bay for Sydney, I was doing my usual rounds of the upper deck to make sure everything was properly secured. As I passed through the starboard, after Ladder Bay, I noticed the Divisional Officer, an ATC Officer, was only securing the ladder alongside and not fully stowing it as I required. When I enquired why it wasn't being fully stowed, he wanted to argue with me. I made it quite clear to him I wanted it fully stowed because previously I had seen a ladder washed away between Jervis Bay and Sydney during a sudden storm that came out of nowhere. When he wouldn't do what I told him, I told his crew to close stow the ladder, which they did.

I was shortly after sent for by the Commander who greeted me with a statement that the Divisional Officer had made an Official Complaint about my overruling him on stowing of the ladder. I pointed out to the Commander that he had made me responsible for overseeing all Seamanship activities as his Mate of the Upper Deck. I explained, that, from experience, I had seen sudden storms arrive during passages from Jervis Bay to Sydney. My long experience as a practical Seaman, and as the Captain of that Top, responsible for a ladder in that position in a previous life, had made me aware of the risks, and that it would only take a few minutes of extra time to fully stow the ladder. Also, I pointed out that the complainer was not an experienced Seaman Officer and would have had little experience of the sea states that can occur between Jervis Bay and Sydney. The Commander accepted the explanation.

The ship returned to Sydney, secured at Fitting Out wharf, progressing maintenance and storing for the coming exercise.

Operational Readiness Inspection (ORI)

Before the month ended *Melbourne* was required to assist as the main body for the Operational Readiness Inspection of HMS *Minerva*. A full day and night flying programme followed, and a replenishment serial carried out with *Minerva*. *Melbourne* later went alongside RFA *Olmena* to fuel.

Fremantle Here We Come

Late on the 28th, *Melbourne*, with HMA ships *Stalwart*, *Swan*, and HM ships *Charybdis*, *Minerva* and RFA *Olmeda* in company set course for Fremantle.

A full passage program was conducted over the next three days including a liquid replenishment programme from *Olmeda* before exiting Bass Strait on the 30th.

HMA ships *Supply* and *Brisbane* joined the Task Group at this stage.

November 1970

Great Australian Bight

As is often the case, the weather in the Bight deteriorated. The second day of a Locating exercise, being conducted with Maritime aircraft from RAAF Pearce, in Western Australia, was cancelled.

Despite the poor weather, four Trackers and three Helicopters carried out a fly past over Albany. Nine representatives from the West Australian press and radio stations were embarked from Albany by helo.

Also, a planned flight by two Skyhawks from Nowra to Pearse (Exercise Nullabor Express) was delayed and rescheduled to take place the 10th.

What I did not know was, about this time in the transit, *Melbourne* embarked rear Admiral D Williams, RN, from RFA *Olmeda*. He remained in *Melbourne* until reaching Fremantle. I believe he was the Executive Officer of HMS *Sheffield* during my first time with the Royal Navy. Unfortunately, I was not able to meet him while he was on board due to my duties. Many years later whilst living in Canberra I did get to meet up with him when he visited as the Chairman of the War Graves Commission.

Fremantle

The day before arriving alongside in Fremantle, five Tracker aircraft carried a fly past over Bunbury, Fremantle and Perth before the ship anchored in Gage Roads. The following day, the 5th of November, the ship entered harbour and berthed at Victoria Quay.

From memory, the Mayor of Fremantle held a Reception during the day. In the evening there was a Fleet Reception on board HMAS *Stalwart*.

The following day the Chief of Naval staff addressed the ship Companies of HMA ships *Melbourne, Supply, Stalwart, Brisbane, Swan, Oxley* and *Otway*, on the flight deck as part of his farewell itinerary. I did not get the chance to say goodbye and apologised for giving him a hard time whilst he was Executive Officer of HMAS *Sydney*.

Later that day, *Melbourne* provided a Colour Party, two Platoons and the Band for a combined march through Fremantle by all the ships present, together with a large contingent from HMAS *Leeuwin*. The salute was taken by his Excellency, The Governor of Western Australia.

All the same day a TV concert was recorded by the local station TVW 7 on the flight deck.

Over the weekend of 7th and 8th, the ship was open to visitors for about four hours each day. Over 12,500 visitors came aboard during these two days.

Exercise Swan Lake

On the Monday, the 9th, the ship sailed for Phase three of this exercise. On the same day, the Commanding Officer designate joined the ship for this phase.

The following day, Tuesday the 10th, saw the arrival of four members of the Kerr Committee who were researching the pay conditions in the Navy. On the same day, *Melbourne* recovered two Skyhawks which had flown across from the East Coast non-stop.

On one of the days, *Melbourne* returned to Gage roads very early in the morning, and embarked over 70 RAAF Cadets and Naval Midshipman aircrew from RAAF Pearce. At the same time, three members of the Kerr committee departed the ship by helicopter. It was a rough trip by boat. Later that day, Rear Admiral Williams RN arrived on board by Tracker and was transferred by Wessex to RFA *Olmeda* before dark. Then it was back to sea.

Later the same day, the ship returned to Gage Roads and anchored to disembark the Cadets from RAAF Pearce.

On Thursday, the 12th, it was reported that a Stoker had not turned up for his duty at 0400. While a search of the ship was going on, a message was received saying a body had been found and this was identified as the missing sailor.

Shop Window

Embarking were nineteen VIPs and five Press men. The Minister of State for the Navy was among the guests. Later they were disembarked by helicopter to HMAS *Leeuwin*. *Melbourne* then returned to carry on with the programmed Serials of Swan Lake. The final tactical phase of Swan Lake was completed in the afternoon of Saturday the 14th. After replenishment the ships in company joined *Melbourne* for night steaming prior to entering Cockburn Sound in column the following morning, Sunday the 15th of November. The ship anchored and began embarking families for Family Day.

Family Day

When the embarkation of families was completed, *Melbourne* weighed anchor and proceeded with HMA ships *Brisbane* and *Swan* in company. A short flying display was given using Wessex and Tracker aircraft.

Escort Duty. One of the Helo pilots was from Kalgoorlie. He indicated that he was sure I would know his dad and asked me to look out for his father as he would be one of the pilots in the Helo demonstration during Family Day.

My mind flew back to the early 1944, when I was required to register for service in the CMF. You may recall I made mention of how I had arrived at the door to the Army Registration Centre just after I had recovered from my 180 degrees out of phase illness, after a bout of Scarlet Fever. The Dad, who worked on the same gold mine as me, and knew me personally, told me it I didn't have to register. He still thought I was the village idiot.

I made myself known to the dad and escorted him to witness the flying demonstrations. I am sure he recognised me as the young lad who worked in the Survey Office of the Lake View and Star mining group. I tried to mention my time in Kalgoorlie; however, he was not interested in discussing the past. Eventually, he went off on his own and met up with his son for lunch.

On completion of the exercises for Family Day, the ship returned to Fremantle, securing alongside Victoria Quay. During the period alongside, the ship refuelled and there were a few receptions for senior officers and others.

Shortly after we arrived in Fremantle, one of our helicopters was sent to medivac a patient from *Stalwart* who was suffering appendicitis. *Stalwart* was 40 miles to seaward passage to Albany. The sailor was landed at HMAS *Leeuwin*.

Whilst in port during a visit to the West, I contacted my uncles, aunts, cousins and some other friends, ex-Navy and civilian.

Return East

Eventually, the time came to say goodbye to Fremantle and on the 19th of November cast off from Victoria Quay, and with HMAS *Brisbane* in company, set sail for Adelaide.

The following day it was necessary to fly a compassionate case from HMAS *Brisbane* to Albany. As the Helo was returning, it was diverted to carry out a medivac from HMAS *Swan* to *Melbourne*. The sailor was returned to *Swan* via a light Jackstay transfer.

During the passage east, lower deck was cleared on the Sunday for prayers and, on completion, the Admiral presented a Leading Radio Operator, a Flag Officers Commendation for initiative in the recovery of a ditched helicopter in November 1969. Long Service and Good Conduct Medals were presented to three Chief Petty Officers from HMAS *Melbourne*.

Flying continued during the passage to Adelaide. Three Trackers carried out a fly past over the coastline embracing Spencer Gulf. Three helicopters flew over Kangaroo Island. *Melbourne* also refuelled *Brisbane* and *Swan* before carrying a formation anchorage off the Fairway Beacon, Outer Harbour, Adelaide.

On the 24th, official guests were embarked for a Shop Window. On completion, the ship proceeded to a berth in Outer Harbour. An official Fleet Reception was held on board *Melbourne* that night.

Whilst alongside, the ship embarked fuel from B.P. Road Tankers.

On the weekend of 28/29th, the ship was open for public inspection for four hours and over 13,000 visitors came aboard over the two days.

On the last day of the month, the ship cast off and set sail for Hobart. *Swan* sailed independently to Sydney. Just before sailing, five members of the Tasmanian Press and TV Media joined the ship for the passage.

December 1970

En route Hobart

As the ship passed down the West Coast of Tasmania a plane fly over of Launceston and Hobart by Tracker and Skyhawk aircraft was cancelled due to the ship's movement and marginal weather conditions.

Melbourne arrived in Hobart on the 2nd of December and secured along Prince's wharf mid-morning. That evening there was an Official Reception on board *Melbourne*.

On the weekend of 5th and 6th, the ship was open to visitors for four hours in the afternoon. Over 13,000 visitors were recorded. This number is not including numerous organised parties who were conducted on tours of the ship.

Sydney Bound

Monday, the 7th of December, the ship sailed and set course for Jervis Bay. As the ship bade farewell to Hobart, it passed through my mind that this would probably be the last time I would visit this city. Memories flooded back of my time as a sailor and officer of the many happy times, and friendships, I had made there. Also, the number of crayfish I had enjoyed. I was not to know then, after my retirement, I would become a Tour Escort and bring a Tour Group to visit the Island. Also, I have returned for several Naval reunions over time.

Jervis Bay

As the ship approached Jervis Bay the weather was such that we could not disembark the Skyhawk Squadron. The Squadron stores, personnel and baggage were successfully transferred to Nowra despite the limited visibility.

The ship headed for Sydney and secured to a buoy and de-ammunitioned.

On Thursday, the 10th, the day after the de-ammunitioning, the ship proceeded to sea for Family Day. HMAS *Swan* came along as plain guard. The Seahawks were launched, and after fly past, returned to Nowra.

After the ship returned alongside, I was able to pack my bags and head home, so I could get ready to arrive at my new appointment in Canberra on the 14th of December.

So ended what I thought would be my last posting to sea. How wrong was that as we will see later in this epistle according to himself.

COMMANDING OFFICERS REPORT

TO MY ENTIRE SATISFACTION

A LOYAL, ZEALOUS, AND HARD-WORKING OFFICER WHO IS MOST DEPENDABLE AND HAS DONE VERY WELL IN THIS SHIP.

Chapter 35

Navy Office (Russell) Canberra

14 December 1970 to 7 April 1974

Navy Office Canberra (Russell)

Joining

I drove the car to Canberra and checked into the HQ building in the suburb of Russell where my new job was to be found. After Security clearance, I was introduced to the team. I then set out to find the house that had been allocated to the family.

I found the Housing Authority and was taken to a suburb called Higgins where there was a Naval Married Quarter. It was a very compact, furnished, four-bedroom house located on the main road leading to the Higgins shopping centre at the bottom of the street. It had a reasonably sized backyard.

I put my gear in the house after accepting the keys and bought a few things at the shop to see me through till the family arrived from Sydney.

Family Arrival

Joan had packed up the family goods and chattels and oversaw the removalist and the arrangements for someone to lease our house in Ashfield, Sydney.

I met the family at the station and introduced them to what was only just suitable for two adults and four children. Our bedroom was very small and the space between the end of the bed and the wardrobe was only wide enough to walk through as the gap was such that your shoulders almost touched the wardrobe and your body, the bed on the other side.

The main thing was the family was together and would be for some time. I looked forward to really getting to know my children and their needs and personalities again.

Shopping was next whilst we waited for the removalist to arrive, and we could unpack and settle in. I think I had the day off to move the family in. I had brought two rabbits and a bird that we had as pets.

And so began our residency in Canberra.

Schools

Eldest son Anthony was enrolled at Daramalan Catholic College in a suburb some distance away and Anne and Peter at the newly opening Higgins primary school.

Church

When we went to the church on Sunday, we were made most welcome and met some of the parents of children who had made friends with our children. It turned out one family lived on the other side of our back fence and were to become close friends.

Joan's Friend

One of Joan's school friends lived in a suburb not that far from Higgins and we became friends and welcome visitors from time to time.

As time went by, we made other friends including the families of my Staff Officers.

Aside. I was not to know at the time, but living in the same street in Higgins, and only a few doors up from us, was the girl I had shared a work bench with at the Kalgoorlie School of Mines all those years ago.

Having settled in, we became part of the Canberra Community. Let me now recount what my job was.

My Work

I won't bore you with a resume of my work, only what it was about and the interesting bits.

I soon settled into the job and found that, after a short time, my boss was leaving, and a new person was taking over. I had met this new boss previously on a ship or in HMAS *Watson*.

Besides reviewing modifications, or other items being introduced, or modified, there was also the requirement to vet draft plans for a new ship that was being considered. The layout, size, and any other item and asset, from our practical experience at sea, if it was suitable and usable in a confined space. It was interesting work.

Drawers. On one occasion I was looking at the size and usability of items in a proposed officer's cabin in the forepart of the new ship design. Something made me look closely at the drawers on the ship's side of the cabin. They were in the section where the hull flared out and on looking at the space in a stack of drawers, found the bottom drawer and a couple above it had so little space as to be almost useless.

Deep Fat Fryer. On another occasion, one of my staff was reviewing an application for a deep fat fryer for an officer's galley in an existing destroyer/frigate. He came to me and showed me the replacement proposal that the Supply people were looking to have approved.

Basically, the cost of the proposed new frier was to be $600 for an AC powered ship and $800 for a DC one. My Staff Officer asked me to look at the proposal and the background to this submission as the Supply branch was pressing for approval to go ahead.

On reading the proposal I found that a ship had bought an off-the-shelf deep fat fryer for use in their galley for $150. A report was written about its use over an eighteen-month period, on that ship now going in for a refit – a second ship had been handed the deep fat fryer to use. After twelve months, this ship also reported on their use of the fryer and suitability. My Staff Officer pointed out the cost difference and that it should be left to ships to buy their own fryer using the captain's fund in each ship.

I agreed and he went off to write up the proposal to cancel the $600/$800 proposal. Next morning, he rang in as he had become quite ill overnight, so I took on the task of cancelling.

I picked up the file and went to the appropriate Department head and asked him if it was necessary for the frier to be able to stand the sea pressure at any depth because that was what seemed to be proposed. His reply was no and said that one using similar materials to a civilian one would suffice. I got him to write that comment on the file. I then went to the Electrical Head and put the same question and got the same answer written on the file.

I then wrote a submission proposing the project be cancelled and that the ships be informed that, if they required a Deep Fat Fryer, to buy it from the Captain's Fund.

Knowing that, if I sent the file back to be circulated with my proposal, it could take months. I took the file with me to the next meeting of the Committee that would deal with the cancellation and put my file on top of those to be considered that day.

Agreement. The Chairman, on opening the meeting, reached for the first file on the top of those to be considered that day. He found my file and exclaimed angrily, "What the hell is this file doing here?" I asked if I could speak and was allowed to give a brief overview and that cancelling the original and agreeing to mine that would get rid of a file forever. Agreed – File closed.

Basically, that was what DUR was all about.

Navy Office Bar

A bar was available at lunchtime and after work. It was a good place to catch up and often have an informal discussion with another on a project or something that was bothering you.

Change of Office

The Hull. Mechanical and Electrical Departments were transferred from the Russell Offices to a new complex at Campbell Park, some distance away. DUR was to transfer to this new location.

Campbell Offices, Canberra

Just before the date of removal, my second Boss left due to compassionate circumstances on the Home Front. My third Boss turned out to be someone I had met during the *Melika* incident whilst serving in HMS *Sheffield* during my Royal Navy time. He was Australian and a Direction Officer Specialist like me. He had come up through the Naval College.

New Boss

My new Boss went under the nickname Weary. He was anything but. On the second day in the office, he came into my office with a large stack of files and dumped them on my desk. They were about 12" to 15" high. He then said, "They are yours to look after."

I asked what they were about.

He said, "Read them and find out."

I did not know what was in those files would affect my future career and life. He was obviously clearing his confidential safe.

Next morning, he walked into my office and said, "Get your coat. We are going to a briefing."

As we went out and got into a car, I said, "What's the briefing about?"

He said, "You will find out when we get there."

The Briefing

The briefing was by the Department of Works and Jerks Representatives from Western Australia, later known as the Department of Housing and Construction. A small team then went on to present their plans for a major Western Australian Naval Facility (WANSF) near Perth.

The Chief of Navy was present and, at most briefings, he usually stayed for the opening session. However, he was still there at lunchtime and that was because this briefing turned out to be not a very detailed outline of the proposed development. On the way back to our office, my Boss then said, "You may even get a trip to the west out of it." I then realised he had done his homework on each of his staff before joining and knew I came from the West.

Lunch-time BBQs

About once a month Weary would send one of the staff to set up a BBQ somewhere appropriate in delightful surroundings in Canberra. It gave all a chance to relax, and no doubt gave Weary a chance to get to know the team well. It also gave the team the chance to get to know one another better. Weary was a great joke teller and regaled us at meetings and BBQs with his wit.

Unsuitability of Married Quarters

It became apparent very quickly that the house allocated to us was most unacceptable for the size of our family and their studies.

I had become aware that many people coming to Canberra would go to the Land Auction and buy a block and have a house built. You could not own the land outright but could lease it for 99 years. I also learnt that a lot of blocks went for $2000 to $3500.

Joan and I decided we would build, as at that stage of my career, it was likely I would spend a lot of time in Canberra. So began the search for a suitable house design with four bedrooms. Picking the house design before selecting a block was prudent so you could identify suitable sized blocks for the house.

I then enquired about the Auction and was given advice of what happened etc. Looking at the next Auction and sites available, there appeared to be only a couple or three blocks suitable for our selected house design. One stood out.

Auction

Auction Day came and we had decided we would offer up to $5000 for the block we wanted. I was advised to stand up and keep my hand in the air until I got the block or decided it was not for me.

It was a very cold morning, and I wore a large outer cold weather coat that probably made me look about half as big again as I was. So once the bidding for our block started, I stood up and kept my hand up. Most other bids dropped off about $3000 to $3500 and I found myself bidding against one other who obviously also wanted the block. As we approached $5000, I began to realise I had to decide if I would stop at $5000. My bid was $4900 and other $5000. I took a punt and bid $5100. The other bidder dropped out. He was to obtain the block next door and he later told me he thought I would keep going. Karma. I was then able to engage the builder and work commenced shortly after.

House Finance

During my visit back to Sydney I took the opportunity to discuss with my Bank Manager that I was buying a house in Canberra and needed access to a loan. He agreed to help and gave me the name of a senior friend in the Bank, who would be reviewing my application, made through my Canberra Branch. He instructed me to make sure the words for attention 'Mr so and so' and title was on the top of the form.

My application was approved, and my Canberra Bank Manager was advised to provide the loan at the normal rate, not at the investment rate.

House Construction

A builder was engaged, and the price agreed for building the design we had selected. Joan and I would visit the site regularly to see how the construction was going.

Soon the fame work was in place for a brick veneer home. The brick layers soon had the walls up. During an inspection, we noticed one of the side wall bricks did not appear to quite match those we had selected. Initially we thought this was due to the wall still being damp from the laying.

However, on our next visit, it was obvious that a slightly different coloured brick had been used on this wall. We approached the builder and he then revealed that due to the building situation he had taken some bricks from those on our block to use on an adjacent house he was building, and he hadn't been able to get the exact match at the time. Obtaining the match was taking time and he had taken a punt that the bricks he obtained would meet the requirement and allow him to complete the building as agreed.

We insisted that the wall be replaced with the correct brick colour. By this time the roof had been put in place. I later learnt that other builders, who became aware of the wall being pulled down and replaced, expected the roof to give way.

Fortunately, it did not move, and the wall was completed with the correct coloured bricks. We had arranged for a suitable insulation to be placed between the bricks and the inner wall.

Knowing how cold it could get we had a gas-fired heater placed in the wall between the kitchen and dining room and in the hallway outside the children's bedrooms.

Finally, the house was completed, and we were able to move in. What a relief to have space, especially for the children in their bedrooms and able to do their homework.

We thoroughly enjoyed living in the house and made friends with the neighbors. One, who worked for the Government Archives, lived next door, and became a great friend. He will be mentioned later in my history.

Birthday Girl

With Joan's birthday approaching in November 1975, I told her I would be taking her somewhere special for her birthday. In fact, I had arranged a surprise party at home for our close friends to come and surprise her.

Our bedroom was at the back end of the house. When all, or most of the attendees had arrived in Ramage Place, they came and rang the doorbell when I gave the signal. Joan certainly was surprised. I had arranged for the food and drinks to arrive soon after.

It was a great party, and I was able to repay Joan for her support during our marriage and particularly having to move so many times.

Work (Liaison)

A WANSF Design team member, Ken, would come to Canberra every two weeks to discuss any item they had a query about or wanted to discuss. My job, as Liaison Officer, was to advise those he wanted to talk to and the subject of the discussion and arrange a time to meet up with the responsible person.

I would meet him at the entry foyer and, once security cleared, I would accompany him during these visits. Sometimes we would arrive at an office and the person to be interviewed would have some excuse as to why he couldn't do the interview at the time he had already agreed to.

Ken was quite large, and on receiving such notice he would say nothing, pull up a chair and sit in the doorway so no one could enter or leave. It always worked a treat.

At other times the officer would plead to be allowed to go to an important meeting where he had to do a presentation. He would be allowed to go, and on return would find Ken sitting waiting for his return. Ken would have gone on to interview others in the officer's absence.

Social Activities

From time to time the family would go to Sydney and stay with Joan's parents for the weekend. They were always ready and glad for us to come.

Other times, we would go to the coast or visit some tourist attraction. There would be children's sports, or we would be invited to visit friends. It was a very pleasant time. No night duties, weekends off and the pleasure of watching my children growing up.

Vinnies

I think I was asked to think about helping with visits to the people needing some form of assistance. Later, I was asked to be an interviewer, then became involved with the Vinnies (St Vincent de Paul) Night Shelter.

Assistance

One of the visits I was with a more experienced helper when we visited a young lady living in a block of units. who had asked for some assistance. My partner interviewed the lady and was able to direct her to where she could get support and help.

Another time we were directed to a home where our information was the father had no help in raising two children and the children were frightened of him. The wife greeted us and led us into the lounge. I noticed she was very well dressed and looked as if she may have just come home or be going out. The husband and children were poorly dressed.

The father and children were happily doing things together and the children were crawling all over him. A bell rang in my mind that something was very different to what we had been told.

One of the children cut his finger and I offered to take him to the bathroom to fix it. When I got to the bathroom there was only a block of soap, and the cabinet was empty. Fortunately, I usually carry a couple of Elastoplast strips in my wallet and so was able to clean up the cut and cover it. On return to the lounge, the father thanked me.

Meanwhile my partner had been trying to assess the needs. I started to study the woman and realised the dress she was wearing was not something off a cheap rack but would have been quite expensive from my knowledge of Joan's outfits. As we were about to leave and were talking to the father, she came into the room with an expensive fur stole. A penny dropped as to where I had seen similar women dressed to the hilts. She was, I believe, a Lady of the Night about to go out for her next conquest and earn some money.

Night Shelter

As I have said, I was asked to help in the Vinnies Night Shelter by being one of two interviewers of men seeking overnight shelter. I was to share the duty with an Army Lt-Colonel who had been doing the interviewing for some time. People could stay up to three nights.

Local Pub Check

There was a pub not far from the Shelter and, after my first duty, I made a habit of calling in and seeing who was in the bars. I would have a cool drink and stay until five or ten minutes before being due at the Shelter. Quite often there were some there who turned up at the Shelter later.

A person would present himself and be questioned about his needs and if he had been drinking or had drugs on him. The answer was invariably no to drinking and if on prescribed medication he would show them. The ones who I saw drinking I would ask if they had a twin brother as I had seen a replica in the Pub on my way to the Shelter. They woke up we knew that they had been drinking and not lie.

My partner insisted they turn out their pockets and one client, had something like fourteen or more prescribed drugs. Occasionally someone would have some drugs that would be confiscated and handed to the manager to give back when they left.

After they had been interviewed, they were given a towel to take a shower and get ready for an evening meal.

One night just before I sat down for the interviews I went to the toilet and noticed a thin rope hanging out the small window. Guessing it would be alcohol or some other not permitted item, I went outside and found a bottle of spirits tied to the rope. There was a piece of rock nearby, so I replaced the bottle and handed it to the Manager of the centre. Later, there was an outburst of swearing and so on from the toilets, so the culprit was identified.

On another occasion, when there was a building strike in Canberra, a young man in his early twenties came in with a most unpleasant attitude and demanded a bed. The L/Col was the interviewer and soon put him in his place and I suggested that if he continued his tirade, he would get a bed for the night, but it would be in the Police lockup. He backed down and was admitted.

Later when I went to get my meal, I noticed him sitting alone having his meal. I sat beside him, and he said he thought my mate was a bit harsh. I pointed out we were volunteers and if he thought the L/Col was hard he was lucky it wasn't me interviewing. He asked what we did, and when I told him, he said he was glad he backed down.

I found out that he lost his job because of a strike, had driven to Melbourne to see if he could get a job in his line of work and found they were also on strike. He had rushed back to Canberra to find his accommodation was no longer available and he was homeless. I gave him some advice on what he should do, and he thanked me.

Old Shipmate

On one occasion I was sent to Melbourne to confer with a section that had made a proposal that needed to be clarified. As I was walking from one building to another, I noticed a man striding towards me on the other side of the road. I recognised him as the Gunnery Chief, who with me, had been the training team in HMAS *Vengeance* all those years ago.

I said in my best command voice, "CPO GI and Name halt and report to me." He halted in the best Navy fashion and looked for where the order had come from. He suddenly recognised me and came and shook my hand and we exchanged details of what we had been doing.

HMAS Sydney Sojourn

Dates of this little diversion are not recorded in my records. Out of the blue I was suddenly told to pack my bag and join HMAS *Sydney*, then preparing for another trip to Vietnam.

I found myself working with the OIC of the Operations Room and my job was the control of the helicopters that were embarked when we sailed from Sydney.

I became aware that there were no escorts available for escort duties on this trip and a detachment of Helicopters from 817C flight were to provide the screen. As we proceeded north and had one of the ship's helo controllers looking after the aircraft on station, I began briefing the lookouts on how to estimate the range of the helo using their binoculars. I would have a range provided from the Ops Room and it was interesting to see how quickly the lookouts picked up what I wanted them to do.

The reason for this training was, if the ship went in radio silence and the radars were switched off, the lookouts could give the range and bearing of the helos to the Ops Room especially if there was a contact made.

Thoughts. As we transited north from Sydney, I had a lot of time on my hands and mused as to why I had been plucked out to come and supervise Helo Ops. My conclusion was that either there was no other Direction Officer available, or it was because of my experience. I couldn't quite decide which it was.

Readiness Upgrade

As the Sydney' entered the likely threat Zone, the readiness of the ship was upgraded, and I was more involved in the overseeing of the Helo Operations.

Finally, the ship arrived at Vung Tau and unloading of troops, equipment and stores began. I was called to report to the Executive Officer's (XO's) cabin.

Family Problem

The XO told me to sit down and handed me a signal (message) that stated my wife had been admitted to hospital following a miscarriage. It also stated I was to return home as soon as possible.

A passage had been arranged in a RAAF aircraft from Saigon. I packed my gear, and a helo flew me to Saigon where I waited 24 hours for the flight. I was fortunate that a fellow Direction Officer was on the staff in Saigon HQ and looked after me until I embarked. I felt a bit naked without a weapon.

I can't remember if the plane landed in Canberra or Sydney. I eventually arrived home and went to see Joan straight away. I looked after the children until she recovered. You can imagine how disappointed we were.

Back to DUR

As soon as Joan was well enough, I returned to work in DUR. I resumed where I had left off and enjoyed myself being with family and friends.

F111 Info

I received a call from the CO (Commanding Officer) of 805 Skyhawk Squadron asking if I could find out details of the F111. I contacted my compatriot in the appropriate Defence section, and he came back to me that, after a thorough search, they had no details of the F111 and in fact did not keep information on friendly aircraft.

This resulted in the Carrier Group deciding to carry out a covet investigation and find out all about the F111 from the crews. They did this by using both Skyhawks and Trackers carrying out Navigation exercises up into Queensland.

They would land at the F111 base for fuel and stay overnight. The RAAF pilots were only too happy to show off their supersonic aircraft and boast about what it could do. Slowly a picture was built up as to its capabilities and any information on its performance and particularly supersonic speed and any liabilities.

By the time they had finished, the Carrier Group had a pretty good idea of the F111's capability and discovered that their detection system may not be able to detect one of the Navy search radars.

The final bits of information of use, to me particularly, was that they had not, at that time, worked on attacking fleet units and had not worked up with Air Force search aircraft.

Later, nearer the exercise time, it was learnt they were restricted from flying below 500 feet and that it was possible their bomb load may cause them to fly subsonic during the exercises.

I had no idea at the time that I was about to be posted to *Melbourne* for some major exercises.

The final question to me, by the Skyhawk Squadron CO, was how hard it would be for a fighter controller to control an intercept with the fighter at 20,000 feet and the F111 at 500 feet. My reply was, providing we could do a few practices to work out the distance, the bomber would move from the time the descent began, there should be no problem.

HMAS *Melbourne* Posting

I received a posting, dated 8th of January 1974, stating I report on board HMAS *Melbourne* on the 8th of April 1974 as the Direction Officer. I wasn't amused. So, I finished up in DUR and joined as directed. However, before I left to join *Melbourne* for the third time, there are a couple of items that I should mention.

New Search and Rescue Centre

During drinks in the Russell Officers Bar, I was talking to an officer who had just been put in charge of the New Search and Rescue Centre that was being set up in Canberra. Enquiring about what it was about, and who worked for him, I realised that he lacked someone with my experience in running an Ops room.

I asked him if he thought he could use me and he jumped at the chance and said to apply for an interview for a Selection Committee meeting So, I applied and was given the date of early January 1975, that suited me as I expected to be in Canberra for leave over the Christmas and New Year period.

COMMANDING OFFICER'S REPORT

To my entire satisfaction.

A competent officer whose wide experience is well applied. He has done an excellent job on the staff of DUR and has been an asset to the naval staff.

Chapter 36

HMAS *Melbourne*

8 April 1974 to 24 April 1975

Joining

At the time of joining, the *Melbourne* was berthed at West Dock Wall, Garden Island, Sydney. It was discharging armoured personnel carriers and other free freight items that had been loaded onto the ship in America on its voyage before I joined. Aviation Fuel was also being off loaded to tankers for transfer to NAS *Nowra* where there was a shortage.

A planned move to the Oil Wharf was delayed two days due to industrial action. Self-Maintenance had begun as soon as the ship arrived back from overseas.

I was duly received back on board and allocated a single cabin that was on 2 decks, one below the flight deck. I found an arrester wire went through near the deck head. As I didn't expect to be sleeping during any flying operations, I wasn't too worried.

My previous two tours of duty in HMAS *Melbourne* meant I had a pretty good idea of everything I needed to know to carry out my duties. Over the days following, I spent time re-familiarising with the ship and checking all the Operation Rooms Equipment.

Duty Officer

I was placed in the duty Lieutenant Commander's Watch Bill with a duty about once a week or so. This duty put me in charge of the ship when the Captain and Executive Officer were absent and generally consisted of ensuring everything was running to plan; also carrying out evening rounds, particularly of mess decks, to ensure they were properly cleaned up for the evening was part of this duty.

At sea, I knew I would be a First Officer the Watch when not employed in the Air Defence Room, or upper Operations Room.

Team Training

Shortly after joining I was involved in a period of Team Training and Tactical games at HMAS *Watson*.

Sea Work Up

On the 22nd of April, the ship proceeded to sea with HMA ships *Hobart* and *Perth* in company. Working up was to prepare for the major exercises the ship was to participate in. Weather conditions were generally favourable for flying training and good progress was made over the next two days. In my area of responsibility, I was kept busy with a variety of exercises, testing the Air Control, Air Defence and all the Surface and Anti-Submarine Air control and plotting that would be needed in the coming exercises. This kept me very busy making sure that the team I had were up to scratch.

During this time, we developed the procedure for interceptions from 20,000 feet on a target at 500 feet.

The ship then returned to Sydney for the weekend, ammunitioning before securing alongside the Oil Wharf.

On Monday, 29 April, it was back to sea to continue the work up for Exercise Kangaroo One. Unfortunately, the weather was unkind with the rough seas preventing flying at sea and much of the qualification deck landing flying was done in Jervis Bay.

May 1974

The ship returned to Sydney on the 10th May and, after ammunitioning and taking on Avgas, the ship was moved to the Fitting Out Wharf for the weekend. Then it was back to sea to continue the Work Up and complete preparations for the coming major exercises. As you can imagine most of my time was spent in the ADR, supervising the Fighter Controllers, Air Control and Air plotting and, from time to time visiting the Upper Operations Room to observe the Helicopter Anti-Submarine Control and checking the anti-submarine and surface plotting teams. On the 22nd May, the ship returned to Sydney having completed the Work Up. The ship remained alongside for the rest of the month.

Exercise Kangaroo One

This Exercise consisted of several phases and provided the opportunity to test all aspects of Carrier operations. The value of organic Naval Air Capability to Naval Surface forces was to be confirmed during these exercises.

June 1974

On the 3rd of June, the ship sailed from Sydney and made its way north recovering the ship's aircraft soon after leaving harbour. However, weather and sea prevented any further flying for the time being, resuming as we headed north towards the Coral Sea.

A4 Skyhawk

HMAS *Melbourne* and Escorts formed the Orange Task Group whose task was to intercept a Royal Naval Blue Force entering the Coral Sea through, I think, the Jomar passage.

A RAAF Maritime aircraft detected the Blue Amphibious Task Group as it entered the Coral Sea. One of the ship's Tracker aircraft then took over tracking and reporting to the Orange Group. I won't reveal the method of the Tracker directing the A4s, the S2 Tracker Orange Strike Aircraft) to a departure point to attack the Blue Force.

Six A4 Skyhawk aircraft were launched for a strike on the Blue Force travelling over 100 plus miles from *Melbourne*, before dropping to sea-top and turning onto the path leading to the Blue Force, the direction being passed to them by the Tracker.

I believe the attack completely surprised the Blue Force, and from memory, their enemy contact report stated three aircraft had attacked the Blue Force. All six aircraft attacked and re-attacked. All aircraft were recovered successfully. They didn't realise there had been six aircraft.

The actions by Orange Air again highlighted not only the initial strike capability but that of flexible restrike capability of Naval Air.

Amphibious Landing

This phase consisted of Air support for the Amphibious Force from a multi threat environment during its passage to the landing assault area of Shoalwater Bay, Queensland.

The landing of troops and the flexibility, time on task and overall effectiveness of the A4 in Close Air Support of land forces was demonstrated. The Close Air Support of troops and strikes on shipping and the Tracker surveillance and strike direction missions showed off the capability of Naval Air.

Remember: In the previous Chapter, I had referred to the obtaining information on the F111 by Naval Air Units conducting Navigation Exercises to Queensland and the collection of information on the F111. The earlier spying by CAG aircraft and loose lips had provided Navy with information they needed on the F111 performance. The fact they could not go supersonic when carrying bombs on the wings, that they were restricted to 500 feet above the sea and that they had not really worked with RAAF Maritime aircraft in the anti-ship role as well as other information allowed us to prepare our defence.

F111 Attacks on Naval Force

An exercise was arranged off the Queensland coast, and I think it was set up to prove that the F111 were more superior to Naval Air. It was all to do with replacing Naval Fixed-wing flying with RAAF shore-based Strike aircraft.

Forward Planning

It was anticipated that the F111 aircraft would fly to where the Maritime aircraft was and be directed towards the Navy group. Another check we made was to know the position of any airline routes in the vicinity of the exercise area and the timetables of any civilian aircraft that might be in those corridors.

Searching Maritime Aircraft

F111 Fighter Bomber

In order to locate the Navy group, who had gone to radio and radar silence, the Maritime aircraft had to come to a height above the horizon. This allowed for the DDG in company, using EW (Electronic Warfare) detection, and one of its radars the Air Force could not detect, to be able to spot this aircraft each time it popped up to see where Navy was. The DDG, with its missiles, was stationed on the bearing of the Maritime aircraft.

Three Skyhawks were positioned at 120° intervals around the Navy group with one aircraft positioned along the line that led to the Maritime aircraft. Their height was 20,000ft.

RAAF Officers were on board *Melbourne* as Observers, and I had at least one in the ADR alongside me,

It was then the waiting game.

A radar contact appeared in the civil air corridor on the edge of the exercise area. This was unusual for the time as no civil aircraft was programmed to be flying there at that time. Here the RAAF strike aircraft made their first mistake by turning towards where we knew the Maritime aircraft to be, thus confirming they were not civil aircraft. They then began descending and passed below the Naval radar envelope. I looked at my watch and said to my team, "Expect them to be here in eight to 10 minutes or so."

The Air Force Observer alongside me asked how I knew that.

I said, "Simple. The Maritime aircraft is at that range from *Melbourne* – aircraft will be departing from that position. By averaging the distance between my radar plots for a minute, and by increasing it slightly to allow for them to be increasing speed, I am estimating how many minutes to get to the Task Group."

Now it was only time to wait for the F111 aircraft to head straight towards the Task Group that was able to track them once they appeared on radar at over 20+ miles. Without their knowledge, the DDG was able to track them with the missile system passively.

The Skyhawks were made aware of the incoming strike and with clear weather, the one on the line to the Maritime aircraft, reported he could see two bogies (enemy aircraft) heading towards the group. As they continued onwards towards the ships, the F111 aircraft suddenly found that their dashboards went red, indicating they were under attack by missiles. They continued over the Navy group, and as they turned for a second attack, they found a Skyhawk alongside them almost standing on his tail with wheels down, flaps down, trying to slow down to the same speed as the Strike aircraft. This was a bit of a shock, I believe, to the RAAF pilots. As they left the Carrier group, another A4 slipped in behind them.

All the attacks by RAAF strike aircraft were engaged before they reached the ships.

Newspaper Report

I am told the Air Force Brass were very unhappy, when an article appeared on the front page of a Sydney newspaper the following day, informing the public that the brand-new RAAF strike aircraft had suffered at the hands of the Navy. I will leave further comment on Air Force versus Navy at sea to a bit later in this Chapter.

Who gave the information to the paper is unknown, and as far as I am aware it was not anyone in *Melbourne*.

Return to Sydney

At the end of these exercises the *Melbourne* returned to Sydney on the 20th of June for maintenance and midyear leave.

Leave

I can't remember whether I was to take the first or second leave period. As you can imagine, being able to take leave and be with the family in Canberra after such a busy time, it was a welcome break. Reverting to family life was delightful after the recent time at sea. Catching up on family, what they had been doing, renewing acquaintances with old friends, and visiting Joan's family in Sydney were welcome distractions before the ship was to go forth and begin another set of exercises.

However, a few other comments before the next trip to sea.

Flag Officer Compliments

In my research for this section, I came across the two following messages from the Flag Officer Commanding the Australian Fleet (FOCAF).

FM Commaustfl Afloat

To HMAS Melbourne

Your strike against the amphibious task group today demonstrated a thoroughly professional performance. Bravo Zulu (Well done)

"FM COMMAUSTFL AFLOAT

TO HMAS Melbourne

Your phase one successes have been followed by continued excellent results meeting flying schedules and by your Operations Room, ADR and Communications departments in controlling operations and exercises.

For a ship of Melbourne's age to come forward with results, reliability is remarkable. Well done.

The reference to the Operations Room and ADR showed that the training undertaken by my team had been very successful.

Club 21

During this period in *Melbourne*, there were some of us officers whose families did not live in Sydney. To break the monotony of living on board when alongside, on some afternoons after work, some of the officers would go out to the Bondi RSL for drinks before dinner. On other occasions they would use the ship's car to take them to top of King's Cross and then visit each of the hotels on the way back, noting the clientele in each. For the uninitiated, it could be an eye-opener.

Early in my posting, my experience in the smaller warships caused me to think about how evenings in the Wardroom could be livened up, especially for those very young officers (Sub Lieutenants) who might like to bring their girlfriend on board for the evening. I felt they could be missing out on what Wardroom life could be.

My mind flew back to my time in HMS *Tumult*, HMAS *Stuart*, and HMAS *Perth*.

The meals at night were not attractive enough to invite any lady friends on board. During dinner one night, an Aircrew Officer, (Bob), left on board, remarked that it would be nice to know what you could expect for dinner on a Wednesday night so we could invite guests and know that the meal would be of a suitable standard. The Mess Caterer was consulted. He agreed to provide a suitable main meal each Wednesday night and to use whatever desserts were left over from lunch.

The first night there were about five or six at the table, I seem to remember, and that instead of having port at the end of the meal we had another alcoholic drink which was passed to the right and not the standard left. I cannot remember whether it was on this first night or the second Wednesday we got the idea of calling it **Club 21.** (The identification number on the side of the ship.)

It was not long before the numbers increased, and people began bringing girlfriends and wives, with a good time being had by all. It was becoming like life on one of the escorts. On at least one occasion, an officer from an escort asked if he could join in as a regular visitor and it was agreed he, and others, could use their ship's mess number provided they paid the bill when received.

Club 21 Night

With the numbers steadily increasing, it was decided that we would have a Club 21 Night with Australian Music and Meal and Aussie attire for the occasion. The Caterer was happy with the idea and promised Aussie food like fish and chips, Chicko and sausage rolls, pies etc., all to be wrapped in paper. It was agreed that wine would be served in a glass, beer in the can. This was advertised in advance.

Came the night, and I had chosen to wear shorts, boots, and a sleeveless Aussie Rules jumper. Others dressed suitability and made the night a great success.

In *Melbourne*, there was the Wardroom with a bar and across the passage was the Dining room. During the pre-dinner drinks there was a knock on the Wardroom door. The Quartermaster had a lady in a long evening dress and a gentleman with suitable tie and evening jacket with him. I found out they had been invited to dinner by the officer who was Duty Lieutenant Commander. At that moment, he was doing rounds of the mess decks.

I welcomed them into the Wardroom and explained that we were having an Australian-themed function, and I was sorry their host had not been so advised. I made sure they had a drink and looked after them with others until the Duty Officer came back into the Wardroom. He was appalled to find everyone dressed as Australian larrikins and to the amusement of his guests, I pointed out he should have read the notices that had advertised the evening.

When we moved into dinner, I invited the well-dressed guests to the head of line. The stewards serving the meal all had T-shirts, with very bald comments. They played their part with comments like "What do you want, love?" and handed over the meal in paper wrapping etc.

The lady guest had hot chicko rolls and fish and chips, one in each hand, so I helped her to a table (no chairs) and made sure she had a glass of wine, as well as her husband. They were a delight and joined in with the mood of the occasion.

Eventually when they were leaving, they both said how much they loved it, and it was much more than they expected as her brother was a bit of a stick in the mud.

Eventually the numbers increased to where we had to move it to the Quarterdeck. As I was about to close the bar at 11 pm, the captain appeared from his run ashore, and joined the gathering, so I made sure he had a drink and kept the bar open. I noticed he was moving among the group and obviously enjoying himself.

After a short time, he left so I called last drinks and he re-appeared and continued drinking so I left the closing of the bar until he left.

Next morning, I was summoned to the XO's (Executive Officer) cabin to explain why the bar was not closed at 11 pm. Obviously someone had reported I had kept the bar open after 11 pm. I explained the situation of the captain arriving, that my training as an officer had been that, if the captain was present, you didn't close the bar until he left. I don't think he liked it but couldn't counter my explanation.

I seem to remember, that on one occasion Joan arrived unexpectedly, having come up from Canberra to see her parents without telling me. I'm sure it was to check if I was up to no good. However, she enjoyed the night and was happy. I guess the going ons in *Melbourne* had become known to our Canberra wife's community and they were suspicious.

The whole of July was spent in Harbour and I was able to get home to Canberra as duties permitted or Joan came up to Sydney for the weekend.

August 1974

Immediate Docking Period

On the 30th/31st of July the ship de-ammunitioned in preparation for the Intermediate Docking Period. However, it was to spend all of August and most of September alongside the Oil Wharf.

My job was planning training, Duty Officer, or as required by the XO.

September 1974

On Tuesday, the 17th of September, the ship was cold moved to the Fitting Out Wharf, and it was decided to defer the docking and prepare for sea. It was then busy, busy, busy, storing, fuelling, and preparing for sea. Finally, it was time to move to a buoy.

Command Team Training

The Command Team spent two days at HMAS *Watson* participating in Tactical floor games. For me, it was like old times being involved with ship team training.

To Sea Again

On Thursday, the 26th of September, *Melbourne* sailed for a shake-down prior to the work up beginning for the next set of exercises just over two months after returning from Exercise Kangaroo One. The weather was uncomfortable due to a large depression off the coast. I think that the ship was reduced to about 4 knots as we made our way to Jervis Bay, arriving there during the forenoon of the 27th. On the last day of the month the ship sailed from Jervis Bay for work up and, if I remember rightly, the Fleet Training Group was embarked. An old classmate on my 1955/1956 Officer Promotion Course in the UK, Dennis, who had transferred to the RAN, was in that team.

During the long period in Harbour, AIO training had continued with Plotting and Voice Procedure exercises to keep everyone up to the mark. However, I was not impressed with the standard of my new senior Radar Plot Instructor due to his lack of time at sea over the years.

October 1974

Continue Work Up

As we passed into the month of October, the ship remained in the Jervis Bay area working up the Carrier Air Group aircraft crews. On Friday the 4th, the ship returned to Sydney for essential maintenance and to drop off students and staff of the Army staff College who had come on board early that morning to witness flying operations during the passage to Sydney.

It was back to sea on the Wednesday, the 9th, to continue the Work Up. At one stage HMAS *Acute* acted as Plane Guard enabling the ship to continue with aircrew qualifications and, as a result, all the Tracker aircrew of 816 Squadron were both day and night qualified, all of 805, A4 Skyhawk pilots were day qualified and three were night qualified as well.

The ship returned to Sydney on Thursday the 17th to embark ammunition, but was unable to berth alongside due to industrial disputes and had to fuel from a lighter.

Returning to sea, the Carrier Air Group personnel and stores were embarked as well as their aircraft. At the end of October, the ship was still working up in the Jervis Bay Area.

Whilst I have emphasised flying operations above, the ship also participated in around ten Anti-submarine exercises, as well as Gunnery, NBCD, Replenishment and transfers at sea. Life is never dull. This kept me busy in the operation rooms making sure my teams were up to scratch.

November 1974 Disaster Relief Exercise

November arrived with the ship as sea operating off Jervis Bay. On the 1st, the Disaster Relief and Internal Security team arrived on board to put us through our paces. All Navy ships had to be ready to provide Aid to a Civil Power, either by way of assistance in the event of Natural Disasters, or on the other hand, Civil Disturbance. In this case it was to test our reaction to a Natural Disaster.

From what I remember we were not the brightest group they had inspected. On completion, this resulted in a complete rethink of the way the manpower would be organised for Disaster Relief. That re-organisation was placed in the hands of my deputy, Tim, and to his credit it worked a treat when tested shortly after.

Further F111 Attack on RAN units

I will comment on another attempt by the F111 to engage Naval units. The first was when two ships were coming back from New Zealand. The RAAF F111 crew decided to not use a maritime aircraft to help locate the ships, a Tanker and a DDG, returning to Sydney from New Zealand.

Having found out the details of the pulse length of the F111 radar was over 80 feet during our previous activities, the two ships travelled close to one another, using a distance line used in replenishments, to maintain a distance apart of 80 feet or less for the whole passage. This meant the two ships would appear as one radar contact. The F111's and Maritime aircraft were looking for two radar contacts. They kept chasing cloud or other ships and cloud contacts.

At the de-brief, the RAAF accused the Navy of sailing the Navy ships outside the proclaimed Exercise Area. They showed the search area and tracks of the F111 and were completely stunned when the Direction Officer of the DDG provided the track of the searching aircraft that matched that of the one the RAAF pilots had presented. At one time, the Navy units were just over ten miles or so from the searching RAAF aircraft.

I will mention a second incident later.

Visitors

Several observers for the exercises varied from the Chief of Naval staff and Air Force Chiefs and their staffs and were on board during these exercises.

Back to Sea

On the 25th of November, after Dead Load trials of the catapult were successful, the ship sailed with HMAS *Brisbane* and *Vendetta* in company for flying prior to Christmas. The Carrier Air Group was embarked on the 27th and the ship proceeded to sea for further exercises.

December 1974

Melbourne returned to Sydney for Christmas, embarking torpedoes and ammunition at the buoy, before berthing at Fitting Out wharf for the Christmas leave period. It was unfortunate that the catapult defect prevented the ship from visiting Brisbane before Christmas.

Christmas 1974

It had been arranged that Joan and the children would come to Sydney and spend Christmas with Joan's mother. I was looking forward to catching up with all the family again and having some seasonal leave with them and associates in Canberra. However, the best laid plans of mice and men are sometimes not realised.

Christmas Day Duty

A few days before Christmas leave was to start, the Executive Officer sent for me and said he had a problem. The Duty Officer for Christmas Day had been sent on Compassionate leave due to a family problem and all other officers on the duty list had also indicated they could not change their arrangements. He asked me if I would be prepared to do the duty. I would be compensated by additional two days leave after Christmas. I gained approval to have my family on board for Christmas lunch.

I rang Joan and she agreed that lunch on board for her mum and the children would be a treat. I accepted the duty. For my sins, as stated above, I had accepted responsibility to be the Christmas Day Duty Officer in HMAS *Melbourne*. This duty meant I was the acting Commanding Officer for that day unless the Captain or XO were on board. However, I got more than I bargained for.

Christmas Lunch, Telephone calls and Cyclone Tracy

My family, and recently widowed mother-in-law, came on board and enjoyed Christmas Lunch, during which time I was getting inklings something was not right. A steward knocked on the door stating the ship's Commander Air was on the telephone in the Wardroom and wished to speak to me. On answering the telephone, I was expecting some pleasantries, but surprised when he asked, "What's happening in the ship?"

My reply was, "Everything is quiet. I was just about to see my family off the ship. What's going on?"

His reply was, "The helicopter squadron has been recalled."

Naturally, my next question was, "Why?"

His reply, "They are going to Darwin. Didn't you know that Darwin has been wiped out?" He followed up with details of a cyclone destroying the place.

My Reaction

I realised *Melbourne* was the only vessel that could take the Helicopters to Darwin and my mind swung into top gear as I realised what was going to happen in the next 24 hours and beyond.

It so happened that, whilst in England in 1956, my first duty as a newly promoted officer was on Christmas day on a ship I had just joined. There was a severe storm, and we were forced to leave the wharf and seek shelter elsewhere.

State of Ship's Engines

As I left the Wardroom, the Duty Engineering Officer was passing in the corridor, so I asked him, "Wat is the state of the engines?"

His reply, "In bits."

Me: "How long to put them together again?"

He: "Three weeks with dockyard assistance."

Me: "What about 8 am tomorrow?"

He: "No way in hell."

Fleet HQ Action

I then rang Fleet Headquarters, identified myself, and asked exactly what the position was concerning the ship and the helicopter recall. The reply was, "We are too busy to talk to you." Just as I hung up the phone, the ship's Captain rang enquiring about what I knew, and I told him what I had done so far, and that Fleet HQ was being most unhelpful. He said he would get back to me.

Reactions

As you can appreciate, I was aware that all hell would be breaking loose very shortly, so I decided to have a quick shower and change into my night uniform. It was now about 5 pm. I decided to take the ship's car and proceed to Fleet HQ and sort out what was required of the ship. Just then the ship's Executive Officer arrived in his car, and I explained the situation so we both went in his car to get a briefing. On return, I did a quick inspection of all the ship's living spaces and found there were no problems in any area and then sat down to my dinner. This was shortly interrupted by the Quartermaster advising me that there was a truck alongside waiting to unload cargo for Darwin.

Cargo for Darwin

I summoned the Duty Watch and crane driver, and while they were mustering, I had a talk with the driver of the lorry, who advised he had to be unloaded as quickly as possible so he could return for another load.

As I was returning on board, a short, slim sailor was approaching the gangway and I noticed he was of the Naval Airmen Branch. I asked if he had been drinking, and the answer was no he did not drink. I then asked if he was a qualified forklift driver, and receiving an affirmative answer. I sent him to acquire a dockyard forklift so we could unload the truck. He came back with an oversized forklift. He seemed like a pimple on a pumpkin in the cabin of the forklift.

Ship's Crane

I climbed up to the flight deck and was informed by the crane driver that, because of limited power, (we were on shore power) that he could only raise the topping lift, turn left or right or lift the load.

To add to the problem, the two ship's lifts were down, and I was unable to get the ship's forklifts to the flight deck due to the power shortage. This meant, when the load reached the flight deck it had to be placed as far as possible from the ship's side. Gradually a semicircle of stores was placed on the flight deck, and with each incoming load, the space available was decreasing rapidly. Fortunately, other people had arrived on board, and it was soon possible to provide full power from the ship's resources. This enabled the two lifts to be raised and the ship's own forklifts to be used to move the items from under the crane onto the lifts and take them down into the hangar.

Bailey Bridge

A Bailey Bridge was finally lifted on board and allowed trucks to drive up onto the flight deck and be unloaded by our own forklifts. I was able to hand over the crane operation and proceeded to get on with things that would be needed for the ship to be ready to sail the next morning.

The rest of the night is a blur as other officers took on various tasks of supervision and it was well past midnight before I was able to get to bed. With the ship sailing as soon as practicable, I was up early the next morning to make sure the two Operations Rooms and Equipment (that I was responsible for) were working and ready for sea.

Sailing for Darwin

At about 8 am on Boxing Day, the order was given to remove the Bailey Bridge using a large crane on the wharf. Nothing happened and my first thought was "Bloody Dockies at it again." The reason for that thought was that previously they had refused to take off the ship's gangways when we were sailing.

However, it was found that there was a blown fuse in the shoreside crane's electrical system that was the problem. When that was replaced, the gangways were removed. Bailey Bridge also was removed, and we were able to sail.

Helicopter Embarkation

We embarked the helicopters as we proceeded to Brisbane to embark members of our own Ship's Company who had not arrived back before we sailed and to embark other personnel to make up the numbers because our personnel on leave interstate had not made it to Sydney by the time we left. Once the helicopters were on board, all their anti-submarine equipment was removed. This allowed up to nine sailors to be airlifted from the ship to shore at the one time.

Reorganisation of Ship's Disaster Plan

As a result of the pre-Christmas Damage Control Inspection and Exercise, the organisation of the manpower had undergone a significant change.

Organization.

Melbourne's reorganisation was rearranging into 30-man teams, divided into three sections of ten, and each section could be sub-divided into five. Each would have a leader with an appropriate rank for the numbers involved. This arrangement served us well in Darwin.

Arrival Darwin

The ship arrived Darwin on the 1st of January, 1975, and anchored in the harbour.

Briefings for Ships Disaster Coordinators

On arrival in Darwin, I, the newly appointed HMAS *Melbourne's* Disaster Relief Coordinator, other senior officers, and other ships Disaster Coordinators were required ashore from briefings of what their ships personnel would be required to do.

Generally, it was to make houses safe, remove debris and place it close to the road for trucks to come and take away. If any valuables were found, they would be placed in a safe area.

As most houses were built on stilts, and destroyed, a safe place could be found under the house or what was left of it. Also, teams were briefed that if any alcohol was found it was also to be placed in a safe place. (Usually there was fridge under the house). Any rotting food was to be removed and placed adjacent to the road.

Engineering and Electrical sailors were employed in repairing equipment and making safe power and re-establishing power lines.

Ship's Company Briefings.

The Ship's Disaster Relief teams were made aware that Darwin's population of women and children had been flown south. It emphasised how they would feel if it was them who had occupied the destroyed home and people were taking their possessions.

Clearing out Delis, Woolworths and Coles refrigerators was the most unpleasant task as there were no proper masks available. You can imagine the stench and the state of some of the food being handled as it was after many days since the cyclone.

Whilst in Darwin, the teams would be called at about 4:30 am so they could shower and have breakfast and collect a packed lunch and water. They would then assemble in the hangar by group and each group were briefed on their task for the day as provided by the Headquarters ashore.

House and Street Scene

Ship's Teams Day-to-Day

They were re-briefed that they must not confiscate any items they found loose in the areas they would be working in clearing rubbish et cetera. It was made clear that this applied to alcohol as well as other items.

Melbourne's Transfer of Men to Shore and Back

As helicopters became ready to transfer people ashore each group would move to the flight deck and embark in the helicopters and be flown ashore. Each person going ashore was checked off against a list. I would be on the flight deck to ensure everything went as planned. On return around 4 pm or later in the day, when the helicopters returned the personnel, they would be checked back on board. Again, I would be on deck to ensure they were okay. Anyone not checked back would be traced if they were on board or still ashore. Also, all returning personnel were searched for any items they should not have taken from shops or a home they were working upon.

This was generally done on the Flight deck. To my knowledge there was only one occasion when somebody tried to bring a bottle of alcohol aboard.

Other ships used their boats to take personnel ashore.

Another Street Scene

Incidents Car

The Naval Officer Commanding, Northern Australia, was driving to a meeting when stopped by an NSW Police Officer pointing a gun. The Policeman stated he was commandeering the car for police use. The Navy guy, a friend and character said, "Okay, but can I drive to my appointment, and you can then have the car?"

The Policeman agreed. The Navy guy drives up to Police HQ where the meeting was to be held and informs the Police of the incident.

The Police Officer with the gun was on his way south within hours.

Archives

On one occasion, I was unexpectedly summoned to the Disaster Relief Headquarters ashore.

A message saying there was a man, who said he was my neighbour in Canberra, wanted to see me. I was given the name and it checked out, so I jumped into the first helicopter going ashore. I found the neighbour at the Headquarters. He was looking for a small work party to help pack and send very important Archival papers south for drying out. The cyclone had unroofed the archival area and drenched most of the papers.

Headquarters advised me that, if I could rustle up a small team from my ship, they would be happy for them to join the Archivist. I made it so on my return to the ship. The Archivist was very appreciative of the help.

Papers Arrival in the South

The papers were a sodden mess, and warehouses had been prepared in both Brisbane and Sydney to dry them out. Imagine the surprise, when the boxes were opened in the south, and it was found all the papers were completely dry.

Miracle or Karma? Apparently in flying south they had dried out with the change of the air pressure or whatever in the aircraft. You learn something every day.

Provision of Fuel

A lesson to come out of Darwin concerned the provision of vehicle fuel. Because the power grid was destroyed, it turned out there was only one outlet in the whole of Darwin that had the ability to pump fuel by hand. So much for the technical age. All the others had to wait until generators could be found or flown in from the south and connected to each petrol station.

Sailors, God Bless Them

Melbourne's band requested they work as a unit. One of the jobs given to them about ten days or more after Christmas day, was the clearance of a small deli's refrigerator. You can imagine the stench. They were accompanied by an Insurance Assessor to record the items being thrown out et cetera.

The first Bandy picks up from the refrigerator a rotting, smelly and slimy bag of barramundi which had five fish in it as noted on the tag. Bandy shows the bag to the Assessor, standing some short distance away, and says "Five Barramundi."

The Assessor states, "No, I want each fish counted."

Bandy: "Really." Bandy opens the bag and holds up one fish saying, "One."

The assessor nods and looks down to mark his paper and finds he has a slimy fish on his chest, and it is very smelly and revolting, as you can imagine.

Bandy says, "Two …"

Panicking assessor: "No, by the bag will do."

Appreciation of Sailors

At the time of Tracy, I had been supervising sailors for something like twenty-nine years, both as a sailor and officer. My appreciation of sailors' 'can do' attitude, was again strengthened by watching the very tired, exhausted men returning each day, having been ashore for a long period in high humidity and heat.

Next morning, they would generally front up, without grumbling, and get on with the job. They did this day in and day out until they were replaced.

Eventually, Army personnel took over; they had gas masks.

HMAS *Melbourne* had to return to Sydney for exercises in Hawaii.

Non-recognition

My greatest disappointment concerning Cyclone Tracy is that no recognition was given to those who participated in Navy help Darwin. There has been no medal or award given, yet a smaller cyclone later saw awards made.

Two days' Leave for Christmas day never eventuated.

Remainder of January 1975

Eldest son Anthony joined the Navy and started officer training school at HMAS *Creswell* on the 20th.

Sydney

On return to Sydney, it was prepared for departure for Hawaii. I was able to get home to Canberra and relax after a very strenuous period since Xmas Day. However, it was not long before it was off to Hawaii for the RIMPAC Exercise.

F111 Second Incident

When transiting to Hawaii the RAAF asked permission to again attack the ships enroute to Fiji. This time they used the RAAF Maritime aircraft to locate the Navy ships. Navy appreciated that the Convergence Zone, (cloudy and rainy weather) would be present on the track and the *Melbourne's* course was set to be under the clouds and rain. In flying an A4 CAP off the ship it would find a clear weather patch to launch and recover.

The cloud cover was from low level to 20,000 feet and solid. The A4 stayed above the cloud. The rain and low cloud made it difficult but not impossible to detect the F111, first by electronic warfare picking up the F111's and Maritime search radars and conversations.

The A4 was kept informed of the location of the F111s in relation to his position. At one stage the airborne A4 happened to be flying over a gap in the clouds and sighted the F111s immediately below him. He dived down through the hole and the shocked RAAF pilots found an A4 alongside of them saying "This way, fellows."

The aftermath of this was the RAAF pilots coming to the American Officers Mess in Hawaii, (which the *Melbourne's* aircrew were using as their mess) and accusing them of cheating. They were very unhappy chappies.

They were told they would have to learn how to get to ships undetected.

Note: At a later date, when back in Australia, the F111s were enlightened by a friendly Direction Officer as to how to attack shipping.

Shore Time Hawaii

I did the usual sightseeing including a very interesting tour of two of the islands during this trip to Hawaii.

RIMPAC EXERCISE

As you can imagine, the almost continuous operation of aircraft saw me spend many, many, hours in the ADR supervising plotters, Air Controllers and in the operation of the Upper Operations Room.

I won't bore you with any detail of Rimpac.

Returning to Sydney

At the end of the Rimpac exercises the ship spent a few days in Hawaii attending a RIMPAC debrief and sailed for Sydney on 27th of May with HMA ships *Vampire* and *Torrens* and US ships *Fort Fisher, Juneau, Alamo,* and *Bristol County* in company.

Cyclone Betty, encountered on the way home, meant the ships had to seek shelter in the lee of an island. Eventually, the ships arrived off Sydney on 11th of April. And, after de-ammunitioning, berthed alongside in preparation for a Major Refit that began on the 21st of April.

Posting

I received notification that I was posted to HMAS *Watson* as the OIC of the Navigation and Direction School to date 25 April and I duly left my last seagoing ship.

I was very disappointed in not being posted back to Canberra where the family was. I made plans to be interviewed for a job in the new Search and Rescue Centre in Canberra that Cyclone Tracy had interrupted.

COMMANDING OFFICER'S COMMENTS

TO MY ENTIRE SATISFACTION

A LOYAL, ZEALOUS AND RELIABLE OFFICER WHO POSSESSES CONSIDERABLE EXPERIENCE AS A SPECIALIST AND WHO OBTAINED EXCELLENT RESULTS, HE SHOULD CONTINUE TO DO WELL IN THE SERVICE

Chapter 37

HMAS *Watson*

21 April 1975 to 14 December 1975

Joining and Duties

This was to be the last time I would walk through the gates of HMAS *Watson* for my last posting in the Sydney area. A disappointment perhaps; I had hoped to return to Canberra and apply for a job at the new Maritime Search and Rescue Centre, where my long experience in running Operation Rooms could be put to the best use of my talents.

My job was Officer in Charge of the Navigation and Direction School and to act as the Flag Officer Commanding East Australia Area's (FOCEA) Navigation and Direction Specialist Staff Officer.

I settled into my cabin and Wardroom life ashore again. I called on the Captain and the Executive Officer and they welcomed me back into the fold.

FOCEA

My next task was to travel to FOCEA's office on Garden Island and report to the Admiral. It just happened that this person had been a Lieutenant Air Controller I had worked with in HMAS *Sydney* in Korea.

After the normal welcome formalities, the Admiral asked me how I was looking forward to being back at HMAS *Watson*. My reply was that I didn't expect to be in the job long because I was thinking of applying for a job in the new Air Sea Rescue Centre in Canberra. I indicated that my home was in Canberra, and with the family growing up, it was time I was home to help my wife who, due to my regular postings to sea, had had to carry a great load because of my absences.

He asked why I would do that. I said I didn't appear to have any chance of promotion because someone had forgotten to place it or maybe suspend it in *Watson's* Scheme of Complement. I considered that my talents could be better used in the new Centre in Canberra.

He thanked me for my honesty, and I returned to *Watson* to do what I'd been doing for many, many years. I was not to know that conversation, and the one I had with the Captain of HMAS *Melbourne*, would see me remain in the Navy until retirement, on the 1st of September 1983.

My Office Building

Aside: I had the privilege of naming this building the "RITCHIE BUILDING" after I had retired. Initially, it was so named above the door. This was changed to reflect its usage; however, it is still known as the "Ritchie Building" with a sign at the top of the steps.

The Rock Spiders

On one of the beaches below this Training building at the northern end of *Watson* is a beach where various types of people would sunbake in the nude on the rocky outcrops.

The Navigation Training Office looked directly down on the beach and, on one occasion as I was walking past the office, I noticed the female Navigator's Yeoman (Assistant) looking out the window down onto the beach. I entered the room unnoticed, and commented, "Where is the most interesting group?" She jumped around quickly and, seeing me, was embarrassed. I told her to relax and not worry about it. I got a broad smile.

Training

The Training facilities that were now available were much better than they had been in the Action Information Training (AITC),

The Operation Room layouts, and the provision of the ship's Bridge for basic training, or those setting out to be trained for a Bridge Watchkeeping Ticket, was interesting to me, particularly as the Bridge could be made to roll just like the ship.

Promotion Notice

Completely out of the blue a letter arrived advising that I was to be promoted to Commander on the 1st of January 1976. Naturally I was delighted and rang Joan with the news.

The Chief of the Naval Service (CNS) at that time was the Lieutenant Training Officer on my arrival at *Watson* in 1946 and had been the Commanding Officer of HMAS *Melbourne* during my second posting to that ship. He was also the only officer to send me a congratulatory note when I was commissioned way back in 1956.

Interestingly, there was a personal message written in green ink congratulating me. (*The CNS uses green ink when writing personally.*)

In my reply to CNS, I decided that, in the thank you, I would add, "Having been kept out of Western Australia for 33 years, now you can send me back to the West."

I had to pay for everyone's drink at the Wardroom bar that lunchtime. I was very happy to do so as I had been quite resigned that I would not be promoted. Promotion meant I would probably be sent to Canberra again.

In congratulating me, the Commanding Officer of HMAS *Watson* suggested that I take on the job of Training Officer for all training being done at HMAS *Watson*. I thanked him for the offer and pointed out that he had to be kidding in asking me, a brand-new Commander, to take on the supervision of more Senior Commanders in charge of other training at *Watson*.

Navy Ball

I can't remember the date; I know it was before I left *Watson* and had yet to find out my next posting.

At the last-minute, I decided to attend the Navy Ball being held in the Trocadero, George Street, Sydney. During the Ball, I needed to go to the toilet, and it so happened I had to pass by the head table where CNS was standing, talking with others at the table. As I passed, he grabbed my arm and said "I want to talk to you." I asked if I could get to the toilet first and he agreed.

My immediate thought was I going to be chided for my comment about posting to the West. However, to my surprise, he said, "You might be right for that WA job."

I thanked him and was very happy and told no one what had been said.

Posting

Eventually, dated the 11th of September 1975, I received my posting to be the Deputy Director of Training, located in the Russell Navy Office, and was to take up that posting on the 15th of December 1975. I thought, *So much for CNS's comment.*

As you can imagine I was very happy that I would now be living at home with the family in Canberra until retirement.

For the rest of the year, I continued to oversee the ND School Operations. Came December, and I bid farewell and made my way back to Canberra.

SO ENDS MY SEAGOING CAREER

COMMANDING OFFICERS COMMENTS

<u>21 APRIL 1975 TO 30 JULY 1975</u>

TO MY ENTIRE SATISFACTION

HIS EXPERT KNOWLEDGE AND EXPERIENCE IN AIO MATTERS IS OF GREAT BENEFIT TO HMAS WATSON

<u>11 AUGUST 1975 TO 15 DECEMBER 1975</u>

TO MY ENTIRE SATISFACTION.

A ZEALOUS ENERGETIC AND KNOWLEDGEABLE OFFICER WITH A KEEN INTEREST IN TRAINING WHO HAS RUN THE N.D. SCHOOL

Chapter 38

Navy Office

15 December 1975 to 14 March 1977

Joining

I was familiar with the Security procedures, and it didn't take long before I arrived at the Directorate of Training. I introduced myself to my new Boss and found out where I was to sit etc. Then I was taken to see the Admiral in Charge of Training.

Meeting the Admiral in overall charge of Training, I realised I did know him personally as he was an Aviator. He welcomed me into the job. I can't remember exactly what he said that caused me to comment along lines of, "I don't expect to be here that long as I understand, that after 30-odd years away, I have been earmarked to go back to the West to assist in the setting up of the WANSF."

He wryly smiled and said, "Yes, I seem to know about that."

Staff Member

Another recently promoted Commander, (John) had arrived a short time before me and had been tasked with looking for a suitable ship for the Sea Training of Junior Officers. We already knew one another as John had been a Direct Entry Officer under training when I was serving in HMAS *Vengeance*. We were to become very good friends right up until his death.

Re-establishing Old Friendships

It was great to resume various friendships that we had developed during my previous time in Canberra. Also, to see the children and how they had grown and developed and for me to become part of the family again.

Accounting Training

I was able to resume my accountancy training as it did not interfere with my duties in the training area. I was very grateful for this.

Training Course

Soon after assuming the role of Deputy Director of Training I was told I had to attend, full-time, a course to make me aware of all facets of training. I protested to my Boss and pointed out I'd been training Sailors and Officers since 1946/47 and if I didn't know how to do my job now there was something wrong.

However, I was directed to attend.

The course was in Victoria. There was a total of 35 Navy Army and Airforce Personnel in the class.

Once the course began it did not take me long to notice that the only teaching aid being used was the overhead projector. I had been marking in my notebook a stroke every time a slide was placed on the projector. I also noted, as I looked around the class that, after about 15 to 20 minutes, there appeared to be a lack of attention because of the total slides being used in each lecture.

My mind raced back to 1946, when a very capable officer of the Schoolie Branch had introduced us to the three Ps to be used in preparing any lesson or speech. Preparation 80%, Presentation 15% and Personality 5%, and the use of various types of aids to make your point. It became obvious to me that the only presentation aid was going to be the overhead projector.

One morning before starting the day, I advised my classmates that I would be standing up and clapping during this session, saying well done and I would like them to join me as for whoever was instructing, would have just put on the 1000th slide. True or false didn't matter.

The instructor, for the first lesson of the day, was a young new Naval Instructor Officer. He began his presentation and after a few slides I jumped up clapping and saying well done with everyone else following. You can imagine the noise and it didn't take long before the Officer in Charge of the School to appear and want to know what was going on.

I pointed out that we had just had the 1000th slide put before us, and I thought there was a need to congratulate the young man for that event. Also, I said surely there was some way to break the monotony of the slide presentation. The result was that the OIC noted the comments and told us to get on with listening.

You all know about good and bad karma.

Towards the end of the course, each student was required to get up and do a presentation on a subject. I can't recall if we were given the subject or told to select one. For one reason or another, I can't remember, I think I was the last one to make a presentation, possibly because I was the Senior Officer in the class.

Remembering the three Ps above, I made sure of what I was going to say, remember the first P (Preparation). I then looked at how I could present it, the second P. (Presentation) without the use of the overhead projector. I found a 35mm projector with suitable slides, I set up an easel and made a few props hidden under a blank sheet, some simple objects related to what I was going to talk about, and a Chinagraph pencil and a stiff plastic sheet.

I had an overhead projector and a stack of files alongside me. I also placed a boat paddle in front of the lectern.

I then proceeded to present my article switching from 35mm, to drop-down sheets, to plastic sheet and pencil etc. As you can imagine everyone was waiting for me to use the overhead projector. A couple of times I made as if to do so.

There was complete silence in the room as I completed my presentation broken by one wag in the class asking what the paddle was for. I just smiled and didn't answer because I thought it was obvious. The class woke up and clapped.

The Officer in Charge of the School stood up and commented, "You have just seen an expert present his case."

WANSF Posting

My posting, as the Pre-Commissioning and Commissioning Executive Office of the WANSF, to be named HMAS *Stirling* on Commissioning, was issued on 25 July 1976 and I was to report for duty on 15th of March 1977.

The first thing I did was to promptly have a steel plate fitted to my back to ensure I was not knifed so someone else could get the job. There were a couple of broken blades.

I wrote to my father a short time later that I was being posted to WA, after over 33 years away from WA, and was bringing the family, except eldest son, Tony, with me. Again, as had happened with my mother, he never got to read that letter and died before it could be delivered.

Pre-Departure

In February 1977, the first thing was to find out what Defence Housing was available around the WANSF. It turned out that we were to reside in a new four-bedroom home that had been built in Kwinana, located some distance from the Base, and not in Rockingham, that was adjacent to the Base entry. (A Political decision to use the Kwinana location.)

Next step was to decide what to take with us and the needs of the children.

Then came the requirement to engage an Agent to manage our Canberra house during our absence. I anticipated I would finish up back in Canberra before I retired in 1981 when I would reach retiring age for rank held.

The planning for our move West was based on leaving Sydney by train on the 18th of January 1977. This meant we could spend our Christmas in Sydney with Joan's widowed mother before embarking on the train.

I seem to remember we had a nice Christmas and were able to say goodbye to family and friends and invite them to come West for their next holiday.

I deposited our car with the appropriate railway person so it could be transported with us on the train.

Departure Sydney

There was great excitement, especially for the three children (Tony was under training in the Navy), and Joan's family shed tears at our moving so far away.

As the train pulled out of Central Station, I remarked from the door, "Goodbye, Sydney; unlike MacArthur, I will not return." Joan gave me a good slap for that comment.

We settled down for the long trip, with the children in one compartment and Joan and me in another. We sat and watched the CBD disappear behind us. Then we saw Ashfield station going by as the train picked up speed, so it was onward to the West.

We were not to know until later in the day that, shortly after passing under the railway bridge at Granville, (a suburb of Sydney), a train crashed into that bridge and closed the line. This was the Granville Train Disaster

For the children it was a great train adventure and for Joan and me a chance to relax. Going to the Dining Room and being able to get off when the train stopped for water, especially out on the Nullarbor section of the journey was fascinating for the youngsters.

As we passed the various watering holes, my mind flew back to when, as a young sailor, I was on troop trains that required train changes at Kalgoorlie, Port Pirie, Melbourne, and Goulburn because of the different gauges of the rail line. (Distance apart of rails.) This journey of ours did not require us to change trains.

I was looking forward to passing through Kalgoorlie again. I think we took a bus tour of the Kalgoorlie area while the train was refuelled and watered.

THEN IT WAS PERTH HERE WE COME.

COMMANDING OFFICER COMMENTS

TO MY ENTIRE SATISFACTION.

CMDR RITCHIE'S DEEP INTEREST IN, AND COMPLETE DEDICATION TO THE SERVICE, IS CONTINUALLY BEING DEMONSTRATED. THE FACT HE IS WIDELY RESPECTED IN THE SERVICE AND HELD IN HIGH REGARD BY HIS COLLEAGUES HAS SIGNIFICANTLY CONTRIBUTED TO HIS SUCCESS IN THIS DIRECTORATE.

Chapter 39

Western Australian Naval Support Facility

15 March 1977 to 27 July 1978

Arrival Perth

I cannot recall much about our arrival in Perth. We arrived at the Rail Terminal in East Perth, and I seem to recall that we were met and directed to our initial accommodation.

I was able to recover the car from the Railway Authority and this provided us with wheels to drive to Kwinana.

WANSF

Kwinana/Parmelia Causeway

Ramage Place
Caribbean Drive
Safety Bay
Fifth Avenue

Our Homes

Our Married Quarter was at 14 Mandfield Way Parmelia in Kwinana. We subsequently built a home at 8 Caribbean Drive Safety Bay and later moved to 20 Fifth Avenue, Shoalwater.

I mention them here for convenience's sake.

Our Married Quarter

This was a new house at Mandfield Way, Parmelia, a suburb in the Town of Kwinana. This was a Defence House with four Bedrooms, an Ensuite and separate Bathroom, a Toilet, a Lounge and Dining Room, a Family Room/Kitchen, Laundry, and a Garage for the car. It was located not far from the Kwinana Shopping Centre, the Catholic Church and school and other amenities, such as a swimming pool near the town centre.

The Removalist delivered our furniture shortly after our arrival and we were able to settle into our new home. It proved to be suitable for our requirements. Its only disadvantage was the distance to the Naval Base Facility in the Rockingham Shire as it was then.

Rockingham Beach

On an early occasion, we decided to take the children for a swim at Rockingham Beach. This is where I had nearly drowned as a young fella. Unfortunately, the Park alongside the beach was full and parking was hard to find. So, we wended our way round the coast to Shoalwater beach, a bit further south. I was not to know then, that in later life, we would buy a house one street back from this beach.

Schooling

The next step was to arrange school for the Children. Eldest son Tony (Anthony) was then at the Naval College at Jervis Bay, NSW, as mentioned previously.

Daughter Anne went to Rockingham High School for her last year. (Year 12)

Son Peter went to Fremantle Christian Brothers Catholic College during 1977. He found a part time job in a fruit and veg store in Medina. He played squash in the Kwinana Recreation Centre competition. He also played Rugby with the Wallaroo's Junior side for the next three years. He also became involved in cricket with Rockingham Cricket Club.

Son Walter was enrolled in the Catholic School in Medina.

Navy Housing

Some comments on the Naval housing provided for the Ship's Company are relevant. There was no married quarter patch where all Naval Houses were in one location.

A decision had been made that no more than three or four houses would be built in a street. In the adjacent street at the back of these houses other Naval Homes were built backing onto the other four. This provided support as a Naval Group and allowed the Naval Families to meet the locals who were much friendlier than I had found in the east.

In my time, I cannot recall there being an incident between the Naval personnel and their neighbours, or local community.

No doubt, because of some political decision, the Naval married quarters for the Base were split between Rockingham and Kwinana townsites rather than have them all in Rockingham near the Base.

Later, a house was built for the Cornmanding Officer in Fifth Avenue, Shoalwater, a suburb almost next door to the beginning of the Causeway to Garden Island. From what I recall it was first occupied by others than the Commanding Officer of the Base.

Below is a picture of the Naval Base on Garden Island, Western Australia. Below is a picture of the Dockyard area. The Accommodation Blocks are located to the right of the picture.

Garden Island

First A Little History Lesson

A comment on the history of Garden Island I think may be appropriate at this point and its name.

In 1500s the Portuguese and Spanish were busy exploring the world and finding new lands. A dispute arose between the two and the Pope, yes, the Catholic Pope, was called on to sort out who should have what. How far we have strayed today.

The Pope decided that they should share equal parts of the World and he divided the world into two. The Spanish would have one half and the Portuguese the other. The dividing line was known as the Papal Line. For all intents it is close enough to what was the Western Border of the colony of New South Wales. It also came very close to Kagoshima in Japan. The Portuguese section of the Papal Line was to the West of the Line and the Spanish to the east.

So, when Captain Cook discovered the Continent that today is known as Australia, he claimed only that portion of the Continent as far west as the Papal Line. This became known as the Colony of New South Wales.

In 1803, Frenchman Commodore Nicholas Baudin had been exploring the local West Australian coast after an earlier visit to the area in 1801. He had anchored in Cockburn Sound near the island he named Ile Buache and a nearby small island to the north, Ile Berthollet.

Before proceeding further, I think it appropriate to provide some background to how the island became known as Garden Island. In 1827, Captain James Stirling had been sent to the West Coast to find a suitable location to establish a settlement, due to a British outpost to the north of Australia becoming unsuitable because of malaria or other tropical diseases. Also, possibly because of the French sniffing around the Western Australian coast.

During this visit Stirling renamed Ile Buache, Garden Island and Ile Berthollet, Carnac Island.

Back to My Story

I think it is appropriate at this stage of my memoirs to comment with a brief summary of why Garden Island was chosen as the site for the Base.

Selection of Garden Island

When the decision was made to construct a new Naval facility in Western Australia, a committee investigated several locations up and down the coast. The final decision made was based on, I believe, the fact that the island was Commonwealth owned and not the State and there would be no acquisition cost in setting up. It would be built on the lee side of the island facing into Cockburn Sound which provided safe anchorage. It was also near major engineering facilities of a Capital city. There was an Interstate Railway Terminal in Perth as well as a major airport.

Holiday Homes

There were holiday homes on the Island, mainly on the Cockburn Sound side, some on the same side to the north, and a few on the west side of the Islands. The owners were given notice to remove these at their cost I believe.

Joining WANSF

When it was time to report for duty, I drove from our new home in Kwinana to Garden Island and, after checking in with the front gate Security, proceeded to the Dockyard area and went into the Guardhouse that controlled entrance to the Dockyard and found my temporary office.

I met the OIC, a very efficient Engineer Officer, also a character. There were another two Officers then working at the facility. One officer oversaw of the Supply Department and the other the Electrical Department. There was also a Warrant Naval Policeman running the Security team of Naval Policeman.

The first thing that struck me was that the four of us officers had come up from the lower deck and believed that this was a great help in the setting up of the Base and its organisation as we were all very experienced in the areas of our responsibility.

Starting My Job

Because of the distance and lack of Public Transport from the Married Quarters in Kwinana, and people in Navy houses and private rentals around Rockingham, a Navy bus would pick up personnel each morning and take them back after work each day. There was a car available in the transport pool for me, as the Executive Officer, and on the second day I caught the bus to work so that Joan could have our car at her disposal.

I met up with the person who was to be my Coxswain. He would be my right-hand man in looking after the Organisational, Management and Disciplinary side of the Navy personnel at the Base.

The Layout of the Base:

The Causeway

To reach Garden Island from the Mainland, the stone Causeway had to be built because there was insufficient steel available for a steel bridge structure.

The distance from the mainland entrance to the southern end of the island is about 4.5km. On the Causeway, there is a two-lane vehicular traffic road, one lane for traffic coming into the Base and the other for off-road traffic. This road continues right up to the northern end of the island.

The western side of the Causeway is built with a rock wall to protect the road and vehicles using it when there is a heavy swell running. However, in bad weather, it was not unusual for a wave to be dumped all over a vehicle, as I was to find out later.

A high bridge was placed over a channel used by small boats exiting or entering Cockburn Sound. Initially, a patrol boat could use this Channel. The silting up of Braun Bay (on the left-hand side of the Causeway, where the Causeway arrived at the island) was expected to reduce the depth of the Channel, and it happened as predicted.

Low Bridge

High Bridge

Naval Base Facilities. (My Knowledge)

In my first posting to Canberra, as the Deputy Director of User Requirement, I attended the first, and very detailed, presentation of what the Department of Housing and Construction (DHC) in WA had prepared to meet the requirements they had been given. Over the next two or so years, I was the Escort for the DHC rep on his regular visits to Canberra to obtain or clarify details from Navy Head Office and Technical/ Stores or other Head Office staff.

Therefore, I had a very detailed knowledge about the Base, etc. The Base was to be manned by naval personnel with some Civilian assistance. The planners set the base up so it could be expanded fourfold within the fenced area of the original buildings.

Layout

The Naval Base layout consisted of five separate and distinct areas on Garden Island. The first of these, as you arrived from the mainland, was the planned Airfield area on the left-hand side of the road running to the north end from the causeway.

The Dockyard area was next on the right, fenced in, with the main access right off the road that ran the length of the island. The entrance to the Dockyard area was through a gate with guard post in the centre of the road to control entry and exit.

On the eastern side of the road into the Dockyard was the Security Building containing office spaces, Naval Police and Security Centre, four cells and a Fire Brigade garage. The Transport Section was on the opposite side of the road leading to the wharves. The next building was the Stores Facilities, then Naval Officer in Charge of WA's HQ, followed by the Base Administration Building. The Powerhouse, Mechanical and Electrical Engineering and a Periscope Workshops were adjacent to the wharf area.

There were two main wharves, one known as the Submarine Wharf and the other the Destroyer Wharf. A third wharf was for Patrol and other small craft. There was a crane on each of the main wharves and Support buildings on each wharf.

(Note: Power was supplied from the Mainland and the Powerhouse provided a backup should the shore power fail.)

Submarine Wharf Power

The original supply of power to the Submarine Wharf was Direct Current (DC) only. Australian submarines at that time used DC. I believe a proposal was made to have Alternating Current (A/C) also on this wharf. However, those back in Head office had opted for DC only. A prudent planner would have had AC and DC at all wharves.

You did not have to be an intellectual pygmy to realise that both wharves would be used by surface ships as well as submarines.

In the event, the first Submarine to use the wharf was an American, A/C powered, nuclear submarine. The team from the DHC, who in what was not to be the only time, showed their skill, and quickly added an AC power supply on the wharf in a short time frame. This was a characteristic of the DHC team involved throughout the construction phase and later.

Small Boat Harbour

There was a small Boat Harbour with berthing facilities inside the fenced Dockyard area. There was a shed and slipway for small boats and the shipwrights workshop formed part of this complex.

The Clearance Diving Section were also in this area until facilities were constructed to address their needs.

Tuck Shop

There was a small, civilian-run Tuck Shop in an area outside of the Dockyard that had originally serviced the Holiday Homes that had previously occupied a considerable part of the area facing Cockburn Sound. Navy personnel used this for lunch if they so needed.

Other facilities

Oil Fuel Tanks

On the left-hand side of the north/south main road, before reaching the third area, there was a Fuel Oil Facility and a small Memorial Area dedicated to 1 'Z' Special Forces, who had trained on the island during World War II.

Note. I will note here, that in Western Australia, the retired Z Special Forces were divided into two groups; they would have separate memorial services on the island each year. I was made an Associate member of one group.

The Accommodation and Living Facilities, Medical, Sports and Recreation Centre, Swimming pool and Sport Grounds.

Except for an Australian Rules Football oval on the right side of the main road leading to the top of the island, the following facilities formed the third area and were inside the northern fence line where there was a gate to the rest of the main road running north-south.

Training, Offices and Submarine Escape Tower

This facility was to train submarine personnel in escape procedures, among other things. It was part of the area outside the Dockyard fenced area. See the picture below.

An Australian Rules oval was located on the left side of the main road. It was part of the area outside the Dockyard fenced area. This facility was to train submarine personnel, including submarine escape procedures.

Escape Tank

See picture below of the escape tower.

Further to the north on the left side of the road was the Base Sewerage Farm outside the fence and a nearby Aerial farm on the right side of the road formed the fourth area.

Submarine Escape Tower

Ammunitioning Complex

This complex was at the north end of the island and was fenced in and made up the fifth area. There was a wharf provided for ships to use for Ammunitioning. It is a short distance on the other side of the north-south road. Also in this area is a Memorial to the first Settlers, facing Cockburn Sound.

On the top of a hill, alongside the road to the memorial is where Captain Stirling had his first house in WA.

Holiday Shacks

At the time of my arrival, there were still some holiday shacks occupying both sides of the North End of the island, and the occupants would remain there until the Ammunitioning complex was ready to be accepted. However, they had to use their own boats to go between the island and the mainland.

(Note: Later I obtained permission for the occupants to remove their goods and chattels and the houses by road instead of having to use their boats).

This area also contained a house, built in 1829 for, Captain James Stirling RN, and he lived on the Island during the early days to set up what became known as the Swan River Colony.

Note: Naval involvement on Garden Island began with Captain Stirling''s arrival. As I write, I have just attended the 190th function celebrating this arrival. I should also point out that the first Government House (shack) was on the top of the hill in this area near the Armament Wharf.

State of Construction (On Arrival)

It's hard to remember exactly what buildings had been completed and handed over to the Navy by the date of my joining. There were three Junior Sailor Accommodation Blocks. All personnel lived ashore, with some single and married personnel in civilian accommodation. Later, one of the blocks was occupied by Junior sailors when the Junior Sailors galley opened.

Junior Sailors Dining Hall/Galley

The completion of the Junior Sailors Dining Hall and Galley, with a Change room alongside, allowed all ranks to initially use these facilities. The changing room was treated like a meeting area, and each lunchtime, people would meet up for a friendly chat.

At that time, it was normal for Shore establishments to have the bar open at lunchtime in each of the three messes (Officers, Senior, and Junior Sailors) to provide refreshments. Following a discussion with the OIC, I agreed to a small bar serving beer and soft drinks to be available at lunchtime in the Change Room each day. This seemed to work reasonably well, and I had no concerns or problems with it.

As previously stated, the small civilian-run tuck shop in the dockyard area provided snacks and soft drinks.

Base Introduction Lecture

Appreciating there would be many Eastern States members and families arriving, as well as Western Australians like me, I decided that all personnel joining the Base should be aware of the purpose of the Base, some idea of why and how it was to operate, the Security requirements, and any other items of importance during the period up to the final Acceptance of the Base by Navy and leading up to the Commissioning that was finally programmed for June 1978.

I produced an introductory Standard Briefing Lecture, given by myself, to all newcomers once a month, or as required, if a large batch of personnel joined the Base.

I emphasised the need to make friends with the locals and made the comment, following my experiences in the east, that the locals could be much friendlier neighbours than in the East.

The first part was to introduce them to the purpose and operation of the Base. The second was to make sure they understood that every one of them was responsible for the Security of the Base. If they suspected something was wrong, like someone unknown or not usually working in the area, they should find out who they were and report the situation. This seemed to work well.

Incident. As it happened, three of the Department of Housing Construction Team leaders were visiting to check up on things, and as they walked through the Powerhouse, the person there, who had only recently joined, intercepted them and asked them who they were and for identification. They identified themselves and produced their DHC IDs and were amused that they, of all people, should be asked for identification. They were permitted to proceed with their inspection. The sailor reported what had happened and asked if he had done the right thing. I thanked him for his efforts. I also advised him to remember them as they would be visiting regularly.

Base Entry Identification

Everyone joining was issued a personal identification card and vehicle registration, so they had no hold-up entering the Base each morning.

First Chance Book

Early on, after my starting the job, I realised the lack of transport to the island could be a problem for personnel getting to the Base, with people arriving late for work because of a car breakdown, family problems, missing the Navy bus or some other reason.

The civilian bus service nearest drop-off point was a considerable distance from the Base front gate.

After the first instance – a sailor taking his pregnant wife to hospital for the birth of a child – was late and charged, I decided that, if I was not to be detracted by having a regular Defaulters table to deal with such matters, I would consult with the Coxswain and have him set up a book to list those people who were late and the reason for the lateness. I delegated to him to warn first-time offenders they had this one chance, and I would not be happy to see them at my table on a second such offence. The First Chance Book system worked well. I had few latecomers to deal with.

My Communications

The telephone in my office connected to the Base exchange. At that time, there was no such thing as a mobile telephone. I had a UHF radio system in my car, which did not allow me to communicate with the Naval Police. I promptly had this changed to VHF so that, when in the car, the Naval Police could contact me, especially if I was off the Base.

I also had a pager so the Naval Police could contact me when I was out of the office and walking around the Base.

Wharf Telephones

At each berthing position at the wharf, a telephone cable connection was available for each ship at that berth so they could be connected through the Base Telephone system. That gave a particular number to the berth and was not changeable.

I appreciated immediately, with ships and submarines going to be based at Stirling, it was quite possible they may not be berthed at the same position on the next visit. I made enquiries of the Electrical Officer proposing, if practical, the same telephone number be available to a particular ship no manner what berth it was placed at. This officer worked with the Telecom people to ensure that what I proposed could be done.

Monthly Luncheons

When the Junior Sailors Recreational Building was completed, I was asked if it would be possible for people to bring their wives on board to have a look around the place. I consulted with the OTC. We decided to give everyone a half day off on a nominated Friday. They could take their wives/partners to lunch on that day. Each visitor was expected to pay a small fee for lunch.

The first lunch, which took place in the Junior Sailors Dining facility, was a success, and so began the Monthly Luncheon routine. This became a regular feature, especially for the Senior Sailors and later the Officers' Mess.

Junior Sailor Club

A short time after my arrival, the Junior Sailors Recreational Building was completed. I can't remember how it came to be named Tamar Tavern. I believe the Junior sailors had set up a committee and put this name forward as appropriate. The OIC agreed.

Tamar was the name of the small kangaroo on the Island. I suppose people thought this cute.

This became the drinking venue for all ranks until the Senior Sailors Mess could be handed over as complete. The drinking area consisted of a long bar with a shorter bar at right angles to the main bar with a Pool Table adjacent. There were the usual tables and stools in the main bar area.

After discussing with the Coxswain whether he thought there was a need to provide some form of screening, where the bar turned at right angles, he agreed that we would not have a screen and see how it worked out. There was occasional banter across the space from main to side bar, but it was nothing that required me to intervene.

Finger Pointing Exercise.

Normally on a Friday, the OIC and I would each buy a jug of beer and take it into the Junior Sailors main bar area and place the jug on two high tables some distance apart. We offered a drink to those present. I was to call this the "Finger Pointing Exercise". Sailors would be invited to make known how they thought things were going and how they and their families had settled in. The sailors were a bit wary at first but soon woke up that we wanted their views on how they were settling in and if they had any problems. On reflection, I believe they appreciated this opportunity to speak.

Occasionally, a sailor would point a finger to emphasise something he thought was wrong. Usually, he had not listened to the briefing or had misunderstood the notice in the Daily Orders.

Sometimes, there was some banter when someone would try to get one over either the OIC or me. They either didn't know or forgot that we had lived on Mess Decks as sailors, and knew most ways of junior sailors, if not all the tricks. It usually ended in a laugh all round when they found out we had a suitable reply.

One thing that came out of it was the OIC and I were aware of how the Junior Sailors were settling in and could cut off any complaints before they were brought forward officially.

When the Senior Sailors Mess was completed and accepted, the Senior Sailors moved out of Tamar Tavern to their own recreational facilities.

It was time for the officers, all five of us, to look at finding a suitable space for a Wardroom, (Officers Mess) as the official building was not quite ready.

First Wardroom

The OIC suggested we use one of the small recreation spaces on the top floor of one of the three Junior Sailor Accommodation Blocks. This contained a fridge, a sink and cupboard underneath, a low table, and some chairs to relax in.

However, whereas the Junior and Senior Sailors Messes received funding from the Canteen System to set up their bars etc., the Wardroom could not access similar funding. So, it was agreed that officers would all put in $20 each to have funds to purchase some beer and soft drinks. We put a markup on sales, recorded each sale and eventually built up funds for when we moved to the Wardroom building.

At each lunchtime, the officers would gather for a drink and informal chitchat or discuss something the other officers needed to be aware of. The Department of Housing and Construction leaders would join us if they were visiting at lunchtime.

Barbecue Area

Having seen the crowds on the Rockingham beachfront, I decided to look at establishing a BBQ area where ships alongside could gather for what was called a Banyan. I also thought it could be used by families.

Facing Cockburn Sound were a few areas where holiday homes had stood before the building of the Base. In one spot, there was a reasonably cleared area facing and adjacent to Cockburn Sound. The house had been dismantled and area cleared. It had a sandy beach, and the water was quite shallow and would allow children to play in the water safely. I decided to put some people to work clearing the area of any debris and setting up a BBQ.

One day the OIC came and asked me "Where are all the hands?"

I replied, "Camp Markham. I have them working on clearing the area."

"What?"

I then explained what I was doing, and he saw that it was a good idea.

It later came to be known officially as Camp Markham in honour of the first OIC and became a memorial for the work he put in during the setting up of the facility. Besides working at WANSF, he also had duties as the Command Engineer at HMAS *Leeuwin*. There is a sign with his name alongside of the road pointing to the site.

Associate Membership

Early on it was decided that we would limit Associate Membership to be no more than the number of full members. I believe the only exceptions were the two civilian doctors who came and provided Medical Services and who were treated as full members and others, what I would call special Associate members. They were the Shire Clerk and one of the Councillors who had served in HMAS *Hobart* in World War II. There were three Housing and Construction Officers that had been very involved with Base Construction who were made Special Associate members also.

The State Director/Overall Manager of Housing and Construction, WA, who was responsible for the overall development of the Base, was married to a Vivian Bullwinkel. She had been shot with a few other Nurses and left to drown, if still alive, off a beach north of Australia. She survived insurmountable horrors until the end of the war in 1945. Most of the people she met along the way didn't make it and are remembered through her testament. It is an astonishing tale that is documented and can be found by writing her name into Google.

The Wardroom was honoured to make her and her husband Associate Members.

Port Service Officer Arrival. (PSO)

The officer who was to run the Port Services duly arrived, and I took him and introduced him to the OIC. Then we had a chat about his job. I briefed him on what was going on and left him to go and look at his area of responsibility. I indicated to him where the Wardroom was and that we all met there at lunchtime. He went on his way while I got on with what I had to do.

Members were having a lunchtime drink in the temporary Wardroom when the new officer arrived at the door. The officer was about to walk in when the OIC said, "Who are you, and what do you want?"

The officer was taken aback, having previously been introduced to the OIC. Fortunately, one of the officers present got up and escorted the new officer away, having realised the OIC was making a point.

A few minutes later, the PSO arrived at the door again, and the OIC repeated his question. The PSO says, "I have just come up through it."

OIC: "Up through what?"

Officer: "The Hawse Pipe."

OIC: "Where was it?"

PSO: "At the end of Submarine Wharf."

OIC: "You'll do," and so the new officer was welcomed into the Special Duties Branch as an Associate member. 'Special Duties' was applied to those officers who had been promoted from the lower deck. The new officer had come up through the Naval Officer training system.

Wardroom Acceptance

Finally, the day came when the Navy accepted the Wardroom and Officers' accommodation. By this time another officer had joined. Members of the mess and all were involved in transferring the drinks from the first Wardroom to our new facility. We were all waiting to have a drink in the new Wardroom.

The day we opened the bar for the first time, our Naval Nurse arrived.

Naval Nurse Arrival

My office was adjacent to the Naval Police Office, as previously stated. Just as I was about to get into my car to go and have my first drink in the Wardroom, I was advised by the Naval Police that the new Naval Nursing Sister was at the front gate with another Nursing Sister from HMAS *Leeuwin* and had been allowed through with directions to the Wardroom. I was advised she was driving a yellow Celica. I decided to wait in my car just outside the dockyard gate and, as they approached, I got out of my car and welcomed them, telling them to follow me to the Wardroom. I should state here it was a terribly hot day, well over the old hundred.

On arrival in the Wardroom, I asked them what they would like to drink, and, from memory, one ordered a brandy and dry and the other nurse a whiskey with suitable mix. I called the order to the person behind the bar, and he held up a beer can. I got the message there was only beer in the bar at that time. I nodded okay.

Shortly after he arrived with three very cold glasses of beer on a silver tray. The new Naval Nurse said in a very haughty tone, "I don't drink beer."

My reply: "Are you thirsty?"

Her reply: "Yes, I am."

My comment was, "You will have to drink beer or water as we only just opened the bar a few minutes before you arrived and we only have beer."

She grudgingly decided to try the beer as did the nurse accompanying her.

Before this little scene, and immediately after, I had listened to a torrent of complaints about how her car, which had accompanied her on the train, had been covered in diesel exhaust fumes and was quite dirty when she went to pick it up. She informed me that she had spent the morning complaining to the Railway Authorities to try to get something done about it.

The tirade stopped when the barman appeared with a silver tray with the whiskey and brandy drinks they had ordered.

The two nurses were impressed.

The barman had rushed over to the nearby Senior Sailors Mess, had obtained brandy and whiskey bottles and mixers. Such was the way we began and carried on the operation of the Wardroom.

Breakfast

I have not mentioned previously that I used to leave home at about 4:30 am and arrive at the Base at about 5 am. The reason for this was that most days, Service representatives on the East Coast rang up and wanted to talk to me. They forgot the three hour time difference (or two in winter) between the East and West Coasts.

The other reason was that visitors from the east wanted to see the Base. My early arrival allowed me to clear my in-tray of anything needing immediate attention before being a Tourist Guide for one or more visitors to see the Base during the day.

I would take a break to have breakfast on board.

New Nurse Complaint

The morning after our new Nurse arrived, she joined me for breakfast. When I asked how she was settling in, she complained that her cabin had not been cleaned properly and that she had spent a long time getting it clean before she could go to bed.

I said I was sorry to hear that.

I had specifically had sailors clean the cabin and I had checked for any dust etc. on shelves, on tops of lockers etc. Later I discovered she was an Operating theatre nurse where everything had to be more than spotless.

Lunch Time

At lunch time it was the custom to meet at the bar and have a drink and discuss anything that needed to be brought up rather than have formal meetings. This arrangement worked quite well and provided me with an understanding of what was happening in the other areas.

On the first lunchtime after her arrival, our new Nursing sister bounced into the bar area and, within minutes, commented that we needed a Social Secretary. One of the others at the bar said,

"What a good idea!" and seconded that.

I asked all to vote by show of hands. All hands went up and when the Nurse asked who it was that had been elected, she was told she was it. I can still hear her words "Men!"

I then pointed out each of us was very busy in our areas and had no time to worry about a social programme and that she would have the least work. She accepted the position with some reluctance and insisted we were all to support her with whatever she came up with. We all promised to support her, and we did.

With the assistance of one of the doctor's wives, she produced some wonderful themes for functions in the Wardroom.

Only this year, 2023, during my customary call to check how she was doing, she informed me that HMAS *Stirling* Wardroom Mess was the best she had been in. I pointed out that it was because of her and a local doctor's wife, who helped her.

Associate Members

Not previously mentioned, before we opened the Wardroom Bar, the Department of Housing and Construction (DHC) managers, and those visiting the Base, would join us for our lunchtime drinks. With the opening of the Wardroom, I proposed to my fellow officers that the DHC Officers be offered Honorary Associate Membership of the Wardroom. I had a seconder. All officers agreed and they proved to be great supporters of the Wardroom and its social functions.

Social programme

As mentioned earlier, I could not have had a better Social Secretary than the Nurse. She soon developed a programme, and from memory, the first item was a formal Mess Dinner so that the wives and girlfriends could get to know one another and the people their partners would be working with.

Mess Dinner

The first Mess Dinner in the Wardroom presented the odd problem in that we didn't have enough stewards, so I arranged that the drinks (bottles) of red and white wine were to be placed on the table and should another bottle be required they would indicate to the steward, and it would be replaced.

Before the dinner started, my efficient Social Secretary came and asked if I was aware that several of the wives were pregnant. I said that, of course, I would make a break available between courses for them.

In reply, I said I was very aware of the pregnant wives, and smiling, said this would be a normal Naval Mess Dinner. The protocol of a Naval Mess Dinner was that no one left the table until after the Loyal Toast at the end of the meal. She took this to mean that I would not be having breaks between each of the courses. She said a few words under a breath and left being very unhappy at my response.

After the first course was served, I advised the gathering, that those who needed to, could leave the table. Smokers, however, were to remain where they were. The Social Secretary came up and made a few uncomplimentary remarks about me knowing I was to make a break and leading her to believe otherwise.

When all had returned to the table, I asked the men to move two seats to their left so they could get to know other members and partners. This was replicated after the main course and worked well. The Social Secretary was happy. However, one officer, who had recently joined, did complain that he was not there to escort his wife from the table when the meal finished. I smiled and asked if he had enjoyed the dinner.

Note: I will name some other functions to give some idea of the standard of the planning that went into entertaining in the mess. I did not take part in the planning or preparation for these functions leaving it to the Social Secretary. She roped in others to assist.

Movie Theme

The instructions for this function were to wear something representing one of your favourite movies. One member came dressed as Doctor Zhivago, another represented a Ribbon around an old Oak tree, and others represented the main or other characters of a movie.

At another function, the organisers had set up an exhibit from tree branches and it formed a sort of pyramid about two and a half metres high. The organisers had placed a full-sized replica of a Cockatoo in the foliage. As people passed by, the Cocky would exclaim "pretty cocky" or "cocky needs a drink" or for some comment about what people were wearing. It startled a few people, who initially thought it was a real cockatoo. However, it was one of the Sub Lieutenants who was inside the tree mock-up.

On another, it was "What were you wearing when the ship went down?"

I'll leave it to you to guess the state of dress. When Joan and I arrived, we found the front door of the Mess locked and in darkness. On walking around the side of the mess there was a gangway that one had to pass over to join the ship (mess). As I entered the Mess, I noticed a black plastic sheeting covering the entrance hallway from the front door. I didn't ask questions.

When the bell rang, advising the ship to be abandoned, a fully inflated life raft appeared from behind the black sheeting. Everyone had to crawl through the raft to the land (three steps to the dining room area). Here, there was no seating, except for the pregnant and unwell Commodore's wife.

The Commodore tried to stop his wife going through the life raft to no available. (A Kalgoorlie Girl from where I come from).

Welcome Back to Crab Day

At the time it was possible to catch blue manna crabs in Cockburn Sound in the area near the Base. Some members and partners would swim behind the dinghy and catch the crabs by hand, passing into the boat the only crabs retained, being male. Females were released. This practice led to the introduction of "the welcome back Cray luncheon". I will note here that once the crabs were caught, they were held in a refrigerator space until the day arrived when they would be cooked along with crayfish and other seafood, mussels, oysters and the like that had been caught or located off Garden Island by Mess members.

Wine and Press Club

I can't quite remember how we came to invite members of the Wine and Press Club to a game of cricket and the sampling of their products.

The cricket match started after welcoming drinks. Each member of the team had to have a bat and bowl three overs. After each three overs, there would be a drink break, if required by the heat, before resuming the game. On most occasions, it ended in a draw or close finish.

It would then be time to return to the Wardroom patio and taste the wines the Press Club had brought. The barbecue worked furiously to provide the food. Some great friendships developed, and I'm sure our Wine Caterer was well looked after during his visits to their businesses and also the selection and price of the wines purchased by the Mess.

Vessels Visiting

On one occasion an American nuclear submarine berthed at Stirling for Rest and Recreation and for some crew changes. For obvious reasons, security was taken to a higher level because of the risk of protesters, etc. I seem to recall that the initial risk area, if there had been a nuclear incident, was just short of the Rockingham shoreline. I cannot recall one instance of any nuclear incident whilst I was at the Base.

One of the Oberon Class, Australian submarines on passage from England to Sydney, stopped over at the Base. The crew were billeted in the Junior and Senior Sailors Accommodation and the officers in the Wardroom. We made them feel very welcome. After a long period at sea, they partied hard. The next morning, I smilingly suggested that I place a cabin number in braille about 25 cm above the passage floor for those who had to crawl their cabin.

As I write this, I wonder how the present-day Navy hierarchy would react. I understand that if you have a drink at lunchtime, you are not supposed to go back to work.

USN Assault Vessel

The Americans requested permission from the RAN for one of their Assault Vessels to berth at the Base and land all their assault vehicles, tanks, halftracks, jeeps, etc. This required a modification at the shore end of the Submarine wharf that was quickly organised and built by DHC in readiness for the visit.

The American officers were entertained in the Wardroom and used the Wardroom facilities; their ship's crew used the Senior and Junior Sailors recreational messes.

Chairman of Housing Complaints Committee

During all that was going on, a letter arrived on my desk stating that I was the Chairman of the Housing Complaints Committee and making me aware of an impending rental rise and that I may have some complaints to deal with. I was quite surprised to receive this letter and to know that I was the Chairman of this Committee as no one had ever thought to tell me about it as part of my job.

I did not expect any complaints from anyone in the Married Quarters as they were all brand new when first occupied by the Base's personnel, whilst others lived in private rentals.

However, the letter caused me to take time out from thinking of the Base and its Commissioning to think about a more permanent home for my family, as I expected to retire in Western Australia when it was time to leave the Base.

House Hunting

Following a discussion with Joan, we went to one of the local Real Estate Agents in the area, trading as Summit Realty. Using our experience of buying a house in Sydney and Canberra, we first looked at the various house plans and visited some of the homes built by Summit. We also were shown some of the land they had for sale and settled on a block at No 8 Caribbean Drive, Safety Bay.

This was a developing suburb, and our house was one of the early ones built in the area.

I don't have the exact details, but from memory, the block cost a little over $11,000, and the house was built for something like $18 - $20,000. Thanks to a friendly Bank Manager (himself a World War II veteran), we were able to get a loan and sign the contract for the house and land.

I can't remember the date the house was completed and handed over to us. (Early 1978)

Cyclone Alby

We were certainly living in it when a Category Five cyclone named Alby passed just off the coast of Rockingham, about the 2$^{nd\ of}$ April 1978. Two things I remember was that the paint on the large H crossbar of the carport was embedded with sand particles from vacant land to the west of our house. The second was that the panels making up the eaves at the front of the house had not been properly secured and, at times, I thought they would be blown away or broken, allowing the wind to get up under the roof. However, a higher authority was looking after us. A late-night call from the Duty Watch had me driving across the causeway to the base at around 2 am, dodging rocks on the roadway with waves breaking over the car.

Water Bore

I was talking to a Senior Naval Policeman from the base and found out that he was prepared to help me set up a water bore to enable me to water the lawns and gardens back and front of the house. When digging the well for the water pump, I found out that the water table was not very far down and in no time at all we had a working bore, and I was able to run distribution pipes to the front and back of the house and soon had the front and back lawns growing and the flowerbeds along the fences coming along nicely.

Joan had settled in quite well. She had become a member of the Ladies Inner Wheel Club associated with the Rotary Club I belonged to. She joined a Mahjong group and the Red Cross group. She was still involved with the Naval Wives Group.

She came to all the functions we ran on the Base and was a great support to me.

COMMISSIONING

Preparation for Commissioning

Let me now turn to Commissioning.

The original Commissioning Date was to be at the beginning of June 1978. However, due to the Chief of Naval Staff's absence overseas at that time, the date was deferred until the 28th of July of that year.

Basic planning began in earnest for the Commissioning Ceremony and Celebrations at the beginning of 1978. At this time, only six or seven officers had been posted to the Base. By the Commissioning date, about fourteen officers had been posted.

During the planning phase, we were advised that the guest list for the Commissioning could be in the order of around 400. That presented a problem in two ways. Firstly, it would be impossible to entertain 400 people in the Wardroom and secondly fourteen officers would each be required to look after 25 to 30 of the guests.

I decided that if we divided the guests into two groups, one of two-thirds and the other one-third, it would be possible to use both the Senior Sailors Mess for the two-thirds and the Wardroom for the one-third.

An option was to ask for officers from HMAS *Leeuwin* to be made available. This would interfere with Junior Recruit training at that facility, and I didn't want to interrupt that training if I could help. Also, it would mean having to brief them on the base.

I wanted to present the Base and its people to the visitors. And it would be necessary to give a detailed brief to these officers before the event.

I had been watching and studying the Senior Sailors who were posted to the Base and had formed an opinion of their various abilities. I decided that they should be given the opportunity to show their potential and be an advertisement for the Base. I approached the Commodore, then Commanding HMAS *Leeuwin*, knowing he would be transferring and becoming the first Commanding Officer of HMAS *Stirling*, the name the Base was to become on Commissioning. I explained the problem of having to split the guests into two groups and that I would have to use the Wardroom and the Senior Sailors mess to avoid overcrowding one venue.

I also asked if I could have the Chief of Naval Staff in the Wardroom group so that he could officially open the Wardroom on the day of Commissioning.

He also accepted my proposal to use the Chiefs and Petty Officers to supplement the fourteen officers. He also agreed that the Chief of Naval staff would be in the guest list for the Wardroom.

Guard

The Commissioning Guard was selected and began training for the occasion. Over time and practice, they were presentable for the proposed gathering of VIPs. However, the Guard Officer, who had little experience of saluting with his sword, had some problems, as he would be looking left as he made the salute.

On the day before Commissioning the Commodore came to check that all was in place for the following day and watch the Guard do their March Past of the VIP saluting position. The Guard Officer's salute was certainly not up to standard, and the Commodore was not impressed and suggested more training for the guard to get it right. My comment was that, because they been practising for some time, it would be better to let them fall out and I would ensure, as much as I could, that the Guard Officer got things correct on the day.

Other Planning

Lunch. The Supply Officer and his Staff organised the meal that would be served for lunch on Commissioning Day.

Commissioning Wines. I discussed with the Wardroom Bar Manager wines for the function, and I agreed for him to go ashore and see if he could arrange a deal for a suitable wine, with labelling, to commemorate the Commissioning.

I allowed him to approach the various wine providers and see if he could come up with a decent wine at a reasonable price. I didn't ask the details of how he got to make his selection. He came back with the information that a particular company had a three-quarter pallet load at a very reasonable price, and they would arrange suitable labelling. However, the cost was quite a bit more than we had in the kitty and that posed a problem.

I discussed the issue with my fellow officers, and I made an offer to provide an interest-free loan of $500 to cover the costs of getting the wine and other incidentals. The conditions were that the loan would be repaid when there were sufficient funds available. After some discussion this proposal was agreed, and we were able to purchase the pallet of wine.

I'll leave it to you to appreciate there was much work to be done to prepare the Base for Commissioning. I've already mentioned the Guard.

Senior Sailors Briefing

This briefing clarified and provided details of what they were being required to do. I emphasised the correct form of address to be used, where appropriate. I also advised them that their wives and partners were considered part of the Stirling complement.

At that time the Navy had not changed the Warrant Officer rank, so it was not the same as the Army and Air Force. The senior lower deck rank was Chief Petty Officer.

Naval HQ Western Australia.

A separate building for the Naval Officer Commanding the West Australian Area (NOCWA) had been provided for in the planning and had been completed before Commissioning. It contained a large auditorium. As commented on earlier,, NOCWA was based at HMAS *Leeuwin*. However, Navy Office hierarchy decreed he was to transfer to the base before the Commissioning Day. That came to pass a few days before the Commissioning, and I think the Commodore was particularly happy to make the move.

Guest Cards

On entering the base, each visitor was given a coloured card with a bus number on it, parking instructions and luncheon venue. There were two colours. One indicated the Senior Sailors Mess for parking and lunch, the other the Wardroom for parking and lunch.

Parking

Planning of guest parking was that, depending on the colour of the card, the guests would be directed to either the Wardroom or Seniors Sailors Mess parking area and a bus would take them to the Commissioning site. On arrival, there they would be led to their seats.

Commissioning Ceremony

This was relatively straightforward and required a dais with microphone, loudspeakers, suitable seating, and the other minor preparation needed. It went without a hitch, and even the Guard Officer got his salute right.

VIP Briefing

A briefing, based on the briefing given to the Ship's Company as they joined the Base, would be given to the VIPs outlining what the Base was required to do. It was delivered by yours truly in the Auditorium of the Naval Officer Commanding Building, a short walk from the Commissioning ceremony site.

This briefing was followed by a bus tour of the Base and Island, with a guide to explain what people were seeing. The coloured card gave the bus number to board. At the end of the tour, they would be disembarked at their allotted luncheon venue as per the card colour stated previously.)

There is one last item to mention before we move to the period after Commissioning.

Senior Officer Query

Late on the afternoon of the day before Commissioning, I received a phone call from Head Office in Canberra, from a very Senior Officer, asking if it was true that Chiefs and Petty Officers would be helping entertain the guests and did the Commodore know.

My affirmative reply was that he was very much aware of it and agreed with the use of those people. I think he was very unhappy at my reply and put the phone down and was no doubt thinking the Commodore was mad to agree to such a situation.

Commissioning Day

It was a beautiful West Australian clear sky day for the Commissioning Ceremony. As I drove to the Base, I went through the whole day's programme in my mind, looking for something I might have overlooked. By the time I had arrived at the Base I was confident that the planning had covered all the bases.

All the Officers and Senior sailors were assembled, and I went through the broad outline of the programme. Each was allocated a task, particularly that of looking after the VIPs. After the briefing, one officer approached me, saying I had not given him a job.

He had recently joined, and I said, "You are the Duty Officer of the Day. Your job is to get a staff car and proceed to a particular hotel in central Perth and get all the Admirals and their wives onto a bus that has been ordered."

After parking his car, and checking the bus was ready, he entered the hotel lobby to find the Admirals lined up on one side of the lobby and the wives on the other. He reported to the senior Admiral and advised that he was there to escort them to the Commissioning Ceremony and the bus was waiting.

The senior Admiral called, "Admirals and Wives, attention, right and left turn, quick march" and proceeded to exit the hotel into the bus. The two lines reached the door of the bus together. The lines were set up so that partners were in the same position in the lines and boarded the bus together. I cannot recall ever hearing of such an incident before. I can't image what the staff and other guests in the hotel lobby would have thought.

Note. Later, this officer and myself were to become good friends, and, as I write this, he could be called my mentor as on each Monday, unless there is an RSL or other meeting, we have coffee after his gym session. It was during one of these coffee times he recounted his getting the Admirals onto the bus.

As we waited for the last two VIPs to arrive, I went and sat in a chair that was some distance to the side of the dais. As I sat back relaxing, a newspaper reporter I knew was passing by me and made a comment along lines of how I was getting on. My reply was that there was nothing I could do now, except keep my fingers crossed that the ceremony would proceed as planned. He laughed and carried on his way to take more pictures of the next two VIPs to arrive.

The Chief of Naval Staff arrived and was shown to his seat. He was soon followed by the Minister for Defence and, once he was greeted and seated, the Commissioning Ceremony began.

Commissioning Ceremony

The Commodore stood and addressed those present and read the Commissioning Order; the White Ensign was hoisted, and the Commodore said a few words of welcome to the gathering.

The next to speak was the Chief of Naval Staff, followed by the defence minister. On the completion of his address, the parade was called to attention, the Guard and Band marched past the dais saluting the Chief of Naval staff and Defence Minister. The Officer of the Guard's salute was quite acceptable and justified my previous day's action.

Briefing

Upon completion of the Commissioning Ceremony, all the guests were escorted to the Operations Room in the Naval Officer in Charge of WA building where there was tiered seating for all the guests.

After an introduction, I began my lecture, and everything was proceeding smoothly until it came for the projector team to show the first slide. For some reason, the projector failed to operate despite having been checked before the briefing.

For the first time and only time, in my many years of standing in front of people, I had not prepared any visual aids in case of such an event. It seemed an eternity before the projector started to work and I was just about to go on without any visual aids when it came on.

(I'm sure that the Supreme Boss upstairs was making a point that he was in charge as he had done many times during my career and continues to do so now from time to time).

Tour of Base

On completion of the briefing, the guests were escorted to the buses, dependant on their luncheon venue. An Officer or Senior Sailor gave them a commentary as they were driven around the Base. You can imagine the number of buses required. I had planned that the buses would start their tour from different points and proceed in a circular path so all would finish back at the appropriate Mess, where they were to have lunch at about the same time. From comments I received, everyone was very happy with the tour and the commentary given by the Officer or Senior Sailor on each bus. The colour code on their invitations worked well in getting the buses and guests to the right venue for lunch.

Wardroom Official Opening

Once all the guests had arrived at the Wardroom, the Chief of Naval Staff officially opened the Mess and unveiled the plaque recording the event.

Everything was going quite well in the Wardroom – everyone had a drink in their hand and mixing well. They were advised of the time that lunch would be served. At that stage, I decided to visit the Senior Sailors Mess to make sure that everything was going well there.

I should make note here that, for very senior VIPs, I had an Officer or Senior Sailor acting as their Shepherd and making sure they had a drink and company to talk to.

As I did the rounds saying hello to people, I noticed that the Secretary of Defence and his wife were seated on a lounge with no drink and no Shepherd. I introduced myself and asked if they were okay and if I could do anything for them. The Secretary smiled and told me that both he and his wife were quite happy, they had been informed what time lunch was to be served, and he had sent my Shepherd to look after others.

I got the impression they were quite happy to watch the passing parade and observe people. With all going well, I then returned to the Wardroom. Shortly after, lunch was served.

Towards the end of my meal, a Steward appeared and said that the Secretary of Defence would like to see me. I was a bit intrigued and wondered if there had been something that had displeased him.

However, when I got to speak to him and asked if something was wrong, he replied no, he had sent for me to ask if it was possible for him to purchase some of the Commissioning Wine. I assured him that was no problem, and he gave me an order, which was for several bottles. I arranged for his Shepherd to collect the number of wines in a box and arrange with his driver to put them in his car. Payment was forthcoming and I thanked the Secretary, who advised me that he and his wife had enjoyed the wine and the day. His contribution helped add to our very small funds available at that time.

While some officers, who lived on board, and others, continued to party, most were quite happy to go home and enjoy a quiet night or party ashore with some of their friends from the Base.

Operation of Naval Support Facility

From the 29th of June, 1978, HMAS *Stirling* began as a Commissioned Naval Support Facility. I am not going to go into the day-to-day activities, except I kept up with the briefing notes I had used from the beginning of my tenure to introduce new arrivals of what the Base was about and their place in the scheme of things.

Perhaps the most important event was the posting out of the Commodore and his replacement.

Commodore Posting

My flimsy shows he finished on the 7th of January 1978, and left for the Eastern States on a new posting. I think that was to lead to his retirement. Yours truly was appointed Commanding Officer from 8th January until 1st February 1979 when the new Commodore would arrive from overseas, where he had been the Naval Attaché in Washington.

COMMANDING OFFICER'S COMMENTS

TO MY ENTIRE SATISFACTION.

AN EXTREMELY DILIGENT AND ZEALOUS OFFICER WITH A RARE DEPTH OF SERVICE KNOWLEDGE AND EXCELLENT ADMINISTRATIVE ABILITY.

IT IS MAINLY THROUGH HIS CONTINUING EFFORTS THAT STIRLING HAS COMMISSIONED AND IS OPERATING ON A SOUND BASIS.

New Commanding Officer

One Sunday, I was relaxing at home with the family when I received a phone call from the Duty Officer. He told me that a sports car, with a bare-chested man with a woman beside him, had arrived at the Police Post at the beginning of the Causeway, informing the Naval Policeman on duty that he was the new Commanding Officer and he wanted access to show the Base to his wife.

When asked for official identification he had none, only a driver's licence with his name. The Duty Officer was concerned that he had done the right thing in allowing him to come on board without the proper identification. He gave me a brief description of the person. I told him it was okay because I recognised the person he described as someone I had served with in HMAS *Vengeance* and HMAS *Watson* when he was a Lieutenant who had recently returned to Australia from England.

The following day, the new Commodore arrived in uniform and with proper identification. He was in his official staff car, driven by one of my sailors. I was able to meet him at the Dockyard Gate and take him to his office.

Later, when I met his wife, we reminisced about Kalgoorlie, where we had both come from. I returned to my role as the Executive Officer.

The Commodore's home was in one of Perth's suburbs. Many of his Naval and Social commitments were in the actual Perth area and he decided that, when he was required to meet any of these commitments, he would remain in Perth on that day. The Courier, usually his driver, would deliver any official correspondence that he needed to deal with.

To ensure proper security of the documents a suitable safe was provided at his home for this purpose.

There were also occasions when he visited outside of Perth. When he was away, the Captain of HMAS Leeuwin would be contacted if necessary. I was left to make sure that everything was running as it was supposed to. That suited me fine. I would contact him should anything arise that he should be informed about.

Commodore's Cuddy

The Commodore had his own Accommodation and Dining area and usually entertained his guests there. These facilities were located on the ground floor at the far end of the Officers Accommodation Building adjacent to the Wardroom.

Induction of a Special Member

One day the Commodore asked if he could have lunch in the Wardroom with a guest. He indicated he would like me to have lunch with them. This request was a bit unusual, as normally he would not come into the Wardroom unless he was invited. I was intrigued and agreed to his request.

On their arrival, he introduced his guest whose name was Leon Goldsworthy, who was one of the most highly decorated Australian Naval Officers of WWII. He had been awarded the George Cross and George Medal for his clearing of mines and the like. I felt very privileged to have him lunching in the Wardroom. During the conversation I learnt that, after leaving the Navy, he had never been a member of a Wardroom Mess. My intrigue was answered.

During the meal, I excused myself and went down to the bar where all the other officers were having a drink and exchanging pleasantries. I indicated to them who the Commodore's distinguished guest was and that he had never been a member of a Wardroom Mess since leaving the Navy at the end of World War II.

I indicated I would be pleased to have him as an Associate Member of our Mess and asked for a seconder to my proposal. This was forthcoming, and all voted to invite him to become one of our members. I promptly asked the Treasurer for a Mess number and returned to my lunch.

I formerly invited Leon to become an Associate Member of the Mess if he so desired. Leon promptly agreed. I then produced his Mess number to use from then on, but not on that day.

After he had finished lunch, I invited the Commodore and Leon to come and meet the other mess members and they made him most welcome. Leon was a character, and his wife was good company. They fitted well as members of the Mess. Each month they came to our monthly luncheons.

I can't remember exactly how many months later, I noticed the wife was a bit terse with Leon. I sat with her and indicated that I sensed a problem and asked was it had anything to do with the Mess. Her reply was no, the problem was that she enjoyed having a drink and socialising and that was constrained by the fact she had to drive Leon to and from to attend the functions. I silently decided to do something about this situation.

We had a courier who regularly drove to Perth to the Department of Housing and Construction HQ to take or collect correspondence. Leon's home was almost on the route the driver took on these runs; I arranged for Leon and his wife to be picked up and brought to the Base on the courier's return trip. One of the other Associate members would take them home after the event. I felt this was the least I could do for an Australian Naval hero and his wife.

Operation of Base

Before commissioning, as previously mentioned in the WANSF chapter, all Departments – Supply Engineering, Port Services and Naval Police – operated broadly as a single entity and people in charge of these departments, and their staff, freely asked one another for assistance if required without the usual formalities of paperwork.

In my case, whenever someone was leaving, I had a plaque or other suitable item made to present to the officers departing. I would arrange with the Shipwright shop to produce what I wanted. I would fill out the necessary form and drop it in the Engineer Officer's tray so he was aware of my request. Sometimes, he couldn't find it because it was in the bottom of his tray.

After Commissioning, things changed. The first officer to be posted to the Base whispered in my ear that in future I'd have to talk to his boss before he could do anything for me. I told him I understood and, from then on, I would have to go and personally consult the Head of that department if I needed something, particularly if it was urgent.

There came a time when I felt I had to clear the air. I went to a particular Head of Department and pointed out that we had to work together as a team if we were to get things done. After some discussion, he agreed, and from then on, things settled down and worked well.

Army and Other Functions

There were several occasions when the Commodore had received invitations that he could not attend because he was already committed elsewhere, and I would be asked to represent him. On one occasion, I had to attend an Army luncheon in Perth on his behalf.

The officer who was looking after me and sat with me at lunch, found out I was from HMAS *Stirling* on Garden Island. He asked me quite a few questions about the island as he had served there during World War II. In particular, he asked if there was still a water bore and tank towards the north end of the island. When I told him yes, he was a bit surprised, and I asked if he would like to come and have lunch with me and look around the Base. He accepted the offer.

When he arrived at the base, I took him in my car to the area where the water bore was. As we walked into the area, he pointed in one direction and said there used to be a creek there that took any overflow away. I pointed out it was still there, a bit overgrown but visible. He then said there used to be a water tank on a tank stand pointing back over his shoulder, and I told him to turn around because the tank and stand were still there.

Over lunch, he made the comment that during WWII, there had been heavy guns placed on the island as part of the Fremantle Port Defence. He regaled me with an incident where a gun barrel was brought over to the island on a barge that came alongside the small wharf that had been built. The mobile crane was hooked on to lift the barrel off the barge. As it strained with the lift, the crane suddenly disappeared over the side of the wharf and landed on the barge. Apparently, someone had forgotten to break the welds holding the gun on the barge.

Other Activities

I will leave it to you to visualise the day-to-day operations of the base with ships berthing and leaving. HMAS *Diamantina*, a Survey ship, was based at HMAS *Stirling* and made regular visits for fuel and stores.

Paydays

Each payday sailors would line up before a table where a Supply Officer would have their pay envelopes. The sailor would approach the table, take off his cap, give his name, and the Paymaster would place the envelope on the top of the cap with the sailor placing his hand over it so it didn't fall off.

Before the pay line began moving, I would stand on a platform and address those present on any matters of concern or anything they should know about that was about to occur. In this way, I was able to keep them informed of what to expect in the coming weeks.

Road Traffic Briefing

Many of the personnel were from the Eastern States and not West Australian natives. With Christmas 1978 approaching I arranged for members of the West Australian Road Traffic Police Section to come and give everyone a briefing and especially emphasise the penalty for drinking and driving with a loss of points as well as any fine.

I sat in on the lecture and everyone was quite attentive and took in what was said. When the police asked if there was any questions on what they had presented, one sailor stood up and had a point or two clarified.

A few days later, my Coxswain informed me that a sailor had been picked up for drink-driving in the Rockingham Beach front area. It turned out to be sailor who had asked the question at the briefing. Apparently, the Police had pulled him over and cautioned him and told him to lock the car and not drive till the next morning. Stupidly, he subsequently unlocked and started driving the car and drove round the block onto the road right on the waterfront and was picked up again. Police couldn't believe it and charged and detained him.

Who can imagine how displeased I was. He was dealt with in accordance with Navy Rules and Regulations.

Here I should mention that the conduct of the sailors was very good and there were not many times that I had to see defaulters. I put this down to the briefings they were given on arrival and on paydays.

Family Activities

My son Peter had become very active with cricket and football and continues to this day. He also had started working as a motor mechanic. Daughter Anne was employed in the health department in Perth and Walter continued his schooling. I was home every night and came to know my children much better than previously.

General Comments

Looking back, all the long hours of planning and organising proved to be well rewarded by the way the Base ran during my tenure.

New Posting

Like all good times, they come to an end. I was coming up with one year to go before I would be retired at the age of 55. Out of the blue came a Posting Note to inform me I was to proceed to Exmouth, about 1200 kilometres north of Perth, and take over as Deputy Commander of the Joint United States and Australian Navies Communications Station run by the United States Navy with the RAN providing the Deputy Commander and supervising the Australian Naval Communication Centre on the Base.

My conversation with the Poster elicited that I had to go. So up bags, and with Joan and Walter in tow, we headed for Exmouth after handing over my duties at HMAS *Stirling* to my successor. My successor was offered my house to rent and took up the offer.

So goodbye, Stirling. Harold E Holt, here I come

Commanding officer's comments

To my entire satisfaction.

His efforts have shown excellent dividends with a very high standard of service being made available from HMAS Stirling. Recommended for promotion.

Chapter 40

Harold E Holt

19 December 1979 to 24 January 1982

Introduction

At the end of 1979, I was posted to the VLF Communication Station Harold E Holt, at Exmouth, named after an Australian Prime Minister. I was to be the Deputy Commander of the Base with a USN Captain in overall Command.

Exmouth

Where is Exmouth and how far from Perth? What was the Base established for?

Before commenting on my family and me, lets have some comments on this Base I was going to.

The town of Exmouth was built at the same time as the Communications Station to support the Base and house the dependent families of US Navy personnel and RAN families.

Family Situation

The only family living with me in Perth at the time of this posting was Walter and he accompanied Joan and me to Exmouth. Daughter Anne and Peter were working and living in Perth.

We were able to let our house, fully furnished, to my relief as XO of *Stirling* and his family. We were happy to have them as tenants.

It was then pack what we needed and store anything else not required in the house. Then with goods and chattels, we headed for Exmouth by car.

Travelling to Exmouth

I drove our car with Joan, Walter and our goods and chattels the 1248 kilometres from Perth. We stayed overnight in Carnarvon before completing the journey the next day.

On the road leading into Exmouth townsite, we passed the Exmouth Airport that had been built/used during WWII. It was near Exmouth that an Australian Air Ace, Bluey Truscott, crashed and was killed when he flew into the sea – a great loss to Australia. However, his name is remembered in the town with the Truscott Club named in his honour.

It is also the place that a Z Force operation began that was to sink ships in Singapore Harbour using a captured fishing boat named Krait.

Our New Home

We duly found the house allocated. A nice modern four-bedroom house with most amenities. No air conditioning but overhead fans in every room. This had been the house occupied by the Civilian Administrator for Exmouth in its early days of development. The town centre was only a short walk from the house. The Naval Base was some distance further away. I was the first Naval Officer to occupy this house.

The Town

The town had grown from basically nothing with construction of the Naval Base. It was a small town, very popular with tourists due to the excellent fishing. There was also a prawn industry based not far from the airport with a processing factory alongside the road leading into Exmouth. It was not unusual, when VIPs were visiting, for the Captain and self to be invited to join in the lunch and drinks on offer.

The two Hotel/Motels were the Pot Shot in the town, in the main shopping centre, and the second, Norcape Lodge, was a short distance away and closer to the beach. There was the usual butcher, baker and grocery Store, tourist Bureau, hairdresser, barber and other shops catering for the population and tourists. There was a racecourse, and races were held often and enjoyed on the day even though you might lose your money.

After arrival we visited the shops and purchased all the essentials.

Entrance to Naval Base

Naval Communications Base

Harold E Holt was a Joint Australian and United States Naval Communications Station located on the north-west coast of Australia, 1248km north of Perth and close to the town of Exmouth, Western Australia. The Base was maintained by the Australian Department of Defence on behalf of Australia and the United Sates.

It provided very low frequency (VLF) radio transmission to United States Navy, Royal Australian Navy and allied ships and submarines in the western Pacific Ocean and the eastern Indian Ocean. The frequency was 19.8 kHz. With a transmission power of 1 megawatt, it was the most powerful transmission station in the Southern Hemisphere.

Communication Centres

There were two Communication Centres, one operated by the RAN and the other much larger facility by the USN. Some Australian sailors worked in the USN Centre.

One of the Communication Channels was made available to the RAN for use in communicating with Australian Submarines. The USN centre had both USN ad RAN sailors working there. The RAN centre was RAN only, manned by RAN sailors under an RAN Communications Officer.

The Base employed Australian civilian support staff and RAN and staff to back up the US employees.

Taking Over

I contacted the person I was to relieve by visiting the Base and making my way to my future office. He broadly explained the working relationship between himself and the captain. He had some problems with the CO which I took on board and we then went and met the other RAN officers.

He took me to meet the captain and the introduction was pleasant and I made the comment that I looked forward to working with and for him. We then left his office, and I was taken to the RAN Communication Centre and met up with the RAN sailors on watch and the other Australian Officers. I visited the Very Low Frequency (VLF) complex and again both RAN and USN personnel worked alongside one another.

VLF Aerial Field

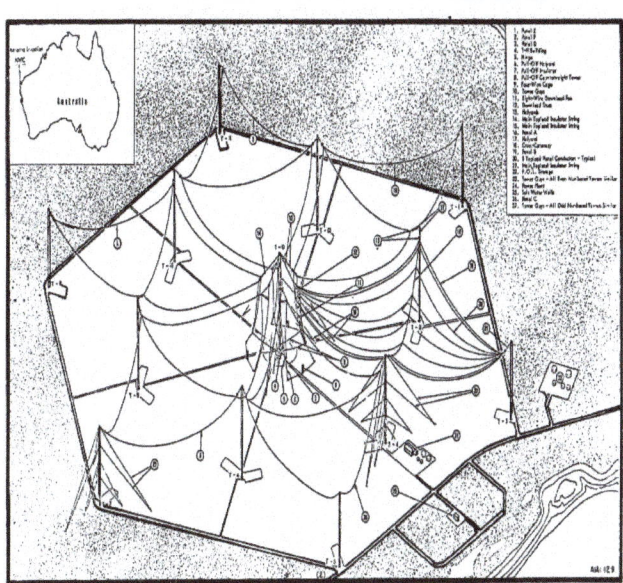

Three views of VLF aerial array layout and comprise three rings of aerials, each ring at a different height. In the upper picture, the control centre for the aerials can be seen. The Water Farm to cool the system was to the right of the upper picture and will be discussed later.

There was another communication equipment centre with High-Frequency (HF) communications and aerials some short distance away.

My Work

The job was that of any Executive Officer, being overseeing the Australian Navy personnel and looking after the cleanliness of facilities, especially the accommodation and other areas. Usually, I was accompanied by the Master Chief (USN) when I went into the USN Sailors accommodation blocks.

All the Australian officers and sailors were married, and to be at Exmouth, you had to be married. Their married quarters were basically fibro-built, while the Americans had brick houses and were located among the local population areas.

Sometime after I left there may have been brick houses for RAN personnel.

Local Community

I asked my predecessor about the locals. He replied he had found them friendly. He had been invited to join Rotary, as his predecessor had been a Rotarian. He suggested that, if asked, I should accept, as it provided access to a great group of people.

I accepted the turnover and bid my predecessor farewell. I also took possession of the Naval Car provided.

At the end of the day, I returned to the new home and relaxed, being very confident that I could do the job well.

Meeting the Locals

It did not take long before Joan and I, with Walter, visited the Pot Shot Inn for a drink and a meal. We were made most welcome, especially by the owner, who I found out later had run a hotel in Kalgoorlie. He was the Shire President and I think it was him who asked me to come along to a Rotary meeting. I accepted and started what turned out to be a long Rotary career and later Probus, where recently (2023), I was made a Life Member. I had run the Probus monthly raffle for something like forty years.

I found it an asset to belong to Rotary, and up until more recent years, I was a 100% attendee both in Exmouth and later, on return to Rockingham, where a new club was forming.

Church

There was a chapel on the base and a Catholic priest said Mass each week. It turned out he was also employed as a refueller at the Airport. Like many others in town, he was a character.

On one occasion, Bishop Witt visited and conducted a service. He was not a Catholic, but the captain insisted I attend. I found his sermon most interesting in what he said and how he delivered it. Instead of staying in the pulpit or on the altar to deliver his sermon, he bounced up and down the centre aisle, and you felt he was directly looking and talking to you.

Sports

Many Australian sailors and some Americans participated in an Australian Rules competition. Invariably, at the end of the game, they would retire to a drinking hole and get merry. I'll refer to an incident at a party later.

Soft Ball was popular. On one occasion I was conned to make up the numbers in a game, RAN v USN. I was fielding in the outfield when a ball was skied my way and I had to run hard to get under it. The wind kept it moving away slightly, and in a final attempt to catch it, I stretched a muscle in my leg and missed the catch. I had a very sore leg for some time.

Fishing

I found that on alternate weekends, a boat was available for fishing: one week, it was for USN use, and the other, for RAN use. I also found out that the captain was an avid fisherman.

Knowing my inability as an angler, I did not take advantage of going out when the Australians had the boat.

When the captain found out, he insisted he take me out. It was a bit on the rough ride, and the boat was close to a reef. Nothing was biting so it was decided to go closer inshore. I suggested we return to shore as there was a race day beckoning. Just then my reel went off and I jumped in the chair and secured the belt and began reeling in. My line was the middle of three over the back of the boat.

However, after a short time, I could not move the line and it was suggested I had caught a fish that had dived into cover. The line was about to be cut when a crewman said I see something. The boat was backed along the line, and I was then making some progress in pulling it in. Eventually, I got it alongside the boat, and it turned out to be a very big marlin. However, instead of removing the hook from its mouth, the hook was imbedded in the side of the fish.

The reason for it being hard to reel in was that it was like a sea anchor. My line was in the middle of three and was less of distance from the boat from the other two. One of the sailors said it must have been going for one of the outside lines and got my hook in its side. The crew managed to get it on board. Everyone was happy for me.

It turned out to be bigger than the one the captain's wife held the record for, and she never spoke to me again.

The finale to all this was when we arrived back alongside. I was helped to take the fish out of the boat onto the jetty and then left with fish and no one to help me. Fortunately, one of the American officers I was friendly with came to my aid. Between us, we carved up the fish on the spot, and I shared the fish pieces with him. Joan and I had beautiful fish for a considerable period. I was never asked to come fishing again.

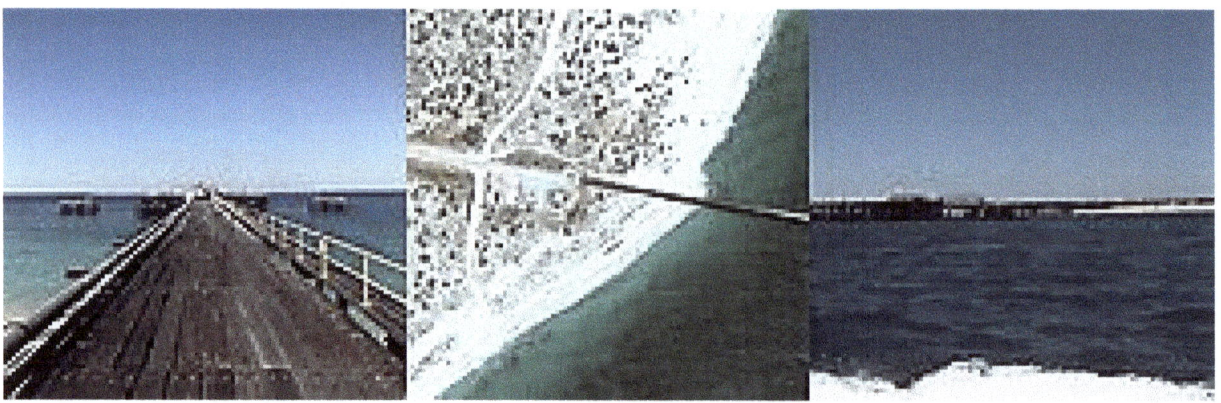
HEH Pier

Ship Visits

From time to time, a US Stores vessel would arrive at the wharf and it was interesting to see the efforts made to unload it as quickly as possible and get the stores and equipment back to the Base.

Occasionally, an RAN ship would visit and hold a Cocktail party on boar,d entertaining VIPs in the Exmouth and USN Community. I enjoyed these visits, especially being able to take Joan to the Cocktail Parties.

Alcohol Counsellors

One of the things I found interesting was that there was a Chief USN who had been an alcoholic and who, on recovery, became an alcohol counsellor. His job was to deal with those with an alcoholic problem. They took steps to refer personnel with a problem to the counsellor and were warned not to drink and to participate in an anti-alcohol programme.

I became aware on the grapevine that those in the rehab programme were required to take anti-alcohol medicine daily. I also learnt that some smart persons, invariably took something that made them throw up the medicine, and they could continue drinking later in the day.

In some ways, I was amused as in most, if not all sailor's cabins, there was a small fridge, and it was not uncommon to see bottles of alcohol on the top of this unit. I kept my mouth shut.

One Incident. The Australians, with some USN sailors, played in the local Australian Rules competition, and, after the match, there was usually a drinks session in the Pot Shot or elsewhere. It was not uncommon for people to overindulge after a match. I usually checked in the Australian Com Centre to ensure my people on watch had not overindulged before coming on watch.

I had found that there were USN sailors who came from an area in America where drinking was frowned on. On one occasion, whilst attending a BBQ, I noticed a very young USN sailor, who I had got to know, had been to a football match and joined in the drinking, probably his first taste. Not being used to alcohol, it didn't take much to affect him. He arrived at the BBQ I was at and was staggering around.

The captain was at the BBQ and noticed this lad and made a comment about him being drunk. I said he was only putting on an act, and the captain didn't say anything. I drew a USN sailor aside and told him to get rid of the drunk quick time, and this was done. Later, I counselled the sailor concerned about alcohol and what would happen to him if he was found to have over-imbibed again.

Truscott Club

From time to time, Joan and I would visit this Club and became part of the regular users. We became friends with those who used the club and enjoyed the company.

Pot Shot

Joan and I were regulars at the Pot Shot for a drink and a meal and became very friendly with the locals and occasionally a visitor or two.

Prawn Factory

The Exmouth area was known for its prawns and there was factory near the airport where you could get some for home use. In addition, VIPs were usually entertained to lunch there. Invariably, the captain, and I would be invited to attend the luncheon. I usually bought some home for Joan, Walter and me to have. Being newly caught, they were excellent to eat.

Race Day

There were regular race meetings at the local racetrack, and Joan and I would enjoy the day and try to pick a winner or two. It was at one of those events that brought back my selling race books at the Kalgoorlie races to earn a bob or two to pay for my attending the Boy Scouts Jamborette in Perth each year.

Report of Proceedings

At the end of March, July, September, and December, I was required to submit a report on the activities of the RAN contingent, equipment, Operations, and the team's Health and Welfare. A copy was given to the captain for information.

In my first report, I mentioned that I had settled in well and had not encountered any problems, as my predecessor had commented. The captain was very displeased, and his officers were told to avoid close contact with me.

During one of my daily walks around the Base, one of the officers made contact and told me of this edict. Basically, the officers I had really become very friendly with ignored the edict off the Base.

Extension of Service

When I was sent to Exmouth and March 1980 came to pass, I had one year to serve before I would be retired at age 55. I found out on the grapevine my posting to Exmouth was basically because all the officers who had been approached had reasons for not coming to Exmouth and, as I had been in HMAS *Stirling* for almost three years, they decided I would be the one to be moved and sent to Exmouth. It was a two-year posting, and I later realised the Posting Authority had not taken that into account that I would be compulsorily retired at the end of my first year at Exmouth.

I asked Joan if she would be prepared to stay for a second year, and she agreed. We decided to send Walter to board in Perth at Aquinas College for that year.

I contacted the Posting Authority and explained that I was due to be retired in the coming year. With my wife's agreement, I would be prepared to serve a further four years to complete 40 years of service but would prefer a three-and-a-half-year extension. That would have given me forty years for pension purposes. They gave me a three-year extension.

So, when the time came, we took Walter to Perth and to Aquinas College as a boarder.

Christmas

There were the usual Christmas get-togethers at someone's home, and Joan and I would be invited. We would be made very welcome by both the USN hosts and the Australian families.

On one occasion the Shire President asked me if I would play the part of Father Christmas on Christmas Day for his young grandchild up from Perth. The child thought, because he was not home, Father Christmas would not leave any presents.

They provided the costume and on Christmas morning I walked up to the Shire President's house, rang the bell, and when the door opened the wife gave me the bag of presents. I had a bell and ringing with the HO HO, HO, I walked through the house and the child came running and I handed out the presents as marked.

However, the Shire President was still asleep, so I went into his bedroom and, with the bell close to his ear, rang it several times causing him to wake up with a start and find Father Christmas giving him his present. His look was something to be seen.

After he had dressed, we sat in the backyard and had a drink or two before I returned home, still in my Christmas outfit. As I left, I noticed the local Bank Manager's house across the road, so I knocked on the door. When he opened the door, I rang the bell loudly and HO, HO, Hoed and wished him a Merry Christmas. He wasn't impressed. I happened to know his wife and family were away for Christmas.

I have forgotten where Joan and I had lunch. I think it was at the Pot Shot.

New Year's Eve.

Before New Year's Eve I was approached by the leader of a small Scots Band and asked to become part of the Band on New Years Eve. I was lent a kilt, jacket and hat/cap etc and given an electric Bagpipe to pretend I was playing.

The routine was to visit various houses around the town, including USN and civilian homes, where a tune would be played and drinks taken before we moved on to the next, playing as we went.

A flat-top truck with eskies full of drinks accompanied us. The timing and route taken was such that we arrived at the Pot Shot just before midnight and that is where the New Year was welcomed.

Airport Pick up/Drop Off Visitors

From time to time, a visitor would come from Perth, and I would be required to meet him/her at the airport and escort them into town. It was not unusual to find a large caravan in the airport car park belonging to a USN Chief who would be seated outside with an esky, etc. I would be invited to come and have a drink. I always had a soft drink instead of alcohol.

On one occasion, a Parliamentary group from Canberra came to the Base, having been flown in by a RAAF plane. After inspecting the Base, etc, they had lunch at the Prawn factory and eventually departed for Canberra in the afternoon. One Western Australian Parliamentary Member had to wait to fly to Perth by the local air service. I had the task of looking after him for the afternoon, and we mainly sat in the Pot shot and discussed the way of the world and he asked me about my service etc. I seem to remember he was the Defence Minister at the time.

Later he was to become the Governor of Western Australia. Many years later, after I had retired, he was the guest speaker at a lunch at my RSL Club. I think us WWII Veterans were recognised as part of the introduction. The next minute, the Governor leaves the VIP party and crosses from one side of the room to the other, stopping at my table with a "Glad to see you again." He shook my hand, and I found a Governor's medallion in my hand.

He never fails to recognise me if I am at a function, and he is the guest speaker or just a guest. Always a nice touch.

Tours of Northwest Cape

Joan and I had many enjoyable times exploring various areas of Northwest Cape and swimming on the weekends.

Cyclone

While I was at Exmouth, several storms and one cyclone occurred. These required me to go around and ensure everyone was prepared for the high winds and rain. Fortunately, the cyclone centre passed the Base down Exmouth Gulf and had, in fact, lost a lot of its intensity. So, as far as I remember, there was no major damage to the Base or the aerial farm.

Public Demonstration

The Tour operators' boats were anchored off the beach alongside the Water Farm, which provided water for cooling the equipment associated with the VLF aerial. There were quite a number of pumps on either side of a cleared area between the pumps. The Tour Operators would pull up alongside the road on the inward side of the Water Farm and use the cleared area to take their clients to their boat off the beach on the other side of the water farm.

The reason for this was that there was no road around the outside of the fenced Water Farm, and it was a long walk around the outside of the farm.

Federal Police consistently warned the Operators that they would be charged with trespassing on Commonwealth Land if they didn't stop using this route to their boats. Eventually, they were given a final warning.

I became aware that a Demonstration was to take place on the Naval Wharf protesting the situation. I rang the Shire President and asked him to come with me and see if I could resolve the situation my way.

On the town side of the fenced Water Farm, there was a significant amount of vegetation and trees that I believed would never be used.

My solution to the impasse was to run a road through this part of the farm with fencing on either side. I asked the President if the Shire would pay for the road and fencing, and he agreed that could be done. I said, "Get the demonstration cancelled and I will get approval for the road."

On my return to my office, I composed a suitable message and sent it off to Canberra. Next thing I knew was the Director of Defence Security, a senior Naval Officer was arriving. I picked him up at the airport, and on the way into town, he wanted to know what the hell my message was all about. I suggested that the last thing the Americans wanted was a demonstration on their wharf, and that could have consequences for our government and the people who used the wharf to fish or take in a view of Exmouth Gulf.

I explained what had been happening and the Federal Police hardline on the security of the pumps in the Water Farm.

I then showed him where I suggested a road could be put through without interfering with the Water Farm and he agreed that was a sensible solution. When he asked who would pay for the road and fencing, I told him I had the Shire President's word the Shire would pay all costs associated with the clearing, road and fencing on either side. He agreed to take my proposal back to Canberra.

I waited with bated breath, and it was not long before the approval came through and I was able to inform the Shire President and captain of the result. All were happy with the result and the Tour Operators owe me.

This saga ended when the Shire President drove up and said to get in his car; he took me to the new road etc. On the way back from the parking area on the bay side of the Water Farm, he said, "Look at the sign directing people onto the road."

It read "BILL'S WAY".

Final Comments.

Eventually the time came to be relieved and my posting for the final period of my service to the Navy and Australia was to return to HMAS *Stirling* as the third Executive Officer. Remember, Walter was at school in Perth, and Joan and I enjoyed a leisurely trip back to Perth, stopping overnight on the way at Geraldton.

My successor at HMAS *Stirling* had vacated our house, so we could move straight in upon our arrival back in Perth.

THE END OF A PLEASANT POSTING WITH THE USN

COMMANDING OFFICER'S REPORT

HE HAS CONDUCTED HIMSELF SUPERBLY IN A PARTICULARLY CHALLENGING POSITION. HE HAS SHOWN HIMSELF TO BE AN ABLE LEADER AND EXPERT ADMINISTRATOR. HE IS DEDICATED, ENTHUSIASTIC, AND PROUD, DISPLAYING OUTSTANDING ZEAL AND ENERGY. HAS CONTRIBUTED SIGNIFICANTLY TO THE ABILITY OF THIS JOINTLY MANNED USN/RAN STATION TO CARRY OUT ITS COMAND AND CONTROL COMMUNICATIONS MISSION

Chapter 41

Return to HMAS *Stirling*

25 January 1982 to 1 September 1983

Introduction

My service at Harold Holt came to an end, and I found I was posted back to HMAS *Stirling* as Executive Officer (XO). The person I was relieving had already left by the time Joan and I had travelled from Exmouth back to our home in Safety Bay.

I cannot recall if we stopped at a motel on the way down or drove straight through to Rockingham. I think we stayed at one of the local motels for the first night and picked up the house keys the next morning.

At that time, son Peter, and daughter Anne, were living away from home, and Walter was a boarder at Aquinas College. We were able to settle back into our home which was exactly as we had left it.

Return to HMAS *Stirling*

All too soon it was for me to report to HMAS *Stirling* and resume the duties as XO. The Commodore was the same as when I left for Harold E Holt. I took the opportunity, during the first few days, to reacquaint myself with the improvements that had been made in my absence.

I found the Wardroom had continued, as when I left. There was a good social programme with lunches as before.

Change of Command

The Commodore was to be relieved, so I arranged the usual farewell dinner for him in the Wardroom, with provision for up to ninety officers to attend. This allowed HMAS *Leeuwin* and ships alongside to send representatives.

A shortage of stewards meant I had to decide concerning drinks during the actual dinner. The arrangement made was that red and white wine opened bottles would be placed at intervals along the tables and it was self-service. When the bottle was empty, the officer at that location would signal the Steward and the bottle would be replaced. This worked well. I had discussed with his wife what would make a suitable farewell present. She advised that he always talked about a travelling clock and one was purchased and presented. The reason for his retirement was a serious illness of his wife.

Death and funeral of Retired Commodore's Wife.

I cannot remember how long after he retired that his wife died. Joan and I attended the funeral service in Cottesloe. There were also several Naval and ex-Naval personnel and their wives who attended. After the Service, the Commodore invited us to his home to have a quiet drink and talk. I recall that I had two glasses of champagne and refused the third. On my way home, I ran into a Breath Testing Police Check Point and, fortunately, was found to be under the limit. It was the first time ever that I had ever been pulled over.

Day to Day

The day-to-day duties were in line with the usual Executive Officer role and this period was largely uneventful.

This posting was particularly fulfilling as I got to see the Naval Base I had spent so much of my later time within the Navy invested in expanding, working, and running as it was designed to be.

Retirement Time

The day 1st September 1983 came. This was the day I retired after 39 years and 39 days of service at the ripe old age of 57 without too much fanfare. A send-off was organised for me, which I greatly appreciated.

Time for me to move into retirement and civilian life for the first time since I was a teenager.

Chapter 42

Retirement

2ᴺᴰ September 1983 – 28ᵗʰ November 2023

Introduction

My retirement would turn out to be much more interesting than I had ever expected. There were to be many twists and turns. I really had no idea what I wanted to do in retirement. I had only undertaken Real Estate training for one month to have a break from the Navy and because some who had retired advised it could be very financially rewarding.

The following pages are set down to cover first, a Retirement Cruise, Rotary, Real Estate Agent, involvement with re-establishing the Rockingham Tourism Centre, attending various Australian Corvettes Association Reunions in different states, establishing a Naval Park in Rockingham, 1986 WA Coordinator for Tall Ships visit to Fremantle, 1988 Bicentennial Chairman for Rockingham, other tours and becoming a Tourist Escort.

One of the last official duties I had to attend whilst in the Navy was to represent the Commodore at the opening of a Tourist Park in the northern suburbs of Perth. I was talking with a chap named Royce, who worked for a Tourist Agency, and I asked him if any cruise ships were coming into Fremantle in the near future. He said he thought there was one coming in shortly, and I asked him, if that was so, to book me a cabin for my wife and me and let me know the cost and date.

Imagine what I thought when I picked up the local *Sunday Times*, and there was the spread of a cruise ship coming in and departing for a six-week Cruise to the Far East sixteen days after I retired. I promptly rang Royce, and he was able to get us a nice cabin with a port hole. Today (end of 2020) Royce is a great friend.

So, let me begin this Chapter.

Shopping

Initially, I accompanied Joan on her shopping trips. She would prepare a list of our requirements. At the shops, I would push the trolley until she had bought everything on the list. I would be heading for the checkout, and she would recall me. We would then proceed up every aisle in the shop, just in case, she had forgotten something. After several shopping trips, I decided I would stay outside the shop and watch the passing parade.

Retirement Cruise

Having retired on 1 September 1983, I was very keen to get away from everything for a while and looked forward to the cruise. This cruise would allow me to show Joan some of the places I had visited for Rest and Recreation whilst in the Navy.

I cannot recall if Joan had ever been to Singapore where the ship was to undertake a Maintenance period whilst we tourists visited other countries.

Embarking in Fremantle, the ship sailed for Singapore for a maintenance period. There was the option of several side tours while the ship was in maintenance.

Nepal Game Park

Our choice was to fly from Singapore to Thailand and then on to Nepal. The flight from Singapore was by normal commercial aircraft to Thailand, and we landed in Nepal's capital, Kathmandu, where we remained overnight. From there, we travelled by small aircraft between and below snow-covered peaks, so we did not need oxygen masks. One of the best views from the plane was of Mount Everest and the Himalayas.

We landed at a small airstrip and were invited to have a drink of very warm Coca-Cola. I do not think anyone took up the offer. A vehicle then took us to a fast flowing river that we had to cross. The means of crossing was by canoe that, when loaded, had little freeboard. I was worried about the new movie camera I was using.

I was impressed by the crew of the canoe when they started paddling upriver, close to the bank, which was much calmer than in the centre of the river. At a certain point, they turned across the river, paddling furiously. At a point, they stopped paddling and used their rudder (oar), turning into the flow, so the boat faced up upriver and neatly and professionally came alongside the landing.

We then boarded elephants to make our way to the accommodation. On the way, we came to another river, where the water was very shallow but with reasonably steep banks. It was interesting to me how the elephants managed to go down and up the slope of this river's banks without tipping us off.

The accommodation was basic, but comfortable, with lanterns or some other form of lighting. There was electric light but this was dependent on the generator being on. It was now getting late in the afternoon and we were summoned to make our way quietly to an observation hide. Here we were able to see a tiger emerge from the forest, come over and kill and remove the small goat that was tethered in the centre of the clearing. I think there was some form of lighting so that we could see this little drama taking place.

Once we'd had enough, we returned to the accommodation area and had dinner, attended a briefing on the activities for the visit before retiring for the night.

After breakfast and a briefing the next morning, we were taken on elephants through the high grass to see wild buffalo and to watch some of the wild animals in the area moving around. We returned to the accommodation area and then explored a bit more of the park before returning for dinner back at the Lodge.

The next day, we reversed the passage back to the runway, using elephants, the canoe and a bus. We returned by the small plane to Kathmandu. Again, we flew between the peaks and the view was spectacular. At Kathmandu, we walked around and observed the activities of any capital city. There were shops selling curios and I think we all felt quite safe. *(There had been some trouble before we arrived.)* Part of the visit was a briefing on ascending Mount Everest. We visited several temples and other places of interest. All too soon, we were on a plane heading for Bangkok.

Bangkok

In Bangkok, we received a briefing on what was to happen during our visit. We visited some interesting temples and other old buildings. We were briefed on the control of country's activities. We also attended a concert showing off their talents with traditional dancing and singing. Later, we moved to a beach area; then it was time to take a flight back to Singapore.

Singapore

As we entered the dining room for breakfast the next day, we noticed that our tour group appeared to be very happy and celebrating. When I asked why I was told we had just won the America's Cup.

Before the ship sailed, we were able to tour the city and its surroundings. From memory, we visited various spots, including the zoo, Boogie Street (well-known to sailors), and a marketplace. We had a drink, a Gin Sling, that the Raffles Hotel was well known for. We took a ride on the train system and returned to the ship for dinner and to prepare for the ship's departure.

The ship had completed its maintenance and was soon sailing to Hong Kong. As far as I can remember we did not visit any other port before Hong Kong.

Hong Kong

I cannot recall the number of times I had been to Hong Kong. On each occasion of sailing into the entrance, my mind always had a flashback to 1945, and I automatically looked up to where there had been a flash of light, like that of a gun firing, that I reported as the port lookout. At that time, as I mentioned earlier in this epistle, we were sweeping for mines to clear the approaches/entry to Hong Kong harbour for the British Pacific Fleet Units to enter and re-occupy the city.

We did the normal tour and walked around the city and other sites, such as the Night Markets. We also took the cable car to the top of the mountain overlooking the city. We took a ferry ride across the harbour to Kowloon. There, we explored the various shops and other touristy places. All too soon, the ship was sailing for Japan.

Japan

What we did on this visit is a little unclear because of my memory lapse. I participated in my naval service in the Occupational Forces during the Korean War, so I was familiar with the people and the surroundings.

I am sure we berthed at Osaka, took a visit to Kyoto and the surrounding areas. These areas showed off the older-style Japanese homes and gardens. I am also sure that we were able to view Mount Fuji from a distance. There was a visit to another site, a prison, where we were shown a static display of the torture and other punishments dealt out to their own people. One of the exhibits was a person hanging by their fingers with their toes fully extended to touch the floor. The second display was a woman kneeling with four or five concrete slabs over her legs.

At one stage I sat on a seat watching the passing parade. Some young ladies and elder Japanese came and asked me if they could have a photo with me. I agreed. I think my beard was the attraction. Japanese men tended to have thin straggly beards. The rest of the tour group were shown other items of interest.

Too soon it was time to sail and turn south, heading for Sydney. My memory of the voyage back is scanty. I recall there were tours of islands to the north-east and east of Australia. One stop I remember was Manila and a tour of Corregidor and the tunnel complex from where General MacArthur left for Australia.

I think another one of the islands was Lord Howe. Then it was time to plan for our arrival in Sydney and disembarkation. We went to stay with Joan's sister, to catch up on both Joan's and my friends. The time passed all too quickly, and a tired pair of travellers were glad to fly back to our Safety Bay home in WA.

Rotary

Soon after arriving home from the cruise, I resumed my activities with the Rotary. On return to HMAS *Stirling* from HEH Communication Station and before I left the Navy, I attended the Rockingham Rotary Club for a couple of meetings. It was suggested that I join a newly forming Safety Bay Rotary club. I had attended several of their formation meetings and attended their Foundation launch. Unfortunately, the list of Foundation members had been sent and, although not one of them officially, I was the first transferee from another club. I was always treated as a Foundation member. From memory there was something like seventy or eighty members. At one stage there were suggestions we put a cap on numbers. I suggested, along with others, that it would be best to wait and see what the future held.

As I write, my Club and the Rockingham Club have merged due to falling numbers.

Outside Visits Coordinator

I accepted the job of organising visits to wineries, tourist attractions, and other places. I also arranged the odd get-together or lunch between meetings.

When I first took the job, my friend Mary from the Rockingham Historical Society, told me that, when organising a 40-seat tour coach for outings, the best way to work out the cost for each person was to divide the total cost by 30 because there would be occasions when not even 30 attended. The profit from over 30 could be used to make up the difference. This worked well.

20 Fifth Avenue, Shoalwater

Among other things, on retirement, one of the items I was considering was growing orchids. Somewhere, I learnt that orchids were coming into Western Australia from Singapore. Many of my sailors in Sydney would tell me about their orchid-growing. I considered perhaps it was a niche market, and I could take a course on growing orchids.

One of my contemporaries in the Navy was selling Real Estate, (when not playing golf) and I asked him to keep his eye open for a block of land in Baldivis, a nearby suburb, where there was grazing and market gardens.

One day he rang Joan and said he had a property to show her. At that stage, I had not discussed with Joan my thoughts. She accompanied them to what were two units that turned out to be much too small for our furniture to fit in and they were also two-storeyed. Joan advised they were unsuitable.

As they were taking her back home, they asked her if she would accompany them as a client to look at a house that had been on the market for eighteen months. They had just acquired permission to try and sell the house. She agreed.

When I arrived home, I received a dressing down for not telling her I was looking for another place to live. I explained the situation and asked what she thought of what she saw. She advised the two flats were too small but the house she could not see anything wrong with. I asked her if she would like to buy it. I pointed out that we had money in the Bank from the sale of our Canberra property and I was losing about 50% of the interest in tax. She insisted I inspect the property first.

I was busy with events taking place at HMAS *Stirling*. I eventually agreed to make the time to have a look at the house. It was one street back from a nice beach, and, using the experience I gained during my time with the Real Estate Agency, I appreciated that it would make a very nice home for us as retired persons. It wasn't far to go for a swim and for a walk along the beach to keep fit, and there was a bus stop outside the next-door property.

My kind Bank Manager, a friend and ex-serviceman, provided an interest-only loan that I could repay with rent from our house in Safety Bay and payout the loan with the extra funds I would have after selling the Safety Bay house.

Knowing it had been on the market for some time, I decided to make what would have been considered a low bid, knowing I could increase the bid as required. Also, we would not really require the property immediately due to our desire to travel, the children's schooling, and their starting work.

Our offer included a clause that they could continue to lease the house for up to a year. They accepted my offer and advised me they would lease it for six months.

At some time after we occupied the house, I found out the previous owners were building a new home down the street from us. Apparently, they were not able to fulfil their desires in the house they had chosen.

Moving In

Eventually, we moved into our new home with son Walter, leaving Peter and Anne to live away from home because of their jobs. We rented and then sold the old house at 8 Caribbean Way, Safety Bay, to son Peter.

Settling in

On the day we moved in, my real estate friend, who had sold us the house, rang to say he and his wife were coming round to help us settle in. They arrived somewhere about noon. We had a cuppa tea on their arrival and generally gossiped about what was going on in the world and around us. I suppose an hour had passed.

After a time, I suggested we have another cuppa tea. My friend then said when we finish that "Let's help you move in."

I smiled and, as we finished the cuppa, he said, "Let's get on with the move in." He did not believe me when I said we had completed the move in by 10 o'clock that morning.

Real Estate

I decided that I should get out of Joan's hair each day and really find out about selling Real Estate. I returned to the agency that I had used during my one month's Resettlement Training. However, I soon realised that I needed to go into Real Estate at a deeper level. I applied for and was accepted for the Real Estate Agents Course. By that time, I had become quite successful at putting a price that the home would sell for, as opposed to its asking price. Later, other agents would ring and ask what I thought the price for which it would sell.

I was able to obtain my Real Estate License to practice. I had decided to concentrate on Business Broking rather than selling homes and land. However, a change in the wind saw another change of tack.

Tourism – A Change of Lifestyle

I cannot remember the actual date I became involved in Tourism. Reading the local paper one day, I saw an article about re-establishing the local Tourist Centre. At the same time, I was invited by the owner of one of the other Real Estate agencies in the area to see if I would care to attend this meeting. I thought it would be interesting to learn about what was being discussed about a Tourist Centre in Rockingham. After all, I had obtained Navy approval for a lone Tourist Coach Operator to regularly tour Garden Island with a member of the Ship's Company trained to give a commentary as they rode around the Base.

The meeting decided to form a small committee. I took the opportunity to put my accounting knowledge into practice and offered to be the Treasurer and part of the Committee. Here, I had forgotten a Golden Navy Rule: **NEVER VOLUNTEER**.

It did not take long for me to realise those on the Committee were leaving it to Muggins to get on and do the job.

The Rockingham Council provided a hall adjacent to the Rockingham Historical Society as a space suitable for the Tourist Centre. It was near the beach and parks on the waterfront and next to the local museum. A request for donations to get the Centre started saw only three businesses in the Rockingham Beach area contribute about $500 each to help set up and fund this new project.

So, for my sins, and forgetting the Navy's never to volunteer, I was basically the Treasurer, Secretary, Manager, and general labourer.

Tourism Assistance

Fortunately, the WA Tourism Agency, responsible for promoting Tourism in WA, had one of its Agents responsible for our local area. His name was John. He contacted me and offered to assist in getting the Centre working. We developed a close working relationship. His help was greatly appreciated.

He discussed a Coastal Drive (known now as Route 202) to start at the Kwinana Beach Park, to the north of Rockingham Beach, travelling south along the waterfront, through the Rockingham beach front and areas to the south showing off the entrance to the Naval Base on Garden Island, Point Peron, past Shoalwater Beach, Penguin Island, Safety Bay, and other beaches to the south. A brochure was designed and published showing the route with a Tourist sign erected at both ends of the drive.

His next help also solved a major headache. I had racked my brain on how to obtain furniture, pamphlet racks, a counter, and chairs as there were no funds to purchase such items. Who was going to pay for it? I also had to organise the Staff to man the centre.

Furniture

One day John rang me and asked if I could get the use of a truck. He told me that the Perth Tourist Centre was being refurbished and the old furniture and pamphlet racks were being thrown out.

I approached the Council's Town Clerk and obtained a Council truck. From a small table with a single brochure rack, we had a full outfit of furniture and only required to obtain brochures to have a fully functioning Tourism Centre. With John's help, we designed a local brochure with a picture of one of the local Fairy Penguins on the front page.

I also arranged brochures that laid out a drive to the historical areas of Kwinana and Jarrahdale, a timber town where logs from their mill were shipped out using the three wharfs that were built on the Rockingham waterfront. This timber was brought from the Jarrahdale Mill by train. My grandfather, Thomas Cope, was the brakeman on the train from time to time.

His job was to apply the brakes on each timber carriage as required. Later, he was to lose his life when he must have slipped and fell under one of the carriers bringing wood in from within the forests.

Staffing

My next problem was to find out how we would pay permanent staff as we had some volunteers willing to man the Tourist Centre once we received the furniture.

One day I received a phone call from a young disabled man who was in the Rehabilitation Centre in Shenton Park. The conversation was that he heard I was employing a disabled person, and he would like to be considered. I put him straight by informing him that the Counsellor who had made that comment was at that stage wrong, as I was not sure that the job was suitable for a disabled person. I asked him for his telephone number with a comment that I would contact him once a decision was made.

About an hour later, while I was attending to a couple seeking ideas about the Rockingham area, a young man in a wheelchair came through the door. Whilst I was finalising details for the couple, the telephone at the other end of the hall rang. The young man picked up the phone and my ears pricked and listened to his conversation. I was impressed by the way he answered the phone, and he said it was for me. I excused myself from the couple whilst I answered the phone; in the meantime, he had wheeled himself to talk with the couple.

When the couple left the Centre, I said I was going to throw him and his wheelchair out the door as I had already told him I would contact him if I considered a disabled person could do the job. The reply was that he had come down to see whether he would be suitable or not. I was impressed by his attitude, especially when he told me he could stand up and walk around without his wheelchair. I tested him on several of the brochure racks and realised he was capable of not pulling the racks over the top of himself.

There was something about his attitude and my experience of handling young men from the age of twenty as an Able Seaman to my then age of 58 suggested I take a punt and give him a chance to prove his capability.

I contacted his Supervisor at the Rehabilitation Centre and she told me they would cover his expenses in all aspects for three months; this included all insurance and wages. I decided that maybe he was the right person to take up the position and it would remove the need to advertise the position and disappoint other disabled people who would be unsuitable. Subsequently, I was able to obtain another three-month payment from the Rehab Centre. That incident occurred something like twenty-seven years or so ago, and he was still doing the job and was Manager of a newer, updated Tourism Centre until he retired on 18 December 2020. I am immensely proud of him and am incredibly happy for him.

Rockingham Memorial Park

The RAN Corvettes Association of Australia, each year, would have a General Meeting and a Reunion, a get-together, in one of the states of Australia. Joan and I would invariably attend these functions no matter what state it was in. A WA Coach operator would either take our group interstate by road or, be at the airport waiting for us with his coach. He would take us to the accommodation he had arranged, and if the reunion programme allowed, we would do some side tours that provided Joan and me the opportunity to see a lot of the Australian land and coastal areas we may never have visited.

On one occasion it was held in Ulverstone, Tasmania. Part of the programme was to hold a Memorial Service for those who had served in the Corvettes during World War II and for those who had *Crossed the Bar (Died)*. At that time, it was held in what was then known as HMAS *Shropshire Park*.

This park contained a central Memorial and a considerable number of smaller plaques on plinths dedicated to various ships. I and other members of the Tour Group were impressed by this park and its presentation. It had been a collection point for garbage and flotsam on the riverbank below where the park was located. A Council staff member, an ex-Corvetter, I believe, had apparently proposed the park.

My imagination was stimulated, and I thought of the long beachfront area beginning at Kwinana Beach and running along the beachfront through Rockingham Beach and areas further south. On return home, I looked for a suitable area where a Memorial Park could be built.

I developed a proposal to put to the Local Council. There was already a large park adjacent to the beach area and was directly opposite the Naval Base on the other side of Cockburn Sound. It was also some distance from the Rockingham beachfront shops, and this may prevent any casual interference with the plaques and Memorial. The proposal was accepted by Council with the proviso that the Naval Association raise half of the cost. At that time, the WA Association in Rockingham had very few funds.

There was a lot of "drawing in of breath" by those at the next meeting of the local Naval Association, who eventually agreed it was a good idea. I suggested that, if the members were prepared to get their hands dirty and lay things like paths, prepare the plinths for the plaques, and any other labouring jobs, our share of the cost could be considerably lowered.

Council provided only half of the area I had requested. However, it was found by Council staff that having only half of the park provided a problem with the reticulation for the lawns of the park. In the end, the whole park initially requested was made available.

The next step was to approach the home owners/occupiers near the park area to see if there were any objections. Three answers were received to indicating no problem and one requesting that no buildings or structures be placed in front of her house that would obstruct the view.

The next step was to consider what the main Memorial would look like. Being in WA, it was a no brainer as to which ship this Memorial would be dedicated to. HMAS *Perth 1* had been sunk during WWII and it was the obvious choice as the centrepiece of the park. I served in the second *Perth* in Vietnam. Guessing there would be a *Perth 3*, I designed it so that the main Memorial would face the main path leading to it. There are two other arms, one for *Perth 2* and one for *Perth 3*, which is still in service at the time of compiling this history.

The entrance to the park would be through an Anchor Cable Archway. The path leading to the main Memorial would be lined with plinths on either side when ships provided a plaque with details of that ship.

Sunk in the same action as HMAS *Perth*, was the USS *Houston*. A member of the Naval Association showed me a picture of the plague he had photographed whilst visiting the Arlington Memorial Cemetery in the United States. The *Houston* was above *Perth* in the wording on the plaque. This gave me an idea that we would use the wording of this plaque and put *Perth* first above *Houston* and leave all the rest of the wording as it was.

Later, I was able to obtain a large rock to which the plaque was attached. Its position is close to the main Memorial.

Since it was opened, the area of Memorials has extended further south down the park. A Submarine Conning tower has since been added. There are gazebos and a barbecues provided by the Council.

The final cost to the Naval Association was $100. The Council staff used Work for the Dole personnel to lay the path, and this saved the Naval Association from having to find $25000.

The park is well used by the general public and for various Naval Remembrance events.

An Aside. On one of our cruises, where our group was made up of many people from Perth and Western Australia, a lady in the group found out I had been in the Navy and lived in Rockingham. She said the family took her mum for outings to the Naval Park in Rockingham. The mum apparently lived nearby.
In jest, I said, "You mean Bill's Park."
She kept correcting me and, after some discussion, I told her I was the person responsible for designing and bringing the Naval Park to fruition.

Yaringa Festival

Sometime after we had opened the Tourist Centre, a young lady named Margaret came in with a proposal for a Festival in one of the two parks at Rockingham Beach. It sounded like a good idea to entertain the public and we were able to obtain the use of a stage from the Rockingham City Shopping Centre. A tent was acquired for the performers to change in and local artists showed off their skill in Churchill Park at no cost to the Tourism Centre.

I cannot recall how many years this program ran for. It was the forerunner of quite a few major events that now occur along the waterfront: horses racing on the beach, a large marquee being provided for a fundraising dinner and other events like musicians and concerts.

Joan and I continued to go cruising visiting other parts of the world and Australia with the Corvettes Association.

Americas Cup

In February 1986, America challenged Australia to try and win back the American Cup. The event was to take place off Fremantle between October 1986 and February 1987. The

Rockingham Town Mayor approached me to be the Coordinator for Rockingham as it was expected there would be some activity involving Rockingham. I accepted as part of my duty in running the Tourist Centre.

Because of a lack of space in Fremantle, one of the large ferries that would take people to watch the Cup races had to tie up at the Palm Beach Jetty in Rockingham and carry out maintenance.

Water Ski Event

The owner of this ferry came up with a proposal that would see 120 water skiers towed by his boat trying to break the record held in Queensland. It was unfortunate that, due to the maintenance on his boat, no practice runs could be done. The event was well publicised with an additional Water Ski demonstration to be held in front of Churchill Park off Rockingham Beach. There were many people from the north of Perth and other areas among the visitors.

The event commenced, and as the ferry increased speed, one of the booms out on either side of the boat broke loose and spilled the water skiers being towed.

Unfortunately, the sea breeze had commenced and proved too much for the Water Ski demonstrations that were to follow and had to be called off.

This meant a significant number of people were taking an interest in Rockingham and its beaches. As they wandered around the Rockingham Beach shopping area and looked in Real Estate windows, they were particularly interested in the price of property in the area. They would have found the price of a house in the area was significantly lower than that being offered in the northern and other suburbs of Perth. Although I was not selling Real Estate, the Tourism activities brought a significant number of people into the area.

Over the Christmas break, I would act as crewman on one of the rescue boats owned by an ex-Corvette sailor during an Annual Regatta. In December 1996, after completing our duty as rescue boat, I was having a drink in the Cruising Yacht Club bar on the Rockingham Beach waterfront when one of the Real Estate salesmen I knew quite well, happened to mention that he had more completed sales at that time than he had ever had in a full year. I smiled, and he asked me why I was smiling, and I told him that it was no doubt due, in part, to the crowd who had come down to the Water Ski events and finding houses in Rockingham were much cheaper than in other areas. Also, the beaches and general areas surrounding would have appeared attractive.

Ferry Race

A Ferry race from the end of the Shipping Channel in Cockburn Sound to Rockingham Beach had been arranged. It so happened that our Yaringa Festival was running in Churchill Park. We encouraged those present to man the beach railing and shout and scream and wave to those on the boats as they slowly sailed near the beach at the end of the race. There was quite a crowd doing this. I later found out that the large crowd, nice beach facilities and many yachts and other boats in the area were a surprise to those aboard the ferries.

Interestingly, this event attracted people on the ferries to come and have a look around Rockingham Beach area. You can guess what happened once they had looked at the Real Estate prices as they walked around. The Ferry Race added to the sale of property in Rockingham. Since that time, Rockingham has grown very quickly and is still expanding as people move into the area.

On my arrival in Rockingham in 1977, there were 16,000 ratepayers. At the end of 2020, it is about 146,000 or more.

WA Tall Ships Coordinator

I received a call from one of the Commodore's, who had been my Boss whilst at HMAS *Stirling*, asking if I would come up to Perth to discuss the Tall Ships Visit to Fremantle. He asked me to join the State Committee and take over setting up the programme for the tall ships visit. I was replacing another person, whom I had worked with at HMAS *Stirling*. I was able to develop a Reception and other activities as well as the likely cost.

As the date of the reception drew near, I found I had not received an invitation and was disappointed. I rang the CEO. He said he thought I had one and he corrected it straight away. I was therefore able to take Joan to this reception and we enjoyed meeting people from the Tall Ships.

On arrival at the venue, Joan and I were walking towards the escalator when I noticed a figure in the car park running towards the building. It turned out to be the person in overall charge for the Tall Ships Visit to Australia. I had to smile because he had not supported my case for the stipend I had been told I would get. It was also the first time I had seen such a Senior Naval Officer running as if his life depended on it.

We both enjoyed the reception.

1988 Australian Bicentenary Celebration

The Bicentenary of the arrival of Captain Arthur Phillip, and the eleven ships of the First Fleet that arrived in what we now know as Sydney Harbour, and founded the Colony of New South Wales on 26 January 1788, was celebrated throughout Australia during 1988.

In 1987, the Town Mayor asked me to chair the local Bicentennial Committee. With one of the members – Mary from the local Historical Society – and others, we began to plan what would happen in the Rockingham area in 1988. One proposal was to arrange to upgrade or replace new plaques on the historical sites around Rockingham. Promoting the history of the area, identifying places of historical interest, recalling the old Turtle factory/Convent in the Point Peron area, the original Shire Offices site, the first school and other still older existing sites proposed by my friend Mary.

Sometime after we began, I became aware that a committee had been set up to arrange for the Town of Rockingham to become a city, as it was expected to reach the 30,000 ratepayers required to become a city during that year.

I immediately realised that our small committee would be probably hard-pressed for funds because of this committee. I wrote to the Town Mayor and suggested that my committee merge with the Bicentenary City Committee, and this was accepted. I pointed out I was happy to be just a member of the one committee. In this way, we were able to complete planning for activities; the central point of the celebrations would be becoming a city.

At the end of the year, I was made the Bicentennial Citizen of Rockingham City for my efforts.

Coral Sea Battle - Commemorative Cruise

In 1991, a tour of WWII sites in the Southwest Pacific was announced and was promoted as a tour for veterans. I was interested as there were some places where I had not served during this war and/or visited during my Naval Service. Joan was interested and we booked our passage to leave from Sydney. We had a few days with Joan's sister before embarking.

We picked up a few more passengers at Brisbane; then it was on to Townsville, where each day, all veterans were recognised in a ceremony at the Town Centre Memorial. We veterans were invited to join the ceremony and be recognised for our service to Australia. Most of us took part in one day or another of our visit.

I cannot remember whether we stopped at Cairns or Thursday Island before heading for Port Moresby. Here, there were various tours, including one to the Kokoda Track, which also included a stop at the Port Moresby Cemetery. Our lunch was to be at a motel after a Memorial Service at Owers Corner, which is at the beginning of the Kokoda Track.

Each morning or afternoon while at sea, briefings would be held on what had happened during the war and the next place to be visited. These were provided by qualified historians and were generally interesting. They also gave details of what to keep an eye out for.

War Cemetery Visit

At the Cemetery, quite a few tourists looked for a relative's grave site. I had visited the cemetery several times and stayed at the entrance. I noticed a lady on her own coming back to the entrance and asked her if she had found what she was looking for. Her answer was No, she could not find the grave. I told her to look inside a small wooden cabinet, attached to a pole, where she would find a book with all the grave positions identified. She did and found the grave number and quickly returned to find the grave. I was also able to help several other people in the same way.

Owers Corner

On arrival at Owers Corner, I proceeded down the track to take a movie of what it was like. However, as I was about to take some pictures, I was summoned back to the Memorial where the Remembrance Ceremony was starting. I was told there would be plenty of time after the service for me to take pictures.

Four PNG soldiers mounted guard over the Memorial. The Service was traditional, and I think I took a few photographs during it.

At the completion of the Memorial Service, I again started down the track to get photographs. One of the ship staff came running after me and told me there was no time for photographs as I had to get on the bus going to the motel for lunch. I was not impressed but did what I was told.

Lunch

Our bus was one of the last to arrive at the motel. As I was recovering from an operation, Joan suggested I sit down at a small table, and she would join the queue. I went to the bar and got a couple of drinks for us. I noticed that the queue and had not moved for a considerable time.

I decided to see what the hold-up was and walked to the serving area and found there were no plates, salads, buns, or other items to put with the mains. The people at the head of the queue had not indicated to the staff there was a problem.

The staff were standing with fork and spoon, all ready to serve the tourists. I asked who was in charge and the person identified himself. I pointed out there was no plates or salads or other items on the table adjacent to the serving area. He apologised and thanked me. Within minutes, everything was available. He handed me two plates with our lunch. Then the queue began to be served.

I walked back to our table and indicated to Joan I had her lunch. As I ate my lunch, I heard a few comments like "never seen anything so brazen in my life!" Eventually, I woke up that the elderly veteran at the end of the queue was talking about me. I was about to go and put him right on how stupid people were to not draw the attention of the motel staff that there were no plates and other things to put with the main meal on. Joan told me to sit down and smile.

Milne Bay

After Port Moresby, we visited Milne Bay where there was to be a Memorial Service, followed by a bus tour of the area by road. It was here that the Australian Forces had forced the Japanese to withdraw. The Japanese lacked the resources to support their landing. The RAAF provided air-to-ground support from a nearby airfield.

This action at Milne Bay was successful because the Battle of the Coral Sea prevented the Japanese from supporting their forces on the ground.

Memorial Service

There were nine Speakers at the Service including a few Pastors/Padres, local and other civil authorities. However, the crowd was permitted to stand right up to where the Speakers were. This stopped most people from seeing the Speakers because of the many heads that were in front of them.

One of the items in the Service was the laying of a wreath at a quite large Cross nearby. The people laying a Wreath had to battle their way through the crowd to get to the Cross.

When the Service ended, we were all invited to board the buses for a tour of the area. Seniors were instructed to form a queue and that they would be taken to the buses. However, the rest of the group were permitted to go and board the buses. When I realised what was happening, I grabbed Joan and we managed to get on board one of the buses where a commentator gave us an excellent presentation as we drove around.

Before the buses left the area, I noticed that elderly people were being lifted into utility vehicles which did not seem to have any cushions or seating.

As we proceeded back to the ship, the driver was asked to stop at a Memorial that was dedicated to an Australian VC recipient. This meant we were late for lunch, and it was being closed off as we arrived back on board.

We visited one other nearby island, whose name I don't recall. We were entertained by a group performing their traditional dances, walked through markets, and generally looked around. We were taken to and from the ship by boat. I believe we then headed for Guadalcanal in the Solomon Islands.

Complaint About Tour

Whilst sailing to the next venue, there was the briefing on what had happened in the battlefield we were visiting next. I was sitting alongside an elderly veteran who was complaining about the cruise being for the benefit of veterans, but the staff seemed to be more interested in associating with non-veterans. I asked him what he was going to do about it; he seemed to think that he could do nothing. I suggested he put his complaint in writing to P&O and he said he would. He then asked if I was going to also write to P&O. As I had been thinking about doing that, I stated that I would also write if he did. I will add here what was to result from my letters to P&O and WA Travel Agent.

When I arrived home and picked up my mail, there was a letter from the said individual that almost burst into flame because of the language he used. As I told him I too would write I took out the notes I had made and, with a covering letter, sent ten or eleven pages that set down what the problem was and how easy it was to fix it with a little forethought and planning. One of the things I pointed out was how it was so easy to throw a piece of rope on the ground some distance from the speakers at Milne Bay and everyone made to stand behind it so that attendees would have been able to see the service properly. I also mentioned that having one of the ship's staff at the Port Moresby Cemetery entrance another at the head of the luncheon queue after the visit to Owers Corner and, there would have been no hold-up like there was, and how I finally went and solved the problem. Another was their organisation for purchasing side tours before arriving in a port.

I gave an example of a small elderly lady who was at the counter being served when suddenly she appeared beside me four rows back. It was like a Rugby scum as people jostled to get to the counter. The staff member serving the lady reappeared and was obviously looking for her and baffled as to where she had disappeared to. The woman was obviously at a loss, so I told her we were going back to the counter. I put my arms around her and elbowed my way back to the counter, and made sure she was served. (Boy Scout Training).

In my report to P&O, I suggested that having four small posts, with a rope between each two and this would have channelled the people in an orderly way to book their tours.

I did not realise, when I posted the letter to P&O, with a copy to the West Australian Tourist Agency, through whom we booked our tour, that my retirement would take another twist. It took P&O about three months to answer my letter. However, the Manager of the WA group we had booked our cruise through was on the phone to me within half an hour of receiving a copy of my complaint. After discussing the complaint, she asked me what I had done for a living. I told her that during my thirty-nine years in the Navy, I had been responsible for young sailors and their employment in various fields. The final remark was that she thought I would make a very good Tour Escort.

I cannot remember what the next tour was about. We attended the Tourist Agency for a briefing on what it would include. While sitting at the table listening to the briefing, the agency manager came in and sat near me. On completion of the briefing, she asked if I had thought about her offer to become a Tour Escort. I finally signed up and was told she would send me with one of her staff to Queensland in about a month's time.

The following week I received a call from her saying she had a slight problem and would I be able to escort a group to New Zealand. Joan and I had already done a tour of New Zealand and I was confident that I would not have any problems. Joan decided she would stay at home. So began my Tour Escort career.

From then on, Joan accompanied me on all the tours that I was to Escort. There was an extensive tour of China, a trip across Canada by rail, a visit to South Africa, another to Norfolk Island, and one taking in a tour of Europe, a visit to Ireland, Norway, and Sweden. We also visited Turkey and Gallipoli.

Probus Club

In the time before going on the European tour, I arranged for the Perth Opera company to come to Rockingham and perform. Unfortunately, it was Thursday night shopping and although we got something like 300 people to enjoy the show we could possibly have had more. I briefed the committee on how to organise a return visit in about a year's time. I took off for Europe, emphasising that they should start organising a return visit. On my return, I found nothing had been done and was told they were waiting for me to come back. By that time, the Opera Company was fully committed. I was not very happy as you can imagine.

On return from our European tour, I found the Rotary Club was setting up a Probus club, and I joined the committee. There were several meetings prior to the official opening of the Club. I became a Foundation Member with something like seventy or eighty members, and that membership continues as I write this. I took on the job of Outside Visits Coordinator and arranged lunches and tours of the local attractions between meetings.

Business Partnership

Son Peter completed an apprenticeship as an Automotive Mechanic in 1982, having been laid off due to his employer being unable to sustain three mechanics and Peter being the least experienced. Peter worked at various casual Mechanic jobs in the local area for the next year or so. Keen to set up his own workshop, he rented various factory units in the old Dixon Road area, eventually with my assistance (and the understanding the deposit I put up would be paid back over time) we purchased a property in Hurrell Way in 1984 and registered and set up business. My role was to do the book work whilst Peter ran the workshop on a day-to-day basis. After approximately seven years and after numerous improvements, including additional units to the property, he started work as a Contract RAC Patrolman. During this time, the business was sold and the property's units leased out, around 1997. Again at Peter's behest, we purchased and developed property in Port Kennedy, which worked out well as the RAC Contract was completed and not renewed in 1998, so Peter again set up a workshop at these premises which he ran for around three years until selling out due to back related issues. From then, we leased the premises out, and from 1984 until 2020, I did the books for all of Peter's business interests, and with all monies paid back, I was happy to hand them over to Peter at the age of 94.

Later Years

With the passing of Joan in 2012, who used to run the house, I had quite a bit of support but surmised that I go back to my military mindset and set myself a routine to follow to enable me to run the house and do the chores previously done by Joan. This worked well, with me cooking and washing etc. As time went on and over time, I had assistance with cleaning and in the last year had personal care a couple of times a week. The house was modified with handrails and an electric recliner etc. I gave up driving in early 2020 at 93. With the onset of Covid and a couple of falls, I became increasingly less agile and less mobile and more housebound. The house was again modified with Anne and Peter's assistance – TV, Air Con, office equipment etc. so I could live exclusively on the upper level. Still being able to get out for church and other functions relied on being picked up and dropped off or catching taxis. I still managed right up to and including 2023 to go over to Sydney each year in May to catch up with son Tony and his family, who all have their birthdays around the month of May. This also gave me time to think back in my mind along with some research to write this story. I lived independently at home with the help, especially of daughter Anne, but also of son Peter, and the aged carers that dropped in regularly right up to my passing.

Finishing Note

Dad, never got to finish writing his recollections of his retirement years, despite much nagging from myself! That said, and after exhaustive checking of his computer and various thumb drives, I have compiled what he had written and tried to complete this period of his life. Where practical, I have edited and added some of the story that he was in the throes of writing.

Son Peter.

Our Poppy

Fields of crimson poppies,
Standing tall and proud.

Your spirit floats over them,
Blessed each stem, you vowed.

In the name of the Father, Son, and the Spirit,
You walk towards heaven's glow.

And as a father, son, and Poppy,
It is to you, we all owe.

Owe smiles and longevity,
Owe identity and success.

Maker of memories and lifeblood,
Your lineage shall progress.

In fields of poppies, your absence we feel,
But in heaven's embrace, your peace is real.

And as the scarlet petals whisper tales untold,
Your legacy blooms eternally; just waiting to unfold.

Vale William Ritchie -
Our Pop amongst the Poppies.

Written by Angelina Ritchie (Granddaughter).

Associations and Memberships

My retirement was partly filled with my involvement with various clubs and associations, attending meetings and functions and assisting with committee positions.

HMAS Stirling Wardroom Mess	Life Membership (Undated)
Rockingham & Districts Tourist Authority	Life Membership 15-08-1988
Rockingham Mandurah District Cricket Club	Foundation-Member 1995
	Inaugural Treasurer
Safety Bay Rotary Club	Certificate of Appreciation in the establishment of Safety Bay Rotary Club 18-06-1996
HMAS *Perth* National Association	Life Membership 13-10-2012
Naval Association of Australia	Life Membership 17-03-2013
Family Historical Society of Rockingham	Loyalty-Award 2015
	20 Years Continuous Membership 1994-2014
Naval Association of Australia	Long Service Cert 18-08-2018
	30 Years Cumulative Service
Combined Probus Club of Rockingham	Life Membership 26-04-2023
Highgate RSL Club	Active Member
Naval Historical Society	Patron

Legacies

Bill's Way Exmouth WA	This is the road to Bundegi Beach off Murat Rd Exmouth
The Bill Ritchie Building	This is the name of the building at HMAS Watson

Appendix

Ships W G Ritchie Served in Ashore and at Sea

July 1944 to 1 September 1983

HMAS CERBERUS

25 July 1944 to 5 January 1944

Initial Training as Ordinary Seaman. On completion of, selected for Radar Operator Training at RAN Station 284 (Later Commissioned as HMAS WATSON)

HMAS PENGUIN for RAN Station 284

6 January to 11 March 1945

Radar Training

HMAS YANDRA

12 March to 27 March 1945

Sea Training as Radar Plotter

HMAS PENGUIN for RAN Station 284

28 March to 10 April 1945

Complete Radar Training

HMAS MORETON

11 April to 17 April 1945

In Transit to New Guinea as spare Radar Operator

HMAS GERARD

18 April to 17 June 1945

Small Supply ships carried much-needed stores in New Guinea and other areas supporting the Land and Naval Operations Coast.

HMAS MADANG

18 June to 5 July 1945

Ashore for short time in jungle environment guarding stores complex waiting for ship to take me further north.

HMAS BROOME

6 July to 20 July 1945

Australian Mine Sweeper operating in New Guinea Waters. Employed as Lookout and Helmsman

HMAS PLATYPUS	**21 July to 10 August 1945**
	Stores and Fuel Ship at Moratai, in Mollucas Islands, for support of small ships operating in the Islands in support of land operations. Part of ship, Storing and Upper deck sentry.
HMAS BATHURST	**11 August to 2 October 1945**
	Minesweeping (retaking Hong Kong) WWII ended during passage to retake Hong Kong.
	Minesweeping operation off entrance to Hong Kong to allow British Naval Forces to enter Hong Kong Harbour and to take over Dockyard. Also, Minesweeping off Chinese coast at Amoy and Swatow after completion of WWII. Participated in return of Women prisoners from Hong Kong's Stanley Prison to Hong Kong Harbour
HMAS PLATYPUS	**3 October to 12 November 1945**
	Return to this ship following Hong Kong operation. Part of ship.
HMAS FREMANTLE	**13 November 1945 to 24 January 1946**
	Minesweeper. Return to Australia via Fremantle, Christmas in Adelaide, and paid ship off in wharf alongside of Spencer Street Bridge in Melbourne.
HMAS LONSDALE	**25 January to 11 February 1946**
	After leaving the ship, I was employed at Fleet Post Office in Lonsdale. On completion of leave headed West by troop train to Perth
HMAS LEEUWIN	**12 February to 14 February 1946**
	Arrived late one afternoon and began Draft In routine. Half was through an RPO met me and handed ticket to Sydney the following day with a sleeper on the train as far as Port Pirie. That ticket was to change the direction of my life.

HMAS WATSON	15 March to 30 August 1946
	Placed on Radar Plot 2 Course on arrival. Ship's Books held at Rushcutter. On completion, employed instructing RP sailors
HMAS MURCHISON	31/8/1946 to 1/12/1946
	Sea Training I/C of Radar Plotters qualifying.
HMAS WATSON	2/12/1946 to 28/7/1947
	Training Radar Plotters and Promoted Acting Leading Seaman Radar Plot 2nd Class (RP2) on the 1/1/1947
HMAS BATAAN	29 July 1947 to 30 September 1948
	(Occupation Force Japan) In charge of Operations Room supervising Radar Plot sailors in Australian and New Zealand waters and anti-smuggling patrolling between Japan and Korea
HMAS WATSON	1 October 1948 to 28 January 1949
	Qualifying RP 1st Class. Promoted to Acting Petty Officer during this period
HMAS ALBATROSS	29 January 1949 to 15 July 1949
	In charge of flight following of aircraft by Radar Plotters and teaching Homing procedures using radio signals from aircraft
HMAS SYDNEY	16 July 1949 to 26 October 1952
	Operated off West and East Coast of Korea during the ship's initial deployment to that War. Working in Air Direction Room in charge of Air Plot and as required. Confirmed Petty Officer 1/10/1949
HMAS WATSON	27 October 1952 to 31 August 1953
	In charge of Training Radar Plotters. Completed advanced Plot and Radar Instructor Course (PRI) Promoted Chief Petty Officer 1/4/1953

HMAS VENGEANCE	1 September 1953 to 5 August 1955
	In charge of Radar Plotters in both Operations Rooms. When flying Operations ceased became one of two Chief Petty Officers running the training for new entry recruits on sea training
HMS DRYAD	6 August 1955 to 17 December 1956
	CPOPRI. Preparing for and commencing Bosun Plot C Radar Course. 27 October to 17 December 1956 Completed course promoted to a/Sub Lieutenant Plot and Radar
HMS TUMULT	18 December 1956 to 16 June 1957
	Period of Cold War in Europe learning to gain a Certificate of Competency to be an Officer of the Watch at sea. Operating from Portland
HMS SHEFFIELD	17 June 1957 to 9 February 1959
	I/C Assistant to Direction Officer and Ship's Boatswain. Period of Cold War in Europe. Operated in North Sea, Mediterranean and as far east as Bahrain. Then sea voyage home
HMAS WATSON	22 April 1959 to 19 June 1960
	In charge of Action Information Training Centre (AITC) training Radar Opera tors and Ships Operation Teams in operation of Operation's Room equipment and Air Control
HMAS ALBATROSS	20 June to 23 June 1960
	Joint Torpedo Anti-Submarine Course (JASC)
HMAS WATSON	24 June to 6 August 1961
	In charge of AITC
HMAS ALBATROSS	7 August 1961 to 11 August 1961
	Joint Torpedo Anti-Submarine Course (JASC)

HMAS WATSON	12 August 1961 to 26 April 1962
	In charge of AITC
HMS DRYAD	11 April 1962 to 21 December 1962
	Training as a Direction Officer and advanced Warfare Training as a Fighter Controller and Air Defence training
HMS ARK ROYAL	7 January 1963 to 18 December 1963
	Period of Cold War in Europe Fighter Controller off British Islands. Sent to East African Coast and then Singapore.
	(during Indonesian Confrontation) Attached to 890 Fighter Squadron. Flown Back to England from Aden to HMS HERON to embark on HMS HERMES
HMS HERMES	January 1963
	Period of Cold War in Europe when embarked with 890 Squadron Fighter Controller for Fleet Exercises off the British Isles
HMAS HERON	30 December 1963 to 18 December 1964
	Period of Cold War in Europe RN 890 Squadron Fighter Controller (Night Fighter Squadron). Completed exchange service and embarked for return to Australia
HMAS MELBOURNE	15 January 1965 to 7 October 1965
	(Malaysian/Indonesian Confrontation) Overseeing Fighter Controllers and Air Defence Room. (2 I/C) Immediately on return from United Kingdom joined ship and sailed for Far East Strategic Reserve
HMAS STUART	7 October 1965 to 30 January 1967
	Indonesian Confrontation/Far East Strategic Reserve. Operations Room Officer and in charge Aircraft Control

HMAS WATSON	31 January 1967 to 17 June 1968
	Training Officer Navigation and Radar School. Promoted Lieutenant Commander 1 April 1967
HMAS PERTH	17 June 1968 to 26 May 1969
	(Vietnam War) In charge of Combat Information Centre and Air Controllers, both Helicopter and Fighters. Received Naval Board Commendation for services in ship during Vietnam operations
HMAS WATSON	26 May 1969 to 31 August 1969
	Training Officer Navigation and Radar Training School
HMAS MELBOURNE	1 September 1969 to 13 December 1970
	(Escort of HMAS Sydney to Vung Tau) In charge of Operations Rooms and particularly Air Direction Room and Fighter Controllers during ship's operations
NAVY OFFICE	14 December 1970 to 7 April 1974
	Deputy Director User Requirements. Involved in Design programme for West Australian Support Facility HMAS Stirling now known as Fleet Base West
HMAS SYDNEY	(No exact dates) Short-term posting.
	Vung Tau trip. Sent to supervise Helicopter Control, Screen Operations, when 817C Flight (Helicopters) sent to ship to provide Anti—Submarine patrols when no surface escorts were available to screen Sydney enroute to Vung Tau
HMAS MELBOURNE	8 April 1974 to 20 April 1975
	In charge of Operations Rooms and Air Direction Room. Christmas Day 1974 and initially responsible for overseeing the preparation of ship for immediate sailing to Darwin after Cyclone Tracy destroyed Darwin. Ship's. Disaster Coordinator

HMAS WATSON		21 April 1975 to 14 December 1975
		OIC Navigation and Direction School
NAVY OFFICE		15 December 1975 to 14 March 1977
		Deputy Director of Naval Training. Promoted to Commander 31 December 1975
HMAS LEEUWIN		15 March 1977 to 27 July 1978
		Pre-commissioning Executive Officer and Executive Officer, HMAS STIRLING on Commissioning, 28 July 1978
HMAS STIRLING		8 January 1979 to 30 January 1979
		Commanding Officer HMAS Stirling
HMAS STIRLING		30 January 1979 to 18 December 1979
		Executive Officer
HAROLD E HOLT		19 December 1979 to 24 January 1982
		Deputy Commander of Naval Communication Station
HMAS STIRLING		25 January 1982 to 1 September 1983
		Executive Officer. Completed Full-time Naval Service and retired to Emergency Reserve List.

NOTE:

Information has been compiled from Navy Office Records provided to W G RITCHIE.

Service During Conflicts

World War II — During 1945

Occupation of Japan — 09/1946 - 1947

HMAS Bataan

Korea — 04/10/1951 - Jan/Feb 1952

 HMAS Sydney 1st Deployment

Cold War - Europe

HMS Tumult — 07/12/1956 - 11/11/1959

HMS Sheffield

Cold War Europe — 07/1/1963 - 18/12/1964

HMAS Ark Royal

890 Squadron

HMS Hermes

HMAS Melbourne — 14/7/1965 - 17/9/1965

Vietnam — 1969/1970

Escort HMAS Sydney to Vietnam

HMAS Stuart — 1965/67 period ???

HMAS Perth — September 1968 - April 1969

Cyclone Tracy

25 December 1974

Introduction

I had accepted the Christmas Day 1974 HMAS *Melbourne* Duty Commanding Officer duty due to the listed officer having to proceed on compassionate leave. It was not until about 3 pm when I received a phone call from the Commander Air of HMAS *Melbourne* asking what I knew about the recall of the Helicopter Squadron and its transport to Darwin. At that stage I had no knowledge that Cyclone Tracy had destroyed Darwin City. I immediately realised HMAS *Melbourne* was the only ship capable of carrying the whole squadron to Darwin.

Subsequent Events

At the time, *Melbourne* was in a main maintenance period, and the Ship's Company was on Christmas leave all over Australia. I rang Fleet headquarters to get the up-to-date situation concerning the ship. I was told they were very busy and couldn't talk to me then and to call back later.

The Ship's Company began to arrive back from all over Australia following the Recall, and, from memory, something like 66% were on board when we sailed the next day. The Ship's Engineers had done a great job on the engines, and they were back operational by about 8 am on Boxing Day.

Stores for Darwin

It wasn't long after I became aware of the situation in Darwin when I was called to the gangway because of a truckload of stores for Darwin arriving alongside and asking to be unloaded as quickly as possible as the driver had to return for a second load. Having summoned the Duty Watch, the Duty Crane Driver said there was a problem with the ship's crane operation due to the ship being on reduced power. He would only be able to do one of three movements at a time. The crane could train left or right, or hoist the topping lift, or hoist and lower a load.

So, I began unloading the truck until full power could be restored. Realising that it may be some time before full power was restored, and we could get the ship's forklifts up from the hangar, it was obvious each item lifted on board would have to be placed as far away from the ship's side as possible. This resulted in a semicircle of stores with subsequent loads creeping closer to the ship's side.

Just as I finished speaking to the driver, I noticed a young sailor with an aircraft handler's badge on his sleeve about to go aboard the ship. I asked him if he had a forklift driver's qualification, which fortunately he had. He also answered that he had not been drinking. I sent him to obtain a forklift from the dockyard facility so we could unload the trucks that would soon appear.

Before we had unloaded the first truck, a second truck appeared. This second truck was unloaded using the forklift from the Dockyard pool.

Eventually, full power was restored, and the use of the ship's lifts and forklifts was available to move stores near the crane for transfer into the hangars.

Later, the wharf crane lifted a Bailey Bridge to the flight deck. This allowed the trucks to come onto the flight deck and be unloaded by the ship's staff using the ship's forklifts and aircraft lifts to send the stores down to the Hangar space. This continued throughout the night until shortly before we were to sail.

As officers and men returned on board, I could pass over some responsibility to others so that they could concentrate on their particular area of operation in getting ready for sea. I was eventually able to pass over supervision of unloading trucks to others so that they could continue to unload trucks and resume other Duty Officer activities. Later, I had to concentrate on getting the two Operations rooms set up for leaving the harbour.

The number of Police and other vehicles delivering members of the Ship's Company back alongside was a sign that the Ship's Company had made haste to leave their family Christmas celebrations and return to the ship as soon as the recall was broadcast. Perhaps the most notable was a Victorian Police car that had brought a sailor all the way from outback Victoria because there was no public transport available.

Before leaving Sydney Harbour, the ship moved to a buoy to refuel and took on stores that could not be transferred at the wharf.

The ship sailed from Sydney later on Boxing Day afternoon and picked up more members of the crew and members of other ships crews at Townsville.

En route Darwin

Planning the days ahead for when the ship reached Darwin, saw the Ship's Company organisation of 30-man teams checked out. Depending on the task required in Darwin, they could be split into five, 10, 20, 30 or any combination within that 30. I was made the Ship's Disaster Coordinator.

The ship's band requested they be used as a unit; this was granted.

Each helicopter had its anti-submarine equipment removed, allowing it to carry up to nine persons at a time.

Darwin

On arrival in Darwin, I was flown ashore to the Disaster Coordination Centre to the briefed on the requirements for the ship's teams. I was sitting in the middle of the back seat in the helicopter as it flew in and was astounded to see the floors of polished wood, with no walls, the whole house having been destroyed. Many of the houses were on stilts and the underfloor areas had debris all around. Occasionally you might see a bath or a toilet still standing.

Work Parties

Each morning the Ship's Company were called about 4.30 to 5 am and had breakfast, collected lunch and water, and assembled in the hangar in their groups. Each group were checked that they knew what their task was. They were briefed that if they found anything valuable or still usable, it was to be placed under the house and secured as necessary. Any alcohol was to be placed in a safe area under the house or in the refrigerator usually located there. They clearly understood what it would be like to stand in the shoes of the Darwin residents, whose house they were clearing the debris from, would feel if they stole anything, no matter what.

Helicopter Transfers.

As soon as it was light enough for the Helicopters to operate a 30-man group would move from Hangar to Flight deck, have their names recorded, and groups of nine personnel would board the Helicopters and be taken ashore. By the second or third day they speedily boarded the helicopters as if they had been specifically trained as assault crews. This allowed the disembarkation of working parties to be completed very quickly.

Clearing Refrigerators.

Some groups were required to help clean up shops and the like. The most daunting task was the clearance of refrigerators of the stinking rotting food. They were not equipped with any type of masks except a handkerchief. You can imagine the smell of rotting food.

The utter devastation and the rubble meant that working groups had to bring all the debris to the roadside where it was picked up and disposed of. Despite the heat and humidity, the personnel got on with the task allocated.

Each afternoon, at about 4 pm, the groups were brought back to the ship by Helicopter. You can imagine they were very tired. Each person was checked back on board to ensure that no one was left ashore and that they were not bringing anything back on board.

Commonwealth Archives

On one occasion, I received a message from the Disaster Coordinator ashore that he wanted to see me. I caught the next helicopter going ashore and checked into the Disaster Centre. Standing there, with the Disaster Coordinator, was my neighbour in Canberra. He worked for the Commonwealth Archives. The coordinator said he had no hands left to assist the Archives representative and was it possible that I could find a small team on board *Melbourne* to assist. I returned the ship and made a broadcast saying I needed up to five people for a job ashore. I quickly had about five sailors present themselves and we took the next Helicopter ashore. They helped the Archivist carefully pack up wet and damp, Commonwealth archives. They helped load records into the aircraft at the airport.

I had ascertained that arrangements were in place for the archives to be dried out in Brisbane. Those receiving the archives were surprised. When they opened the boxes, the records were all dry. Apparently, they had dried out during the flight, an unexpected Bonus.

Summary

Every day during HMAS *Melbourne's* stay in Darwin, I witnessed the going and coming back of the various teams sent ashore to help in the clean-up, following Cyclone Tracy. I witnessed their assembly each morning and the return each night following a day in high humidity and temperatures. Though tired and worn out by the effort they had made that day, they fronted up the next day ready to do it all again. I also spent some time checking on site the various tasks they were doing. I was very proud to have been their Coordinator and, except for some good-natured banter from time to time, I never heard a sailor or officer complain.

They had been called during their Christmas leave and celebrations with their family and many had travelled long distances once they received the Recall. I cannot recall, during my long service in the Navy, how the personnel very willingly turned to every morning without someone grumbling. On their return I would ask each group whether anyone had any problems that needed attention and the answer was always no.

From my personal observations, on board and during inspections of work parties on the job, I have no hesitation in stating that the performance of all those involved was way, way, above any other task I had been involved in 30-odd years in the Navy, 28 of them instructing and managing men at sea in the Royal Australian Navy and during two three year stints with the Royal Navy during the Cold War, that involved operations from near the Arctic Circle and as far east as East Africa and Singapore.

Award of National Emergency Medal.

I believe that the efforts of all Navy personnel who participated in the relief of Darwin after Cyclone Tracy, went way and above by a considerable amount, the effort required to be recognised for an award and that they should be recognised with the award of the **National Emergency Medal.**

Those in Cyclone Yasi were awarded a medal so let's be fair and honourable and change the Regulation. As I said in my letter to which this Appendix is attached "Rules were meant to be Broken." Arguments that it was too long ago are irrelevant, in my opinion, because the system should have recognized the personnel soon after the event. This implies incompetence on those who should have recognised the need for such recognition.

If an award can be made for Cyclone Yasi, the effort made by Naval personnel involved in Navy Help Darwin after Cyclone Tracy, was far more involved than that for Yasi. Also, Cyclone Tracy was far more damaging and affected far more people than Yasi. The Naval personnel gave up their Christmas with family having already spent a considerable amount of time at sea in 1974. The Engineering Staff, in particular, did a great job in restoring the engines to operational standard, as did all those involved in the storage and stowage of the stores coming aboard.

WHERE IS THE JUSTICE for the personnel involved?

WHERE IS THE AUSTRALIAN FAIR GO in the decisions not to support the application?

Any comments about not being able to find the names of those involved is irrelevant as records of those on board all the ships involved should be available for each ship.

I fully support Captain Brian Swan in his approach to seeking recognition and justice for Navy Help Darwin personnel – especially as I was at the front line from the recall to the final day in Darwin.

OBN Details - Bill Ritchie

A Kalgoorlie boy, he joined the Australian Navy in 1944 as a very Ordinary Seaman Second Class, retiring in 1983 as a Seaman Commander. After basic training, qualified as a Radar Plotter. Unlike all his classmates who went to ships, Bill was sent to the SW Pacific Area as a replacement Radar Operator for Australian Ships operating in the SW Pacific and further north. On arrival in New Guinea, one of his first duties was night guard, with three others, on a Stores Complex some distance from the Base. It came to pass that as a result of this duty, he began the first of many appearances before his superiors, from Ordinary Seaman to and including Commander. Not Guilty of course.

Whilst on Guard duty, on a clear and very still night, there was a loud crack as if someone had stepped on some rotting foliage and some rustling. Bill challenged in accordance with the orders, and not receiving a reply, dropped the rifle to his hip and fired a slightly elevated shot.

A very frightened Banshee screaming 'Stop Firing,' the Officer of the Guard appeared from behind a large tree where he had been hiding. Bill was relieved of his duty and charged with deliberately trying to kill the Officer of the Guard. When questioned Bill explained he had challenged and had received no reply and, as he had been taught by Old Soldiers in The Volunteer Defence Corp before joining the Navy, fired a warning shot. The OOG kept insisting it was deliberate and Bill was questioned why he fired from the hip. Again, he had been taught to use the pointer finger along the barrel and fire with the middle finger as invariably the finger would be pointing in the direction of a suspect intruder. Case dismissed. It appears that Bill's shot had snapped a branch above the OOG and it fallen on him hence the OOG being upset as he thought he had actually been shot.

By the time Bill returned to Australia, he had served in a small stores ship, twice in a Repair Store ship, and three Corvettes, including one of the lead mine sweepers clearing the way into Hong Kong for the British Pacific Fleet. Total Radar operating time was 20 minutes. Lookout, many, many hours.

Bill decided to stay in the Navy and signed to complete a twelve-year engagement. He quickly rose up the command chain and as No Badge Leading Seaman was in HMAS Bataan, a Tribal Class Destroyer, during the Occupation of Japan and later as an acting Petty Officer welcomed the First Carrier Group to HMAS Albatross so beginning an association with the Fleet Air Arm. From Albatross he went to HMAS

Sydney and the Korean War. In 1956, Bill was sent to England for Officer training. The Royal Navy tended to treat Australians as being in the Royal Amateur Navy. Bill outshone his RN counterparts coming in first in Class. Promoted to Bosun Plot and Radar (in 1957 changed to Sub Lieutenant) he served his first of two stints with the Royal Navy in HMS Sheffield, a six-inch cruiser, that operated from just outside the Arctic Circle to Bahrain in the Gulf. While acting as a Russian Heavy Cruiser in an exercise against a crack RN destroyer group, led by a distinguished WWII Captain, Bill was responsible for disrupting the attack. Instead of an angry Captain assailing him for not following the exercise orders that had nothing about electronic warfare in it, the Captain was surprised to find Bill was an Australian and congratulated him on teaching the Captain a lesson.

In all, Bill served in carriers eight times, six times in the Australian Carriers, (Sydney x 2, Vengeance and Melbourne x 3. He also served in the British Carriers HMS Ark Royal and HMS Hermes being the Fighter Controller for 890 Sea Vixen Night Fighters. He upset a V Bomber crew when he put two night fighters on their tail without them detecting the fighters. The RAF had never done that apparently.

He served three times in the Indonesian/Malaysian Conflict and twice in Vietnam in HMAS Perth and later during his second trip in HMAS Sydney when there were no surface escorts and helicopters were embarked. HMAS Perth during her second deployment was the last RAN ship to be fired on by a shore Battery.

In between sea time, Bill was at HMAS Watson in Sydney as Instructor and became the OIC of the Navigation and Direction School. **The Ritchie Building** at Watson is named after him.

In 1970 Bill was sent to Canberra as Deputy Director of the Directorate of User Requirements. The third Boss in as many months dumped a 400cm high stack of files saying they are your responsibility. Asked about the files he was told to read them and find out. So began an over eight-year association with the Western Australian Naval Facility known today as HMAS Stirling or Fleet Base West. Four years in Canberra in the Development and Planning stage and over four years as Pre-commissioning and First Executive Officer, Second Commanding Officer and third Executive Officer. Bill smiles as he looks on the Base today: there were three attempts to stop the project or put it into Care and Maintenance. Nothing like seeing the look on the face of a Chief of the Defence asking how many people Bill had.

"Eighty," was the reply."

"How many can you reduce to?"

"120," was reply.

This scenario was repeated three times before Bill informed the General, who thought

Bill was raving mad, that he was 40 short as it was. In the event the Base was allowed to continue thanks to Colonel Frank Statham and his group who convinced the Navy it was cheaper to complete than stop. He was made a Member of the Order of Australia for his services to the Navy and particularly HMAS Stirling.

Since retiring Bill qualified as a Real Estate Agent and, when in 1986 he was about to commence operations in Rockingham, became involved in the Setting up and running the very successful Rockingham Tourist Centre as a volunteer. This he did for three plus years. In about 1989 or 1990 he trained a very young, disabled man to take over as paid manager and that person is still managing the Centre today.

Bill continues to be involved wherever there is a need.

Bill's wife of 57 years died in 2012. He has four children; one served ten years as a Submarine Weapons Electrical Officer. A daughter works for Defence on Garden Island, and another son Works for ASC. His last son has worked in Stores Warehousing. He has ten grandchildren, only one of which is a boy. **"Lousy plumbers," Bill says.**

Highgate RSL Sub Branch – OBE Luncheon.

Name: Bill Gray Ritchie, born Kalgoorlie.

Brief ???? Service History: Joined Navy in 1944 as Ordinary Seaman second class and retired 39 years later in 1983 as a Commander. Trained as a Radar Operator he was sent to New Guinea as spare operator for any ship needing one. On arrival in New Guinea one of his first duties was night guard, with three others, on a Stores Complex some distance from the Base. **It came to pass that as a result of this duty he began the first of many appearances before his superiors from Ordinary Seaman to and including Commander. Not Guilty of course.**

On arrival in New Guinea Bill was given Guard duty. It was a clear and very still night, there was a loud crack as if someone had stepped on some rotting foliage and some rustling. Bill challenged in accordance with the orders, and not receiving a reply, dropped the rifle to his hip and fired a slightly elevated shot.

A very frightened Banshee screaming "Stop Firing," the Officer of the Guard appeared from behind a large tree where he had been hiding. Bill was relieved of his duty and charged with deliberately trying to kill the Officer of the Guard. When questioned Bill explained he had challenged and had received no reply and, as he had been taught by Old Soldiers in The Volunteer Defence Corp before joining the Navy, fired a warning shot pointing in the direction of a suspect intruder. Case dismissed. *It appears that Bill's shot had snapped a branch above the OOG and it fallen on him, hence the OOG being upset as he thought he had actually been shot.*

By the time Bill returned to Australia he had served in a small stores ship, twice in a Repair Stores ship, three Corvettes, including being in one of the lead mine sweepers clearing the way into Hong Kong for the British Pacific Fleet. Total Radar operating time 20 minutes. Lookout, many, many hours.

He transferred to the Permanent Navy in 1946 and was rapidly promoted through the Ranks to Chief Petty Officer Radar Plot.

Whilst serving in the Carrier HMAS Vengeance he was sent to England in 1955 for Officer training and in 1956 promoted to Bosun Plot and Radar. In 1957 this was changed to Sub Lieutenant Special Duties. He served in the Destroyer, HMS Tumult and 6-inch Cruiser HMS Sheffield. After three years overseas he returned to HMAS Watson as OIC Action Information Training Centre for three years. Off to England for Navigation and Direction Officer training and another two years with RN. He served in Carriers HMS Ark Royal and HMS Hermes as the Fighter Controller for 890 Night Fighter Squadron. These posting were during the Cold War.

On returned to Australia he was immediately posted for the first of his three postings to HMAS Melbourne. He later served in HMAS Stuart and HMAS Perth in Vietnam and later HMAS Sydney when a Helo Flight was embarked to cover for the absence of escorts.

Bill spent three trips during the Indon/Malaysian Emergency.

In between sea time Bill was at HMAS Watson in Sydney as Instructor and became the OIC of the Navigation and Direction School. **The Ritchie Building** *at Watson is named after him.*

In 1970 Bill was sent to Canberra as Deputy Director of the Directorate of User Requirements. The third Boss in as many months dumped a 400cm high stack of files saying they are your responsibility. Asked about the files he was told to read them and find out. So began an over eight-year association with **The Western Australian Naval Facility known today as HMAS Stirling or Fleet Base West.** *Four years in Canberra in the Development and Planning stage and over four years as Pre-commissioning and First Executive Officer, Second Commanding Officer and third Executive Officer. Bill smiles as he looks on the Base today: there were three attempts to stop the project or put it into Care and Maintenance.*

Nothing like seeing the look on the face of a Chief of Defence asking how many people Bill had.

"Eighty," was the reply.

"How many can you reduce to?"

"120," was reply.

This scenario was repeated three times before Bill informed the General, who thought Bill was raving mad, that he was 40 short as it was. In the event the Base was allowed to continue thanks to Colonel Frank Statham and his group who convinced the Navy it was cheaper to complete than stop. He was made a Member of the Order of Australia for his services to the Navy and particularly HMAS Stirling

Civilian Achievements: *Whilst in Canberra, he studied to be an* **Accountant** *so he could understand facts and figures. On Retirement he studied and obtained a Real Estate Agents License.*

However in 1986 he became involved with the setting up of a very successful **Tourist Information Centre** *in Rockingham as a Volunteer. He trained a very young man to run the place as Manager and he is still running the place today.*

He was very active as a 100% Rotarian and the only surviving member of the originals of the Safety Bay Probus Club.

For some years, he worked as Volunteer Tour Escort, taking people on Ship Voyages and Overseas and Interstate.

He is Patron of the Naval Historical Society in Western Australia. For his services, he is a Life Member of the original HMAS Stirling Officers Mess, now Sir James Stirling Mess, a Life member of the Naval Association, the HMAS Perth National Association and the Rockingham Tourism Authority.

Bill's wife of 57 years died four years ago. His eldest son served as a Submarine Weapons Electrical Officer, a daughter works for Defence on Garden Island, a second son works for Australian Submarine Corporation and a third son has worked in industry on the Kwinana Strip. He says they are lousy plumbers as he has ten grandchildren and one great-grand child and only one is a grandson.

MEDAL # ON MOUNT	MEDAL SERVICE	PICTURE
1	ORDER OF AUSTRALIA MEDAL (A.M.)	
2	1939-1945 STAR	
3	PACIFIC STAR	
4	WAR MEDAL 1939-1945	
5	AUSTRALIA SERVICE MEDAL 1939-1945	
6	AUST ACTIVE SERVICE MEDAL 1945-1975	
7	KOREA MEDAL	
8	UNITED NATIONS KOREA	
9	GENERAL SERVICE MEDAL 1962	

10	VIETNAM MEDAL	
11	AUSTRALIA SERVICE MEDAL 1945-1975	
12	DEFENCE FORCE SERVICE MEDAL	
13	NATIONAL MEDAL	
14	AUSTRALIAN DEFENCE MEDAL	
15	VIETNEMESE CAMPAIGN STAR	
16	PINGAT JASA MALAYSIA MEDAL	
17	NAVY MERITORIOUS UNIT COMMENDATION	

www.ingramcontent.com/pod-product-compliance
Lightning Source LLC
Chambersburg PA
CBHW040123130526
44590CB00051B/4349